Business Ethics and Values

Business Ethics and Values

Individual, Corporate and International Perspectives

Fourth edition

Colin Fisher

Nottingham Business School, Nottingham Trent University

Alan Lovell

Former Dean, Glamorgan Business School

Néstor Valero-Silva

Nottingham Business School, Nottingham Trent University
with a case study by Shishir Malde

PEARSON

Harlow, England • London • New York • Boston • San Francisco • Toronto • Sydney • Auckland • Singapore • Hong Kong
Tokyo • Seoul • Taipei • New Delhi • Cape Town • São Paulo • Mexico City • Madrid • Amsterdam • Munich • Paris • Milan

Pearson Education Limited
Edinburgh Gate
Harlow CM20 2JE
United Kingdom
Tel: +44 (0)1279 623623
Web: www.pearson.com/uk

First published 2003 (print)
Second edition 2006 (print)
Third edition 2009 (print)
This edition published 2013 (print and electronic)

The Financial Times. With a worldwide network of highly respected journalists, *The Financial Times* provides global business news, insightful opinion and expert analysis of business, finance and politics. With over 500 journalists reporting from 50 countries worldwide, our in-depth coverage of international news is objectively reported and analysed from an independent, global perspective. To find out more, visit www.ft.com/pearsonoffer.

ISBN: 978-0-273-75791-7 (print)
          978-0-273-75793-1 (PDF)
          978-0-273-78128-8 (eText)

British Library Cataloguing-in-Publication Data
A catalogue record for the print edition is available from the British Library

Library of Congress Cataloging-in-Publication Data
A catalog record for the print edition is available from the Library of Congress
10 9 8 7 6 5 4 3 2 1
16 15 14 13 12

Print edition typeset in 9.5/12pt ITC Stone serif by 73
Print edition printed and bound by Ashford Colour Press Ltd, Gosport
NOTE THAT ANY PAGE CROSS REFERENCES REFER TO THE PRINT EDITION

Brief Contents

Contents

Chapter 8   Compliance and integrity: an organisation's internal accountability   299

Chapter 9   Corporate Social Responsibility   332

Companion Website

ON THE WEBSITE

For open-access **student resources** specifically written to complement this textbook and support your learning, please visit **www.pearsoned.co.uk/fisherlovellvalerosilva**

Lecturer Resources

For password-protected online resources tailored to support the use of this textbook in teaching, please visit **www.pearsoned.co.uk/fisherlovellvalerosilva**

Introduction

The fourth edition of this book has undergone substantial updating and restructuring to ensure that the balance of its content matches the current priorities and issues. We recognize that the issues encompassed within the field that we still refer to as 'business ethics' have, since the first edition, been labeled as corporate social responsibility (CSR) and that more recently the term sustainability has become the all-embracing term for the subject of this book. Néstor Valero-Silva and Shishir Malde have joined with Colin Fisher and Alan Lovell in the task of bringing these new themes to the fore in this new edition of the book.

Corporations represent the arenas within which most people spend much of their waking lives and the sheer scale of some of their operations makes many multinational corporations more influential in world affairs (not just business affairs) than some governments. Hence the actions of corporations, whether judged 'good' or 'bad', can affect many, many people, both within the organisations and outwith. Minimising the negative effects of corporate behaviour thus becomes an issue, not just for business, but for the political and social spheres of human activity.

However, the simple labels of 'good' and 'bad' will often represent gross oversimplifications of what could be complex and dynamic issues and situations. We are often faced with dilemmas, with the options available to us containing both positive and negative aspects. This book has been written not only to allow you to understand the ethical underpinnings of such complex situations, but also to allow you to determine where the weight of evidence might lie in any given case or situation.

At the time we wrote the first edition of the book the bankruptcies of Enron and WorldCom were just beginning to unfold. As we applied the finishing touches to the second edition, the senior officials of Enron had yet to stand trial, but Bernie Ebbers, the chief executive of WorldCom, had been found guilty of an $11bn fraud. He was sentenced to 25 years. Jeffrey Skilling of Enron received a 24 year jail sentence. As we finish the third edition, we knew that Kenneth Lay, the Chief Executive of Enron had died in 2006 without having been sentenced, However, for the companies who were part of these organisations' supply chains, the company's employees, their investors and other involved groups and individuals, these outcomes were scant consolation. Many had lost their livelihoods, with the personal turmoil and distress that invariably follows. As we prepare the current fourth edition of the book new scandals have emerged, the latest in the line of Enron type scandals was the admission by Olympus the Japanese camera and optical company that it had been disguising losses for many years. Perhaps the revelations of these scandals suggest that the business, or economic, sphere of human activity cannot exist for long without an ethical base. Mistrust, cheating, conniving, deceit and fraudulent behaviour are the quicksand upon which no business system can be built.

Far more than many other books on business ethics we have devoted considerable attention to business ethics at the individual level, without underplaying the need also to look at business ethics at the corporate level. The reason for this attention to the individual is that ultimately the actions taken in the name of corporations will in fact be decisions made by individuals, acting either in groups or alone. This is not to deny that corporations can develop a form of persona, what we might call ethical culture, which can be transmitted and maintained through stories, myths, legends and artefacts, which we explore in Chapter. The effects of these actions and cultures will be felt by (other) individuals, either collectively or singly. It is for these reasons that we give to the individual such attention.

A second major feature of our approach is to stress the centrality of argumentation within business ethics. At its heart the subject is devoid of facts. It is a collection of theories, beliefs and arguments. It is no less important because of this; indeed we believe it to be profoundly important. With its roots set in argumentation we need to help you gain confidence in understanding the various ethical perspectives or stances. Most ethically charged situations are arenas for competing arguments, even if some of the arguments are judged weak, or fraudulent. Dealing with controversial issues must inevitably involve debate and argument and we believe that a primary aim of a book on business ethics should be to develop the skills of argumentation, or what are known as rhetorical skills. A new web-based toolkit for shaping such debates has been added to this new edition of the book.

We do not advocate particular positions in the book, for that would be hypocritical as educators. However, we do advance, in the closing chapter, a tentative manifesto for affecting ethics in business as a way of crystallising the issues and arguments raised in the book. Such a proposal also plots a possible way forward.

We make the case throughout the book that, whilst there are competing arguments concerning where the ethical high ground might be on particular issues, the competing arguments are unlikely to be equally valid or meritorious. Our objective has been to provide you with the knowledge and understanding necessary to be able to form your own reasoned arguments and ethically informed positions on the many varied and complex issues that permeate business life.

The opinions we may each hold and the behaviours we may display in different situations are likely to be affected by a range of issues, including the support of others, our dependents, the risks associated with the issue, where power lies and our respective values. Indeed, we devote time to the subject of values as reflected in the title of the book, because we believe values to be important elements in understanding both ethical reasoning and moral behaviour. Values can be said to act as filters and triggers for stimulating responses to ethically charged situations and we devote a whole chapter to considering the nature of values and their roles. However, we do not claim certain values to be superior to others. This is a matter about which each of us should come to our own conclusion. Our task, as authors, has been to help you analyse, explain, interpret and interrogate ethical situations, but not to prescribe how you should view the situations.

Our emphasis upon argument explains another feature of the book. As well as providing you with the basic material you would expect to find in a textbook on business ethics, we also develop new arguments that are subject to challenge and dispute. Consequently the book is not designed as a definitive work of reference (although where the material is standard we have treated it as authoritatively as we can). Instead, the book is intended to provide thoughts, ideas and provocations to stimulate your own thinking.

The book is designed for both undergraduate and postgraduate students; each may take from it what they need. The materials on ethical theories and ethical reasoning should be of use to both undergraduate and postgraduate students. These theoretical materials are provided to give you resources for developing arguments for and against particular positions on issues in business ethics. Undergraduate students tend to have limited business experience to draw upon when considering different ethical stances and theories. Thus, we have provided many case studies which are designed to illustrate the application of the various ethical theories. Postgraduate students may like to extend the case studies featured in the book by referring to their experiences in handling, or being aware of, ethically complex business situations. The case studies perform two roles. First, they provide practical applications of ethical theories and arguments, making the arguments more accessible and understandable. Second, they show, unequivocally, the relevance of business ethics for both individuals and societies by illustrating the pain and anguish that can ensue from corrupt, deceitful or other practices that might be judged immoral.

In addition to the case studies within each chapter, there are small tasks to undertake or challenges to respond to. At the close of each chapter we have provided suggested assignment briefs and activities that can be undertaken by groups, probably in seminar rooms.

The book provides more material than might be possible to cover in either an undergraduate or a postgraduate programme, thereby making a helpful complement to lectures and seminars, taking the subject beyond what might feasibly be explored in the time available for lectures and seminars. Thus, you should follow your tutor's guidance on which parts of the book are critical to your course, and where you can usefully extend your studies by studying parts of the book not able to be covered in the required depth during lectures or seminars. For postgraduate students and practising managers, the book should aid reflection upon personal and organisational experience.

The benefits offered by the study of the book are:

- a comprehensive review of standard/classical ethical theories, complemented by new perspectives to equip you for the challenges of organisational environments;

- a wealth of diagrams and charts that present overviews and contexts of the subject, which also act as useful study aids;

- 'definition' boxes that highlight and explain key themes;

- Cross-reference boxes, which make links between ethical theories that are considered in one part of the book with particular applications or arguments featured elsewhere in the book;

- real-life case studies that contextualise theory and provide springboards for debate;

- simulations and exercises that encourage you to reflect upon your own values and ethical standards;

- several of these activities have been converted into web-based interactive activities that makes them esaier and more fun to use;

- activities for group and seminar work that enliven study; a blend of academic theory and concrete issues that reflect the challenge and excitement of the subject; and

- a tentative proposal, offered by the authors for affecting ethics in business, as a way of 'making sense' of the many issues and arguments considered in the book and as a possible schema for debate.

The structure of the book

The book is divided into four main parts, each representing an important subset of business ethics.

Part A – Business ethics matters: what is it and why does it matter?

This opening section groups together the chapters that lay the foundation for the book.

Chapter 1: *Perspectives on business ethics and values.* This scene-setting chapter considers a range of issues, in preparation for the more focused chapters that follow. The chapter opens with the way values can be created, maintained and communicated via the medium of stories. The chapter moves on to provide an early exposure to the 'business case for business ethics'. There follows a consideration of stakeholder theory and then four dominant theories of the firm, each with its own underpinning set of assumptions as to what constitutes ethical behaviour. The chapter closes with a review of other theoretical positions, namely descriptive, normative and reflective approaches.

Chapter 2: *Ethical issues in business.* The purpose of this chapter is to move from the big questions to the particular issues. A 'map' is used to identify the range of ethical and moral issues to be found in business, organisations and management. Detailed case studies are provided to give you a clear understanding of the issues, many of which are referred to throughout the book.

Chapter 3: *Ethical theories and how to use them.* Having presented you in Chapter 2 with the range of ethical problems, this chapter describes the formal ethical theories and principles that are available for use in analysing them. The theories are largely drawn from the history of western philosophy (other philosophies are considered in Chapter 11). Few of the theories were developed with reference to business and so the chapter draws out the implications of the theories for organisations and the people within them.

Part B – Individuals' responses to ethical issues

A feature of our approach is our consideration of ethics in business from the perspective of the individual. This section groups together Chapters 4 to 6, with each chapter dealing with an important aspect of this broad focus.

Chapter 4: *Personal values and heuristics*. This chapter deals with the subject of values and decision making which we show to be a multifaceted subject. Five distinct perspectives on values are introduced and discussed to provide a thorough understanding of the issues involved.

Having presented an introduction to personal values we consider here how people might think through an ethically charged situation. We argue that personal values can be seen as filters through which the elements of any ethically charged situation are sieved (along with other filters such as perceptions of power, and the support of others), as an individual wrestles with an ethically complex situation. Heuristics are a form of 'cognitive short-cut', allowing us to handle complex, ill-defined and/or incomplete information in ways that have a logical rationality, at least from the perspective of the individual.

Chapter 5: *Individual responses to ethical situations*. Here we consider how an individual might define, or 'label', an ethical situation. The two dominant processes involved in 'labelling' are categorisation and particularisation and the choice will be heavily influenced by an individual's personal values. Categorisation, for example, would describe the situation where someone decided that an issue was a matter of following the core values set by an organisation, or that an issue was a question of loyalty. However, the particulars of a situation might make that person think that the categorisation is not right. It is the details of a situation that make people debate under which value an issue should be categorised or indeed whether it should be put in a separate category of its own.

Chapter 6: *Whistleblower or witness?* The concluding chapter in Part B considers ethical behaviour and specifically the employee who rails against an organisational practice to such an extent that, following failure to achieve resolution within the formal organisational structures, s/he reveals their concerns to another individual, whether inside the organisation or outside.

Part C – Organisational responses to ethical issues

This group of chapters moves our focus to the organisational level of analysis and considers the ethical obligations and accountabilities of corporations.

Chapter 7: *Corporate Governance, an organisation's external accountability*. Whether an organization is in the private, public or voluntary sectors it is important that it is held to account for its actions. The reasons why good corporate governance are important are explored. The chapter also looks at the standards of corporate governance that are expected and looks at its role in the areas of corruption and corporate manslaughter.

Chapter 8: *Compliance and Integrity, an organisation's internal accountability*. In this chapter we discuss the internal mechanisms that organisations employ to try to inculcate and maintain particular ethical practices and to identify those practices that are unacceptable. The most common of these mechanisms are codes of conduct and codes of ethics. Such codes can be developed by organisations to apply to their own internal processes and contexts, but codes are also developed by external bodies, sometimes in collaboration with large corporations to whom the codes relate, but sometimes without their co-operation. The chapter also considers ethical leadership and its role in developing an ethical organizational culture.

Chapter 9: *Corporate Social Responsibility*. Most organisations say they are committed to behaving in a socially responsible manner, and the chapter rehearse the big argument about the relative importance of meeting shareholders and stakeholders expectations. The chapter looks at Fairtrade, organisational diversity and CSR reporting as particular arenas of socially responsible behavior.

Chapter 10: *Sustainability.* In this chapter we consider the issue of sustainability from a variety of perspectives, including, but not limited to, environmental sustainability. We debate the current preference for a market-based 'business' solution to the problem of greenhouse gas emissions and the more general case of ethical egoism being the underpinning assumption of human behaviour in developing policy responses to the challenges of sustainable corporations and societies.

Part D – The international context

This section considers the international context of business ethics, but in Chapter 13, we bring the individual perspective back into consideration within both the international and the corporate contexts.

Chapter 11: *Global and local values – and international business.* It is a cliché to say that values and cultures vary, but recognition of the notion of 'difference' is an important issue for international organisations as they endeavour to operate in various cultural contexts without offending a wide range of sensibilities, values and laws. This chapter provides insights and comparisons between western operating contexts and those in the Asia, notably China and India.

Chapter 12: *Globalisation and international business.* Globalisation is a term that can arouse considerable passions, often negative. We consider the full gamut of issues that corporations operating at a global level face: their potential as forces for positive developments, and also their involvement in cases that illustrate the issues that trouble many concerning their power and their practices.

Chapter 13: *Moral agency at work and a modest proposal for affecting ethics in business.* This is much more than just a 'summing-up' chapter. Whilst we draw upon many of the issues, arguments and theories we have discussed in the preceding chapters, we take these forward by initially worrying about the implications of democratic ideals of what is termed 'globalisation', but more than this we also offer a tentative proposal for affecting ethics in business. The latter is a risky venture because it smacks of prescription, as if 'we know best'. That is why we have qualified our proposal with the adjective 'tentative'. However, the proposal addresses two important issues for us as authors. The first is that it pulls together into a coherent framework the key issues that we have highlighted and discussed in the book. Second, it provides a framework around which debates and arguments can be framed and possibly moved forward.

Chapter 14 *Concluding integrative case studies*

Two major case studies are presented, one focusing on social responsibility and the other on corporate governance, that provide the reader an opportunity to look at ethical issues within a realistic context.

A range of support materials is available to lecturers and students on the website for this book at www.pearsoned.co.uk/fisherlovellvalerosilva.

Acknowledgements

We are grateful to the following for permission to reproduce copyright material:

Figures

Figures 1.1, 1.2, 1.3, 1.4 from *Does Business Ethics Pay?*, Institute of Business Ethics (Webley, S. and More, E. 2003); Figure 5.1 from *Strategic Human Resources. Principles, Perspectives and Practices*, Leopold, J. Watson, T. J. and Harris, L., Pearson Education Limited, © Pearson Education Limited 1999; Figure 9.2 from 'Toward a theory of stakeholder identification and salience: defining the principle of Who and What Really Counts', *The Academy of Management Review*, 22, 4, p. 874 (Mitchell et al. 1977), The International Academy of Management and Business; Figure 10.1 from *Good News & Bad: The Media, Corporate Social Responsibility and Sustainable Development*, The Beacon Press (2002) p. 7, SustainAbility 2002; Figure 11.1 from *Culture's Consequences,* 2nd edition, Sage (Hofstede, G.H.)

Tables

Table 4.2 from *Simple Heuristics that Make Us Smart,* Oxford University Press (Gigerenzer, G. and Todd, P. 1999) p. 87; Table 11.6 from Boxing with shadows: competing effectively with the overseas Chinese and overseas Indian business networks in the Asian Arena, *Journal of Organisational Change Management,* 11, 4, p. 308 (Haley, G. T. and Haley, U. C. V. 1998), Emerald Group Publishing Limited; Table 14.1 after data compiled by S. Malde from Mergent Online, http://www.mergentonline.com; Table 14.2 after Birmingham City Business School.

Text

Case Study 2.14 after 'Professor quits over tobacco firm's £3.8m gift to university', *Guardian*, 18/05/2001 (Meikle, J.), Copyright Guardian News & Media Ltd 2001.

Photographs

Alamy Images: © Ace Stock Limited/Alamy 527; **The Art Archive:** 526.

In some instances we have been unable to trace the owners of copyright material, and we would appreciate any information that would enable us to do so.

PART A

Business ethics matters: what is it and why does it matter?

CHAPTER 1

Perspectives on business ethics and values

Chapter at a glance

Chapter contents

- Learning outcomes
- Introduction
- Stories and business ethics
- The business case for business ethics
- Stakeholder theory
- Business and organisational ethics
- Boundaries of jurisdiction or spheres of justice
- Defining the boundaries of the economic sphere
- Reflections
- Summary

Case studies

- Case study 1.1 The *News of the World* story
- Case study 1.2 Biography and philosophy

Activities and exercises

- Activity 1.1 Is it ever ethical for a newspaper to use illegal means to expose political or commercial wrongdoing?
- Podcast 1.1 The limits of the economic sphere – post offices and the McCann story
- Typical assignments
- Group activity 1.1
- Useful websites

Learning outcomes

Having read this chapter and completed its associated activities, readers should be able to:

■ Identify the good, tragic, comic, satirical and farcical elements in the way in which people and organisations deal with matters of ethics and morality.

■ Explain the basic features of stakeholder theory.

■ Evaluate the business case for business ethics and the validity of its claims.

■ Give an account of the various arguments about the moral status of business, organisations and management.

Introduction

This chapter lays down the foundations of the book. Many of the foundations are stories and we start with stories that identify some of the issues, problems and dilemmas that form the subject of business ethics. We then tell one very important story about business ethics (at least in the UK and in the USA but not necessarily in other countries) in which there is a 'business case' for business ethics. In this moral tale, behaving well as a company has the fortunate consequences, according to the story, of increasing profits. The stories of business ethics have many characters, or in business speak – stakeholders; they are identified and their relative importance discussed in the next section. Finally there is a debate about whether all the stories of business ethics are about economics or whether moral, cultural and social perspectives should be included in the narratives.

Stories and business ethics

The study of business ethics begins with stories. Families and societies have always used stories to illustrate and reinforce their sense of values, justice and fairness. And so it is in business and organisations. There are the stories often found in organisational glossy newsletters of good deeds done by staff volunteering to work among disadvantaged groups and the benefits that the organisation has brought to the communities it works within. Then there are the more gossipy stories that are told, and half told, as episodes are interrupted by work or authority figures, that tell of jealousies and spites, corruption and abuse, lying and distortion.

Czarniawska (2004: 21) pointed out that there are four types of dramatic story in the European classical tradition – romances, tragedies, comedies and satires, each of which has its characteristic figure of speech. Each of them can represent different kinds of business ethics issues.

Figures of speech

Metaphor

Makes comparisons by referring to one thing as a different thing. So calling all the employees in an organisation 'assets' is a metaphor. If you said of a chief executive officer 'she is a Branson among business leaders', this would be a use of metaphor and a means of making a hero of the CEO. It could also be a kind of paralipsis in which attention is drawn to something – that the CEO is a woman and Branson a man – while pretending to pass over it. As a form of irony this paralipsis could be taken as a criticism of the CEO.

Metonymy

Uses an attribute of something to represent the thing itself. Chairpersons sit in a chair when they hold a board meeting. The chair is their attribute, so they become known as chairs. In tragedy a single attribute can undermine a person's integrity; a good person is often brought low because of a part of their behaviour or character.

Synecdoche

Uses a part of something to represent the whole. Business people wear suits and so that particular aspect of them comes to represent them and their role. Others refer to them as suits, as in 'are the suits arriving today to check us out?' Suits are also a means by which business people present a good image of themselves. In comedy synecdoche points out the comic pretensions between ambition and reality. The smartness of the clothes can emphasise the vacuity of the wearer.

Irony

Speaking or writing in such a way as to imply the opposite of what is being said. Often used to imply mockery or jest. It is therefore the basis of much satire.

Romances are based on the quest of a single individual to achieve some noble goal that is only achievable because human beings have an innate, if sometimes well disguised, goodness. The Quaker heroes of the past such as Joseph Rowntree, who built model factories and villages for model workers, or more modern heroes such as Anita Roddick, who sought, against the odds, to make selling beauty products a beautiful process, are good examples. Such heroes become metaphors for their particular brand of ethical management.

Tragedies tell of people who try to behave well but who, by challenging fate, come to personal grief. The stories of whistleblowers who reveal corporate wrongdoing but in so doing lose their families, their homes and their livelihoods are a good example. Tragedy is based on metonymy, as in the film *The China Syndrome* (Bridges, 1979) in which Jack Lemmon plays an engineer in a malfunctioning nuclear power station who is the only person to be troubled by a vibration felt as a test procedure is conducted. The vibration is a metonym for the potential cataclysm that is waiting to happen.

Comedies are stories about how human imperfections and weaknesses make the achievement of a happy ending difficult. The ways in which companies operating in a new country often get their attempts to integrate wrong are a strong source of comedy. The western businessmen, for it is mostly men who would do this, who ignorantly offend their Arab business partners by putting their feet up on their desk after concluding a deal in an attempt to show that the formal business is over and everyone can relax, and so revealing the soles of their shoes, have a degree of comic potential. The dirty soles of the shoes act as a synecdoche, a part of the businessman that stands for the unwholesomeness of the whole man.

Satires work ironically. By contrasting people's behaviour with their words, or by defining the context in which the words are said, it is made clear that people meant the opposite of what they said. When corporations are accused of not taking care of

- customers, by not closing the doors on the *Herald of Free Enterprise* (*see* p. 288), or

- employees, as in the Bhopal incident in which 20,000 people were killed or harmed by a chemical leak from an American owned chemical works in the city (*see* p. 465) (the leak could have been prevented if procedures, management and maintenance had been rigorous), or

- the environment when the oil companies are accused of despoiling the Niger Delta (*see* p. 471),

organisations often reply by saying that the objects and subjects they have damaged are in fact their top priority. They thereby make themselves the object of satire. People then take such claims as ironies. In the film *Super Size Me*, Morgan Spurlock (2004) tested McDonald's claim that its food is not intrinsically unhealthy by living for a month on its products. Of course such a diet made him an unhealthier person (that is irony).

Cross reference	The ethical issues raised by the film *Super Size Me* are discussed in Case study 2.24 (p. 93).

There is, in business ethics as in life generally, a narrow point of balance

- between romance and satire
- and between tragedy and comedy.

These tensions are the narrative dynamic behind business ethics issues. The heroes of romances can easily become the subject of satirists' scorn. In the struggles between heroes and villains the heroes can overreach themselves and believe they really do have magical powers, in some cases literally. In 1999, in the oil producing delta region of Nigeria members of a cult known as the *Egbesu* began a violent campaign against, as they saw it, the despoliation of their homeland by the oil companies (Ibeanu, 2000: 28). Members of the cult believed that the charms they wore made them impervious to bullets. The heroes may then become ridiculous and the villains begin to look more benign. Tragedy can, uncomfortably, have comic elements. As Marx (1963: 1) pointed out, history repeats itself, 'first time as tragedy, second time as farce'. Just as commonly comedy can descend into tragedy. The difference between an organisational comedy of incompetence and a tragedy may be no more than the operation of chance. If luck remains with the organisation then we can all laugh at its bumbling, but if luck runs out the story can become tragic, for some. In December 2004 (Harding, 2004) a Delhi schoolboy from one of the elite schools, doubtless anxious to show off his new mobile phone with built-in camera, used it to take a video clip of his girlfriend providing him with oral sex. Unfortunately for him within a few days the video clip was on sale on Bazee.com, the Indian version of eBay, and indeed owned by eBay. The company took the item off the website as soon as it became aware of it but nevertheless an uproar ensued in India and a mildly, if in poor taste, comic event turned serious. The boy was taken to juvenile court and expelled from school. Avnish Bajaj, the CEO of Bazee.com and a US citizen, was arrested and thrown into the notoriously overcrowded Tihar gaol. For three people at least tragedy was a tale of prosperity, for a time, that ended in wretchedness. The matter was debated in the Indian parliament and the Bharatiya Janata Party (BJP) denounced the incident as the result of American 'interference'. The American government in its turn was taking a serious interest in Mr Bajaj's imprisonment. Condoleeza Rice, the soon to be American Secretary of State, was reported to be furious at the humiliating treatment meted out to an American citizen. The Indian software industry association called for Bajaj's immediate release.

It would seem that the issues and problems that form the subject of business ethics can appear in different forms, sometimes as romances, sometimes as tragedies, sometimes as comedies and sometimes as satires. It follows that stories are a good mechanism through which business issues can be studied and understood. If we can understand how the plots of these stories can lead to either good or bad outcomes we can develop an intuitive knowledge of how to encourage more happy endings than bad ones. Or at least the stories might palliate, or help us come to terms with, the dilemmas we face (Kirk, 1974: 83).

| Case study 1.1 | The *News of the World* story |

One of the major business ethics stories in Britain during 2011 concerned its leading Sunday newspaper, the *News of the World* (*NoW*). The newspaper's success might be related to its focus on publishing stories of scandal amongst the rich, the powerful and the ranks of media celebrities. It was famous for one of its reporters disguising himself as a rich Arab from the Gulf in order to lure the naïve and the famous to do things that would make a good story when published in the newspaper. The paper was part of *News International*, which in turn was the UK arm of *News Corporation*, which is Rupert Murdoch's international media company. This example can be used to illustrate business ethics stories as examples of romances, tragedies, comedies and satires.

The story had begun several years earlier when the newspaper's royal correspondent, Clive Goodman, was accused of employing a private investigator to hack into voice messages on the phones of members of the Royal Family. Such invasion of privacy is a crime. Both the private investigator and the reporter were found guilty and were given prison sentences. Andy Coulson, the editor of the paper at the time, said that he had no knowledge of this illegal hacking and that this case had been a one-off aberration. The story refused to go away, however. There was continued speculation that instead of being an aberration, phone hacking was in fact a normal

▶

part of the paper's working practices. A number of prominent people such as John Prescott, who had been deputy prime minister, claimed that their phones had also been hacked. Other prominent people in the media industry came to out-of-court settlements with News International and dropped their allegations that their phones had been hacked in return for a sum of money. The story rumbled on and Coulson resigned as the paper's editor whilst still claiming that he had not known of, or authorised, the hacking.

Although the phone hacking story remained alive it did not attract wide concern amongst the general population; that is until 4 July 2011 when *The Guardian* newspaper published the story that the *NoW* had listened to, and deleted, messages on the phone of murdered schoolgirl Milly Dowler whilst the police investigation into her disappearance was ongoing. Ironically, given that *The Guardian* was reporting journalistic malpractice, it had later to admit that the messages may have been deleted automatically and not by agents of *NoW*. However, at that time, that a newspaper had acted so crassly led to a wave of public disgust that had massive repercussions for News International. This was a particularly difficult time for News International. It was already a major shareholder of BSkyB the major subscription TV company in the UK and was seeking to acquire a controlling interest in the company. As News International's newspapers were seen as having great influence over the electoral prospects of political parties many felt that the company already had too much influence and were unwilling for it to accumulate more by gaining complete control over BskyB. In July 2011 the government was about to decide whether to accept News International's compromise proposal, that it would float the news operation as a separate entity from the parent company to ensure its editorial independence if it was allowed to acquire control of BskyB. It was anticipated that the deal would be accepted by ministers. The Milly Dowler story changed all that. In turn News International published a public apology and made a private apology to the Dowler family for its actions; it closed down the *NoW*, although Rebekah Brooks the CEO of News International, and one-time editor of *NoW* kept her job. Later the company withdrew its compromise deal related to the BSkyB purchase and therefore the government referred the deal to the competition authorities. As the public furore strengthened, Rebekah Wade retired and she, together with Rupert Murdoch and his son, were questioned by a Parliamentary Select Committee. Later Rebekah Wade, Andy Coulson and others were arrested and questioned by the police investigating whether crime has been committed.

Only the bare outlines of the story have been recounted above, and particular aspects of it can be drawn out to illustrate the different types of business ethics stories.

A Romance: a hero as a metaphor for ethical behaviour

A romance is a story that lauds a hero. There are those involved in the phone hacking story for whom the metaphor of hero can be used. They are, amongst others, Nick Davies a reporter on *The Guardian* newspaper and Alan Rusbridger the paper's editor. They deserve to be seen as heroes because they continued to investigate and report upon the phone hacking story despite pressure from many to drop the investigation. In particular they came under pressure from senior officers from the Metropolitan Police to change their reporting about the claim that, after the initial Goodman hacking case, the police had dropped the investigation rather than following up the evidence that they had gathered that suggested that the hacking had been more widespread. It was implied that the decision to drop the case had been made to avoid making life difficult for the *NoW*. The Commissioner, Assistant Commissioner and Director of the Metropolitan Police had meetings with Rusbridger in December 2009 and February 2010. They sought to convince the editor that the reporting of the story was 'over egged and incorrect' and that 'Nick's (Davies) doggedness and persistence in pursuing the story was displaced' (Dodd, 2011a).

After the revelations about the Dowler phone hacking *The Guardian* and Nick Davies received praise for their persistence.

A tragedy: a metonym tarnishes a hero

Associated with the romance story is a related tale that has the character of a tragedy. Sir Paul Stephenson was appointed as Commissioner of the Metropolitan Police in 2009. He was regarded as a safe pair of hands and someone who would bring stability and disinterestedness to the Metropolitan Police after the enforced resignation of the previous Commissioner. He had had an impressive career working his way up from constable to the most important job in the police service. However in July 2011 Neil Wallis, who had been a deputy editor of *NoW*, was arrested as part of the Metropolitan Police's re-opened investigations into the phone hacking case. It then emerged that after his resignation Wallis had been appointed as a part-time PR consultant to the Metropolitan Police; and that he had dined many times with senior officers from the force. This revelation identified that at the time that Stephenson and his colleagues were trying to persuade *The Guardian* to change its reporting on the *NoW* story the Metropolitan Police was employing a former *NoW* employee who had been at the paper when it was using hacking to source its scoops. It was claimed that Wallis had not been involved with the Metropolitan Police's dealings with *The Guardian* but there remained the problem that the Commissioner and his assistant had not revealed to *The Guardian,* or to the politicians responsible for the police, that the appointment had been made. The allegation was that the Metropolitan Police's relationships with the *NoW* were too close; in part perhaps because police officers were afraid they would be made the subject of critical news stories. A further revelation that the Commissioner had recuperated at a health spa, free of charge, after an operation on his leg, and that Neil Wallis was also a PR consultant for the spa added to the pressure on him to resign (Dodd, 2011b; Boffey & Townsend, 2011). On 17 July he did resign, saying that he had not acted improperly but that the media pressure was distracting him from doing his job; and that it would be better if he resigned and allow someone else to take forward the important work facing the Metropolitan Police. This work included preparing the security arrangements for the 2012 London Olympics. A successful career was tragically ended when aspects or parts of his behaviour, metonyms of his wider role, undermined his broader reputation as a policeman of integrity.

A comedy: a synecdoche points up the humour of a situation

An ethics story as comedy can be illustrated by a different aspect of the hacking scandal. The comedy arises from the contrast between those parts of a journalist's arguments that express a commitment to high-flown principles and other parts that relish the publication of seedy details about the lives of celebrities. The journalist in question is Paul McMullan who at one time was deputy features editor at the *NoW*. The celebrities are Steve Coogan, a British comedian, and Hugh Grant, a film actor. McMullan had been responsible for publishing stories about these two, most notably the story of Hugh Grant's encounter with the prostitute Divine Brown in Los Angeles in 1995, which, Grant and Coogan believed, invaded their privacy. McMullan thought it was legitimate to publish stories about the private lives of celebrities who avidly sought publicity to advance their fame and wealth, and that phone hacking was not wrong in every case. He argued that the public were not critical when it involved a 'game' between celebrities and the popular media (*Daily Telegraph*, 2011). During the *NoW* scandal Grant's car broke down and a passing driver stopped and gave him a lift. The driver was Paul McMullan. Grant said he would return and have a drink with McMullan, who by then was running a pub, to thank him. When Grant met McMullan he was wired and managed to record McMullan saying that he thought phone hacking was quite routine

▶

at the *NoW*. The story was published in *The New Statesman* and the tabloid journalist was humiliated by the same underhand techniques that he himself advocated (Greenslade, 2011). Further humiliation occurred when Steve Coogan and Paul McMullan came face to face on a BBC *Newsnight* programme, McMullan looked every inch the stereotype of a seedy hack – stubbled, necktie loosened, his shirt collar open; perhaps this late evening TV show was just the last of many interviews that day? Steve Coogan mounted a ferocious attack calling McMullan 'risible… morally bankrupt' and someone who published gossip and claimed this was necessary to defend the freedom of the press. McMullan attempted to fight back. He argued that without invasive techniques there would be no freedom of the press and corrupt politicians would remain undetected. But under pressure he expressed a further motive in a feature that is common in British culture; delight in a famous person being brought down. As he put it: 'You (Coogan) were in the Green Room talking about the number of houses you have bought this year. Oh, we all feel terribly sorry for you . . . we do these [kiss & tell] stories and five million people read the newspaper, and then when a good story comes along, when bad guys get exposed, five million people read it'. Coogan replied sarcastically 'Oh I didn't realize you were on a moral crusade. I am sorry' (Thorpe, 2011).

A satire: exploiting irony

A final aspect of the *NoW* scandal illustrates a satirical aspect of the story. As *The Sun* newspaper also belonged to News International there was speculation in the media about whether the bad habits practised by *NoW* reporters were also practised by *Sun* reporters. There was no evidence that this was the case, and on 20 July Trevor Kavanagh, the associate political editor of *The Sun* went on the Radio 4 *Today* programme to say so (BBC, 2011). He was asked whether, as associate editor, he had asked questions or made enquiries to discover if hacking was practiced at *The Sun*. He said that he had not and that no one senior in the company had asked him to do so. He explained that, as there were no accusations or information that suggested reporters were hacking, there was no need to investigate. In any case he believed that '*The Sun* did not do it' and so there was no need to investigate. He would expect to be told if it became known that someone was hacking phones. In any case, he said, his title was an honorary one and that he had no executive role in *The Sun* and did not work in the office. Therefore he could not know what was happening in the paper's newsroom. The irony, which makes the interview a self-satire, is that reporters are meant to be investigators who delve and question to discover the truth yet in this instance Kavanagh, a well-respected political reporter, saw no need to question what was happening even though problems had been identified in a sister paper.

Activity 1.1	Is it ever ethical for a newspaper to use illegal means to expose political or business wrongdoing

There are always arguments for and against, when deciding whether an action is ethical or not; unless of course you are a person whose values and standards, however eccentric they may be, cannot be challenged by evidence or argument. Can there be circumstances when it is right for the media to use information obtained illegally or dubiously? In recent times there have been many examples of issues being brought to light by information obtained in such a manner. The British MPs expenses corruption scandal, when some Members of Parliament were discovered to be claiming expenses falsely and improperly, only became known because confidential Parliamentary data had been leaked to *The Telegraph* newspaper. On a wider scale there is the example of Julian Assange and *Wikileaks*.

In what, if any circumstances would it be right for the media to use improper or illegal means to obtain information to publish a story? Identify the arguments for and against the practice.

One of the long-running business ethics stories concerns a moral decision that faces profit-seeking organisations. It is a conflict between public duty and self-interest. Should they only exercise their social and environmental duty if it coincides with the financial interests of their owners? In this case they will be heroes in the stories of the owners but villains in the tales of everyone else. Or should they prevent the organisation harming society and the environment, beyond the demands of the law if necessary, even if it will hurt the owners' immediate interests? In this case their ascription to the roles of hero and villain in the stories will be reversed.

Following the Asian tsunami in 2004 many Australian companies made donations to the appeal fund. Stephen Matthews, a spokesman for the Australian Shareholders' Association (ASA), criticised the companies, saying that they had no approval for their philanthropy. He implied that companies should not make such donations without expecting something in return.

> Boards of directors don't have a mandate from their shareholders to spend money in this way. [ ] There is a role for business to make a contribution in relation to the tsunami, particularly those businesses who have activities up in South Asia. [ ] Where their businesses are dependent on those sorts of markets there could possibly be a benefit for shareholders in them making donations to relief.
>
> (ABC News Online, 2005a)

Later the Association's chief executive tried to limit the damage of the ensuing public disdain by clarifying the statement. The ASA was not opposed to companies making donations because 'it is in everyone's interests that the affected communities and economies recover as soon as possible'. Companies should, however, disclose to the shareholders the extent of their giving (ABC News Online, 2005b). Some commentators thought, uncharitably, that the rapid donations of cash and goods to the affected regions by some large companies was an attempt to have their brands associated with humanitarian good works (Simpson, 2005).

The story illustrates the question of whether a business case should be proven for acting in a socially and environmentally responsible way before it is necessary for an organisation to adopt the role. This is dealt with in the next section.

The business case for business ethics

Should private, profit-seeking organisations behave in a socially responsible and moral way, beyond the requirement of the law, because it is the right thing to do or because it pays them to do so? This might be seen as a moral dilemma; indeed in many ways it is the central issue in business ethics. If it is true that corporations that behave in a responsible and ethical manner do in fact make better returns for their owners than do those organisations that cut corners or behave badly, then the philosophical question of whether organisations ought to behave well is redundant. Do the well-behaved hero companies actually achieve their reward and despite their tribulations win through and enter into a successful long-term relationship with their investors and reach the top of the corporate financial performance league tables, or, in folk story terms, marry the princess and ascend the throne (Czarniawska, 2004: 78)? Several people have sought to answer this question.

There are sensible arguments that can be used to suggest that corporate bad behaviour can be bad for business. It would be logical to assume that a business that was seen to behave badly would lose the esteem and respect of its customers and so lose sales and profitability. A poor image would counteract the large sums that companies spend on developing their brands. Conversely if a company is associated with good behaviour, using renewable resources, not employing child labour in its factories in developing countries, and providing good training and development opportunities for its staff, this should be good for sales.

However, these benefits of good behaviour are not guaranteed. A brand untarnished by a poor reputation is most likely to affect the buying decisions of consumers, but less likely to influence business purchasers, who will rate a good deal before a sense of social responsibility. Bad corporate behaviour will only diminish reputation, and good behaviour boost it, if it becomes known. Many companies of course have PR departments and corporate communications departments that are designed to prevent harm being done to their brands and reputation. Making bad behaviour known requires that wrongdoing is seen and made public and that there are ways of measuring good behaviour so that credit can be given to those corporations that score well on some kind of ethics scale. There are measures of social, ethical and environmental performance, but these are mostly designed to meet the needs of the ethical investment community rather than consumers and purchasers.

Measures of corporate social, ethical and environmental performance

There are a number of standard measures, or more properly indices, that are available for assessing the social and environmental performance of corporations.

1. FTSE4Good
This index is calculated from a number of fators that cover the three areas of:

- working towards environmental sustainability;
- developing positive relationships with stakeholders; and
- upholding and supporting Universal Human Rights.

The factors are sometimes but not always measurable things. Judgments about whether a company is complying with international ethical standards are also included. A panel of experts meets to decide whether companies' performance entitles them to be included in the index.

2. Dow Jones Sustainability Indices

The DJSI tracks the financial performance of companies that have committed to long-term sustainability. It is a guide for those who wish to invest in companies that are ethical or that profess a philosophy of sustainability.

3. SERM Rating Agency

SERM rates companies on a scale of AAA+ to E according to how well the companies manage their environmental and socio-ethical risks. Twenty-five dimensions are used in three fields: environment, health and safety, and socio-ethical. The last category includes items such as use of corporate power, business practices and regard for human rights.

4. Ethical Investment Research Service

EIRIS carries out research on companies worldwide and provides information for those who wish to invest ethically. It is a charity set up in 1983 by churches and charities that did not wish to invest any of their money in ethically dubious organisations.

The indices are all professionally designed and include checks and tests to ensure that the judgments they contain are valid; this, however, makes starker the fact that they are judgments rather than measures of social and environmental outcomes.

Webley and More (2003) have sought an empirical answer to the question whether business ethics pays. They faced the technical problem that there is no single and definitive measure of ethical performance. They happily admit that they have had to choose proxy or surrogate measures that are indicative of whether a company is behaving in an ethical and environmentally protective way but not conclusive proof that they are. (Commentators have taken a satirical delight in the fact that Enron was often commended for its ethics policies.) Webley and More chose the following measures:

1. Whether a company has a published code of ethics that has been revised within the past five years.

2. Companies' SERM rating.

3. Companies' ratings on *Management Today*'s 'Britain's Most Admired Companies' survey, which is carried out by Michael Brown of Nottingham Business School.

Their analysis showed that companies that had a code of ethics had better ratings on both SERM and the 'Most Admired Company' league tables than those that did not. Therefore, to keep things simple all they needed to check was whether companies with a code performed better financially than those that did not.

It might have been anticipated that when Webley and More (2003) came to consider how to measure the financial performance of companies the task would be easier, but there is a wide range of possible measures. They chose:

1. Market value added (MVA) – This is the difference between what investors have put into a company over a number of years and what they would get from it if they sold it at current prices.

2. Economic value added (EVA) – This is the amount by which investors' current income from the company is greater or less than the return they would get if they had invested the money in something else of equal risk. In other words it is the opportunity cost of placing money in a particular company.

3. Price earnings ratio (P/E ratio) – This is the market value of a share in a company divided by the shareholders' earnings.

4. Return on capital employed (ROCE) – This is a measure of the return that the capital invested in a company makes for its owners.

The results of their research into the relationship between a company's ethical standing and its financial performance is shown graphically in Figures 1.1, 1.2, 1.3 and 1.4.

Two cohorts, each a little short of 50, of large companies were chosen from the FTSE 350 for the study. The results indicate, *prima facie*, that companies within the sample that have a code of ethics (and hence score better on the SERM ratings and the 'Most Admired Company' tables than those who do not) also achieved a better MVA and EVA over the four-year period 1997–2000. Between 1997 and 2000 companies without a code had a greater ROCE than those that did, but by 2001 the position had reversed and those with a code performed better. The P/E ratio was more stable over the period of the study for companies with codes than it was for companies without. There is a strong indication that having a code, managing the non-financial risks of a company (as measured by SERM), and being rated by one's peers as a reputable company are associated with higher and more stable financial returns.

1. **Is having an ethical code consistent with the generation of more added value?**

Chart 1:   Average Economic Value Added (EVA) by year for major UK quoted companies

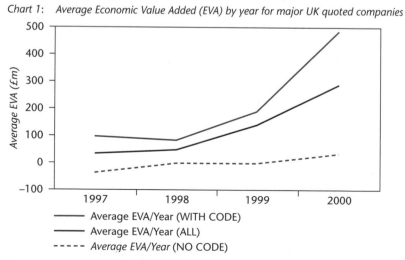

——— Average EVA/Year (WITH CODE)
——— Average EVA/Year (ALL)
- - - - - *Average EVA/Year* (NO CODE)

Figure 1.1 Does business ethics pay: does it add value?

Source: Webley and More, 2003

three-year time lag. The Institute of Business Ethics research could not be expected to identify this time lag because their key indicator, the presence or absence of a code of ethics, is not one that would fluctuate year on year, but the index that Moore used would. This direction of causation, from financial to social, is known as the Available Funding Hypothesis (Preston and O'Bannon, 1997). However, giving attention to these new social projects causes companies to take their eye off their main objective, making money. This distraction of attention, plus the fact that these projects can cost a lot of money, causes the financial performance to worsen. In response, companies return their efforts to financial performance. Commentators within the supermarket industry anticipated that as Sainsbury's and Marks and Spencer were performing less well financially, their social and environmental efforts would decrease.

These same commentators also speculated whether social and environmental performance might be related to the social class of customers (Moore and Robson, 2002: 27). Tesco and Morrisons served lower socio-economic groups (on average) who were less likely to be conscious of social and environmental concerns and so there would be no advantage to the company in taking a lead on such matters. The higher status groups who shopped in Sainsbury's and Marks and Spencer were more likely to be careful conservers of the natural and social world, and might begin to boycott the stores if they were not seen to be sufficiently interested in sustainability.

In a later study (Moore and Robson, 2002: 28–9) a more detailed statistical analysis was carried out between the 16 social performance indicators (instead of the aggregate result as in the first study) and an extended range of financial performance indicators. Negative, and statistically significant, correlations were found between growth in turnover and the league table rank of:

- the mission statements compared with those of others;

- the proportion of women managers compared with other companies;

- the environmental policy;

- the environmental management systems; and

- the social performance total.

In summary, this suggests that as companies increase their turnover their social performance worsens, or the obverse, that as their social performance improves their turnover declines. This adds support to the second part of the cycle suggested above, that social performance endangers financial performance, but does not of itself support the first part of the cycle, that companies flush with profits are inclined to spend some of the profits on social performance, even though, as we saw above, this is precisely what Sir Richard Branson says they should do. These results of course only apply to one industry – retailing and supermarkets.

There is an association between good social performance or ethical business practices and good financial returns. It is not clear, however, that it is the good social performance that increases profits. It may be the other way around. This conclusion is not necessarily dismissive of all concerns with business ethics from an organisational point of view. There may not be a financial case for actively and purposefully seeking to make a better social and environmental world. This does not mean that companies should not seek to minimise the potential costs of being found to have acted unethically or improperly. If a company or government department is sued for damages arising from its negligence or its bad behaviour, the costs of the case and the costs of the award can be very high. It may be wise to seek to avoid those actions and practices that could cost dearly; this management function is known as risk management. If a company can be shown through its risk management procedures to have taken every reasonable precaution to identify a potential malpractice or problem and to do what is reasonable to prevent it, then, even if the problem or malpractice happens and damages others, the company will have a legal defence.

So, unfortunately (although fortunately for textbook writers for if otherwise we would have to close the book at this point), it is not clear that there is a business case for business ethics, although on the defensive principle there is one for managing the financial risk of unethical or improper organisational behaviour. It is necessary to turn to other ways of deciding whether companies and organisations should act ethically and responsibly. This comes down to the question of whose interests companies and organisations should exist to serve. Should they serve the interests of society generally? Or should they serve the interest of particular groups within society? If so, which groups should they serve? It is the answer to these questions we now turn to.

Stakeholder theory

Cross reference	Stakeholder theory is a key and recurring theme in this book because ethics is concerned with the harm or good done to people. As different people may be affected differently by the same action then it is important to take these various impacts, some good and some bad, into account. The simplest way of doing this is to use stakeholder theory. The theory will be used and discussed in Chapters 9, and 11.

If we continue with the storytelling metaphor it is important to know who the characters in the story are. In terms of business ethics stakeholder theory provides an answer. It might be more accurate to say stakeholder theories, since there are various interpretations of what the term means. They share one attribute, however, which is that for any organisation there are a number of definable groups that have an interest, or a stake, in the actions of that organisation. There is more disagreement about what constitutes a stake. It is clear that the shareholders, the owners if it has any, have a legitimate stake in an organisation. So do its employees. At the other extreme the 'phishers', who fraudulently try to gain customers' bank account details through fake, spammed e-mails, obviously have an interest in the banks they attack; but it is hardly a legitimate one. So the issue is threefold:

- What responsibilities or duties, if any, does an organisation owe to its stakeholders? The fact that a stakeholder group may have a legitimate interest does not, of itself, mean that the organisation owes anything to it. At one extreme of the spectrum of possibilities an organisation may be obliged to do what its stakeholder group requires. If that group is society at large, as it expresses its will through legislation, then the organisation should submit to it. At a level below this, stakeholders could have the right to participate in the organisation's decision making. This might be accepted in the case of employees who are expected to commit to the organisation's objectives and decisions. It might not be right in the case of a judicial system's obligations to those being tried in a court. A lesser obligation might be a stakeholder group's right to be consulted before major decisions are taken. If not this, then at least the group might expect the organisation to give it an account of why it did what it did. At the other extreme, the organisation might owe the stakeholder group nothing.

- How should an organisation decide between its obligations to two or more stakeholders if they demand incompatible things from an organisation? What criteria should the organisation use when deciding which stakeholder group's wishes it should prioritise? Often in public service organisations the criterion used is a crude one – the group that shouts loudest is the one listened to. There is an interesting issue involved here. What if a constituency is not a person or persons but a thing or collection of things or ideas (these are known in sociological jargon as actants) such as rivers, nature reserves, spirituality? How can these things be given a voice? An easy answer might be that their voices are those of the lobby groups that support each particular cause. There is a problem here though. Some research indicates that, when lobby groups cause too much irritation to the organisation they are trying to influence, their reward is not to be listened to but to be shut out. If the cause of environmentalism is voiced by over-aggressive agitation then an organisation might close its ears to the problem when the cause itself is more deserving than its supporters' actions.

- What legitimate interests justify a group of people being regarded as a stakeholder in an organisation? A criterion often proposed is that stakeholders are any group that is affected by an organisation's actions. But this would give a commercial company's competitors a voice in its activities because their performance would be affected by the organisation's performance, which would not seem fair.

So far the discussion has focused on fair and open debate of ethical matters. But the question of who should have a voice in the debate is also an important ethical matter. This question can best be considered by looking at the application of stakeholder theory to ethical matters. This theory proposes that, for every organisation, stakeholder groups can be identified:

- who are affected by,

- who can affect, or

- whose welfare is tied into the actions of a corporation. It may be necessary to add a criterion of legitimacy to the identification of stakeholders. As Whysall (2000) pointed out, a shoplifter's welfare may be affected by a retailer's actions but that does not make them a legitimate stakeholder.

Donaldson and Preston (1995) presented four perspectives on the roles of stakeholder management.

- *Descriptive* – that the stakeholder theory describes what corporations are, i.e. constellations of interconnected interest groups.

- *Instrumental* – that if corporations adopt stakeholder management they will, all other things being equal, be more successful than those organisations that do not.

- *Managerial* – that the theory enables managers to identify options and solutions to problems.

But underpinning each of these roles was the fourth *normative* one: stakeholder theory can be used to develop moral or philosophical guidelines for the operations of corporations. In particular it forces corporations to make a broad ethical appreciation of their actions that considers their impact on communities as well as on the profit and loss account. Whysall used the case of companies that retail goods, at premium prices to affluent consumers, which were manufactured in sweatshop conditions in Third-World countries. A traditional management approach would only consider the benefits of the business model to the corporation and its customers. A stakeholder approach would also involve consideration of the impact upon the workforces, the communities and governments of the countries involved as well as activists and lobbyists.

The subject matter of business ethics is an attempt to answer these three questions. In the next section we consider four different answers, or perspectives, that are given in modern western, capitalist societies.

Business and organisational ethics

In this section four broad theories of the firm, and the assumptions and implications of these perspectives for prioritising the various stakeholders' needs and for the exercise of moral agency, are considered.

> **Moral agency** within organisations is the ability of individuals **DEFINITION** to exercise moral judgment *and behaviour* in an autonomous fashion, unfettered by fear for their employment and/or promotional prospects.

Organisation, in the sense we are using the term here, refers to any configuration of people and other resources that has been created to coordinate a series of work activities, with a view to achieving stated outcomes or objectives. At this stage we make no distinction as to whether an organisation is profit seeking, located within the public sector or is a charitable/voluntary organisation. The issues we discuss are largely, but not exclusively, sector-blind, although the intensity with which the issues are experienced may vary significantly between organisational types.

As will become evident as we progress through the chapters, the location of an organisation within the public sector does not make it immune from economic constraints, even economic objectives. Likewise, there is a growing body of opinion that argues forcibly that profit-seeking organisations should be more accountable to a body of citizens that extends considerably beyond shareholder-defined boundaries. While the distinctions between private sector and public sector, profit seeking and non-profit seeking, have become less clear-cut in recent years, we do not argue that all organisations are equivalent, and that the sector of the economy in which an organisation is located is irrelevant to understanding the ethical, political, economic and social constraints within which it operates. Penalties or sanctions for poor performance are possibly more obvious and severe in the profit-seeking sectors, but it can be argued that the multiplicity and complexity of the objectives managers are required to achieve in certain parts of the public sector make managing in such a context a far more demanding and ethically fraught role. Although each perspective assumes that organisational relationships are largely, if not exclusively, mediated by market dynamics, the extent to which 'the market' is relied upon as an exclusive mediating mechanism does vary.

Table 1.1 presents the schema of four perspectives to highlight the point that different imperatives and assumptions may underpin market-based, capitalist economies.

Within the four categories in Table 1.1 different assumptions are made about the relationships between:

- organisations and the state;

- organisations and their employees;

- organisations and their various stakeholder groups (i.e. beyond the employee group).

We need to understand these perspectives because they are helpful in appreciating the potential for, and the constraints we each face in exercising, moral agency within business contexts.

With the exception of the 'classical-liberal' category, each of the categories is an amalgam of a variety of theories, ideas and practices. The corporatist approach is referred to by Crouch and Marquand (1993) as 'Rhenish'. This latter term refers to a particular (German) approach to a market-based, capitalist-oriented economy, although the writers broaden their consideration beyond Germany to take in a wider group of non-Anglo-American market-based economies. Whilst the German approach displays important differences from the Japanese and the Swedish approaches, they have, for our purposes, been grouped together as representing a more corporatist approach, where the overt involvement of the state and employees in the running of individual organisations is an accepted practice.

This is not to say that the Anglo-American approach to economic development can be simply categorised within the 'classical-liberal-economic' group. Notwithstanding the rhetoric of various UK and US governments, state involvement has been required and forthcoming on many occasions in these two countries, often to overcome what is known as market failure. However, the common belief in the UK and USA leans towards the need for less, or minimal, government interference in business, and a drive towards market dynamics to facilitate organisational coordination.

Table 1.1   Theories of the firm and their ethical implications

Issue	Classical liberal economic	Pluralist (A and B)	Corporatist	Critical
Status of the category	1. For its advocates it is the only game in town, not merely the most efficient, but the most ethically justifiable	1. Type A. A stakeholder perspective is advocated in corporate decision making, with key interest groups physically represented on decision-making boards	Refers to the business relationships in countries such as Germany, Sweden and Japan (although the approaches adopted are not identical). The interests of employee groups, non-equity finance, and sometimes the state, are represented alongside the interests of equity shareholders, on senior decision-making boards	Ranging from descriptive theories category of the firm that portray how organisations appear to be (or are), rather than how they should be, to critical theorists who portray an organisational world beholden to the demands of capitalism or managerialism (these terms are not the same). Both approaches reflect messier and more ethically fraught worlds than tend to be suggested in the other three categories
	2. For others the 'pure' model must be tempered by interventions to (a) minimise problems of short-termism, or (b) correct power imbalances	2. Type B. Individual managers weigh the full ethical and social considerations of their actions and decisions. Stakeholder groups would not necessarily be present at decisions		
	3. Whilst for others the neo-classical model is a corrupting chimera that acts as a cover to camouflage the interests of the powerful			

Number of objectives recognised	One – meeting the demands of equity shareholders	Multiple – reflecting an array of stakeholder perspectives, although the actual mechanics remain problematic	A mix of equity shareholder, employee and non-equity finance perspectives, although the long-term economic interests of the firm are dominant	Multiple – reflected by the various coalitions and power groups within an organisation, particularly economic interests
Status of financial targets	Regarded as the organisation's primary or sole objective, because they will reflect the efficiency with which resources are being employed	Important, but do not dominate all other considerations. Ethical as well as multiple stakeholder perspectives are weighed in decision making	Important, but greater attention paid to longer-term implications of decisions than appears to be the general case in Anglo-American corporations	In highly competitive markets, or during periods of crisis, likely to be the dominant, although not the exclusive, organisational consideration. During periods of relative stability, other considerations will gain in significance and could dominate
Significance of ethical behaviour (both individual and corporate)	Defined by national and international laws, which are seen as both the minimum and maximum of required ethicality. The neo-classical model is argued to be the only approach that allows the primacy of individual interests to be reflected in economic and social coordination	At the heart of the debate for those who bemoan what is seen as the exclusive, or overly dominant, economic orientation of organisations	No clear evidence that ethical considerations feature more strongly in corporate decision making, although the lack of an exclusive shareholder perspective might offer greater potential for a broader societal perspective	An important, but variable, element in defining the reputation of the organisation. Will be shaped by the power of influential individuals and groups within and external to the organisation
Role of managers	Portrayed as functionalist, technicist and value neutral	Type A. Managers come into direct contact with specific sectional interest groups, which should affect decision making. Type B. Individual managers are required to have internalised a societal ethic into their decision making	The structures of organisations reflect a formal involvement of employee representatives, non-equity financiers and sometimes state representatives, alongside shareholder interests, on corporate decision-making boards	Complex, with competing and sometimes/often mutually exclusive interests and demands being required to be satisfied, including the managers' own agendas

Table 1.1 Continued

Issue	Classical liberal economic	Pluralist (A and B)	Corporatist	Critical
Status of employees	Resources to be used by the organisation in its quest to satisfy shareholder interests	Employees represent an important interest/stake-holder group within the organisation, although economic considerations are not ignored	Employee representation is guaranteed on some of the organisation's senior decision-making boards, e.g. supervisory boards in Germany	Operating within a capitalist mode of production, employee interests will vary between organisations, depending upon the power of individuals and groups of individuals
Values	Competition seen as the bulwark against power imbalances. Efficient re-source allocation facilitated by profit-maximising behaviour	Inherently societal in orientation, but the views of those actually making decisions will be important	Those of the shareholders, employees, non-equity financiers (possibly the state) are likely to dominate	A complex interaction of mul-tiple individual and corporate values. Critical theorists would single out the values that underpin capitalism
The possibilities for moral agency in organisations	The individual as consumer, as chooser, is the personi-fication of moral agency, but the individual as moral agent when selling his or her labour is troublesome. The atomisation of society, which appears to be an inevitability of this form of individualism, is seen by many as leading to feelings of alienation and anomie	Type A. Multiple perspec-tives offer heightened possibilities, but medium to long-term organisation-al survival will dominate concerns. Type B. Very similar to Type A, but the confidence and integrity of individual managers becomes a critical issue	With employee represen-tatives on the supervisory boards of organisations (as in Germany), the possibilities again appear stronger than with the liberal-economic perspec-tive. However, economic considerations will remain dominant	Empirical evidence indicates that the suppression of moral agency might be more than minor and isolated aberra-tions in an otherwise satisfac-tory state of organisational affairs. Critical theorists would see these problems as an inevitable consequence of the demands of capitalism

The following is a closer examination of the four theories of the firm and their implications for moral behaviour within, and of, organisations.

The classical-liberal-economic approach

A classical-liberal theory of the firm places the organisation within an economic system that is made up of a myriad interconnecting but legally separate parts, and where relationships between these many parts are defined in terms of free exchange. Money acts as the facilitator of exchange, thus performing the role of the oil that greases the economic system's wheels. The 'invisible hand' that Adam Smith spoke of is the force that drives the mass of individual transactions. The argument is that, with no individual person or company able to affect price, the resulting transactions, and the prices that draw both suppliers and customers into the marketplace, reflect people's wishes. This is the strength of the claims for the ethicality of 'free' markets as espoused by writers such as Milton Friedman, Friedrick von Hayek and Ayn Rand. Individual choice, free of government coercion, is seen as the only ethical influence in shaping economic and social development.

Rand is probably the least well known of the three advocates of free markets mentioned above, although her advocacy appears to have been influential. She is reputed to be a favourite writer (she wrote novels rather than philosophical monographs) of Alan Greenspan, the Chairman of the American Federal Reserve from 1987 to 2006. Friedman's arguments in defence of a business world free of government or social obligations beyond those defined in law are considered in more depth in Chapter 8, so a little more time will be given here to consider some of the key thoughts of Rand on the subject of markets as the basis of economic and social coordination.

Ayn Rand was born in Russia in 1905, but she emigrated to America when she was 21, nine years after the 1917 Bolshevik uprising in Russia and four years after the civil war that followed the uprising. On arriving in America, Rand took a variety of low-paid, menial jobs. She is quoted as saying: 'I had a difficult struggle, earning my living at odd jobs, until I could make a financial success of my writing. No one helped me, nor did I think at any time that it was anyone's duty to help me'. Such snippets of historical and biographical features are helpful in understanding some of the factors that might explain an individual's philosophical position on key issues. Rand depicted man as 'a heroic being, with his own happiness as the moral purpose of his life, with productive achievement as his noblest activity, and reason as his only attribute'. Two of her novels have been recently republished (Rand, 2007a, 2007b). *The Fountainhead* first published in 1943 tells the story of Howard Roark, a ground-breaking, genius architect who has a clear vision of how buildings should be. He refuses to dilute the purity of his vision to suit the demands of clients and so business is bad and he becomes a manual labourer. But no matter, his integrity is preserved. He has many further setbacks. One of his buildings is built in ways that deviate from his design and so he blows it up. At his trial he expounds Rand's theories and is acquitted. As a recent reviewer (Crees, 2007) pointed out:

Rand's characters make stands, but they rarely question themselves, and introspection is almost regarded as a form of serious thought-crime.

Her novel *Atlas Unshrugged* is was made into a film in 2011 but stars, such as Angelina Jolie, who were slated to be in it, were not.

Randianism (the term used by followers of Rand) rejects government in anything other than its minimalist form, i.e. that which can be justified to protect individual rights, such as the police, the law courts and national defence forces. All other functions can and should be operated by 'the people', preferably via market mediation, and paid for (or not) by choice.

Rand is credited with developing the philosophical position that is known as objectivism. Objectivism has three key elements:

Case study 1.2	**Biography and philosophy**

Bauman (1994) contrasts two philosophers, Knud Logstrup and Leon Shestov. Logstrup lived a tranquil and civilised life in Copenhagen. He wrote of human nature, 'It is characteristic of human life that we mutually trust each other . . . . Only because of some special circumstance do we ever distrust a stranger in advance . . . initially we believe one another's word; initially we trust one another' (Bauman, 1994: 1). Shestov, on the other hand, experienced great persecution during his life, under both the tsarist and anti-tsarist regimes and as a consequence had a far more pessimistic view of human nature, portraying the individual as one who is vulnerable and must at all times be ready to be betrayed. 'In each of our neighbours we fear a wolf . . . we are so poor, so weak, so easily ruined and destroyed! How can we help being afraid?' (Bauman, 1994: 2).

1. *'Reason* is man's [*sic*] only means of knowledge', i.e. the facts of reality are only knowable through a process of objective reason that begins with sensory perception and follows the laws of logic. Objectivism rejects the existence of a God, because it lacks (to date) empirical support. However, in America, some of the most strident advocates of free markets come from politically powerful religious groups.

2. *Rational self-interest* is the objective moral code. Objectivism rejects altruism (i.e. the greatest good is service to others) as an unhelpful and illogical human attribute. Individuals are required to pursue their own happiness, so long as it does not negatively affect anyone else's. This is compatible with negative freedom, one of Isaiah Berlin's two forms of freedom. It relates to a 'freedom from' approach that grants people a right to be free from interference by others, including, and in particular, government.

3. *Laissez-faire capitalism* is the objective social system. It is important to recognise that laissez-faire capitalism is referred to by its advocates as a social system, and not just an economic system. This is an important issue and one towards which critics of the approach feel unified in their opposition, although such opponents have differing views on how to respond. Some would argue for an overthrow of the capitalist ethic and practice, whilst others would retain a market-based framework, but define boundaries of relevance and ethical justification for markets. The latter is exemplified by writers such as Walzer (1983) and is discussed below.

> **Laissez-faire** means unrestricted. So laissez-faire capitalism refers to a preparedness to let markets 'sort themselves out', even during periods of disequilibrium and apparent malfunctioning. The belief is that a 'market' will self-correct in time (a natural law, or Darwinist view within economics). Self-correction rather than external intervention is deemed infinitely preferable in the long run for all concerned.
>
> **DEFINITION**

The attachment of modern-day libertarian-economists to a myopic focus upon competition can be criticised for ignoring two other significant elements of economic systems, which are:

- *Command* (the extent to which power, coercion and hierarchy affect economic relationships), and
- *Change* (the way that capitalism effects change and is itself affected by change).

These three central elements of capitalism – competition, command and change – have ethical and moral implications and it is argued here that they are interconnected, not subject to easy and simplistic separation. However, the classical-liberal perspective eschews these arguments and presents a schema in which the operations of the firm, both those within the firm and how it interacts with its external environment, are treated as if they are value neutral.

Within the simple competitive model of economic behaviour managers are expected to behave in ways that reflect what is known as economic rationality. This normative theory is open to challenge in terms of its descriptive rigour, hence the existence of alternative theories of the firm. Supporters of the neo-classical-economic perspective would accept that actual practice is likely to be variable around the preferred norm, but it is argued that economic rationality is the goal towards which organisations should strive. They argue that those organisations that get closest to the normative position will prosper, with competitors having to respond in a similar fashion, or wither on the economic vine.

The corporatist approach

The corporatist approach does not deny the primacy of competitive market forces, but an exclusive equity shareholder perspective is eschewed in favour of a broader-based set of perspectives in some of the organisation's decision making. These additional perspectives are those of employee representatives, debt financiers, and in some cases state interests. This broadening of the decision-making base is claimed, and appears to offer, a longer-term view to certain aspects of corporate decision making. For Crouch and Marquand (1993: 3):

> The system as a whole trades-off losses in the short-term efficiency on which the Anglo-American tradition focuses against gains in consensual adaptation and social peace. It owes its extraordinary success to its capacity to make that trade-off … In a high skilled – or would be high skilled – economy, consensual

adaptation and social peace are public goods, for which it is worth paying a price in strict allocative efficiency.

The sphere of inclusion reflected in this approach goes beyond the exclusivity of the shareholder orientation of the classical-liberal perspective espoused by most Anglo-American corporations. Evidence suggests that the corporatist-type approach has avoided, or minimised, many of the worst effects of short-term economic 'adjustments' in world trade that have been experienced since about 1960. This is not to say that countries such as Germany, Sweden and Japan (examples of the corporatist perspective) can be immune from significant movements in world economic activity, but it is argued that significant economic lurches have been avoided in these countries, thus minimising significant rises in unemployment levels, with the attendant impacts upon social cohesion. The significant economic downturns experienced by a number of Asian economies in the late 1990s, including Japan, were associated more with structural factors within these economies than with inherent weaknesses in Japan's more corporatist approach to market coordination.

Whether the corporatist approach is preferred by some because it offers a greater likelihood of economic, and thus political, stability, with the greater apparent value placed upon the interests of individual citizens/employees merely an ancillary benefit, or whether the rationale for employing this approach is reversed (i.e. the ethics of the corporatist approach are argued to be the main reasons for its adoption), is not critical for our discussion. What is relevant is that both the 'classical-liberal-economic' and the 'corporatist' approaches can cite ethical justifications for their superiority as economic and social systems. The former can do so because of the primacy attaching to the notion of individual choice, the latter because of its attachment to social cohesion and the desire to avoid, or minimise, what might be deemed unnecessary social disruption and distress to individual lives during periods of economic correction or recession.

The pluralist perspectives

There are two main pluralist perspectives. The first (referred to as Type A pluralism) sees broad stakeholder interests being represented (as far as this is possible) by elected or appointed members of corporate boards. This is a development of the corporatist perspective, but with the stakeholder groups being drawn more widely. The corporatist approach is evident in the countries cited above on a reasonable scale, whereas the two pluralist perspectives currently exist as arguments and debates, rather than as practice. Companies such as The Body Shop are very much the exceptions that prove the rule.

In Type A pluralism stakeholder groups are required to do more than argue their particular, vested-interest, case. They are expected to be representative of societal interests. Clearly the extent to which the latter are adequately represented will depend upon the composition of the stakeholder groups. Thus, as compared with the classical-libertarian-economic perspective, where the unconscious forces of individual decisions are deemed to give expression to society's preferences, within

Type A pluralism societal preferences are given voice by the presence (or not) of stakeholder groups on company boards or committees.

The second pluralist perspective (referred to as Type B pluralism) does not dispute the possibility of stakeholder groups being physically represented within corporate decision-making processes, but this is neither a prerequisite, nor part of the basic arguments. This second variant of pluralism sees economic rationality being moderated by concerns for, and recognition of, wider social implications of corporate decisions, with these factors being weighed by individual decision makers. Type B perspectives can be presented as a continuum, with writers such as Casson (1991) at one pole, and Maclagan (1998), Maclagan and Snell (1992) and Snell (1993) at the other.

The perspective argued by writers such as Casson is that competition via market-based economies is the preferred economic system, but that reliance upon unadulterated economic rationality as the sole explanation of individual behaviour is both naïve and unhelpful. For the discipline of economics to retain relevance Casson argued that it must recognise behaviours that are explained by drives other than, or in addition to, economic rationality.

> These professional prejudices must be overcome if economics is to handle cultural factors successfully. They are the main reasons why, in spite of its technical advantages ... economics has not contributed more to the analysis of social issues.
>
> (Casson, 1991: 21–2)

Classical-libertarian economics retains a view of human behaviour that sociologists would describe as 'under-socialised' (i.e. unrepresentative of the complexity and variability of actual human behaviour). Type B pluralism argues for a recognition of the realities of everyday market conditions, but also a more socialised set of assumptions of human behaviour. Whilst a market-based economy is seen as the foundation upon which organisational coordination takes place, structural issues and problems within markets are recognised, e.g. power imbalances between competitors; information asymmetry between producers and customers; and the capricious nature of (the owners of) capital. Greater responsibility, ethicality and humanity are required of corporate decision makers.

In a similar vein, but with less of Casson's implicit instrumentalism, Etzioni (1988) employed a moral justification for an overt recognition of broader perspectives beyond short-term profit motives. In the following quotation Etzioni used the term 'deontological'. This is an important word in any consideration of business ethics and it is considered in more depth in Chapter 3. However, we offer a brief definition of the term here to allow you to understand the argument that Etzioni was making.

A **deontological** approach to moral behaviour is one that believes **DEFINITION** that moral reasoning and action should be guided by universal principles that hold irrespective of the context in which an ethical dilemma might exist.

Instead of assuming that the economy is basically competitive, and hence that economic actors (mainly firms) are basically subject to 'the market' possessing no power over it (monopolies are regarded as exceptions and aberrations), the deontological 'I & We' paradigm evolved here assumes that power differences among the actors are congenital, are built into the structure, and deeply affect their relationships. We shall see that power differentials are gained both by applying economic power (the power that some actors have over others, directly, within the economy) and by exercising political power (the power that some actors have over others, indirectly, by guiding the government to intervene on their behalf within the economy). These fundamentally different assumptions make up what is referred to here as the I & We paradigm (one of the larger possible set of deontological paradigms). The term [I & We] highlights the assumption that individuals act within a social context, that this context is not reducible to individual acts, and most significantly, that the social context is not necessarily wholly imposed. Instead the social context is, to a significant extent, perceived as a legitimate and integral part of one's existence, a whole of which the individuals are constituent elements … The deontological paradigm evolved here assumes that people have at least some significant involvement in the community (neo-classicists would say 'surrender of sovereignty'), a sense of shared identity, and commitment to values, a sense that 'We are members of one another'.

(Etzioni, 1988: 5)

Etzioni continued:

The issues explored here range way beyond the technical, conceptual matters of what constitutes a workable theory of decision-making in economic and other matters. At issue is human nature: How wise are we, and what is the role of morality, emotions and social bonds in our personal and collective behaviour.

(Etzioni, 1988: xii)

Progressing along the continuum, past Etzioni's position, one moves towards those who argue for Type B pluralism on the grounds that a broader ethic than that required by classical-liberal economics is desirable, even essential, on the grounds that society as a whole needs organisational decision makers who understand and can exercise moral judgment in complex situations (Maclagan, 1996, 1998; and Snell, 1993). These writers see management practice as essentially a moral practice, set in a complex and challenging arena (business organisations), for individual moral development.

Thus, our pluralist continuum moves from writers, such as Casson, who argued for theories of decision making to recognise actual human behaviour and instincts in order to make economic theorising more relevant and realistic, to the arguments of writers such Maclagan and Snell, who justify the inclusion of the moral dimensions within business decision making on the grounds of the ethical demands of society as a whole.

The critical perspective

The critical perspective is composed of many different theories about human and collective behaviour, including the politics of organisations (Simon, 1952, 1953 and 1955); expectation theory (Vroom, 1964); the use of ambiguity and hypocrisy as managerial tools (Brunsson, 1986 and 1989); the theory of coalitions (Cyert and March, 1992); the exploitation of people (Marcuse, 1991); the benefits that people seek at work and the importance of these benefits (Maslow, 1987); power and identity in organisations (Knights and Willmott, 1999); and the range of strategic resources that individual managers draw upon to allow them to cope with managerial life (Watson, 1994). This is far from an exhaustive list, but it gives a flavour of the range of research and theories that have been developed to explain actual behaviour within organisations. What these works share is a picture of organisational life that is far more complex and messy than classical-liberal economics would prefer to work with. The behavioural and critical theories are not normative theories (i.e. theories of how things should be, such as the classical-libertarian-economics perspective), but what are referred to as descriptive theories, i.e. theories of how things actually appear to be. However, behavioural theorists and critical theorists do vary in terms of the intentions of their respective arguments.

Behavioural theories are amoral in their stance in that, unlike the liberal-economic, corporatist and pluralist perspectives, they do not put forward a preferred ethical foundation for their theorising. They might, however, highlight examples of laudable, contentious or downright immoral behaviour. They do so by acting as organisational windows through which we can observe the ways in which employees at all levels in organisations appear to react, and behave, when faced with ethically complex situations. For example, you become aware that a friend and work colleague, who you know has a very difficult financial situation at home, unlawfully takes a small toy (a company product) home to one of their children. Such situations could involve divided loyalties between either colleagues or concepts, where the ethics of a situation are not clear-cut or neat; or where moral agency is compromised by power imbalances that jeopardise future employment and promotional prospects.

Critical theorists, however, have an avowed commitment to societal change, for the emancipation of employees from the shackles of capitalism. However, critical theorists make different analyses (for example, Foucaudian perspectives, e.g. McKinley and Starkey, 1998, and neo-Marxist perspectives, e.g. Alvesson and Willmott, 1996) and there is no consensus on the preferred replacement for market-based societies. Habermas (whose ideas are discussed in Chapter 3) does, however, outline the necessary conditions for a societally acceptable economic set of relationships to develop.

Boundaries of jurisdiction or spheres of justice

The fear of market-based relationships as the bedrock upon which all societal and interpersonal relationships are based is articulated by a number of writers. Walzer (1983), for example, wrote:

> One can conceive of the market as a sphere without boundaries, an unzoned city – for money is insidious, and market relations are expansive. A radically laissez-faire economy would be like a totalitarian state, invading every other

sphere, dominating every other distributive process. It would transform every social good into a commodity. This is market imperialism.

(Walzer, 1983: 119–20)

Taking his cue from Walzer, Keats (1993) argued that:

> It is as if their [liberal economists'] theoretical energy has been so fully utilised in demonstrating the virtues of the market that little has been left to deal with the arguably prior question of what it is that defines the nature – and hence limits – of that 'economic' domain with respect to which market and state are seen as the chief rival contenders.

(Keats, 1993: 7)

As a way of handling this problem Walzer argued that societal life should be seen as a series of spheres, which contain and constrain differing elements of societal existence. One of these spheres is the economic, in which markets are recognised as the most effective mediating mechanism, and competition the most defensible form of organisational coordination. Whilst markets, contract and competition are seen as appropriate mediating elements, their relevance is largely constrained within this sphere. Within the spheres representing non-economic interpersonal relationships we find notions of trust, care, welfare, sharing, friendship, leisure and possibly even altruism (although this is not highlighted by Walzer). There is some similarity between Walzer and the earlier work of the German philosopher Hegel (1770–1831) who also used the notion of spheres to conceptualise the social world (Singer, 1983). Hegel spoke of the spheres of state, family and civil society, and to these Walzer adds the economic as worthy of consideration.

McMylor comments upon the development of market-based capitalism from feudal societies. He presented the development from non-market societies as a process whereby the economic moved from being enmeshed 'within other domi-nating frameworks' to a situation in market societies when:

> the economy, with a capital 'E' is no longer so embedded. The market means that there is in some sense, a differentiation of economic activity into a sepa-rate institutional sphere, no longer regulated by norms that have their origin elsewhere. The individual economic agent is free then to pursue economic self-interest, without 'non-economic' hindrance.

(McMylor, 1994: 100)

From a moral perspective one of the problems with dividing the human world into separate spheres is that it might suggest the spheres are independent to the point of allowing differing forms of behaviour to prevail within each. Behaviour might be accepted, or at least tolerated, in one sphere that would not be acceptable in anoth-er. It has been argued that this is a recognition that people sometimes act (or feel they need to act), when in 'business mode', in ways that they would not employ within their private, domestic lives. Walzer recognised this and argued that the spheres should not be seen as totally autonomous and independent. Rather, he por-trayed a dynamic set of relationships between the spheres in which shifts between spheres of particular facets of societal life do happen, and that a sphere's scope and importance may wax and wane. Boundary conflict thus becomes endemic:

> The principles appropriate to the different spheres are not harmonious with one another, nor are the patterns of conduct and feeling they generate. Welfare systems and markets, offices and families, schools and states are run on different principles: so they should be.

> (Walzer, 1983: 318)

However, Walzer went on to say that 'the principles must fit within a single culture' (1983: 318). This is highly problematic, unless the single culture is one that recognises difference, a multiplicity of cultures. Within such a complexity of perspectives, the notion of wisdom becomes an important mediating factor, but this has to be an active wisdom, i.e. it is always in a state of emerging through dialogue and debate. Within this perspective the dynamic of change is recognised, is debated and matures through processes that are demanding but which, it must be stressed, are subject to 'social capture' by active groups and voices if participation is shirked by the general polity.

Social capture is a term used to describe a mechanism, e.g. a **DEFINITION** committee, a regulatory body or a political process, which is established to oversee a particular facet of social life, but which becomes dominated by, or heavily influenced by, the very sectional interests the mechanism was intended to monitor or control. The original intentions behind the creation of the mechanism thus become at best neutralised, and at worst subverted.

To minimise the risk of social capture and other such distorting influences within political, economic and social systems requires an active citizenry, prepared to be interested in, even involved in, micro- and macro-level debates about equity and justice – the very morality of life's various spheres. Hegel spoke of the dialectic, the processes of debate and argument that are required to surface and (possibly) resolve differences of view and contradictions. The dialectical approach is to be found in the teachings of Socrates, certainly in the way that Plato presents the work of his master. Billig (1996) makes a plea for a resurgence of the practice of rhetoric, not in the pejorative sense in which the term tends to be viewed in contemporary society, but as a return to an engagement in debate and argument, for these are the mechanisms and processes by which civilised societies develop and progress.

Podcast 1.1

The limits of the economic sphere – Post Offices and the McCann story

Podcasts explaining how today's business news relates to the topics discussed here will be updated in an ongoing process. Podcast 1.1 refers to two current issues to illustrate the drawing of boundaries between different moral domains or spheres. To listen to this podcast, other archived podcasts or recent additions, please visit the companion website at www.pearsoned.co.uk/fisherlovellvalerosilva.

Defining the boundaries of the economic sphere

One of the principal virtues of competitive markets, as the mechanisms by which business and social interaction is mediated, is that the 'invisible hand' of the market is amoral, i.e. value neutral. Although some may suffer as a result of market-based outcomes, through unemployment or loss of capital, the outcomes are not intended from the start. They are simply the unintended consequences of the multitude of transactions that comprise a free market. Sir Keith Joseph, a notable politician of the 1970s and 1980s and an architect of the political period and philosophy referred to as Thatcherism, was a devotee of Hayek and Friedman. As Heelas and Morris (1992: 19) observed:

> Policies designed to effect more equal distribution of resources, Joseph claims, are not only coercive and threaten individual liberty but are counter-productive and give rise to a series of negative consequences (economic, psychological, moral and political). . . . Liberty is primarily to be exercised by the self-interested consumer in the market place, including the political, educational and medical 'markets'.

Plant (1992), taking up the theme of markets being the most appropriate mediating mechanism for medical services, explored the possibilities for a free market in body parts (human organs), as well as the justification for a market-based ethos replacing a service ethic in non-voluntary, public service organisations. With regard to a market for human body parts Plant (1992: 91) observed:

> On a strictly capitalist view of market principles, it is very difficult to see why there should not be such a market. The scope for a market is clearly quite wide. There could be a market in blood and blood products; in kidneys; in sperm; in renting out a uterus for surrogate pregnancy; and so forth.

Plant argued that, from a market perspective, at least three principles would favour a market in these areas:

1. There is a clear demand.

2. The current donor system is failing to meet demand.

3. Ownership of the human organs is clear and would not be undertaken by the donor if it were not in their personal interest.

Despite strong advocacy for such markets, broad public support was (and appears to continue to be) lacking. Plant argued that this reluctance reflected a boundary being drawn by society, with human organs currently residing outside the boundary that defines the limits of market application.

Titmuss (1970), in a seminal work on the marketisation/commercialisation of blood donor services, observed, when responding to arguments that blood should be seen as a commodity and thus private blood banks should be introduced to improve the productivity of the blood giving process:

In essence, these writers, are making an economic case against a monopoly of altruism in blood and other human tissues. They wish to set people free from the conscience of obligation. Although their arguments are couched in the language of price elasticity and profit maximisation they have far-reaching implications for human values and all 'social service' institutions . . . . The moral issues that are raised extend beyond theories of pricing and the operations of the marketplace.

(Titmuss, 1970: 159)

Titmuss worried about the wider implications of commercialising the blood donor service in the UK. If the altruism that, it is argued, is reflected in the voluntary and unpaid giving of blood is replaced by a commercial relationship, what, asked Titmuss, fills the space that used to be occupied by the sense of community inherent within the existing system?

There is nothing permanent about the expression of reciprocity. If the bonds of community giving are broken the result is not a state of value neutralism. The vacuum is likely to be filled by hostility and social conflict, a consequence discussed in another context . . . the myth of maximising growth can supplant the growth of social relations.

(Titmuss, 1970: 199)

Titmuss discussed four economic and financial criteria, excluding the much wider and unquantifiable social, ethical and philosophical aspects to concentrate upon those aspects that economists (the focus of his criticism) would recognise. These were:

1. Economic efficiency.

2. Administrative efficiency.

3. Price – the cost per unit to the patient.

4. Purity, potency and safety – or quality per unit.

On all four criteria the commercialised blood market fails. However, paradoxically ... the more commercialised a blood distribution system becomes (and hence more wasteful, inefficient and dangerous) the more will the GNP be inflated. In part, ... this is the consequence of statistically 'transferring' an unpaid service (voluntary blood donors, voluntary workers in the service, unpaid time) with much lower external costs to a monetary and measurable paid activity involving costlier externalities.

(Titmuss, 1970: 205)

The discussion so far in this chapter has laid out the arguments for claiming that the market system is:

- The only defensible economic and social system for protecting the freedom of the individual to exercise personal choice, which allows the development of economic and societal relationships that are free from government coercion and intervention. This is the liberal-economic perspective.

■ Something that is preferable to alternative economic systems, but which needs to be carefully watched and, if necessary, modified from time to time to ensure that the economic system is compatible with broader societal aims. This incorporates the corporatist and pluralist perspectives.

■ An intrinsically corrupting system that pits human beings against each other, with only an elite few dictating the life chances of the many. This is the critical perspective.

The argument has been about the place of ethics in business life, and the place of business in the ethics of life.

Descriptive, normative and reflective approaches

Two ways of discussing ethical matters, normatively and descriptively, are often proposed. Normative discussion is concerned with rules and principles that ought to govern our thoughts and actions. Normative arguments are focused in particular on how such prescriptive claims can be shown to be legitimate or valid. Descriptive discussion focuses on how things *are* rather than how they should be. A descriptive approach to ethics would give an account of the values and ethics of particular groups and try to explain how they have emerged. It would analyse value systems to look for norms and the tensions between them. The word normative is troublesome in a subject such as business ethics, which spans both philosophy and sociology. In sociology, normative refers to that which is the norm within a group or society. The term is both descriptive – the norms are those of a particular group, and also normative – they define right and wrong within that group. In philosophy normative and descriptive are seen as opposing terms. In this book normative will be used in its philosophical sense.

Many business ethics textbooks take a normative approach. They identify ethical difficulties in business, rehearse the arguments about what should be done about them and then present a resolution or a set of principles. Rather than taking a normative and prescriptive approach this textbook takes a descriptive and analytical approach. It attempts to describe how people in organisations interpret and respond to ethical issues at work. It does not propose solutions to the many ethical dilemmas and problems that face managers and organisations. However, by explaining how others think about and respond to ethical matters, and by providing you with the appropriate tools for thinking, we hope the book will enable you to analyse the issues and to come to your own conclusions.

The intention of the book brings us to a third way of talking about business ethics, the reflective and reflexive approach. Reflection implies careful consideration of ethical issues. Reflexive means to turn back on one's own mind and to consider one's own values and personality. This textbook therefore tries to help you examine your own positions and thoughts. This can be done in part by reflecting on the material in this book and other publications. But this is vicarious learning, piggybacking on the experiences of others. Reflexive learning occurs when you use your values to challenge your actions and your experiences to challenge your values.

Reflections

One of our concerns in this book is the possibility of the existence of moral agency and ethical practice within organisations. Integrity is one of the concepts that would form part of any definition of business ethics. The importance of integrity within organisational life in general, and executive decision making in particular, is discussed by Srivastva and Cooperrider (1988), although they stress that the way forward is not easily mapped. It can only be navigated and negotiated through dialogue, reflection, learning, tolerance and wisdom.

> Executive integrity is dialogical. Executive integrity is more than the presence of morality or the appropriation of values; integrity involves the process of seeing or creating values. Whereas ethical moralism is blindly obedient, integrity represents the 'insightful assent' to the construction of human values. In this sense, organisation is not viewed as a closed, determined structure but is seen as in a perpetual state of becoming. Dialogue is the transformation of mere interaction into participation, communication, and mutual empathy. Executive integrity is, therefore, a breaking out of a narrow individualism and is based on a fearless trust in what true dialogue and understanding might bring, both new responsibilities and new forms of responsiveness to the other.
>
> (Srivastva and Cooperrider, 1988: 7)

The big weakness of a heavy reliance upon the notion of a dialectic transformation of society is that the associated processes are subject to the risk of social capture. The best chance of minimising this possibility is for all of us to take ourselves seriously and to believe that our individual voices count in shaping the societies in which we live.

We end this opening chapter on a qualified, optimistic note. Spaemann (1989) refused to accept that conscience is either purely instinct or exclusively a function of upbringing:

> In every human being there is the predisposition to develop a conscience, a kind of faculty by means of which good and bad are known.
>
> (Spaemann, 1989: 62–3)

However, Spaemann went on to say that conscience has to be nurtured and supported – shown good practice in order for it to flourish and mature. Fail to do this and the development of a strong conscience becomes 'dwarfed'. The term 'dwarfing' is used by Seedhouse (1988) when discussing the growing attention to a 'business mentality' within UK health care, at the expense of a prioritising of the individual. Both Spaemann and Seedhouse saw the individual as central to any challenge to the primacy of business interests, although, as you will see in Chapter 6, conscience is often the victim of the need to maintain organisational and personal relationships.

Hannah Arendt (cited in Bauman, 1994) also placed the individual at the centre of any developments towards making ethics a live and legitimate subject for debate within organisations. Arendt wrote, 'there are no rules to abide by ... as there are no rules for the unprecedented'. Bauman continued

in other words, no one else but the moral person themselves must take responsibility for their own moral responsibility.

(Bauman, 1994: 14)

With this in mind, this book is intended to inform your understanding of some
of the key issues that bear upon this critical element of modern society – the possibilities for business ethics.

Summary

In this chapter the following key points have been made:

- Business ethics issues can be illustrated through stories; sometimes these are expressed as romances, as tragedies, as satire, as comedies and sometimes as farces.

- Many writers, and indeed organisations, argue that there is a business case for
companies to behave ethically and responsibly. There is an association between
the two, but whether good companies are profitable because they are good,
or good because their profitability means they can afford to be, is not easily
proven one way or the other.

- Many business ethics issues are best understood by using a stakeholder approach.

- Four different perspectives: the classical-liberal, the corporatist, the pluralist
and the critical, on the question of whether organisations, and their role within
market systems, are ethically proper.

- The doubts about the classical-liberal model place a premium on the role of the
moral agency of individuals within organisations. Moral agency involves reflection on what is right and wrong and working for the good within organisations.

Typical assignments

1. Is there an effective 'business case' for corporations acting in a socially, ethically and
environmentally responsible way?

2. Compare and contrast the four approaches to the involvement of stakeholders' business decision making (classical-liberal, pluralistic, corporatist and critical) outlined
in this chapter.

3. How should a company decide which interest groups should be treated as stakeholders and which should not?

4. What can we learn about business ethics issues at work by studying the stories in
which they are reported?

Group activity 1.1

A delphi exercise on reasons to be an ethical organisation

Delphi is a technique for creating a consensus on difficult matters of prioritising or forecasting. In this instance it will be used to answer the question:

Why should organisations choose to behave ethically and socially responsibly?

The exercise needs the group to divide into groups of between five and eight people. Each group should then follow these steps.

1. Each person, working on their own, should think of as many reasons as they can why an organisation should behave ethically and socially responsibly. Write each reason down on a Post-it note and make a pile of them.

2. Everyone then posts their Post-its in random order on a convenient board.

3. The group should gather around the Post-its and sort and cluster them, putting similar points together, until the mass of Post-its has been reduced to about five or six clusters of reasons.

4. The group should then write a simple, one-page questionnaire that lists the five or six reasons and asks respondents to score each reason according to its importance. The scoring should be done using percentages, the larger the percentage the more important the reason. Photocopy a batch of the questionnaires (or, if you are inclined, create a small spreadsheet).

5. Each member of the group then completes the questionnaire on their own.

6. The scores are then totalled and averaged and presented to the whole group.

7. Each group member then completes a new questionnaire taking into account the average scores of the whole group.

8. The process continues through cycles of individual scoring and group feedback until the group reaches a consensus, or nearly does, on the scoring and importance of the five or six reasons.

9. You will then have decided why organisations should behave ethically and socially responsibly.

10. Discuss in the group how the arguments you have identified are similar to or differ from those presented in this chapter.

Useful websites

Topic	Website provider	URL
Global business ethics issues.	World Economic Forum	http://www.weforum.org/issues
Business ethics and etiquette guide	Youngstown State University	http://maagblog.ysu.edu/business-ethics/web/
A useful website for keeping up to date with business ethics issues	Institute of Business Ethics	http://www.ibe.org.uk
FTSE4Good Home page	FTSE	http://www.ftse.com/index.jsp
Assessing firms' sustainability performance	Dow Jones Sustainability Indexes	http://www.sustainability-indexes.com/
Another ratings agency for sustainability	Ethical Investment Research service (EIRIS)	http://www.eiris.org/

CHAPTER 2

Ethical issues in business

Chapter at a glance

- Case study 2.16 Economy with the truth when dealing with the tax authorities
- Case study 2.17 Fraudulent corporations – Parmalat, Satyam and Madoff
- Case study 2.18 Lord Black and Hollinger International
- Case study 2.19 BAT and allegations of cigarette smuggling
- Case study 2.20 The retention of dead babies' organs in hospitals
- Case study 2.21 British Airways and Virgin Atlantic
- Case study 2.22 The hospital consultants
- Case study 2.23 Supermarkets' treatment of their supply chains
- Case study 2.24 The *Super Size Me* sales promotion
- Case study 2.25 Sexual harassment
- Case study 2.26 The Firestone Tire recall issue
- Case study 2.27 Huntingdon Life Sciences

Activities and exercises

- Video clip 2.1 Bullies on the job
- Video clip 2.2 Fired for being fat
- Discussion activities 2.1–2.27 Discussion points arising from the case studies
- Typical assignments
- Group activity 2.1
- Recommended further reading
- Useful websites

Learning outcomes

Having read this chapter and completed its associated activities, readers should be able to:

- Describe the range of ethical and moral issues that arise in management, business and organisations.

- Distinguish between ethical, moral and legal wrongdoing and assess the importance of a particular misdeed.

- Analyse the complex consequences and motives that typically attend ethical and moral issues in management, business and organisations.

Introduction

Identifying the range and variety of ethical issues in business and management is the main focus of this chapter. It includes many case studies and so is longer than the other chapters. The case studies are provided because understanding theoretical issues, which are not dealt with until the next chapter, is made easier if the reader first has some concrete examples to which to refer. They also provide resources that will be referred to in other chapters. When reading this chapter it is not necessary to read all of the case studies. Only read those that have taken your interest or where you feel you need to think some more about the general issues raised. To make the chapter more manageable it has been divided into five parts.

- Part one: The map of business ethics issues

- Part two: Encouraging goodness

- Part three: Creating a level playing field, benignness

- Part four: Preventing indifference to others

- Part five: Discouraging badness

Part one: The map of business ethics issues

If the variety of business ethics issues is going to be explained we need a map, and that in turn requires a set of coordinates to explain how the range of issues relate to each other. In practice the field of business ethics has been divided into specialist fields dominated by academics and consultants with backgrounds in different forms of knowledge.

- Corporate social responsibility (CSR) – dominated by social policy experts and environmentalists

- Corporate governance – largely dominated by lawyers and accountants

- Corporate citizenship – lawyers

- Sustainability – environmentalists

- Ethical investment – market analysts

- Employment rights and human rights – human resource management specialists and lawyers

- Fair trade and the regulation of international trade – economists

- Risk management – accountants

- Reputation management – marketing and public relations specialists.

We will not divide the issues between these sub-fields because it prevents the holistic approach that business ethics issues commonly demand. Our map will use two coordinates:

- Degree of morality, or from bad to good.
- Legality, illegality and justice.

Good and bad

The semiotic square

The semiotic square, under the name of the square of opposition (Parsons, 1999), has been used by philosophers since classical times as a tool for logical analysis. It was reinvented in the twentieth century by Greimas (1987) as a method for analysing the structures in stories and narratives. We will use it to identify the structures within stories about business ethics matters. It has been popularised in the UK by Chandler (2001). All semiotic square analyses begin with a key theme and continue by plotting three types of relationships that necessarily stem from it (*see* Figure 2.1). As we are dealing with ethics we will begin the semiotic square with the notion of good.

The first type of relationship is opposition or contrariety. If we begin with good its opposite is bad. Both of these two terms then has its contradiction – the second form of relationship. Contradictions are represented by the diagonal lines in Figure 2.1. In the semiotic square opposites and contradictions are not the same thing. Contradictions occur through particulars and practicalities that negate formal, universal terms. An example is the poet Edna St Vincent Millay's remark 'I love humanity but I hate people'. In other words, in formal, general terms Millay approved of humanity, but her dislike of individuals in all their, sometimes unpleasant, diversity contradicted that belief. If the good is negated we are left with an absence of good, which is not the same as the bad; it may be mere indifference. Indifference however, in its connection with 'bad', represents the third kind of relationship – complementarity – because, as in the quotation famously (but probably incorrectly) attributed to Edmund Burke, 'the only thing necessary for the triumph of evil is for good men to do nothing'. Indifference may permit badness but is not the whole of it. It is, to use the term of the original square of opposition,

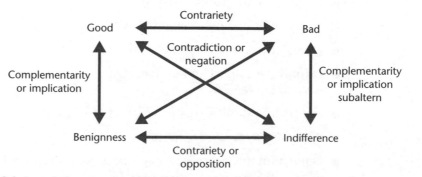

Figure 2.1 A semiotic square analysis of the concept of 'good'

subaltern to it. The most complex relationship is now left, which is the contradiction of 'bad', the negation of the negation. If we absent the bad we are left with benignness (as incorporated in the famous precept 'first of all do no harm'). This is the opposite of indifference. Benignness allows the good to occur and avoids the bad, but on its own does not constitute the good. Benignness may only consist in avoiding the doing of harm and not concern itself with doing good.

The semiotic square identifies four degrees of rightness and wrongness in behaviour, which in order of goodness are:

- the good;

- benignness;

- indifference; and

- the bad.

These four categories, which form a scale from good to bad, are the first dimension in Table 2.1, which will be used to illustrate and explain the range of ethical issues facing businesses, organisations, managers and those affected by them. The scale from good to bad may also be seen from a different perspective. In terms of moral action what is required at the 'good' end of the spectrum is encouragement, or prescription, while at the 'bad' end distraint, or proscription, is necessary. Some writers (Vardy and Grosch, 1999, Taylor, C., 2001) distinguish between the terms ethics and morality to point up this contrast. Ethics is focused on doing good. It deals with defining the good life for humankind. Morality in contrast is a concern for justice, which is about preventing wrongs and making restitution if wrongs are done. Ethics, in these terms, can be thought of as developmental whereas morality is judgmental. In Christian terms the Ten Commandments represent morality but ethics is represented by the Beatitudes. The Ten Commandments specify what it is wrong to do, for example commit murder or adultery (Deuteronomy, 6). The Beatitudes are the virtues that Jesus commended in a sermon to his followers. They include meekness, mercy, pureness of heart and peacemaking (Matthew, 5.7). Just to confuse the issue some writers make the same distinction, between the effort to prevent bad behaviour and the effort to encourage positive behaviour, but use different terms to describe the two ends of the spectrum. Caza et al. (2004: 172) describe a focus on the positive as ethos and virtuousness but use the terms ethics and integrity for the other pole of the spectrum; thereby giving the word ethics an entirely opposite meaning to that ascribed to it by Vardy and Grosch (1999). Despite the confusion of vocabulary the distinction is an important one.

Legal, illegal and just

The second dimension in Table 2.1 is based on the following categories, which can be used to judge the rightness of actions:

- things that it is legal to do but which the law does not require to be done;

- things that must be done or not done according to law; and

- things that are illegal but that may well be justified (i.e. a requirement of justice).

Table 2.1 Illustrative cases of the major issues in business ethics

Ethics → Morality
Prescribing the good life → Proscribing bad actions

	Good Positive action for good or to prevent harm being done		**Benign** Avoiding doing harm, supports the doing of good but takes no positive action to do good		**Indifferent** Ignoring harm done by or to others and disregarding the rights of others		**Bad** Taking action to do harm / Taking no action to prevent harm being done	
	Social development and caring	Social responsibility and supporting	Reciprocity	Fairness	Lying and dishonesty	Cheating and selfishness	Bullying and social irresponsibility	Harming and social and environmental disengagement
Legal, but not a legal obligation	The Nationwide Foundation. Case study 2.1, p. 52	AIDS drugs and patent rights in South Africa. Case study 2.4, p. 56	Paying for staff's professional training. Case study 2.7, p. 62	Providing new drugs for MS sufferers. Case study 2.10, p. 67	BAT, Nottingham University and the honorary professor. Case study 2.14, p. 78			
Legal	British Sugar and Sunday trucking. Case study 2.2, p. 53. Farepak. Case study 2.3, p. 54	Child labour in developing countries. Case study 2.5, p. 58	Executive fat cats. Case study 2.8, p. 63. The oil companies and the 2000 fuel crisis. Case study 2.9, p. 65.	The British railway system: priorities, profits and governance. Case study 2.12, p. 70	Economy with the truth when dealing with the tax authorities. Case study 2.16, p. 80	The retention of dead babies' organs in hospitals. Case study 2.20, p. 87.	The hospital consultants. Case study 2.22, p. 90. Supermarkets' treatment of their supply chains. Case study 2.23, p. 91.	The Firestone Tire recall issue. Case study 2.26, p. 95. The Super size Me sales promotion. Case study 2.24, p. 93.
Illegal				Discriminating against employees. Case study 2.11, p. 68.	The case of Shell's missing oil barrels. Case study 2.13, p. 75. The Lord Browne. Case study 2.15, p. 78.	Fraudulent corporations – Parmalat, Satyam and Madoff. Case study 2.17, p. 81. Lord Black and Hollinger International. Case study 2.18, p. 83. BAT and allegations of cigarette smuggling. Case study 2.19, p. 85.	British Airways and Virgin Atlantic. Case study 2.21, p. 88. Bullies on the job. Video clip 2.1, p. 88.	Sexual harassment. Case study 2.25, p. 95. Fired for being fat. Video clip 2.2, p. 95.
Illegal but just?	David Shayler and whistleblowing on MI5. Case study 2.6, p. 58.							Huntingdon Life Sciences. Case study 2.27, p. 97.

Legality and illegality are defined by the criminal or civil law. A criminal offence is one so grievous that the state takes action to protect society. Civil law is concerned with the compensation that people who are damaged by others (by tort or breach of contract) may seek. Four combinations of legality and justice are identified.

1 Actions that are good and legal but not a legal obligation

Some actions may raise ethical issues because, although they are good and legal, people do not take them because the law does not require them to do so. The question is whether people, and corporations, should do them even though they are not obliged to do so.

2 Actions that are wrong and illegal

In the next category ethical or moral questions arise because an action is both wrong and illegal. Such actions ought to be straightforward to condemn. However, on issues that many would place in this category, others might argue that the action is neither wrong nor illegal.

3 Actions that are legal but not necessarily just

Another category includes actions that may be legal but are also, arguably, bad. Many of the moral and ethical issues that affect business and management fall into this category. They are a reflection of the big question, raised in Chapter 1, of whether business has moral obligations beyond the proprietary claims of the shareholders. The claim that there are no ethical obligations on a private company other than to obey the law and meet the demands of their shareholders was most famously articulated by Milton Friedman (1970).

Cross reference	Milton Friedman is an economist who is one of the major participants in debates about business ethics. His views are discussed in Chapter 9.

Friedman's position can be criticised from several perspectives. Solomon's (1993) critique is based on the Aristotelian idea of virtue (*see* p. 131). He argued that the belief that business is simply about the financial 'bottom line' is untrue. However, he claimed this misconception has generated many false metaphors for business that hide the truth from people. The idea of cowboy entrepreneurs who are driven by greed and profit and who see themselves as loners in competition with all others is one such metaphor. Rather, he argued, the purpose of business is to provide for the prosperity and happiness of the community. This cannot be achieved if people make a distinction between their business and their personal lives. People are social animals but their social needs are ignored if their business lives are focused on the individualistic pursuit of profit. The problem is intensified if working lives are associated with necessary drudgery in contrast to the pleasure that can be had from personal and social lives. Virtues, according to Aristotle, are formed from the ability to find a sensible mean between such extremes as dreary work and pleasurable personal lives.

The bottom line of the Aristotelian approach to business ethics is that we have to get away from the 'bottom line' thinking and conceive of business as an essential part of the good life, living well, getting along with others, having a sense of self respect, and being part of something that one can be proud of.

(Solomon, 1993: 104)

There is a religious objection to the Friedmanite view of business that can be exemplified from the Roman Catholic position as expressed in the encyclical *Centesimus Annus* (John Paul II, 1991). Humans, it argued, have a capacity for transcendence – the ability to give themselves away to others, and to God. The role of capitalism and profit seeking has to be seen within this context.

The church acknowledges the legitimate role of profit as an indication that a business is functioning well. When a firm makes a profit, this means that productivity factors have been properly employed and the corresponding human needs have been duly satisfied. But profitability is not the only indicator of a firm's condition. It is possible for the financial accounts to be in order and yet for the people, who make up the firm's most valuable asset, to be humiliated and their dignity offended ... In fact the purpose of a business firm is not simply to make a profit, but it is to be found in its very existence as a community of persons who in various ways seek to satisfy their basic needs and who form a particular group at the service of the whole society.

(John Paul II, 1991: §35)

Large companies, such as Shell, are adopting forms of accounting that attempt to balance traditional financial accounting with a concern for environmental sustainability and social justice. This is known as triple bottom-line accounting, which provides output and performance measures in the, potentially contradictory, fields of financial, social and environmental performance. The idea, similar to that of the balanced scorecard, is to make it obvious if financial success is only being achieved at a social and environmental cost. The technical problem of identifying measures that can illuminate a company's performance on environmental quality and social justice is difficult. Comparing the many possible measures against each other and against financial performance is a matter of judgment rather than of accountancy calculation (Elkington, 1999).

Cross reference	The triple bottom-line reporting concept is discussed in more detail in Chapter 9.

The issues that arise from legal, but unethical, managerial and business actions all reflect one or more of these criticisms of the Friedmanite perspective.

4 Actions that are just but illegal

The final category of the dimension is one that will always generate controversy. It concerns actions that may be illegal but are morally or ethically good. It concerns the perennial question of when a law can be said to be immoral and when it is justifiable to break or defy it. Campaigning against a law one disapproves of is acceptable within a democratic system; the ethical problem only emerges when a person moves from campaigning to disobedience. The dilemma is twofold.

The first problem is to define the conditions or circumstances in which it would be proper to defy the law. In a democratic system does a general acceptance of governmental authority imply that it is never acceptable to disobey a particular law? Political obligation does not exhaust moral obligation. This is the case with conscientious objectors, for example, who refuse to take a combatant role in a war. But before refusing to obey a law the person needs to consider carefully the balance between their political and moral obligations (Raphael, 1970: 115–16). If in general the state seeks to achieve justice and the common good, and if the law has been passed with the assent of the majority and according to the rule of law, then there is a presumption in favour of complying with the law. Conversely where laws are arbitrary and the state is not just, the contrary presumption may hold. Lyons (1984: 214) argued that the presumption should be that a legal system does not automatically deserve respect. Respect has to be earned. Greenawalt (1987: 222), however, pointed out that there are no plain rules available to guide people on when it is proper to disobey a law.

The second problem is the nature of the defiance, which can extend from passive civil disobedience through to violent direct action. Gandhi, in his campaigns against British rule in India, practised passive resistance. His belief was that people should disobey immoral laws but should not resist when the forces of the law took action in response. His concept of *Satyagraha* was based on the Hindu Vaishnavite principle of *ahimsa* (or non-violence) and the importance of suffering (Brown, 1972: 6). He believed that passive resistance would eventually cause the authorities, through shame, to right the injustices. This increasingly appears to be the position of the Catholic Church. The Pope wrote, concerning the fall of the Soviet bloc:

> It seemed that the European order resulting from the Second World War and sanctioned by the Yalta Agreement could only be overturned by another war ... Instead it has been overcome by non-violent commitment of people who, while refusing to yield to the force of power, succeeded time after time in finding effective ways of bearing witness to the truth.
>
> (John Paul II, 1991: §23)

At the other extreme some anarchist and other radical groups argue that harming property, and in some cases people, can be justified by the importance of their cause. As will be seen in Case study 2.27 some animal rights activists argue that the evil of vivisection, practised by some pharmaceutical companies, justifies violent action against those companies, their employees and backers.

Deciding when, if ever, violence against an organisation is justified is similar to arguing about which circumstances can make war just. The concept of the just war has concerned theologians since the time of St Augustine. St Thomas Aquinas set down the main tests of a just war in the thirteenth century. They were:

- The war must be declared by a lawful authority (*auctorprincipis*).

- The cause must be just (*justacausa*).

- Those going to war must intend to advance the good and avoid evil (*recta intentio*) (D'Entreves, 1965: 159).

- The test of 'proper means' (*debitomodo*), which requires that minimum force be used in accordance with the rules of war and that peace should be established at the end of the conflict, was added to the list later.

An additional requirement, that all other means of resolving the issue should have been exhausted before resort is made to violence, seems to be a twentieth-century addition.

In considering the question of the justness of violent action against organisations, rather than war between states, the first criterion does not apply. If the actions that people condemn as immoral also happen to be legal then the state could not be expected to take action against the company. However, the criterion does alert us to the dangers of validating violent action that is not carried out in the name of some legitimate body. Allowing self-legitimating groups the right to define who is evil and to use force to attack them could lead to the intolerance displayed by fascism. Sometimes civil associations or non-governmental organisations (NGOs), such as Greenpeace, take this legitimating role upon themselves.

The cause of militant animal rights activism can illustrate the impact of the other criteria. Even if the cause, for sake of argument, were just, its narrow focus on destroying an alleged evil, rather than the creation of a peaceful solution, violates the requirement that the violence should serve the establishment of long-term peace. Nor do the movement's tactics meet the requirement for minimum use of force and adherence to the 'rules of war'. Actions have included intimidating 'civilians' such as investors and bankers who had only an indirect connection with vivisection. These also violate one of Greenawalt's (1987: 235) considerations for disobeying a law: that the law objected to and the laws being broken are closely connected. The final criterion has not been met in the case of violent actions in support of animal rights because, in a democratic society there are always non-violent means of protest that can be adopted. Pacifists of course object to the notion of a just war and would claim that, as violence begets violence, its use to stop evil is never justified.

The business world of Russia since the collapse of the Soviet Union provides an example of the issues that surround behaviour that may be illegal but just. Tax evasion (not just legal tax avoidance) is rife among companies in Russia. Corporations evade their tax liabilities by constructing the accounts so as never to show a profit, by transferring the company's income to a third-party organisation a few days before the tax is due, providing loans and insurance cover for employees to reduce the taxable revenue and so on. These practices are clearly illegal, but in a study into Russian executives' views on these practices Meirovich and Reichel (2000) reported that 36 out of 40 interviewees regarded such practices as ethical while the remaining four took the neutral position that the practices were neither ethical nor unethical. Their arguments in support of this view were that:

- the legal and environmental conditions for businesses in Russia are draconian and businesses would not survive if they paid tax at 90 per cent on all their profit;

- the government itself is corrupt and inefficient and it merely wastes or embezzles the taxes received, therefore it is good to deny the government the money and instead direct it to society at large by enabling economic growth.

There are, of course, suitable counter arguments such that the illegal behaviour of private organisations further encourages the growth of corrupt institutions. Also the loss of revenue to the government prevents it from meeting the many pressing social needs of the Russian population.

Cross reference	The battle between the Russian government and the oil company Yukos is instructive on this matter. It is described in Chapter 12, p. 466. Some see it as a proper attempt by the Russian government to make large corporations pay their taxes, which can then be used for the good of society at large. Others see it as an attempt by the Russian government to renationalise a major industry and curtail the growing political power of the oligarchs – businessmen who have become very rich after they bought many state enterprises during the time of privatisation.

The cases

Table 2.1 plots some classic, and some recent issues in business against the two dimensions just discussed. The cases (presented later in this chapter) are located in positions on the grid according to whether, on the face of it, they are examples of goodness, benignness, indifference or badness and whether they represent actions above and beyond legality, conformance to the law, illegality or unjust legality. These grid positions are not indictments of the people and organisations discussed in the cases. The cases are located at certain coordinates in the grid because it forces us to ask questions about legality, morality and ethicality, not because they are definitive illustrations of good or bad behaviour.

Part two: Encouraging goodness

Social development

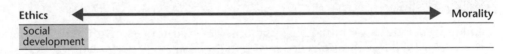

Social development is defined as actions taken by an organisation or company that are designed to improve the social, economic, cultural or environmental conditions of a society. In an earlier period such actions would have been termed philanthropy. Andrew Carnegie, who was a poor Scottish immigrant to the USA in the nineteenth century, provides a classic example. He built an industrial empire and when he sold his business he was thought to be the richest man in the world. He disposed of his wealth philanthropically. A particular interest was the public libraries, of which he founded 2,509 throughout the English-speaking world. He thought libraries important because of the role they could play in helping the poor to participate in what he saw as a meritocratic society in which people could become successful through learning. He also saw libraries as a means by which immigrants such as he could learn about the countries in which they had chosen to live.

Between 1985 and 2000 the generosity ratio of UK companies (the percentage of their philanthropic donations to their pre-tax profits) rose from 0.10 per cent at the start of the period to 0.40 per cent at the end (all statistics are from Moore, 2003). This rate of growth in the ratio was much faster than it had been in the previous decade. There is a Percent Club in the UK, an association of corporations committed to giving 0.5 per cent of their pre-tax profits to good causes, though none of the members has yet achieved this. In the USA where there is a form of social contract, which requires low corporate tax rates to be offset to some degree by higher levels of philanthropy, the average level of donations is five times higher than in the UK, although the generosity ratio is in decline there.

A company's social development activities need not be directly connected with its business activities. However, even if they are not it may be argued that organisations are hoping to improve the standing of their business indirectly as a result of their good works. Motives, corporate and philanthropic, are nearly always mixed and this should not detract from the value of development activities. Other organisations, such as NGOs, have social development as their prime purpose.

Corporate citizenship is sometimes used as an alternative term for social development. British Airways, for example, define its citizenship objective as 'To succeed in partnership with the communities in which we work, not at their expense' (British Airways, 2000: 26). It has provided high-profile sponsorship, in the tourism field, for the Millennium Dome (which probably did little for BA's reputation) and the British Airways London Eye (which probably did much for the company's reputation). BA's (2000) corporate social responsibility report mentions, among other things, charitable work in Kenya and Bangladesh, and its Community Learning Centre at Heathrow. Many of its initiatives stem from voluntary work by its staff and volunteering is an important theme in its activities.

Case study 2.1 reports on an organisation that is seeking to respond to social problems and raises the question of whether philanthropy necessarily must arise from altruism or whether the point is to bring social good from strategic necessity.

Case study 2.1	The Nationwide Foundation

Building societies are mutual organisations. Their customers own them. This reflects their origins as self-help organisations designed to help people buy their own homes. In the 1990s, and into the twenty-first century, there was a move to demutualise building societies. This process involved converting a society into a public limited company (plc). The new plc would give the previous owners (the customers) shares in the new company to compensate them for their loss of ownership. The new owners could either keep or sell these new shares. If they sold them they would make a windfall profit. They would receive a cash sum for a property that had cost them nothing except the constraint of saving with, or accepting a mortgage from, that particular building society. Some building societies wished to remain as such. The pressure to demutualise is more keenly expressed by their customers.

The Nationwide Building Society wished to remain mutual. In 1997 it created the Nationwide Foundation to become the channel for its charitable giving. Everyone who became a member of the society from November 1997 onward also became a member of the foundation and agreed to assign to the foundation their rights to any future conversion payments. This meant that should the society demutualise or be taken over in the future then any connected payment of any sort, which would otherwise be received by the society members, would be passed to the foundation to create a fund for charitable giving. Bluntly, there would be no windfall payments. A number of the society's members who had been members since before 1997 also agreed to become members of the foundation.

None of the building societies that became banks by demutualising survived the financial collapse of 2007–2008. They were either obliged to merge with other banks or become part nationalised. The Nationwide, however, survived and continued as a building society and its Foundation supports schemes throughout the UK using money donated by the society, its staff and its members. Its strategy for 2009–2012 focuses on addressing the housing and financial capability problems of the survivors of domestic abuse and disadvantaged elderly people.

(*Source for further information:* www.nationwidefoundation.org.uk)

Discussion activity 2.1

Does the use of the fund as a means of meeting the society's own purpose, of remaining a mutual institution, detract from the worth of its activities?

Case study 2.2 is about a company that was accused of disengaging from the largely rural community within which it operated. Although its plans were legal it drew back from implementing them because people objected to the disruption they would cause to the pattern of weekend life in East Anglian villages.

Case study 2.2 — British Sugar and Sunday trucking

East Anglia is sugar beet territory. There is an annual sugar beet harvest that lasts for five months when the crop has to be taken to British Sugar's factories for processing. For many years there had been an agreement between British Sugar and the National Farmers Union (NFU) that deliveries would take place for five-and-a-half days each week with no lorries on Saturday afternoons or Sundays. Most residents in the villages through which the large and heavy beet lorries rumble accept the beet harvest as part of country life. In 2000 British Sugar in an attempt to diminish the queues of lorries that formed during the mornings at the factories, decided to switch to seven-day-a-week deliveries and it came to an agreement with the NFU to do so. There was immediate outcry. As a resident in one of the affected villages said, 'We do appreciate that they have a job to do. The noise of these lorries is quite considerable. All we want is for them to leave us in peace for one day of the week.' The hauliers who delivered the beet met at Peterborough and came out against seven-day deliveries. As one of them said, 'Imagine big sugar beet lorries driving past country churches on a Sunday morning while people are trying to worship. It simply won't work – we won't do it.' The campaign against the additional deliveries carried on and within a few weeks British Sugar announced that it was suspending its agreement with the NFU to deliver beet for seven days each week.

(*Sources*: Moore, 2001; Bradley, 2000; Pollitt and Ashworth, 2000)

Discussion activity 2.2

Was British Sugar right to forgo the efficiency and cost benefits that could have been gained from a seven-day working week?

The next case study considers whether a bank should have been more generous in the name of social responsibility.

Case study 2.3   Farepak

Farepak was a part of the savings economy that people had forgotten about; but which was very important to the many people on low incomes or benefits for whom it was a way of saving for Christmas. It began as a Christmas Club in a butcher's shop in 1969. By 2007 it was part of the European Home Retail (EHR) group. Customers made monthly or weekly cash payments to self-employed agents, who were often their relatives as well as being savers within the scheme themselves. In return before Christmas the customers received hampers and vouchers to spend in high-street stores. By 2006 the EHR group was in financial difficulty. Money that Farepak customers had paid in was not protected or ring fenced as would have been the case with deposits in banks or other regulated institutions. Instead the money went into EHR's accounts, from where it was used to offset the company's overdraft with HBOS (Halifax/Bank of Scotland). Eventually in October 2006 HBOS refused to extend the overdraft and EHR called in the administrators. As Farepak's funds had been drained away its 150,000 customers looked as if they would receive as little as 4p in the pound when the company was wound up; and, of course, there were no Christmas hampers or presents. There was much argument over who was to blame. The Farepak management said it was HBOS for refusing to accept rescue plans and extend the overdraft. Others blamed HBOS for insisting that EHR use customers' savings to pay off the overdraft, even though this was perfectly legal. Some commentators pointed out that savings clubs were one part of the financial industry that was unregulated. The government did not see it as their job to protect club customers' savings; although a year later when Northern Rock collapsed it moved swiftly to protect that bank's customers' deposits. The MP Frank Field claimed that HBOS had a 'pivotal role' in the collapse of Farepak. He argued that the bank had been acting as a 'shadow director' and therefore bore responsibility; HBOS argued that they were 'bankers to EHR, we did not run the company'. A public fund was opened to provide some compensation to those who had lost their savings. By the end of November 2006 £6m had been saved by the administrators. As savers had lost £40m they would receive about 15p in the pound from this fund. HBOS donated £2m to the fund without admitting liability and said it would pay no more. One Scottish MEP demanded that other banks should donate to the fund. One big bank, the Royal Bank of Scotland said it would not.

However, five years later the claims had still not been settled and in 2011 it was reported that there was a fund of £5.53m to pay compensation to customers but the cost of winding up the company had been greater at £8.2m.

(*Sources*: BBC News Online, 2006a; Warwick-Ching, 2007; Bolger, 2006)

> ### Discussion activity 2.3
>
> Did the banking sector generally, and the banks in particular, have a responsibility for this unregulated savings industry? Should they have paid more into the Farepak compensation fund? Does the fact that Farepak's customers were often from the poorest groups of society make a difference?

Social responsibility

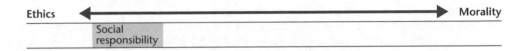

Social responsibility, in the way the term is used in this chapter, covers a narrower canvas than social development. It can be defined as conducting the business of an organisation in a manner that meets high social and environmental standards. It differs from social development in not requiring organisations to do good works beyond the commercial purposes of the organisation. Also social responsibility affects fewer arenas than social development. Social responsibility excludes the social and cultural good works that are appropriate to social development. Social responsibility is important to organisations 'not least because of the devastating impact that even isolated acts of wrong doing can have on an organisation's reputation among its stakeholders' (Arthur Andersen and London Business School, 1999). Many large companies report their performance as socially responsible organisations; for an example see British Petroleum's social and environmental report (BP, 2001).

The nature of a socially responsible approach to redundancy illustrates some of the factors that distinguish social responsibility from social development. It is possible to argue that redundancies, especially on a large scale, are morally wrong because they harm individuals, families and communities. The counter argument is that the welfare of families and communities is not the concern of a company or organisation. Another possible defence is that the loss of some jobs protects the jobs and livelihoods of many more. Social responsibility would suggest a middle position. It would argue that redundancy may be justified but that a responsible organisation will take trouble to help those affected. This might involve using outsourcing consultants to provide counselling and career advice to those losing their jobs. It could involve setting up agencies or funds to encourage the introduction of new businesses in affected localities, or helping those made redundant to start their own companies. Social responsibility is an obligation to minimise the collateral harm caused by the organisation's actions and decisions.

Case study 2.4 provides an example of assertive public and governmental opinion, which judged companies' protection of their patent rights as socially irresponsible. The pressure of global media scrutiny became such that the threat to the companies' reputations became greater than the economic loss caused by the challenge to their patents.

| Case study 2.4 | AIDS drugs and patent rights in South Africa |

There is an epidemic of AIDS in southern Africa. There is therefore a great need for drugs (anti-retro-viral – AVR) with which to treat the disease. One of the drugs, Ciprofloxican, cost South Africa's public health sector 52p for each pill when bought from the company that had developed it and that held the patent. A generic version of the drug could be imported from India for 4p a pill. The cost of these drugs was a heavy burden on the health service and the South African government proposed a new law that would allow the cheaper generic drug to be imported. The world's largest pharmaceutical companies opened a lawsuit against the South African government to claim that their property and patent rights were thereby put at risk. However, in May 2001, as the case was about to commence in the South African High Court, the pharmaceutical companies withdrew the claim.

The following article from the *Financial Times*, which includes an interview with the chief executive of one of the major pharmaceutical companies, rehearses the arguments.

FT Very sick people need drugs. The world's largest pharmaceutical companies charge plenty for them but they channel that money into research to find new medicines. The companies, now suffering an unprecedented onslaught over the prices they charge and lack of access to their medicines, want to refocus public attention on what they see as the main issue. 'You can kill the golden goose', says Hank McKinnell, chief executive of Pfizer, of demands for lower prices. 'You'll eat well today but the cupboard will be bare in future.'

Mr McKinnell is a staunch defender of the prices that his company, the world's largest drugs group, charges. He is also very aware that a humanitarian and economic disaster is unfolding in Africa, where 27m Africans are now HIV-positive and only a fraction of them have access to or can afford even deeply discounted western AIDS medicines. But in an interview he points out that AIDS was first identified by medical researchers in the early 1980s. By 1987, he says, there was one treatment. Now, 64 AIDS drugs are available and more than 100 are in development. 'What was the right thing to do in 1981?' asks Mr McKinnell. 'Say the prices are too high and take away the incentives for the research? That doesn't help patients or their families.'

But many believe this is an argument the drugs industry will never win. Companies are supplying AIDS drugs in Africa at up to 90 per cent discounts but they face demands for larger cuts. This is on the grounds that the products are still unaffordable for almost all HIV-positive patients or their governments. Meanwhile, companies in countries such as India and Thailand are making cheap, often illegal, copies of western drugs and promising to save thousands of lives at a fraction of the cost. And in the US there is speculation that it will not be long before patients lose patience and refuse to pay up to 10 times the price for treatments. Whichever way they turn, Mr McKinnell and his peers will be accused of placing a different value on the lives of people on different continents.

Pfizer's chief executive concedes the industry appears to have lost its way trying to formulate a response to the unprecedented wave of bad publicity. Changing that is one of his new responsibilities. This month he became chairman of the Pharmaceutical Research and Manufacturers of America, the industry's most powerful lobby group. Drugs companies have been caught off-guard by the sheer size of the attack. As well as being criticised for their drugs pricing policy in sub-Saharan Africa, they have endured closer scrutiny of pricing and patent regimes worldwide.

Federal and state regulators in the US have been investigating abuses of marketing to physicians and consumers. Influential Washington politicians have proposed revisions to US patent law that make it easier for cheap copies of drugs to come on the market. Meanwhile, Mr McKinnell says, Indian companies have been lobbying the World Trade Organisation to preserve their ability to break patent laws being ushered in as part of the WTO's Agreement on Trade Related Intellectual Property. He has little sympathy: 'The Indian companies have been making billions of dollars stealing our technology and selling it, not only in India but any place around the world they can get away with it.'

He believes the pharmaceutical industry has convinced people it genuinely wants to help, particularly in Africa. Last week, in a high-profile dispute, 39 pharmaceutical companies abandoned their case against the South African government in which they had said their patent rights were in danger. Bad publicity was an important factor behind the decision to drop the case and the companies have escaped a disastrous legal situation. Mr McKinnell says the companies have also been increasing their efforts to work with aid agencies, non-governmental organisations and local governments to improve distribution.

'Unfortunately, we haven't expanded them rapidly enough', he says. 'But there is now a realisation that if we don't provide access, we're going to stay as part of the problem ... I think we've been pretty successful in becoming part of the solution.'

But prices are still too high in countries where any price is unaffordable. The answer, says Mr McKinnell, is to forge partnerships with agencies and governments to bring in more resources. 'If the sole problem is the high price of drugs, you give up. But the industry has been smart enough to take that off the table. When the drug is free or at cost, now what's the problem? It's national will, it's distribution, and it's medical treatment.' In other words, drugs companies have knocked 90 per cent off the price but it is up to someone else to find the rest and to help deliver the drugs.

(*Sources*: Inside Track: Big pharma and the golden goose, *The Financial Times,* 26 April 2001 (Michaels, A.), Copyright © The Financial Times Ltd.; McGreal, 2001; Clark and Borger, 2001)

The main pharmaceutical companies began to cut their prices for ARV drugs in developing countries. Glaxo SmithKline reduced the price of its main drug three times in 2003. The large companies also began to come to understandings with the generic drug producers in India and began to license generic producers in South Africa (Dyer, 2003a). In some cases regulatory bodies such as the South African Competition Commission argued that the international companies were breaking competition rules by over-charging and threatened to force the companies to grant generic licenses to local producers (Dyer, 2003b). Much of the movement on the issue was attributed to pressure from institutional investors, who were worried that the damage being done to the reputation of the pharmaceutical industry might reduce its ability to charge premium prices in industrialised countries. The focus of the debate shifted more to the ability and commitment of governments in some African countries to take action against AIDS. It took the South African Government, for example, a long time to agree to a programme to provide free ARVs and in 2004 there were criticisms that the roll-out of the programme was being delayed (DegliInnocenti and Reed, 2004).

New drugs, known as 'second line' treatments, have emerged since the pharmaceutical companies started providing AVRs to Africa at not-for-profit prices. The supply of these new drugs has again been hampered by patent problems; a situation exacerbated because India has tightened up on its patent laws and so the supply of generic new drugs from Indian companies is restricted. However, several African countries are now establishing their own pharmaceutical companies in an attempt to reduce their reliance on international pharmaceutical companies (BBC News Online, 2006b).

Discussion activity 2.4

What are the arguments for saying that knowledge that is medically beneficial to humanity should not be private property?

Case study 2.5 raises similar issues to those discussed in Case study 2.3 as it reviews why a company acted more responsibly than was required by law.

Case study 2.5   Child labour in developing countries

The use of child labour by multinational companies in their factories in the Third World to produce cheaply the products they sell in western markets became an international issue in the 1990s and the first decade of the new millennium. The United Nations' Convention on the Rights of the Child and the International Labour Organisation's Declaration of Fundamental Principles and Rights at Work (United Nations, 1989) condemn the use of child labour. NIKE in particular has been the subject of public campaigns against its labour practices in South East Asia.

Although the issue has been high on the agenda for many years problems still occasionally emerge. In 2007 a 10-year-old boy was filmed in India by *The Observer* newspaper making clothes for the fashion chain Gap. The newspaper was told that the boy had been sold to the factory owner by his family in payment of a debt; that he had worked without pay for four months and would not be allowed to leave the job until his family's debt had been paid off. Gap has a code of Vendor Conduct (Gap Inc., 2007), which states in relation to child labour, that factories which supply goods for Gap:

- will employ only workers who meet the applicable minimum legal age requirement or are at least 14 years old, whichever is greater; and
- must maintain official records that verify the workers' dates of birth.

The code also encourages factories to provide apprenticeships and educational programmes for its younger workers. Once the company became aware of the problem it investigated and discovered that the vendor had subcontracted the production of one particular garment to an unauthorised subcontractor (contrary to the Vendor Code). The order for the garment, a smock blouse, was withdrawn and the product was withdrawn from sale and destroyed. The company also said that it would hold meetings with its suppliers in Asia to reinforce its policies (BBC News Online, 2007a).

Discussion activity 2.5

What action do you think companies should take when they find their suppliers use child labour contrary to their company policy? Why do you think Gap destroyed the garments made by the unofficial subcontractor?

The next case introduces a new aspect of social responsibility, which considers when it is proper for a person to break their duty of confidentiality to their employer if they know that their employer is acting irresponsibly.

Cross reference	This issue, also known as whistleblowing, is discussed in detail in Chapter 7.

Case study 2.6	**David Shayler and whistleblowing on MI5**

David Shayler is an ex-employee of MI5. He alleged that the service had plotted to kill the President of Libya. Having made the allegation he fled to France where attempts by the British government to extradite him were unsuccessful. However, he decided to return to Britain where he was arrested and charged. As a member of MI5 he had signed the Official Secrets Act of 1920, which banned him from revealing official secrets for life. The Public Interest Disclosure Act (*see* p. 285), which gives some limited protection to whistleblowers, does not apply to the security services. Shayler's intention was to use the Human Rights Act 1998, which incorporated the European Convention on Human Rights into English law, in his defence. The Act provides a right to freedom of expression and if a court makes a declaration of incompatibility between the Human Rights Act and a particular piece of legislation, such as the Official Secrets Act, the government would have to consider amending the law. Some of the issues are raised in the following leading article from the *Financial Times*.

FT Here's a paradox for Britain's spymasters. Three years ago, David Shayler, the former secret agent, fled to Paris after claiming that the security service had tried to kill President Muammar Gadaffi of Libya. Robin Cook, the foreign secretary, said the allegation was 'pure fantasy'. Yesterday on his return to Britain, Mr Shayler was arrested. But he would only be guilty in relation to the Gadaffi affair under the Official Secrets Act if what he said about his former employment was fact, not fiction.

The authorities seem to have avoided this difficulty by charging him with unauthorised disclosure related to his other allegations of mess-ups and impropriety in the service. Even so, the case shows up a huge problem for spymasters in dealing with former agents who talk too much. In James Bond's world, the solution was easy – perhaps something nasty with an exploding cigar, or a shark.

Outside spy fiction, the authorities face harder options. They may dismiss mud-slinging agents as mercenary fantasists. But then some of the mud may stick. If the authorities prosecute the agent for a serious disclosure, they risk giving credence to his allegations. If they bring charges for a technical breach, they look heavy handed. If they mount a full investigation into the agent's allegations, they risk further embarrassing revelations – even if the allegations prove false. If true, the agent faces huge difficulties in proving them in court.

Clearly the secret services must be allowed to keep their secrets. But such secrecy is only tenable in peaceful democracies if the agencies are seen to act within the law and the principles of civil liberty. This requires a good deal more openness than they have shown in recent decades – and more vigorous scrutiny by the parliamentary committee set up to watch over them 11 years ago.

In the present case, the authorities must show that they have not done a shabby deal by promising to soft-pedal charges in exchange for silence. If Mr Shayler has revealed important secrets – as the authorities appear to believe – he must be prosecuted vigorously, however embarrassing his defence might prove.

▶

Equally, the police, who are now investigating his charges against the service, must find ways to demonstrate that they are doing the job properly. Mr Shayler's accusations may be found eventually to be insubstantial or wildly exaggerated. But if the authorities take Mr Shayler seriously enough to prosecute him, there must be a presumption that his allegations against the service deserve, at the least, serious investigation.

(*Source*: Leader: Spy Trap, *The Financial Times*, 22 August 2000, Copyright © The Financial Times Ltd.)

Shayler appeared in Court in August 2002 and was charged with passing on information without the consent of his employers. He pleaded not guilty but was found guilty and sentenced to six months in prison. He appealed on the grounds that he was acting in the public interest but he was denied this defence by the Court of Appeal and by the House of Lords.

Discussion activity 2.6

Was David Shayler's whistleblowing justified?

Were the British authorities acting in a socially responsible way in choosing the offence David Shayler was charged with?

Part three: Creating a level playing field, benignness

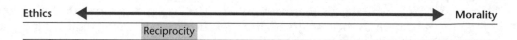

Ethics ⟵——————————————————⟶ Morality
Reciprocity

Reciprocity

If the avoidance of doing good and behaving well is irresponsibility, then selfishness is doing harm through a pursuit of self-interest. This section discusses human beings' inclinations to act either selfishly or altruistically. The assumption that selfishness is the norm in the behaviour of human beings may be unsafe. Research into the evolution of insects and animals suggests that altruism, sacrificing oneself to benefit others, may be the result of evolutionary selection. Reciprocity is perhaps a more appropriate term than altruism because such behaviour anticipates a future benefit for the individual's near relatives, if not for the individual. One form of reciprocity is called kin selection. It accounts for the altruistic behaviours found among ants, bees and wasps. Individuals in these species, it is suggested, forgo their own opportunity to breed in order to support the queen, their sister, in rearing large numbers of offspring. By doing this they will increase the total number of offspring that are born bearing genes similar to their own. This characteristic is particularly noticeable among bees, ants and wasps because their odd genetic system means that they are more closely related to their sisters than they are to their offspring. Reciprocity can also be a successful evolutionary allele (genetic trait) in animal evolution. Some writers, such as Dugatkin (2000), have argued, controversially, that studies of altruism in animals and insects can provide clues for improving human cooperation. Of course, this behaviour will only develop if in the long run 'cheats' (individuals who accept but do not return the favour) are 'punished'. This issue is most often studied through the medium of a game theory scenario known as the Prisoners' Dilemma.

The **Prisoners' Dilemma** involves two imaginary prisoners who have jointly committed a murder. They have been arrested by the police and put in separate cells. They have not been able to talk to each other since the murder and the police make sure that they cannot communicate in the police station. The police have inadequate information to charge them with murder but they could charge both of them with possessing illegal weapons. The two prisoners are interrogated separately. They have a choice of two options, to confess or to keep silence. The consequences of each option, in terms of number of years in gaol, are shown in the pay-off figure (Figure 2.2).

If both prisoners confess they will each receive the normal sentence for murder of six years' imprisonment. If they both keep silent the police have insufficient evidence and they will be charged for the weapons offence for which the sentence is two years in prison each. This is the best option for both of them. However, if one confesses after doing a deal with the police, he will only get one year in prison, while the one who keeps silent will have the book thrown at him and will receive the maximum penalty of 10 years. Neither prisoner knows what the other will do because they cannot communicate. If each prisoner feels they can trust the other then neither will confess and both will receive a relatively light tariff of two years' prison each. However, if one keeps silent, but the other 'cheats' and confesses, the silent one will receive a harsh 10 years. If a prisoner feels he cannot trust the other then the best bet is to confess. The worst that can happen is six years in prison but the worst that can happen if he does not confess is 10 years. This is the Prisoners' Dilemma, whether they can trust each other enough to achieve the best outcome for both of them by both not confessing.

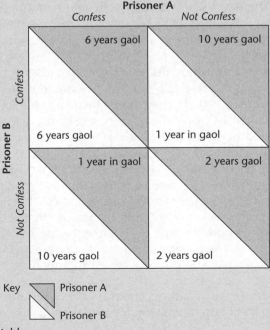

Figure 2.2 Pay-off table

The Prisoners' Dilemma can only be avoided if the players exist in a continuing community in which cheats are punished. In these circumstances the players have to continue to meet, which enables trust to develop. Selfishness will occur, on this analysis, where there is a lack of trust or where people do not see themselves as being in the same community as those whom they harm by their selfishness.

These issues can be seen in the following case studies. In Case study 2.7 altruism was present because all the players saw themselves as part of the same community and there were opportunities for the altruism to be reciprocated. But even in this situation the person explaining the situation found it hard to decide whether the recipients were trustworthy and who was likely to reciprocate his altruism.

| Case study 2.7 | **Paying for staff's professional training** |

Extract from an interview with a partner in an accounting firm responsible for the professional training of new staff

Well, treating people properly and fairly is always an interesting one; it is a very subjective area. In my role as training partner there are undoubtedly incidents every time anybody doesn't pass an exam; we have to decide what to do about it. Whether to terminate their contract, or whether to pay for absolutely everything. There is a whole spectrum of solutions. Yes, and there is never, I don't think, a right or wrong answer. Well, we had a situation a few weeks ago where we had two students, sat the same exams, got very similar results, both marginally failed.

One of them had cruised through the year, not really done enough, but was a bright lad. The other, a girl, had sweated blood throughout the year and still wasn't quite good enough. Then you get a situation where, some people would think, well, Claire deserves another chance because she worked so hard, some people think you should treat Chris better, he is the brighter one, he will be the more marketable one, he will be more use to us. Some people think you should treat them the same. Some people think that people should be allowed to keep sitting exams at our expense for as long as it takes. Some people think we should just terminate people's contracts for failure.

So, I suppose, I take a business decision basically, rather than a moral judgment when anyone fails. I would say that in practically no instance would more than a small minority agree with my decision, some people think they should be treated harsher, some people think they should be treated more leniently. I gave them both a week's study leave and I paid for their exams, so it gave them both another week and a half to find out of their holiday and about £200 to find for the course. It was a close call, it was a difficult call.

But what you have to do as well is consider the impact on the other students, what message it sends to them. I will have a dilemma within the next year, because I have only been training partner for just over a year. The exam results here; I don't believe they are good enough. I don't think they have been good enough basically because there has been tolerance of failure in the past and I have said repeatedly that in certain circumstances I will terminate people's contracts for failing. That has not happened here for about five years. Sooner or later I am going to have to do it, otherwise people won't believe me. I will only have to do it once. The difficulty is, one person has got to pay the price.

Everyone knows the rules but no one will believe the rules. Now the brighter one of those two, the one who had cruised, the Monday when I spoke to them about it, I was in a foul mood.

I didn't terminate his contract – the only reason I didn't – I was sorely tempted to, because (a) I think he deserved it and (b) it would have made an example of him – the reason I didn't was because I was in a bad mood and I thought, there is a risk that I could let my mood take my decision. Had I been in a good mood, I think I would have terminated his contract.

(*Source*: Research interview conducted by the authors)

Discussion activity 2.7

Why do you think the training partner acted altruistically when, by not supporting the trainees, he might have better met the (selfish) needs of the firm?

In Case study 2.8 it is clear that highly paid executives do not feel they need to act altruistically towards the generality of employees because they see themselves as belonging to a small elite group of world-class CEOs. This is the market argument, which holds that executives are entitled to whatever salary they can command on the international market. This argument only holds good of course if the market is an open and fair one. The second argument in support of high executive rewards is that it can be justified if they secure good performance and results for the organisation. Researchers from two Business Schools (Erturk et al., 2004 cited in Caulkin, 2004) studied chief executive pay in a sample of FTSE 100 companies. They reported that between 1978/9 and 2002/3 CEO pay in those companies rose by 536.9 per cent but net profits only increased by 118.9 per cent. At the same time the differential in remuneration between the CEOs and average employees rose. CEOs now earn on average 50 times as much as ordinary employees but 20 years ago the figure was only nine times average pay. Case study 2.8 was written at a time when the question of executive pay had long been a matter of public concern and debate.

Case study 2.8 — Executive fat cats and bankers' bonuses

The question of whether corporate executives are being paid too much, which has always been referred to as the 'fat cat' issue, has been a topic of debate since the late 1990s (Skapinker, 2001). It became an even more explosive topic when bankers seemed to retain their large bonuses after the financial collapse of 2007–8.

In 2006 The Trades Union Council (TUC) in the UK reported that from 2000 to 2006 the remuneration of directors of FTSE 100 companies rose by 105 percentage points above the rate of inflation. The earnings of other employees rose by only 6 percentage points (Taylor, 2006). In 2011 the median pay of the CEO of these companies had increased to £3.5m when most of their employees had received either no, or only very small pay increases. The gap between the median pay of the average worker and their top managers has been increasing and continues to increase. Top managers also have greater opportunities than normal employees for avoiding paying tax on their incomes. They can become non-domiciled (a non-dom), even though working in the

▶

UK, for tax purposes and thereby reducing liability for UK tax. In 2012 it was reported that some top public sector managers were having their salaries paid into private companies that they owned, thereby paying the lower rate corporation tax on their income rather than the higher rate income tax.

Such practices highlight the first ethical concern with high executive pay. It can be argued that too big a gap between the pay of the average employee and that of the top managers is unfair. Directors and executive are not the owners of a company (though as individuals they may well hold shares in the company) and like all other employees are servants of the company. This essential equality would mean that if the company can afford to increase earnings then it would be fair for all grades of employees to benefit in the same proportion. Large discrepancies between top and median pay can also be seen as unethical because they diminish any sense of community and common purpose within the organisation. Others would argue that this is just envy and that people should not worry about the rich getting richer. The more common argument is that as most companies operate in a global market they have to constrain average salaries and increase top salaries. The claim is that there is a limited pool of executive talent that they have to compete for in the world market and if top remuneration is not offered companies will not obtain the leadership they need.

A further ethical consideration is whether the pay increases are actually justified, or not, by the performance of the office holder or the organisation they are managing. Following the financial and banking crisis of 2007–8 the level of banker's bonuses did fall but soon began to return to previous levels (see Table 2.2) even though the banks were not often performing well and the rest of the economy was still coping with the recession that the banks had triggered. In 2011, under Project Merlin, the British Treasury reached an agreement with four of the largest UK banks that the size of the annual bonus pot should fall. The Office of National Statistics reported that in 2010–11 the financial and insurance sector (a broader sample that that reported on in Table 2.2) paid out £14bn in bonuses, unchanged from the year before (Groom, 2011).

Table 2.2   City bank bonuses 2001–9 and projections for 2010–12 (£m.)

2001	2002	2003	2004	2005	2006	2007	2008	2009	2010	2011	2012
3.921	3,329	4,893	5,695	7,130	10,059	10,241	4,008	6.012	6,654	7,098	7,546

(*Source*: CEBR, 2009)

Another trend is to pay executives a bonus for completing a one-off transaction, such as an acquisition, or as a retention payment to keep them with a company whilst it goes through a major change. In 2007 Tesco announced plans to give its chief executive 2.5m in shares for the success of its American 'Fresh & Easy' chain. Many investors were concerned that a chief executive should receive a bonus for one part of the business when he was already remunerated for running the whole business. There was a protest vote against the package at the AGM but the vote was not binding (Rigby, 2007). In March 2008 there were reports that sales at the Fresh & Easy stores were falling short of expectations. Tesco denied the reports (Birchall and Braithwaite, 2008). A particular issue arises when an executive achieves a target in one year but the bonus for their success is paid in arrears; and it is actually distributed in a subsequent year when the company's performance is poor. A sensible senior executive always ensures that they have a good severance deal included in their contract should they fail and the company wishes to replace them quickly (Donkin, 2007).

Discussion activity 2.8

Are chief executives inclined to selfishness? If they are, is that a problem?

Is the high pay of top ranking professional footballers more morally accept-able than that of CEOs and bankers? If so, why?

Does it matter if the gap between top incomes and average incomes widens if everyone is earning more?

Case study 2.9 raises questions about whether there is an obligation on companies to avoid selfishness in times of national crisis.

Case study 2.9 — The oil companies and the 2000 fuel crisis

The UK experienced an oil crisis in July 2000. A combination of self-employed lorry drivers, owners of small haulage companies and farmers objected to the high price of petrol (the bulk of the price of which in the UK is determined by the excise duty). In a Poujadist protest they used their mobile phones to create a network of supporters, who blockaded the country's oil storage depots and led slow-moving convoys up and down motorways causing traffic queues. Any modern country depends on the internal combustion engine and the shortage of fuel caused by the action soon threatened chaos. The National Health Service was put on red alert and businesses could not carry out their normal business. There were fears that food would not be delivered to the supermarkets.

The government was caught unawares. The Prime Minister declared that the situation would be back to normal within 24 hours; but it was not. It looked for scapegoats and blamed the international oil companies for selfishness. The government argued that the oil companies should take strong action to break the blockades and ensure that oil was delivered to the nation's petrol station forecourts. The oil companies argued that it was not their responsibility to take risks with the safety of their employees. They would not order their drivers to drive through the pickets if there was a danger that they might be hurt. The oil companies were suspected by some politicians of secretly agreeing with the protestors. It was reported that there was a 'chummy camaraderie' between the protestors blockading a refinery and the management within in it; even to the extent that the protestors were served tea and bacon sandwiches from the canteen within the refinery (Weaver, 2000). The oil companies claimed to make only small profits of a penny a litre on retailing petrol, and if the protest led to a reduction in excise duties it could only be of benefit to the industry. Oil transport was outsourced to small independent companies and self-employed drivers (some of whom had been sacked by the companies only to be re-employed as independents for less pay) who did have real complaints about the cost of the diesel that fuelled their lorries. The oil companies had little leverage to force these drivers to break the blockade. The view of the *Observer* (2000) leader writer was that the oil companies were too concerned with maximising their shareholders' returns by carrying low contingency stocks of oil and using a just-in-time logistics system, which meant there was no buffer in the case of a crisis. There was a view that the companies owed an obligation to the wider community when they traded in a material that was so vital to the functioning of society.

▶

The blockade melted away as quickly as it had formed as people began panic buying at the supermarkets. The Prime Minister said he would not be forced into cutting the duty on fuel.

There was a minor replay of this issue in April 2008 when rising world oil prices and a strike at an oil refinery caused some truck drivers to protest in Whitehall about increasing fuel prices. Again in 2012 tanker drivers voted to go on strike for better pay and conditions. The government responded by saying that it was training soldiers so that they could take over fuel deliveries if the strike went ahead.

DEFINITIONS

Poujadism is a set of political beliefs named after Pierre Poujade, a small-town shopkeeper in France in the 1950s. It objects to state interference such as taxation, the investigation of tax evasion and any regulation of small businesses. It also opposes big corporations and large-scale labour organisation.

Discussion activity 2.9

Do the oil companies have a moral obligation to maintain fuel supplies in a country?

Fairness

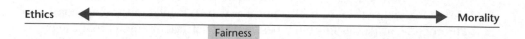

Fairness concerns the proportions in which resources are distributed between people or causes. The resources can be money, respect or any possession that a community can allocate among its members. Aristotle expressed the central concern, about the appropriateness of the proportions, in a system of distributive justice. He saw it as a matter of algebra in which there are at least four terms: two persons and two shares. A just distribution is one in which the ratio between the first person and the first share is equal to the ratio between the second person and the second share. If Fred is twice as worthy as Jane then Jane's portion should be half of Fred's. In this case the two ratios will be the same. The arithmetic is fine but the question is how the two people involved are to be assessed. Aristotle said it should be done by assessing their merit. But he admitted that people define merit in different ways.

> People of democratic sympathies measure degrees of merit by degrees of freedom, oligarchs by degrees of wealth, others judge by good birth, those who believe in the rule of the 'best' go by moral and intellectual qualifications.

(Aristotle, 1976: 146)

This does not exhaust the possibilities. Marx measured it according to need, 'From each according to his ability, to each according to his needs' (in Marx and Engels, 1962: 24). Others might measure merit by personhood and insist that, since all are equal in this particular aspect, then everyone should receive equal shares.

The debates under the ethical heading of fairness concern the appropriate measure of a person's merit and the fairness of the ratios between one person's merit and share and those of others. The case studies in this section give examples of these debates. Case study 2.10 focuses on need, 2.11 on personhood and 2.12 contrasts the property rights of shareholders with the needs of customers.

Case study 2.10	Providing new drugs on the NHS to people with multiple sclerosis

Multiple sclerosis is a debilitating and incurable disease. A new drug, with the generic name of beta interferon, has been shown to alleviate the effects of the disease but it costs £10,000 per patient per year. The National Institute for Clinical Excellence (NICE) in the UK investigated the drug to see whether, on clinical and economic grounds, it should be made freely available on the NHS. The belief of those who suffer from the disease, and of those who support them through membership of lobby groups, is that it would be unfair to deny this drug to sufferers. The following article from the *Financial Times* identifies some of the politics and anger that surround the issue.

FT The National Institute for Clinical Excellence has put off a decision on the use of beta-interferon, the drug for multiple sclerosis sufferers, until at least July next year. The decision to delay has been taken to allow a publicly available economic model of the costs and benefits of the drug to be built. The delay brought a furious reaction from the Multiple Sclerosis Society that accused the institute of putting back the decision to ensure that it came after the likely date of the general election. Peter Cardy, the society's chief executive, described the decision to delay as 'astonishing' and 'breathtaking bungling' given that beta-interferon and glatiramer, another MS drug, have been reviewed by the institute for almost a year.

Mike Wallace, a former managing director of Schering, which manufacturers beta-interferon, said: 'I find it appalling. You have to wonder what these guys are playing at. I feel desperately sorry for the people with MS who have had their hopes raised and dashed and raised and dashed again by the NICE process.'

The institute initially judged that MS drugs were not cost effective and should be supplied only to patients already receiving them. Appeals led to that decision being reconsidered, but the institute is unhappy with the economic models that Schering and Biogen have supplied. The appeals committee described as 'flawed' a model built by Biogen that claimed the drug might save money when the cost of working days lost by patients and carers was taken into account. Schering has submitted a new model, but has told the institute that it is commercially sensitive – a stance which appraisal committee members say makes it difficult for the institute to explain its objections to the model's conclusions.

The committee has, therefore, decided to build its own model – an approach that may force manufacturers to reveal more of the assumptions behind their results. Mr Cardy said it was 'impossible to understand why NICE has only now decided to look at the cost effectiveness of these drugs in a different way'. He demanded that Alan Milburn, the health secretary, 'sort NICE's ineptitude out'. Andrew Dillon, the institute's chief executive, said: 'The evidence relating to the cost effectiveness of these medicines is critically important in this appraisal.' It

▶

was 'of the utmost importance that the institute's guidance is both evidence-based and seen to be fair', and the delay to achieve that was in the best interest of those with MS. The appraisal committee originally said that a big price reduction would be needed before the drugs became cost effective. The process of deciding what would go into the institute's model, and the commissioning and evaluation of its results would be transparent, said Mr Dillon. The results would be published in full, with interested parties free to comment on it.

(*Source*: National News: Medicines arbiter delays decision on beta-interferon: Clinical Excellence Multiple Sclerosis Society angry that drug ruling is only likely after election, *The Financial Times*, 23 December 2000 (Pilling, D. and Timmins, N.), Copyright © The Financial Times Ltd. Additional material from Barlow, 2001; NICE, 2001 and 2002.)

In 2002 NICE decided it would not recommend beta interferon or glatimirer for the treatment of MS.

Discussion activity 2.10

Should the decision whether or not to provide these drugs to MS sufferers be based solely on clinical grounds or should cost-effectiveness criteria also be considered? What influence should powerful lobby groups have on such decisions?

Case study 2.11 raises the issue of unfair discrimination at work. In the last three decades of the twentieth century this was one of the major areas of ethical concern in business and organisational life. In the UK discrimination on grounds of race has been illegal since the Race Relations Act 1975 was passed. The Sex Discrimination Act came into force in 1975; it was amended and broadened in 1986. The Equal Pay Act took effect in 1975 and was amended in 1984. In 1995 an Act of Parliament made discrimination on the grounds of disability illegal. There is currently much debate about discrimination on the grounds of age but at the time of writing this was not illegal.

Case study 2.11   Discriminating against employees – the Metropolitan Police Service

One of the most high-profile cases of race discrimination at work involves the Metropolitan Police. It was accused of institutional racism by the McPherson report into the police's investigation of the murder of Stephen Lawrence (Burns & Shrimsley, 2000). This case had a major impact on the force, which sought to establish that it was an equal opportunities employer in practices as well as in policy. Many thought that the service had worked hard to become multicultural and to reduce racial discrimination.

The issues of discrimination later became focused on the case of Superintendent Ali Dizaei, who was Iranian born and one of the most senior officers in the Metropolitan Police from an ethnic minority background. In 1999 he became officer in charge of operations at Kensington Police Station. The Metropolitan Police made him the subject of an undercover operation called 'Helios', which investigated suspicions that he was involved in drugs and prostitution. This enquiry became the most expensive ever undertaken against a single officer. Dizaei was suspended from office in 2001. He was eventually charged with attempting to pervert the course of justice, misconduct in public office and submitting false expenses claims. In April 2003 he was found not guilty of perverting the course of justice and in September of the same year the prosecution withdrew the expenses charges. His lawyers claimed that the prosecution had been a 'witch hunt' and a campaign of 'Orwellian proportions' (Tait, 2003).

The criminal proceedings being concluded, the Metropolitan Police service then began a disciplinary process against Dizaei. In 2003 nine allegations were identified and an investigation began. Subsequently the National Black Police Association (NBPA), of which Dizaei was once president, called for a boycott of the Metropolitan Police Service by anyone from the ethnic minorities who might have considered joining the service. This was something of a blow when the service was intent on increasing the proportion of its officers from the ethnic minorities. Before the investigation was completed the Home Secretary urged Dizaei and the Metropolitan Police to come to a settlement. A deal was brokered by the Arbitration and Conciliation Advisory Service. Under this deal Dizaei admitted that his conduct had fallen 'far below the standards expected of a police officer' and he agreed not to take his employer to an employment tribunal. In return he received £80,000 compensation, a statement that his integrity was intact and a return to work (BBC News Online, 2004a). The NBPA dropped its boycott. However, the Police Complaints Authority (PCA) was unhappy that the disciplinary process had not taken its proper course and had been pre-empted by a private agreement between the parties. The chairman of the PCA stated,

> Every police officer should face a consistency of treatment as far as the disciplinary process is concerned – we can't have one officer getting special treatment because he is a senior black officer and because there are concerns about race in the police service.

> (*Source*: BBC News Online, 2004b)

The Metropolitan Police resisted the demand to continue disciplinary action against Dizaei and in March 2004 the PCA directed the Metropolitan Police to take disciplinary action. However, the PCA was then replaced by a new body called the Independent Police Complaints Commission (IPCC). This organisation reconsidered the issue. It was also unhappy about the private deal but thought it not in the public interest to pursue the disciplinary action. It beleived the charges against Dizaei were capable of proof but that if he were found guilty any penalty would likely be modest. It pointed out that he had admitted errors and was to receive 'Words of Advice from his Chief Officer'. It therefore revoked the instruction to continue the disciplinary proceedings (IPCC, 2004). A separate enquiry by another Police Force into Operation Helios continued.

Dizaei said his re-integration into the Met would not be easy – he thought there might be some backlash from others in the service; but that he had never had an easy time in the force (Dodd, 2011a). Nevertheless in 2008 he was promoted to Commander. There continued to be tensions between him and other senior managers. He became involved in the case of Inspector Ghaffur, who was accusing the Commissioner of racism. The situation became confused when it emerged that Ghaffur's solicitor, a Mr Mireskandari, had a criminal conviction and his practice was shut down by the Solicitors' Regulation Authority. It emerged that Mireskandari was Dizaei's best man when he married his third wife and there were claims that Dizaei had advised Mireshkandari's clients, including a Russian millionaires who killed a man in a hit-and-run crash. Dizaei was cleared of any wrongdoing.

▶

Further problems arose when Dizaei was involved in a brawl over an invoice for work on his website, and he had his protagonist Mr al-Baghdadi arrested. Allegations were made that he had 'fitted up' al-Baghdadi. Dizaei was tried, convicted and dismissed from the Metropolitan Police in 2010. Dizaei's wife investigated al-Baghdadi's background and discovered that he had lied to the court about his identity and had been defrauding the social benefits system. On appeal Dizaei's conviction was quashed and he was released from prison after having served a year. However the appeal judges recommended a retrial. Dizaei said 'When I clear my name it is my intention to go back to the Metropolitan Police and serve my time" (Dodd, 2011b). In September 2011 he was reinstated but then was immediately suspended. His retrial started in 2012 and resulted in Dizaei being sentenced to three years' imprisonment.

In a link with another business ethics issue in 2011 it was claimed that Dizaei's phone had been hacked into by the *News of the World* (See Case study 1.1).

The story of Ali Dizaei is picaresque; a series of accusations and challenges. Each time he is cleared there are claims that he is the victim of racism.

Discussion activity 2.11

It is probably impossible for those without detailed knowledge to come to a definitive view on the Dizaei case; but it does raise a range of interesting issues.

Does an individual case, such as that of Ali Dizaei, suggest that an organisation is institutionally racist despite its policies and principles?

To what extent do formal process of discipline and grievance exacerbate rather than solve problems of discrimination?

Case study 2.12 considers whether Railtrack, the company that oversaw the operations of the British railway system, was fair in its treatment of its stakeholders, in particular the travelling public, in relation to its solicitude towards shareholders.

Case study 2.12   The British railway system: priorities, profits and governance

In May 2001 Railtrack, the company responsible for running the infrastructure of Britain's rail system, published its financial results. It made a worse than expected loss of £534m. This was largely due to the cost of renewing the permanent way after the Hatfield crash in 2000. Despite a disastrous year the company maintained the dividend payment to its shareholders. It was argued that it had to keep the confidence of the financial markets because it would need to borrow millions of pounds in the future to invest in the rail system.

The following leading article was published in the *Financial Times*.

 That profits conflict with safety on the railways can no longer be in doubt. The draft report of the official inquiry into the Hatfield derailment reveals a catalogue of management and engineering failures.

After privatisation in 1996, the top executives of Railtrack, the infrastructure company, focused too much on immediate value for shareholders and too little on maintenance of the track. This might have been predicted; for although the rail regulator set targets for infrastructure improvement, every pound saved on maintenance helped to increase dividends.

Railtrack would have been entitled to keep such savings if they had resulted from extra efficiency. But the inquiry shows that it lacked managerial and technical skills, was slack in its maintenance discipline and communicated poorly with subcontractors. New management brought in after the fatal crash has admitted past failings and has made some progress towards putting them right. But broader remedies are needed. The company must be subject to a new set of incentives that more explicitly recognises its status as a public service utility in receipt of large government subsidies.

At the time of privatisation, it was decided to adopt the regulatory model used in the gas, electricity and telecommunications industries. This sets a price that the utility may charge, leaving an incentive to make extra profits from greater efficiency.

It is now obvious that this was a bad model for the railways – partly because of the importance and unpredictable costs of safety and partly because the fragmented structure of the industry creates perverse incentives. If Railtrack closes a line for unexpected safety work, for example, it must pay penalty charges to train operating companies.

Regulation should move closer to the US model. That would involve tighter supervision and replace the profit motive with the guarantee of a 'fair' rate of return – provided the company does its job properly. There are disadvantages: the spur to efficiency is blunted and, when the return is assured, managers may try to over-invest.

But since Railtrack has failed to convince its shareholders, the markets and the general public that it can find the right balance between profit and maintenance expenditures, stronger regulation must be the way ahead.

(*Source*: Leader: Changing track, *The Financial Times*, 9 May 2001,
Copyright © The Financial Times Ltd.)

The case raises the question of whether public utilities, which are necessities of a civilised life, are ethically different from other products and services. The chairmen of UK regulated utilities, according to a survey (Brigley and Vass, 1997: 164), thought they were not, and that the ethical obligations on a private utility company should be no different from those placed on any private company.

In 2001 Railtrack plc was declared insolvent and placed into administration. The shareholders demanded that they should be compensated by being paid the value of the Railtrack shares when the company was floated on the stock exchange. The government retorted that taxpayers' money would not be used to spare shareholders the consequences of their poor investment.

The successor body is called Network Rail. It is a not-for-profit public interest company. It has no shareholders but it does have 116 members. It was thought that a company devoid of shareholders would be run for the benefit of the whole railway network and its customers and not simply for the financial benefit of the shareholders. The members have no financial interest in the company and receive neither dividends nor capital. Nevertheless they are expected according to Network Rail to ensure that 'Network Rail is managed in line with high standards of corporate governance' (House of Commons, 2004). Two-thirds of the members are members of the public who were appointed from those chosen from 1,200 applicants by a membership selection panel that was appointed by Network Rail. The public members therefore are the appointees of Network Rail. Some public members represent special interest groups, such as The Royal Society for Disability and Rehabilitation (Gosling, 2004). In addition the key industry stakeholders, franchise holders who actually run the train services,

▶

railway undertakings and operators of railway assets who look after the rolling stock and property such as stations are represented. The Parliamentary Select Committee on Transport (House of Commons, 2004: §59) argued that this structure would create no strong account-ability to the public interest.

> We were also concerned that the industry members were virtually self-appointing. These members include contractors [to Network Rail] and while members may have a duty to the company, there was always some possibility of the appearance of a conflict of interest. Finally the public members are appointed by the Board of the company and represent no one but themselves.

There was much scepticism regarding whether members without a financial interest would have sufficient influence on the Board. The rail regulator thought the members would not have the motivation to drive down costs. It is arguable that such a consequence reflects a better balance of influence between stakeholders, and between the demand for profit and other demands such as safety. If this argument is correct then the governance of Network Rail might be a powerful new model of governance. In 2008 the Office of the Rail Regulator fined Network Rail £14m after it failed to complete engineering works on schedule and caused massive delays for rail passengers.

Iain Croucher left his job as chief executive of Network Rail in 2010 after he had been the subject of criticism that reflected on the corporate governance of the organisation. The allegations were that there was not enough constraint on the chief executive's power. One illustration of this was the debate about executive bonuses that many thought were excessive. The Board approved the payments by 37 votes to 31. Fewer than half of the 'public' members of the Board voted for the bonuses. The chairman of Network Rail said that the decision had been a good demonstration of the management being held to account (BBC News Online, 2010).

Discussion activity 2.12

What is a fair balance between interests of the owners of a company that provides a public utility and the interests of the customers? Was Railtrack right in its approach? Will the structure of Network Rail, which has no shareholders, redress the balance?

Part four: Preventing indifference to others

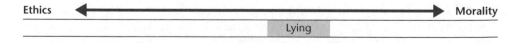

Ethics ⟵⟶ Morality
Lying

Lying

Lying is wrong; except that in everyday usage it is not always so. The acceptability of a lie depends partly on the context in which it is made. Perjury, lying under oath in a court of law, is not acceptable; indeed it is a crime that carries heavy punishment. In the context of business negotiations lying, in the form of bluffing, may be acceptable as Carr argued (1968) in a classic article. Lies, in such a context, may be no more than putting a spin on an unpalatable truth.

> **DEFINITION**
>
> Winston Churchill used the phrase **terminological inexactitude** in a speech on Chinese labour in South Africa. The phrase was not actually used as a euphemism for a lie. He argued that although the labourers' contracts might not be proper or healthy they could not be classified as slavery without 'some risk of terminological inexactitude'. However, Alexander Haig, the American politician, is credited with saying, 'It is not a lie, it's a terminological inexactitude'.

The reprehensibility of a lie may also depend upon its nature. Telling an absolute untruth is often worse than failing to tell the whole truth. A cabinet secretary to a British government famously objected to a suggestion that he had lied. He had, he claimed, merely been 'economical with the truth'. Managers often find difficulty when they have to keep silent about privileged or confidential information, as when they know there are proposals to make people redundant but have been required to say nothing until the plans are finalised and can be announced. Their loyalty to their staff conflicts with their commitment to their company's needs. Conflicts of interest are a particular problem for professionals and public officials whose judgment should be seen to be free of private or opposing interests. They should be open about any such conflicts. Recruitment consultants finding new jobs for staff being made redundant would be regarded with suspicion if they received fees from both the organisation buying the out-placement service and the company in which they placed the redundant staff. The Nolan Committee's (1995) seven principles for public life are all focused on ensuring that private or sectional interests do not prejudice people's decisions on matters of public interest.

> ## The Nolan principles
> **DEFINITION**
>
> **Selflessness**
> Holders of public office should act solely in terms of the public interest. They should not do so in order to gain financial or other benefits for themselves, their family or their friends.
>
> **Integrity**
> Holders of public office should not place themselves under any financial or other obligation to outside individuals or organisations that might seek to influence them in the performance of their official duties.
>
> **Objectivity**
> In carrying out public business, including making public appointments, awarding contracts, or recommending individuals for rewards and benefits, holders of public office should make choices on merit.

▶

Accountability

Holders of public office are accountable for their decisions and actions to the public and must submit themselves to whatever scrutiny is appropriate to their office.

Openness

Holders of public office should be as open as possible about all the decisions and actions that they take. They should give reasons for their decisions and restrict information only when the wider public interest clearly demands.

Honesty

Holders of public office have a duty to declare any private interests relating to their public duties and to take steps to resolve any conflicts arising in a way that protects the public interest.

Leadership

Holders of public office should promote and support these principles by leadership and example.

Another test of the dishonesty of a lie is its purpose. There is a range of names for acceptable lies, including fibs and white lies, that are intended to avoid giving offence or causing distress to individuals. Not all managers see such lying as acceptable, as one told us in a research interview.

> I think for me the most important thing is honesty and what I find difficult is when managers maybe are doing something for one reason but are telling staff it's for another reason. Something like that I would find, and do find, quite difficult. Rather than actually saying to staff, you didn't get the job because your performance isn't as accurate or whatever else; what they give is fairly obscure reasons rather than actually facing the real reason.

A lie involves intent to deceive; if there is no such intent there is no lie. We fill our conversations with figures of speech such as hyperbole ('I'm so hungry I could eat a horse') and metaphor ('That man is a pig'), which do not lead people to accept the literal truth of what we are saying. Advertising is a common area in which companies may seek to deceive their customers. The Advertising Standards Authority, in a typical example, criticised Virgin Trains for claiming in their advertisements that all fares were half price when conditions meant that many were not (Milmo, 2001).

Sometimes organisations simply lie. In 2007 Southern Water, which provides water and waste water services in the south-east of England, was fined £20.3m by the water industry regulator. Water companies have to provide performance information to the regulator and it was discovered that Southern Water had deliberately misreported information, to make its performance look better than it was, on its response times, billing enquiries and service complaints. Because the industry is a regulated one, and because the increase in retail prices it is allowed by the regulator partly depends on its performance, the company had been able to increase its prices more than was justified. It had to pay back £500,000 to its customers (BBC News Online, 2007c).

The case of Shell's missing oil barrels

The Royal Dutch/Shell company, or rather group of companies, has been accused of being over-large, out of control, secretive and hidding behind a bland façade. These claims have centred on the story of Shell's missing oil reserves.

The problem began in the late 1990s. One of the figures used by observers of the oil industry is the reserve replacement ratio (RRR). Shell's RRR was one of the poorest in the industry. It was not finding new sources of oil fast enough. Managers assumed that the policy for 'booking' new reserves was too restrictive. There was a fashion in management at the time for using problem-solving teams to come up with radical and creative solutions, and Shell established four such teams to improve the exploration and production function, which was led by Sir Phillip Watts. New guidelines for booking reserves were implemented. In Shell's 1998 annual report there was a brief note reporting that 'Estimation methods have been refined during 1998'. The RRR consequently increased by 40 per cent and the director was rewarded for improving the efficiency of his directorate. Shell had adopted the system of determining senior managers' rewards and bonuses according to their performance against critical performance indicators. Rewards were triggered by numbers and targets, and not by the rounded judgments of appraisers.

In 2001 the American Securities and Exchange Commission (SEC) published new guidelines for assessing the commerciality of new oil discoveries. These were to be used to determine whether finds were certain enough to be accounted as a reserve. Shell's booked reserves in Australia, Norway and Nigeria did not comply with the new SEC guidelines. However, there was great pressure within Shell to keep the RRR as high as possible. Nor was there much internal auditing pressure to review the reserve figures, the auditing of which was done part-time by one engineer who had no staff to back him up.

It is clear that several top executives within Shell knew of this problem by 2002. However, nothing was made public. This was largely a result of feuds between senior managers, particularly between Sir Philip Watts (who had been promoted to chairman) and Walter van de Vijver, head of exploration. After what van de Vijver considered an unfair performance appraisal from Sir Philip Watts the former sent the latter an e-mail stating 'I am becoming sick and tired about lying about the extent of our oil reserves issues and the downward revision that needs to be done because of far too aggressive/optimistic bookings'.

On 9 January 2004 the Shell group announced through its investor relations staff that they had downgraded their reserves by 20 per cent, or 3.9 billion barrels of oil. The markets were not happy and the stock market valuation of Shell dropped to £2.9bn. That the announcement had not been made by Sir Philip Watts personally increased investors' anger. The pressure led to Watts and van de Vijver resigning. At first it was reported that Watts left by mutual consent, although later it was admitted that he had been pushed. Nevertheless he received a £1m compensation package for the breaking of his contract. Jeroen van der Veer from Royal Dutch became the new chairman. There was some negative comment in the business press that the new chairman was an insider, although given the reported friction between the British and Dutch wings of the group Shell insiders would be more likely to see the appointment as a Dutch *coup d'état*. The finance director resigned in July. There was no question of financial impropriety on her part but there were questions about her effectiveness in ensuring compliance with good accounting practice.

▶

Shell argued that the differences between its criteria for booking reserves, and those of the SEC, are largely a technical matter. It pointed out that the de-booking of reserves does not mean that the oil is not there and it anticipates that 85 per cent of the missing barrels will prove to have been there all along. Shell's approach to internal control is on a risk assessment basis, which is designed to manage rather than to eliminate the risks to achieving the company's objectives. In September 2004 Sir Philip Watts announced that he planned to challenge the UK Financial Services Authority (FSA) in the Financial Services and Markets Tribunal (the appeal court for FSA decisions). He was claiming that he was treated unfairly by the FSA, which criticised him implicitly in its report, although not by name, and did not give him an opportunity to rebut the criticisms (Hosking, 2004).

Shell's audit committee instigated an internal review, which was carried out by external accountants. There was pressure for an independent inquiry both in the UK and the USA. In the UK the charge was that the company had breached Stock Market regulations by not reporting in good time matters and information that could have an impact on the share price. The FSA started an investigation, as did the SEC in America.

Shell cooperated fully with the investigations. In August 2004 the FSA fined the company £17m and the SEC fined it £66.29m. The FSA accused Shell of 'unprecedented misconduct' and a failure to put internal controls in place to prevent misleading information being given to the market. In its agreement with the SEC Shell did not admit any illegality but it did agree to spend nearly £3m on developing better internal compliance systems. These official punishments may be only the start of the problem for Shell as lawyers in the USA are clamouring to start class actions against the company on behalf of various pension funds, which believe that the misinformation caused them financial losses. Shell may be one of the first cases to feel the weight of the Sarbanes–Oxley Act, which was passed in the USA following the Enron and WorldCom cases. Under this Act's provisions the senior managers of the company signed a declaration concerning the 2002 annual report that 'based on my knowledge, this annual report does not contain any untrue statement of a material fact'.

Royal Dutch Shell has an unusual, but not unique structure. It is a dual listed company. This means that the Shell group operates as a single organisation but legally it is two organisations: the Royal Dutch Petroleum Company, which is based in Holland and listed on the Dutch Stock exchange, and the Shell Transport and Trading Company, which is based in London and whose shares are listed on the London Stock Exchange. These two companies are the parent companies. The shareholders of Royal Dutch are mostly Dutch and those of Shell Trading mostly UK based, although there is a substantial block of American depository receipts (ADR) held in the USA. A series of legal agreements governs the relationship between the two parent companies. This arrangement dates from 1907 when Shell (which was founded in 1833 as a shop selling seashells to naturalists) merged with the Royal Dutch Company for the Exploration of Petroleum Wells in the Netherlands East Indies. Under this deal Royal Dutch controls 60 per cent of the group's assets and Shell Trading controls the remaining 40 per cent.

Royal Dutch and Shell Trading do not undertake any operations. Instead they own the shares of two holding companies, Shell Petroleum NV and the Shell Petroleum Company Ltd. These in turn own the large number of companies that carry out the group's operations around the world. The two parent companies each have a board of directors (Royal Dutch has a supervisory board as well) that have different memberships. The combined group is overseen by an executive board known as the committee of managing directors (CMD). The members of the CMD are appointed by the boards of the parent companies. In such a structure there is clearly tension as to who has the greatest influence and who carries oversight and responsibility for the organisation's compliance with laws and conventions. It appears that Royal Dutch is the dominant partner. The supervisory board of Royal Dutch controls a number of foundations that own 'priority shares', which confer voting rights but no economic benefit. These enable the supervisory board to control nominations to both parent company boards and thus to the CMD. The CMD is not formally covered by the joint venture agreement, which defines the merged company, and so it has no formal authority over the parent companies' assets.

Investors have complained that the legal structure of Royal Dutch/Shell makes it difficult for shareholders to gain information from the group and to influence its policy. This, taken together with the divisionalised structure of the group, which leads to a high level of decentralisation, raises questions about the effectiveness of internal control. This said, the group has the full panoply of policies, codes of ethics and operating principles, which all large companies have, to ensure good governance. Economists have studied the tensions between insider ownership and insider control (through such devices as priority shares) in dual class companies. Some have suggested that when the insiders, in this case the Dutch boards, have great voting muscle they use it to support their own position as against the interests of outsiders such as shareholders. This tendency itself would make it difficult for shareholders to hold the company to account. Although it can equally be argued that the system in Royal Dutch/Shell, which gave the managers low ownership but high voting rights, contributed to the development of a strong and flexible corporate culture.

The reserves revaluation has led to calls for changes in corporate governance of Royal Dutch/Shell to prevent the reoccurrence of similar problems. Shell has now adopted a single board structure. In 2005 Shell announced the largest profit ever made by a British based company, largely attributable to the increase in world oil prices in 2004.

(*Sources*: Doran and Mansell, 2004; Gompers et al., 2004; *The Guardian*, 2004a and 2004b; Harrington, 2003; Harris and Michaels, 2004; Morgan, 2004; Plender, 2004; Shell Group, 2004; Watchman, 2004)

Discussion activity 2.13

- In your opinion did Shell lie?
- If you believe it did what were the factors and influences that may have caused it to lie?
- Is this a good news story because the regulatory agencies punished Shell?
- Why did Shell's shareholders get so vexed about the corporate governance issues?
- What changes in corporate governance, if any, might be necessary?

Refusing to be true to one's own beliefs can be a form of self-deception. This can happen when a person justifies continuing their connection to an organisation even though they object on ethical grounds to the organisation's behaviour.

| Case study 2.14 | **BAT, Nottingham University and the honorary professor** |

In 2011 Nottingham University accepted £3.8m from British American Tobacco (BAT), the world's second biggest tobacco company, towards setting up an international Centre for Corporate Responsibility. There was, of course, nothing illegal about the gift but many individuals and groups thought it was wrong. The problem was that Nottingham University carried out medical research into cancer and its treatment, some of it funded by medical charities. This was thought to fit badly with accepting money from a company that sells products known to cause cancer.

Richard Smith was editor of the *British Medical Journal* (BMJ) and an unpaid honorary professor of medical journalism at Nottingham University. He believed the university's acceptance of BAT's money was a 'serious mistake'. He polled readers of the BMJ to discover their views on whether he should resign from his post at Nottingham University. Of the 1,075 votes cast 84 per cent said the university should return the money and 54 per cent said that Professor Smith should resign if the university did not do so. The latter vote was closer than had been anticipated and this was because some argued that the professor should stay within the university and argue his case internally. The professor did resign, both because he said he would abide by the result of the poll and because he firmly believed the university was wrong in its actions.

(*Source*: Meikle, 2001)

| **Discussion activity 2.14** |

Is it better to retreat and live to fight another day or to take a stand on a matter one sees as an injustice?

The next case study concerns a senior manager who told what was, of itself, an inconsequential lie; but one that nevertheless had great consequences because of the context in which it was told.

| Case study 2.15 | **Lord Browne of Madingley** |

Lord Browne was appointed chief executive of British Petroleum (BP) in 1995 when the company was valued at £24.4m. By 2007 it was worth £108.3bn. He was an internationally respected executive with access to senior politicians. He was due to retire, and be lauded with praise at the end of 2008. However, on 1 May 2007 he announced his immediate resignation. Lord Browne had been in a four-year relationship with Jeff Chevalier. Lord Browne supported his partner by encouraging him to enrol for a postgraduate course, helping him set up a business and taking him to BP functions. When the relationship ended in 2006, Chevalier found the transition from a luxury lifestyle to a more normal existence difficult. Chevalier offered to sell his story to the *Daily Mail*. This story included a number of allegations, such as that Lord Browne had allowed Chevalier to use his BP laptop computer for his personal e-mails and that he had talked openly about issues he had discussed with senior politicians. BP and Lord Browne denied the allegations. Lord Browne applied for an injunction to prevent publication of the story and it was granted on 6 January. He announced the following week that he would be retiring in July 2007 instead of the end of 2008. Even the date in 2008 was earlier than Browne had originally wanted but was the result of a battle with the chairman of BP over succession. The *Daily Mail* took the case to the House of Lords. During the hearing Browne lied when he said that he had met Chevalier whilst exercising in Battersea Park. The judge said he was not prepared;

> to make allowances for a 'white lie' told in circumstances such as these – especially by a man who prays in aid of his reputation and distinction.

Once the judgment had been published and the judge's comments became known, Lord Browne resigned. By resigning before the end of his contract he lost a pay package worth nearly £16m. The lie may have been a small one, and Browne's sexuality of no relevance to his job; but lying in court was a diminution of his honesty and integrity. The CEO's integrity would have been an issue had he stayed on; especially as there were legal proceeding taking place against BP in the USA over the Texas City oil refinery explosion that killed 15 people. In October 2007 BP admitted being guilty of a felony in not maintaining proper safety standards and paid fines of $373m (Grant et al., 2007).

(*Sources*: Crooks, 2007; Hawkes, 2007)

Discussion activity 2.15

Can a white lie be acceptable to protect one's privacy?

In the Lord Browne case, the judge's remarks that Lord Browne was willing to lie and 'trash' the reputation of Mr Chevalier to protect his reputation and avoid personal embarrassment hints at what was known in ancient Greek tragedy as hubris.

Hubris, nemesis and catharsis   DEFINITION

The first two terms represent the themes of Greek tragedy and the third is the experience of the audience watching the play. **Hubris** is a great pride and belief in one's own importance. **Nemesis** is a deserved punishment that cannot be avoided; and **catharsis** is the release of strong emotion caused by the experience of fear, albeit only expressed on the stage. These terms can be illustrated by the story of Jonathan Aitken, a prominent politician and one-time Minister of State for Defence. In 1993 he stayed at the Paris Ritz. *The Guardian* newspaper took an interest in this visit and enquired why a cabinet minister was staying at a very expensive hotel at someone else's expense. Aitken said he had paid for the stay himself. He lied. But at the time there was no proof he had. *The Guardian* kept running the story, believing the weekend was connected with an arms deal involving Saudi Arabia, and Aitken, saying that he was going to fight 'the cancer of bent

▶

and twisted journalism . . . with the simple sword of truth', sued the newspaper for libel – his hubris. He persuaded his wife and his daughter to lie in support of the claim that he had paid for the stay himself. When documents were presented that showed that he had lied on oath in the court the libel case collapsed. He was charged with perverting the course of justice and perjury in 1998 and sent to prison in 1999 – his nemesis. That the public found this cathartic is suggested by his availability as a public speaker (SpeakersUK, 2005). Rumours that Aitken was planning to become a priest after finishing his 18-month sentence were denied by him. He did enrol to study theology at Oxford. This may be his catharsis.

(*Sources*: *The Guardian*, 1999; Harding, 1999; Wilson, 1999)

Many of the issues related to lying, as in the following case study, concern the failure to tell the whole truth rather than the telling of falsehoods.

Case study 2.16	**Economy with the truth when dealing with the tax authorities**

Extract from an interview with the finance director of a private company

Most of the ethical issues revolve around disclosure to the revenue and tax authority. The issues are whether we should disclose all the material facts and secondly, when arguing a case with the revenue, whether we should make a case even when we know it is weak. The rule is 'we will make a case as long as we have one argument – however obtuse'. As long as we have an arguable position we won't be embarrassed.

I have just had a conversation with someone on an issue . . . actually tax again, on whether we give the Inland Revenue a letter or not at this particular point in time. It could be slightly prejudicial, only slightly, to our case, and as we are going to have a meeting and it may settle it, do I need to give it to him [the tax inspector] now? This is a question of timing. If I can settle it without giving it to him I might do.

It's just to do with tax planning and why we actually had done a transaction. It may make the revenue renege on something they have just agreed. Unlikely, but you don't want to raise doubts in somebody's mind who has actually spent some time looking at it. Tax is always slow anyway, so why shouldn't I delay sending the letter? We are likely to have a meeting in July. I would see how that went and if they decide they still want the correspondence – we'll give it to them. It is actually the fact that we know we have got a meeting due that enables us to prevaricate.

(*Source*: Research interview conducted by the authors)

Discussion activity 2.16

In what circumstances might it be right not to tell the whole truth?

Cheating

This category of ethical issues concerns keeping the rules. However, for many in organisations the important question is whether the benefits of bending the rules are high enough, and the chances of being caught low enough, to justify taking a risk. This ethical calculation can be made both at a corporate level and as a matter of individual discretion.

Rules are not always bent to benefit the person doing the bending. In bureaucratic systems rules are often bent to protect people who would otherwise be harshly treated by the system. One example we came across during our research concerned a production-line worker in a factory that made prepared foods for supermarkets. The employee was diabetic and, on the day of the incident, had been careless of his diet. Consequently at work he felt the start of a hypoglycaemic attack and took, and ate, one of the products from the production line. This prevented him from collapsing. But he was threatened with dismissal because company rules made theft of company property punishable by instant dismissal. The personnel officer thought the man had been foolish but thought it unjust to sack him. The rules were ignored.

In many cases, however, rules are broken and lies are told by people who simply seek their own benefit at others' expense. The case of the rise and fall of Parmalat provides a major example. The Tanzi family, who were the major shareholders, benefited themselves to the cost of bond holders and other investors. More recently there have been the cases of Bernie Madoff and Satyam.

Case study 2.17	Fraudulent businesses – Parmalat, Satyam and Madoff

This case study considers three examples of fraudulent accounting by companies.

In 1961 Calisto Tanzi started a milk pasteurisation plant to supply milk to the Italian city of Parma. From that starting point it grew to become a multinational, publicly owned corporation in the food and milk business. Until December 2003 Tanzi led the company, which employed 36,200 people in 146 plants in 30 countries on five continents. In December 2003 Parmalat defaulted on payment of a €150m bond despite having €4.2bn of liquidity. Tanzi handed over control to a company doctor. Then the Bank of America announced that the claim that Bonlat, a Parmalat subsidiary, had an account in the Cayman Islands with €2.95m was untrue and that Parmalat had a €4.9m hole in its accounts. Parmalat sought bankruptcy protection and the Italian Prime Minister Silvio Berlusconi said he found the revelations 'almost unbelievable' but pledged to save the company, which was Italy's eighth largest corporation (CNN International, 2003). As time went on the financial hole in the company was discovered to be larger – €14.8bn (Kapner 2004a). Parmalet had created false accounts to hide the losses

The company's operating principle seems to have been that ensuring the long-term survival of the firm by acquiring influence among local politicians was more important than making a

▶

profit. In this, of course, it was proved wrong. However, it applied this system in countries other than Italy. A *Financial Times* investigation identified that Parmalat considered, but never completed, a deal to buy a near-bankrupt Nicaraguan Bank in 2001 in an effort to 'build influence in Central and South America' (Barber and Parker, 2004).

A letter writer to the *Financial Times* generously saw Parmalat's policy of subsidising European farmers (by making a loss of between €350m and €450m per year in the late 1990s) as more efficient than the European Union's Common Agricultural Policy. He pointed out that the farmers received a subsidy at no cost to European taxpayers because the financial strain was being borne by largely American Parmalat bond holders. So the farmers were better off, as were the taxpayers, and the consumers were no worse off (Carter, 2004).

When this policy proved expensive and the company was making losses the Tanzi family, several of whom apart from Calisto were arrested, tried a number of devices to cover up the losses and protect their own interests. One technique was to transfer money from the publicly owned Parmalat to family-controlled companies, such as the travel firm Paratours (Kapner and Minder, 2004). They also used sophisticated and legal financial devices. In one deal with a bank called Buconero (black hole in Italian) the bank made an 'investment' in Parmalat of €117m in return for a share of the company's net profit. By setting up the loan as an investment Parmalat's borrowing costs were made to look smaller than they were (ExecutiveCaliber, 2004). On occasions the company resorted to plain lying and forgery. When the auditors enquired about the money in the Cayman Islands branch of the Bank of America they received a reply from the bank, confirming the existence of the account, which had in fact been forged at Parmalat's headquarters.

Calisto Tanzi was sentenced to 10 years imprisonment for market rigging. He remained free while other legal processes took place. He was subsequently charged with fraudulent bankruptcy and criminal association and was given a sentence of 18 years in 2011. However while he appeals against the sentence he continues to live on his estate near Parma. It is in any case unusual for elderly people, Tanzi is in his seventies, to go to prison in Italy. Sixteen other Parmalat executives were found guilty on various charges.

Satyam Computer Services is an international information technology services company based in Hyderabad, India. It was presented as a paragon of the new Indian outsourcing industry that was successful, innovative and focused on developing its employees. In four years it had increased the number of its employees from 9,000 to 42,000. Satyam is structured around 1,773 business units, each headed by its own chief executive. Ramalinga Raju the founder and chairman of the company argued that innovation is the key to satisfying the customer and that learning, at both the individual and at the organisational level, is what drives change. The company had a strong official culture known as the Satyam way, which is made available to all associates as a book.

On 7 January 2009 Raju published a letter in which he admitted that he had falsified the company's accounts. He had entered fictitious assets, equivalent to $1.5bn. He said that it had started with an initial cover-up of one quarter's poor performance and then escalated. He wrote in the letter:

> It was like riding a tiger, not knowing how to get off without being eaten.
> I sincerely apologise to all Satyamites and stakeholders, who have made Satyam a special organisation, for the current situation. I am confident they will stand by the company in this hour of crisis.

(Times Online, 2009)

By 2011 Raju was in judicial custody and his repeated appeals to be granted bail had been refused. Satyam's American Depository Shares had been traded on the New York Stock exchange and in 2011 Satyam, which by now was trading under new management, and its former auditor PricewaterCoopers agreed to pay fines to the SEC in the USA of $17.5m.

Bernie Madoff was a highly rated financial advisor and investor. He used his charm to attract investors and his fame became such that people were begging him to invest their money in his company. He took deposits, not only from individuals, but also from financial institutions and hedge funds. However in December 2009 his sons reported that Madoff had confessed to them that his business was a massive Ponzi scheme. (Both Raju and Madoff eventually confessed their crimes – is this a feature of fraudsters who believe they are about to be found out?) A Ponzi scheme is a very simple scam. The conman takes in deposits but does not invest them. Instead new deposits by new investors are used to pay the dividends and capital gains to earlier investors. As the scheme grows the conman can find no new investors and at that point the whole inverted pyramidal structure collapses. Few of Madoff's investor queried how he managed to provide consistently better returns than the market average. It was this misplaced confidence that kept the scheme afloat for many years. Investors lost an estimated $18bn. In 2009 Madoff pleaded guilty to various charges and was sentenced to 150 years' imprisonment.

Discussion activity 2.17

Neo-institutionalism is a theory which argues that societies have templates of formal and informal rules, values and acceptable ways of behaving; and that organisations in those societies fit in with, and organise themselves to fit in with, those institutional templates. The technical name for this process is isomorphism. Can the story of Parmalat be interpreted using this theory? Can it be argued that Parmalat's way of operating by keeping local politicians and others happy reflected the institutional world of a small company in Italy in the 1960s, but that it was too risky to sustain when Parmalat had become a huge multinational corporation?

The next case study tells a similar story but the history and motivations were probably very different from those seen in the Parmalat case study.

Case study 2.18   Lord Black and Hollinger International

At the beginning of 2004 Conrad Black, Lord Black of Crossharbour, was chairman and chief executive of Hollinger International, an organisation based in the USA that owned many newspapers including the *Daily Telegraph* in Britain and the *Chicago Sun-Times* in the USA. On 3 March 2008 he started a six-and-a-half year jail sentence in Florida after being convicted on three counts of fraud and one of obstructing justice.

The group has a complex structure. Hollinger International Inc. is the holding company that oversees the group's assets and operations. Hollinger Inc. (a Canadian registered company) holds 18.2 per cent of the equity in Hollinger International; and 80 per cent of Hollinger Inc. is held by Ravelstone which is a private company belonging to Lord Black. One particular feature of

▶

the structure is that although Hollinger Inc. only owns a small part of Hollinger International it owns 68 per cent of the voting rights. This was possible because Hollinger International has a dual class of shares. Those held by Hollinger Inc. were super-voting shares carrying more votes per share than ordinary shares. This discrepancy between ownership and control gave Black control of the main company and control over appointments to the board.

This situation led to a conflict between Lord Black and the rest of the board of Hollinger International. In 2003 Lord Black lost his position as CEO of Hollinger International but remained chairman. However, Lord Black's announcement in January 2004 that he had made a deal, to sell the *Daily Telegraph* to the Barclay brothers, which prevented the ordinary shareholders of Hollinger International benefiting from the sale, brought the crisis to a head. The 'non-interested' board members challenged the deal by setting up a corporate review committee to scrutinise the deal. Lord Black responded by using his controlling interest to change the company's by-laws by written consent, a technique that bypassed the other shareholders. The new by-laws abolished the review committee and put practical constraints on the board's freedom to act. The matter went to court in Delaware and Lord Black lost the case.

After these battles the board of Hollinger International commissioned a detailed investigation into Lord Black's business affairs in relation to Hollinger International. The investigation was conducted by Richard Breeden, a former chairman of the SEC. The Breeden report, which arose from the investigation, was published in September 2004 and accused Lord Black of 'fiduciary abuses' and fraudulent acts. According to Breeden, Black had taken £223m from the company in a six-year period up to 2003. This represented 95.2 per cent of its entire adjusted net income. Most of this money, it was claimed, came in the form of excessive management fees paid to Black and his associates and in expense claims. Lord Black challenges these claims and has hired forensic accountants to work on his case. He argues that there was no misconduct and that his actions were approved by the board.

One of the main accusations was that Lord Black and Mr Radler, a former deputy chairman, broke their fiduciary duties to the company's shareholders by causing Hollinger International to pay them unjustifiable management fees through Lord Black's private company Ravelstone. This matter was the cause of Lord Black losing his position of CEO in 2003 when he was found to have overcharged for his services by $32m, a sum that he subsequently repaid to Hollinger International. Some of the fees were paid to shell companies registered in Barbados, which does not tax dividends and charges only 2.5 per cent income tax. One particular device that was used by Black was non-compete payments that were made between 1999 and 2001. When Hollinger International wished to sell one of its publications Black and his associates would demand a fee to sign a non-competition agreement with prospective purchasers, which ensured that they would not enter the competition to buy the titles. The Breeden report considered this a conflict of interests because, as a board member of Hollinger International Black had responsibilities to maximise the sale price of the company's assets. If these non-competition deals had not been made then the fee paid to Black (as compensation for not acquiring the assets) would most likely have gone to pay a higher purchase price to Hollinger International.

The second main charge against Black made by the Breeden report was that Black and Radler and their families had used Hollinger International as a 'piggy bank'. The company paid for much of their living expenses, their housing expenses and their personal travel. Radler was given a private aircraft by the company, worth $11.6m, and Black had a Gulfstream IV leased for him at a cost of $3m–$4m a year. The running costs of these aircraft between 2000 and 2003 were $23m. Two of the more high-profile items mentioned in the report were $43,000 spent by the company on Lady Black's birthday party and the $2,436 handbag she was given as a gift.

KPMG, who were auditors for Hollinger International, Hollinger Inc. and Ravelstone, did not initially question or raise with the company's audit committee the matter of whether the management fees and non-compete contracts contradicted Lord Black's fiduciary duties to Hollinger International. However, it did so in late 2003 and resigned as auditors in December.

Some of the journalists who worked and socialised with Conrad Black saw him as an intelligent and scholarly man, who acted with propriety in editorial matters concerning the papers he controlled. Some saw him as leading a revival of newspapers in Canada. The journalist who uses the pseudonym Taki (2004) wrote:

> Conrad Black took the *Telegraph* company, which was moribund, and turned it into a powerful weapon for the values we conservatives believe in. He was a great proprietor, but more important, a great visionary. He and his wife should get their good name back and the sooner the better.

Black was rewarded in 1999 when he was made a British peer, though the Canadian Prime Minister forced him to renounce his Canadian citizenship in order to accept the honour. Black was also a generous host.

> (*Sources*: Burt (2004); Hollinger International Inc. (n.d.), Investor Responsibility Research Centre (IRRC) (2004); *Observer* (2004); Paris et al. (2004); Parker (2004); Rees-Mogg (2004); Rubin (2004))

Discussion activity 2.18

- Can a greedy person be a good visionary and corporate leader?

- What ethical problems might flow from dual-voting structures and 'super shares'?

- Conrad Black was the effective owner of Hollinger International; could he not do as he wished with his property?

- What rights, if any, did or should the minority shareholders have in such companies?

- Have you ever manipulated your expenses or used organisational resources for personal benefits?

Case study 2.19   BAT and allegations of cigarette smuggling

An oddity in the world market for cigarettes was discovered in 1997. When global exports were compared with global imports one-third of the total inventory was unaccounted for. The reason was not hard to find. Up to one-third of cigarettes sold are smuggled. The charge made by investigators and journalists against BAT was that it colluded with tobacco smuggling and factored the sales of smuggled cigarettes into its strategic planning. The charge was not that BAT employees actually took cigarettes across borders without paying the excise duties. It was that they sold

▶

cigarettes to distributors whom they knew would avoid paying tax. This conclusion was drawn from a study of BAT's internal documents, which were made public as a result of legal cases in the USA and in the UK.

BAT used a series of euphemisms for smuggling in its documentation. They included DNP (duty not paid), GT (general trade) and transit goods. Legal goods were known as DP – duty paid. One extract from the documentation illustrates the process. It concerns a 1995 dispute in Colombia between BAT and Philip Morris over the ownership of a cigarette brand called Belmont. One memorandum proposed a contingency plan to be used in the event that BAT lost the case. The plan was 'to launch a new brand in DP and maintain Belmont in a GT channel'. One problem with selling Belmont through GT was that the 'company could not support Belmont in GT through advertising'. Advertising a product that was not officially imported might have caused the revenue authorities to ask questions.

Kenneth Clarke, the deputy chairman of BAT, and a one-time Chancellor of the Exchequer who had been responsible for UK duties on tobacco, responded to these criticisms when they were published in *The Guardian*. He pointed out that smuggling was a major problem in the tobacco business. Cigarettes are easily transportable and of high value. These factors, combined with the high rates of duty and the high differentials between the taxes of neighbouring countries, provide incentives for smuggling. He pointed out that BAT was always willing to cooperate with governments that wished to crack down on smuggling. He added:

> However, where governments are not prepared to address the underlying causes of the problem, businesses such as ours who are engaged in international trade are faced with a dilemma. If the demand for our brands is not met, consumers will either switch to our competitors' brands or there will be the kind of dramatic growth in counterfeit products that we have recently seen in our Asian markets. Where any government is unwilling to act or their efforts are unsuccessful, we act, completely within the law, on the basis that our brands will be available alongside those of our competitors in the smuggled as well as the legitimate market.

Audrey Wise, a Member of Parliament and a member of the House of Commons Health Committee, said of BAT's policy:

> If there was ever a case of being within the letter of the law but clearly outside the spirit of the law then this is a gem. Smuggled goods are illegal goods, so if you're deliberately making your goods available for smuggling knowingly and deliberately you are an accessory to the fact.

(*Sources*: Center for Public Enquiry, 2000; Clarke, 2000; Maguire, 2000)

Discussion activity 2.19

Should companies accept being placed at a competitive disadvantage by following the spirit as well as the letter of the law?

The next case study raises a large number of ethical issues. One is whether doctors used people's ignorance of the law and the regulations to 'cheat' parents grieving for their dead children.

Case study 2.20	The retention of dead babies' organs in hospitals

When a child dies in the UK the coroner can order a post-mortem examination to discover the cause of death. A hospital can also order a post-mortem with the parents' consent to study the disease that killed the child. After post-mortems, organs from the child are often retained for research or educational purposes. Doctors assumed, wrongly, that a coroner's request for a post-mortem allowed them to retain organs. In other cases the law merely required that the parents should not object. Over a period of years a collection of 50,000 organs from dead children was established in a number of English hospitals. The general public were unaware of these collections; more importantly the parents of the children were not aware the organs had been retained. Even where parents had given consent to post-mortems they were not necessarily aware that the hospital could remove and retain the organs. The parents had not been given the opportunity to give full and informed consent. This is a form of cheating that arose, as Professor Kennedy argued, 'from a type of professional arrogance that ignored – indeed did not acknowledge, the views and voices of parents'.

The issue exploded into the public's consciousness because of the Alder Hey hospital case. Professor van Velzen at that hospital had developed an obsession with organ retention. The Redfern report into Alder Hey found that van Velzen had ordered illegal retention of children's organs, had falsified records and had failed to catalogue the specimens. The identification of this particular example of illegal activity triggered the investigations that revealed a culture of mendacity over organ retention in many hospitals. The issue released raw emotions, as parents who believed they had buried their dead child requested that they be allowed to bury their child's retained remains.

The impact of these new stories was a tightening-up of rules for organ retention and an unwillingness of the public to allow organs to be retained. Researchers began to complain that research into cancers was being prevented because of the difficulty of obtaining human material for use in trials and experiments. The pharmaceutical companies were removing clinical development from UK to Europe because of the difficulties in obtaining materials for work on breast and prostate cancers.

(*Sources*: Anon., 2001; Boseley, 2001a; Boseley, 2001b; Redfern Report, 2001)

Discussion activity 2.20

Was the general practice (rather than the particular practice of Dr van Velzen) of retaining organs without proper consent a case of actions being ethical but illegal?

Part five: Discouraging badness

Bullying

In organisations bullying is the misuse of power to abuse, humiliate or cajole others. Unlike bullying in the school playground, which may also involve physical harm, organisational bullying is more likely to be social. Some bullying may be too insignificant or transient to be turned into an issue. But where should the line between the insignificant and the significant be drawn? At what point does proper assertion, within a negotiation for example, become an improper use of aggression? The problem is made worse by people's differing perceptions of acceptable, and unacceptable, behaviour. What may be harassment from a supervisor, from a subordinate's point of view, may be an effective example of leadership from the team leader's perspective.

Video clip 2.1	**Bullies on the job**
	The clip deals with bullying and harassment at work.
	To view the video clip please visit this book's companion website at www.pearsoned.co.uk/fisherlovell.

One answer to the problem of bullying is to allow the victim to define it. This empowers the weak against the strong by accepting that if someone says they are being bullied then they are. If a legal perspective were to be taken this would put the burden of proof on the accused and not on the victim. The accused would have to prove they were innocent. This, of course, is the opposite of the legal custom that the accused is innocent until proved guilty.

The following case may not look like bullying but it is an example of a company using its dominant position to control the actions of its agents. It raises the question of when assertive marketing and selling practices cross the line and become illegal.

Case study 2.21	**British Airways and Virgin Atlantic**

British Airways (BA) and Virgin Atlantic have for many years been in intense competition. In 1993 Virgin had accused BA of 'dirty tricks' that discouraged customers from buying tickets from Virgin. In the subsequent libel proceedings BA paid Richard Branson, the chairman of Virgin, £610,000 to settle the case. Virgin started proceedings in the United States courts seeking damages for BA's unfair and illegal marketing practices.

The core of Virgin's complaints was that BA, by far the larger of the two airlines, was using its dominant position in the market to coerce travel agents to sell its flights. This was done by only paying agents certain commissions when they had sold a quota of BA flights, and by packaging discounts on flights. People who travelled to destinations where BA had little competition were offered additional discounts if they bought BA connecting flights in areas where there were many alternative carriers. In November 1997 Virgin formally complained to the European Commission that these 'illegal' practices were in breach of Article 86 of the Treaty of Rome, which covers abuse of dominant market position.

In 1998 BA accused Virgin Atlantic, in its in-house magazine *BA News*, of using similar marketing techniques to those that BA was accused of using. In November of that year Sir Colin Marshall, chairman of BA, apologised to Richard Branson for the accusations and destroyed all copies of the magazine.

In 1999 the European Commission fined BA £4.5m for operating an anti-competitive loyalty scheme with travel agents. The Competition Commissioner said, 'It is well established in community law that a dominant supplier cannot give incentives to its customers and distributors to be loyal to it, so foreclosing the market from the dominant firm's competitors'. BA announced it would appeal. In October of the same year a New York judge threw out Virgin Atlantic's claim against BA. One lawyer pointed out that the notion of a 'dominant company' did not exist in American law.

At the end of 1999 it appeared that BA's ticketing practices were illegal in the European Union but legal in the United States.

(*Sources*: Anon., 1997; Anon., 1999a; Anon., 1999b; Skapinker, 1998)

The story entered the mythology of business and Sir Richard Branson did his best to keep it fresh; especially as in one version first published in 1994 (Gregory and Rufford, 1994) he was presented as a hero – a combination of a 'corporate Peter Pan' and a 'misty eyed Corinthian' (Tilney, 2000). (Unfortunately Corinthian has a range of meanings from 'a wealthy sports enthusiast', through 'a fashionable man' to 'someone given to elegant dissipation'.) Virgin republished the book in 2000. In 2003 Richard Branson sought to take over the operation of Concorde from BA when the latter announced it would be taken out of service. BA announced this intervention as a 'stunt' and Branson retorted that BA was acting in ways reminiscent of its dirty tricks campaign in the 'bad old days' (Done, 2003).

The ill feeling between the two companies has also had significant commercial effects. The case of airline routes to India is an example. The commercial flights between India and the UK have long been constrained and controlled by a bilateral treaty. Consequently the supply of direct services was much less than the demand. In 2004 the two countries agreed a new deal that would increase the number of flights between them from 19 to 40 a week. BA had held the rights to all of the flights under the old treaty and Virgin only provided a limited service to Delhi through a deal with Air India. The Civil Aviation Authority held a competition for the new services because BA had applied for all 21 and Virgin for 18 (Done, 2004). BA were awarded seven, Virgin ten and British Midland four.

For 17 months from August 2004 and January 2006 it looked as if the two companies were collaborating. Executives from both companies met to agree the prices they would charge for the fuel supplements that were necessitated by increases in fuel prices. Of course, this was against competition law because they should have been competing on fuel surcharges and not making life comfortable for each other by ensuring one did not undercut the other. It appears that both companies were willing participants in the cartel. Then Virgin blew the whistle and informed the competition authorities about the collusion. Companies who blow the whistle on such practices are given immunity against prosecution. The result was that Virgin escaped all penalties whilst all the opprobrium was laid at the door of BA, which was also fined £121.5m by the Office of Fair Trading (BBC News Online, 2007b).

Discussion activity 2.21

Is corporate bullying as common as personal bullying? Is it more or less of an ethical wrong than personal bullying?

This next case involves powerful individuals within an organisation exploiting their strength.

| Case study 2.22 | The hospital consultants |

Extract from an interview with an accountant in a hospital

You will be aware I am sure, through the media, that the government this year has made available an extra £500 million or £600 million for trying to reduce the waiting lists [of patients awaiting treatment]. What that means with a hospital like this is that suddenly you have got to do an extra lot of work, very quickly over a short period of time and it doesn't really give you time to get additional staff employed. You are really talking about expecting either existing staff to do overtime or to get some agency staff in to help. Also we haven't had confirmation that this money will be recurrent, although it is likely to be. But because we haven't had that specific guarantee, hospitals are reluctant to employ people on open-ended contracts.

One of the problems we then face is with consultant surgeons, a lot, if not all, of whom have private work as well, and there are some of them who say, 'Right, I will do this extra work, provided I am paid such and such a rate'. The rates that they are inclined to quote will be what they would charge privately. I think they forced the hospital's arm into agreeing to it. They got what they wanted then ... They will see their job probably in a wider context than just their work in the NHS, because it is regular, their private work. What their stance of course is, if you are wanting me to do this extra NHS session, in theory I am foregoing doing a private session somewhere else, so I want to be compensated at least somewhere near the level of income that I would have earned.

It causes me some unease. I suppose in terms of unfairness. If we haven't got additional nurses in the hospital prepared to do extra hours, then we won't get the operations done because it needs a team in the operating theatres, both the consultants and the nurses. But, of course, the nurses haven't got the option of doing private work and being able to earn more money so they haven't got the clout. Yeah, I think, I am sure whoever you speak to, they will see it is the consultants who have got the most clout in the hospital. It is them who can bang the table. Why is it that they can do this? Is it right that they should do this? Don't get me wrong, I am not saying that every surgeon in the hospital has taken a slider, some think the stance taken by most people is totally wrong and unjustified. I know that when there was a meeting of surgeons to discuss it, one particular [consultant] said 'well, he didn't think that any of the surgeons should get additional money for this extra work because they all earned quite enough anyway'. In some ways it can be helpful, because in theory you can maybe marginalise those that have taken a more extreme stance, but that depends really if they are very forceful personalities within the hospital; it depends then whether the hospital management wants to stand up to them.

(*Source*: Research interview conducted by the authors)

Discussion activity 2.22

Were the consultants exercising their market power legitimately or were they bullying the hospital management?

The bullies in the next case study were organisations rather than an individual or a group.

Case study 2.23 — Supermarkets' treatment of their supply chains

In recent years there have been many criticisms of the power that the major supermarket chains exercise in the UK. Among these criticisms were the charges that they were using oligarchic power to keep prices to the consumer high and that, by building large out-of-town stores and requiring people to drive to them, they were damaging the environment. The Competition Commission investigated several of these arguments. They found that the market was competitive and that profits were not excessive. However, they did uphold the claim that the big supermarkets did bully (to use our word, not theirs) the farmers and smaller companies locked into their supply chains. The following extract from a *Financial Times* article rehearses some of the arguments.

FT The relationship between food suppliers and retailers will again come under the microscope. In the meantime, ministers want to use a new code of practice between supermarkets and suppliers, one of the recommendations of the Competition Commission report, to clamp down on some of the extreme practices, such as retailers imposing retrospective price cuts to contracts.

A draft code has been drawn up by the Office of Fair Trading with the supermarkets. Food suppliers are being consulted on the results and have signalled their dissatisfaction with what they have seen so far. Instead of calling a halt to some of the practices criticised by the Competition Commission, such as asking suppliers to meet the cost of shop refurbishment or staff hospitality, the code suggests retailers should not 'unreasonably' ask suppliers to foot the bill. But Whitehall officials expect the code to be toughened up during the consultation process. 'The code has to be robust. It has to end the practices the Competition Commission criticised, not just say it would rather they didn't happen. If there is no confidence in the new code, a future government may have to consider further legislation,' said one. Colin Breed, Liberal Democrat agriculture spokesman, believes the code will not help suppliers stand up to supermarkets. 'The only sensible way to proceed is to appoint an independent retail regulator who would not be in the pockets of the supermarkets,' he said.

The industry may also come under the scrutiny of the [House of] Commons' trade and industry committee. Members have praised the sector for helping to deliver lower food prices through fierce competition, but say they are aware suppliers further down the chain often pay the price. Martin O'Neill, committee chairman, said there could be room for an inquiry around the time of the planned sweeping review of the farming industry. 'I would hope that review will spark off a broad debate about the future of retail and the protection of consumer choice just as much as consumers' rights', he said.

▶

Retailers are, of course, keen to avoid any inquiry that focuses directly on their role, although all say they are happy to take part in any wider-ranging review of the supply chain. Inquiries are costly and time consuming. They can also depress share prices across a sector. For many retail analysts, constant carping about supermarket profits risks damaging the industry, leaving it susceptible to overseas predators. 'One day people are weeping and wailing about the fact that Marks and Spencer does not make £1bn profits any more,' said one analyst. 'The next thing, they are complaining that Tesco does just that. Do they want a successful retail industry in this country or not?'

(*Source*: Supermarkets facing more scrutiny after election, *The Financial Times*, 11 April 2001 (Bennett, R. and Voyle, S.), Copyright © The Financial Times Ltd.)

A few years later the Competition Commission did undertake a full-scale investigation and its provisional findings were published in 2007. They again found that overall the market and competition in the grocery trade were working to the consumers' advantage. They did identify some areas of concern. They concluded that the buying power of the large supermarkets was a contributory factor to the decline in farm profitability but that other factors were equally important. However, they found that large suppliers with powerful brands could counter the supermarkets' buying power. They reported that supermarkets adopted various supply chain practices, which transferred risk and unexpected costs from themselves to their primary producers. Although if the code of practice discussed in the above article had not been in place the situation would have been worse (Competition Commission, 2007: § 8.25, § 9.5). In their final report the Commission proposed that an Ombudsman be set up to deal with complaints about purchaser/supplier problems.

A Code of Practice for regulating the relationships between supermarkets and their suppliers was developed by the Competition Commission and the Government agreed in 2010 to establish an independent adjudicator to investigate breaches of the code. However, in 2011 the debate continued as a committee of MPs claimed that the sanctions available to the adjudicator were too weak.

Discussion activity 2.23

How easy is it for supply chain partnerships, which are proposed as a new and better way to manage procurement, to become abusive relationships? How might this tendency, if true, be prevented?

Harming

This category involves questions of harm to individuals, animals, institutions, organisations or the environment. One area of controversy is whether a degree of harm is acceptable if the overall results of the harmful action are good. Another concerns the accuracy of the forecasts of the amount of harm and good a particular action will do. An interesting case, which involved such judgments, was that of the Brent Spar oil platform. The issue was whether it was safe to dump the disused platform at sea or whether it would be better to take it ashore and dismantle it. Some time after the issue had been resolved the environmental group Greenpeace admitted that it had exaggerated the amount of environmental harm the sinking of the platform would have done.

Many of the examples of harm being done within or by organisations concern harm to individual employees, as in the following case study.

Case study 2.24	The *Super Size Me* sales promotion

The film *Super Size Me* was directed by Morgan Spurlock (2004) and gives a cinematic account of the results of living for 30 days by eating only the food he bought from McDonald's. The question of whether a sensible person would eat such a monotone diet is at the centre of the ethical issue raised by the film. It was a question that had been considered by the American courts in 2002. Ashley Perelman, aged 14, and Jazlyn Bradley, aged 19, were both obese and had many of the health problems associated with the condition. They also ate hugely at McDonald's restaurants. They blamed the McDonald's Corporation and sued it. The judge pointed out that this was a conflict between personal responsibility and public health, and thought the girls were sufficiently knowledgeable and rational to realise that eating too much of what they fancied would not do them good. But the judge's rejection of the girls' claim was not an unalloyed victory for McDonald's (United States District Court, Southern District of New York, 2003). He pointed out that in certain circumstances it could be possible to show that McDonald's might be responsible for its customers' obesity-related ill health. If restaurants do nothing to encourage people to overeat, and provide all the proper nutritional information, then if the customers still decide to eat more than they should that is the customers' problem. If, however, it was shown that any restaurant intended and encouraged customers to eat its food at dangerous rates then 'proximate cause' could be established. Many American restaurants do encourage gluttony by offering a free dessert if a customer can eat, for example, an impossibly sized steak. If it could be shown that McDonald's staff were encouraging people to eat a meal far larger than anyone should eat at a single sitting then the legal situation might be very different. The judge commented,

> The plaintiffs fail to cite any advertisement where McDonald's asserts that its products may be eaten for every meal of every day without any ill consequences [and] if plaintiffs were able to flesh out this argument in an amended complaint, it may establish that the dangers of McDonald's products were not commonly well known and thus that McDonald's had a duty towards its customers.
>
> (United States District Court, Southern District of New York, 2003: 12, 17)

This comment must have acted as the trigger that led Spurlock to make his film, in which there were three rules he chose to follow.

1. He had to eat everything on the McDonald's menu at least once.

2. He could only consume what was on offer at McDonald's, including the water.

3. Whenever McDonald's offered him the option to super size his meal by the addition of extra French fries and sodas he had to take it.

▶

At the start of the month he was fit, healthy and slim; he was checked by doctors who confirmed his healthy condition. Thirty days later he was 35 pounds heavier, with a liver in poor condition and all the symptoms of addiction – twitches, chest pains, headaches. He was also impotent. Some of the latter symptoms, it may be supposed, could have been reinforced by his need for a good film narrative. As one reviewer pointed out,

> Obviously the more rapidly his health deteriorates; the better it is for his career. [ ] When one of his doctors tells him that his liver is malfunctioning and he must stop the diet at once, he keeps a straight face; but we can tell that inwardly he is cheering.

(Wilson, 2004: 17)

The film was a critical success and McDonald's felt it necessary to take out advertisements in the daily newspapers in the UK arguing that it was irresponsible for anyone to eat such an imbalanced diet; and that no sensible person would eat their products alone. They pointed out that eating at McDonald's, if part of a balanced diet, would not cause people problems. They also pointed out that the company had introduced healthy options into its menus, though others pointed out that if the dressings provided with the salads were eaten then the meals had as many calories as the burgers. The messages were reinforced by a special website set up to counter the film's claims (*www.supersizeme-thedebate.co.uk*). It did, however, cease the *Super Size Me* promotion. As Wilson concluded her review of the film,

> The best the food giant can do is to accuse Morgan Spurlock of having acted 'irresponsibly' – by eating too much of its own food.

(Wilson, 2004: 17)

Discussion activity 2.24

1. To what extent should people be protected against their own ignorance and frailties? (This by the way is a standard revealing question because it gives away the feelings of the writer – so you might wish to reframe it.)

2. Is there a litigation culture developing in other regions of the world following US precedents? Is it a bad thing?

Case study 2.25 — Sexual harassment
Extract from a research interview

I mean I haven't had it personally but a very close friend of mine was a secretary in a very large organisation in London and worked for the Assistant Chairman and she felt she was being harassed. Well she was being harassed and when she actually spoke to her personnel department they said, 'Well yes, you're probably right, we've had complaints before but nobody in this organisation will remove the Assistant Chairman. We will help you find another job.' So their compassion went to the individual in getting her another job because their knowledge was, what could they do? The organisation would not support [her], whatever claim she put in, at the end of the day it would not result in his dismissal. It may have resulted in a rap over the knuckles but she could not work for him and . . . sometimes you know that that is the approach you are going to have to take. Fortunately I've never been in that sort of situation of something quite as clearly wrong.

(*Source*: Research interview conducted by the authors)

Discussion activity 2.25

What are the longer-term consequences of not confronting behaviour such as that discussed in the case study?

Video clip 2.2

Fired for being fat

The clip considers whether it is acceptable to fire cocktail waitresses and waiters if they become too fat and no longer match the company's image and values.

To view the video clip from the interview please visit this book's companion website at www.pearsoned.co.uk/fisherlovell.

The next case describes the harm that can be caused by corporate inaction, although in this example there is a dispute as to which of two corporations was culpable. It also raises the question, to be discussed in Chapter 8, of when harm done by corporate indifference can, or should, invite criminal charges as well as civil liabilities.

Case study 2.26   The Firestone Tire recall issue

In August 2000 Ford and Firestone announced the product recall of 6.5 m tyres used on Ford's sports utility vehicle (SUV), the Explorer. The recall was limited to tyres made at Firestone's plant at Decatur in Illinois. Tyres made at other plants were not recalled. The problem was that the treads on the tyres were prone to separate in hot weather; this could cause a loss of control of the vehicle, which could result in a rollover accident. Over 180 people had died in such accidents in the USA and 700 people had been injured.

It was alleged by commentators that Firestone knew the problem was not simply a quality systems fault at Decatur but a general problem that affected all of Firestone's SUV tyres. It was therefore alleged that Firestone, far from putting things right, was replacing the faulty tyres with equally dangerous ones.

The situation was made more complex by the desires of both Ford and Firestone to blame each other for the rollover accidents and the deaths. While Ford blamed Firestone, Firestone

▶

partly blamed design faults in the Explorer. In a report on the accidents Firestone identified some problems for which it was responsible, but also claimed that Ford's recommendation that the tyres should be inflated to a pressure significantly below the tyres' maximum capacity (to overcome a design fault in the Explorer) increased the temperature of the tyres and increased the possibility of tread separation. Ford, in its 'root cause' report, claimed that design problems played no role in the crashes and that under-inflation was not a contributory factor. The argument continued during 2000 and was the subject of Congressional hearings.

On 22 May Firestone announced that it would no longer be a supply partner of Ford, ending a relationship that had lasted nearly a century. On the same day Ford announced that it was recalling 13 m tyres at a cost of $2.1 b. On the previous day it had recalled 47,000 of its SUVs because of fears, unconnected with the Firestone issue, that tyres had been damaged on the production line.

The case paralleled that of the Pinto model, which exercised Ford in the 1970s (De George, 1999: 240–1). The Pinto was a car produced in a hurry. When it was tested for rear-end impact it was found to be below the standard of comparable cars. There was a danger, because of the positioning of the fuel tank, that the tank could be punctured in a crash and the car would explode. Ford undertook a cost-benefit analysis. They estimated that the cost of inserting a protective baffle was greater than the cost of legal claims that might arise from deaths attributable to the design fault. The design of the car was not changed between 1971 and 1978 and the customers were not informed of the potential problem. Between 1976 and 1977 13 Pintos exploded after rear-end crashes. The cost of the legal compensation proved to be much greater than the cost of the alteration and in 1978 the cars were recalled and protective baffles were fitted.

(*Sources*: Turner, 2001; Firestone Tire Resource Center, n.d.; Bowe, 2001)

Discussion activity 2.26

Had Ford's strategic attitude to safety fears concerning its vehicles changed in over 20 years?

This last case study concerns when it might be right to break the law to prevent an organisation doing harm. It also, as it centres on the issue of the moral status of animals, questions the definition of harm.

Case study 2.27   Huntingdon Life Sciences

This case raises questions about whether there are situations in which it is appropriate to take illegal action because either the law is immoral or the law has to be broken to prevent some greater harm being done. This case study concerns Huntingdon Life Sciences (HLS), a company that carries out pharmaceutical testing on laboratory animals. The company's activities are highly regulated by government agencies and the testing it does is legal.

Animal rights activists argue that testing drugs on animals is cruel and immoral. The case raises difficult questions about whether animals have rights. The traditional view was that animals are not accorded moral status or rights because they lack the power to reason. The obvious response is that this does not prevent them from suffering. This argument may justify minimising the pain caused during experiments, but it does not necessarily mean that the experiments are bad in themselves, especially if they contribute to a greater benefit for humanity through the development of better drugs and medical treatments. The arguments around this issue, which are not primarily the concern of this text, can be explored in Tester (1991) and Scruton (2000). When people claim the existence of rights they may be exhibiting emotivism. This simply means claiming something is right because it feels right. Moral judgment becomes a subjective emotional reaction to a situation.

Animal rights activists believe they are justified in using violence, or the threat of violence, to stop vivisection. The shareholders of HLS, as well as its managers and employees, have been intimidated. The activists threatened to identify and protest to the shareholders. Various institutional shareholders decided in consequence to cease investing in HLS and a number of brokers advised shareholders to sell after threats from activists. Two of HLS's market-makers had also withdrawn and this made it difficult for investors to trade their shares. The company responded by proposing to set up a rarely used shareholding structure to keep investors' identities anonymous and to protect them from intimidation. The proposed corporate nominee scheme is within the rules set out by the FSA.

The government felt it had to take action, as described in the following article from the *Financial Times*, to protect a legitimate business.

FT The authorities on Thursday stepped up their fight against animal rights activists with the launch of a police hit squad and a top-level government committee. The two measures are aimed at preventing violent attacks against companies that carry out medical research, their customers and financial backers. The police announced the creation of a squad 'to target the ringleaders of animal [rights] extremist activity who are organising and taking part in serious criminal offences'.

The group will draw officers from different police forces and will work under the National Crime Squad. It aims to prevent attacks such as those suffered by directors, staff and customers of Huntingdon Life Sciences, the drug-testing group. Over the past year, activists have set fire to Huntingdon workers' cars, sent hate mail to staff and assaulted Brian Cass, its managing director. No one has been arrested in connection with these attacks.

The Association of Chief Police Officers denied that the police had acted slowly in dealing with animal rights extremists. It would 'not say [the squad] was late. We felt this was the right time to act.' The squad will liaise with the new government committee, which includes five ministers and is chaired by Jack Straw [at the time, Home Secretary]. The committee will co-ordinate government action against the activists. The home secretary, who on Thursday visited Huntingdon's laboratories in Cambridgeshire, said: 'We will not tolerate a small number of criminals trying to threaten research organisations and companies.' Some 15 protesters stood outside the gates but were denied a meeting with the Home Secretary. Greg Avery of Stop Huntingdon Animal Cruelty said the campaign group had no involvement in the violent attacks.

(*Sources*: Hit squad to tackle animal rights activists by F. Guerrera, www.FT.com, 27 April 2001, Brands feel the impact as activists target customers by E. Alden, *The Financial Times*, 18 July 2001. Copyright © The Financial Times Ltd.)

> ### Discussion activity 2.27
>
> In what situations do you think it might be justified to break, or defy, the law, to end an injustice?

Reflections

This chapter has presented a panorama of the ethical and moral issues that affect managerial and organisational life. Some patterns can be seen to emerge from plotting the case studies on the matrix in Table 2.1. Many of the issues that cause difficulty and controversy in the business and organisational world concern actions that are, arguably, wrong but legal. These cover the range of matters from the ethical to the moral. Issues that centre on actions that are wrong and illegal mainly concern questions of morality rather than ethics. They are about stopping organisations doing harm. Conversely, issues arising from actions that are good and legal, but are not legal obligations, rest mostly at the ethical end of the spectrum in Table 2.1. The most contentious issues, and perhaps the least common, are those concerning illegal actions that are ethically and morally justifiable.

All the case studies are matters of controversy; every claim that an act is illegal or wrong can be challenged. As Watson (2002: 455) argued, ethical ambiguity and ethical dilemmas are inevitable in organisational and managerial life.

Summary

In this chapter the following key points have been made:

- The major virtues of corporate and organisational behaviour are:
  - **Doing good**
    - social development
    - social responsibility

  - **Acting benignly**
    - reciprocity
    - fairness

- The major vices are:
  - **Ignoring harm done to others**
    - lying and dishonesty
    - cheating and selfishness

  - **Doing harm**
    - bullying and social irresponsibility
    - doing social and environmental damage

- Under each of these headings issues at work may raise questions about what is right and what is wrong. What is right may in many cases also be legal but not necessarily a legal obligation. In other cases what is right may not be legal. Conversely, things that the law allows might not be right.

- Ethical issues are not easy to categorise. They appear as dilemmas in which arguments can be made for all sides. The protagonists in the cases, however, may see and present only a single point of view.

Typical assignments

1. In what circumstances might it be right to break the law in an effort to prevent a company behaving in a way that is legal, but, in the eyes of some, immoral?

2. Discuss the proposition that companies should behave in a socially responsible manner but are not obliged to contribute to social development.

3. Are there degrees of lying? Can some forms of lying be acceptable in business and management practice?

4. Should dual class share systems (in which some shares carry more voting weight per share than others) be made illegal? Illustrate your reasons from recent cases.

Group activity 2.1

Locating issues on the grid shown in Table 2.1 is not straightforward. An issue may involve several of the moral and ethical problems identified. It might, for example, exhibit an unfair distribution of resources as well as lying and bullying. It might also be possible to argue about which categories of rightness and legality the issue best fits. Different readings of the facts of the case might lead to different opinions about whether an action was, *prima facie*, illegal or not.

In class identify current business ethics issues that are being discussed in the media. Identify as best you can the facts of the issue and discuss where, on the grid in Table 2.1, the issue might best be placed. It might be necessary to plot different aspects of the issue in different places on the grid.

Recommended further reading

A good review of issues in business ethics is P.W.F. Davies (ed.) (1997) *Current Issues in Business Ethics*, London: Routledge. Allhoff and Vaidya (2008) *Business in Ethical Focus: An Anthology*, Ontario: Broadview, is a more recent review of business ethics topics. D. Winstanley and J. Woodall (2000) *Ethical Issues in Contemporary Human Resource Management*, London: Macmillan, is a very useful guide to ethical issues related to human resource management.

Useful websites

Topic	Website provider	URL
A business ethics blog	Chris McDonald	http://businessethicsblog.com/
A website that reports on current business and human rights issues	Business and Human Rights Resource Centre: a charitable not-for-profit organisation set up to promote discussion of human rights issues in business	http://www.business-humanrights.org/Home
John Entine is a controversialist who first came to prominence by criticizing the business ethics of *The Body Shop*	An online magazine edited by John Entine	http://www.ethicalcorp.com/
Most of EIRI'S services are subscription based but it does provide press releases which identify emerging business ethics issues	EIRIS (Ethical Investment Research Service)	http://www.eiris.org/publications.html
A London-based organisation concerned with human rights in business	The Institute for Human Rights & Business	http://www.ihrb.org

CHAPTER 3

Ethical theories and how to use them

Chapter at a glance

Chapter contents

- Learning outcomes
- Introduction
- A map of ethical theories
- Applying ethical theories
- Reflections
- Summary

Activities and exercises

- Video clip 3.1 Interview with the Canon Precentor of St Paul's Cathedral, London. Priorities and human flourishing
- Discussion activity 3.1 Conscience
- Discussion activity 3.2 Kantian ethics
- Discussion activity 3.3 Rawlsian justice
- Discussion activity 3.4 The 'do no harm' perspective
- Discussion activity 3.5 Utilitarian ethics
- Discussion activity 3.6 Corporate Social Responsibility
- Discussion activity 3.7 Ethical egoism & objectivism
- Discussion activity 3.8 Virtue ethics
- Discussion activity 3.9 Decency
- Activity 3.1 The Ethical Corporate Decisions Toolkit
- Activity 3.2 Prioritising your ethical principles
- Activity 3.3 The TI Ethics Quick Test
- Typical assignments
- Group activity 3.1
- Recommended further reading
- Useful websites

Learning outcomes

Having read this chapter and completed its associated activities, readers should be able to:

■ Compare and contrast 10 approaches to ethical thinking.

■ Describe the implications of different ethical theories for businesses, organisations and management.

■ Apply the theories to ethical issues in business, organisation and management.

Introduction

In Chapter 2 the range of ethical issues that can affect businesses, organisations and managers was plotted and examples were given that you were invited to think about. This chapter will give you tools for ethical thinking that you can use to analyse such issues. We have called them ethical theories because they are speculations or mental conceptions about how one should think about ethical matters. They should help you to move from an intuitive response to ethical matters to a systematic and analytical approach; a shift from system 1 to system 2 thinking as Kahnemann (2011) terms it. However, the theories do not provide an easy resolution. One reason for this is that there are many theories and it may not be obvious which should be applied to any particular set of circumstances. A second reason is that the theories are general. It is not always clear how they should be applied or interpreted in specific cases. The fact that some of these theories have been the subject of philosophical debate for many centuries implies that there is no consensus, or final resolution, to be had on these questions. It may be best to consider that the theories provide means of legitimating the stances you take on an issue rather than as sources of definitive or authoritative solutions.

A map of ethical theories

A map or framework of ethical theories is shown in Figure 3.1. Any fans of Madonna may recognise the form of the diagram as the Ten Sefirot of Kabbalah, of which Madonna is, or was, an enthusiast. Kabbalah is a system of medieval Jewish mysticism that in the twenty-first century has been revived as an aspect of New Age philosophies. The authors of this book are not New Agers. We have not adopted the diagram of the Sefirot for mystical reasons but because it expresses a convenient logic for explaining how the various ethical perspectives that we shall use in this chapter link together. Towards the end of the chapter this framework will be used as the basis of a corporate ethical decision-making tool.

In Figure 3.1 each of the ovals represents a particular ethical perspective or way of thinking. Each of these will be explained in detail in this chapter. At

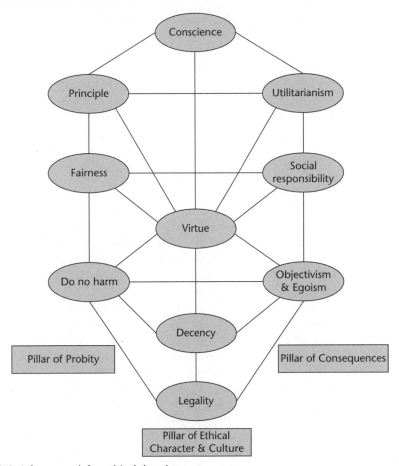

Figure 3.1 A framework for ethical theories

the end of the chapter they are used as the foundation of a toolkit designed to help people make ethical corporate decisions. The 10 ethical perspectives are divided into three columns or pillars. On the left is a pillar of probity, on the right a pillar of consequences and in between them a pillar of ethical character and culture. The two outer pillars are in tension with each other. As in the original Kabbalah version of the diagram the left-hand pillar is concerned with constraint and proper behaviour. In the terms developed by Dworkin (1977: 48) this pillar includes standards that have to be observed, not because they will advance an economic, political or social situation, but because they are a requirement of fairness or justice or some other dimension of morality. They take no regard of the consequences of an action as in 'let justice be done though the heavens fall', a maxim of Roman law that was famously used in 1772 by Lord Mansfield during a legal case concerning slavery. Whereas the right-hand column is focused on action and impact. It is a policy-focused pillar and is defined by considering the goal to be reached, generally an improvement in some economic, political or social feature. The middle column has the function of mediating between these opposing imperatives. The balance is achieved by people, either as individuals or as participants in an organisational culture, exercising their ethical judgment and moral imagination in deciding what the right thing to do is, and willing it into action. These three pillars can also be associated with a commonly made distinction in ethics between:

- Deontology – the pillar of probity
- Teleology – the pillar of consequences
- Virtue ethics – the pillar of ethical character and culture

Deontology is the study of the right action, which it is it is it is the duty of all to do, even if there are sometimes bad consequences. Teleology derives from the Greek word *telos*, which means an end to be achieved. Therefore teleology means that the rightness or goodness of an action is not intrinsic to that action but can only be judged by its consequences. These theories are sometimes therefore called consequentialist. Virtue ethics is concerned with finding a balanced position between extremes.

A brief description of the framework can be started by looking at the middle pillar of character and culture. At the top and bottom of this pillar are conscience and legality, respectively. All the pillars are hierarchical in that the higher positions exhibit a higher level of ethics than the lower ones. For example simply conforming to the law shows a lower level of ethical development than acting according to conscience. In between these two positions are virtue ethics proper, and below that, but above legality, is decency. Decency is a minimal form of ethical behaviour. A decent person does not seek to constrain or harm others but neither do they show any positive concern for other's welfare. The pillar of probity has a sequence of standards of behaviour. The lowest one requires no more than that a person does no harm. The next position up, fairness, requires as a principle that those who are worst off in a society should not be made worse off to the benefit of the best favoured in society. At the top of this pillar is principle, which is the most demanding expectation on this column, and which obliges people to apply certain universal principles in all their actions. At the apex of the pillar of consequences is utilitarianism, which seeks the greatest good of the greatest number. Below that is corporate social responsibility, which is also concerned with a balance of beneficial consequences but with a narrower remit, concerned only with those parts of society with which a company or organisation is involved. At the lowest point on this pillar is objectivism, which is narrower still and only concerns what is good for the organisation, or perhaps narrower yet what is good for the owners of the organisation.

Each of these ethical perspectives will be discussed in turn.

Legality

At the bottom of the ethical framework in Figure 3.1 is legality. This subject has already been discussed in Chapter 2. Legality is at the bottom of the framework because it requires someone to make only a minimal ethical effort. When evaluating or proposing an action a person simply has to discover whether that action is legal or illegal. Laws of course seek to be definitive but the complexity of actions and society means that sometimes it is not known whether something is legal or not until it has been tested in the courts. Again, should the situation arise, the ethical choice is made by the courts and not by the individual. It can be argued that the principle of the Rule of Law reinforces individual's lack of responsibility for thinking through the ethics of a thing themselves. The Rule of Law means that no one is above the law, as long as the law has been promulgated in a legitimate and transparent manner. The principle developed out of the need to protect individuals against arbitrary government. However, it also implies that people should not disobey a law even though they think it wrong or bad. They do though have the democratic right to use legitimate processes to seek to change a law of which they disapprove.

In terms of business ethics legality can be extended to include the rules, regulation and policies of the organisations within which people work. These do not have the same force as national or international laws and therefore the grounds on which organisational rules can be broken, if they are considered unethical, will be slighter than those needed to justify disobeying laws on the grounds of their immorality.

Conscience

Conscience can be seen from a psychoanalytical perspective but in this section conscience is viewed as a way of reasoning about whether a particular act is ethical or not. For this purpose it is placed at the top of the framework in Figure 3.1. It is also in this position because all the other ethical perspectives in the framework are subordinate to conscience. To illustrate the type of thinking conscience may involve we will use, what Arjoon (2007) names, triple-font theory. This is not a new approach but is closely based on the theology and philosophy of St Thomas Aquinas who lived between 1225 and 1274. His philosophy, called Thomism, is at the core of Roman Catholic teaching.

Cross reference	You can find a discussion of conscience from a psychoanalytical perspective in Chapter 5 p. 202.

The three fonts that are used to judge whether an action can be taken in good conscience are:

- moral object;
- intention; and
- circumstances.

The test of moral object asks whether the end or purpose of a proposed action is good. Moral object is concerned with the moral form or kind of the act as determined by some absolute moral precepts. Intention refers, not to the object of an action but to the motive of the person who proposes carrying it out. Intention is concerned with people's will to act and whether their intentions are moral. Finally circumstances may change the moral nature of an act. By circumstances is meant the particular setting and context within which an act is being considered. These can include the condition of the person, whether for example they are suffering a mental illness, or whether they are being prevented from acting morally by some insuperable force. Some circumstances are aggravating factors that do not change whether an action is moral or immoral but simply either increase or decrease the degree of goodness or badness. There are also specifying circumstances that change the ethical nature of an action rather than simply emphasise its goodness or badness. The reason why someone plans or undertakes an act is a specifying circumstance, although this is seen as separate from the person's intention (Smith, n.d.: Arjoon, 2007: 399–400). A company seeking its own self-interest by cutting costs, of itself, is a matter of moral indifference; but the circumstance of doing it in a way that does harm, by say bullying partners in a supply chain, would make it unethical.

A consideration of circumstance may identify that an action will have a mixture of both good and bad consequences. The double-effect principle is proposed by Arjoon (2007) to deal with situations where an action can have both good and bad consequences. If four conditions, developed by Aquinas, are met an action that has bad effects as well as good effects can be ethical. The conditions are that the action itself must be moral, the good effect must not be achieved through the bad effect, the bad effect must not be an intention and finally, there must be sound reasons for tolerating the bad effect. The principle of double effect allows the aggravating, mitigating or justifying circumstances of an action to be taken into account when judging the action's morality.

Cross reference	A particular example of this manner of reasoning, applying the princicple of double effect, is Aquinas' discussion of the Just War. This is discussed in Chapter 2 p. 50.

Trolleyology and the double-effect principle

The trolley problem is a thought experiment that can be explained by the double-effect principle. It was developed by Phillippa Foot and Judith Jarvis Thomson and its study has expanded so much as to become an 'ology'. Imagine there is a fast train racing down a track towards five people who will certainly be killed. But before the train reaches them there is a spur track that will divert the train from its otherwise inevitable victims; and you have the button that will switch the points. The only snag is that on the spur there is a man chained to the rails. So, here is the ethical dilemma; do you switch the points and so condemn one man to death but save five others or do you do nothing and stand back as five die? Then consider a slightly different situation. This time there is no spur track, but standing beside you on a bridge over the rails is a fat man who, if you push him onto the track, will stop the train and so save the lives of the other five who are still in danger further down the track. Although the cold morality of the two situations is the same;

should you sacrifice one life to save five, most people say they would throw the points but they would not push the fat man onto the track (Edmond, 2010). The double-effect principle can be used to explain this preference. If you switch the points in the spur line scenario the act is good, even though there is also a bad effect (the death of the individual man), because it is not your intention to kill him, because and because the overall effect of the act is good. In the fat man scenario, however, the act of pushing your neighbour onto the track requires an intention to kill him. The double-effect principle therefore says this act cannot be moral. Some people have argued that the double-effect principle is a neurological imperative that we cannot easily overcome; which is, conveniently, quite a good definition of conscience.

Amongst Catholic philosophers there is a debate about the impact that circumstances can have on the nature of moral norms. The proportionalists argue that ethical rules cannot be absolute if they are influenced by circumstances. The Papacy declares that there are absolute moral principles and that the proportionalists are guilty of error. This orthodoxy argues that circumstances may change a person's culpability for a bad act but they cannot make a bad act good. They also claim that the proportionalists focus on intention and circumstances but ignore moral object. However, this argument requires claiming that circumstances may not always be circumstances; but may be a part of the form of the moral object (Smith, n.d.). It can be claimed that the orthodox start from the position that there are absolute moral norms and then struggle valiantly to interpret Thomist philosophy in a way that supports that view. If it is believed that there are, at least some, absolute values then conscience cannot be above principle, as it is shown in Figure 3.1; and it ought to have been included in the next section that deals with principle. If principles have to be weighted, or put into proportion, in response to circumstances then conscience involves judging object, intention and circumstances to come a conclusion about the morality of an action.

Discussion activity 3.1	Conscience

Apply the triple-font test to Michael Shayler's whistleblowing described in Case study 2.6. Was the action a moral one? If it was were there circumstances that diminished his culpability?

Principle; Kantian ethics

One of the most important western philosophers of duty and principle was Immanuel Kant who came from Konigsberg in Germany, now known as Kaliningrad in Russia, and lived between 1724 and 1804. His ethical principles are the basis of the highest position on the column of probity in Figure 3.1

Kant's ethical philosophy was that actions must be guided by universalisable principles that apply irrespective of the consequences of the actions. In addition an action can only be morally right if it is carried out as a duty, not in expectation of a reward. From a Kantian perspective, principles exist *a priori*. By this is meant that, knowing what to do in a situation will be determined by a set of principles that have been established by deductive reasoning, independent of, or before, the specifics of the decision in hand have been considered. Indeed, for Kantian ethics the context and consequences of a decision are irrelevant. Lying, for example, is invariably employed to illustrate the inflexibility of Kantian ethics. Lying, irrespective of the context, is wrong. So, for Kant, truth telling, even if the telling of a lie would save a human life, has to be strictly adhered to – no deviations, no exceptions.

For Kant actions have moral worth only when they spring from recognition of duty, and a choice to discharge it. The 'duties' to which Kant refers were a response to the question, 'What makes a moral act right?' They were formulated around the concept of the 'categorical imperative'.

Categorical imperative

DEFINITION

Categorical means unconditional (no exceptions), while imperative means a command or, in Kantian terms, a principle. Thus a categorical imperative refers to a command/principle that must be obeyed, with no exceptions. If the categorical imperative is conceptually sound we should be able to will all rational people around the world to follow this particular law. This is the concept of universalisability.

The Ten Commandments of the Old Testament are written in the form of categorical imperatives, i.e. 'Thou shalt not . . .', although the extent to which they are universalisable is problematic. (The commandment 'thou shalt not kill' is debated below.)

For Kant an act is morally right if it can be judged by all reasoning people to be appropriate as a universal principle of conduct, irrespective of whether they are to be the doers, receivers or mere observers of an act. The issue of putting oneself in a state of ignorance as to one's own position within a situation is an interesting one, and one to which we will return when we discuss the ideas of John Rawls.

The 'Golden Rule', which is normally expressed as 'do unto others as you would have done unto yourself', is an example of a categorical imperative. It is a rule that can be willed as universalisable. Indeed, Shaw and Barry (1998) cited the scriptures of six world religions, which go back over millennia, identifying quotations from each that are examples of the 'Golden Rule'.

Bowie (1999), in his proposal for business organisations built upon Kantian principles, provided three formulations of the categorical imperative.

1. The first is that universalisability provides a theory of moral permissibility for market interactions. Interactions that violate the universalisability formulation of the categorical imperative are morally impermissible. This might appear reasonable, but it must be remembered that under this rule someone who is prepared to allow others to exploit, harm and cheat him could, within the universalisability principle, proceed to exploit, harm and cheat others. Bowie tackled this issue when he cited Carr (1968), who argued for a different set of rules and morality for business. Carr observed:

The golden rule for all its value as an ideal for society is simply not feasible as a guide for business. A good part of the time the businessman is trying to do to others as he hopes others will not do unto him . . . The game [poker] calls for distrust of the other fellow. It ignores the claim for friendship. Cunning, deception and concealment of one's strength and intentions, not kindness and open-heartedness, are vital in poker. And no-one should think any worse of the game of business because its standards of right and wrong differ from the prevailing traditions of morality in our society.

(Carr, 1968: 145–6)

A further example of this attitude is provided by Pava (1999) who, drawing upon the work of Badaracco (1997), referred to the case of the pharmaceutical company, Roussel-Uclaf, and its chairman, Edouard Sakiz. The case concerned the abortion drug, RU 486. Sakiz wished to market the drug, but a range of powerful interest groups opposed the drug's sale, including Roussel-Uclaf's majority shareholder, the multinational Hoechst organisation. One of Hoechst's drugs (Zyklon B) had been used by the Nazis in their pogrom against the Jews in the Second World War. Since then the company had committed itself to 'placing our energy, our ideas and our dedication to the service of Life' (Pava, 1999: 82). Sakiz is claimed to have employed a devious and high-risk strategy, in which he forced a vote of the executive committee on the drug's launch, voting against the decision himself. However, in so doing he compromised the French government, which was keen to see the drug launched. The French government threatened to move production of the drug to another company, which forced Roussel-Uclaf to reconsider its decision. This it did, but now 'under the seeming protection of the government' (Pava, 1999: 83). Pava observed:

Sakiz obtained his ultimate goal and avoided the pitfall of publicly proclaiming his real intentions. Badaracco justifies such seeming hypocrisy by stating that public leaders must follow a 'special ethical code', one that differs from their private morality and from Judeo-Christian ethics. Badaracco elaborates that 'only a naive manager would think otherwise'.

(Pava, 1999: 83)

A Kantian refutation of this argument would avoid a consequentialist assessment, that businesses could not work effectively if lying and deviousness was the universal norm, on the basis that Kant refused to allow considerations of consequences to enter into issues of ethics. Instead a Kantian refutation would take the form of a rebuttal of the logic of the attempted categorical imperative, 'always lie, always be devious'. If everyone always lied or was devious, there would be no point in listening to what anyone had to say. Conversation, language even, would be meaningless and would therefore become redundant. Thus, 'always lie, always be devious' cannot be universalised. Because categorical imperatives are derived deductively, they can be successfully challenged, if flawed.

2. Bowie's second formulation of the categorical imperative is 'respect for humanity in persons'. This is normally taken to mean treating fellow human beings as ends not means. However, Bowie's formulation is looser than this, and might fail to achieve this objective. Bowie's argument is that this formulation provides the basis for a moral obligation in the employment of people. Employees would cease to be commodities. Everyone involved in market transactions – employees, suppliers, customers and indeed all stakeholders – should be treated with respect. However, this presupposes that it is not possible to treat a commodity with respect. If it is possible to do so, then this formulation fails to achieve its stated aim – to treat people as ends not means. The ultimate test of this formulation would be the reaction of the Kantian organisation to a dramatic fall in demand for its goods or services. If the economics of the situation demanded cost-cutting measures for the firm to survive, with redundancies high on the agenda, the people-as-ends-not-means philosophy is severely tested. It is possible to show respect to those who are being made redundant, for example by providing as generous a financial severance package as is feasible, providing counseling sessions and assistance in interviewing techniques, but, in the end, the redundant employees are redundant because they are judged to be a resource that can no longer be justified (economically) by the firm. They are ultimately a means, not an end.

This particular circle can only be squared if it is acknowledged at the outset that a market-based economy is the backdrop against which the Kantian firm is located. Thus, it is within the actions permitted by market dynamics and economic logic that the Kantian perspective is being argued. In which case, short-term pressures from financial markets to protect the company's share price are likely to take precedence over desires to accept lower profit figures in order to protect employment levels. Any significant deviation from this set of relationships would require a different set of institutional arrangements between a business and its significant investors from that which currently exists. These issues are taken up further when we discuss the stakeholder perspective later in the chapter.

3. The third formulation is an attempt to further minimise or remove the 'people-as-means' accusation. It is an argument for greater democracy in the workplace – the moral community formulation. For example, by involving all employees (or at least their representatives) in corporate decision making, as with the 'Type A' pluralist model discussed in Chapter 1, the Kantian firm will seek out the most equitable solution when faced with a severe downturn in its markets, arriving at a 'way forward' that reflects the views of the employees. Whether this will be the majority view, or some other formulation, would presumably be left to the firm to decide.

The criticisms leveled at Kantian ethics, over the rigidity of the categorical imperative, are challenged by both Beck (1959) and Bowie (1999). Kant is partly to blame for the criticism, argued Beck, because of the examples he used to illustrate his principles (Kant actually argued for truth telling in a situation in which a lie would save an innocent life). One possible way out of this cul-de-sac is to create a hierarchy of categorical imperatives. In this way the categorical imperative of 'always tell the truth' would be inferior to the categorical imperative of 'lie if it will save an innocent life'. Whether this form of hierarchical formulation is permissible, within a strictly Kantian categorical imperative perspective, is debatable. The notion of categorical imperatives being ranked contains a logical inconsistency. If categorical imperative 'A' can be overridden on occasions by categorical imperative 'B', then it cannot be a categorical imperative because it is not universalisable. We will return to this issue when we discuss *prima facie* obligations, but for the moment we will concentrate upon those writers and arguments that have sought to stay true to an undiluted version of the categorical imperative, but have offered ways of overcoming its rigidity.

De George (1999) offers one such resolution. The scenario depicted by De George addresses the truth-telling categorical imperative. It involves the shielding of an escaped slave who is being pursued by his slaveholder. For De George an untruth that might be told to the slaveholder to throw him off the scent would *not* be construed as a lie, on the basis that slavery is immoral, irrespective of what the law of the land might say. The slaveholder is not judged to have a legitimate interest in the information being sought. Under this interpretation the telling of an untruth is not lying if the person seeking information has no legitimate (ethically acceptable) interest in the information.

This approach is arguing that the telling of an untruth to someone who does not possess a morally legitimate interest in the information being sought is not merely acceptable, but accordingly not actually a lie. The enquirer's lack of moral legitimacy does not warrant the same level of truthfulness from the respondent, as would be required if the enquirer had possessed a legitimate interest.

Kant's use of truth telling has created many problems for the principle of categorical imperatives. The above, rather tortuous, attempts to try to overcome them are not altogether convincing. Purposely misconstruing known facts is a lie, to whomever the lie is to be told, and whatever the justification for the lie. By adopting a pure Kantian perspective, the concealer of the slave is left with no option but to reveal the whereabouts of the slave. However, if the protection of an innocent person is judged more important than telling an untruth, at a *universalisable* level, then there is something wrong with making truth telling a categorical imperative.

The critical question with regard to the truth-telling example used by Kant thus becomes: is the flaw within the principle of a categorical imperative, or is the problem the use of truth telling as an example of a categorical imperative? Whilst Kant did indeed cite truth telling as an example of a categorical imperative, this is not to say that the example is an appropriate or helpful one. If the way out of this difficult situation is simply to reject truth telling as an example of a categorical imperative, then further questions arise, namely:

(a) Is it possible to identify a categorical imperative? and/or

(b) Is it not possible to think of at least one exception to every categorical imperative that might be suggested, thereby nullifying its claim to being universalisable?

You might, for example, suggest 'one should not kill another human being' as a categorical imperative. But would a mother be morally wrong to respond to the pleas of her child who was being attacked by someone intent on taking the child's life? The killing of the assailant might be unpremeditated, unintentional even, but in an unequal struggle between mother and crazed assailant, how does the mother defend her child and herself? This is not to say that the killing of the assailant is the only outcome possible from such a scenario, but what is the status of a categorical imperative of 'no-taking-of-life', if the mother does ultimately stab or shoot the assailant? This is an extreme example, but a categorical imperative is intended to be universalisable and must therefore be able to withstand such tests.

Writers such as Ross (1930) have felt the need to develop a more flexible form of principled reasoning, but remaining emphatically within a non-consequentialist perspective. Ross employed an approach known as *prima facie* obligations.

DEFINITION

A literal translation of the Latin term *prima facie* is 'at first sight' or colloquially 'as it seems'. '*Prima facie* evidence' is a legal term that refers to evidence that is deemed sufficient to establish a presumption of truth about an incident, unless or until counter-evidence is discovered. Thus, we can define a *prima facie* obligation as one that should be respected in one's practice, unless and until a different *prima facie* obligation, with a superior claim for adherence, is presented.

Thus, whilst supporters of *prima facie* obligations would see truth telling as a *prima facie* obligation, in a situation where truth telling would lead to the probable death of an innocent human being (e.g. by revealing the whereabouts of an innocent fugitive), the *prima facie* obligation of 'lying to protect a wrongly or unjustly accused person' would override the obligation to tell the truth.

Discussion activity 3.2   Kantian ethics

Employing a Kantian perspective, briefly analyse Case study 2.20 (*The retention of dead babies' organs in hospitals*).

1. Can you develop a categorical imperative that would be appropriate for this case?

2. Would *prima facie* obligations be more helpful? If so, what would they be?

Notwithstanding the above problems, Kant and others who argued for principle-based ethics did so out of a belief that there are certain principles upon which societies need to be based if they are to develop in positive ways. With the emphasis on the atomised individual in modern society, non-consequentionalists feel that principle-based ethics are particularly relevant in the present day. At the root of consequentionalist concerns are the issues of justice and human rights. It is to these issues that we now turn.

Fairness; justice as fairness

In 1971 John Rawls published a book (revised in 1999) that has had a significant impact upon debates about theories of justice. His theory of justice as fairness is the basis of the middling position on the column of probity in Figure 3.1.

While Rawls does not argue that his theory is a practical one for everyday decision making, it presents a normative approach to deciding what a just society would look like in what he describes as 'the original position'. It offers a reference point against which contemporary social, political and economic systems can be contrasted. We then have to decide, as individuals and as societies, what we want to try to do about the differences between these two states – the should-be and the actual.

The original position is an artifice of Rawls that allows each of us to contemplate a 'just' society without the burden of our life experiences and prejudices tainting our views. We are required to envisage a situation in which we have no knowledge of who we are. The distinctive personal characteristics that we will ultimately possess (assuming we will actually have some bestowed upon us) are unknown within the original position. We have no knowledge of any natural or social advantages, or disadvantages, we might ultimately possess. We do not even know where in the world we would live, and therefore under which type of political system we might be governed. We do not know our ethnic origins; whether we will have a privileged or deprived upbringing; whether we would be intelligent or slow-witted; male or female; be sexually abused or lead an idyllic childhood; be short or tall; born with profound physical disabilities or be an Olympic-grade athlete; or experience a very poor or excellent educational system. We are placed behind what Rawls refers to as a 'veil of ignorance'.

From this position of total ignorance we are then asked a series of questions about the type of society we would like to live in. We are expected to employ actual knowledge of the chances of being placed within a privileged or elite position when answering a series of questions relating to issues such as social, political and economic governance; health care; education; social norms; wealth distribution and hereditary wealth; race, gender and religious equality; and employment opportunities. It must be emphasised again that the world we construct from the original position is a world in which we do not know where we will ultimately fit.

Faced with this challenge, Rawls argued that the rational person would adopt a maximin strategy. This is a risk-averse strategy that works on the basis of studying all the worst-case scenarios that exist within each option before us. Having identified all the worst-case possibilities, we then select the one that is the least worse. Thus, we opt for the option that gives us the greatest possible benefit, assuming we were unfortunate enough to be dealt a position at the bottom of the economic and social ladders in any of the choices with which we are confronted. The following illustrates the approach.

The veil of ignorance

You are in the 'original position' and the choice of political systems in which you will live are feudal, dictatorship, democracy and anarchy. You can imagine a range of outcomes for yourself in each system. In a feudal state, a dictatorship or a centrally controlled state, history has shown that the lives of those in power can be privileged ones, and that such an outcome is a possibility for you. However, maybe only a few can be expected to enjoy such lives. For the rest of the population, life is likely to be miserable. In a democracy the distribution of power will be far greater, going beyond political democracy and taking in workplace democracy. The opportunities to exercise moral agency should be higher than in the other options, although the opportunities to enjoy the sumptuous lifestyle of the elite of the feudal or dictatorship systems would be slight. Anarchy might possess certain attractions, but the uncertainty surrounding the notion of anarchy is likely to prove unappealing to you. Remember, Rawls anticipates that you are a calculating, risk-averse individual. Thus, considering the options before you, Rawls assumes you will judge that if you were to be one of the general members of the public (and there is a 90–99 per cent chance that this will be the case), it would be better for you to live in a full democracy.

A way of rationalising Rawls' original position is to see it as a mechanism to free each of us from our personal prejudices and life experiences. By removing us from the shackles of the inequities of how things are, it can enable us to focus upon what we believe distributive justice would/should look like, without the distortions born of history or fate.

Flowing from the assumption that the individual in the original position will desire not to be dealt a station in life that is unpalatable, Rawls argued that there are two guiding principles that will explain the reason for each choice made. These are:

1. Each member of society would be entitled to the same civil and political rights; and

2. Open competition for occupational positions exists, with attainment being based upon merit, but with economic inequalities being arranged so that 'there is no way in which the least advantaged stratum in the society could as a whole do any better' (Barry, 1989: 184).

The second principle is referred to as Rawls' difference principle. This is because Rawls was not arguing that everyone could be or should be the same. He recognised that differences relating to qualities such as intelligence, acumen, technical skills, physical abilities and so on will exist. However, he viewed the arbitrary and random distribution of social and natural attributes as no justification for the individuals blessed with these attributes prospering to the detriment of others less fortunate. Rawls thus rejected Nozick's entitlement theory. As Shaw and Barry observed,

Rawls' principles permit economic inequalities only if they do in fact benefit the least advantaged.

(Shaw and Barry, 1998: 114)

In dealing with differences in personal attributes and qualities, Rawls argued that contingencies must be set in place to handle the issues raised by such differences. These contingencies would be mechanisms, established at the original position, built upon cooperation and mutual respect.

> We are led to the difference principle if we wish to set up the social system so that no-one gains or loses from his arbitrary place in the distribution of natural assets or his initial position in society without giving or receiving compensating advantages in return.

(Rawls, 1971: 101–2)

Thus, before you would be asked questions about your preferred political system, education, corporate governance, etc. (and still in a state of ignorance about your personal position), you would have to identify the mechanisms that would need to be in place to minimise the worst effects of the differences that would exist between individual members of society, and between societies, when the final allocation of roles was made.

You may have detected a form of schizophrenia within Rawls' theory, inasmuch as the first principle has a strong socialist egalitarian moral perspective, while the second principle clearly assumes market-based, self-interest-driven behaviour. Rawls has been challenged on this 'inconsistency' from a variety of sources. Meade (1973) observed:

> In my view the ideal society would be one in which each citizen developed a real split personality, acting selfishly in the market place and altruistically at the ballot box . . . [It] is . . . only by such altruistic political action that there can be any alleviation of 'poverty' in a society in which the poor are in the minority.

(Meade, 1973: 52)

Rawls also acknowledged that there have to be limits to what people can reasonably be expected to do on behalf of others less fortunate than themselves. He termed this limit the 'strains of commitment'. In doing so Rawls accepted that there would be boundaries to the demands that the least privileged could make of those more fortunate than themselves. However, Rawls' theory does demand far more of individual citizens than that advocated by free-market theorists. The 'hidden hand' of Adam Smith delivers an impoverished form of justice from a Rawlsian perspective. Incentives are acknowledged, albeit in a reluctant way. As Barry observed:

> Inequalities are not ideally just, but . . . once we concede the need for incentives, inequalities permitted by the difference principle are the only defensible ones.

(Barry, 1989: 398)

Discussion activity 3.3

Briefly analyse Case study 2.4 (*AIDS drugs and patent rights in South Africa*) from a Rawlsian perspective.

The principle of 'do no harm'

The lowest point on the pillar of probity is the principle of 'do no harm'. It is at the bottom of the pillar because it is a default principle, to be used in the absence of any higher imperative. It requires that, if you cannot act well, you should at least avoid acting badly. The principle is historically associated with Hippocrates, the Greek philosopher (c460 BCE – c370 BCE) who is often called the 'Father of Medicine' because he has given his name to the Hippocratic oath, which it is commonly believed that all medical doctors take. The oath is the subject of many myths; not least that it is required to be taken by doctors, though some do take a modern version. Nor does it contain the words 'First, do no harm' that are attributed to it (National Institute of Health, n.d.). It does however include pledges amongst other things, not to give medicines that may do harm or not to take the knife to patients (surgery) when one does not have the skill to do so.

The principle takes the form in business and policy matters of the precautionary principle, which is expressed through the techniques of risk management. The concept emerged out of concern about environmental pollution but it is now seen as a useful guide to ethical behaviour in many different fields. The principle focuses on the prevention of harm rather than rectification after the harm has been done. It also requires that action should be taken to stop or limit the likely causes of a harm, even if there is a lack of definitive scientific knowledge that they are the true causes of the harm. The World Commission on the Ethics of Scientific Knowledge and Technology (2005: 14) give the following working definition of the precautionary principle:

> When human activities may lead to morally unacceptable harm that is scientifically plausible but uncertain, actions shall be taken to avoid or diminish that harm.

The failure to diminish the risks of exposure to asbestos by industry and governments identifies the damage can be done if the precautionary principle is not applied. Evidence that exposure to asbestos was injurious to health was known, if not proven to be so, and was available as early as 1898–1906. It was not until 1993 that asbestos was banned in the European Union. One Dutch study suggested that in that country alone 34,00 people could have avoided harm if the ban had been introduced 18 years previously (The World Commission on the Ethics of Scientific Knowledge and Technology, 2005: 11).

Discussion activity 3.4	**Do no harm**

Briefly analyse Case study 2.26 (*The Firestone Tire recall issue*) from the point of view of the precautionary principle and the need for risk assessment in industry.

Utilitarianism

Utilitarianism, which is at the top of the pillar of consequences in Figure 3.1, accepts utility, or the greatest happiness principle, as the foundation of morals. It holds that actions are right in proportion, as they tend to promote happiness, wrong, as they tend to promote the opposite of happiness. Or as Jeremy Bentham, the eighteenth-century philosopher who proposed the principle, put it:

> The greatest happiness of the greatest number is the foundation of morals and legislation.

(Bentham, 1994: 142)

The term utilitarianism, however, was coined by John Stuart Mill, a nineteenth-century writer, and not by Bentham. One interesting question that arises from utilitarianism is, 'What is happiness?' Most philosophers were at pains to suggest that it is not simply sensual pleasure. As J.S. Mill argued, 'It is better to be a human being dissatisfied than a pig satisfied' (Mill, 1998: 140). The importance of the higher pleasures over the lower has long been a theme in western ethics. St Augustine recognised that worldly pleasures were not of themselves bad but that they were insufficient to achieve an admirable life. He saw the sensual, material world as but part of human experience that has to be understood within the wider context of the intelligible world, which is one of clear and enduring ideas. Utilitarianism, according to Mill, who took a similar view, is not concerned only with material and sensual pleasures.

Utilitarianism is a calculating approach to ethics. It assumes the quantity and quality of happiness can be weighed. Bentham (1982) identified the following features of happiness that ought to be considered when measuring it:

- Intensity.
- Duration.
- Certainty – the probability that happiness or pain will result.
- Extent – the number of people affected.
- Closeness (propinquity) – pleasure or pain now or deferred in time.
- Richness (fecundity) – will the act lead to further pleasure?
- Purity – is the pleasure unalloyed or is it mixed with pain?

It is often assumed, in a business context, that maximising happiness is the same as maximising profit or return on capital invested. Plainly, improved profitability will generate happiness for some. But to apply the utilitarian principle properly one must consider the possibility that the pleasure derived from increased profitability has been achieved at the cost of a greater pain to other people. Mill (1998: 151) pointed out that most of the time someone applying the utilitarian principle need only concern themselves with their private interest. This is not necessarily so when the 'person' in question is a corporation.

Cost-benefit analysis is a natural tool of a utilitarian approach because it measures not only the direct costs and benefits to an organisation but also externalities. Externalities are defined in economics as social costs and benefits that are not reflected in the price of a product because they do not accrue directly to the organisation concerned. When people smoke the cigarettes produced by a tobacco company they are more likely to fall ill and so create costs for health-care systems. But the costs of that health care are not reflected in the costs of the cigarettes because the medical bills are not the tobacco company's responsibility. In the USA, however, the claim that tobacco companies misled their customers as to the harmful effects of smoking led the courts to require the companies to reimburse states with the cost of the medical treatment of smoking-related diseases. In this case an externality was converted into a private cost of the companies.

Cost-benefit analysis is a form of project appraisal. The costs and outputs of the project are identified and priced. If the outputs will arise over an extended period of time, and inputs are needed over a similar time span, the benefits and costs are discounted. If the benefits are greater than the costs then investment in the project would be sensible. If the project were, for example, a malaria control programme in a poor country, it is clear that the benefits would be widespread. Many lives would be saved; the health of the population would be improved. But these benefits are intangible and difficult to measure in financial terms. It might be thought that the costs of such a project would be easier to identify. Some, such as the cost of the labour and the insecticide, would be. But there may be wider, and less easy to measure, costs such as increased costs of education because more children survive and are fit enough to attend school.

DEFINITION

Cost-benefit analysis is based on the premise that both elements in the equation can be measured in monetary terms. To do this some limitations have to be accepted. An example of a study undertaken by Lambur et al. (2003) illustrates the point. The question was whether a programme of nutrition and health education in schools created more benefits than costs by altering children's eating habits in ways that made them healthier and less prone to illness. The costs of the programme were tangible and could be measured. Three main types of benefits were anticipated:

1. Direct tangible benefits – the savings on medical treatment of people who would have become ill had they not changed their eating patterns. These benefits could be measured financially because the costs of treating medical conditions are known.

2. Indirect tangible benefits – the additional economic productivity that is achieved by preventing or delaying the onset of illness.

3. Intangible benefits – these are such things as the improved quality of life and improved self-esteem associated with healthier eating. The analysts in this case, as do all cost-benefit analysts, listed the intangible benefits but did not measure them or include them in the quantitative analysis.

Analysts have to make further, technical, choices, about how to conduct the analysis. There are three main issues:

1. Cost-benefit ratio. This is the monetary value of the benefits per pound or dollar or euro spent. If the ratio is greater than one then benefits exceed costs.

2. Discount rate. The value of money to be spent or received at some future time is less than money spent or received in the present. In cost-benefit analysis it is necessary therefore to choose a rate at which future income will be discounted.

3. Net present value. This is a way of showing the result of a cost-benefit analysis in present-day values. The streams of benefits and costs in future years are discounted, using the chosen discount rate, so that all costs and benefits are presented in terms of their present value.

In the study we are looking at it was decided that the cost-benefit ratio was the appropriate method and it was found to be $10.64 worth of benefits for every $1 spent. There are two problems that emerge from this form of analysis.

1. So many assumptions have to be made, and so many things have to be left out of the calculation that the validity of the results is brought into question.

2. A cost-benefit analysis may show, as indeed the example given does, that the expenditure would be worthwhile. But it does not show whether that expenditure is affordable or what its priority is in relation to other projects that could be undertaken, unless the simple criterion is used that priority should be established according to the cost-benefit ratio, with projects with higher ratios having the greater priority. Fisher (1998) has argued that establishing priorities is a more complex matter.

One danger of utilitarianism, which cost-benefit analysis is designed to address, is that organisations seek to maximise *a good* rather than *the good*. In the British National Health Service, for example, the government set a target for reducing the size of the waiting lists for treatment, maximising a good – the number of patients treated. However, many hospitals achieved this by treating patients with minor problems that could be quickly and cheaply resolved and leaving those who needed lengthy and difficult treatment at the back of the queue, and so they failed to maximise the overall good.

In the case of public policy, public, and not simply private, good has clearly to be taken into account. Kemm (1985) used a utilitarian approach in a discussion of the ethics of food policy. He was interested in the ethical issues involved in modifying the eating habits of the population through regulation, facilitating measures (such as differentially taxing foods) and education. He argued that a policy is ethical if it produces more beneficial outcomes than harmful ones. But his suggestions about how policy makers might analyse issues sheds light on the limitations of technical means such as cost-benefit analysis.

Kemm stressed the interconnections between subjective and objective thinking in assessing the outcomes of policies. The three stages in this process are:

1. Determining the inherent goodness or badness of an outcome. This is a subjective value decision such as that involved in stating that dental mottling is less bad than carcinoma of the colon.

2. Measuring the probability that the desired outcome will be achieved. This is a scientific and objective activity.

3. Assessing the degree of certainty with which the probability of the outcomes has been estimated. This is a matter of judgment rather than measurement.

The subjective element can be illustrated by an example from the first item in the above list. Utility's concern for populations makes these subjective judgments difficult. How, for example, should moderate good for the majority be weighed against great harm to the minority? Fortifying chapatti flour would provide some health benefit for most chapatti eaters, but for the rare individual with vitamin D sensitivity it might cause serious vitamin D toxicity. The ethical problem can be exacerbated by the fact that the majority may not be aware that they have received benefits from the fortified flour. To give another example, if food policies increase the amount of fibre in the diet this will benefit people by protecting them from diverticulitis. However, they will not be aware of this. But those who suffer from flatulence as a result will be in no doubt that they have suffered, albeit the pain is not critical.

> Most would take the view that a very small harm to a very few individuals could be outweighed by a sufficiently large benefit to a sufficiently large number of individuals.
>
> (Kemm, 1985: 291)

One of the criticisms of utilitarianism is that it is unconcerned with equity. As Sen said:

> The trouble with [utilitarianism] is that maximising the sum of individual utilities is supremely unconcerned with the interpersonal distribution of that sum.
>
> (Sen quoted in Barr, 1985: 177)

The problem of forecasting future consequences, as identified in the last two items of Kemm's list, is a general difficulty with utilitarianism. If people cannot make accurate predictions about the consequences of particular actions then it is hardly worth the bother of weighing the anticipated pleasures and pains. Common experience, as expressed in Murphy's Law (if it can go wrong it will), suggests that people's forecasting skills are not to be overestimated. There is psychological evidence that people are overconfident when they make predictions. Fischoff, Slovic and Lichtenstein (1977) asked people a series of general knowledge questions (e.g. is absinthe (a) a liqueur or (b) a precious stone?) and found that when people said they were 100 per cent certain they had given the right answer they had in fact only done so on 80 per cent of occasions.

The form of utilitarianism that has been discussed so far is known as act utilitarianism, which calculates the net pleasure or pain to be obtained from a particular act. One of the practical problems with it is that the calculations it would require are too many and too complex. Let us consider a decision over whether 25 per cent of a company's employees should be made redundant to reduce costs and prevent the company going into insolvency. Table 3.1 lays out the calculations that might be required. The example is fictitious and the numbers are invented; the purpose of the table is to explain the nature of the calculations required.

The first step in the calculation is to identify the groups, stakeholders, who would be affected by a decision to make people redundant and the ways in which they might be affected. The following have been chosen although doubtless other groups could be identified.

- The shareholders who own the company. If the company becomes bankrupt they face losing their investment. If making people redundant saves the company then their capital is secured and they might even make slightly higher returns on it in future. Even if the company is saved from insolvency the situation would have increased their worries about the long-term future of the company.

- The managers will have to decide who to make redundant and also tell people that they have lost their jobs. The psychological effect of this on some managers will be to cause them much anxiety and worry because they dislike inflicting distress on others. Some managers, however, will gain a psychological boost from the event because it will confirm their self-impression that they are strong managers capable of making tough decisions.

- Those employees who will keep their jobs will have a weight of worry lifted from their shoulder but this may be balanced by feelings of guilt that they kept their jobs while their friends and colleagues lost theirs. They may also feel less confident about the long-term prospects of keeping their jobs. There would also, of course, be pleasure that they are still receiving a salary and in response to both these feelings they may work harder.

- The people made redundant would suffer a degree of psychological trauma and suffer a loss of self-esteem. Some may find a new and better job quite quickly, or discover that a different lifestyle not based on employment is more to their liking. These people would gain some pleasure from having been made redundant. Those who only find a worse and less well-paid job or remain unhappily unemployed will only experience pain.

- The families of those who lost their jobs will also share some of the psychological and economic impact. They may all become more stressed yet not be able to afford a holiday to help them relax.

- Finally, in this list, the taxpayers may have to pay for additional social security benefits for those who have lost their jobs.

Table 3.1 A utilitarian calculation concerning making employees in a company redundant to prevent bankruptcy

Stakeholder	Impact Positive (+) or Negative (−)	The probability that the impact will happen	Amount of pleasure or pain (JOLLIES) per person	No. of people who might be affected	Intensity and duration Scale 1–5	Propinquity Scale 1–5	Purity Scale 1–5	Fecundity Scale 1–5	Net totals (millions of JOLLIES)
Shareholders	Insolvency is avoided (+)	0.6	5	2,000,000	2	5	3	1	66
	Financial returns are increased (+)	0.4	3	2,000,000	2	3	4	2	26.4
	Worry about long-term future of the company (−)	0.7	−2	2,000,000	3	1	2	3	−25.2
Managers	Psychological pain at dismissing staff (−)	0.7	−20	150	3	5	2	2	−0.0252
	Psychological benefit from seeing oneself as able to make the tough decisions (+)	0.3	20	150	2	5	4	4	0.0135
Employees who keep their jobs	Removal of worry and anxiety (+)	0.5	30	60,000	2	5	1	4	10.8
	Continued receipt of salary (+)	1.0	50	60,000	2	5	1	3	33
	Work harder in gratitude (+)	0.6	5	60,000	3	5	1	3	2.16
	Sense of guilt at having kept their job (−)	0.7	−20	60,000	2	4	3	2	−9.24
	Fear that may lose job in future (−)	0.3	−10	60,000	4	1	3	4	−2.16
Employees made redundant	Psychological trauma (−)	0.9	−50	20,000	5	5	4	4	−16.2
	Quickly find a better job or lifestyle (+)	0.15	100	20,000	3	3	5	4	4.5
	Find a job that is worse than the one you lost	0.50	5	20,000	4	2	1	4	0.55
	Find no job and suffer a loss of income (−)	0.35	−100	20,000	5	5	5	5	−14
Families of those made redundant	Psychological and economic impact on families of those who lost jobs	0.8	−40	50,000	3	5	2	4	−22.4
Taxpayers	Additional social security benefits paid and loss of revenue	1.0	−0.001	29,400,000	2	2	3	1	−0.2352
								TOTAL	

The JOLLIES calculator

The next two tasks involve identifying the number of people in the stakeholder groups who may experience the impact of the downsizing; and the probability that they will. Some of these groups are large. In the UK, for example, there are 29.4 million income tax payers and it is certain (a probability of one) they would all have to bear a portion of the increased public expenditure on social security caused by the redundancies. Other groups are quite small. In this fictitious example, there are only 150 managers who have to make the redundancy decisions. The fictitious company has 80,000 employees and the proposal to make 25 per cent redundant would result in 20,000 job losses. In the table it is estimated that 90 per cent of them would suffer symptoms of psychological trauma. It is also estimated that 15 per cent would find a better job, 50 per cent would accept a new job that was less good than their previous one and 35 per cent would fail to find a new job (accounting for 100 per cent of those made redundant).

A further element needed in the calculation is a unit of measurement for pleasure and pain. We will have to invent one. In cost-benefit analysis in health care, health economists created a measure called QALYs (Gudex, 1986) to measure the consequences of medical and surgical interventions. In a similar spirit we have invented the JOLLIES (Judged, Outcome Leveraged, Life Improvement Expected Sum – OK, we admit – it is a joke). Pleasure is measured by positive JOLLIES, the greater the pleasure the more JOLLIES. Pain is measured in negative JOLLIES. In Table 3.2 the number of JOLLIES per person caused by each consequence of the redundancies is assessed. Some consequences are obviously high but some are very low. For example, because there are so many taxpayers, the extra amount of tax an individual would have to pay to cover the cost of extra social security payments would be so low that it might not even be noticed. Consequently, the pain caused to an individual is very small.

Utility   DEFINITION

In economics the measure of happiness or satisfaction received from an act – mostly goods and services – is known as utility. It is the formal term for what we have jokingly called JOLLIES, which would cover a wider range of acts than simply the provision of goods and services. Utility is of course difficult to measure and so economics is largely based on preferences, which can be measured. In plainer language there is no objective way to measure the happiness I get from a shot of vodka. It is, however, possible to measure whether I prefer vodka to tequila. So it is not possible to measure the amount of happiness gained from the drinks, which is what utilitarianism requires, but preferences can be put into rank order even though we cannot know the happiness gaps that separate them.

The other economic approach to the problem of measuring utility is to use money as a proxy measure. In other words we can assume that the more money we have the more it enables us to put ourselves into positions that make us happy. This assumption is the basis of much cost-benefit analysis because it allows things that cannot be measured directly to be incorporated into formal economic analysis. The problem is that there are disputes about what the exact relationship between the intensity of happiness and money is. It is generally thought not to be a straight line; increase of wealth suffers from diminishing marginal returns in the amount of pleasure it delivers but the shape of the relationship is not proven (Lane, 1995: 276–8).

The first calculation to be done is to multiply the number of people who might be affected by the probability that they will be affected. This number can then be multiplied by the number of JOLLIES to identify the amount of pleasure or pain caused by the redundancy decision. This is not the end of the calculation, however. As we have seen, pleasure and pain have different qualities (*see* p. 129) intensity, duration, certainty, extent, propinquity, fecundity and purity. The total, raw quantity of pleasure and pain has to be weighted by these factors. In Table 3.2 each of these factors is assessed on a five-point scale on which one equals very low and five equals very high. We will give a few examples.

- The intensity and duration of shareholders' relief at the avoidance of insolvency is marked but it will not last long as their minds move on to other issues and concerns. The psychological impact of redundancy on those made redundant, however, is likely to be intense and last a long time and so this has been scored high at five.

- Propinquity is concerned with whether the pleasure or pain is felt immediately or only occurs at some future time. The managers' delight at confirming their self-estimation as tough managers will be close in time to the decision. Contrarily, the psychological impact of redundancy may only emerge some time after the family member has been made redundant. The guiding principle involved is similar to that of discounted cash flow – pleasure and pain deferred to the future carry less weight than that experienced immediately. Future pleasure and pain carry lower weighting therefore in the calculation.

- Purity is concerned with the degree to which pleasure and pain are alloyed with each other. The pleasure those who keep their jobs feel will be mixed with anxiety about how much longer their jobs will be secure, and so this scores low on purity. Those who find themselves in a better position since being made redundant will experience a relatively pure pleasure and so this is scored high at five.

- Fecundity concerns the extent to which an act will create future pleasure or pain. The psychological stress caused to the job losers is likely to create more problems for them in the future and so this is scored high, whereas the typical short-sightedness of investors will mean that their pleasure at receiving increased dividends will not produce much future pleasure because they will be hungry for the next reward.

In the next stage of the calculation the raw total of JOLLIES is multiplied by all the weighting factors added together (and then divided by a million to keep the numbers manageable). As the purpose of a utilitarian analysis is to balance the total amount of pain caused against the total amount of pleasure, the final calculation is to add up the total JOLLIES, remembering that the pain JOLLIES are negative to get the net impact. If the result is positive then the pleasure outweighs the pain and the act is ethical; if the total is negative the act would result in more pain than pleasure and so would be unethical. In Table 3.2 the total is positive and so the redundancies would be an ethical act.

We have written a simple Excel spreadsheet to do the calculations in Table 3.2 and it would not be too difficult to devise a small program that prompted users

3: Ethical theories and how to use them   **125**

to make the various judgments needed and then perform the calculations. The example also identifies some of the limitations of this approach to ethics.

- If all the stakeholders and all the impacts that an act may have upon them were included then the matrix of data and calculations would become very large. One obvious one that has been ignored in the example is the impact on local businesses and economy of making 20,000 people redundant.

- People are not good at judging the consequences of actions and so it is quite likely that the probability figures in the third column are wrong.

- There are many problems in creating a measure of pleasure and pain because these are essentially subjective. The system of QALYs mentioned earlier used a matrix of pain and mobility to make the assessment and a large sample survey. A real measure such as a QALY or a fictitious one such as JOLLIES can only give an average value for the pain or pleasure caused by a particular event and cannot capture the individual experience.

- The weighting scales for the features of pleasure and pain are also subjective and so will suffer the problem of inter-rater comparability; in other words different raters may make different assessments on these scales. The overall problem is that it is difficult to identify precise and agreed numbers to put into the calculations. This means that each number has a large margin of error and if calculations were done using one extreme of the range the act might be calculated as ethical, yet if numbers at the other extreme were used the act might be shown to be unethical.

Cross reference	It seems unlikely that managers go through such a complex calculation whenever they have to make a decision. Indeed, psychological research suggests they use an intuitive, heuristic approach that reduces the complexity of decisions and restricts the amount of information that is brought to bear upon it. Heuristics in decision making are the subject of Chapter 4.

Some writers have tried to overcome this difficulty by proposing rule utilitarianism. This approach looks at the general consequences, in terms of pleasure and pain, of particular rules of conduct. The rule, the following of which produces the best results, is the best rule to follow. This approach does not, however, necessarily make matters simpler. A rule such as 'you should always keep your promises' would probably have to be followed by so many exceptions that it would be no simpler than act utilitarianism.

A further criticism of utilitarianism is that it is implicitly authoritarian. This tendency can be illustrated by the public debate, in the early part of the nineteenth century, over the sources and mechanisms of revenue collection in the Indian provinces ruled by the East India Company. James Mill, the father of John Stuart Mill, was at the centre of this debate and through him the utilitarian philosophy of Bentham became a dominant theme in the argument. The utilitarians argued that the company had a duty to decide how best to spend the tax revenue of the country. As Holt Mackenzie argued in 1820:

Holding 9/10ths of the clear rent [revenue] of the country as a fund to be administered for the public good, the government may, I think, justly be regarded as under a very solemn obligation to consider more fully than has hitherto been usual, how it can dispose of that fund so as to produce *the greatest sum of happiness*.

(Stokes, 1959: 113, emphasis added)

There was a clear authoritarian and paternalistic strand in the thinking of these utilitarians. They believed they had a mission to transform India, but this mission could only be achieved by strong government. They would decide how the revenue should be spent. Utilitarianism requires the presence of a powerful figure who can calculate where the happiness of the country lies and then take the necessary action to bring it about. This strain of thought can be found in Bentham's own writings in which he argued that the will of the executive should not be checked by constitutional or popular devices (Stokes, 1959: 72, 79). It can also easily take root in companies and organisations where management become the judges of utility.

Despite the criticisms that can be made of utilitarianism its core ideas are commonly expressed by managers when they talk of 'business cases'. These are arguments that a thing should be done because it would be good for the business; the good of the wider society is not always considered.

Discussion activity 3.5	Utilitarian ethics

Briefly analyse Case study 2.10 *(Providing new drugs on the NHS to people with multiple sclerosis)* from a utilitarian perspective.

Corporate social responsibility

The notion of corporate social responsibility (CSR) is discussed in detail in Chapter 10. In Figure 3.1 CSR is positioned in the middle of the pillar of consequences. The CSR perspective is subsidiary to utilitarianism on the pillar because organisations can expand or restrict their areas of responsibility. A company's commitment to act responsibly only requires it to consider the consequences of its own actions and it is not responsible for the actions of others. Whilst a company may have a social responsibility to its employees, for example, it does not have an obligation towards those employed by other, independent organisations.

On occasions the emphasis may be on palliating or mitigating harm caused by organisational actions rather than on doing positive good. It may be necessary for an organisation to downsize its work force by making people redundant. In broad utilitarian terms this may produce the best balance of good and bad outcomes. However a socially responsible organisation would take action to minimize the disadvantages to those who lose their jobs by, for example, training those made redundant for new jobs or helping them establish small businesses. In this section we want to look at CSR as a criterion for judging whether a proposed action or decision is ethical or not.

As a yardstick for evaluating actions CSR is concerned with whether the actions of a company or organisation assists with the development and sustainability of individuals, communities and the environment. Ideally this implies that organisations should

- form themselves so that they are learning organisations in which the individuals within it can develop to their own potential;

- help the communities in which they operate develop and grow;

- increase the sustainability of the environment they draw upon. This will be dealt with in chapter 10.

What role should organisations have in helping its employees develop? Covey's (1992) *The Seven Habits of Highly Effective People* can stand as an example. He argued that people develop their character ethic through a process of deep self-reflection. He distinguished character ethic from personality ethic (Covey, 1992: 18–21). The character ethic proposes basic principles of effective living, things like integrity, fidelity, humility, courage and so on. These are hard precepts to live by. In contrast the personality ethic proposes 'quick-fix solutions' drawn from a public relations approach, which aims to present a good image of oneself and easy behavioural tricks used to manipulate others. It is the character ethic that people should concentrate on, and which responsible organisations would encourage employees to develop. Covey (1992: 36) adopted the 'principle of process' of personal growth in the spheres of emotion, human relationships and character formation. These processes cannot, he argued, be short-circuited; people have to go through the necessary stages to achieve greater effectiveness. He applied these lessons not only to people's personal lives but also to working lives. His book became a very popular guide for managers.

Senge, in his book *The Fifth Discipline* (1990), also stressed the importance of individuals' learning, which he saw as necessary for the development of learning organisations. These, he argued, were the only kind of organisation that will be successful. For Senge learning is not simply an acquisition of useful information; it is a personal moral development. He used the classical Greek term *metanoia* (Senge, 1990: 13–14) to describe the sort of learning that learning organisations should aspire to. It means a shift of mind. The word was used by the Gnostics who, in the early years of Christianity, saw gnosis, or knowledge, as an awareness of a person's relationship with God. Gnosis involves relating to the divine power of creativity by truly learning to know oneself (Pagels, 1982: 133–4). Senge's view of organisational development parallels this view of learning as ethical and spiritual growth.

> Real learning gets to the heart of what it means to be human. Through learning we recreate ourselves. Through learning we reperceive the world and our relationship to it. Through learning we extend our capacity to create, to be part of the generative process of life.
>
> (Senge, 1990: 14)

Individual growth and learning is not simply learning how to use new leadership or financial appraisal techniques. It is a process of becoming aware of one's ethical potential. Learning becomes an ethical end in itself that responsible learning organisations support

The communitarian approach to ethics is a reaction to the liberal view that sees the individual as more important than social groups. The communitarian approach argues that people are inherently social and that they can only achieve their moral potential by being part of growing and developing communities. By contributing to the ethical growth of a group people also become ethical individuals. These communities may be based on place, such as a neighbourhood, on shared group memories, such as in immigrant communities, or on a host of voluntary associations such as golf clubs, parent teacher associations, churches and so on. A tenet of the communitarian perspective is that different communities might be expected to develop their own values and moral principles. The universalism of liberalism's claim, that democratic, free market systems are the correct solution for all societies, as argued by Fukuyama (1993) in his book *The End of History*, is false. This acceptance of particularism or relativism will become important when we discuss international business in Chapter 11. Amitai Etzioni (1993) is the most high-profile advocate of a communitarian approach.

It follows from a communitarian point of view that anything that limits the potential for communities to grow and be responsible for themselves is reprehensible. Such threats may come either from the political left, with its concern for creating centralised, bureaucratic welfare structures for dealing with social problems, or from the right, whose protagonists do not see why granting rights such as flexible working hours, parental leave and childcare facilities to support families should be tolerated in a free-market system.

Communitarian ethics raises a number of questions for businesses and organisations:

- Should business try to create a homogenous world in which everyone consumes the same products and shares the same values? This would maximise industry's efficiency. Or should business respond to the particularities of different societies and groups by diversifying their products and business models?

- To what extent should businesses and organisations contribute to the growth and development of local communities? Should they provide resources and managerial expertise to encourage the development of self-help groups in the communities in which they work? Should such support be philanthropic or be part of commercial sponsorship deals? The development of 'family friendly' employment practices (Elshtain et al., n.d.) is important from a communitarian perspective. These matters of corporate citizenship are considered in Chapter 8.

- Should organisations attempt to create themselves as communities? The Foster Architectural Partnership has long sought to design office buildings that encourage the development of community bonds, as well as employment relationships, between the staff. Their buildings include 'streets', cafés, restaurants, swimming pools and games areas so that in one building the staff described working in the building as 'homing from work' (Foster, 2001: 206). The commercial pressures on organisations mean that such facilities are often converted to a more directly productive use.

Discussion activity 3.6　　A CSR perspective

Briefly compare Case study 2.1 (*The Nationwide Foundation*) with Case study 2.3 (*Farepak*) from a CSR perspective.

Objectivism or ethical egoism

J. S. Mill praised those who would sacrifice their personal happiness to gain a greater happiness for others. Ethical egoists would not understand such an act. They argue that an individual should pursue their own interests by applying their reason to the task of identifying and achieving their own best interests. Objectivism is located, in Figure 3.1, at the bottom of the pillar of consequences because this viewpoint only considers the benefits of an action to an organisation and its managers. We will consider this view by looking at the ideas of Robert Nozick and the objectivist philosophy of Ayn Rand.

Robert Nozick (1974) was a leading advocate of the libertarian position on justice and rights. The libertarian perspective adopts the notion of negative freedoms. That is, it holds as its primary tenet the individual's right of 'freedoms from'. The most significant of these is freedom from government interference in all but the most critical of property rights protection systems, for example, police forces for private property and military forces regarding property of the realm. From a libertarian perspective, there is little outside the maintenance of property rights that represents legitimate government activity. Differences in personal wealth, talent, physical attributes and intelligence are seen as being obtained in the 'natural' sense, in that their ownership owes nothing to social or political institutions. If they are obtained in this way, nothing can deny the owner possession of them, or the value that derives from that ownership. Differences caused to the life-chances of individuals by the possession, or not, of these qualities/characteristics are not seen as justifying the meddling of governments in attempts to redistribute some of the associated benefits.

Within the libertarian frame of reference, and as long as what an individual wishes to do is within the law, then nothing should prevent the individual from fulfilling those desires. It is for this reason that taxation (and particularly the taxes levied on inherited assets) is such a vexed subject. From a libertarian perspective, taxation is the forcible, involuntary withdrawal of economic resources from individuals to be spent by governments in ways that might fail to satisfy or be compatible with the desires and values of the taxed individuals.

Nozick coined the term 'entitlement theory' to express the view that what has been acquired legally and fairly (although fairly is an ill-defined concept) cannot be taken away within a libertarian concept of justice. This is despite the fact that practices that are regarded as immoral and illegal today, for example, slavery, have not always been so, yet they represent an important factor in explaining the present distribution of wealth that shapes so many people's life-chances. Interestingly, in his later works, Nozick recognised the problems associated with resources obtained or lost by dubious methods and modified his views a little with respect to inherited wealth, an example being the plight of the American Indians. However, inherited resources and life-chances remain central issues within this debate.

Entitlement theory attempts to draw a veil over the means by which wealth may have been acquired. The ramifications of being denied an equal opportunity to education, health care, legal justice are seen as irrelevant within a libertarian conception of justice, or at least a greater injustice would be to transfer 'legally' acquired assets from those that have to those that have not. With no limits attached to what individuals can achieve in a liberal society, it is for every individual to improve their own life chances.

Objectivism gained popularity in America during the twentieth century through the novels of Ayn Rand (1905–1982), who has already been discussed in Chapter 1. Her ethical stance is known as objectivism. It gives primacy to people's capacity for rational thought. This facility, when applied to knowledge of the world gained through the senses, leads to an objective understanding of the world that leaves no room for the sceptical belief that all knowledge is mere opinion. The theory's ethical position is that each individual should seek their own happiness through a productive independent life in which their own rational judgment is their only guide. The main virtues of objectivist thought are independence, integrity, honesty, productiveness, trade and pride. It encourages a robust belief in self-help and accepts that people who cannot or will not take responsibility for themselves would have to bear the consequences. They should not expect the state or society to bail them out. An individual should not sacrifice themselves to others or expect others to sacrifice themselves for him.

We will illustrate the main themes of objectivism through Kirkpatrick's (1994) defence of advertising. He used objectivism to counter the social criticisms made of advertising, which are that advertising can be manipulative and offensive. His broad argument is that laissez-faire capitalism is good because, according to Rand, the principle of trade is the 'only system consonant with man's rational nature' (Kirkpatrick, 1994: 28). If capitalism is good then advertising, which is a necessary part of it, must also be good. Kirkpatrick blames Kant for the common mistake of seeing advertising as unethical. He attributed to Kant the ideal that human reason cannot objectively comprehend reality because reason is always affected by the innate structures of a person's mind. If this were so then human reason would not be adequate to cope with the blandishments of advertising. But he argued that Kant is wrong and Rand is right. Objective knowledge is possible and human reason is capable of properly evaluating the advertisers' messages. As to the charge of offensiveness, he argued that values are not intrinsic to objects. So a cigarette for example is not in itself a bad thing; only the way people use it can make it good or bad. If cigarettes are not intrinsically immoral and individuals have free will then 'tobacco advertisers defraud no one' (Kirkpatrick, 1994: 80).

The only necessary constraint on advertising is the common law one against fraud. 'Anything less than that turns both marketers and consumers into victims of subjective law, that is, of "rule by men" *[i.e. by bureaucrats]* rather than the "rule of law"' (Kirkpatrick, 1994: 51). The American-ness of the argument was emphasised when he quoted Daniel Boorstin arguing that advertising is the American epistemology – the way in which Americans learn about things. Kirkpatrick's argument for advertising only stands, of course, if objectivism is held to be objectively true.

The difficult question for ethical egoism is how far self-interest would cause individuals to give away some of their independence in order to accommodate others. Kirkpatrick argued that obeying the common law should be the limit of the surrender. Hobbes, who wrote in the seventeenth century, identified the key problem. People are very similar in wit and strength and therefore,

> If two men desire the same thing, which nevertheless they cannot both enjoy, they become enemies; and in the way to their end, which is principally their own conservation, and sometimes their delectation only, endeavour to destroy, or subdue one another.
>
> (Hobbes, n.d.: 81)

Self-interest, therefore, would cause people to

> be willing, when others are so too, as far-forth, as for peace, and defence of himself he shall think it necessary to lay down this right to all things; and be contented with so much liberty against other men, as he would allow other men against himself.

(Hobbes, n.d.: 85)

Of course, in modern business terms, it is a matter of dispute as to the degree of liberty a person, or a company, would rationally agree to forgo.

Discussion activity 3.7	**Ethical egoism**

Briefly analyse Case study 2.22 *(The hospital consultants)* from an ethical egoism perspective.

Although this discussion has largely focused on individuals, which is intrinsic to an egoist philosophy, Rand does acknowledge the importance of organisations. Corporations, Rand argues, should be associations of individuals who freely choose to cooperate together on the basis of shared rational ideas and principle (Rand, 1995). In the world that we are focusing on in this book therefore objectivism becomes a concern for meeting the needs of the owners of a corporation, normally a focus on shareholder wealth.

In the toolkit at the end of this chapter a focus on the self-interest of organisations and companies is considered from both a short-term and a long-term perspective. From a philosophical objectivist point of view only a long-term orientation is appropriate for a person seeking the rational development of their potential. A fixation on the short term would be a degenerate, if not uncommon, form of objectivism.

Virtue ethics

Virtue ethics is located on the central pillar of character and culture in Figure 3.1, below conscience but above the perspective of decency.

Virtues are not 'ends'; rather they are 'means'. They are personal qualities that provide the basis for the individual to lead a good, noble or 'happy' life. Whilst the notion of what is virtuous behaviour has changed over time, the person most associated with virtue ethics is Aristotle, a philosopher of great eminence who lived in Greece between 384 and 322 BC. Not only have the characteristics of a virtuous life undergone significant changes, but the meanings attached to the terms used to describe particular characteristics are also a source of difference.

The Greek word, εύδαιμονία (eudaemonia) is loosely translated as 'happiness'. However, as MacIntyre (1967) pointed out, in Greek the term actually embraces the notion of both behaving well and faring well. Its use in ancient Greece was not concerned with hedonistic notions of happiness. It concerned itself with the individual's behaviour, and thus the way others perceived the individual. The latter was an essential ingredient to personal happiness. The 'good life' had, and retains, strong connotations of a 'whole' life, and places the individual within a social context. Even though social structures were deeply class-ridden during Aristotle's life, within the social and political elite there was a strong sense of being part of a whole.

Aristotle, reflecting the ideas of his age, placed the 'great-soul-man' on a pedestal. As you will see, the great-soul-man displays those virtues that were regarded as of the highest order. In ancient Greece the views of one's peers were critical to feelings of self-worth. Whilst the individual is the focus of Aristotle's attention, it is an individual within a society. Some social commentators, like MacIntyre (1967, 1987), have argued that since the eighteenth century liberalism has placed the individual outside of society. In this latter context, society is at best the sum of its parts. At worst, in Margaret Thatcher's famous words, 'there is no such thing as society'.

Virtue ethics is not a system of rules, but rather a set of personal characteristics that, if practised, will ensure that the individual is likely to make the 'right' choice in any ethically complex situation. Thus, the question for the individual, caught in the maelstrom of an ethically complex situation and appealing to virtue ethics as a guide for action, would ask, 'What would a virtuous person do in this situation?'

Plato, Aristotle's teacher, had identified four virtues, those of wisdom, courage, self-control and justice. For Aristotle, justice was the dominant virtue, but he expanded upon the number of personal qualities that could be regarded as virtues. Thus, into the frame came qualities such as liberality (the virtuous attitude towards money); patience (the virtuous response to minor provocation); amiability (the virtue of personal persona); magnanimity, truthfulness, indifference (in relation to the seeking of public recognition of achievement) and wittiness. It must be stressed that these virtues were not seen as of equal merit. The original Platonic virtues were seen as central to the attainment of a 'good' life, whereas the other virtues were seen as important for a civilised life. To understand the nature of a virtue we must understand how they are derived, and to do so we introduce the concept of the 'mean'.

For Aristotle, those personal qualities that were regarded as virtues were reflected in behaviours that represented a balance, or mean, in terms of the particular personal quality being considered. Thus, if the response of an individual to the threat of 'danger or significant personal challenge' was being considered, we can envisage a continuum with cowardice at one extreme and recklessness at the other (as in Table 3.2). Neither of these personal qualities (what Aristotle termed 'dispositions') is appealing as they are both likely to lead to detrimental outcomes in the long run. In the face of danger the 'noble' or 'great-soul-man' (and it was always the male that was considered in ancient Greece) would have to overcome his fears (i.e. suppress feelings of cowardice), but avoid acts of rashness, which would be likely to reduce the chances of success. Thus, an intermediate-point is required. This mean, or disposition, in this context is termed 'courage'.

Table 3.2 Aristotle's moral virtues

Context	The vice of deficiency	Virtue (mean)	The vice of excess
Danger or a significant personal challenge	Cowardice	Courage	Rashness
Physical pleasures	Indifference (being unable to recognise the joy that physical pleasures can offer)	Self-control (knowing when and where to enjoy oneself)	Greed
Wealth	Meanness	Liberality (discriminating generosity)	Profligacy
Money	Miserliness	Magnificence (knowing when to spend, how much and on what)	Spendthrift
View of self	Meekness	Magnanimity (being able to feel and display personal pride when it is deserved, but without vanity)	Vanity
Personal recognition	False modesty	Indifference (good deeds are done for their own sake and not for personal recognition)	Careerist
Minor irritants	Defeatism	Patience	Irascibility
Personal demeanour	Obsequious (fawning and grovelling)	Amiable	Quarrelsome
Sincerity in expression	Self-deprecating	Truthfulness	Boastfulness
Sociability	Boorishness	Wittiness	Buffoonery

Video clip 3.1

Interview with the Canon Precentor of St Paul's Cathedral, London. Priorities and human flourishing

The Canon Precentor discusses the notion of human flourishing. To view the video clip from the interview please visit this book's companion website at www.pearsoned.co.uk/fisherlovellvalerosilva.

Aristotle also considered modesty (used by Aristotle to mean 'respect', or 'sense of shame') as a possible virtue, but he dismissed it, other than as a virtue in the younger man. In the latter case, Aristotle saw it as a curb on youthful indiscretion, but he considered that the virtuous mature man should not require modesty for he should not commit acts of which he could be ashamed.

For Aristotle, the 'great-soul-man' was magnanimous, which was defined as 'possessing proper pride, or self-control' (Aristotle, 1976: 153). It is not surprising that, in the class-ridden society of ancient Greece, the virtues described by Aristotle were only available to the elite of society. McMylor (1994), citing MacIntyre, observed:

> Certain virtues are only available to those of great riches and high social status, there are virtues which are unavailable to the poor man, even if he is a free man. And those virtues are in Aristotle's view ones central to human life.

> (McMylor, 1994: 103)

Wealth, however, was not a necessary prerequisite of a magnanimous man.

> It is chiefly with honours . . . that the magnanimous man is concerned; but he will also be moderately disposed towards wealth, power, and every kind of good or bad fortune, however it befalls him.

> (Aristotle, 1976: 155)

Indeed when discussing the virtuous approach towards wealth Aristotle identified liberality as the virtue (the mean). Illiberality or meanness was one extreme vice, while prodigality or profligacy was the other. However, Aristotle did not regard the two extremes as vices of equal unacceptability, judging profligacy as less objectionable than meanness. This ranking of profligacy over meanness underscores the slightly lower importance attached to money and wealth, although this is not to say that wealth was unimportant.

Magnanimity was not equated with self-deprecation or undue humility. These were seen as approximating to vices, but so too were vanity and boastfulness. Being *rightly* proud of who you were, or what you had achieved, was not a vice; only unjustified high self-esteem was unacceptable.

> A person is considered to be magnanimous if he thinks that he is worthy of great things, provided that he is worthy of them; because anyone who esteems his own worth unduly is foolish, and nobody who acts virtuously is foolish or stupid.

> (Aristotle, 1976: 153)

The point about this statement is that it is the perception of others that determines whether behaviour is vain or deserving. In one sense a person can be both vain and deserving, but for Aristotle vanity implied a degree of exhibitionism above that which could be justified by one's achievements or social standing. Thus, vanity becomes a relative term in this context, relative to the state of deservingness attached to the achievement of the individual or his position in society.

Virtue and justice

Aristotle gave justice prominent consideration, but the notion of justice in ancient Greece was quite different from that which we articulate today. As is further explored below, the accepted standards of ethical behaviour are a product of their times, notwithstanding that notions of justice feature in most philosophies of ethics. Aristotle, while he spent some time differentiating between differing forms of justice, nonetheless offers a less than precise definition of justice, with the notion of the 'mean' again featuring strongly.

> To do injustice is to have more than one ought, and to suffer it is to have less than one ought and justice is the mean between doing injustice and suffering it.
>
> (Aristotle, 1976: 78)

This concentration upon the notion of justice as the bedrock of ethical behaviour is not universally shared, with the invisibility and muteness of women within such debates a cause for concern.

The role of women in ancient Athenian society did not register on political and social seismographs. Thus, the virtues as articulated by Aristotle can be said to be virtues from a masculine perspective. This is a relevant observation when we consider, as we do later, the work of psychologists, such as Lawrence Kohlberg, who developed a hierarchy of moral reasoning, based upon the assumption that justice is the ultimate test of the superiority of one form of moral reasoning over another. Within this framework, hard choices can be made between competing claims using justice as the decision criterion. The hypothetical scenarios employed by Kohlberg during his studies presented research subjects with choices to be made, but compromises were not available. Under this approach, one claim could be successful, while all others would fail.

Gilligan (1982), a former student of Kohlberg, has taken issue with the use of justice as the pre-eminent determinant of moral reasoning. Within Kohlberg's studies fewer females than males have displayed the form of moral reasoning that has allowed them to be classified as reasoning at the highest levels of Kohlberg's hierarchy. Gilligan has argued that this should not be interpreted as a lower level of reasoning than is possible, rather that the form of reasoning often displayed by women is *different* from that held by men. It is argued that women's early socialisation processes (particularly observing their mothers) encourage them to seek out compromises, not to allocate blame exclusively to one side or another, nor to distribute prizes or plaudits exclusively to only one member of a group. Rather the resolution of competitions, games or arguments is achieved with a sense of 'everyone gets something'. This approach is adopted with one eye on the medium to long term, that is, if a family is to develop cohesively there must be give and take from all sides at one time or another. From Gilligan's perspective the wisdom of Solomon involves more than the simple application of all-or-nothing justice to resolve a family dispute. Gilligan's argument contains a strong sense of the wisdom of the female perspective that she referred to as 'care'.

The need for wisdom to temper justice is possibly best exemplified in recent times by the approach adopted by President Mandela's government in South Africa when, on coming to power, it established the Commission for Truth and Reconciliation. The Commission was charged with investigating the myriad of stories and accusations of atrocities, murder and brutality inflicted upon the black and coloured communities by individuals, the police and the army during the apartheid years. Under the chairmanship of Archbishop Desmond Tutu, the Commission for Truth and Reconciliation continues to investigate a wide range of cases, with the accused giving evidence in the knowledge that they will not be prosecuted for their crimes. It is hoped that the truth relating to each case will thereby emerge (a critical issue for the bereaved), and gradually the nation's shame will be exorcised. In the process a potential bloodbath of retribution will have been avoided.

Whether the Commission's work has satisfied everyone is a moot point, but it represents an understanding that justice, if exercised exclusively in the form of retribution ('an eye for an eye'), would be unlikely to serve the longer-term interests of the people of South Africa.

Gilligan argued that the concept of 'care' should be regarded as highly as justice when interpreting responses of research subjects to moral reasoning scenarios. This is not care (which is too often interpreted as compromise) born out of an 'anything-for-a-quiet-life' approach. Rather, care is reflected by an approach that seeks to find a way forward that not only provides some form of equitable resolution to a conflict (although not necessarily reflecting 'full' justice in an Aristotelian or Kohlbergian form), but also holds out the possibilities for maintaining a working relationship between the protagonists, so that future cooperation might be possible. This is not to deny that there are times when guilt or success should be identified with individuals, to the exclusion of all others. Gilligan's argument is that such an approach is undoubtedly appropriate on occasions, but not as a universal maxim.

If we think about this issue from an Aristotelian perspective, we can employ the notion of a mean as in Figure 3.2. You may wish to consider this perspective when you tackle Activity 3.1.

Changing perceptions of virtue

The notion of virtue is heavily dependent upon the period in which the concept is being considered. As MacIntyre (1967: 174) observed,

> it [virtue] always requires for its application the acceptance of some prior account of certain features of social and moral life, in terms of which it has to be defined and explained.

As centuries have passed, so shifts can be detected in what becomes regarded as virtuous behaviour.

- In the time of Homer (who lived some 400 years before Aristotle and during a period of constant hostilities), the warrior was the model of human excellence and achievement.

- During the Greece of Aristotle's time, with its relatively stable Athenian city-state, the virtues embodied in the privileged, Athenian gentleman were paramount.

- From a western perspective, the rise of Christianity, as reflected in the New Testament, brought with it a fundamental shift in the perception of virtuous behaviour. Contra Aristotle, the New Testament presents an image of goodness that is unattainable by the wealthy and the privileged. Only the poorest are

Vice of deficiency	Virtue/mean	Vice of excess
Inflexible rule following	Care/wisdom	Appeasement

Figure 3.2 Care and wisdom as a virtue

deemed worthy, with slaves (the lowest class within Aristotle's Athenian society) more likely to be seen as virtuous than the rich.

■ The coming of the Industrial Revolution, in the eighteenth century, found new personal qualities becoming valued. Benjamin Franklin, for example, espoused the virtues of cleanliness, silence and industry, as well as punctuality, industry, frugality, plus many others, but always with utilitarian motives (McMylor, 1994).

■ Solomon (1993: 207–16) identified honesty, fairness, trust and toughness (having a vision and persevering in its implementation) as the important virtues for managers in modern corporations.

The Aristotelian and Christian perspectives recognise different virtues but both link means and ends. Unethical means cannot be justified by good outcomes. A good deed is not a good deed if it is done with bad motives, for example, to avoid pain, or to ingratiate oneself with the recipient. In Aristotelian terms, a virtuous life is one that allows individuals to achieve their *telos*, or end, to its full potential. Practice of the virtues makes this potential realisable. The emphasis is thus upon both means (virtues) and ends (*telos*). From this perspective the relationship between means and ends is an internal one, not external. Both are within the control of the individual.

For Franklin, however, virtue was dependent upon some specified notion of utility. Achievement of socially acceptable ends (which have increasingly become articulated in material terms) can justify less than virtuous means. Understanding the values, social structures and key discourses of an era is crucial to understanding what will be regarded as virtues.

Within the Franklinian conception of virtues we have some of the seeds of what troubles many people about juxtaposing ethics and business. Some of the virtues articulated by Franklin can be achieved most effectively by the suppression of individual rights, for example, silence and industry, whilst others, for example, punctuality and cleanliness, are regarded as virtues, not primarily because they benefit the individual concerned, but because they contribute to the economy and efficiency of business. Thus, whilst the ends (punctuality and cleanliness) can be regarded as beneficial in themselves, they would not be regarded as virtues from an Aristotelian perspective, because they are driven by a concern with ends and not means.

| Discussion activity 3.8 | Virtue ethics |

Briefly analyse Case study 2.15 (*Lord Browne of Madingley*) employing a virtue ethics perspective.

1. Which virtues would you prioritise?

2. Are there any personal characteristics that so far have not been mentioned that you would regard as virtues and that might contribute to addressing the issues raised in the case?

Decency

Decency is one of those words that in English carries great emotional power but is hard to define. The decency of behaviour is intuitively judged. It is placed below virtue ethics, but above legality, on the pillar of character and culture in Figure 3.1. Decency is the minimum degree of respect that we should give to others in our dealings with them. It is the basic expectations that we need to have of others in order to be able to do business with them.

Elaine Sternberg (2000) has argued strongly that private companies' ethical responsibilities only extend to serving the interests of the shareholders, or owners; and that it is unethical for them to dissipate their energies trying to meet the contradictory demands of the large range of interest groups, often called stakeholders, who are involved with companies. But she does not argue that companies should be wholly unrestrained in seeking their own interests. She argues that companies must act in a decent manner. She attributes two qualities to decency. The first is acting in a legal manner. This is dealt with elsewhere in this chapter; and so in this section we shall deal only with the second quality of decency, which is acting in a manner that establishes and maintains trust between the company and its customers, suppliers, distributors and all the others it comes into contact with. She defines decency as the honesty, fairness, and the avoidance of coercion or threat, that are necessary for an organisation to earn profit over the long term.

Discussion activity 3.9	Decency

Briefly analyse Case study 2.23 (*Supermarkets' treatment of their supply chains*) to assess whether the supermarkets treat their supply chain partners decently.

Applying ethical theories

As you are now aware there are many ethical theories. Even if you find it easy to discount some of them, because you think them trivial or ill-founded, several will remain. This raises a question for someone who wishes to think ethically. Should all or several theories be applied when thinking about an issue or should one approach be adopted that seems best suited to the matter in hand? Petrick and Quinn (1997: 55–6, 63) argued that those managers who are temperamentally attached to one of the theoretical perspectives on ethics 'fanatically rush to judgement'. They claimed that there can be no 'quick fixes' when dealing with matters of managerial integrity and that managers ought to use the ethical insights to make balanced ethical decisions.

If all, or at least several, ethical perspectives need to be applied when trying to make a decision that is ethical then debate and discussion is inevitable. It may be that debates between a group of people are necessary or it may simply be that an individual needs the debate the issues with themselves within their own heads. This brings us to the topic of discourse ethics and in the next section an account of it will be given. Discourse ethics has not been included in the diagram in Figure 3.1 because it is the approach to ethics that frames Diagram 3.1 and so it cannot also be an element within Figure 3.1. This next section is followed by an introduction to a toolkit for making ethical decision that you can access on this book's companion website.

Discourse ethics

Discourse ethics is a normative approach that deals with the proper processes of rational debate that are necessary to arrive at a resolution of ethical questions. It does not lay down what is right and wrong but it does distinguish right and wrong ways of arguing about right and wrong. It is an ancient idea that the process of argument, or rhetoric, is key to discovering the truth. Some, such as Protagoras, argued that there are always two sides to any argument (Billig, 1996: 72). This implies that dialogue cannot lead to a definitive truth because there are always arguments to be made for or against any proposition. However, Protagoras was prepared to argue, as reported by Socrates, that although opposing arguments could be presented some were more useful than others. Whether or not argument and debate can lead to true or useful statements about what is right and wrong, these classical concerns established an importance for forensic debate, and the classification of rhetorical techniques, that has remained in western culture.

The approach in modern times is most closely associated with Jürgen Habermas, of the Frankfurt school of critical theorists (Pusey, 1987). Habermas built upon the philosophical heritage of Kant. However, he breaks with Kant, in his belief that knowledge develops through social interaction and discourse. Knowledge is not, as Kant argued, a matter unaffected by social and cultural processes. Habermas holds that disagreement can be resolved rationally through debate that is free of compulsion, in which no disputant applies pressure to another, and in which only the strength of the arguments matters. This calls for linguistic skill but it also requires a critical self-reflection in which those involved in a debate challenge their own arguments at:

- The objective level – at which a statement is tested against an observed state, checking for example whether the statement that 'the balance sheet does not add up' is true.

- The inter-subjective level – when a statement is made and heard it creates a social relationship between the hearer and the speaker. At the inter-subjective level it has to be questioned whether this relationship is legitimate. If the statement that the balance sheet does not add up implies, without evidence, that the listener is accused of cooking the books the relationship may be unfair, especially if the speaker is the listener's boss.

- The intra-subjective level – at which a speaker has to consider whether their speech sincerely or authentically mirrors their internal thoughts and values.

It is these processes of validation that Habermas refers to as discourse. The application of these in organisations would be very difficult. However, writers have attempted to put these ideas into operation. Some have focused on the skills of debate. Schreier and Groeben (1996) looked at the advice, given in popular books on how to persuade and influence people, about which tricks of presentation were unfair. They asked a panel of experts to categorise 84 of the rhetorical tricks against four ethical categories that are used to assess whether an argument in a debate was proper. Using the results they were able to identify some possible rules or tests for assessing the ethical integrity of any debate. A few examples follow.

- **Formal validity** – Are the arguments logically rigorous? *e.g. do not select only those cases to use in your argument that support your point of view.*

- **Sincerity/truth** – Are the arguments intentionally misleading, inconsistent or economical with the truth? *e.g. misrepresenting an opponent's position or exaggerating a point.*

- **Content justice** – Treating your opponents unfairly or imposing impossible requirements on them. *e.g. ad hominem attacks on an opponent in which the opponent is vilified rather than his or her arguments criticised. Making mutually exclusive demands on an opponent.*

- **Procedural justice** – Preventing an opponent from fully and freely participating in the debate. *e.g. unnecessary use of technical jargon in a way intended to confuse the opponent.*

Steinmann and Lohr (quoted in Preuss, 1999: 414) also propose the use of discourse to achieve a consensus on ethical business issues. They simplified the characteristics of ideal discourse, against which actual discussions may be assessed, as:

- impartiality;
- non-coercion;
- non-persuasiveness; and
- expertise.

They had an opportunity to put these guidelines into practice when they organised and chaired a series of corporate dialogues within Procter & Gamble on the question of self-medication by selling over-the-counter cold medicines. Others have proposed rules and procedures for debate. This has been particularly common in the field of public policy making. Fischer (1983) made a case for forensic skills to be applied to the process of evaluating public policy options through ethical discourse. He drew upon a method he called normative logic. This was based on studies of how people discuss and decide normative issues in everyday speech and life. He concluded that despite the lack of final ethical truths, people resolved value matters by combining questioning based on empirical knowledge with a lawyer-like process of marshalling a supportable case, by drawing upon their knowledge of:

- the consequences of the different positions or actions they may take;
- the alternative positions and actions open to them;

■ established norms, values and laws;

■ the facts of the situation;

■ the network of circumstances that preceded the situation; and

■ the 'fundamental needs of humankind'.

People can construct defensible cases for taking particular actions or positions by answering the questions just listed. However, according to some philosophers this process is untenable because it requires decisions, about what ought to be, to be derived from descriptions of how things actually are, and this they claim is illogical.

Cross reference	In philosophy this argument is known as the naturalistic fallacy, as is discussed further on p. 432. Fischer's response is argued from the point of view of pragmatism, which is explained on p. 160.

Fischer's response was to say that the purpose of drawing up guidelines for debate is not to establish ultimate values but to arrive at pragmatic resolutions through a rigorous, if ungrounded, process that is not anchored in immutable values.

The mention of pragmatism brings us to the basis of the toolkit for making ethical decisions that will be discussed shortly. Pragmatism can be contrasted with Habermas' theories of discourse that have just been discussed. Habermas was not so much concerned with everyday decision making, which he called pragmatic discourse. In his writings this is the lowest of the forms in the hierarchy of discourse. He was interested in how, through discourse, a community could establish fixed and general ethical principles that would form the framework for the resolution of specific ethical conundrums. Such a consensus may not commonly exist in organisations, which are the focus of this book, and it cannot be assumed that organisations are moral communities with agreed moral standards. The pragmatist philosopher Richard Rorty takes a different view of discourse; and it his view that informs the ethical decision-making toolkit. As can be seen from the discussion of pragmatism later in the book (see p. 160) the pragmatists argue that it is not possible to define a fixed and valid objective truth. The nature of language disbars such an achievement. Rorty argues that because of this humans need to maintain a dialogue. If there is no definable objective truth then, without dialogue societies will either lapse into cynicism or allow fundamentalists, who believe they do have the truth, to dominate all others. Therefore, as Mounce (1997; 185–9) noted we must keep the conversation going. According to Rorty the absence of absolute truth or standards does not prevent people living in a civilised and well-mannered condition, as long as dialogue is kept open. He calls this a re-educative process in that people's desire for validated norms and standards should be replaced by a wish for solidarity for others; something that Habermas regards as inadequate (Habermas, 1999: 348). Rorty's retort is that Habermas should drop the idea of the 'better argument' and accept that there is only 'the argument which convinces a given audience at a given time' (Rorty, 1985: 162).

The toolkit for ethical decision-making builds upon Rorty's ideas. It takes the form of a maze. The toolkit user is asked a series of questions about the action or decision they are thinking of taking. These questions are based upon the different ethical perspectives that have been outlined in this chapter. The answer the user gives leads to further questions. In a Rortyean sense this sequences of question, answer and subsequent question might continue endlessly; but as Rorty points out it is only necessary to convince a given audience, perhaps temporarily, at a given time, and so at certain points the toolkit makes a recommendation about whether the action or decision should be accepted or rejected.

Activity 3.1	The ethical corporate decision toolkit

The Ethical Corporate Decision Toolkit is based on the framework shown in Figure 3.1. You can access it at www.pearsoned.co.ukfisherlovellvalerosilva. In order to use the toolkit you have to frame the action or decision you want to evaluate. The toolkit does not compare a series of options at a go; rather it evaluates single options against a set of ethical criteria. At the start of the maze you will be asked a few questions about the context of the decision. Then you will be asked to consider the action from a number of ethical perspectives.

Like many aids to ethical decision making the Ethical Corporate Decision Toolkit uses a screening process by which decisions are tested against a sequence of ethical positions. There are various such decision aids you can explore. Cavanagh et al. (1981) proposed three criteria in their process, namely, utility, rights and duties, and justice. In response to feminist criticism they added (Cavanagh et al. 1995) a fourth test of caring. Post et al, (1996: 125) reverted to the three-test model in their framework. Carroll & Buchholtz (2000; 157) also used a threefold screen, but in their framework the tests were, firstly, conventional (is the proposed action acceptable to a range of conventional norms and standards) secondly, principle and thirdly ethical tests (is the action acceptable to one's conscience or sense of oneself as a good person). The apparent simplicity of the Carroll & Buchholtz three-test model is undermined by the presence of a variety of sub-tests within the categories. The principle test for example incorporates a diverse set of criteria such as justice, rights, utilitarianism and the 'Golden Rule'. Brooke Hamilton et al. (2009) developed a specialist decision aid for companies considering whether they should remain or quit a country that did not allow them to operate to their own, higher, ethical standards.

An alternative to the screening approach to making difficult ethical choices is to choose one ethical approach and to ignore others, or at least to put the approaches into rank order of preference. Carroll (1990) proposed a simple exercise (Activity 3.2) for people who wish to reflect on the relative importance they give to a range of ethical perspectives. The list of principles he proposed included both normative approaches, methods for thinking about the right response and norm approaches, which invite a person to accept the values and standards of a particular group. The categorical imperative, the Golden Rule and the utilitarian principle are all methods for normative thinking whereas the disclosure rule, the organisation ethic and the professional ethic concern decisions about which social group one wishes to belong to. These norm-based questions could be seen as an application of a stakeholder analysis.

| Activity 3.2 | **Prioritising your ethical principles** |

Here are a number of 'principles'. Identify your top three and rank them 1, 2, 3 in order of importance/relevance to you and your decision making. Then mark your least relevant 9, 10 and 11.

Principle	Description	Rank
Categorical imperative	You should not adopt principles of action unless they can, without inconsistency, be adopted by everyone else	
Conventionist ethic	Individuals should act to further their self-interest so long as they do not violate the law	
Golden Rule	Do unto others as you would have them do unto you	
Hedonistic ethic	If it feels good, do it	
Disclosure rule	If you are comfortable with an action or decision after asking yourself whether you would mind if all your associates, friends and family were aware of it, then you should act or decide	
Intuition ethic	You do what your 'gut feeling' tells you to do	
Means-ends ethic	If the end justifies the means, then you should act	
Might equals right ethic	You should take whatever advantage you are strong enough and powerful enough to take without respect for ordinary social conventions and laws	
Organisation ethic	This is an age of large-scale organisations – be loyal to the organisation	
Professional ethic	You should only do that which can be explained before a committee of your professional peers	
Utilitarian ethic	You should follow the principle of 'the greatest good for the greatest number'	

Source: Principles of business ethics: their role in decision making, *Management Decision,* Vol. 28, No. 8, Fig. 2, p. 21 (Carroll, C. B. 1990), © Emerald Group Publishing Limited, All rights reserved.

Carroll used the list in Activity 3.2 as the basis of a research project and found that the Golden Rule was given the highest ranking by his respondents. The disclosure rule came second in the study.

Some ethical checklists, such as the Texas Instruments Ethics Quick Test, emphasise the social acceptability of an ethical decision rather than the philosophical correctness of the mode of thought used to achieve it. Use the questions of the Quick Test to decide whether an action you are planning to take is right.

Activity 3.3	The TI Ethics Quick Test

- Is the action legal?

- Does it comply with our values?

- If you do it, will you feel bad?

- How will it look in the newspaper?

- If you know it's wrong, don't do it!

- If you're not sure, ask.

- Keep asking until you get an answer.

(*Source*: Texas Instruments, 2001)

Reflections

This chapter has provided the formal, philosophical tools that can be used when you have to think about an ethical problem. These tools are not, however, easy to handle. There is first the problem of which theories you are going to use. If all the theories were to give the same answer to a problem then admittedly there would be no problem. But this is not always the case and then you have the difficulty of choosing which theories to ignore or deciding how much weight to give to the various theories. Once you have chosen a theory there remains the difficulty of applying it to the particular circumstances of the issue confronting you. It may be these problems that make the TI Ethics Quick Test (Activity 3.3) look so attractive. The 'quick and dirty' approach it uses leads us into the matter of how people actually decide about ethical issues – which is the subject of the next chapter.

Summary

In this chapter the following key points have been made:

- Ethical issues at work might be best approached by concentrating on developing people who are virtuous and have the judgment to be able to make moral decisions and act upon them when faced with ethical problems.

- Ethical issues at work might best be approached by seeing organisations as networks of individuals who learn personally and collectively through experience, reflection and the sharing of that learning. Learning about learning, learning how to deal with ethical issues, is more important than learning pre-packaged solutions.

- Ethical issues at work might best be tackled by applying sound moral principles, which should guide our actions.

- Ethical issues at work might best be tackled by forecasting which actions will bring about the greatest amount of good.

Typical assignments

1. How relevant to business and management is a Kantian approach to ethics?

2. Discuss the use of child labour in factories in developing countries from two different ethical perspectives (you might choose between virtue ethics, Kantian ethics, Rawls' theory of justice or utilitarianism).

3. It is sometimes argued that a major flaw of utilitarianism is that it is only concerned with maximising the total amount of good and is not concerned with the distribution of that good between people and groups. Is this true?

4. How might an organisation implement the practices implied by discourse ethics?

Group activity 3.1

Form into groups. As a group, choose one of the case studies from Chapter 2. Each member of the group should then choose a different ethical perspective – utilitarian, fairness, ethics of care and so on, and individually produce an analysis of the case from that perspective. Come back together as a group and debate the issue.

Recommended further reading

P. Vardy and P. Grosch (1999) *The Puzzle of Ethics*, London: Fount, is a good introduction to the main ethical theories. Simon Blackburn's (2001) *Being Good. A Short Introduction to Ethics*, Oxford: Oxford University Press, is an elegant reflection on the main issues in ethics. Anne Thomson's (1999) *Critical Reasoning in Ethics*, London: Routledge, is a good guide to the application of theories to issues.

Useful websites

Topic	Website provider	URL
Ethics Updates. This site provides some helpful materials on all the major ethical theories and perspectives. It is a general ethics site rather than a business ethics site.	Edited by L.M. Hinman, The Values Institute, University of San Diego	http://ethics.sandiego.edu/about/editor/index.asp
Some useful material and quizzes on ethical decision making	Centre for Ethics and Business, Loyola Marymount University	http://www.ethicsandbusiness.org
A website on virtue ethics, and a pdf file on virtue ethics. The website provides a link to a virtue ethics scale	A website provided by Michael Cawley III, James Martin and John Johnson, Penn State University	http://personal.psu.edu/faculty/j/5/j5j/virtues/Virtue.pdf & http://www.personal.psu.edu/faculty/j/5/j5j/virtues/
An ethical decision-making tool. Other toolkit items are available on this website	The Ethics Resource Centre, a non-profit research organisation	http://www.ethics.org/resource/plus-decision-making-model
A fan site for Ayn Rand	Centre for Ethics and Business Leonard Peikoff	http://www.peikoff.com/
The Bentham Project, University College London Jeremy Bentham's auto icon (his embalmed and preserved body, although the head is waxen, the original having decayed), bequeathed in his will for the inspiration of future generations, can be seen in the south cloisters of the main building of University College. Use the link for an image of the auto icon.		http://www.ucl.ac.uk/Bentham-Project
A framework for ethical decision making	Markula Center for Applied Ethics, Santa Clara University	http://www.scu.edu/ethics/practicing/decision/framework.html

PART B

Individuals' responses to ethical issues

CHAPTER 4

Personal values and heuristics

Chapter at a glance

Chapter contents

- Learning outcomes
- Introduction
- Perceptions of values
- Values and ethical thinking
- Heuristic thinking
- Decision-making heuristics
- Values as heuristics in ethical reasoning
- Value heuristics and priority setting
- Integrity and loyalty as value heuristics
- Discussion of the *Dilemma* simulation
  in Activity 4.4
- Reflections
- Summary

Case studies

- Case study 4.1 Chris's managerial
  development: A fable

Activities and exercises

- Video clip 4.1 The Dilley six pack
- Activity 4.1 Terminal and instrumental values
- Activity 4.2 Analysing Chris's managerial development
- Video clip 4.2 Nepotism
- Video clip 4.3 Ethical communication
- Activity 4.3 *Monksbane and feverfew*: a diagnostic instrument about values and priority setting
- Activity 4.4 *Dilemma*: a diagnostic inventory of managers' ethical horizons
- Typical assignments
- Group activity 4.1
- Group activity 4.2

■ Recommended further reading
■ Useful websites

Learning outcomes

Having read this chapter and completed its associated activities, readers should be able to:

■ Define values and distinguish them from attitudes and beliefs.

■ Explain the idea that a set of values may be fragmented or integrated.

■ Explain how traditionalists, modernists, neo-traditionalists, postmodernists and pragmatists may have different perspectives on their values; and consider which position might explain their own stance.

■ Understand how values, acting as heuristics, affect decision making and judgement about what is ethical.

Introduction

It is difficult to discuss ethics in a business and organisational context without talking about values. As both are central themes in the book, it is necessary to distinguish one from the other.

The broad distinction we wish to make is that ethics is a branch of philosophy and is therefore concerned with formal academic reasoning about right and wrong, but values are the commonsense, often taken-for-granted, beliefs about right and wrong that guide us in our daily lives. Imagine a situation at work where you have to decide whether to take action against a manager who you know to be fiddling their expenses. Ethics provides principles and arguments, drawn from ethical theory, for thinking about the issue. The emotional force of your values in contrast would lead you to an intuitive feel for the right thing to do. Of course, how much weight you give to your analysis and your emotions is another matter.

Ethics and values have different sources. Ethics are drawn from the books and debates in which philosophical theories about right and wrong are proposed and tested. Ethics have to be studied. Values are acquired informally through processes of socialisation. We acquire values from our interactions with our friends, family and colleagues and, most importantly for our purpose, from the organisations we work for or belong to. Values are learned, not studied. It is true that our employing organisations may make formal attempts, through induction courses and corporate videos, to inculcate their formal values. We are not required to study them, which would involve a critical engagement with them; we are simply required to 'buy into them', to 'mark, learn and inwardly digest' them. If values are learned rather than studied, they must be few and simply expressed so that all in a society can understand them. Ethics in contrast need to be studied, not simply learned, because they are more complicated.

Video clips 4.1	**The Dilley six pack** The clip deals with the impact of nature and nurture on human personality by considering a family of sextuplets. To view the video clip from the interview please visit this book's companion website at www.pearsoned.co.uk/fisherlovellvalerosilva.

There are overlaps between ethics and values. The processes through which values are formed, adopted and modified within groups and societies may be influenced by debates between philosophers. Equally the rational discourses of ethics may be swayed by the emotional undertow beneath the participants' arguments. Within a group of philosophers social learning, conforming to the group's norms may be more emotionally comfortable than challenging it. Conversely, critical study and the reading of books may challenge the values people have acquired through life. Nevertheless the distinction between learned values and studied ethics is still a useful one.

It follows from the above argument that values are social. They exist and are communicated through social connections. Rokeach defined values as:

> a small number of core ideas or cognitions present in every society about desirable end-states.

> (Rokeach, 1973: 49)

DEFINITION

Values are core ideas about how people should live and the ends they should seek. They are shared by a majority of people within a community or society. They are simply expressed generalities, often no more than single words such as peace and honesty. As they are very broad, they do not give guidance on how particular things should be evaluated.

Attitudes, like values, are evaluations of whether something is good or bad. But unlike values they are evaluations of particular things, issues, people, places or whatever. Attitudes, because they relate to specific circumstances, are more changeable than values.

A **belief** is an acceptance that something is true or not. This acceptance does not imply any judgment about whether that thing is good or bad.

Rokeach's work is helpful because it distinguishes between different types of values that might affect thinking about ethical issues.

- *Moral values* – concern interpersonal behaviour, e.g. being honest is desirable.

- *Competence values* – concern one's own valuation of one's behaviour, e.g. behaving imaginatively is desirable.

- *Personal values* – concern the ends, or terminal states, that are desirable for the self, e.g. peace of mind.

■ *Social values* – concern the ends that one would desire for society, e.g. world peace is desirable.

The first two items in this list concern instrumental values that are about how a person should live and behave. The second two items are terminal values that concern the ends or purposes that we should be striving for. Table 4.1 lists the instrumental and terminal values identified by Rokeach's survey of a sample of Americans.

The rank orders in Table 4.1 are averages, and individuals will, to a greater or lesser extent, have different views on the proper order of the values. Billig has also pointed out (1996: 240) that Rokeach's view of values is positive and aspirational. He argued that values may be negative. We may, for example, all agree that cruelty is bad.

Table 4.1   The instrumental and terminal values of Americans

Terminal values	Rank order (females)	Rank order (males)	Instrumental values	Rank order (females)	Rank order (males)
A comfortable life	13	4	Ambitious	4	2
An exciting life	18	18	Broadminded	5	4
A sense of accomplishment	10	7	Capable	12	8
A world at peace	1	1	Cheerful	10	12
A world of beauty	15	15	Clean	8	9
Equality	8	9	Courageous	6	5
Family security	2	2	Forgiving	2	6
Freedom	3	3	Helpful	7	7
Happiness	5	5	Honest	1	1
Inner harmony	12	13	Imaginative	18	18
Mature love	14	14	Independent	14	11
National security	11	10	Intellectual	16	15
Pleasure	16	17	Logical	17	16
Salvation	4	12	Loving	9	14
Self-respect	6	6	Obedient	15	17
Social recognition	17	16	Polite	13	13
True friendship	9	11	Responsible	3	3
Wisdom	7	8	Self-controlled	11	10

Note: 1 represents the highest value and 18 the lowest.

Source: From *The Nature of Human Values,* The Free Press (Rokeach, M. 1973) p. 58. Adapted with the permission of The Free Press, a Division of Simon & Schuster Adult Publishing Group, from *The Nature of Human Values* by Milton Rokeach. Copyright © 1973 by The Free Press. Copyright© renewed 2001 by Sandra Ball-Rokeach. All rights reserved.

Activity 4.1	**Terminal and instrumental values**

Put the two lists in Table 4.1 (terminal values and instrumental values) into rank order according to your personal preferences. Compare these with the American average scores (male or female as appropriate) by subtracting the American ranking from your ranking (and ignoring whether the result is positive or negative). For example, equality is ranked 9 by American men. If my ranking was 12, the difference is 3. Then total up all the differences. The smaller the number, the greater the similarity between my ranking and that of Americans. If the difference is zero, then the two sets of rankings are almost certainly (but not entirely, because there may be differences that cancel each other out) identical. Ask some friends or colleagues to do the ranking. Compare their average score with yours.

Consider: Is the difference between your ranking and the American's ranking greater or lesser than that between you and your friends?

Different organisations, different groups, different cultures and different countries may have different values. Ethical theory, however, is disdainful of societies. It does not matter to the validity of a theory if it is not accepted by the generality of people. The truth of an ethical theory cannot be judged by an opinion poll. It will be a constant theme of this book that in business and organisation there can be great tensions between how an ethical theory says people should behave and how their social values incline them to behave.

Cross reference	The diversity of values relating to business and management in different countries and societies is explored in Chapter 11.

Perceptions of values

Just as in the first chapter we discussed different views on whether there is a normative ethical order that applies to business so we can ask similar questions about the nature and role of values. It is convenient to do this by using the notion of fragmentation to explain the nature of values. Fragmentation is the idea that things in the social world are disordered and disconnected. A fragmented view of values would see them as diverse, various and expressed through conflict between different views and opinions. There are no wholes in a fragmented social and ethical world, only discordant parts that clash against each other. The philosopher Thomas Hobbes expressed this view in the seventeenth century. He argued that even a single person's view could be fragmented.

> Nay, the same man, in divers times, differs from himself; and one time praiseth, that is, calleth good, what another time he dispraiseth, and calleth evil: from whence arise disputes, controversies, and at last war.

(Hobbes, n.d.: 104)

The contrary view is the one we have already noted that Rokeach expressed. He claimed that values, far from being fragmented, are simple and whole. Billig (1996: 240) agreed that the values of a group or society are simple and whole. But he pointed out that this makes them difficult to apply to particular situations. A society may have clear views on the importance of telling the truth and on loyalty. However, there may be situations in which such simple nostrums do not help much. There are two reasons for this.

1. The demands of truth telling and loyalty may conflict in a particular case. Should a government spokesman tell the truth about a military operation if it would cause danger to the soldiers who might expect him to show them loyalty? In such cases, the simplicity and wholeness of values is broken by not knowing which value should be applied.

2. Simple and whole values can only provide general guidance. When it comes to dealing with specific situations, values need interpretation. Can there be situations, as the behaviour of politicians often implies, when truthfulness can be interpreted as not telling lies but equally as not telling the whole truth? Once interpretation is necessary, values that were simple and whole become fragmented.

Ambiguity can arise in organisations when simple values are inadequate because they cannot deal with new circumstances or are in conflict with other values. When ambiguity occurs, those who seem to offer a resolution gain power and they bring with them their new values and ideologies (Weick, 2001: 47). Weick sees this as a process of sense-making in which, through communication and interaction, people interpret and construct a view of their organisation and their roles within it. From this perspective, values do not exist prior to and separate from organisational life (as Rokeach would suggest); instead they emerge and become pervasive in organisations as a consequence of a dynamic process within organisations. In his earlier book, Weick (1995) identified seven properties of sense-making. These can be illustrated by considering how values about telling the truth (or not; manipulating performance measurement information for example) might emerge from a sense-making process.

- **Identity construction.** When someone considers deceiving others at work by manipulating performance statistics, they will consider how they see themselves: whether they believe themselves to be macho managers, who will change the management information to give a better impression of their efforts, or whether they value themselves as truthful individuals who can bear the truth even if it hurts them.

- **Retrospective sense-making.** According to Weick, sense-making will occur after people have acted – in other words, values follow actions and do not precede them. The case of the Russian business people (*see* p.00) who justified their avoidance of taxes by arguing that they only did this because the state was too corrupt to be the rightful guardians of tax revenues is a good example.

- **Sense-making is done through enactment.** People make sense of things by taking action. If people decide to manipulate performance management information, they do so by choosing an action that fits with their environment (they might decide that to actually change the performance numbers might be unacceptable), but by their choice of method of deception (say, hiding the poor figures in a great many other numbers), they also change the environment by creating a climate where that particular form of deception becomes acceptable.

- **Sense-making is social.** If people talk with their colleagues about what they have done then the practice may become accepted through use. It has been discovered that different occupational groups have different perceptions of right and wrong. Different occupational groups as a consequence may have different views about what is and is not acceptable behaviour. Some groups of programmers, for example, think it more acceptable than other groups to violate intellectual property rights (Stylianou et al., 2004), probably because they are great users of the Web, which diminishes the idea of property rights in knowledge by making it so accessible.

- **Sense-making is ongoing.** As situations change, for example, if a member of staff is dismissed for violating intellectual property rights, then people will reformulate their position on the matter in discussion with each other.

- **Sense-making is focused on 'extracted cues'.** This means that people in an organisation will concern themselves with some things in the daily stream of events and ignore others. Those cues become the raw material from which a view and actions are taken. The vicarious experience of others (e.g. whether others who are known to have deceived the performance management system flourish or are caught and punished) will become part of the sense-making process.

- **Sense-making is driven by plausibility.** The process of sense-making is based on personal assessments of risk and benefit. It is not a process of fine judgment based on incontrovertible facts. In other words, people take a calculated gamble. When deciding to manipulate performance management systems, they are chancing that the benefits of doing so will be great enough to outweigh the probability of being caught and the severity of the punishment.

This brief review would suggest that values can be seen as something that emerge from dynamic processes of sense-making as well as being one of the process inputs. Agreed sets of values in organisations can be changed through this process. Values express a potential tension between wholeness (wanting a consensual set of values) and fragmentation (the value sets are broken up and reformed). People's responses to this tension and their method of making sense of it can be classified under five headings:

- Traditionalist;

- Modernist;

- Neo-traditionalist;

- Postmodernist; and

- Pragmatist.

The traditional view of values

From the traditional viewpoint, a group – whether a work group, an organisation, a profession or a country – is defined by its possession of shared values. The idea of value fragmentation therefore is considered anathema and a contradiction in terms. A group's values either derive from the ancient traditions of the group or are presented as if they did. In organisations these traditional values are often presented as those of the firm's founder. In companies that were not blessed with a charismatic founder, a mythical one is sometimes created for public relations and advertising purposes and to act as a fount for the values the company wishes to present (Mr Kipling of Kipling's Cakes is an example). A group based on traditional values sees them as a whole. By turning their gaze inwards and not outwards to other groups and societies, they fail to recognise the fragmentation and diversity of values that surrounds them.

This inward-lookingness identifies a disapproval of questioning as a feature of traditionalism. Education and training are seen as the processes of attaining knowledge burnished by age. To challenge that knowledge by asking why it should be so is unacceptable. In broad historical terms it can be argued that the Enlightenment, which occurred in Europe in the eighteenth century, was a time when thinkers began to challenge with empirical observation and study things that had long been accepted as unchallengeably true because they were stated in ancient religious and classical texts (Sloan and Burnett, 2004). A consequence of the lack of questioning is that traditionalism is often experienced as a moral traditionalism that defines which behaviours are acceptable in and beyond organisations. This may be seen in the movement in the Bible Belt of the USA to run businesses according to fundamental Christian precepts. Riverview Bank in Minnesota, for instance, was set up as America's first evangelical bank. Its founder believed it to be a good commercial proposition because born again Christians do not smoke or gamble or drink and are dedicated to their families, all of which make them a good credit risk (Doran, 2004).

The Enlightenment   DEFINITION

This was a historical period during the eighteenth century when academics and writers began to question truths and beliefs that had been long held because they were sanctified by the Church or by the ancient writings of Greek philosophers. Traditionally it was thought to have been dominated by European philosophers such as Immanuel Kant (*see* p. 000) who defined the Enlightenment (*die Aufklärung* in German) as emancipation from humankind's self-incurred immaturity. But it was also seen in the work, for example, of antiquaries and amateur geologists who began to discover and collect fossils, rocks, minerals and finds from what we would now call archaeological sites. The study of these objects began to raise doubts about the previously accepted fact that the world was created in 4004 BC, a date that Bishop Ussher had calculated from the Bible. From such practical activities, rational analysis based on observation began to undermine traditionalism's criteria of antiquity and the Bible as the tests of truth. It was also a period when morals drawn from these sources were challenged by rational analysis in such works as Mary Wollstonecraft's (1995) *Vindication of the Rights of Women* published in 1792.

The modernist view of values

The modernist position is that the twentieth and, so far, the twenty-first century have been characterised by value fragmentation. However, this is seen as a transitory phase and it is thought that, through the application of reason, the pieces can be put back together and true values defined. Those who take this position believe that values are tangible, and can be unambiguously stated and defined through formal and rational debate. They accept deductive reasoning that allows truths to be logically developed from first principles. The modernist believes that values can be determined by ethical study. Jürgen Habermas, for example (Pusey, 1987: 78ff.), constructed a complex theory of communicative action that defines how the validity of spoken understandings between people can be tested. Modernism sees this as an individual task. Progress, both moral and technical, is thought possible through individual effort and rationality.

> [modernist identity] is epitomized by the notion of the self-developing individual, rootless yet constantly evolving to new heights.
>
> (Friedman, 1994: 39)

At the least, other modernists believe that values can be defined and clarified (Kirchenbaum, 1977; Smith, 1977) as a preliminary to rational discussion about an organisation's mission and core values.

Cross reference	Habermas' idea of communicative action is discussed within the general framework of what is known as discourse ethics in Chapter 3, p. 139.

The rationality that Habermas talks about is not the same as that spoken of by many managers. The former can be labelled as critical and emancipatory whereas the latter is instrumental rationality. Instrumental rationality is focused on achieving a set of given aims. Much managerial effort, for example, goes into maximising return on capital or increasing the number of hospital beds without giving much thought to whether these ends are in themselves the right ones. Questions about whether growth at all costs is a good thing, or whether, for example, a focus on preventive health measures might not be better than simply building bigger hospitals, are forgotten. Emancipatory or critical rationality (Legge, 1995: 288) asks these deeper questions. It challenges the conventional wisdoms of modern life so that people become aware of the constraints that deform their lives. Both forms of rationality have a place in the modernist perspective. Between them they develop the 'cognitive adequacy' (Giddens, 1985: 100–1) that organisations and societies might use to improve and unify their values.

The neo-traditional view of values

The neo-traditional approach emphasises the function of culture as a device for mediating the tensions between fragmented values and the need of societies and organisations for a common purpose and mutual understanding. Neo-traditionalists see values in the context of organisational and social cultures; indeed, cultures are defined by the values that characterise them. They argue that the fragmentation of values can be overcome and that organisations and societies can have unified values. But such an end cannot be achieved by rational analysis, which sees values as objects for analysis and not as shared myths, which is how neo-traditionalists view them. Myths can act as the glue that holds an organisation or society in unity because of their simplicity (which needs no sophisticated explanation) and because of their ability to finesse dilemmas. Sometimes the glue is weak and sometimes strong. There is agreement, however, among neo-traditionalists that values, presented as vision and myth and not as cold rationality, are the keys to overcoming fragmentation. This perspective is a form of 'back to basics' and traditional values. Historically, this may be dated to the publication of Peters and Waterman's (1982) *In Search of Excellence*. This book advocated replacing the 'paralysis by analysis' of modernism, with an emphasis on values and organisational culture. Those who take this approach stress that organisations are culture-creating mechanisms and that cultures can change. This thought leads to the notion that culture may be a critical lever or variable with which managers can lead or direct their organisations. As Smircich put it,

> Overall the research agenda arising from the view that culture is an organisational variable is how to shape and mould the internal culture in particular ways and how to change culture, consistent with managerial purpose.

> (Smircich, 1983: 346)

Values, from this view, can be deliberately used as a means of overcoming fragmentation and improving organisational effectiveness. As Smircich also pointed out, there is an alternative view that cultures are too complex for managers to be able to mould them into a desired form.

A second form of neo-traditionalism can be seen in the wave of interest in 'New Age' therapies and philosophies that encourage the spiritual growth of individuals through the rejection of materialism. It might be thought that this would fit ill with the self-interest of organisations but Covey's work (1992 see p. 127) has led to many agreeing that concerns with individual and organisational growth can be combined.

The postmodern view of values

The postmodern stance sees nothing in the social and intellectual world as tangible or fixed. At this vantage point, fragmentation is accepted as part of the human condition. In Lyotard's (1988: 46) famous phrase, there is 'incredulity towards metanarratives'. This means that the large ideological schemes, such as capitalism and communism, that used to dominate people's thinking no longer have credibility. In the postmodern view there are no eternal truths or values. What we think of as objectively true emerges through discourses that are embedded in power and knowledge relationships where some have more influence on the outcomes of the discourses than others. But what emerges is in any case uncertain because the language we use is opaque and carries no single, clear message (Legge, 1995: 306).

The words we use to express our values have no fixed meaning. Statements of value have to be treated as texts and deconstructed. *Différance* is Derrida's device for exploring the limitless instability of language. One aspect of *différance* is that no word has a positive meaning attributed to it; it only has meaning to the extent that it is different from other words. Another aspect is deferral because the meaning of one word is always explained by reference to another and the search for meaning can involve a complex chain of cross-references as one chases a word through a vast thesaurus. Let us take an innocuous statement about public management:

> The first steps to achieving accountability for performance must be to clarify objectives and develop a recognised approach to measuring and reporting performance.
>
> (Dallas, 1996: 13)

This is enough to cause a deconstructionist to salivate. Most of the words in the sentence do not have an unambiguous or uncontested meaning. Accountability, for example, can only be defined by relating it to other words such as hierarchy, responsiveness, transparency and so on. Accountability may be viewed from different discourses such as political accountability, audit and accounting, consumer rights, and investigative journalism. If we had the time to explore this sentence in detail and to plot its webs of signification, we would find that the sentence could mean almost anything.

The search for meaning may not be endless; but the end will be terminal confusion rather than clear understanding. The function of deconstruction is to reach a final impasse. This can be seen in Derrida's view of ethical decision making. He recognises that decisions have to be made but points out that any decision is 'haunted by the ghost of undecidability' (Painter-Morland, 2011: 130). By which is meant that sense of discomfort that remains after any decision we make because we know we may have misunderstood the issues, or are simply aware of the impossibility of having made a fully rational decision because we chose between options which themselves will have been incomplete or poorly founded.

Deconstruction is not intended to overcome fragmentation but simply to map the instabilities, paradoxes and aporetic states that define it. From this position, there is no hope that the fragmented values can be put back together again. As Harvey (1989: 45) expressed it, disapprovingly, postmodernism

> swims and even wallows in the fragmentary and chaotic current of change as if that was all there was.

The political passivity of postmodernism annoyed him:

> The rhetoric of postmodernism is dangerous for it avoids confronting the realities of political economy and the circumstances of global power . . . metatheory cannot be dispensed with.
>
> (Harvey, 1989: 116)

This form of postmodernism could be called hard postmodernism because it seems to lead to the impossibility of business ethics, or any other kind of ethics, in a world that desperately needs it. However, as Derrida (Derrida with Bennington, 1985: 221) said, to deconstruct the enlightenment project (which seeks to raise humanity's moral status through the application of reason) is not necessarily to criticise it. Just because someone points out that the language used, when people attempt to analyse the realities of global power, is inadequate does not mean the task is unworthy. As Gustafson (2000: 648) emphasises, Derrida does not say that all ways and options are of equal value, though it is not possible to say that there is one best way. This softening of the stereotypical view of postmodernism does allow postmodernists to have an ethical agenda, but this will be described in the next section under the more suitable heading of pragmatism.

The pragmatic view of values

The pragmatism of this stance is that of the American philosopher Richard Rorty (1989, 1990). He shares the postmodernists' scepticism about the possibility of an objective truth and of a fixed hierarchy of values. In this circumstance, the issue for Rorty is not how to represent, or mirror, the world in our thinking but how to cope with its ambiguity:

> All descriptions (including one's self description as a pragmatist) are evaluated according to their efficacy as instruments for purposes, rather than their fidelity to the object described.

> (Rorty, 1992: 92)

The notion of usefulness is a hermeneutic one. If a belief helps us to interpret our other beliefs and vice versa then it is useful. The justification of belief is therefore conversational. A dialogue between developing beliefs is necessary, not because it will bring us to an ultimate truth, but because it keeps the conversation going (Mounce, 1997: 185–9). The line taken by pragmatists is that the inability to ground our values in some grand overarching theory such as Christianity, Marxism, Islam or capitalism does not prevent people making sensible and practical arrangements for living a civil and well-mannered life. As Rorty expressed this view,

> No such metanarrative is needed. What is needed is a sort of intellectual-analogue of civic virtue – tolerance, irony and a willingness to let spheres of culture flourish without worrying too much about their 'common ground', their unification, the 'intrinsic ideas' they suggest or what picture of man they presuppose.

> (Rorty, 1985: 168)

He argued that the lack of a metanarrative could be overcome by dealing with the concrete and practical concerns of a community and by finding ways of harmonising, but not abolishing, the conflicts of values within the community.

Zygmunt Bauman (1993) developed a pragmatic notion of ethics that he called, adding to the confusion surrounding the term, postmodern ethics. (The title of one of his other books – *Life in Fragments* (Bauman, 1995) – reinforces the importance of the idea of fragmentation in a postmodern sensibility.) He saw the techniques of rational analysis and technological development, as proposed by modernism, as part of the problem of business ethics. Organisations take a bureaucratic approach to the matter by defining rules and regulations that deny and quash employees' natural tendency to act morally towards each other. Such rules enable them to settle for the lower standard of obeying the regulations rather than aspiring to the higher level of behaving well. The failure of rationality to solve ethical problems does not mean that we should not continue to try to solve them. The contribution of postmodern ethics, however, may lie more in asking important questions than in finding the answers.

Gustafson (2000: 652–4) identifies a number of characteristics of postmodern (though we would prefer to call it pragmatic) ethics.

- Not separating personal values and principles from those applied at work. Dividing one's life into a series of disconnected boxes is a typical modernist way of reducing complexity and ambiguity to a seeming sense of order. A postmodernist would much rather face up to the conflicts between their personal values and those they are called upon to apply at work.

- As postmodernists do not accept any grand metanarrative ethical theories, they have to look instead at particulars and circumstances. These can only be expressed in stories and myths that express humanity's fears, confusions and expectations. Concrete illustrations of moral issues are a more assured route to ethical awareness than mental abstractions divorced from substance. Some people have gone as far as to recommend that we should return to meditation upon the lives of saints to help us deal with the ethical dilemmas and tensions that we experience (Wyschogrod, 1990: xiii). As the medieval historian Gervase of Canterbury wrote in the twelfth century:

There are many people whose minds are induced to avoid evil and to do good more easily by example than by prohibition and precepts.

(Bartlett, 2000: 629)

- A disbelief in Utopian ideas. As Bauman expressed it, a postmodern thinker uses history (particularly that of the twentieth century and even more specifically of the Holocaust) as evidence of modernists' belief in instrumental thinking and technological development is wrong. Even on a more mundane level the belief held in the 1960s that technological development would lead to a world in which everyone would have huge amounts of leisure has proved false.

- Finally, Gustafson sees postmodern ethics as a 'tempered quest'. By this he means that the search for ethical answers to the problems of business ethics is conducted with the one item of knowledge that is certain – that no definitive answer can be found.

Living in an ungrounded ethical system may call upon people's resources of humour and tolerance. These are needed because value conflict will be endemic in such a situation. Irony is helpful because people's purposes may require them to act in ways that seem naïve in the absence of a metanarrative that justifies simple behaviours. Let us explain this point by quoting Umberto Eco (1985: 67). In his reflections on his best-selling novel, *The Name of the Rose*, he used the example of the pragmatist lover. The lover wishes to say to his partner, 'I love you', but he cannot do so because everyone is aware that the proliferation of romantic novels has devalued that particular metanarrative. He would feel too naïve and unsophisticated if he said that simple sentence even though it is the emotion he wishes to express. Being a pragmatist he does not give up, and stalk away undeclared. Instead, he says, 'As Barbara Cartland would say "I love you"'. He has thereby expressed his purpose but in a way that reveals his knowledge that such sentiment can no longer be justified by reference to transcendental values. Irony, by which an apparently straightforward statement is undermined by its context, is essential to the pragmatist's stance.

From a pragmatic view, in summary, it is recognised that there is confusion and conflict over the ends of a good organisation or society and that the meanings people ascribe to values change and develop as they debate and discuss issues with others. Nevertheless the pragmatist believes that by maintaining the conversation with good humour and irony it is possible to make organisations and societies more bearable.

The five stances can be characterised in relation to their position on ethical fragmentation. A traditionalist sees a unified world united by time-hallowed values. From the other four positions, the ethical world is seen as fragmented but with different responses to this perception. The modernist believes that unity can be restored through rational development of individuals. The neo-traditionalist believes unity can be restored only by a return to concern for neglected values. The postmodernist accepts the inevitability of fragmentation and enjoys it. Pragmatists learn to live with fragmentation. The following exercise is designed to test your understanding of the five stances. Read Case study 4.1. Although it is an invented case study, many of the incidents have been taken from interviews with managers. Then answer the questions in Activity 4.2.

Case study 4.1	Chris's managerial development: a fable

Chris is a newly qualified social worker. She didn't start training until she was in her late twenties but she had much previous experience of acting as an unpaid worker with a voluntary agency. In her first role as a field social worker, she brought much of the enthusiasm and motivation that she developed during her early experience and training. She liked to see her clients as whole persons and she tried to spend as much time with them as possible so that she could come to a proper understanding of their situation from their point of view. It is important, she believed, not to take action without the full and active consent of the client.

After some years the pressure of Chris's caseload made it difficult to find the time she needed to spend with clients. She often felt frustrated that she had to foreshorten important discussions with them. On occasions this frustration caused her to be short and less than helpful with those clients who seemed to enjoy creating their own misfortune and yet were ungrateful for any help she provided. Although some of her clients were often short-changed on the service they received because of this reaction, it did not undermine her essential belief in the need to work with her clients in a way that maintained and developed their dignity.

After a few years, Chris was promoted to team leader and she became responsible for the management and professional supervision of a team of workers. In a small way, her attitude towards the clients changed. She no longer spent the bulk of her time working face to face with them. She also had the managerial responsibility of dividing her staff resources between all the clamouring demands for service. Her attitude towards clients was more objective. She made sure that careful, measured and objective assessments were made of all clients so that those with the greatest needs received priority.

A few years later, Chris was appointed as a services manager for a particular category of clients in the northern area of the county. Two important themes within her new job were service quality (as expressed by performance indicators) and budgets. Cost-effectiveness became a worrying issue. She had to convince her managers that she was providing value for money and this caused her to question whether the range of services was not too wide and whether some of them could be ended or reduced. There was talk within the department about only providing the high 'value added' services. She came to the view that better IT, better information and more rational decision-making processes would improve the service's effectiveness. She was studying for an MBA and its heavy emphasis on IT and management science convinced her that the department needed to put more effort into producing a computer-based needs profiling and resource allocation system. She started, in a small way, to produce such a system for use within her own locality.

A few years later Chris was still a services manager, but she had moved sideways and was now working with a different client group. The move made her realise the differences in professional values between people who worked with different client groups. It was the failure to address these differences, she thought, that was at the root of organisational conflict within the department. She came to believe that it was very important that everyone in her area subscribed to a central vision and mission that would motivate and inspire all staff. To this end she organised a couple of away-day sessions at which she and her fellow managers tried to hammer out some key goals and core values for the service as a whole. The software she had developed in her previous job had proved very valuable but it had failed to deliver easy solutions to the resource allocation problems. As a result of this experience, Chris thought that focusing the department on some basic core values was a better way of managing than relying too much on IT systems.

After a few years in this job, Chris was more aware of its political dimension. Managers seemed to spend their time fighting their corner and the person who shouted loudest got the most. For example, whilst the IT system optimised the allocation of staff to clients, it caused as many problems as it solved. It gave some groups of clients a very low priority ranking. Some managers felt that this was correct ('it would be more effective to pay for them all to go to Lourdes', as one senior manager put it) but there was a powerful and critical lobby from the relatives of the clients.

When she was trying to develop core values she began to see it as a game. People were trying to control the language that was to be used in framing the values. It was also clear that when they wrote a core value everybody bought into it while retaining the right to define it in their own way. Everyone was smart enough to play the language games of anti-oppressive practice but there was no consensus about its meaning. Indeed at meetings Chris thought they were playing a circular word game in which *client focus* was identified with quality of service, which in turn was defined as providing equal opportunities, which in its turn was seen as responding to the diversity of clients. The debates' ends were their beginnings. The inconclusive debates over policy documents often led to a point where everything seemed ineluctably confused.

▶

Some years later Chris was a senior manager. Her enthusiasm for the importance of social services was undimmed but her expectations were less ambitious. She was aware that things in organisations do not always work as planned. She no longer believed that the answer to organisational management was more and better computers; nor did she think that the publication of a nicely printed and laminated card proclaiming the Mission Statement actually meant that everyone shared the same values. She saw the organisation as having many stakeholder groups, internal and external, and the task of managers was to keep them sweet. But this ironic awareness did not mean that Chris became cynical, although this is precisely what has happened to some of her colleagues. Chris continued to work for improvement (whatever that is) but perhaps in a different way. She came to believe in proceeding on a Ready – Fire – Aim basis. This meant trying things out in a small way, without too much prior planning, and building on them if they worked, and modifying or abandoning them if they did not. No more rational master plans. She no longer believed in acronyms (such as CFI – Clients First Initiative) any more. Truth lay in aphorisms not acronyms. Aphorisms are a statement of a general principle memorably expressed in a condensed form. For example, 'He who is too busy doing good finds no time for being good' (Tagore quoted in Gross, 1987: 197). Aphorisms make you think about fundamental issues, acronyms just require blind acceptance. Chris accepted both the fragmented nature of the managerial role and the plurality of values within the organisation, and she could become a little manic-depressive as a result. Nevertheless, Chris tried to maintain manners and tolerance when managing the service. Her attitude was 'pessimistic wishful thinking'.

Activity 4.2	**Analysing Chris's managerial development**

The fable implies that managers' responses to value issues at work may change as their careers progress. In this fable can you detect the periods when Chris's approach was:

(a) traditional,

(b) modernist,

(c) neo-traditional,

(d) postmodern, and

(e) pragmatic?

We will give one possible interpretation of the fable in Case study 4.1. You may have made a different reading of it. Chris starts her career as a field social worker as a traditionalist. She had acquired a set of values about how social work clients should be treated. To some extent these would have been absorbed as she grew up and from her voluntary work. They would have been reinforced by her social work training. She had picked up the traditional values that are associated with her chosen profession. As her workload pressures increased, she found it increasingly difficult to apply these values. Her next two jobs gave her responsibility for setting priorities, managing budgets and achieving performance targets. In response she began to adopt a more modernist stance. She had to assume that clients' needs can be objectively measured and ranked in order of importance so that she could make sure the neediest would receive services. She extended this view into a belief, fostered by doing a master's degree in management science, that the difficult decisions about the rationing of services, when need exceeds the resources available to meet it, could be made easier by more data and more rational decision making. Up to this stage in her career, Chris had been working in the same specialist field. Her next job took her into a different one and she realised that different groups have different values and norms. This, together with the failure of more data and better software systems to solve the management problems, led her to take a neo-traditionalist stance and to try to make the service more effective by developing an organisational set of values that everyone could 'buy into'. However, this proved to be more difficult than she had expected as attempts to create a unified organisational culture floundered on organisational politics. Chris began to view things from a postmodern perspective and observed wryly the games playing with language that went on in the organisation. However, by the time she had become a senior manager she had become a pragmatist, who saw no quick fixes to organisational problems, but nevertheless continued to work to improve things, even though progress, even if everyone could agree it was progress, was slow and piece meal. Success, she felt, lay in maintaining the importance of concern for others and for good manners even though this seemed an endless task.

Values and ethical thinking

The next part of the chapter considers how people think about and make ethical decisions in practice. It is in contrast to Chapter 2, which considered how philosophers and writers on ethics argue that people should think about ethical matters. The central theme of the chapter is the role of heuristics in human thinking. The argument is that people do not use a comprehensively rational process when they come to a view on moral matters. Rather, it will be argued, people use heuristics to ease the process of arriving at a view or taking a decision, and to simplify the mass of competing views and information that surround any issue.

The account of ethical thinking provided in this chapter is to some extent speculative. It presents an argument about how people might make up their minds on ethical matters. The argument is based on well-established ideas as well as on newly emerging theories, but their application to thinking on ethical matters is incomplete. Unusually for a textbook therefore it remains for you to make up your mind on the arguments presented.

Heuristics are a means of discovering or finding out something. **DEFINITION** They are mental tricks of the trade or rules of thumb that are used, almost unconsciously, to simplify the process of decision making. They are cognitive devices that limit the need to search for, and evaluate, further options. The term also carries with it the idea of discovering things by trial and error rather than by systematic analysis of all appropriate information.

Heuristic thinking

The idea of heuristic thinking can be illustrated by contrasting it with a rational approach to making a non-ethical decision such as choosing a car to buy. If this decision were to be approached from an analytical and rational position, you would have to go through the following stages.

- Identify all the cars available on the market.

- Identify all the factors that are important to you in a car, such as cost, reliability, acceleration, colour and so on.

- Decide on the relative importance to you of the above criteria by either putting them into rank order or assigning weights to them.

- Research each car on the market and decide how they score against each of the criteria.

- Calculate the degree to which each car would satisfy your wishes by combining the cars' performances against each criterion with the criterion's importance, so that cars that do well against the more important criteria will have the higher scores.

- Choose the car that scores highest in these calculations.

The process just described is called subjective expected utility. This is because the decision maker makes a personal (subjective) assessment of both what is important to them about a car (utility) and the chances (expected) that any particular car would actually provide that value.

This is obviously a time-consuming process. A heuristic approach would simplify it. A large number of heuristics could be involved in deciding which car to buy. Here are just a few. To begin with, you would probably not evaluate every car available on the market but simply focus on those you have been made aware of by advertising. This is the availability heuristic. The recency heuristic might mean that a pleasurable trip last weekend in a friend's new car weighs heavily in your preference for that model. Your dislike of the colour purple might mean that the purple car you have been considering seems to have a lot of factors that turn you against it. This is an example of the halo and horns heuristic that is explained on p. 169. The application of one or more of these heuristics will leave you with a narrow range of cars from which to choose and an intuitive inclination to buy one particular car.

Let us move on to consider decision making about ethical matters. Benjamin Franklin proposed, in the eighteenth century, the use of a moral algebra to resolve such issues (Gigerenzer et al., 1999: 76). This was similar to the rational and analytical model, described above, for choosing a car. He would divide a sheet of paper into two columns and head one 'Pros' and the other 'Cons'. He would then identify the factors for or against a particular course of action. On further consideration, he would strike out some pros and cons because they cancelled each other out. If two cons were, in his view, equal to one pro he would strike out all three.

As a result of this process he would come to a balanced view about the right thing to do.

If we applied moral algebra to an ethical question we might find, but not necessarily, deontological pros ranged against consequentialist cons. Rights would have to be weighed against justice and equity and the virtuous mean might be hard to find. Giving equal consideration to potentially mutually exclusive ways of thinking about ethical questions may lead to confusion. Some writers (Kaler, 1999) suggest that the way business schools teach business ethics ('well, you could look at it from a deontological viewpoint or alternatively from a consequentialist position') encourages such confusion. It will be argued, contrarily, that people tend not to combine all the ethical perspectives on an issue but choose one and use it in a heuristic manner.

It is further argued in this chapter that values and emotions can perform the role of decision-making heuristics. Two examples of the role of values as heuristics in ethical decision making are provided to illustrate the process.

- The first example focuses on priority setting and uses the case of resource allocation in health-care management.

- The second example concerns ideas of integrity and loyalty as decision-making heuristics. Each of these is explained, and illustrated by an activity.

Decision-making heuristics

The idea has long been recognised that people do not possess the capacity to obtain and process the amounts of information necessary in order to take a rational approach to decision making. Herbert Simon's (1983) concept of bounded rationality is the classic formulation of this viewpoint. Search behaviour is the process of looking for the information and options necessary to make a decision. Bounded rationality sets limits on the extent of such searches. He introduced the concept of satisficing, which is the process of searching for and evaluating options until one is found that is good enough. He accepted that this solution may not be the best or optimal one. If the decision maker had continued to identify and assess options, better ones might have been found. But, he argued, once a solution has been found that will do, the psychological and practical costs to the decision-maker of looking for the best solution outweigh the additional benefits of a best solution that may not, in any case, be found. Simon's work emphasised that fully rational decision making was at best an aspiration and that the way people actually made up their minds about things was less analytical and was based more on trial and error – which is one definition of a heuristic.

Some examples might give a clearer understanding of heuristics. In the 1970s, psychologists, among them Kahneman et al. (1982), studied the exercise of judgment. In particular, they investigated how people made estimates about the probability or likelihood of situations and events. The research was carried out using questionnaires. The box below presents an example of the questions they asked.

Blue taxi or green taxi?

A taxi was involved in a hit-and-run accident at night. Two taxi companies, the green and the blue, operate in the city. You are given the following data:

(a) 85 per cent of the taxis in the city are green and 15 per cent blue.

(b) A witness identified the cab as blue. The court tested the reliability of the witness under the same circumstances that existed on the night of the accident and concluded that the witness correctly identified each of the two colours 80 per cent of the time and failed 20 per cent of the time.

What is the probability that the cab involved in the accident was blue rather than green?

(*Source*: Kahneman et al., 1982: 156–7)

This example identifies a heuristic (known as base-rate neglect) that leads people to pay more attention to immediate sources of information (the witness's statement) and to ignore background information (such as the relative frequency of the two types of cabs). The correct answer, derived from Bayes' theorem (which takes both items of data into account), is 0.41.

DEFINITION

Bayes theorem includes both prior and current information when calculating a probability. It is not necessary for you to know the mathematics but for those who are curious there is a useful Bayes' theorem calculator on the Web at http://faculty.vassar.edu/lowry/bayes.html.
If you put into this calculator:

■ the probability that the taxi will be blue, which is 0.15 ($P(A)$),

■ the probability that the witness will correctly identify the taxi as green if it is green, which is 0.68 ($P(B|\sim A) = 0.8 \times 0.85$), and

■ the probability of the witness identifying the taxi as blue if it is blue, which is 0.12 ($P(B|A) = 0.15 \times 0.8$)

it gives the probability of the taxi being blue as 0.41.

Most people, when asked to answer this question, however, ignored the data in point (a) because they were considered too general and distant from the event, and produced an answer around 80 per cent, which was based on the information given in point (b) alone.

In this classic research conducted by Kahnemann and his colleagues, the research questions were constructed so that if a heuristic were present respondents would misuse or neglect important information and give incorrect answers. The inference was then drawn that heuristics were a source of bias and prejudice in judgment. In hind sight it can be objected that the questions were so deviously constructed that they did not represent the kinds of judgment people have to make in real life. If so, the possibility remains that in everyday situations the heuristics might not be a cause of error.

A large number of heuristics are identified in Hogarth (1980). Just a few will be mentioned here. The recency effect was mentioned in the example of the car-buying decision mentioned above. This heuristic causes people to put more weight on information they have collected recently and to undervalue things they may have learned in the past. The halo and horns heuristic has long been known to selection and recruitment specialists. This heuristic leads people to latch on to one aspect of an interviewee to which they have a strong like or dislike. It may be the fact that the interviewee has a moustache or is wearing blue suede shoes. This one feature then dominates the recruiter's whole assessment of the individual. They might think that a man with a moustache cannot really be trusted, or that anyone who wears blue suede shoes must be just the sort of creative person the company needs. The heuristics-and-biases programme of research established the existence of heuristics in judgment but suggested that they were a problem.

A more recent programme of research led by the ABC research group, based in Berlin, has revisited heuristics and come to the conclusion that far from being a distortion of decision making, they are both necessary and effective. The programme is intended to 'capture how real minds make decisions under constraints of limited time and knowledge' (Gigerenzer et al., 1999: 5). It rejects the rational, subjective, expected utility model as a description of decision making and instead proposes the idea of fast and frugal heuristics. These are rules for limiting the search for information and options, and for making choices, that employ a minimum of time, knowledge and computation. It argues that fast and frugal heuristics are bounded rationality in its purest form.

The working of fast and frugal heuristics can best be explained by an example. One of the heuristics is the recognition heuristic that applies to situations where a person has to decide which of two objects has a higher value on a particular criterion. The heuristic is defined as follows: 'If one of the two objects is recognised and the other is not, then infer that the recognised object has the higher value' (Gigerenzer et al., 1999: 41). In an experiment students at the University of Chicago and the University of Munich the question, 'Which city has more inhabitants: San Diego or San Antonio?' Sixty-four per cent of the Chicago students got the answer right, but 100 per cent of the Munich students gave the correct answer. Why did the German students do better? They had heard of San Diego but not of San Antonio. They applied the recognition heuristic and got it right. The American students recognised both cities and could not apply the recognition heuristic. They had to search their memories for further clues as to the right answer. The additional information merely confused them. There is of course logic to the recognition heuristic; cities of which you have heard are more likely to be bigger than those that are unknown to you. The heuristic uses this logic as the basis of a very simple decision rule. But because of the logic the heuristic is not only simple; it is effective.

Of course there are many situations in which the recognition heuristic cannot be used because both of the options are recognised. Gigerenzer et al. (1999: Chapter 4) used a computer simulation to evaluate some simple heuristics for searching through data for solutions in such circumstances. As in their work reported above, the simulation was based on the task of deciding which, of pairs of cities, was the larger. They built into the simulation a series of 10 cues or clues about each of the cities. Whether a city was a capital or not was one clue. In the database of information, which was to be searched in the simulation, the cue was recorded as positive (if it was a capital city) because a capital city was likely to be larger than a city that was not, as negative (if it was not) or as a 'don't know'. Some additional information was included about the reliability of each cue (how often its use could give the right answer) and how often it would prove useful (as only one city can be a capital city you will not often have an opportunity to use it to discriminate between pairs of cities). In the simulation, six search strategies were tested. The first three were based on heuristic principles.

1. *Minimalist.* Choose one of the 10 cues at random. If one of the pair of cities you have to decide between scores a positive on this cue and the other a negative, then choose the positive city as the larger one. If not go on trying cues randomly in turn until one provides an answer.

2. *Take the last.* Choose whichever cue worked well last time this kind of decision had to be made.

3. *Take the best.* In this strategy, some of the information about the reliability and usefulness of the cues is used to decide which cue is likely to provide the most accurate answer.

The other three search strategies were all based on the rational model. They were:

■ Franklin's rule

■ Dawe's rule

■ Multiple regression.

We will not explain each of these in detail. It is sufficient to point out that they all shared one common feature, that, when choosing between two cities, they aggregated all 10 cues about each city in order to decide which was likely to be bigger. The heuristic strategies, in contrast, only used cues one at a time and when a decision had been reached ignored all the other cues.

The results from the simulation are shown in Table 4.2. The results suggest that not only are heuristics efficient because they give answers by using less information than the rational strategies, but they are also as accurate as the rational techniques. The fast and frugal researchers see heuristics as (generally) effective strategies for making decisions. This leaves open the possibility that ethical thinking, as well as judgment, might be a heuristic process.

Table 4.2 The results of the simulation comparing heuristic and rational research strategies

Type of strategy	Strategy	Frugality (no. of cues looked up)	Accuracy (% of correct answers)
Heuristic	Take the last	2.6	64.5
	Minimalist	2.8	64.7
	Take the best	3.0	65.8
Rational	Franklin's rule	10.0	62.1
	Dawe's rule	10.0	62.3
	Multiple regression	10.0	65.7

Source: From *Simple Heuristics That Make Us Smart,* Oxford University Press, Inc. (Gigerenzer, G. and Todd, p. 1999) Table 4-2, p. 87, Copyright © 1999 by Oxford University Press, Inc., By permission of Oxford University Press, Inc.

Values as heuristics in ethical reasoning

In this section, we want to move away from what is established in the literature and to speculate about how the fast and frugal heuristics may apply to ethical decision making. The argument is that heuristics operate in ethical decision making and that values are the basis of these heuristics.

Gigerenzer et al. (1999: 30) pointed out that, while most of the fast and frugal research concerns cognitive heuristics, emotions and social norms can also act as heuristics. For example, a social norm such as 'copy the choices made by your social peers' acts as an efficient heuristic for stopping further searching for other options. This heuristic might be particularly powerful in academic recruitment procedures in which academics apparently appoint those whom they think their colleagues would approve of. Emotions, such as love for one's child, prevent wasteful ethical dithering. If a child screams in the night, the emotional response forces the parent to get out of bed and comfort the child. Such parents do not calculate whether the greatest utility is achieved by this action or whether staying in bed so that they might be fresher for work the next day might do greater good. Kahneman (2011) has written in his new book that in the past the role of emotion as a decision-making heuristic has been underrated and that the affective heuristic is one of the most important amongst heuristics.

Four categories of moral emotions have been identified (Haidt, 2003) that, once elicited by some event, act as a trigger or create a tendency to act in a particular way. They are:

■ Other condemning – contempt, anger and disgust.

■ Self-conscious – shame, embarrassment and guilt.

■ Other suffering – compassion.

■ Other praising – gratitude and elevation.

If emotions and social norms can act as heuristics, then it is possible that values can also do so. This is because values are closely related to emotions and social norms. Values are like emotions because people find it hard to give a rational account of why their values are important to them; they just are (Eden et al., 1979). The link with social norms derives from the fact that values are acquired as part of the process of growing up and becoming socialised in a society. It is this early acquisition of values, according to Rokeach (1973: 17–18), that makes values simpler and more robust than attitudes.

Values acting as heuristics

The ways in which values may act as heuristics can be illustrated by considering a well-known management development exercise called *Cave Rescue* (Woodcock, 1979, 1989: 81). In this exercise, groups have to decide how to allocate scarce resources between people who are described in thumbnail sketches, which are deliberately brief and partisan. *Cave Rescue* concerns six volunteers in a psychological experiment that requires them to be in a pothole. The cave is flooding and the research committee in charge of the experiment has called for a rescue team. When the team arrives, it will only be able to rescue one person at a time because of the narrowness of the cave's entrance. The committee has to decide the order in which the volunteers will be saved from the cave when the rescue party arrives. The exercise provides a good opportunity to study the values that are articulated in such debates.

Observations of people doing the exercise suggest that they used their preferred values to select the information from the thumbnail sketches that they consider useful. Each of the characters in the *Cave Rescue* exercise has positive and negative aspects included in their thumbnail sketches. Some material about each of the characters has to be edited out for other information to become useful in making the necessary ranking decisions. A number of different values are used that include:

- Maximising the number of people who are saved by rescuing first those likely to panic and hamper the rescuers.

- Maximising the happiness of society by rescuing first those who can make the greatest contribution to society (utilitarianism).

- Rescuing first those who have the most family or other dependants.

- Rescuing the youngest first because the oldest have already had their opportunity for life.

- Rescuing the morally worthy before the morally unworthy.

The heuristic use of values can be illustrated by reference to volunteer Paul who, according to the information given to the participants, has been convicted of indecent assault. But he also has, in his working notes, details of a cheap cure for rabies. People who used the morality criterion to choose whom to rescue assumed that the cure could be understood from the working notes (and that in any case he was bound to have a research assistant who understood and could continue the work) and that there was, consequently, no barrier to using his behaviour to decide his order of rescue. Other people, using a utilitarian value, assumed that it was impossible to make sense of the working notes. This allowed them, when making their decision, to ignore Paul's criminal activities and concentrate on his potential contribution to society. People edited out, or rationalised into insignificance, that information which inhibited the application of their preferred values.

How values are used as heuristics

So far, the argument seems straightforward. Values are simple but strongly held beliefs such as the importance of honesty. People, it is suggested, use values as filters to reduce the amount of information they take into account when making a decision. Values may act as a fast and frugal heuristic for limiting the amount of search behaviour. To the three heuristic search strategies proposed by Gigerenzer et al. (1999, see p. 87) might be added another one: choose a cue that you like because it fits with your values.

If people do not change their values, ethical decisions ought to be easy. But it is not. Ethical issues are often seen as dilemmas that are not easily resolved. According to Billig (1996: 238–47), values may be simple in themselves but in at least two ways they are complex matters of controversy.

- The first concerns the interpretations of the values. Their very simplicity makes them banal. This in turn means that they have to be interpreted before they can be of use in making decisions. An example can be taken from health-care management. Everyone in the field would agree that patients come first. But different health-care professionals may make sense of this value in different ways. For some it would mean improving the patients' clinical condition. Others might say it is empowering the patients to take control of their treatment and their condition. Yet others might claim it means making the patient physically comfortable and at psychological ease.

- The second source of argument and conflict over values is the multiplicity of conflicting values in any given society. Ambition, for example, may clash with honesty. Ethical issues are often difficult because it may not be certain which value, from a variety of contradictory values, should be applied in any given situation.

The problem for someone faced with an ethical matter is to choose which of many values to apply to the situation. This brings us back to a feature of fast and frugal heuristics as described by Gigerenzer et al. (1999: 30). They proposed that people are equipped with a psychological adaptive toolbox that is filled with a jumbled collection of one-function tools. Just as a mechanic manages to choose the right tool to repair a car, so people choose the best heuristic to hand to help them make their mind up or take a decision.

Video clip 4.2

Nepotism

The clip deals with nepotism – taking family connections into account when recruiting staff. Is this a good and appropriate value to apply or not?

To view the video clip from the interview please visit this book's companion website at www.pearsoned.co.uk/fisherlovellvalerosilva.

In the next two sections we explore the ways in which particular values might be used.

Value heuristics and priority setting

Resource allocation is a particular form of priority setting. It involves deciding which things are more important and which less. In this section, it is argued that right answers to problems of priority setting cannot be found by technical means. Priority setting is a matter of values. The person setting the priorities has to decide which values they will use to determine relative importance. Whether a particular set of priorities is right or wrong depends upon the values used to judge it. This makes that priority setting an ethical matter.

This section explores the use of values as heuristics for making decisions in ethical matters, using a simulation exercise called *Monksbane and feverfew*. The exercise is based on a problem in health-care management. A limited budget has to be divided between two health-care programmes, one aimed at the diagnosis and treatment of monksbane and the other at the diagnosis and treatment of feverfew, both dangerous, if fictitious, diseases. The problem is to decide which programme should be given priority. Fisher (1998) identified six values concerning priority setting in the allocation of resources. They are listed here but will be defined later in the chapter:

1. utility

2. individual need

3. deservingness

4. ecology

5. fairness

6. personal competence and gain.

In *Monksbane and feverfew*, there are opportunities to apply each of these values in setting your priorities between the two programmes. Whichever you choose will lead to a different allocation of resources. It may be that you will change your mind as you work through the simulation. Do Activity 4.1 now and then the different values will be explained.

Activity 4.3	**Monksbane and feverfew: a diagnostic instrument about values and priority setting**

Go to the companion website for this book (www.pearsoned.co.uk /fisherlovell) where you will find both an interactive, web-based version of the activity as well as a hard-copy version that you can print off. The interactive version calculates your scores for you. If you use the hard copy you will have to do the scoring yourself.

Transfer your score from the *Monksbane and feverfew* exercise to the grid to the below by placing ticks in the appropriate cells.

Heuristic	Low	Medium	High
Utility			
Individual need			
Deservingness			
Ecology			
Fairness			
Personal competence and gain			

Source: Fisher (1998)

The value heuristics of resource allocation

Each of the six value heuristics for resource allocation will be explained by reference to the information provided to the decision maker in *Monksbane and feverfew*.

Utility

Utility is a value concerned with allocating resources in a way that maximises the common good (or the beneficial impact of services). Utility values the maximisation of the quantity of good done. It is a form of utilitarianism.

In Section 1 of *Monksbane and feverfew*, you are given enough information to apply utility as a value. If the graph is studied carefully it is clear that at any point money spent on feverfew will always save more lives than will be saved by spending it on monksbane. The way to save the most lives is to spend all the money on feverfew and none on monksbane. Those who make this decision are using the utility value. Not everyone can bear to do this. Those who know that rationally any money spent on monksbane costs the lives of feverfew sufferers, who might otherwise have been saved, may still find themselves unable to spend nothing on monksbane at all. They therefore decide to spend a small amount on its treatment. This suggests that they are not entirely at ease with the utility value.

Utility is the heuristic that underwrites much management theory, and management science in particular. The development of QALYs, in health-policy studies, provides an illustration of this approach. QALY stands for quality-adjusted life years (Gudex, 1986) and is a measure of the benefit, to the average patient, of a medical treatment in terms of additional years of life and of the quality of life. Once the benefit of a medical intervention is measured, its cost can be calculated to produce a ranking of treatments in cost-effectiveness terms. Haemodialysis produced a cost per QALY of £9,075 while for scoliosis surgery the cost was £194. The latter treatment will therefore produce more benefit for any given sum of money than the former. There have been many criticisms of the utilitarian QALY approach, as reported in Pereira (1989) and Baldwin et al. (1990), but it is still persuasive to many.

Cross reference	The heuristic of utility relates to the general ethical tradition of utilitarianism that is discussed in Chapter 3, p. 117.

Individual need

Individual need is a value that can be triggered by the cues and information given in Section 2 of *Monksbane and feverfew*. This value holds that resources should be allocated in proportion to people's needs. Needs can of course be attributed to groups of people but those who adopt this value prefer to consider people as individuals. Needs are not the same as wants or demands, however. A need can only be defined by an expert in the field, in the cases of monksbane and feverfew by a doctor. Needs have two further characteristics: they can be objectively described, which means that it is possible for someone to have a need they do not know about, and, secondly, they can be ranked so that some are seen as more pressing than others.

The information provided in Section 2 of *Monksbane and feverfew* suggests that people who suffer from monksbane have greater need than those ill with feverfew. Monksbane patients are much more likely to die if not treated than feverfew patients. The information in Section 2 also highlights another aspect of individual need. It is the belief that if there are the means and the technology to improve people's lot, then we are obliged to use them. In a medical setting it is the belief that everything that can be done, that has some chance of providing some benefit to the patient, should be done. It is to be noted that more can be done to treat people with monksbane than can be done for those with feverfew. If someone adopts the individual need value therefore, they will decide to spend significant sums of money on the treatment of monksbane.

The problem with individual need as a value is that it wills the expenditure of money without any regard for the availability of that money.

Deservingness

The deservingness heuristic, which is made available in Sections 3a and 3b of Activity 5.1, divides people into two moral classes, the deserving and the undeserving. When resources are being distributed according to the deservingness heuristic, the favourable allocation is given to the former and the unfavourable portion to the latter. Deservingness is an Edwardian concept. This traditional view saw the provenance of poverty and need in individual moral failure and indolence. The growing depersonalisation and alienation of social life, caused by nineteenth-century industrialisation, made this view untenable, and a distinction was drawn between the deserving poor, brought low by social and economic factors beyond their control, and the undeserving poor, whose failure was of their own doing. New possibilities for morally classifying people have emerged since Edwardian times. People can be allocated to moral categories according to whether they are, on the one hand, greedy, truculent and ungrateful or, on the other, meek, humble and full of gratitude. A further moral criterion of deservingness is group membership. The deserving person is one of us; the undeserving person is an outsider.

In more recent times, the debate about the funding of treatment for sufferers from AIDS suggests that the distinction between the morally deserving and the undeserving is still current, and indeed is experiencing a renaissance. Academic writing on the subject has been concerned with whether the treatment of AIDS sufferers is cost effective (Eastwood and Maynard, 1990). But there were arguments put forward, particularly in the press, which suggested that AIDS patients should be seen as 'less eligible' for treatment because they had visited the illness upon themselves through homosexual behaviour or drug abuse. It is, perhaps, the effect of deservingness that accounts for the different public perceptions of the plights of haemophiliacs, who acquired the disease through the necessary treatment of their primary illness, and that of homosexuals who, more likely, acquired it as a result of chosen behaviours. Whilst the UK government was initially curmudgeonly in the question of compensation for haemophiliacs, who had become HIV positive from being treated with infected blood products, public opinion clearly thought they should be compensated quickly (Mihil, 1990). There was a popular temptation to see haemophiliacs as deserving, and homosexuals as undeserving, and to fund their programmes accordingly.

In *Monksbane and feverfew*, you are informed that people with the disease to which you have given the biggest share of the budget are ungrateful and truculent and that their behaviour has contributed towards their condition. If you are attracted to the value of deservingness, you will have little patience with these people and decide to spend less on their treatment. However, if you do not hold this value, you will probably regard all the information given in this section as irrelevant to the problem and decide to leave the budget allocation unaltered.

Cross reference	The heuristic of deservingness has some connections with the largely American philosophy of objectivism that is associated with Ayn Rand, whose ideas are discussed in Chapter 3, p. 130. This philosophy emphasises the moral independence of individuals. Those who do not rise to this challenge are undeserving.

Ecology

The apologists for the ecology heuristic take a very different approach. They see clients as morally autonomous agents who are not passive recipients of services but actors within the resource-allocation process. Put simply, the ecology value states that the voices of all the parties interested in a decision should be heard. Those who value this perspective are pluralists who assume there will be many different points of view that have to be accommodated.

The ecology heuristic is concerned with identifying the different perceptions of the many groups involved with a service and trying to create a consistent policy from that variety. Ultimately, this concatenation is achieved by giving more weight to the views of those who are most closely involved with the service. Some groups, particularly the most powerful with respect to the decision makers, will be listened to more intently than others. In other words, an ecological resource allocation is one that meets the expectations and aspirations of the most significant interest groups. But such allocations also have to meet the minimum requirements of all the interest groups. If they do not, then those disregarded groups will seek to make themselves more significant to the organisation and so reach a condition in which the decision makers have to listen to them.

Section 4 of *Monksbane and feverfew* provides enough clues for people who adopt this value to act upon it. Some very powerful interest groups are pressing for more money to be spent on the monksbane programme. People who accept ecology respond by putting another five or ten thousand pounds into the programme. Most of those who reject ecology as a value simply ignore the demands of the pressure groups. Some respondents, however, are so incensed by what they see as bullying by the pressure groups, that they reduce the expenditure on monksbane to punish those who would seek to bring pressure to bear.

Fairness

Fairness is concerned with impartiality between individuals. Fairness emphasises the importance of giving everyone equal access to services or at least an equal chance of access. This makes the use of arbitrary mechanisms for allocating scarce resources possible. Some managers, for example, when faced with too many job candidates, all of whom fit the employee specification, believe the only fair way of choosing the successful candidate is to draw lots. People who apply the fairness heuristic are interested in the standardisation and consistency of services to customers and clients. One of the clearest definitions of fairness, as it is defined here, can be found in a medieval Islamic story.

> A child and an adult both of the True Faith are in Heaven, but the adult occupies a higher place. God explains that the man has done many good works whereupon the child asks why God allowed him to die before he could do good. God answers that he knew the child would grow up to be a sinner and so it was better that he die young. A cry rises up from the depths of Hell: 'Why O Lord did you not let us die before we became sinners?'
>
> (Russell, 1985: 85)

The Lord was obviously working on an ad hoc basis, dealing with individuals as they appeared before him for judgement. For some reason this child was noticed and saved while many others were not, a lapse on God's part that those in Hell naturally thought unfair. Fairness therefore must operate according to universally applied rules. Either all potential sinners die young or none.

Fairness is only concerned with equality of access and opportunity, not with equality of outcomes. In Section 5 of *Monksbane and feverfew*, the table shows that if £10,000 is spent on feverfew and £60,000 on monksbane then 30 per cent of sufferers from feverfew and 30 per cent of sufferers from monksbane would be identified and treated. This would be fair because, irrespective of which disease a person had, their chances of treatment would be the same. This does not of course mean that they would all have the same chances of being made well. Some people favour the value of fairness but would not wish to impose it by dividing up the budget 10:60. Section 6 of *Monksbane and feverfew* therefore provides another option for applying the fairness heuristic. In this section you are given the opportunity to leave the allocation of resources between the two treatment programmes to chance. This is done by treating patients as they present themselves, irrespective of their diagnosis, and by stopping all treatments when the budget is spent. This alternative puts everyone in a queue and so everyone is dealt with in the same way – fairly.

Personal competence and gain

Personal competence and gain is a heuristic which, when applied to the allocation of resources, causes decisions to be made to the decision maker's benefit. The benefit can be of two different kinds. The first is the sense of worth and self-esteem that can come from having done a job properly. This implies that the decision has been made using appropriate methods and that no short cuts, which offend against the decision maker's beliefs, have been used. The second sense relates to personal advantage. In this sense, the decision makers allocate resources in a way that brings some material or personal benefit to them – this may be an increase in organisational influence, professional satisfaction, something which eases the burden of daily life, cash or a bottle of whisky. Personal gain does not necessarily imply gain for the decision maker because they may value being able to help their friends or family, but it does imply that decisions are made according to private rather than public considerations.

In *Monksbane and feverfew*, respondents are invited to respond to this value in Section 7. It suggests that someone very dear to the respondent is suffering from the disease that is being given the smaller amount of money. Clearly that person's chances of recovery would be better if more money were spent on the screening and treatment for that disease. If the respondent increases the money allocated to the disease of the person close to them, they are using the personal gain value. A range of other factors could of course trigger this value. The person making the decision might, for example, have a research or clinical interest in the treatment of one of the two diseases. We do not necessarily think people will answer this part of the simulation honestly. We suspect people do not know how they would behave in such a situation until they are in it. However, Section 7 does illustrate how this value could be used as a heuristic for making the decision.

We are suggesting that *Monksbane and feverfew* illustrates how values can operate heuristically in the way that people search for solutions to a priority-setting problem. It is suggested that the six value heuristics identified in this chapter can be seen in any priority-setting or resource-allocation decision. They can be seen, for example, in decisions about the allocation of budget cuts or increases between departments, in deciding whom to make redundant in a round of downsizing and in decisions about responding to different market segments. Although it does not prove that people use values heuristically when making real-life decisions, it does provide some interesting issues for you to think about.

Integrity and loyalty as value heuristics

There are two other values that, it will be argued, can play an important role as heuristics for deciding what to think, say or do in an ethical matter. They are integrity and loyalty. A commitment to either loyalty or integrity can act as a heuristic for deciding what should be done in a situation. The process may be related to the extent of a person's ethical horizon, which is a personally set boundary within which a person seeks to act with integrity. When dealing with those considered to be beyond that boundary, a person shows loyalty to those within their ethical horizon. All of these issues need to be explained in more detail.

Defining integrity and loyalty

Integrity is defined as basing action on sound judgment and seeking a unity or wholeness of thought and action. The medieval scholar Aquinas, after Aristotle, argued that the practice of virtue requires people to act knowingly, voluntarily and according to a fixed principle or habit (D'Entreves, 1965: 147–8). Winstanley and Woodall reflected these ideas when they argued that

> The development of integrity [is] based upon ethical judgement and a sense of responsibility, the development of appropriate virtues.

> (Winstanley and Woodall, 2000: 285)

Integrity therefore is defined by its possessor's self-reflection and awareness. As C.P. Snow, quoted by Adair (1980: 171), epigrammatically expressed it:

Give me a man who knows something of himself and is appalled.

Video clip 4.3

Ethical communication

The clip deals with the importance and nature of integrity in business communication. To view the video clip from the interview please visit this book's companion website at www.pearsoned.co.ukfisherlovellvalerosilva.

A sense of self-doubt, as well as the tension between integrity and loyalty, can be illustrated by an account of an incident given during a research interview we conducted. The interviewee was a senior manager. His company required all managers to attend a series of development workshops that were designed to apply the precepts of an eastern mystical tradition to modern management practice. The respondent was a man of strong Christian belief who believed the philosophy of the seminars was contrary to his Christian principles. He felt that he should not in conscience attend the seminars. He was aware that taking this stance to maintain his integrity was at odds with his sense of loyalty. His loyalty was not particularly directed at the company but was focused on the rest of the management team who would be going to the seminars. The other team members told him that they thought him an important team member and they wished him to attend the seminars. The respondent reported that the issue caused him to think deeply about his beliefs and his responsibilities to others. His final position on the issue spoke of a self-conscious attempt to meet the demands of both integrity and loyalty. He attended the seminars but made a personal statement at the commencement in which he stated his personal objections to the values that informed them.

In contrast to integrity, loyalty is an unthinking faithfulness to a person, group or purpose. If a loyal person were to reflect on their actions they would have to question whether they were being loyal to the right thing. As Snell (1993: 82) characterised it, loyalty can range between a high commitment, analogous to a marriage, and a low level, which requires only the performance of actions contractually agreed. In a situation where high loyalty is demanded, but there is no opportunity for developmental openness (which would allow an individual to develop their own values and ethical reasoning),

Unquestioning conformity is expected of members: one must suppress individuality, ignore one's own arguments and perspectives and accept what one has to do.

(Snell, 1993: 82)

The unreflective nature of loyalty can be illustrated by another account of an ethical issue given by a manager in a finance department. When he moved to a new job he asked a colleague, with whom he had previously worked, to move with him and to support him in his new role. The manager was aware that the colleague was a discharged bankrupt who had invested unwisely when he had worked in the City. The financial accountant, who also reported to the manager, warned him of suspicions about the colleague's use of the credit card that the company had given him for business expenses.

> I had to take a view whether to expose him or to bring him to account, make him pay it back, and to carry on . . . Either to keep it to myself and the financial accountant, or to let other people know. I think there was enough going on that could have cost him his job: and I chose the latter. I had known him for a number of years, he was an extremely hard working individual, played hard as well, and played hard sometimes in my time. But if someone is working for me I take a balanced view. I don't expect them to work like an automaton . . . He was always getting phone calls at home in the early hours of the morning from the department, 'can't do this and can't do that', and he solved it . . . he was also being hounded by the CSA [Child Support Agency] so he wasn't having an easy time. All this encouraged me to take a lenient view. I also knew of his background and he was probably finding life a bit tough.

The colleague had spent £600 improperly using the credit card. The manager challenged him privately and, instead of starting disciplinary proceedings, made him pay the sum back within two weeks. The manager's loyalty towards the employee was at a cost to his honesty and integrity. He thought the colleague reciprocated the feeling of loyalty:

> I felt that as he was working for me he would behave himself and he would not wish to implicate me. I thought I was entitled to more consideration than somebody he didn't know.

However, within a short space of time the colleague had found himself a new, better-paid, job with a different company and in his last few weeks of his old employment he again misused his credit card.

> And so I felt as if I had paid my dues . . . I had no loyalty to him then once he had done it twice . . . On many occasions I have gone back and questioned my initial judgment. I find it quite difficult to think of abstract examples and decide what I would do, *because most things are instinct*. I am nearly forty-six years of age and so I have had a fair amount of experience; I am not sure I would do the same thing again.
>
> (Research interview: our emphasis)

Loyalty, in this account, is seen as a matter of instinct and experience and not as a matter of self-reflection. The instinctive wish to act loyally can easily be destroyed, as here, by an act of betrayal by the person to whom loyalty is given.

Ethical horizons

People in organisations may experience conflicts between behaving with integrity within a group they belong to and their inclination to defend this chosen group to those beyond it, even if that group has acted badly. Let us imagine that someone is a member of a professional body that has acted unethically. Within that group, they may well seek to put right the thing badly done, in short to act with integrity; but when someone outside of that body challenges it for its wrong doing, that same person could well defend the body, even though they know it has done wrong. The issue is well illustrated by a conversation imagined by Watson (1998: 266).

> *David:*   Alright for the sake of argument, imagine we set up a business to murder people.
>
> *Colin:*   Murder Incorporated.
>
> *David:*   OK; it's been done. But say we did this and we followed all the culture and empowerment stuff. We could have democratic management, lots of trust and all that. There's good pay for everybody, welfare arrangements, good pensions, and Christmas parties for the kiddies. There's a moral code – just like the Mafia – that holds everything together. Everything we have said so far makes this a moral business. But it is not. Murder isn't moral is it?

Legge expressed the dilemma, raised by this thought experiment, in a more formal way when discussing human resource management (HRM):

> If capitalism is, or has the potential to be viewed as ethical, then HRM similarly has a good chance. If not, it is difficult to imagine how an ethical system for managing people at work can emerge from an essentially unethical economic order.
>
> (Legge, 1998: 166)

The dilemmas in these two quotations hinge on the question of ethical horizons. An ethical horizon represents a person's belief about the extent of their ethical world. For some the horizon may be very close and focused on themselves alone or their immediate family and associates. For others their ethical horizon might be so wide as to include global society as a whole. Within the ethical horizon, people seek to act with integrity; beyond the horizon, they believe, it is not necessary to act with integrity but it is important to show loyalty to those within the ethical horizon.

The concept of an ethical horizon can be used to explain the issues in the examples of the fictitious conversation about organised crime, and Legge's discussion of capitalism. To take the mafia conversation first. If people's horizon is local and only encompasses the organisation, then they are only required to act with integrity within the organisation. Outside of the organisation, they are not required to act with integrity and can engage in criminal activities, as long as they show loyalty to the organisation. However, if the ethical horizon is drawn very broadly to include society as a whole, then such criminality would be unacceptable because people would be expected to display integrity in all their actions. In the example of Legge's

The Cynocephali

An example from the Middle Ages can illustrate the idea of an ethical horizon. In medieval maps of the world, there can often be seen on their margins images of people, normal in all respects, except that they have dog's heads. They are the cynocephali. It was thought they lived far to the east. Theologians were worried about how to treat the cynocephali when contact was eventually made with them. Should they be treated the same as the rest of humanity, with respect and with care for their souls? Or should they be seen as less than human in which case they could be treated as chattels and be exploited for humanity's benefit? Their problem was where the horizon of the ethical universe should be drawn. Should the cynocephali be within it or beyond it? If they were beyond it then the normal moral standards would not apply to how they should be treated.

analysis of HRM, she makes a similar point. If the ethical horizon is drawn widely then HRM is not ethical if capitalism is not; but if it is drawn only around the function of HRM then integrity is not required in the wider capitalist system. It is argued therefore that whether people think they should show loyalty or integrity, when it is not possible to do both, is affected by the extent of the subject's ethical horizon. A simplified analysis of the range of ethical horizons is shown in Box 4.1.

The ethical horizons of loyalty and integrity

Four levels of ethical horizon

1. The ethical horizon is drawn around the self and close associates

   - When people are acting within this narrow horizon, people are expected to focus on themselves, family and associates. Within the horizon they are expected to treat others properly and with integrity, as defined by their social norms. This may be represented by the alleged judgment on many East End gangsters that they were essentially good because they 'were good to their mothers'.

2. The ethical horizon is drawn around a person's networks and associations within civil society

   - Within this horizon, people are expected to act with integrity within their civil associations. When they are acting in the space beyond this horizon, they must defend and show loyalty to those associations. This is perhaps exemplified by E.M. Forster's (1975) remark, 'If I had to choose between betraying my country and betraying my friend, I hope I should have the guts to betray my country'.

3. The ethical horizon is drawn around a person's employing organisation

   - A person who perceives the organisation as their ethical horizon should act in an ethical manner within it but show loyalty to it if it is criticised or attacked from beyond the horizon. As the Civil Service code of ethics states, 'Civil servants owe their loyalty to the duly constituted government' (Cabinet Office, 2004).

4. The ethical horizon is set at its widest extent to include global society

■ When the horizon is drawn at its widest, there is no space beyond the horizon so that loyalty has to exist within rather than beyond the horizon. This means that loyalty and integrity become one. To be loyal to global society you have to act with integrity.

The first level in the hierarchy of ethical horizons in Table 4.3 is the broadest one and encompasses a concern for the well-being of society as a whole. At this level, people see themselves as parts of the whole, as flakes of rock chipped from the mountain. Such a sense of personal inconsequence, yet commitment to society, creates a willingness to sacrifice the self for the greater good. As, when the horizon is drawn this wide, integrity and loyalty are one, a person would be willing to resist any wrongdoing. Such an action would exhibit both integrity and loyalty to wider society.

When ethical horizons are set around membership of a civil association or an organisation, people seek to behave integrity within the organisation or association but will sacrifice their integrity in order to show loyalty to that body when acting in the world beyond it. Imagine a situation where someone has discovered that the organisation or association has done something seriously wrong. Within the horizon people will try to act with integrity and put the wrong right, or at least to convince others in the organisation to put things right. However, when dealing with people outside of the organisation, the same person will put their concerns to one side and protect and defend their organisation against criticism. In short, they will show loyalty. The degree to which they will sacrifice integrity to show loyalty will vary with the degree of their emotional identification with the organisation or association. At a minimal level, loyalty may just be keeping silence about the wrongdoing. At a further level, people may be prepared to lie to protect the organisation. At the extreme a person may be willing to become a scapegoat for the wrongs of the organisation or association. In the biblical origin of the term the scapegoat is not killed but is allowed to escape into the wilderness. This is an appropriate image for the ways in which modern organisations 'let go' those who carry the taint of organisations' bad behaviour.

When the ethical horizon does not extend beyond the self, the focus of actions will be on the protection and improvement of the self's position. Protecting the self's integrity can be achieved in two ways. The first involves drawing the ethical horizon so tightly around the self that any wrong action is kept beyond it. In plainer terms the subject claims or feigns ignorance of the wrongdoing. This approach to integrity has similarities with the concepts of ethical closure and ethical bracketing (Jackall, 1988; Kärreman and Alvesson, 1999). However, if the situation makes this stance untenable then people can maintain their integrity, not by attempting to put things right, but by removing themselves, by resigning from the organisation. When a person acts with integrity, by resigning from an organisation that they cannot prevent from behaving unethically, they sacrifice their material well-being, their job and their salary, to protect their ethical well-being. Loyalty to the self involves sacrificing integrity for material benefits. In the scenario described in Activity 4.4, it is represented by using knowledge of the organisation's wrongdoing to gain advantages for the self. The subject believes their integrity justifies self-seeking behaviour, and that the self-seeking legitimates their integrity.

In summary, what has been argued is that a focus on a particular ethical horizon can act in a heuristic manner. A person's ethical horizon constrains the range of actions open to them. How then does a person choose between them? You can see which values you favour, at least under simulated conditions, by completing Activity 4.4.

Activity 4.4	**Dilemma: a diagnostic inventory of managers' ethical horizons**

Go to the companion website for this book (www.pearsoned.co.uk /fisherlovellvalerosilva) where you will find both an interactive, web-based version of the activity and a hard-copy version that you can print off. The interactive version calculates your scores for you. If you use the hard copy you will have to do the scoring yourself. Have a go at the activity.

Discussion of the *Dilemma* simulation in Activity 4.4

The exercise you have just completed has been tested on a sample of undergraduate business students. Studying the sequence of choices they made as they worked their way through the action maze can identify their ethical horizons. In the first section of the maze, just over half of the respondents chose integrity in the organisational arena and tried to convince the management to admit the tax liability and to regularise the situation. Nearly 30 per cent continued with this position when the management at first refused to concede. A small percentage of respondents (5.8 per cent) found themselves in a closed loop, by continuing to suggest, despite the management's intransigence, that the tax liability should be admitted. But most of the respondents, when rebuffed by the management, chose integrity at the level of self and resigned from the organisation. Twenty-five of the 30 respondents who chose resignation subsequently took a position of integrity at the civil-association horizon, by whistleblowing on the organisation, when urged by their professional peers to do so. The most common route through the maze took, at every opportunity, a path of integrity rather than loyalty, but the ethical horizon changed as circumstances changed. Practising managers may not share undergraduates' commitment to integrity.

A minority of respondents took the route of loyalty but changed the focus of their loyalty. Nineteen per cent of the respondents initially opted for loyalty to self, by using their knowledge of the tax liability to gain advantage for themselves. But in Section 5 of the maze, most of those who had chosen loyalty to self changed their focus to loyalty to the organisation as they helped in the cover-up.

People's commitments to the sometimes competing demands of loyalty and integrity illustrate the importance of values as heuristics in decision making on ethical questions.

Cross reference	The issue of whistleblowing, raised in Activity 4.4, is explored more fully in Chapter 6.

Reflections

Our values are our ethical anchors. However, we each may find our values difficult to pin down. Schein (1993) has argued that we each have a 'career anchor', a value that is so important to us that we would rather lose our jobs, or in some other way be disadvantaged, rather than offend against it. The problem is that we may be uncertain about what that anchor, among our many professed values, may be until we are actually tested by some crisis or hurtful dilemma. At the same time, we have argued in this chapter that when we fail morally at work we tend to fail in a way that is characteristic of our temperament and our stance. In other words, it is not just what our values *are* that matters, but also how important those values are to us. Cathexis is a term from psychoanalysis; it refers to the strong sense of attachment that people may have towards their values and it is this commitment that drives people to act in the world (Young, 1977). The nature of a person's emotional attachment to a particular value may have many forms. A particular value may be:

- something we keep to ourselves and use only to manage our personal lives (a stance known as quietism);

- things that we are aspire to for others (a modernist stance);

- straightforward truths that we do not question (traditionalists and neo-traditionalists);

- things over which we agonise and debate (the position of pragmatists); or

- things that we can conveniently and playfully use to persuade people in arguments at work (as postmodernists think).

All of these possibilities indicate that our connections with our values are not straightforward. This suggests that the belief, often put forward by management writers, that the role of senior management is to promulgate a mission and a set of values that everyone can accept, looks naïve. People's response to their organisation's published values will be complex. They may accept them, for example, as ones they can work with even though they are not the same as their personal values. Or they may accept them ironically or mockingly such that their listeners are not sure whether they actually agree with them or not. More commonly they may agree with the values but doubt whether the top managers who published them have committed to, and are willing to act in accordance with, them. Such qualified acceptance of an organisation's values by managers and staff might not be a bad thing. As has been argued in the case of Enron, the over-enthusiastic acceptance of an organisation's values may give it the characteristics of a cult, and that carries its own dangers. The Enron case also reminds us that there is no particular reason to believe that people who reach the top of organisational career ladders will be particularly ethical and therefore capable of being ethical leaders.

The complexities of people's connections with their values and with those of their organisations also raise doubts about the value of ethical leadership. Employees may consider their leader a good ethical role model who exhibits, what Blanchard and Peale (1988) argued were, the cardinal virtues for organisational leaders: the five 'Ps' – pride, patience, prudence, persistence and perspective. The employees may not follow their leader's example to the extent of becoming role models themselves, or indeed even follow their leader's good example. The very act of putting a leader on an ethical pedestal may indicate that such good behaviour is only for those special enough to be leaders, and who can aspire to such ethical behaviour, and that other more ordinary people cannot possibly emulate them.

People do not simply 'have' values. Their values are constantly being redefined and prioritised as they find themselves in different situations and talking to different people. It is rare for people to be driven to such extremes that they discover what their value anchors, to misquote Schein, actually are. This analysis means those who believe an organisation should and can be managed so that everyone accepts the organisation's values are misguided. The term often used for such acceptance – buy-in – suggests a limited form of engagement. You only buy into something because you think it will be advantageous, not because you think it is right.

Many textbooks on business ethics have relatively little to say about values. When they are discussed, it is in the context of corporate codes of ethics or statements of organisational core values. The materials and arguments put forward in this chapter suggest that values may be central to people's thought processes when they are deciding what to say or do in response to an ethical issue. There is a paradox, however. Values can be used heuristically to *simplify* the process of making up one's mind, but the problem of which particular value to apply to an issue, when there are many values within organisations and society, all of which are valued but which conflict with one another, is *complex*.

The account of values as heuristics in this chapter may provide a good description of how people make decisions on ethical issues. This does not imply that this is how such decisions should be made. Indeed, if heuristics are more a matter of habit than conscious thought, they may merely be ways of avoiding complex value and ethical choices. Choices involve thinking about what we ought to do, not recalling what we normally do. In the next chapter we will explore these tensions between taking habitual stances on ethical issues, bred from our upbringing and experiences, and having to knowingly challenge our habits because the ethical matters we face contain novel circumstances or inconvenient facts.

Summary

In this chapter the following key points have been made:

- Ethics represents an intellectual approach to matters of morality at work whereas values represent a response based on beliefs that people hold with emotional attachment. Both perspectives need to be considered when dealing with business ethics matters.

- People may take one of five viewpoints on the role of values in business ethics: the traditional, the modernist, the neo-traditional, the postmodernist and the pragmatist. The position they take will reflect their responses to ethical issues at work.

- Which of these they adopt will depend, among other things, on their career history and experiences in organisation and on their education and training.

- Rational and analytic theories explain how decision making ought to be done.

- Heuristic theories probably explain how people make decisions in practice.

- Research into heuristics used to see them as sources of bias and distortion; the fast and frugal research programme sees them as efficient and effective procedures for decision making.

- Values probably act in a heuristic manner in decision making about ethical matters.

- Values can be used to limit and stop decision makers' searches for further information and options.

- In decisions such as setting priorities and deciding how to respond to wrongdoing in an organisation the problem is to choose which of many mutually exclusive values should be applied.

Typical assignments

1. Compare the traditional view of values, as exemplified, for example, by the work of Rokeach, with the view that values emerge from a process of sense making. Which view might be more helpful in understanding the role of values in management?

2. How might people with different sensibilities (traditional, modern, neo-traditional, postmodern and pragmatist) understand the nature and role of values in organisations?

3. What criticisms can be made of a postmodern view of organisations and management? Are they justified?

4. 'The commonly accepted idea that management should define and publish a set of organisational core values may create as many problems as it resolves.' Discuss vigorously.

5. Compare rational and heuristic models of decision making (that is to say contrast system 1 – thinking fast, with system 2 – thinking slow, as Kahneman (2011) terms them). How might the heuristic model be applicable to decision making on ethical matters?

6. Loyalty or integrity: which should be the most important to organisational employees?

7. Analyse a resource allocation decision that has been taken in an organisation by reference to the six resource allocation heuristics.

8. What role do emotions and value play in an individual's decision making on ethical matters?

Group activity 4.1

The Rice Orientation Test (ROT)

This test was devised by our colleague Chris Rice. It is designed to alert you to your approach to ethical issues. It uses a distinction between hedonism, moralism and pragmatism. It is not a statistically validated test and so its results must be used as a trigger for reflection and no more.

Think about each of the headings in the boxes in turn. Decide whether that term causes you to think in terms of:

A – right and wrong

B – pleasure or pain

C – success or failure

Then decide whether the concept (A, B or C) that you have chosen is of High (Hi), medium (Me) or low (Lo) importance in your thinking about the headword in the box.

Then place a tick in the appropriate cell of the grid within the box. If you think about the lottery in terms of pleasure or pain but that this is only of medium importance in your thinking, then place a tick in the central cell in the grid.

Carry on to complete all the boxes.

The National Lottery

	Hi	Me	Lo
A			
B			
C			

Trades Unions

	Hi	Me	Lo
A			
B			
C			

David Cameron

	Hi	Me	Lo
A			
B			
C			

Competition

	Hi	Me	Lo
A			
B			
C			

Richard Branson

	Hi	Me	Lo
A			
B			
C			

Management

	Hi	Me	Lo
A			
B			
C			

Higher education

	Hi	Me	Lo
A			
B			
C			

Manchester United FC

	Hi	Me	Lo
A			
B			
C			

Profit

	Hi	Me	Lo
A			
B			
C			

Gordon Brown			
	Hi	Me	Lo
A			
B			
C			

The Welfare State			
	Hi	Me	Lo
A			
B			
C			

Parliament			
	Hi	Me	Lo
A			
B			
C			

Scoring Instructions

Add up the number of ticks placed in each of the cells in the above matrices and transfer the totals into the table below. Calculate the weighted totals, and their percentage of the grand total, for each of the three rows in the table. The percentages show the relative importance to the respondent of moralism, hedonism and pragmatism.

Scoring ROT						
	Hi (N × 3)	Med	(N × 2)	Low (N × 1)	Total	%
A = Moralism						
B = Hedonism						
C = Pragmatism						

Discuss your results with your colleagues in the group.

Group activity 4.2

Obtain a copy of the *Cave Rescue Exercise*, which can be found in Woodcock (1979, 1989: 81) and in the appendix to Fisher (1998). Another version of this exercise can be found in Francis and Young (1979). Both are variations on a classic management game theme, of which *The Kidney Machine* is another popular version (Jones and Pfeiffer, 1974).

Divide into groups of between six and ten people and do the exercise.

Recommended further reading

Milton Rokeach's (1973) *The Nature of Human Values* is the classic work on the subject but pages 239–47 of Michael Billig's (1996) *Arguing and Thinking* provides a contrary view on the subject. The whole book is worth reading because it offers a new perspective based on the idea that thinking is entirely an argumentative process in which there are no fixed points, only constant debates, both within our heads and with other people. An implication of this is that the arguments never come to a definitive end, although people might have the last word on a particular occasion. This view has interesting implications for the role of values in business ethics that are followed up in Chapters 5 and 6. Terry Eagleton (1996) is not a management writer but he provides an intriguing introduction to postmodernism, *The Illusions of Postmodernism*. It is particularly relevant to the themes of this chapter because he treats postmodernism as a sensibility, a particular way of looking at the world, rather than as a set of philosophical ideas, although he also discusses many of these with a degree of humour. If you want to read a critique of the more (mostly French) extreme writings in a postmodernist mode then Sokal and Bricmont's (2003) *Intellectual Impostures* is good fun. An interesting book that explores management issues from a postmodern perspective is Gibson Burrell's *Pandemonium: Towards a Retro-organizational Theory* (1997, London: Sage). It has the distinction of being capable of being read back to front as well as in the normal direction.

For a wider account of how values can be fragmented or integrated in societies, see Jonathan Friedman's (1994) *Cultural Identity and Global Process*. On the topic of the role of values in management, see Paul Griseri's (1998) *Managing Values*. There is an excessive number of 'how to manage with values' books. Two worth looking at are Rabindra Nath Kanungo and Manuel Mendonca's (1996) *The Ethical Dimensions of Leadership* and Stephen Covey's (1991) *Principle-centred Leadership*.

If you are interested in the role of heuristics in decision making, see G. Gigerenzer, P. Todd and the ABC Research Group's (1999) *Simple Heuristics That Make us Smart*, Oxford: Oxford University Press. Daniel Kahneman, who won a Nobel prize for his work on heuristics has published a book on the topic for the general reader; D. Kahneman (2011), *Thinking Fast and Slow,* London: Allen Lane Penguin. On the topic of the role of values in management, see P. Griseri (1998) *Managing Values*, London: Palgrave.

Useful websites

Topic	Website provider	URL
A useful overview on values and the issues of moral education and development	Huitt, W. (2004). Values. Educational Psychology Interactive. Valdosta, GA: Valdosta State University	http://www.edpsycinteractive.org/topics/affect/values.html
Home page of the ABC Centre, which researches heuristics and decision making	Centre for Adaptive Behaviour and Cognition	http://www.mpib-berlin.mpg.de/en/forschung/abc/index.htm
A good interactive guide to heuristics and decision making	Elliott Hammer	http://cat.xula.edu/thinker/decisions/heuristics/
Thinking about risk. Information on some of the heuristics of judgment	Centre for Informed Decision Making	http://www.cygnus-group.com/CIDM/risk.html
A very simple interactive questionnaire for identifying your personal values	MAS Management Advisory Service	http://www.mas.org.uk/quest/ivp2.htm

CHAPTER 5

Individual responses to ethical situations

Chapter at a glance

Chapter contents

- Learning outcomes
- Introduction
- Categories of response to ethical issues
- Competing stances: the possibility of cognitive dissonance
- Influences on choice of stance
- Reflections
- Summary

Case studies

- Case study 5.1 Disabled access
- Case study 5.2 Particularisation and categorisation

Activities and exercises

- Podcast 5.1 Visa frustration
- Discussion activity 5.1 Discussion based on Case study 5.1
- Activity 5.1 Downsizing: An instrument on perceptions of ethical considerations in human resource management and management accountancy
- Activity 5.2 Examples of particularisation and categorisation
- Activity 5.3 Scoring the locus of control scale
- Typical assignments
- Group activity 5.1
- Recommended further reading
- Useful websites

Learning outcomes

Having read this chapter and completed its associated activities, readers should be able to:

- Explain the different ways in which people may respond to ethical issues at work.
- Use this understanding to think about their own reactions to ethical issues.
- Explain the processes of categorisation and particularisation in ethical thinking.
- Explain the range of factors that influence how people respond to ethical issues at work.

Introduction

This chapter concerns people's responses to ethical issues at work. Such matters are not uncommon. A survey conducted by CIMA (2008: 20) reported that 27 per cent of finance professionals reported experiencing pressure to compromise ethical standards. The previous chapter dealt only with ethical thinking. Responses to ethical situations obviously involve thinking about the issue but also go beyond it. Responses include what people say, how they say it and how they behave. There are two main cognitive processes involved in choosing responses, categorisation and particularisation (Billig, 1996). The first of these involves putting an issue into a box or category and saying, 'That is the way in which I will deal with this matter'. These categories are often based on values. Someone might decide, for example, that an issue is a matter of following the core values set by an organisation, or that an issue is a question of loyalty. However, the particulars of a situation might make someone think that the categorisation is not right. It is the details of a situation that make people debate under which value an issue should be categorised or indeed whether it should be put in a separate category of its own.

The first section of the chapter describes and explains different categories of ethical response. Later the chapter explores the possibility that people do not adopt a single categorisation but debate with themselves and with others about a range of competing possible categorisations. The exercise in Activity 5.2 later in the chapter also raises the possibility that people's categorisations may change over time as they become aware of new information and different perspectives on the issue. The third section of the chapter discusses the range of factors that may influence how someone chooses to categorise an issue. The final section summarises the arguments of the chapter and gives the reader opportunities to reflect upon them.

Categories of response to ethical issues

In this section, we will use a matrix to describe the categories, let us call them stances, that people at work may use to classify ethical issues. The model is shown in Figure 5.1. Before the eight categories it contains can be described, we will explain the two dimensions that form the matrix.

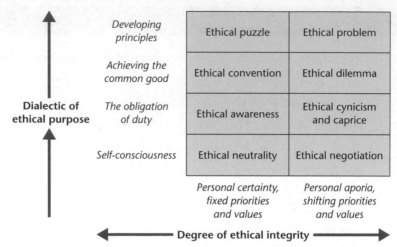

Figure 5.1 Managers' perceptions of ethical issues – a framework
Source: Fisher and Rice (1999)

Ethical integrity, the horizontal axis in Figure 5.1

The dimension of ethical integrity will be described first. The position at the extreme left of the horizontal axis in Figure 5.1 represents clarity and certainty about values. A person at this point on the scale sees moral issues in a straightforward way, which helps them to know what should be done in a situation or how an issue should be analysed and resolved. A person at the extreme right of the dimension, however, is more likely to be confused or even aporetic (aporetic means finding a situation so intrinsically contradictory that it is not possible to know what to do). A person in this condition will find the plurality of views on an issue difficult to reconcile and they will often change their minds. If integrity is defined as the congruence, or fit, between a person's thoughts on an issue, then the left-hand column in Figure 5.1 represents a high degree of integrity and the right-hand column a low degree of integrity.

The dialectic of ethical purpose, the vertical axis in Figure 5.1

The vertical dimension represents stages in the dialectical development of a personal and conscious view of right and wrong. It models a developing personal responsibility for recognising the presence of ethical issues at work and addressing them. In the initial stage, at the origin of the framework – self-consciousness – a person sees their moral universe as a personal one. They accept responsibility for themselves but wish to remain apart from ethical issues in the wider world. They show this unwillingness to accept a moral responsibility by turning a blind eye. This position is termed quietism, which is the resignation of self to achieve contentment. It is a disengagement from the ethical problems of the world. But an individual's moral isolation is an ideal: it cannot be sustained; it is contradicted by the clamorous demands from others, bosses, colleagues, customers and so on, that they become involved.

> **DEFINITION**
>
> The **dialectic** is a method of analysis (associated with the German philosopher Hegel (1770–1831)) in which an initial, formal concept (thesis) is challenged by practical contradictions contained within it (antithesis) until a synthesis comes about that overcomes, or transcends, the tensions between thesis and antithesis. The thesis is a blank ideal because it has not been expressed in reality. It is when it confronts social reality that the messy detail of life negates the formal ideal. The synthesis negates this negation and the dialectic moves to a new, positive stage. The synthesis does not abolish the tensions but moves beyond them. The synthesis becomes a thesis and the cycle begins again.

Cross reference   A detailed example that shows how the dialectic works is given on p. 440.

The contradiction at the self-consciousness stage is between a person's sense of their own moral worth and their defensive refusal to take a moral stand on ethical issues. Ethical duty is the synthesis of this contradiction. People at this stage take a stand and, without much critical reflection, do what their backgrounds and their consciences tell them is their duty. However, doing one's duty can lead to an awareness that others have contrary conceptions of what their duty is.

> Unreflective duty can take its imperatives from the dooms of Zeus, from priest or parent, from the custom of a tribe or city, and act in peace and faith. But the first conflict unveils an Antigone and the question 'Whose standard?' soon brings down all standards.
>
> (Mabbott, 1967: 44)

Antigone, in Greek myth, followed her conscience by giving a ritual burial, against custom and the decree of King Creon, to her brother Polynices, who had tried to usurp the throne. The formal idea of doing one's duty is undermined by uncertainty about what that duty is in any particular circumstance. This tension causes this stage to be expressed either as a sincerely, but uncritically, held principle or its opposite – cynicism.

The lack of grounding, or legitimisation, of the idea of duty leads to the next stage in the dialectic, which is the search for the common good as a basis for moral certainty. In this phase, people try to reconcile competing ethical demands by using such notions as organisational values and mission statements, economic utility or the public interest. This stage involves difficult debates about values and priorities. Consequently attempts to create a consensus or a common ethical convention constantly threaten to dissolve into ethical plurality and dilemmas.

When, and if, attempts at consensus building stumble or fail, a person may move into the final phase of the vertical dimension. In this phase, through self-analysis and debate, people create their own set of moral precepts and values. At this level on the dimension people are aware of the plurality and fragmentation of the moral world and make choices about how to respond to it. They may either take a postmodern route, and learn to live with an ungrounded moral plurality by playing with problems, or they may seek to reintegrate the fragments by reason and categorisation, as if they were doing a jigsaw puzzle.

Now that the dimensions in Figure 5.1 have been described, the eight categories of ethical issue can be defined in relation to them. The categories are important because they define the range of possible reactions to a moral issue.

The ethical categories

Ethical neutrality

People put ethical issues into the category of ethical neutrality when they argue that nothing should be done about an issue that troubles them. There may be many reasons for this response. People may have applied ethical bracketing (Jackall, 1988) or ethical closure (Kärreman and Alvesson, 1999: 10–11). This causes them to suspend their normal ethical standards when these would obstruct them in getting the job done. This may lead people to argue that an issue, such as redundancy for example, has no moral dimension and should be seen as a practical question. De George (1999: 112) identified the range of excusing conditions that people may use to justify their neutrality. These included the arguments of inability (you cannot be expected to save a drowning person if you cannot swim) and ignorance (you cannot be culpable if you were unaware of the consequences of not taking action). Though sometimes neutrality can just be an expedient refusal to engage.

Ethical awareness

Ethical awareness is a category of ethical responses that causes a person to feel uncomfortable because an issue offends against their instinctively held values. At this stage the individual has an intuitive knowledge of what their duty is. As Mabbott (1967: 45) argued,

> everyone knows what in any particular set of circumstances his duty is. . . . I know my duty in each particular case and that I can give no reasons, nor are there any, why I should assert this act or that to be my duty, except the self-evidence of every particular instance.

In the stage of duty a person knows what is right but cannot say why. Their reaction to an issue may only involve making their feelings known but it may extend to active opposition to the proposal under consideration. Ethical awareness is the same as emotivism, which is discussed in Chapter 2. A feature of emotivism, which is important in the context of ethical awareness, is the apparent irresolubility of moral disagreements as one person's statements of their values, in relation to an action, person or situation, contradict others' value statements.

Ethical convention

An issue is allocated to the category of ethical convention when it is thought that it can best be resolved by applying accepted norms to it. They may be social norms, the expectations and standards of professional behaviour, or the constraints of organisational cultures and subcultures. A feature of conventional ethical norms is that they are informal and unwritten or, if they are written, they are expressed in general terms and not as detailed prescriptions. In one incident that was described to us the respondent, a personnel manager, believed there was a norm in her organisation that one should not turn against people who had come looking for professional advice and assistance. She consequently felt a little guilt when she suspended a manager who had initially come to seek her help in disciplining a member of his staff, but who was later ensnared in the investigations he had initiated.

Ethical puzzle

A puzzle is a conundrum, such as a mathematical teaser or a crossword puzzle, to which there is a technically correct or best answer. Arriving at the correct solution may be no easy matter, involving much hard thought and work, but the effort is justifiable because a best answer can be obtained. A puzzle can only exist in a clear moral context in which there is little argument about the values appropriate to its resolution. The wish to transform ethical difficulties into puzzles can be illustrated by those who argue that if only we had, in the National Health Service in the UK for example, better information (on clinical effectiveness, public views on medical priorities, costs and hospital activity rates) and better decision-making software to process the data, then questions of medical priorities could be settled technically, optimally, without recourse to messy political arguments about competing values in which, quite commonly, the one who argues the loudest gets the most resources (*see* Case study 2.10, p. 65).

A decision to see an issue as a puzzle requires the puzzle solver to place the issue within a coherent moral framework and to ignore the demands of contrary values and perspectives. This often enables a puzzle solver to construct detailed mechanisms and steps (rules, procedures and techniques) for resolving an issue.

Ethical problems

A problem is a conundrum to which there is no optimum solution. It may be necessary to take action on a problem, but the action will not remove the difficulty. A problem may be ameliorated or modified but it is unlikely to be resolved. Problems are complicated entities that form, develop and disappear according to their own dynamics. An issue is likely to be categorised as a problem because it involves many different values, and principles which, when taken in isolation, make perfect sense, but which, when taken together, fall into conflict. In these situations, there has to be a debate between the differing conceptions of value, and part of the difficulty, for people who see issues as ethical problems, is to ensure that the arguments in the debate are conducted rigorously and fairly. The discussion of discourse ethics in Chapter 3 is relevant to this stance.

Ethical dilemma

A dilemma is a perplexing state involving difficult or unpleasant choices. The options presented by a dilemma are often unpleasant because they demand a choice between conventions. If the person decides to act according to one set of conventional norms or rules then they will break another set of expectations. As conventions are social constructs, it follows that dilemmas are essentially social and political issues. Breaking out of a dilemma necessitates choosing to support one group, by accepting their rules and values, but annoying another group by offending against theirs. It is not unsurprising therefore that categorising an issue as a dilemma can lead to indecision and inaction.

Ethical cynicism and caprice

Cynicism emerges when ethical duty turns bitter. In the category of ethical awareness a person tries to do what their conscience tells them is right. The cynical person, however, has given up on this aim and become, as in the original definition of the word, like a surly dog. The cynic believes that all ethical issues will be resolved in ways that primarily meet the personal and private interests of those involved. Sometimes, the cynic thinks, it would be better to leave matters to capricious chance than to try to improve things. The cynics' aim, apart from maintaining their safely detached position, is to cast blame on those who are trying to deal with an issue.

Ethical negotiation

Ethical negotiation is the process followed when someone is seeking to protect their self-interest (keeping their heads down and getting on with their work), by remaining ethically neutral, but find themselves caught between powerful groups with different views and values. Ethical negotiation therefore is a search for consensus or compromise between differing positions. This category is not concerned with the rightness of a decision but with the correctness of the process used to arrive at it. Put another way, the morality of an action is ignored; only a broad acceptability of an action, as determined by voting, opinion polling, consensus seeking, deal cutting and negotiation, is required. Responding to opinion becomes more important than doing the right thing. This was a barb frequently thrown at the Labour Party during the 2001 election campaign as it responded to feedback from focus groups. This category involves defending oneself by responding to the demands of competing interest groups.

The stances in practice

The model presented in Figure 5.1 represents a range of stances or reactions to an ethical issue at work. However, the descriptions of them are very general and summary. They would be difficult to identify in everyday life. Table 5.1 identifies the sorts of arguments and values, arising from each of the stances, that people would use in their discussions.

Competing stances: the possibility of cognitive dissonance

It would be convenient to claim that people opted for one of the eight categories just described, when dealing with an ethical issue, and kept to it. In practice, people may change their categorisation of an ethical issue; indeed they may hold conflicting views in their minds at the same time. This latter possibility will be explained first.

Table 5.1 A summary of the eight categories of ethical response

Stances	Ethical perspectives based on this stance	Way of thinking about the issue	Likely actions
Ethical neutrality	Keeping out of trouble/jobsworth	People decide to ignore what they see as an injustice because to raise the issue would cause them trouble.	Inaction and keeping quiet.
	Getting the job done	For example, a team leader might choose not to respond to concerns raised about the unethical behaviour of some staff working on a contract, because it would have disrupted the staff scheduling that had been planned with much difficulty.	
Ethical awareness	Dignity of persons	A sort of pop Kantianism, which is triggered when it is thought that people are used as means and that their proper dignity is not respected.	Assertion of, and acting upon, one's values. Expressing surprise that others may see things differently.
	The importance of truth	The moral imperative of always telling the truth.	
	Just desserts	Rewarding people according to their merits. A form of deservingness. One respondent, working in government, regarded the catering management as feckless and shed no tears when they were threatened by competitive tendering; but he thought it unjust when the laundry, which the respondent believed provided an excellent service, lost out to an external bidder.	
Ethical convention	Professional norms	The argument that people should adhere to professional and organisational norms and standards.	Seeking advice and help from others on what the normal and acceptable response would be. Applying norms and conventions.
	Fairness	Keeping a level playing field and being fair, treating all the same.	
Ethical puzzle	Policies, rules and procedures	The belief that things are best kept ethical procedures and proper by sticking to the rules and regulations and not bending them to allow for special cases.	Applying the rules of an organisation or institution.
	Utility	Belief in the maximisation of an objective or of utility. This is the philosophy of utilitarianism.	Calculating the consequences of an action. Acting to resolve the issue on the basis that they have the correct or best solution. The assumption is that, the correct action having been taken, this will be an end to the matter.

▶

Table 5.1 Continued

Stances	Ethical perspectives based on this stance	Way of thinking about the issue	Likely actions
Ethical problem	Moral judgment	The application of moral judgment rather than the moral calculation of utility. Moral judgment, the ability to define the ethical mean proportionately is acquired through the development of virtues. One respondent argued that ethical codes were unnecessary because the organisation's staff were virtuous and honest.	Clarifying how the conflicts between different values would lead to different actions or decisions. Acting upon one's best judgment.
	Learning from moral exemplars	The argument that ethical lapses can be temporarily tolerated if people have the opportunity to learn new and better ways.	
Ethical dilemma	Personal relationships	In a wicked world one should concentrate on the development of personal relationships. See Case study 6.1 for an example.	The emphasis of action is on maintaining discussion about the issue rather than seeking closure on it. When conflicts about issues are serious, it is important to maintain good manners and interpersonal relationships.
	Ironic liberalism and pragmatism	This notion is taken from Rorty (1989). It is a view on how sanity can be maintained in a world where values are ungrounded. The key techniques are the separation of private and public domains and giving priority to 'keeping the conversation going' (Mounce, 1997: 197, 207).	
	Relativism	The argument that different cultures have different moral precepts and that what may be unethical in one culture, or organisation, may not be so in another.	
	Holism	Trying to take the whole position into account. At its most extreme it is like the Buddhist belief that great effort is needed to see beyond the illusion of fragmentation to the unity beyond (Kjonstad and Willmott, 1995: 457).	

Table 5.1 Continued

Stances	Ethical perspectives based on this stance	Way of thinking about the issue	Likely actions
Ethical cynicism	Façadism	One person thought others wanted to be seen to follow the proper recruitment procedures even though the person they wanted to have the job had been decided beforehand. This grid includes being economical with the truth and the belief that business involves games playing and bluffing (Carr, 1968).	The cynic will withdraw from any action or decision but will snipe from the sidelines at any action or decision that others may have taken.
	Personal gain and selfishness	The argument that people are distorting selfishness situations and procedures to their own private advantage.	
Ethical negotiation	Complex politics	'There are high-level politics concerning this issue to which I am not privy – so I keep my own views to myself.' A person working with this perspective tries to steer a compromise route through the competing demands of different groups. The problems of allocating scarce car-parking spaces at work are often a good example.	Seeking out others' views and supporting or acquiescing in the wishes of the most powerful.
	'Dodgy deals'	Bending rules, or acquiescing in rule bending, to accommodate the interest of powerful groups.	

Let us consider how someone might hold conflicting views. When someone is thinking about an ethical issue it can be speculated that there are at least four perspectives from which the issue can be addressed:

■ What is it that is ethically or morally wrong about a situation? What has triggered the recognition of the issue as an ethical one? What in other words has triggered their *conscience*?

■ What ideally should be done about the situation? When they apply their ethical reasoning to the situation what will they think is the proper course of action?

■ What do they think all the other interested persons and parties think about the situation? What are the demands and expectations of the other stakeholders in the situation? Consequently, what, in practical terms, can be done about it given all the constraints and complexities of the 'real' world? What are their *options for action*?

■ What action do people actually take, or do they decide to do nothing?

The theory of cognitive dissonance claims that people try to make all their perspectives fit neatly together in their own minds. Instead it will be argued that people may hold contradictory views. Each of these perspectives can be discussed in more detail.

Conscience

Aspects of an issue might cause some pain or difficulty because they are thought to be wrong. This feeling may be termed conscience, defined as an anxiety caused by the belief that a thought or act is wrong. Conscience is the starting point for the analysis of people's response to ethical incidents. It is conscience that causes, as one of our interviewees phrased it, 'the ethical twinges' that lead us to identify an issue as an ethical one. Conscience, or the superego, to use a psychoanalytic term, is the function that keeps bad impulses in check. It does this by drenching the mind with anxiety whenever temptation is on hand and by creating feelings of remorse and humiliation when bad impulses are succumbed to. Conscience does not, however, tell us what is right; that is more the province of social norms and ethical reasoning.

Ethical reasoning

Ethical reasoning is a person's rational, or rationalised, analysis of what they think should be done in relation to an incident or issue (Snell, 1993). If conscience defines the problem then ethical reasoning identifies the solution. It is the actions (or inactions) that the person thinks, on the basis of their values and analysis, they should take.

The demands and expectations of others and options for action

From the perspective of the demands and expectations of others, a person undertakes a mini 'stakeholder analysis'. They attribute motives to others from their speech and actions; and these influence the options for action thought to be available. It is important to note that this perspective cannot pretend to know what the other's motives actually are. It is focused on what the person thinks the others involved in the story are thinking and why they are thinking it. If conscience is the expression of the superego then the perspective of options for action represents the ego. In psychoanalysis, the ego is the instinct for self-preservation. It is the aspect of the self that is aware of the external world and rationalises how one should act within it. This aspect of ethical decision making therefore is about deciding and willing an action.

Action

The final perspective is the action that people take and their justification for taking it. Of course, the position taken may be to take no action.

These four perspective can be mapped, broadly, onto Rest's (1986) model of ethical decision making. His four stages are:

- recognising the ethical aspects or significance of a situation. This is similar to the triggering of conscience.

- thinking about what should be done in the situation in order to be ethical. This is much the same as the ethical reasoning perspective.

- ethical intention, which is the willing of an action or in other words determining to take an action. This is similar to the perspective proposed here of choosing an option for action based upon a consideration of the demands imposed by all the other groups involved.

- ethical action, which of course is the same as the final perspective of ethical action.

These four perspectives in Figure 5.1 and the eight categories of ethical response can be used to analyse someone's (or one's own) position on any particular ethical issue. An illustration of how this might be done is shown in Figure 5.2 – an

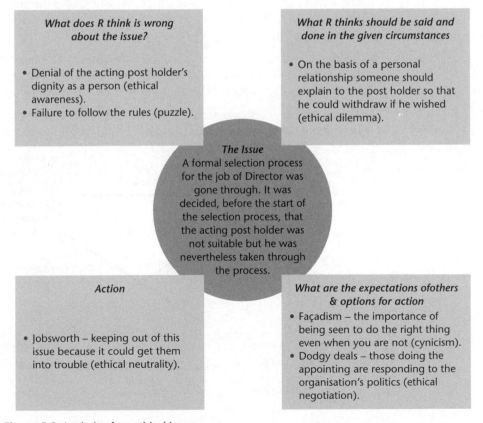

Figure 5.2 Analysis of an ethical issue

example of an ethical incident described by a research interviewee (R) and analysed using the four perspectives.

Conflicts between perspectives

The above example illustrates how a person can hold different views on an issue at the same time. People may think that something is wrong, and suffer pangs of conscience about it, but simultaneously believe that it may not be ethically proper to do anything about it. It is also clear, as Snell (1993) pointed out, that just because someone is capable of thinking at an advanced ethical level it does not mean that this will be reflected in his or her actions. There is no necessary connection between reasoning and action.

When people experience conflict because they adopt contradictory stances at some or all of the four perspective points, they may experience a number of states, as shown in Figure 5.3. We argue that if people adopt different stances in the four perspectives, which clash with each other, then certain consequences can be predicted. Six types of conflict have been identified and they are shown in Figure 5.3.

■ Type 1 conflict occurs when conscience and ethical reasoning are at odds and this produces feelings of anxiety. There was no type 1 conflict in the illustration in Figure 5.2 because, although there are differences between the respondent's conscience and ethical reasoning (denial of personal dignity and personal relationships), a personal approach would have restored the personal dignity of the acting director.

■ A type 2 conflict could be seen in the illustration. The respondent took a position of neutrality on an issue her conscience told her was wrong and this might be expected to produce feelings of guilt, shame or remorse.

■ The illustration also suggests a type 3 conflict because there was disagreement between what the respondent thought should be done and the position of those

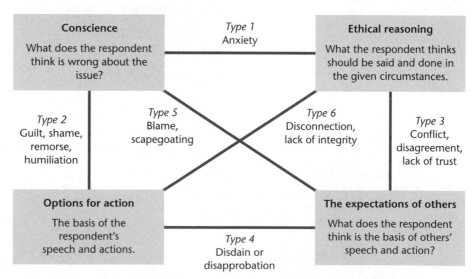

Figure 5.3 The consequences of conflicting perspectives: six types of conflict

conducting the selection process. The respondent thought the selection procedure should have been properly applied with no prior decision being taken about the suitability of any candidate. The senior managers, however, were happy to maintain a façade of keeping the rules and spirit of the recruitment policy while ensuring that the acting director did not get the job. This conflict might be expected to reduce the respondent's trust of the senior managers. If they were capable of 'shafting' one individual then they might just as easily do it to others.

- The respondent's position, in the illustration, of neutrality in the 'action' box prevented a type 4 clash with the views of others.

- There was a type 5 conflict in the illustration because the respondent blamed the others for behaving wrongly.

- Type 6 conflict, in which a person acts contrary to their ethical reasoning, will damage people's sense of integrity because they cannot consider their thoughts and actions to be of a piece. This was the situation in the illustration because the respondent did not do what her ethical reasoning told her to do.

Podcast 5.1	**Visa frustration**
	Podcasts explaining how today's business news and issues relate to the topics discussed here will be updated in an ongoing process. Podcast 5.1 uses an everyday business problem, obtaining a business visa, to explore the use of the model in Figure 5.3. To listen to this podcast, other archived podcasts or recent additions, please visit the companion website at www.pearsoned.co.uk/fisherlovellvalerosilva.

Festinger's theory of cognitive dissonance (1957) held that the consequences of holding conflicting ideas in our heads were so unpleasant that we jerk our attitudes and actions into line so that they all fit comfortably together. Billig (1996: 202) pointed out that dissonant thoughts are not in themselves a cognitive problem. They only become an issue if an external opponent makes a public criticism of them. Even in this case, it can be argued that, if the dissonances are trivial and not to be taken seriously, then the contradictory thoughts need not be a problem to the possessor of the ambiguity. Many may find little difficulty in taking different stances from each perspective.

Case study 5.1	**Disabled access**

Extract from an interview with a personnel manager
The fact [is] that both sites are not access friendly in a way that they would need to be for a lot of disabled people. So we've had a small audit of access and mobility type issues. You think it's small when you start out and then you get into it and there are major changes that would be required and therefore the money comes into it and how much we should be spending. So there's fairly wide-ranging discussions going on at the moment about whether any of those changes should be made up front of employing anybody, or whether we wait to be pushed along that line ▶

by the employment of somebody. The law says you can obviously wait for the latter. There're two distinct camps. Those in slightly more senior positions, those with the clout, are favouring small changes now and delaying big spend on bigger changes until there's a need because we already employ a couple of individuals who fall into the definition of disabled, and both are perfectly well able to carry out their jobs with the arrangements that we have currently. But then we do have some people who strongly believe that we should make ourselves more overtly accessible and as a result we would attract a greater range of people.

Well, we have a working party set up and there are some people on it who are motivated by different things. Some are not often invited on to a working party and have taken the issue to heart so strongly that they feel that you should do something with it. Others have members of their family, or people that they know, who have disabilities and are therefore fighting from a particular corner for it. You do get into a moral argument with some people about, you know, it's the proper thing to do, we should do it. But there's quite a lot of proper things to do and at some point in time they have to be slotted into some sort of order, to deal with them. I would argue that there are a number of lower cost areas that could be addressed that would make us [more accessible], for instance we do not have ramp access to our reception. Now that wouldn't be a big deal but would be very visible and would then allow those with access problems to get into us. We could then move from there. We tend to have a lot of people that make assumptions about the nature of disabilities of people and assume that anybody with [a] disabled nametag is in a wheelchair and therefore everything should be wheelchair related. When we know it's not like that at all. So I would much rather get into some of the more obvious things like somewhere to park that's not too far away from the front. A ramp so that people can actually get in. Some of the problems we have are huge, like upstairs [you have to go] round goodness knows how many corridors, downstairs and back up again to get to the canteen. And that's the only place where people can buy food. But on the basis that we employ a couple [of] males already who have fairly strong disabilities we can get round it. No I don't think it's easy. It's particularly difficult. I recently popped back from work to attend a conference at which one of the lads, who is disabled, was arguing very, very strongly for spending all this money – big sums of money; and it's a very sensible argument. He delivers it with force. I mean at the end of the day [he was] saying that you have your independence and you should therefore do everything to ensure other people have independence because all a disabled person wants is independence. You should therefore facilitate that however you can. Yes it is hard to argue against but at some point things have to take their place. It's hard to argue against the fact that the best person for the job could cost ten grand a year more than you've actually got available. You know you could get the value for that person but somewhere it's got to stop. It is hard and I don't sit on the working party personally but obviously I've got quite a lot to do with what they're up to. I do know that they go round in circles on that one quite a lot and they will do. We have a policy decided and we don't have a disability budget. Budgets are set for the next twelve months and have been for quite some time so it is a question of saying well if you spend the money on X it doesn't get spent on Y. Or finding it from somewhere else, well we're always looking for money from somewhere else for something.

Discussion activity 5.1	Discussion based on Case study 5.1

Describe, using the categories in Table 5.1, the respondent's view of the problem described, in the interview above, under the headings of conscience, ethical reasoning, the positions of others involved and practical action. The issue concerned making a building appropriate for disabled people to use.

A suggested analysis is shown in Figure 5.4. In this figure, the informant's perspectives on the central issue of access improvements have been shown by quoting her words and then by categorising them using the eight ethical stances and the list of values shown in Table 5.1. The analysis could have been done more simply without recourse to the eight stances, but their use clarifies any conflicts between the four perspectives.

The contradictions between the respondent's perspectives are indicated by the arrows in Figure 5.4, which shows type 1, 2, 3 and 4 tensions. Her conscience informed her that there was a major wrong that ought to be righted, but her ethical reasoning suggested that it would be wrong to do everything that needed to be done. Her conscience had sympathy for the views expressed by the member of staff but her ethical reasoning did not. So her actions (in sympathy with her reasoning rather than with her conscience) contradicted what she thought the staff were telling her. This pattern of conflicts and congruencies might be described as melancholic acceptance. With regret she thought it wrong to do what her conscience, and the consciences of others, demanded (Fisher, 1999).

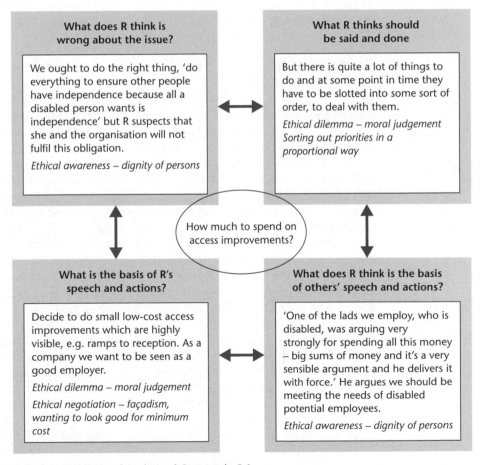

Figure 5.4 A suggested analysis of Case study 5.1

Activity 5.1	*Downsizing*: An instrument on perceptions of ethical considerations in human resource management and management accountancy

Go to the companion website for this book (www.pearsoned.co.uk /fisherlovellvalerosilva) where you will find both an interactive, web-based version of the activity as and a hard-copy version that you can print off. The interactive version calculates your scores for you. If you use the hard copy you will have to do the scoring yourself. You can plot your scores on the scoring matrix in Figure 5.5.

Shifting stances

The discussion in the previous section has illustrated how a person might take potentially conflicting perspectives on an ethical issue and hold them simultaneously. In the changing circumstances of a working life it might be that people give emphasis to different perspectives as the situation develops and more particulars become known. Others, of course, might adopt an initial stance and then keep to it without distraction. This is the issue that is explored in Activity 5.1.

Some research findings from the use of *Downsizing*

Downsizing has been completed by a large sample of financial professionals and accountants and by a smaller sample of human resource (HR) managers (Fisher and Lovell, 2000). The results are shown in Figure 5.6. You might wish to compare your results with those of these two samples.

The great majority of both accountants and HR specialists began by taking a neutral position in Section 1. The inference would seem to be that redundancy is a common part of organisational life and there is no reason to suspect there are any particular moral issues arising from the situation. In Section 2, doubts are sown about the ethical status of the organisation in the case study. A narrow majority of the HR specialists changed their view of the case, took a position of ethical awareness and began to protest against the redundancies. The majority of accountants continued to take a neutral stance although a minority shifted to the ethical awareness position. In Section 3, respondents were given the opportunity to adopt a conventional response to the situation (reducing numbers through voluntary redundancy) and the majority of both accountants and HR specialists took this option.

The opportunity for a conventional response is removed in Section 4 when Chris withdraws his offer to take voluntary redundancy. The respondents are given sufficient information to treat the problem as a puzzle. A number of criteria that can be used to select candidates for redundancy are provided and all the team members are ranked against each of the criteria. These can be used to make a rational choice of who should be made redundant. Over 80 per cent of the accountants, and over three-quarters of the HR specialists, took this opportunity and used the information provided to choose the most suitable candidate for redundancy. A small percentage of respondents (although fewer accountants than HR specialists) recognised that it was not possible to identify an optimum candidate for redundancy when all of the proposed criteria were applied. Put simply, there was no candidate who was the best choice on all the criteria. These respondents took an ethical problem stance that recognised the conflicts between the values represented by the different criteria.

Further information is provided in Section 5 of the exercise. This reports a clash between incompatible values. Those respondents who chose a candidate for redundancy on apparently rational grounds are told that the choice raises other problems and ethical difficulties. Some accountants, as a consequence, did move their stance to that of ethical problem but most ignored the new complexities and continued to see the issue as an ethical puzzle. The majority of HR specialists, however, did take a new, ethical problem, stance. Further complexities are introduced in Section 6. Most of the accountants still saw the issue as a puzzle. A fifth of the HR specialists now saw the issue as a dilemma; a third saw it as a problem but the single biggest group of the HR specialists returned to a puzzle stance. The pattern was the same in the last section of the exercise, in which some information was provided that was intended to encourage some to take a position of ethical negotiation. Only a small proportion of respondents did so.

In the latter half of the exercise, most accountants stuck with their ethical puzzle stance, no matter what ethical difficulties they were presented with. Most of the HR specialists did initially respond to these difficulties but they subsequently returned to a pragmatic ethical puzzle stance. You can see from the scoring matrix (Figure 5.5) that the results for the second part of the exercise are labelled 'forced hard choices', whereas those in the first part are termed 'espoused stances'. Espoused values are those that people would wish others to think that they hold. These are often contrasted with those values that people use in practice, especially when under pressure.

Categorisation and particularisation and the eight stances

The results from *Downsizing* suggest that some people pigeonhole an issue under one category, and do not change their minds; other people change their views as the issue unfolds. This phenomenon can be explained by using the concepts of categorisation and particularisation that were mentioned at the start of the chapter. The emphasis in this chapter so far has been on categorisation but the idea of particularisation will be useful in explaining the processes that cause people to take different stances on ethical issues.

Categorisation is the process of placing an object within a general category or schema. Psychologists have claimed it is the fundamental process of thinking. As Cantor et al. (1982: 34) claimed:

> Categorisation schemes allow us to structure and give coherence to our general knowledge about people and the social world, providing expectations about typical patterns of behaviour and the range of likely variation between types of people and their characteristic actions and attributes.

The terms category and schema are similar in meaning. However, it is generally claimed that schemata are more general and complex than categories. It is

Use the decision rules in each box to allocate responses to an ethical category

Espoused stances and values

Forced hard choices: stances and values in practices

	Section 1	Section 2	Section 3	Section 4	Section 5	Section 6	Section 7
Ethical Cynicism				If 10 ticked	If 15 is Chris	If 19 ticked	If none of 22/23/24 or 25 is ticked & if 26 ticked
Ethical Negotiation							If 22, 23, 24 or 25 ticked & if 26 ticked
Ethical Dilemma						If 18 ticked or if 17 is different from 15 or if 20 ticked	If 26 ticked, or if 21 is the same as 17, or different from 15
Ethical Problem				If 14 ticked	If 16 ticked, or 15 different from person chosen in section 4, or if 14 ticked	If 17 is the same as 15, or if a choice is made after choosing 14	If 21 same as 15
Ethical Puzzle			If 08 ticked	If 10 or 11 or 12 or 13 ticked	If 15 the is same as person chosen in section 4	If 17 is the same as person chosen in section 4	If 21 same as person chosen in section 4
Ethical Convention			If 09a ticked	Name of person chosen	Name of person chosen	Name of person chosen	Name of person chosen
Ethical Awareness	If 03 ticked	If 06 ticked	If 07 ticked				
Ethical Neutrality	If 02 ticked	If 05 ticked					
Ethical Cynicism	If 01 ticked	If 04 ticked	If 09b ticked				

Figure 5.5 Scoring matrix for Downsizing

possible, for example, to see schemata as formed from collections of categories. On its own, however, Billig (1996: 154) argued, categorisation can lead to bureaucratic and prejudiced forms of thinking. The story (which may be an urban myth) of the doctor who would not give emergency treatment to a person who had a heart attack on the pavement in front of the hospital, because his employer's liability insurance did not extend beyond the hospital premises, illustrates the typical ethical costs of bureaucracy. The research finding (Galton and Delafield, 1981), that primary school teachers' ways of talking to and questioning pupils they had judged to be low performing led such pupils to do less well than they ought, identified the prejudicial impact of categorisation.

Illustrations of the bureaucracy and prejudice that can emerge from categorisation were found when we interviewed people about ethical incidents they had experienced at work. In some cases, the rigidity of bureaucracy was at the organisation's (rather than the employee's or customer's) cost. In one incident a young marketing manager had been partly disabled by a stroke that prevented him from driving. His job required him to work on two widely separated sites and the company paid his taxi fares and overnight costs. In other circumstances, a manager of his seniority would have had a company car with free petrol. The week before his summer holiday he asked personnel to hire a car for him so that his wife could drive him about on their continental holiday. He argued that other managers were able to use company cars and petrol on their holidays and that he should be treated the same as them. Most of the personnel department, for they all became involved in discussing the case, tended to the view that the manager was trying it on, manipulating the bureaucratic rules to gain a personal advantage. They thought that the bureaucratic rules were being used to achieve an unfair and undeserved benefit for the marketing manager.

Other interviewees gave accounts of many instances in which an injustice may have resulted from the way in which people were categorised. In one case an employee was appointed to a post but was denied membership of the company pension scheme because he was too fat. In other cases managers refused, illegally, to appoint young women to jobs in case they later caused disruption by becoming pregnant and taking maternity leave.

Billig proposed that categorisation, because it can lead to distorted responses, should be understood in the context of the tension with its opposite – particularisation. Particularisation is the process of recognising the specific and unique features of a situation, which mean that it cannot be categorised. At the least, particularisation causes controversy about how an issue should be categorised. It provides a counterweight to categorisation. Those whose powers of particularisation are diminished may become bureaucratic and prejudiced in ways that deny justice, or at the least provide a dulled and mechanical response to ethical issues.

Comparison of the *Downsizing* results of the accountancy and HR specialists (Figure 5.6) suggests that categorisation, evidenced by an unwillingness to change one's categorisation of an issue, need not be the dominant way of thinking about ethical issues in organisations. The HR managers were more likely than the financial specialists to change their categorisation as they worked through the instrument. They were readier to change their categorisation in response to new particulars. The greater proportion of women in the HRM profession could account for the relative strength of particularisation in the HR sample. Some research (Helson and

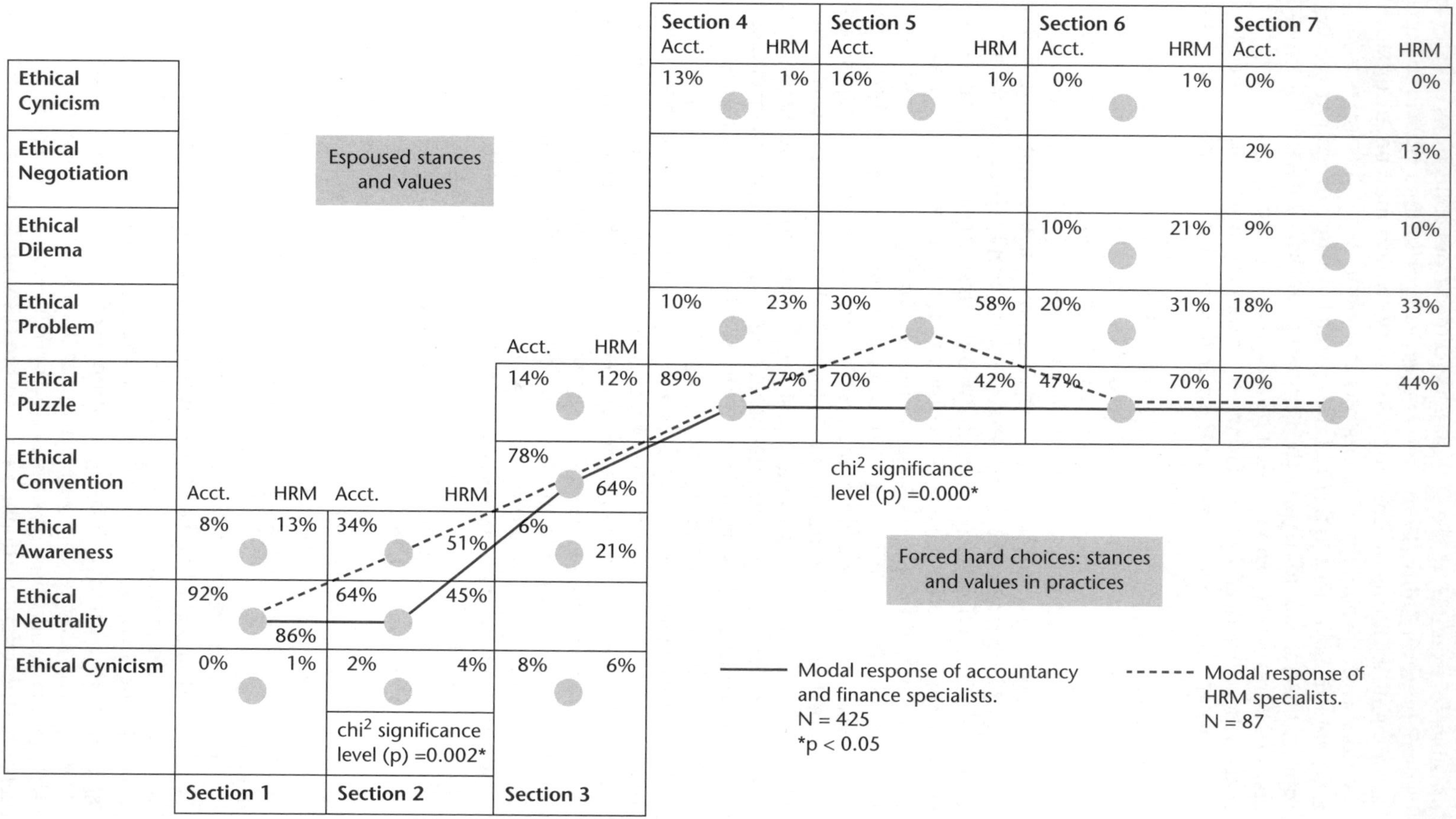

Espoused stances and values

	Section 1		Section 2		Section 3	
	Acct.	HRM	Acct.	HRM	Acct.	HRM
Ethical Convention	8%	13%	34%	51%	14%	12%
Ethical Awareness			6%	45%	6%	21%
Ethical Neutrality	92%	86%	64%		78%	64%
Ethical Cynicism	0%	1%	2%	4%	8%	6%

chi² significance level (p) = 0.002*

Forced hard choices: stances and values in practices

	Section 4		Section 5		Section 6		Section 7	
	Acct.	HRM	Acct.	HRM	Acct.	HRM	Acct.	HRM
Ethical Cynicism	13%	1%	16%	1%	0%	1%	0%	0%
Ethical Negotiation							2%	13%
Ethical Dilemma	10%	23%			10%	21%	9%	10%
Ethical Problem			30%	58%	20%	31%	18%	33%
Ethical Puzzle	89%	77%	70%	42%	47%	70%	70%	44%

chi² significance level (p) = 0.000*

—— Modal response of accountancy and finance specialists. N = 425 *p < 0.05

----- Modal response of HRM specialists. N = 87

Figure 5.6 Results from the *Downsizing* instrument: the percentage frequency with which Accounting and Finance specialists and HRM specialists chose ethical positions in the seven sections of the instruments

(*Source:* Fisher and Lovell, 2000)

Wink, 1992) has suggested that women have a greater tolerance of ambiguity as they get older. This tendency, if related to a greater ease with particularisation, contrasts with men's inclination to see things in the puzzle mode more often as they get older (Fisher and Lovell, 2000).

The point is not which mode, categorisation or particularisation employees ought to be encouraged to adopt, rather that they should be helped to use both. As Winter puts it (1989: 53), dialectical critique means looking for 'unity concealed behind apparent differentiation and contradiction concealed within apparent unity'. People should be helped to challenge, and argue about, how ethical issues at work should be categorised. Particularisation and categorisation need to be operated in combination because particularisation is the trigger for challenges to habitual categorisation. Billig (1996: 171) discussed

> the rhetorical strategies which turn around our schemata and unpick our categories. It will be seen that these strategies are not based upon a simple process of particularisation. Rather they are located within a continual argumentative momentum, oscillating between particularisation and categorisation.

There are two aspects to this momentum: arguing about which category it is appropriate to use in a particular case; and arguing about what the categories are, or what they mean. An issue from our research interviews can illustrate this. A company that trades with developing countries had relieved its managers of wrestling with the ethical problems associated with accepting gifts from overseas agents. It required that any employees who were offered gifts by an overseas agent should accept them (thereby avoiding giving offence to the agent), but hand them over to the company. During the year such gifts were auctioned and the proceeds donated to charities. Thus, the need to think or worry about how to handle such situations is removed from the individual manager involved by the adoption of an ethical code. Whilst managers' lives were made easier by the code it also took away from them their personal moral responsibility. For this reason the categorisation of the issue as a matter of rule following should have been challenged. It could, for example, have been recategorised as a matter of ethical awareness, and the view taken that nothing that could be seen as corruption should be tolerated. In this case no gifts should be accepted. Or, by way of redefining the categorisations, it might have been argued that it was a question of following ethical conventions, but not those of the company's home base. Instead the norms of the country in which the business was being conducted (where giving bribes was accepted) should be followed. There is another possibility. Texas Instruments' (1999) code argued that a gift is improper if it is expected to provide the giver with an advantage. The impropriety of a gift is not judged by its scale, which customarily differs between countries, but by the intention of the gift giver. This approach categorises the issue as one of moral judgment within a problem perspective. These possibilities lead to the conclusion that ethical behaviour in organisations requires employees to balance their tendency to categorise or 'label' ethical issues by using the particularity of a situation to challenge their categorisations.

Case study 5.2 shows how particulars can suddenly challenge categorisations as one particular feature of a case acts as an epiphany that causes a major realignment in a person's view of an issue.

Epiphany was originally a Christian term for the manifestation of God's presence in the world. James Joyce (1996, but actually published in 1914–15) took the term over, in his novel *The Portrait of an Artist as a Young Man*, to mean a commonplace object or gesture that provides a sudden insight.

DEFINITION

Case study 5.2

Particularized and categorisation

The following incident was recounted by one of our research interviewees, a senior personnel manager in a food processing company. The company had a van sales force, which sold and delivered the product to small shops and catering businesses. She became indirectly involved in discussions about the fate of a van salesman who had been accused of theft. She was told that on his rounds the salesman had seen a bike on waste ground outside a shop he was delivering to, and had put it in the van to take it home to give to his son. The police had stopped him and accused him of theft and the question was whether the salesman should be summarily dismissed in line with the company's disciplinary policy. The man's manager, realistically in the personnel manager's view, said that he was loath to dismiss the salesman because he was good at his job and, in any case, 'Wouldn't we all take the bike in similar circumstances; pick up an abandoned bike?' The manager also reported that the police had said it would be unfair to dismiss the salesman. Despite this the police had decided to prosecute, which seemed a little odd to the personnel manager.

The personnel manager thought it important to maintain the reputation of the van sales force for trustworthiness.

They are out on the road on their own and we trust the van sales people. Your sales reps have to be honest because the shopkeepers have a degree of mistrust and it's important that we build up a reputation as an honest company.

This thought inclined her to dismiss the van salesman. However, there had been a number of recent cases where staff had been involved in minor theft and had been let off with a caution because they had been good employees. It seemed sensible to show leniency to the salesman especially as there was some doubt about whether it was a case of theft or simply a matter of 'finder's keepers'. On this basis, the personnel manager was inclined to accept the manager's wish to retain the salesman.

Out of curiosity she asked:

'What sort of shop was it where the bike was taken from?' The manager replied, sheepishly, 'It was a newsagent's early in the morning'. Suspicions aroused she asked, 'Was it a newspaper boy's or girl's bike?' 'Yes it was', came the resigned response. 'It was leaning against the side wall of the newsagents – but it was on waste ground. It was just alongside the newsagents.'

This fact was enough for the personnel manager, who insisted that the employee be dismissed. The manager was annoyed because he had lost a good salesman and recruiting new ones was not easy. The sudden revelation of a few particulars about the nature and position of the bike were enough to settle the personnel manager's mind on how the issue should be categorised. It was a clear puzzle, which could be easily resolved by applying company rules, not an ethical problem that called for fine moral judgments.

Activity 5.2	**Examples of particularisation and categorisation**

This small example provides an illustration of how particulars may serve to challenge categorisations. Can you think of other examples?

Cross reference   The implications of particularisation for making decisions on ethical questions are explored in Chapter 13, p. 515.

Influences on choice of stance

So far, this chapter has concentrated upon identifying the categories people use to label ethical issues. It has also highlighted the importance of allowing categorisations of an issue to be challenged and changed by particulars. It is now necessary to look a little more closely at these particulars. The emphasis in this section will be on the factors and influences that bear upon people's choices of the stance to be taken on an ethical issue. Some of the influences upon these choices have been pre-empted in the description of the two dimensions in Figure 5.1. The vertical axis suggests that the adoption of a stance will depend upon the sophistication of a person's ethical reasoning. The horizontal axis indicates that a person's certainty about their values will also affect their choice of stances.

There are many other factors that have a claim to influence ethical categorisation and decision making. Models of the antecedents influencing ethical decision making often include four broad areas as detailed under the following headings.

1 Cultural factors

The importance of an organisation's ethical culture or ethos is discussed in Chapter 10. Trevino and Youngblood (1990) identified a link between an organisation's culture and the ethical position adopted by organisational members, which they called vicarious reward and punishment. They hypothesised that people's actions would be influenced by whether they saw the wrongdoing of others being punished and whether others' ethical actions were praised. The conclusion was that vicarious reward and punishment influenced ethical decisions if they were greater than expected. It was argued that people expected wrongdoing to be punished and ignored this effect unless the punishment was stronger than they had anticipated. Conversely they did not expect good to be praised, and when they saw it was, it did have a positive effect on their assessments of the probability that their own good actions might attract praise and reward.

2 Situational factors

The specifics of a situation can also affect someone's response to an ethical issue. Some people's jobs and organisational positions make it easier for them to take a moral stand than do those of others. The degree of closeness to an ethical problem, or their formal responsibility for resolving it, is an important factor. The closer one is the greater the obligation to act. Stewart (1984) defined this as the Kew Gardens Principle. (The geographical reference is to the public gardens in New York where passive bystanders witnessed a murder and did nothing, and not to the British botanical gardens.) This principle proposed an obligation to take action against an ethical wrong where:

- there was a clear case of need;
- the agent was close to the situation in terms of 'notice' if not space;
- the agent had the capability to help the one in need; and
- no one else was likely to help.

Cross reference	The Kew Gardens case is discussed more extensively in Chapter 13, p. 520. As well as defining the conditions under which people have a moral obligation the case also raises the problem of why people do not act on the obligation. This is a particular problem for the American ethical objectivism based on the work of Ayn Rand (see Chapter 1, p. 25.) The objectivists argue that ethical good comes from reducing government interference in people's lives and giving them the maximum autonomy. If, as the Kew Gardens case would seem to show, people cannot be trusted to act well then the moral case for objectivism is undermined.

In our research interviews, people often claimed their 'distance' from an issue, in terms of their managerial responsibility, justified taking a position of neutrality on some example of organisational wrongdoing. Equally a person's general situation, in terms of their responsibility for others, for family, or their degree of economic independence, will also affect their willingness to move beyond neutrality. The specific circumstance of the ethical issue will also affect a person's response to it. Most people's response to the theft of a box of paper clips from work will be different from their response to serious misuse of a company credit card.

3 Psychological factors

Trevino (1986) suggested a number of individual variables that could affect a person's response to an ethical issue. They included ego strength, which is the tendency to stick to one's convictions. People with high ego strength are less likely to be swayed by circumstances or impulses into changing their mind. Field dependence was another possible variable. This refers to the degree to which someone depends on information given by others when faced with an ambiguous situation. A person with high field dependence, if asked by their superior to take a possibly unethical action, would be influenced by the superior's assurances that they will not be blamed and that the action is not really improper. A person with low field dependency would wish to make up their own mind independently of the advice from others. Other writers (Verbeke et al., 1996) have suggested that Machiavellianism, as a personality trait, may affect someone's response to an ethical issue.

Machiavellianism is named after Niccolò Machiavelli (1469–1527), whose name (rightly or wrongly) has become synonymous with cunning, amoral, devious and manipulative behaviour. The reputation is based on his book, *The Prince*, in which he gave practical advice on statesmanship. He saw democracy as the best form of government but recognised that it was not always possible to behave in the most virtuous way. The dictum that 'the end justifies the means' is attributed to Machiavelli. By this he meant that there is no moral distinction between ends and means so that any badness in a proposed means can be balanced by the goodness of the outcome. It does not mean that good ends can justify any means no matter how wicked (Mackie, 1990: 159), but, as Machiavelli (1950, Ch. XVIII) put it, 'the prince must have a mind disposed to adapt itself, according to the wind, and as the variations of fortune dictate . . . not deviate from what is good, if possible but be able to do evil if constrained'.

DEFINITION

Rotter's (1966) internal-external locus of control scale is another psychological construct that may affect ethical choices. It measures an individual's perception of how much control he or she exerts over events in their lives. Some people believe that most things in life are within their control. They do not believe in luck; they believe people make their own luck. Others do not believe they control their own lives. They believe in luck, fate and happenstance. Trevino's analysis found there was a relationship between this factor and people's ethical choices. It showed that people who felt in control of their actions were more likely to make ethical rather than unethical decisions than those who believed themselves influenced by external factors. To some extent this relationship was reinforced by the tendency of people with an internal locus of control to believe that they can bring about the beneficial consequences of their actions that they hoped for.

Activity 5.3   **Scoring the locus of control scale**

Versions of the locus of control scale for you to fill in, and obtain your own score from, are to be found in plenty on the World Wide Web. Go to one of the following sites and see how you score.

Locus of control questionnaires on the World Wide Web

http://uhddx01.dt.uh.edu/~avenf/locus.html

http://www.psych/uncc.edu/pagoolka/LocusofControl-intro.html

www.ballarat.edu.au/bssh/psych/rot.htm

4 Cognitive factors

The seminal work on levels of moral development was conducted and published by Lawrence Kohlberg (1969, 1984). His theory originated in the field of developmental psychology. He researched the development of children's capacity for ethical reasoning and it was only later that the model was applied to adults and people in organisations in particular. Whether the focus is on adults or children, the key idea is that people pass through an invariant and hierarchical sequence of three stages – the pre-conventional, the conventional and the post-conventional – in the development of their ethical cognitive ability. However, it is not quite as simple as this. Kohlberg originally proposed that each of the three stages be sub-divided into two, giving a total of six stages. Subsequent developments have led to this being expanded to eight or possibly nine stages. We will take you through these one at a time.

Pre-conventional stages

Stage zero

At this stage, a person has no capacity for moral reasoning. They simply act impulsively and respond to any urge no matter what the consequences.

Stage one

People at this stage, and certainly all young children, have no innate sense of morality but they have learned that certain actions bring praise and others bring punishment. They can respond to the carrots and sticks without knowing the rationale for their subsequent behaviour. This stage of development consists of unwitting compliance with the demands of those with the ability to praise and punish. Parents clearly have this power but so do managers and supervisors in organisations.

Stage two

Personal gain, and the wish not to miss out on good things, characterises moral thinking at this stage. People evaluate options according to the benefits that they might gain. This is a selfish stage at which a person cannot, when considering a situation, think beyond what might be in it for them. In an organisational context, only the prospect of higher pay, promotion or some other benefit would be of weight.

Conventional stages

Stage three

It is at this level of development that a person responds to their social role by thinking about morality in terms of being, to use the phrase always used of this stage, a 'Nice Boy/Good Girl'. At this stage, people accept as legitimate the social norms and expectations of the groups they belong to. This stage does not involve ethical thought about the issues. People abide by the social norms not because they have analysed them and concluded they are correct but because they wish to be socially accepted.

One of these social norms is the obligation to be caring towards others; and this lowly positioning of care (level three when eight or nine represents the highest level of morality) has been the source of a major criticism of Kohlberg's model. Gilligan (1982) showed that girls' moral development differs from that of boys (*see* p. 107). Girls place more emphasis on relationships, responsibility and caring for others than boys. Gilligan argued that care is more than a response to social norms, that philosophically it is the equivalent of the cold abstraction of justice, which, as we shall see, Kohlberg placed at the apex of his model. Kohlberg responded to this criticism by placing welfare higher in his model, but many argue (Snell, 2000: 274) that this response is inadequate.

Stage four

At this stage, the conventions that frame a person's morality are not social but organisational and institutional. Sometimes this stage is further divided into two. At the inferior of these two stages morality is framed within the rules and regulations of a specific organisation, such as a company or a professional association that has defined rules of conduct and ethics. At the superior level the adherence is to the wider institutional rules of society. Some people argue that rule utilitarianism (*see* p. 137) is the guiding morality of this stage. The critical factor in both stages, however, is that the commitment to 'law and order' is a knowing one. People have chosen to apply the rules by choice because they believe them to be good for themselves individually as well as for the wider institutions of society.

The post-conventional stages

Stage five

At the post-conventional stages, people are capable of questioning and reflecting upon the systems and principles of morality that they follow. At this stage, which is referred to as the social contract stage, people challenge the prevailing morality and seek to change it in accordance with their own reflections. They might, for example, campaign to change the law on cigarette advertising because they think it would advance social justice to do so.

Stage six

At stage six, which in some versions is the final stage of the model, there is an acceptance of the existence of universal principles of justice (and in later versions, *pace* Gilligan) welfare. This knowledge of universal principle is not easily come by but gained through intellectual struggle and practical confrontation with injustice in the world. A person at this level takes risks to bring justice wherever they find injustice. Kohlberg's definition of level six is Kantian (*see* p. 109). It is austere and concerned with abstract principle. Not all of Kohlberg's critics were at ease with this.

The postmodernists in particular had trouble with the notion of justice as a metanarrative. Snell (1993: 20) reported, and to some extent accepted, the arguments of those who see stage six as a capacity for principled relativism rather than irrefragable justice. This mirrors Rorty's views (Mounce, 1997: 185–9) in stressing the need for continuing conversations, a celebration of doubt and paradox and a playful sense of irony when dealing with complex moral matters.

Stage seven

This stage we find hard to define because of its transcendental nature, which means you have to achieve it to know it. It does in general draw themes from many of the world's major religions including Christianity, Buddhism and Judaism. One such is the idea of the unity of all creation, the belief that in some way all things are part of a single whole. The idea of morality at this highest level is linked with the idea of becoming at one with the whole of creation. This is the final stage in the nine-fold developmental sequence (remembering that the first phase is called stage zero and that stage four can be subdivided).

There have been many criticisms of Kohlberg's model but it has proved robust and remains a core theory. It has been pointed out that the stages may not be hierarchical. One particularly relevant form of this argument is that even though people may have acquired a capacity to think morally at one of the higher levels, there is no guarantee that they will choose to do so. Nor is such a capacity a guarantee that people will act according to the highest level thinking that they are capable of. Nevertheless it is clear that a person's capacity for moral reasoning will have an impact on which of the ethical stances is chosen.

Reflections

This chapter has presented a classification of eight stances that may be taken in response to an ethical issue at work. The question has to be asked whether some stances are more ethical than others. It might be considered in two parts. The first is to consider whether, in Figure 5.1, the stances higher in the matrix are more ethical than those lower on the vertical scale. The second part is whether those stances on the right-hand side of the matrix are more ethical than those on the left-hand side.

Kohlberg has made the case that ethical cognitive development is hierarchical. On this basis, it could be argued that the ethical puzzle and problem stances are better than neutrality or negotiation. However, such a claim would suggest that people should always aspire to the higher stances. This might lead to some odd consequences. Would it be sensible to apply the relatively complex stances of ethical puzzle or ethical problem to a relatively simple matter such as the casual theft of office stationery? This question implies that a contingency approach might be sensible in which the 'higher' and more complex stances would be more appropriate for major and difficult ethical dilemmas. Snell made a suggestion of this type in relation to Kohlberg's stages of moral development. He argued that an ethical difficulty arises when a level of ethical development creates rather than solves a problem. If someone is thinking at level three (nice boy/good girl), then they will be in a dilemma if the people they want to like them are tugging them in contradictory directions. It is the level of thinking that is causing the difficulty. Snell

(1993: 62) recommends overcoming such difficulty by shifting the level of ethical thinking up at least one stage. If the demands of social peers are incompatible then the difficulty can only be overcome by thinking in terms of the rules and regulations of the organisation (stage four). The general principle is that one should use the minimum cognitive level, or stance if we move from cognition to action, which is required to overcome an ethical difficulty.

The second part of the question is whether the left-hand stances are ethically better than the right-hand stances. The two sides of the matrix in Figure 5.1 can be described in terms of categorisation and particularisation. The left-hand stances give priority to categorisation. They all operate by pigeonholing issues so that their commonalities may be stressed and standard responses applied. The right-hand stances give more emphasis to particularisation. They all emphasise the complexity and ambiguity of issues, which are things that make it difficult to categorise an issue. These stances do not dictate particular solutions to issues though they do suggest ways of dealing with or coping with the uncertainty (debating judgments, keeping the conversation going, cynical withdrawal or negotiation with stakeholders). The trade-offs between the left-hand and right-hand stances are clear. If the left-hand stances are taken, actions can be decisively chosen and implemented, but they may be inappropriate or unfair. The right-hand stances might be more responsive to the nuances and complexities of an issue but they may also lead to prevarication and inaction. The results from the *Downsizing* exercise (Activity 6.1) suggest that many managers and professionals were uncomfortable with the right-hand stances (the accountants being more uncomfortable than the HR specialists). This may be dangerous because it is the neglected right-hand stances that provide the critical element necessary to limit the left-hand stances' propensity for inflexibility and unfair discrimination. As has been suggested earlier in the chapter people at work may need to develop a momentum that swings them between the left-hand stances and the right-hand stances – between categorisation and particularisation.

Summary

In this chapter, the following key points have been made:

- There are eight stances that people may take in response to an ethical issue at work.

- People may take different stances on an issue, depending on their consciences, ethical reasoning, perceptions of others' views, and in their actions.

- Tensions between a person's conscience, ethical reasoning, perceptions of others' views and their actions can cause psychological discomfort and interpersonal conflicts.

- The particulars of a specific ethical issue will also have an influence on the stance a person chooses and their inclination to change stances.

- Their choice of stances will be affected by a number of factors such as their level of cognitive development and the values they share with a group or society.

Typical assignments

1. Analyse an ethical issue that you have experienced at work using the categories, conscience: ethical reasoning: expectations of others: options for action framework presented in Figure 5.3.

2. Discuss the ethics of downsizing using the framework of stances presented in Figure 5.1. Illustrate your arguments by reference to particular cases of downsizing.

3. How effective is Kohlberg's model of moral development, which was based on studies of children, to understanding the behaviour of managers when faced with ethical issues?

4. What range of factors might influence how a manager responds to an ethical situation at work? How important are the cultural factors in relation to other influences?

Group activity 5.1

The following is an extract from an interview with a personnel manager. It gives two examples of situations where an organisation's senior managers wanted to dispense with employees whom they thought no longer fitted with the official culture and values of the organisation. The personnel manager, who was an intermediary in both of these situations, took a different stance in each case. In the first case, she was in favour of parting with the employee but in the second case she thought it would be wrong to part with the member of staff.

Read the interview and discuss how the respondent might explain why she took different stances on issues that seem to involve the same matter of principle.

1. Should employees be let go if they do not fit with an organisation's official culture?

2. What particulars might have triggered different categorisations in each of the incidents?

The most recent example is a retail business manager who has got a consistently high appraisal rating, high performance rating over the last few years. But what is required over the next three years? Has this person the ability to move forward? Therefore there is a big question mark over where that person goes. Because we're talking about somebody who's perceived by the organisation as a high performer. Yet in terms of everything they do everyday we can see that they have the inability to change, to move forward with the change in an emerging brand.

Well, the whole style of the operation is changing. We have a new director and general manager and senior management team for a start. They have a different way of working. The emphasis is on empowerment. The emphasis is moving away from control culture, control type management to a more loose management culture and more sales oriented and building on development in sales. This person is not interested in development and growing sales. He's more about the old control culture. Hit them with a big stick and sack them if they don't do what you tell them mentality. But he has an excellent performance record, and if you look in terms of actual year on year profit performance he's the best achiever in the company.

Also the difficulty is because he has a reputation throughout the company for that tough management style nobody else wants to face him. So the fact is that we'll end up losing somebody [*said ironically, meaning the manager*] from the organisation. Which will also cause or create a huge employee relations issue. Because he will take us to tribunal. Rightly so in terms of performance.

Well, we've decided he's got to go. Well it will be a severance. He'll have to go. We've looked at the other alternatives and there aren't any.

I think in terms of the organisation's culture it's absolutely right but actually this guy has worked for the company for some time and in his own way has been committed. So I think there probably is a view that maybe over the years this person hasn't been managed properly in the past and maybe if he'd been managed better in the past then maybe we wouldn't be at this point now. Yes we've worked on him, we've been working on it for the last six months. It's not even a runner. We're basically saying, up yours, you know, as good as. Well, I've dealt with so many [severance cases] that I always think that if I go home at night and sleep, my conscience is relatively clear. I have a job to do and I believe when it comes round and it's right for the business, then it's part of the job. I think so, yes.

I quite often won't do something if I don't agree with it being morally right, or I'll look for a compromise. Yes, somebody who works for me who, one of the directors felt, wasn't committed enough to the organisation because they didn't work seven days a week. He told me that I needed to do something about that person and I refused point blank. I said that they actually worked more effectively than anybody else here and no I don't intend to get rid of him. I refuse to do that. At the end of the day, just because you [the director] believe that we should work seven days a week it doesn't prove that they're not committed. So I actually did dig my heels in and said no I'm not going to do it. I refused and we've worked around that. I did then talk to that person and let that person know how he [the director] felt about it and said you know you just need to think about raising your profile and meeting part way. Well, I think I responded as I did because that person is an extremely effective member of the team and actually the output is far higher than the average. And really it was more about profile. In terms of the organisation, it's the nature of the business and because our business does operate seven days a week, then it becomes the accepted norm. If you've got pressure from a senior manager then it makes life difficult for you and then ultimately it forces somebody out. The director was being unreasonable, totally unreasonable, absolutely.

It's settled down again now but it was very difficult at the time. It put me in a difficult position. I'm a great believer in sticking to your guns and I'm a spade or shovel person.

Recommended further reading

Many of the key themes and ideas of this chapter are taken from M. Billig (1996) *Arguing and Thinking. A rhetorical approach to social psychology*, 2nd edn, Cambridge: Cambridge University Press. It is not an easy read but it is very rewarding. R. Snell's book provides a good introduction to Kohlberg and has convincing case studies that relate the theory to resolving ethical problems at work: R. Snell (1993) *Developing Skills for Ethical Management*, London: Chapman and Hall.

Useful websites

Topic	Website provider	URL
The official centre for purchasing the Defining Issues Test for assessing stage of moral development	Office for the Study of ethical development, University of Alabama	http://www.ethicaldevelopment.ua.edu/
Interactive games provided by BT, which illustrate decision making in the context of social responsibility and sustainability	BT	http://www.btplc.com/Responsiblebusiness/Ourstory/Interactivegames/index.htm

CHAPTER 6

Whistleblower or witness?

Chapter at a glance

Activities and exercises

Learning outcomes

Having read this chapter and completed its associated activities, readers should be able to:

■ Examine the various issues that relate to the act of whistleblowing.

■ Debate the role that whistleblowing potentially has to play within corporate governance processes.

■ Discuss possible explanations of the whistleblower's plight.

■ Evaluate the legislation that seeks to protect whistleblowers in the UK.

Introduction

Chapter 5 considered possible stances or ethical positions that people facing ethical challenges may move through. The stances are ways of labelling the different forms of responses people might display in ethically complex situations. In this chapter, we discuss the issue of those employees, who, for a variety of reasons, come to a position where they are so uncomfortable with a particular practice or activity within their employing organisation that they feel no alternative but to raise the matter with another person. This other person might be a work colleague, a senior member of the organisation, a family member, or a non-related third party who is external to the employing organisation. The person to whom the revelation is made can be important because in the UK, for example, it can affect the degree of legal protection that is available to the concerned employee. However, regardless of to whom the concerned employee confides, the act is the same. It is often referred to as whistleblowing and the people who whistleblow are usually referred to as whistleblowers. However, this can be a pejorative term and some writers prefer other descriptions, e.g. Beardshaw (1981) described such employees as 'conscientious objectors at work', while Winfield (1990) preferred 'principled dissenters'. Borrie and Dehn (2002: 5) offered some thoughts on how whistleblowers might be viewed in the future and in order to help change people's perceptions they suggested the alternative nomenclature of 'witness', not 'complainant'. This is an interesting suggestion because changing people's perception of those who whistleblow is an important stepping stone in altering the likely outcomes experienced by those who reveal organisational malpractices.

The words we use to describe people or things are important because they create an initial context and orientate our emotions towards the discussion that might follow. Thus, if the term whistleblower brings to mind the notion of a snitch, or

| Cross reference | The issues and arguments discussed in this chapter build upon Chapters 4 and 5 by focusing attention upon those individuals who encounter an issue within their organisation that challenges their personal values and ethics in a profound way, but for which they can find no satisfactory resolution. |

a grass, then you are more likely to be inclined, initially at least, towards a negative view of a whistleblower with regard to any discussion of a particular whistleblowing case. If, however, you prefer the descriptions proffered by writers such as Winfield, Beardshaw or Borrie and Dehn, because that is how you see most whistleblowers, then your interpretation of the 'rights' and 'wrongs' of a particular case is likely to lean towards the position of the whistleblower. Our quest in this chapter is to consider the issue of whistleblowing and whistleblowers, using the terms neither pejoratively nor exaltingly, but merely descriptively.

In this chapter we will present you with the arguments surrounding whistleblowing, but also with evidence of the pressures within organisations that can constrain potential whistleblowers and the implications of such 'muteness'. We will use actual cases to illustrate the arguments, reflecting the messiness that is often to be found in organisational life, and the organisational impotency that many employees feel, irrespective of their position within the organisation. This is not to justify or to recommend an uncritical acceptance of the messiness and personal impotency that can be experienced in ethical dilemmas. The tools of analysis and the implications of the differing philosophical positions discussed in Chapters 3 and 4 will allow you to form reasoned judgments on the questions, issues and cases relating to whistleblowing that you will now consider.

However, before we progress, we would like you to work through Activity 6.1.

Activity 6.1	**Responses to whistleblowing**

On the scales shown, identify your feelings towards the person raising the alarm.

Case A

You are playing in a team and a player on your side fouls a player on the opposing side, but the referee misses the incident. However, one of your teammates suddenly stops the game and brings the foul to the attention of the referee.

Extremely supportive   Extremely angry

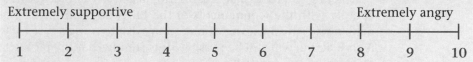

1   2   3   4   5   6   7   8   9   10

Case B

You read in the newspaper that an employee of a building company has provided evidence to a national newspaper of practices on building sites that contravene health and safety legislation and that have resulted in fatalities and serious injuries during the past two years.

Extremely supportive   Extremely angry

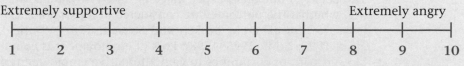

1   2   3   4   5   6   7   8   9   10

▶

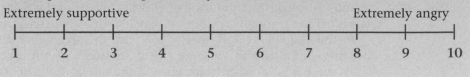

Case C

You work for a car manufacturer and a fellow employee, whom you do not know personally, releases information to the press of a design fault in one of the company's best-selling models that is potentially life threatening. Sales of the car plummet and significant layoffs are announced.

Extremely supportive   Extremely angry

1   2   3   4   5   6   7   8   9   10

When is a whistleblowing act performed?

A commonly held understanding of a whistleblowing act is the release of confidential organisational information to an external third party, often, but not exclusively, the media. However, as suggested above, a whistleblowing act can be a conversation, a remark even, to a work colleague or a family member in which organisational information, unknown to others participating in the conversation, is revealed. If these concerns are relayed back to 'management' before the employee concerned has raised the issue through the company's formal procedures (assuming they exist), and they are dismissed as a result of the revelation, then, in the UK, they are likely to lose the protection of the law that was introduced to protect whistleblowers. This is the Public Interest Disclosure Act 1998 (PIDA), which is discussed in more detail later in the chapter.

The PIDA was designed to provide protection to those who raise awareness of an act or practice that poses problems for public safety, or threatens other specific areas of public interest. From the above it is clear that, whilst whistleblowing is normally a purposeful and intentional act, it might also be unintended and innocent. The law makes little, if any, distinction between intended and unintended whistleblowing.

Reacting to a particular organisational activity or practice in a way that does not comply with the requirements of the PIDA does not mean that legal recourse is denied to a whistleblower, should they wish to bring a case for wrongful dismissal. A civil action will still be possible. It is simply that the protection afforded by the PIDA will not be available.

Why whistleblow?

The personal outcomes experienced by many whistleblowers have been damaging, whether the outcomes are considered at a psychological, financial or social level (*see*, for example, Soeken and Soeken, 1987; Winfield, 1990; Miceli and Near, 1992; Hunt, 1995, 1998). Loss of employment is common for the whistleblower, with opportunities to gain alternative employment often limited. Some whistleblowers have become unemployable as their names have been circulated among employing organisations as 'troublemakers'. Borrie and Dehn (2002) refer to such an example.

Case study 6.1	**Paying a heavy price**

Robert Maxwell, who was chief executive of Maxwell Communications, stole $1m from the pension funds of the company, which included the pension funds of the *Daily Mirror* group of newspapers. He sacked a union official who had challenged what he was doing with the pension money at a Scottish newspaper. Maxwell, a powerful businessman, was able to ensure that the man could not get another job in the industry. Subsequently the claims of the union official were found to have been accurate, but that was little consolation for him as his career in the print industry had been ruined.

The whistleblower and his or her family often experience great financial and emotional hardship, with break-ups in marriages or partnerships frequently reported. Suicides of whistleblowers have also been attributed to the financial and psychological fallout from their whistleblowing experiences (Soeken and Soeken, 1987). However, not all whistleblowing cases end in such unhappiness, although it is difficult to overplay the trauma that is likely to be experienced while the scenario is unfolding, even if the final outcome shows the whistleblower both vindicated and adequately compensated. Sherron Watkins was an accountant and a former vice-president at Enron before she 'blew the whistle' on the corrupt practices there. Watkins has enjoyed something of a celebrity status since her whistleblowing act, but this might have something to do with the scale of the fraud at Enron and the ease with which it was possible to identify key individuals at the top who were directly implicated in the fraud. A less clear-cut scenario, with slightly less media scrutiny, can find the potential whistleblower in a more vulnerable and exposed position. As it was, Watkins was faced with some hostility from her work colleagues. It must be recognised that the revelation of an organisational malpractice, however corrupt and indefensible it might be, risks damaging the employing organisation's share price and standing in its various product or service markets. This could place jobs at risk, the jobs of one's work colleagues and perhaps their pension funds.

The situation at Enron was complicated by the fact that many of the employees had invested heavily in the stocks and shares of Enron, believing that the phenomenal growth in the share price that had been experienced over the previous seven or so years would continue, allowing their portfolio to be converted upon retirement into a sizeable pension fund. Thus, anyone blowing the whistle at Enron would be putting at risk both jobs and personal retirement/pension funds. Without minimising the courage displayed by Sherron Watkins, her position was possibly eased slightly because she first formally raised her concerns in an internal letter to Kenneth Lay (CEO and chairman) on 15 August 2001. This was only two months before Enron made a public announcement that it was making significant write-offs and only three-and-a-half months before it filed for bankruptcy. The scale of the fraud and the perpetrators became evident quite quickly, a state of affairs not often experienced by whistleblowers.

The PIDA does appear to have made a difference in some cases, and with compensation claims now having no ceiling (which was not the case when the act was first introduced), the compensation awards to some wronged whistleblowers have been significant. The organisation Public Concern at Work has undertaken a review of the first three years' working of the act. During this period employees lodged over 1,200 claims alleging victimisation for whistleblowing. Of these two-thirds were either settled out of court or withdrawn without a public hearing. Of the remaining one-third, 54 per cent of claimants lost, 23 per cent won their case, but under a different employment or discrimination law, and the final 23 per cent won their case under the PIDA. The highest award made was for £805,000 and the lowest £1,000. The average value of award made during this first three-year period was £107,117.

Although the protection afforded by the PIDA may encourage some potential whistleblowers to become actual whistleblowers, whistleblowers have followed their respective consciences for millennia without the protection of the PIDA, so what might explain such acts? The answer may be found in a number of tragedies, but we will focus upon only those of recent times. In these instances we often find evidence of employees who have raised concerns prior to the final incident occurring. Had these concerns been acted upon the tragedy in question might not have happened. Whether we look at examples such as the Piper-Alpha disaster or the Zeebrugge (*Herald of Free Enterprise*) tragedy, BCCI, Maxwell Communications, Barlow Clowes, the Lyme Bay canoeing tragedy, the Southall rail crash, the Clapham rail crash, or the incidence of high fatality rates among operations on young children at Bristol Royal Infirmary, we find evidence of the ignored concerns of employees.

These were tragedies in the Greek sense. They could have been predicted from their specific circumstances yet the final dénouement appeared inexorable. The circumstances in question often related to lax controls and practices and/or a failure to listen to the concerns of employees. The concerns had either been reported to management, but not acted upon, or unreported due to oppressive and authoritarian management practices or misguided feelings of loyalty. An example of the former is the case of the *Herald of Free Enterprise*, which capsized as it left Zeebrugge harbour because its bow doors had been left open, resulting in the deaths of 192 passengers and crew. A more detailed account of the case is provided in Chapter 7 in Case study 7.4 (*see* p. 288), but some relevant details are provided here. The inquiry report into the disaster, concluded,

> If this sensible suggestion . . . had received the serious consideration it deserved this disaster might well have been prevented.

> (Lewis, 2000: 3)

The suggestion in question was the fitting of lights to the bridge, which would have indicated whether or not the bow doors were closed. On five occasions prior to the *Herald of Free Enterprise* capsizing, P&O staff had experienced ferries leaving port without the bow doors being fully closed and had expressed their concerns, but these were not acted upon. The concerns, although communicated to the ferries' management, had not been conveyed to the company's top management. The concerns appear to have become lost in the middle management tiers of the organisation. Tragedies, such as those mentioned above, created a sufficiently supportive socio-political climate to allow the PIDA to be passed as an Act of Parliament in 1998 and to become operative in 1999.

| Case study 6.2 | The Lyme Bay canoeing tragedy |

Once again the term 'tragedy' is appropriate, because this appears to have been an accident waiting to happen. The company OLL Ltd offered outdoor adventure holidays, breaks and vacations for younger people. However, two of the instructors were concerned at the lack of attention to safety issues within the company. They became exasperated at the refusal of the owner of the company to take their concerns seriously, so that they felt compelled to resign, although not before they wrote to the owner, detailing their concerns. Not long after their resignations a group of school children were taken canoeing in Lyme Bay, England, by the company, but the weather and sea conditions changed and four of the school children lost their lives. Because there was evidence that the safety failings in the company had been brought to the attention of the owner, 'the guiding mind' (which is discussed in more detail in Chapter 7), a case of corporate manslaughter could be brought. The company was fined £60,000 and the owner was jailed for three years.

The penalties imposed upon the corporations and individuals found complicit in the injuries or deaths of others are not necessarily adequate to influence adherence to health and safety regulations. Slapper and Tombs (1999) cite a couple of cases that illustrate this point. The first relates to Mr Roy Edwin Hill, who was a director of a demolition company. In 1994, the company won the contract to demolish the former Lucas Building in Brislington, which is near Bristol. The factory was demolished with an excavator, but, in violation of health and safety legislation, no precautions were taken to prevent the spreading of asbestos and asbestos dust contained in the roofing and pipework lagging. In 1995 Mr Hill received a jail sentence of three months and a fine of £4,000. While these penalties might be surprising, what is possibly more surprising is that Mr Hill's sentence was the first custodial sentence under health and safety legislation in 193 years!

| Case study 6.3 | Dickensian practices, but in modern times |

A 19-year-old man, Michael Pollard, was employed as a heavy goods vehicle mechanic by a company that manufactured fibres that were used in carpet felt. Mr Pollard was not employed to maintain the equipment in the factory, but on the day in question he was instructed to correct a problem on one of the factory machines. A safety gate was not working and this allowed Mr Pollard to enter the machine while it was still operative. His arm became trapped between spiked rollers and was torn off at the shoulder and shredded in the machine. The Health and Safety Executive immediately maintained that a Prohibition Notice, which was served on the company to prevent the use of the dangerous equipment, had been ignored by the directors. Two of the company's directors were sent to jail for ignoring the Prohibition Notice, but the maximum sentence under the legislation is six months.

The next case has some gruesome details, but it reveals the types of practices that are still prevalent.

The next case provides further evidence of the calculative approach companies can adopt in weighing up whether it is cost-effective to comply with legislation.

Case study 6.4	**What is a life worth?**

James Hodgson was 21 years old. In 1996, while cleaning the chemical residues from a road tanker, Hodgson was sprayed in the face with a toxic chemical and died. The company was found guilty of gross negligence in the supervision, training and the equipment it supplied to handle dangerous chemicals. The company was found guilty of corporate manslaughter and fined £22,000 (£15,000 of which related to the corporate manslaughter) and the owner of the company was sent to prison for 12 months (subject to early release for good behaviour).

So, in response to the question 'why whistleblow?', examples, such as those above, can be cited of situations in which (many) lives might have been saved, had the concerns of employees been listened to and acted upon. Alternatively the concerned, but ignored employees might have taken their worries on to a broader public platform and made the general public aware of their concerns. So does this type of evidence make the general argument in favour of whistleblowing correct, justifiable, and to be encouraged? If so, why is the act of whistleblowing and of a whistleblower so often portrayed and perceived as a negative force within society?

A contributory factor in explaining why one person might choose to whistleblow in a given situation, while another, when faced with the same circumstances, would opt for a different strategy, is associated with the issues we discussed in Chapter 3. With concepts such as justice, honesty and integrity normally included in any set of virtues, a virtue ethics orientation (shown in the central pillar of Figure 3.1) would also suggest that someone possessing such an orientation would be more likely to resist pressure to compromise themselves should an ethical issue prove insoluble. Likewise, for a Kantian-oriented person, whistleblowing would be a likely outcome to an intractable ethical issue.

This contrasts with someone whose ethical orientation reflects consequentialist thinking, i.e. whose decision making will be determined by a thinking through of the consequences of the available options before choosing a course of action. With this orientation, the course of action chosen will depend upon the circumstances of each situation. Given the history of whistleblowing cases (and not just the negative outcomes for the whistleblowers, but also for other employees and the organisation concerned), whistleblowing becomes a far less likely outcome if the concerned employee displays a consequentialist orientation.

The above discussion assumes, of course, that the individual is free to adopt the ethical reasoning that reflects their personal orientation. This, however, is often not possible, due to powerful pressures upon individuals to suppress personal values and to compromise their principles. We discuss the implications of these pressures in the case examples that follow.

Activity 6.2	**What would you do?**

If your knowledge of an organisational malpractice could, if revealed, cause job losses among your colleagues and possibly harm their pension funds, do you believe that you could undertake a whistleblowing act?

What, if any, organisational issue would be likely to force you ultimately to whistleblow?

When might whistleblowing be justified?

Some writers have set out what, for them, are the essential conditions that make whistleblowing acts justifiable. De George (1999) argued that there are six such conditions. De George's position on whistleblowing is a consequentialist one. Because any whistleblowing act is likely to do harm to the employing organisation, the act can only be justified if the overall effects of it are likely to be positive. There is no reference to principles or virtues. For De George, it is the overall consequences of a whistleblowing act that determine its justification. The first three conditions (shown below) are argued to make whistleblowing permissible, but not obligatory. If conditions 4 and 5 can be satisfied then whistleblowing becomes a far more persuasive option, in De George's terms, morally obligatory. Another way of interpreting these conditions is to say that, without them, an act of whistleblowing cannot be morally justified as the likely outcome will be painful and probably fruitless for the whistleblower, and detrimental to the organisation. The conditions are as follows:

1. A product or policy of an organisation needs to possess the potential to do harm to some members of society.

2. The concerned employee should first of all report the facts, as far as they are known, to their immediate superior.

3. If the immediate superior fails to act effectively, the concerned employee should take the matter to more senior managers, exhausting all available internal channels in the process.

4. The prospective whistleblower should hold documentary evidence that can be presented to external audiences. In this condition De George argues that the evidence should show that the product or policy 'poses a serious and likely danger to the public or to the user of the product' (De George, 1999: 255).

5. The prospective whistleblower must believe that the necessary changes will be implemented as a result of their whistleblowing act.

6. The sixth condition is a general one and it is that the whistleblower must be acting in good faith, without malice or vindictiveness.

These conditions will now be considered to assess their defensibility, but first we would like you to ponder their appropriateness and helpfulness.

Activity 6.3	Challenging the conditions for justifiable whistleblowing

The six 'conditions of whistleblowing' mentioned above suggest that, if they cannot be fulfilled, then a whistleblowing act cannot be justified. Develop arguments against as many of the six conditions as possible to justify acts of whistleblowing.

A consideration of the conditions

1. *A product or policy of an organisation needs to possess the potential to do harm to some members of society.*

   At first sight it might seem difficult to find fault with this requirement, because if no public safety or public concern issue exists, where is the public interest in 'the problem'? What can be the justification for any revelation? An important caveat would be that harm must be interpreted widely and not confined to physical harm. Economic harm, as in the cases of Enron and WorldCom, or psychological harm in the form of race or gender discrimination can be just as damaging as physical harm.

2. *The concerned employee should first of all report the facts, as far as they are known, to their immediate superior.*

3. *If the immediate superior fails to act effectively, the concerned employee should take the matter to more senior managers, exhausting all available internal channels in the process.*

These two conditions are considered together because of their obvious linkage. Some would argue that organisations should view internal whistleblowing procedures as important mechanisms within their corporate governance processes. It might seem common sense that organisations would wish to be informed about practices that threaten the well-being of their customers, or the public at large. After all, reputations and brands can take years and considerable expenditures to build, but be destroyed in a very short time by adverse publicity. Thus, enlightened self-interest would seem to dictate an interest in encouraging internal whistleblowing. So why are many organisations not more receptive to the concerns and criticisms of their employees?

The roots of the explanation are complex, but they have to include personal reputations and relationships. By suggesting that 'organisations' would wish to be informed about unsafe practices or products gives a physical status to the term 'organisation' which is, in this context, inappropriate and unhelpful. Criticisms made of products and practices will invariably be criticisms of people, usually more senior than oneself. Condition 2 implies that one's immediate superior within the organisation should be consulted, even if they are part of the problem, hence condition 3. The PIDA also recognises this potential problem and allows the whistleblower to bypass their immediate supervisor if this can be shown to be warranted.

Condition 3 assumes that some form of internal whistleblowing process exists and is operated with integrity. A good example is Nottinghamshire County Council's website, from which you can access a report prepared for the Council on its whistleblowing procedures. The County Council employs an external organisation to operate its anonymous whistleblowing procedure. This is a laudable approach and the County Council operates a refreshingly open policy to its procedures.

However, it is quite possible that the cause of one's concerns lies with the policies or practices of the senior management. For example, budgetary pressures to achieve improved output targets within existing or reduced resources might compromise quality, including safety checks. Alternatively, managers at differing levels within their organisation might each, unknown to the others, impose planned efficiency savings on budgetary forecasts in order to impress senior management (De George, 1999: 244, cites such a scenario). In the process a final budget is created that might involve production outputs and cost levels that are wholly unrealistic. As a consequence, corners are subsequently cut to try to approach the agreed output or cost budgets. Any expression of concern by an employee may become 'lost' within the management hierarchy. Finding out where the blockage exists might be a far from simple task. Expecting employees who are employed 'at the coal face' to have the awareness or confidence to express their concerns higher up the management tree (assuming one can identify how far one needs to go to escape the vicious circle of partially implicated managers) could be an unrealistic assumption. In real life, raising one's concerns internally can simply mean that management can identify which employees are likely to reveal problems that are of the managers' making.

A number of cases reported on the Public Concern at Work website (www .pcaw.co.uk) illustrate how the PIDA has been used and several cases relate to whistleblowers being victimised following internal disclosure of concerns.

Returning to De George's conditions, it might be argued that conditions 2 and 3, while initially suggesting a way for concerned employees and enlightened

| Case study 6.5 | **Victimisation and its consequences** |

In the case of *Fernandes v. Netcom* (2000), Fernandes (F) was the finance officer of a subsidiary of a large US telecoms company. F became concerned at the level of expenses claimed by the CEO of the subsidiary company. F was initially told by his contact in America to 'turn a blind eye', which initially F appears to have done. However, when the CEO's expenses went above £300,000, F took his concerns to the US Board. F (not the CEO) was immediately put under pressure to resign, but he refused. F was disciplined and then sacked for authorising the CEO's expenses. F brought a claim using the PIDA. Contrary to the claims of the American parent company, the UK Employment Tribunal found that F had been dismissed for his whistleblowing, not for authorising the expenses, and because he was 58 and unable to secure similar work he was awarded £293,000.

organisations to operate open channels of communication, might in fact be more reflective of a desire to keep the problem within the organisation, as experienced by Fernandes. This implies an emphasis upon loyalty to the organisation, loyalty which history would question in terms of reciprocated loyalty and commitment.

So far we have shown that a number of circumstances can exist that make conditions 1, 2 and 3 problematic. Yet these are only considered to be conditions that would make a whistleblowing act permissible. They are argued to be insufficient on their own to constitute the necessary conditions for an act of whistleblowing to be morally obligatory. To achieve this, De George argued that conditions 4 and 5 need to be satisfied.

4. *Documentary evidence should be in the possession of the prospective whistleblower that can be presented to external audiences.*

Here it is being argued that, without hard evidence of your concerns, you are not obliged to reveal them to an external (or internal) audience. The rationale is that without strong evidence you may risk the negative outcomes experienced by many whistleblowers, without being able to expose the bad practices that concern you. This has to be a sensible, cautionary note for any potential whistleblower to weigh in their deliberations about expressing their concerns, but it does not address the moral dilemma that the concerned employee faces.

Obtaining the evidence one requires to substantiate one's concerns can be extremely difficult. First there is the problem that ownership of the information is likely to rest with the organisation. The law of property rights would make the photocopying of such evidence a criminal offence. However, to blow the whistle without such evidence would be naïve in the extreme. Most whistleblowers obtain as much evidence as they can and let the courts decide whether accusations of stealing company property are an adequate defence by the employing organisation.

The other major problem is that sometimes incriminating evidence is either too difficult to obtain or simply not available. In the example of the misappropriation of pension fund monies by Robert Maxwell, the case was so complex, due to the interlocking nature of so many of the subsidiary companies within the Maxwell Communications empire, that the task for one, or a few, employees of obtaining sufficient corroborating evidence to support their concerns was simply impossible. It took a team of accountants nearly two calendar years, and many more person years, to unravel the web that Maxwell had woven.

So if one has deep concerns about a particular issue (say the use of pension funds as in the Maxwell case), but a lack of hard evidence, is one absolved from one's civic responsibilities? The financial loss suffered by the pensioners of the Maxwell companies, as was experienced by the employees of Enron and World-Com, were significant. These were not minor financial scams. A lot of people were financially hurt; in a significant number of cases their lives were damaged irrevocably.

While it is wise to counsel caution to prospective whistleblowers if their corroborating information is not strong, society as a whole might be the lesser if this condition was used as an ethical loophole, through which individuals could escape their personal dilemma, i.e. to divulge or not to divulge. It is unlikely that sufficient corroborating evidence will be gathered in many cases to prove irrevocably that a particular revelation is watertight. This is why the PIDA uses phrases such as the whistleblower should 'reasonably believe' and should believe the accusation to be 'substantially true'. UK law does not require that the accusation be 'true', only that it was reasonable to believe that it was true.

5. *The prospective whistleblower must believe that the necessary changes will be implemented as a result of their whistleblowing act.*

The emphasis here is again on the protection of the whistleblower. Given the negative personal outcomes that the majority of whistleblowers have experienced, this condition is merely saying, 'If the probabilities are that nothing will change as a result of your action, you are not duty bound to make your revelation'. Although the condition is expressed in a positive sense, i.e. 'if conditions 1–5 exist and you are of the view that your revelation will cause the offending or dangerous practice to cease, then you are morally obliged to make your revelation', the condition can be reinterpreted as possessing a negative slant. In its negative form the condition is effectively offering an escape route to the uncertain whistleblower.

6. *The whistleblower must be acting in good faith, without malice or vindictiveness.*

This is a contentious condition. It begs the question, 'Why are the motives of the whistleblower important or relevant?' If, say, the whistleblower can be shown to have grounds for harbouring resentment at being passed over for promotion at some time in the past, or for being disciplined for an organisational infraction, why should this invalidate or undermine any revelation that they might make about an organisational malpractice? If, as some managers claimed in our research interviews, the disgruntled employee was lying, out of spite, about an alleged wrongdoing, then clearly the claimed whistleblowing act would not, in fact, be one, because no wrongdoing took place. Such acts are simply lies, not whistleblowing.

We might prefer that those revealing organisational malpractices do so for honourable reasons, and the purity of the whistleblower's position is an oft-cited requirement for acceptable whistleblowing, but it is a doubtful argument. As you will see when we discuss the PIDA, one of the requirements of the act is that, for a whistleblower to gain its protection, they must not profit from the whistleblowing, e.g. being paid as a result of publishing their revelations in a newspaper or book. While it might not be wholly desirable for whistleblowing to be stimulated by thoughts of personal gain, it has to be asked whether the public interest is served by denying such whistleblowers legal protection. Practices for encouraging whistleblowing are followed when rewards are offered for information leading to the successful prosecution of criminals in cases of robbery, murder, hijacking and so on, and nothing is judged to be untoward in these circumstances. One must ask what the distinctions are that make whistleblowers of organisational malpractices less valued by society than whistleblowers of other crimes?

The 'crime' of revealing corporate malpractices is sometimes seen as greater than the corporate malpractices themselves. Whilst offering rewards for the capture of, say, criminals who have robbed a bank is acceptable, the offering of rewards for evidence against companies who have 'robbed' shareholders and employees is somehow seen in a different light.

Whistleblowing: a positive or negative force within society?

The tragedies referred to earlier in the chapter might suggest that organisations would be wise to institute internal whistleblowing procedures to allow employees to raise their concerns and thus create early warning systems upon which the employing organisations could act. Indeed, internal whistleblowing structures can be seen as essential to good corporate governance. So is whistleblowing a characteristic of a healthy, self-aware and self-critical society, with those who reveal organisational malpractices regarded as performing positive civic acts? The evidence would suggest that as a society we are some way away from such a position, although Borrie (1996) observed that the development of organisations such as *Childline* might be heralding a changing view in relation to those who reveal evidence of abuse, recklessness, and disregard for the integrity and sanctity of fellow human beings.

Sternberg (1996) argued that companies should look upon whistleblowing processes as critical elements within good corporate governance practice, and Borrie and Dehn (2002: 5) have also discussed the development of a whistleblowing culture in which, the whistleblower would be seen 'as a witness, not as a complainant'. They argued that, 30 years ago, it was rare to find a company seeking the views of its customers about the quality of the company's products or services. Now it is regarded as central to staying competitive. Borrie and Dehn suggested that perhaps by, say, 2030 whistleblowing processes will not merely be the norm, but seen as essential elements of a corporation's information gathering processes.

A more serious concern for the development of supportive whistleblowing cultures is that, if their justification is based upon economic rather than ethical grounds, then if the economic justification ceases to exist (i.e. the costs of operating a whistleblowing process are judged to outweigh the benefits being derived), then whistleblowers will once again be seen as impediments to organisational competitiveness.

As mentioned earlier, incidents such as the Lyme Bay canoeing disaster and the *Herald of Free Enterprise* disaster created the social and political conditions that allowed the Public Interest Disclosure Act to become law, but history is replete with examples of individuals who have revealed organisational malpractices, invariably to their own personal cost. Peter Drucker (cited in Borrie, 1996) referred to whistleblowers as informers and likened societies that encouraged whistleblowing as bearing some of the characteristics of tyrannies such as those of Tiberius and Nero in Rome, the Spanish Inquisition and the French Terror, a view that not all would share. Others see the acts of whistleblowers as equivalent to referees who maintain 'the rules of the game'. However, the analogy of the whistleblower as a referee in a sporting contest is flawed and a closer examination of the acts of whistleblowing within the context of a sporting event goes some way to explaining the antipathy that some feel towards whistleblowing and whistleblowers.

A whistleblower in a sporting event would not be the referee, but a member of one of the opposing sides who, upon seeing an infringement by one of his own side, stops the game and calls the referee's and the crowd's attention to the incident. This would be referred to as displaying a Corinthian spirit, i.e. placing the ideals and integrity of the sport above the mere winning of the immediate contest.

Whether the supporters and fellow team members would see the incident in exactly the same light is debatable.

The sporting analogy should not be taken too far, because whistleblowing cases involve far greater consequences than the result of a game. The point of the analogy is that whistleblowers are not the appointed referees of organisational affairs. Neither do they claim to be so. They are usually unfortunate individuals who become ensnared in the maelstrom of a situation, which for a variety of reasons becomes irresolvable, at least to their satisfaction. They are then faced with the predicament of either allowing their concerns to subside and to 'keep their heads below the parapet', or to seek to get the issue resolved by revealing their concerns to either an internal or external audience. Some have described whistleblowing acts as heroic acts, because the outcomes for many whistleblowers tend to be so negative. But why are whistleblowers so often maligned and cast as the wrongdoers, in situations where others have created great potential harm?

Besides the unpleasantness of being seen as a 'snitch' or an informer, the prospective whistleblower has to weigh the implications for an organisation of news reaching its critical markets about the practices in question. These markets include both product markets and securities' markets. In competitive markets, ground lost to rival organisations can be difficult to make up, and confidence lost by investors in the organisation difficult to restore. The threat of lost jobs can mean that even long-term colleagues may not support the whistleblower. Whilst the architect of such a situation is the person/s who have committed the malpractice, the innocent employee who becomes knowledgeable of the malpractice is placed in a complex, vexed situation. In some respects they could be damned if they do (i.e. whistleblow) by their colleagues, but damned if they don't (i.e. stay silent) by members of the public who might subsequently be harmed as a result of the malpractice.

The following example, which is taken from a study conducted by the authors (Fisher and Lovell, 2000), indicates that such bad practices are not confined to small, back-street operators who exploit the vulnerability of a low-skilled workforce. The company concerned was a large, internationally known engineering organisation.

None of the claims about the foreign government could be validated, but, assuming they were accurate, what did the actions of the senior management of the company say to the employees of the engineering company? Whatever the rights and wrongs of the situation, the engineering company was employing criteria and a decision process that sanctioned law-breaking activity.

Interestingly, Tony Blair, the then British Prime Minister, made the problems of Africa one of the major challenges of his 2005 G8 presidency. Having previously established the Commission for Africa, one of the principal areas of focus of this was the issue of fraud within African governments and between those governments and multinational corporations. If progress ensues from the work of the Commission then the type of incident portrayed in Case study 6.6 might become a thing of the past, but history would suggest that progress may be slow and uneven. This is particularly so if the account provided by Evans (2004) is indicative of the UK government's commitment to the principles of the Commission for Africa. Evans reported that secret documents, which were revealed in the high court on 22 December 2004, showed that the Trade Secretary, Patricia Hewitt

Case study 6.6	The engineering company and its overseas markets

This company operated in a range of domestic (UK) and overseas markets. In at least one of the overseas markets 'arrangements' were sometimes negotiated with overseas agents that involved exported goods being artificially reclassified to reduce the level of import duties in the overseas country. For example, a £1m order for engineered products would be reclassified for invoice purposes as £700K engineered products and £300K consultancy services. In this particular overseas country consultancy services were not subject to import duty.

The engineering company did not suffer as a result of the reclassification, and the importing agents acquired the goods at a lower cost (taking import taxes into account) than they would otherwise have had to pay. The only losers were the governments of the countries concerned. When these situations arose, the unofficial, but well-understood, procedure within the engineering company was for the requested 'arrangement' to be passed directly to the sales director and managing director of the engineering company. This ultimate decision-making unit would weigh the risks, the returns and the implications of the decision and then decree whether the proposed deal with the agent would be sanctioned. Clearly this act was illegal, yet it was argued that such behaviour was necessary in order to stay in the markets concerned and to protect jobs in the UK. Other operators in these markets were claimed to offer similar 'arrangements'. Here the consequentialist argument that all the implications of a decision should be weighed in order to identify the decision that offers the greatest good to the greatest number might be tabled. The waters become further muddied when the management of the engineering company argued that the government of the overseas country operated a repressive regime, employing punitive import taxes in order to shore up excessive government expenditure on military equipment and government largesse.

overruled her civil servants to water down rules to curb corruption by companies after lobbying by the Confederation of British Industry (CBI) and Rolls Royce, BAE Systems and the Airbus aircraft maker, . . . previously confidential documents showed that the CBI had appreciated the 'full engagement and (continuing friendliness) on this very important issue' shown by Mrs Hewitt and 'our friends at the Department of Trade and Industry' . . . the government and business were 'really playing together now on this'!

If the argument is raised that business is not a precise and neat ethical practice and that one has to accept that in certain cases the ends justify the means, one is accepting a situation where different rules are known to apply in different contexts. No part of a code of behaviour can be seen to be inviolate and every organisational value has its price. This is not to suggest that all laws have to be respected, however repressive and immoral, but the behaviour of the engineering executives was not lawbreaking born from high ideals, but rather lawbreaking born of organisational or personal gain and/or prejudice.

An obvious question regarding the engineering company is why the employees we interviewed tolerated their organisational environment. The answer to this question is not explained by one single factor, but it did appear that the most

Case study 6.7	**A postscript to Case study 6.6**

An interesting development to the previous case was that the practice involving the reclassification of exported products had come to the attention of an overseas government and the major operators in this market (including the UK engineering company) were making provisions for substantial repayments of undeclared import taxes. There was also the possibility that a number of the operators could be barred from selling in the overseas market in the future. This development does not suddenly make the decision-making procedures employed invalid, when previously they could be justified on an ends-means basis. An action does not acquire the status of being ethical or unethical merely on the grounds that its existence is either publicly known or unknown.

senior managers of the organisation were implicated in the practices. Fear that any form of dissent would be quickly suppressed and impair future promotional prospects was the overriding reason offered by the interviewees for their muteness. There were no whistleblowers within this organisation. Was this a state of affairs to be applauded or encouraged, and how and why can middle and senior managers possess such feelings of organisational impotence?

Within the engineering company many understood the practices, but no one possessed the courage, the will or the independence (as a result of the need to retain their employment) to raise their concerns, either within the organisations or to external agencies. The extent of the malpractices acted like a cancer, corrupting others who might otherwise have exercised moral judgment. There appeared to be a view among certain middle and junior management levels of 'what is sauce for the goose (senior management) is sauce for the gander (themselves)'.

The engineering company might seem an extreme example of modern organisational life. However, the continuing evidence of unacceptable organisational practices and whistleblowing cases (*see*, for example, Hartley, 1993; Hunt, 1995, 1998), and the work of organisations such as Public Concern at Work and Freedom to Care, do not provide much support for benign assumptions about respect for the moral agency of individual employees.

Podcast 6.1	**Whistleblowing by corporations – a new trend?** Podcasts explaining how today's business news relates to the topics discussed here will be updated as an ongoing process. Podcast 7.1 discusses the emerging trend of corporations blowing the whistle on each other. To listen to this podcast, other archived podcasts or recent additions, please visit the companion website at www.pearsoned.co.uk/fisherlovellvalerosilva.

Suppressed whistleblowing

For the concerned employee, there are not only potential costs associated with re-vealing organisational malpractices; there are also costs associated with suppress-ing whistleblowing. The latter costs tend to be emotional and psychological and are associated with a loss of self-esteem. This is illustrated in Figure 6.1. A fuller account of the issues relating to this framework is given in Lovell (2002).

The framework possesses two layers. The first of these is concerned with two non-organisational factors that are significant in shaping the third element, that of the individual's personal autonomy. The three elements of layer 1 are:

■ The individual's personal value system, born of past experiences, including family values and perspectives (both nature and nurture are included).

■ Broader societal values, which are unlikely to be homogenous or consistent.

■ The feeling of personal autonomy held by the individual.

Layer 2 also possesses three elements, which are context specific. These are:

■ Values derived from within the organisation.

■ The ethical intensity of a situation or problem felt by the concerned employee.

■ The support from others, normally organisational colleagues, both peers and hierarchical superiors, and family, but also support groups, professional asso-ciations, etc.

In Figure 6.1 the six cells are shown as the same size. However, the figure can be used to describe the relative importance of the six elements in different potential whistleblowing situations. The relative size of the cells is contingent on the specif-ics of each case.

The emboldened lines of Figure 6.1 represents an inflexible organisational boundary. If an ethically charged situation develops in which the position of the troubled employee is at loggerheads with the senior management, it is likely that the organisational mores/strength of practices will flex and grow in scale. With the boundaries of Figure 6.1 fixed, either one or more of the other elements has to shrink, or a fracture in the boundary will occur. If this happens, then confinement

LAYER 2	Intensity of problem	Organisational values/ strength of practices	Support of others
LAYER 1	Personal values	Personal autonomy	Societal values

Figure 6.1 Elements of ethical complexity

of the problem within the organisation will have ceased and an external whistle-blowing situation could follow.

If the troubled employee wishes to retain employment within the organisation, but retains a belief that the organisational practice is wrong, their personal autonomy will need to shrink to accommodate organisational/managerial interests. As a consequence of this diminution of personal autonomy, the ability to exercise moral agency is driven out.

Effectively an individual's personal autonomy acts as a type of shock absorber, allowing confinement of the issue within the organisational boundary. As a consequence, however, the confidence of the suppressed whistleblower can be severely affected. This was particularly so with respect to the individual featured in Case study 6.6. The shrinking of personal autonomy is also significant in Case study 6.8.

Case study 6.8	The charity

G possessed a strong religious faith, which reflected his family upbringing. He worked for an internationally known charitable organisation, whose *raison d'être* was love, understanding, tolerance and forgiveness. During the initial interview G revealed that he had an interesting example of principle that was live at the time of the interview. Having recently attended a seminar on value added tax (VAT), G had realised that a practice operated by the charity was liable to VAT, but the practice had never been declared for VAT purposes. On returning from the seminar G brought the matter to the attention of the directors, believing that the correct approach would be to notify Customs and Excise and to discuss the issue with them. G was very aware that the charity could not afford to repay the sums that were now clearly owing to Customs and Excise, but G believed that Customs and Excise would agree that the VAT rules were never intended to apply to charities like his own, and at worst the charity would need to lobby Parliament and the Treasury to get the rules changed retrospectively. Being an internationally known charity that attracted widespread public support, G believed this would be possible.

At a subsequent meeting with G, he was clearly less buoyant than at the first meeting. He described how the charity's solicitors had been contacted to obtain a legal ruling on the practice in question and they had confirmed G's assessment. However, the attitude of the senior management towards G was not one of gratitude, but rather coolness, even a degree of wariness. At the third meeting with G, he revealed that the affair had been a sickening experience for him. The legal advice had been that the practice should be terminated immediately, but that no mention should be made to Customs and Excise. The belief was that Customs and Excise would demand a refund of the unpaid taxes and that the probability of the Treasury seeking a change to taxation legislation to exclude the charity from future liability was low, with no chance of retrospective legislation. G's wishes to be honest and 'come clean' with Customs and Excise were dismissed as naïve. What particularly vexed and troubled him was that he was now, in his own words, 'perceived as a potential whistleblower'. His relationship with members of the charity's board of directors had changed from a close and friendly one to one characterised by considerable wariness and mistrust. He had no intention of whistleblowing (out of loyalty to the organisation, not to the senior management), but it hurt greatly to come face-to-face with his organisational impotency, when he had thought that he and his work were highly valued.

At the start of his ethical dilemma, G carried with him a set of values that, he argued, reflected a strong commitment to notions of fairness, equity and justice. These underpinned his initial reasoning of the problem. These were values that he believed corresponded with those of the broader society and the charity in question.

For G, the intensity of the problem was initially high, but he quickly realised that the support of others did not exist, particularly at a very senior level. This mix of level 2 elements (high problem intensity; total resistance from senior management and low support from others) transformed the issue from one, in G's eyes, capable of resolution within notions of justice and equity, to an ethical dilemma. G's preference to discuss the issue with Customs and Excise put him at variance with the charity's board of directors. G became isolated and was seen as a deviant. He had a loyalty to both the organisation, whose values and mission he wholeheartedly believed in, and to his fellow employees, whose livelihoods would certainly be affected if the tax authorities did demand a repayment of back taxes.

G expressed the view that, if he really believed that Customs and Excise would be successful in demanding repayment of back taxes, he too would support concealment, as the work of the charity would be affected to the point of ruin. However, he simply could not accept that this would be the ultimate outcome. He believed that the board of directors did not wish to be seen as having made a serious error in the decisions they had taken over the configuration of the organisation that had led to the practice in question attracting VAT liability, a ramification they had overlooked.

G considered that the concealment decided upon by the directors reflected an avoidance of pain motive on their part, the very lowest stage of reasoning within Kohlberg's hierarchy. The values imposed upon the situation by the board of directors effectively challenged G. He either stayed and kept quiet or he left. Due to family commitments and a strong belief in the work of the charity G stayed, but his personal autonomy was severely diminished and he viewed the future with sadness and apprehension. Figure 6.2 reflects an application of the elements of ethical complexity to the case.

If a whistleblower reveals an organisational practice that they consider to be against the public interest, such a whistleblowing act could be considered a civic act. In the sense used here, civic describes an act that an individual citizen carries out as a member of a community or state. The term citizen is an inclusive term. It locates the individual within a community of others. It stresses relatedness,

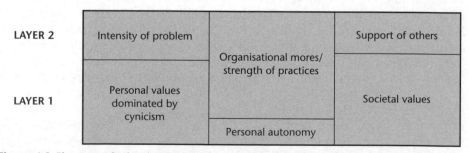

Figure 6.2 Elements of ethical complexity (Case study 6.8)

Cross reference	*Kohlberg's hierarchy of moral reasoning* G's apparent willingness to 'break the law' is not necessarily a reprehensible position to hold. In G's view the particular VAT law in question represented a failing in the legislation's drafting. It was 'bad law', and could be corrected once its failings were brought to the attention of the relevant authorities. This form of reasoning would normally be considered to reflect high levels of moral reasoning, that is, 5, possibly even 6, within Kohlberg's hierarchy (*see* p. 218), depending upon how hard G was prepared to fight for his convictions.

without the integrity and specialness of the individual being lost in the blandness of a crowd. The citizen is both part of a community, but identifiable and separable within it.

There is no suggestion that in such a society every individual is perpetually and desperately seeking to achieve a utopian form of communitarian existence, a form of societal nirvana. What the term civic describes is a context in which justice and understanding are at the bedrock of social relationships. Thus, when a (potentially) significant injustice is observed, the civic-minded individual does not walk away from their civic responsibilities by ignoring the injustice or public hazard. They seek to change the practice, and if this is unsuccessful they seek to bring the problem to public attention. They act in an autonomous way, i.e. they act as free people. They act with moral agency. This is what many whistleblowers would claim for their acts. This is not an argument for a form of societal or organisational chaos that would encourage everyone to challenge everything. As with all aspects of human relations, rights should normally carry with them responsibilities. As a consequence the right to exercise moral agency requires that individuals also respect the beliefs of others insofar as they represent commonly held views.

The whistleblower can be portrayed as a somewhat heroic figure, and some writers do argue this position. While no attempt will be made to suggest that whistleblowing is a saintly act, there is no doubt that particular whistleblowing cases portray individuals who have displayed personal courage and determination to overcome legal, financial, psychological and physical obstacles in their attempts to stop a particular organisational practice, or to bring it to public attention (*see* Hoffman and Moore, 1990; Matthews et al., 1991; Miceli and Near, 1992; Lovell and Robertson, 1994; Hunt 1995, 1998 for examples). But, for some, there can be an exhilaration associated with whistleblowing. Paul van Buitenen (2000) was the EU employee whose revelations about the misuse of EU funds contributed to the resignation of the entire European Union Commission in 1999. His autobiography reveals that, although his whistleblowing damaged him, he also relished the excitement of the clandestine meetings and the media attention that arose from it.

Returning to our consideration of the societal role and defensibility of whistleblowing, we consider Case study 6.9. This case provides further evidence of the psychological damage that can be inflicted upon an employee who rails against an organisational practice. The person in question occupied a senior position within the organisation concerned, but was judged to pose a threat to certain key individuals within the organisation.

Case study 6.9	The costs of whistleblowing

W had worked for the organisation concerned for seven years and had risen to a senior position, effectively being the joint deputy head of finance. However, his unease about certain accounting 'adjustments' he was being asked to make and the obstacle that he represented to the advancement of a junior colleague whom the chief executive appeared to favour, meant that W suddenly appeared to be a 'persona non grata'. This was surprising to all those who were interviewed to corroborate this case, because, without exception, they all held W in very high esteem. A decision appeared to have been made by the chief executive that W had to go, and considerable psychological pressure was exerted on W to encourage him to resign. W's last annual appraisal spoke about his failing performance, despite glowing previous appraisals. W finally resigned, although he appeared to have been 'constructively dismissed', and an out-of-court settlement was made to remove the threat of an industrial tribunal hearing for wrongful dismissal. The words of W are illuminating:

. . . they drag you down to such an extent that your confidence is absolutely rock bottom. You have no confidence in your own ability and it takes you a long time to realise that you didn't deserve this. You hadn't done anything wrong.... in the back of your mind you're thinking, did I do something wrong to deserve this? Until now, I have not said anything about my case. . . . You want a career and you're not quite sure what influence they have in the rest of the public sector – I still haven't got a permanent position.

The governance structures of W's organisation were clearly deficient.

Whistleblowing was not on the agenda of any of the central characters within the cases considered in this chapter because of their fear for their respective employment prospects. Many of those who, in a study of accountants and HR managers (Fisher and Lovell, 2000), expressed disgust over certain organisational practices felt impotent and unable to do anything to put things right.

The words of a hospital's deputy director of finance reveal behaviour that might surprise some.

'I haven't done anything wrong.' These are words to ponder.

Thus, against the six criteria H would have found a degree of support for an act of whistleblowing, although the belief that little if anything would change as a result of a whistleblowing act (condition 5) does provide a justification (within De George's framework) for 'keeping quiet'.

A further consideration was that H feared that the adverse publicity that such a revelation would attract would do the hospital great harm, at a time when hospitals across the UK were under considerable media scrutiny due to revelations about the concealment of negligent practices by clinicians (*see* Case study 2.20). It is not just organisations operating in the profit-seeking sectors that can suffer from adverse publicity and falling 'client' confidence. H's concerns over the ramifications for 'his' hospital of any disclosure about the greed of a significant number of consultants were real.

Within this account of H's case, there are a number of issues that need to be explored further. The first is the harm that can be caused by an act of whistleblowing.

Case study 6.10	**The hospital case**

This case was recounted to the researchers by a range of middle-ranking HR managers and accountants within a hospital, as well as by H, the deputy director of finance. It was a situation that troubled many in the hospital (see Case study 2.22 for another interviewee's perspective).

The case relates to the waiting lists initiative instigated by the Department of Health in 1998. The intention of the initiative was to provide additional funds to hospitals to allow them to reduce hospital waiting lists in key areas. The following are the words of the deputy director of finance.

The government has just put all this money into the waiting list initiative to treat patients and get them off the waiting list. It's taxpayers' money – the spirit of that money was not to line consultants' pockets. In theory, it's NHS money, health sector money. A number of the specialties reacted as one would hope. However, the ophthalmologists said, 'Yes, we will do this, if you pay me something like £750 per case. We will pay the nurses time and a half . . . And if you don't pay us that rate we won't do the list.' So ophthalmologists got their way – a very dirty deal – nurses get a bit and porters and cleaners get nothing. The ophthalmologists are getting about £15,000 extra per list.

In addition to the ophthalmologists, ENT specialists and anaesthetists at this hospital also negotiated their own special deals with regard to the waiting lists' initiatives. When asked how particular specialties could drive through such arrangements, the response was, 'They confronted the organisation. The chief executive is frightened of the power of these groups, so he is prepared to do deals, rather than risk not getting patients done.'

When asked to describe his own feelings towards this situation, H replied, 'Perhaps I am naïve, but I wouldn't have let it happen. I think all staff should be treated equally and I would have waged war with the consultants and said, I am sorry – we are not playing.'

Had H ever been tempted to blow the whistle at any time? The answer was yes and the above situation was such a time. He had not because, 'I have to respect the chief executive's decision. My loyalty to him, my accountability – I haven't done anything wrong.'

Notwithstanding the existence of unacceptable organisational practices, or shortcomings in quality and/or safety, the whistleblowing act itself may inflict harm upon individuals and organisations including individuals known personally to the whistleblower. To present whistleblowing situations as always clear-cut, with 'good guys' and 'bad guys' clearly demarcated, and issues neatly packaged with 'right' and 'wrong' labels attached, would be misleading. Life is messy, and organisational life is particularly messy on occasions. However, this is not an excuse to do nothing. Judgment has to be a major factor in shaping personal decision making, but when that judgment is constrained by employment fears, moral agency is undermined and impoverished. This takes us to the second point, that of floating responsibility (Bauman, 1994).

H's closing words 'I haven't done anything wrong' could be seen as an example of floating responsibility. It becomes an organisational defence against individual conscience. In this way the following of rules and adherence to the commands of superiors make identification of responsibility difficult to isolate. 'I was only following orders' is a plea heard from junior clerks to senior military officers.

| Cross reference | Using De George's six criteria for justifiable whistleblowing (*see* p. 234) it is possible to argue that H could have responded positively to conditions 1, 2, 4 and 6. |

- H would have been acting honourably, assuming he did not sell his story to the press, if he had chosen to go public with his knowledge (condition 6).

- It was disgust with the way senior consultants were using their organisational power to 'line their pockets' with public money that was at the heart of H's angst (condition 1).

- H had also discussed the issue with the finance director (condition 2), although the latter seemed resigned to the realities of organisational power within the hospital.

- H also had the documentary evidence to substantiate his case, had he chosen to use it (condition 4).

- However, H had not taken the matter to the chief executive because the chief executive was a central figure in the affair (condition 3).

- He doubted whether a whistleblowing act would change much, after the initial furore had died down (condition 5).

Floating responsibility   **DEFINITION**

Floating responsibility refers to the situation where all the individuals that were potentially involved or implicated in a particular incident or problem are all able to explain that responsibility for the problem was not theirs. Responsibility becomes impossible to pinpoint. It appears to fall between the cracks of job descriptions and roles.

The third point to consider is H's expressed loyalty to the chief executive. 'I have to respect the chief executive's decision. My loyalty to him, my accountability.' Besides loyalty to the chief executive, H was also thinking of his other work colleagues. As the case indicates, H was not alone in his knowledge of the affair, yet H indicated that no one else would 'rock the boat'. These others preferred to 'keep their heads down' for fear of the personal consequences. Colleagues (and their families) who choose to ignore the implications of a malpractice could be significantly affected by any revelations. These are heavy considerations to weigh in the decision of whether or not to whistleblow. The vulnerability and aloneness of the potential whistleblower, but also those who adopt a 'not my business' stance, need reflecting upon. Jos (1988: 323) argued that,

Modern organisations require workers to do things they might not otherwise do . . . [they] undermine the capacity of workers to make their own judgement about what they should do. By uncritically deferring to others, workers may become party to immoral or illegal activities and policies. In short, it is the worker's autonomy, his status as a chooser that is at stake.

Jos's lament over the demise of moral autonomy needs to be juxtaposed with the celebration of 'the individual' as evidenced in much political and corporate rhetoric. The wishes of the individual consumer are claimed to be sovereign. Citizen charters abound, and organisations, both public and private sector, claim to dance to the tune of consumer preferences. Nisbet (1953), while addressing issues of political economy, offered some thoughts that are relevant to this debate.

> The political **enslavement** of man requires the **emancipation** of man from all the authorities and memberships . . . that serve, one degree or another, to insulate the individual from the external political power . . . totalitarian domination of the individual will is not a mysterious process, not a form of sorcery based upon some vast and unknowable irrationalism. It arises and proceeds rationally and relentlessly through the creation of new functions, statuses and allegiances which, by conferring community, makes the manipulation of the human will scarcely more than an exercise in scientific social psychology . . . there may be left the appearance of individual freedom, provided it is only individual freedom. All of this is unimportant, always subject to guidance and control, if the primary social contexts of belief and opinion are properly organised and managed. What is central is the creation of a network of functions and loyalties reaching down into the most intimate recesses of human life where ideas and beliefs will germinate and develop.
>
> (Nisbet, 1953: 202, 208, emphasis in the original)

Thus, Nisbet argued that the freedom inherent within current conceptions of individualism is a particular and partial form of individualism, located precisely in the economic sphere. This ideology has, however, facilitated the neutering of people as political actors. Yet in the economic sphere, individualism is again prescribed, with certain forms of action almost proscribed. Sarason (1986) commented on a society in which individuals affected by social dilemmas perceive their dilemmas as their, and only their, responsibility. Paraphrasing Sarason,

> If **your** ethical dilemma is **your** responsibility according to **my** morality, this is quite consistent with the increasingly dominant ideology of individual rights, responsibility, choice and freedom. If I experience the issue as **yours**, it is because there is nothing in my existence to make it **ours**. And by **ours** I mean a socio-cultural network and traditions which engender an obligation to be part of the problem and possible solution.
>
> (Sarason, 1986, emphasis in the original)

What we hope is becoming evident is that whistleblowing is a complex, many-sided debate that cannot be removed from the social, cultural and economic contexts to which it relates.

Whilst individual attitudes might be difficult to change, certainly in the short term, maybe the least that might be expected of a civilised society is that those of its members who do act in ways that reflect a civic orientation in their whistleblowing should enjoy the protection of the law. Thus, it is appropriate that we now progress to a consideration of the law relating to whistleblowing in the UK, the Public Interest Disclosure Act, 1998.

The Public Interest Disclosure Act (1998) (PIDA)

There are two central elements to the PIDA to recognise from the outset. The first is that it does not give a right to an employee to whistleblow. The act has been constructed upon the premise that confidentiality of corporate information is the primary principle, from which there a few exceptions. It is to these exceptions that the act speaks. It offers protection to those who speak out (in the parlance of the act, make a 'disclosure') against specific types of organisational malpractices, as long as certain conditions are met. The act's construction encourages disclosure to be kept within the employing organisation's boundaries by increasing the conditions that have to be satisfied if one makes a disclosure outside the confines of the employing organisation.

The second element that lessens the act's potential from the perspective of the concerned employee is that the burden of proof is upon the employee to show that a malpractice has occurred, although the burden of proof does vary depending upon to whom a disclosure is made. In circumstances where the work environment is intimidatory and oppressive, obtaining supporting evidence, such as corroboration from current employees, could prove extremely difficult.

The term 'protected disclosure' relates to the type of whistleblowing act that falls within the protection of the act. The malpractice must normally relate to the employing organisation. However, in certain, restricted situations a protected disclosure can be made against third-party organisations. Interestingly, auditors, with the exception of matters relating to terrorism and money laundering, do not have a duty to report wrongdoing, and neither are they protected by the PIDA if they do make such a revelation. It could be argued that this exclusion from protection by the act and the omission of a duty to report wrongdoing, other than in the two areas mentioned, suits the practising members of the accountancy profession, as it avoids their coming into conflict with their clients. Audit income is but a part of the income that most practising accountancy firms earn from their audit clients. It is not in the interest of practising accountancy firms to be required to play the role of society's watchdog on the activities of their clients.

For a disclosure to fall within the protection of the act, the disclosure itself must relate to a specified set of malpractices. These are:

- A criminal offence.

- A failure to comply with any legal obligation.

- A miscarriage of justice.

- Danger to the health and safety of any individual.

- Damage to the environment.

- Deliberate concealment of any of the above.

To comply with the PIDA (and thus to stay within its protection), an ethically concerned employee must use to the full the organisation's internal procedures for handling such concerns. Such procedures can be avoided only if:

- at the time the disclosure was made the employee reasonably believed that they would be 'subject to a detriment' by the employer if a disclosure was made to the employer;

- the employee is concerned that evidence relating to the malpractice would be concealed or destroyed by the employer;

- the employee has previously made a disclosure to the employer of substantially the same information.

> **Detriment** is defined in the act as being penalised by the employer, e.g. being fined, demoted, sacked or denied promotion.　**DEFINITION**

Internal procedures can be sidestepped if they are shown to be seriously flawed, because of legitimate fears of information being confiscated or destroyed. Other fears, such as the existence of an oppressive and threatening employment environment, can be more difficult to substantiate. This is because obtaining corroborating evidence from fellow employees (who might be fearful for their own jobs) can be extremely difficult to obtain.

One concern about the act is that it addresses the circumstances of the employee once that employee has made a disclosure. It is possible that, if only the *threat* of disclosure is made by the concerned employee, the act would not protect the employee in the event of the employee being sacked before a full disclosure was made. In addition, whilst expressions of concern by one employee to another employee about a particular organisational (mal)practice might constitute a breach of confidentiality (and thus create the possibility of dismissal), the PIDA would not be available to the sacked employee if he had not raised the issue with the organisation's management.

While the establishment of an internal whistleblowing procedure may, at first sight, be a laudable development by any organisation, in the hands of unscrupulous employers it might be a mere device for complying with the letter of the law but not the spirit. Warren (1993) questioned the rationale for American firms introducing corporate codes of conduct. The same might be said of internal whistleblowing procedures.

There is also the issue of gaining sufficient evidence to feel able to lodge a concern. Raising a concern within the employing organisation requires that the concerned employee must satisfy two tests. The first is that he must 'reasonably believe' that one of the above-mentioned malpractices has occurred. Secondly, the disclosure must be made in 'good faith'. However, the process of gaining evidence, as mentioned in relation to the Maxwell affair, can be a big problem. In such situations, being able to prove that sufficient evidence existed to allow individuals to 'reasonably believe' there were malpractices afoot could be extremely difficult. In addition, the use of internal procedures could prove unattractive to an employee (as in the Maxwell case). This would leave the concerned employee with only external whistleblowing to contemplate. However, the burden of proof required to stay within PIDA protection increases as soon as one raises one's concerns with external third parties. If information is revealed within the firm then the 'reasonably believe' test applies. However, if concerns are expressed to an external third party then the test becomes, 'the employee . . . reasonably believes that the information and any allegation contained in it are *substantially true*' [emphasis added]. Thus the concerned employee must be able to show that there were reasonable grounds for them to believe that the allegation being made was 'substantially true' – a far more rigorous criterion than 'reasonably believe'.

Even if this condition is met, the concerned employee loses protection of the PIDA if the employee is rewarded for disclosing the wrongdoing, e.g. receiving payment from a newspaper. Thus, motive for the disclosure affects the protection provided by the PIDA. As mentioned earlier, rewards for information (including that provided anonymously) that leads to the successful prosecution of a criminal are quite acceptable. So why the different treatment of those who report the criminal activity of organisations?

If the internal whistleblowing procedures of an employing organisation are judged to be unsafe by a concerned employee, they will normally be expected to use the offices of a 'prescribed body'. Such a prescribed body is likely to be a regulatory body of an industry (e.g. OFWAT for water companies, or the Financial Services Authority for financial service companies). Within the public sector, such prescribed bodies are less likely to exist. It will be important for the concerned employee to establish whether a 'prescribed body' exists to handle their concerns. Failure to follow the required procedures might take the complaint outside the protection of the PIDA. Notwithstanding this, there exists no requirement on the part of a regulator to act in response to the information supplied by a concerned employee, other than the rules under which the regulator normally acts.

The above uncertainty over the 'actual' protection afforded by the PIDA is at the heart of concerns expressed about the act. The evidence provided by *Freedom to Care* on those cases it has investigated is that the PIDA would not have provided the protection the whistleblowers needed to withstand losing their jobs.

Employees working in areas covered by the Official Secrets' Act are also not protected by the PIDA. There are many examples of classified information within central government and (to a lesser extent) local government that are of dubious sensitivity, yet the information is covered by the Official Secrets' Act. There is a need for a concerned employee to check whether any information that relates to the cause of their concern is of a classified nature.

If all the requirements of the PIDA are satisfied (including the requirement that the alleged malpractice be deemed to be a sufficiently serious offence, plus all the other requirements mentioned above), the act does provide protection that previously did not exist. Additional features of the PIDA are:

1. Gagging clauses. Gagging clauses are restrictive clauses in employment contracts that prevent the mentioning of anything of an organisational nature to anyone outside the employing organisation. These were a very real problem for many employees prior to the PIDA, but they appear to be void under the act – other than those covered by the Official Secrets Act.

Whilst gagging clauses appear to be outlawed by PIDA, it must still be remembered that an implied term of employment contracts is the duty of confidentiality to the employing organisation on the part of the employee. It is this 'duty of confidentiality' that explains the considerable restrictions that have been placed upon the definition of a 'protected disclosure'. Only when the conditions of the PIDA have been judged to have been complied with, can the 'duty of confidentiality' be usurped by the PIDA in the specified situations identified above.

2. Interim relief (keeping one's salary if dismissed for whistleblowing). Under section 9, the PIDA extends one of the provisions of the Employment Rights Act (ERA). If an employee suffers dismissal as a result of making a 'protected disclosure', they should make representation to an Employment Tribunal within seven days of dismissal. This aspect is known as interim relief. If the Employment Tribunal considers that the disclosure is likely to fall within the definition of a protected disclosure, it *may* order the employer to reinstate the employee. If the employer fails to comply with such an order, 'the employee is deemed to remain in employment until the hearing and entitled to continue to be paid as such'. However, before these conditions are activated on behalf of the employee, three further conditions must be met:

1. The claim for an interim relief must be lodged within seven days of dismissal.

2. The Employment Tribunal must first decide that the employee is likely to be found to have made a protected disclosure (not an obvious decision without studying all the relevant information).

3. An order is likely to be made to the employing organisation to reinstate the employee (and this ruling happens relatively infrequently).

Thus, an interim order, while appearing to be a positive aspect of the PIDA, is likely in practice to be much less frequently activated than it might first appear. For example, in the case, *Bladon v. ALM Medical Services ET*, reported by Myers and Dehn (2000), an application for interim relief was rejected by the chairman of the Employment Tribunal without hearing evidence. The basis for this judgement was that the tribunal chairman considered the claimant's (the whistleblower) case to be 'implausible'. Yet, when the case was finally heard, the whistleblower's actions were upheld and he was awarded damages. However, in the many months between the application for an interim relief and the actual tribunal hearing, the whistleblower was denied any salary from his former employer.

If an employee's case falls within the protection of the PIDA, then:

- The employee will be entitled to a compensation payment if victimisation is experienced as a result of the whistleblowing act (e.g. the employee stays within the employing organisation but suffers demotion). The level of compensation will depend upon the specifics of each case.

- If dismissed, the employee will be entitled to a compensation payment in line with the awards available through Employment Tribunals. These rates change over time, but, as mentioned earlier, the ceiling has now been removed.

Reflections

This chapter has considered various aspects of whistleblowing. Although examples can be cited of revelations of organisational malpractices that have been shown to be both accurate and serious, as well as examples of where the concerns of employees have been ignored or 'lost' in managerial structures and disasters involving loss of life have followed, the prospects for those contemplating whistleblowing remain uncertain. Employment law and the PIDA are written with the primary intention of protecting the commercial confidentiality of organisations that operate in legally compliant ways. There is thus a fundamental tension between, on the one hand, the need for employees to feel able to exercise moral agency and raise awareness of issues that have a genuine public interest and, on the other hand, the need for organisations to retain commercially sensitive information, and be protected from malicious and ill-founded accusations by disgruntled employees. The extent to which the balance between these competing requirements is acceptable and appropriate needs to be revisited regularly.

In modern times strong economies and vibrant business sectors are essential if political and social goals are to be achieved. It is difficult to refute the centrality of a strong economy to many societal aspirations, whether the economy is located in the so-called developing or developed worlds. As a result, businesses, and pressure groups representing business interests, act as powerful influences in the creation and maintenance of the legal frameworks that govern business activities. In this context it is perhaps not surprising that the PIDA was framed in the way that it was, if it was to receive sufficient support in the UK Parliament and thereby become law. Yet the very necessity to support and protect business interests creates loopholes for unscrupulous organisations to use. In addition there are those situations in which organisations flout the laws that society has passed, and the question then arises as to how and when society should be made aware of these infractions.

There are also questions about the relationships between business, environmental and societal interests, with the latter relating as much to future societies as to present ones. It is important that assumptions regarding the roles and power of organisations are challenged – not taken for granted. Related to, but separate from, these assumptions are the issues relating to notions of individualism and civic perspectives that have been alluded to in this chapter. These need revisiting on a regular basis to ensure that the issues and debates are themselves comprehended, and not overpowered by the pre-eminence of business interests.

Summary

In this chapter the following key points have been made:

- Whistleblowing includes, but is not limited to, the revelation of an organisational issue to an external party.

- Whistleblowing help-lines can be both important organisational mechanisms for the raising of ethical concerns, and early warning systems of unacceptable practices.

- Protection offered to whistleblowers by the PIDA is constrained and cannot limit the trauma that tends to accompany whistleblowing acts.

- The pejorative connotation of whistleblowing needs to be reflected upon and understood. Whilst perpetual whistleblowing is an unattractive proposition, the organisational impotence reflected in the case studies cited is equally unpalatable.

- Viewing whistleblowers as witnesses rather than snitches would be a positive development.

- If it is right to reveal the identity of those who break the law outside organisational life, why is it less right to reveal those who break the law or who endanger human life in their capacities as organisational employees?

Typical assignments

1. Debate the strength of the arguments that seek to change the terminology for describing those who reveal organisational malpractices as whistleblowers.

2. To gain the protection of the Public Interest Disclosure Act, those who reveal organisational malpractices have to satisfy a number of conditions that witnesses in other criminal investigations do not have to satisfy, e.g. deriving no financial gain from the case and not having been involved in the crime at any stage. Critically evaluate the merits of these conditions.

3. Evaluate the argument that internal whistleblowing procedures are an essential part of any learning organisation.

4. Assume that a person has responded to Activity 6.1 in the following way. He has indicated:

   - an extreme level of anger (point 10 on the scale) in response to Case A;

   - a high level of support (point 2 on the scale) in Case B; and

   - a fair degree of anger (point 6 on the scale) in Case C.

   Discuss the factors that could explain these variations in the responses to the questions posed and what this might say about ethical principles.

Group activity 6.1

Consider the PIDA and make recommendations to reduce or add to the scope of the act. Your proposals should be able to withstand critical appraisal at both a practical and theoretical level. Divide a sheet of paper into four columns. In the first column list your proposals. In the second column state against each proposal why you believe the amendment is justified. In the third column you should identify the principal objections or problems associated with your proposal. The final column should reflect your thoughts on the strengths of the objections/problems identified in column three, and whether you believe they are surmountable.

Recommended further reading

The two main authors writing on the topic of this chapter are Borrie and Hunt. We recommend that you read Borrie (1996) 'Business Ethics and Accountability', in Brindle, M. and Dehn, G., *Four Windows on Whistleblowing*, pp. 1–23, Public Concern at Work. Also Borrie, G. and Dehn, G. (2002) *Whistleblowing: The New Perspective*, Public Concern website, http://www.pcaw.co.uk/. Hunt's books (1995) *Whistleblowing in the Health Service: Accountability, Law & Professional Practice*, Edward Arnold and (1998) *Whistleblowing in the Social Services: Public Accountability and Professional Practice*, Edward Arnold are also useful. A more recent work is by Lewis, D. B. (2000) *Whistleblowing at Work*, Athlone Press.

Useful websites

Topic	Website provider	URL
The website of the leading charitable organisation providing advice to both individuals and organisations on whistleblowing issues/ organisational hotlines	Public Concern at Work	http://www.pcaw.co.uk
An impressive organisation, which acts as an advocate for those who stand up for freedom of speech in the workplace. Publishes an extremely thought provoking and important newsletter	Freedom to Care	http://www.freedomtocare.org

PART C

Organisational responses to ethical issues

CHAPTER 7

Corporate governance: an organisation's external accountability

Chapter at a glance

Chapter contents

- Learning outcomes
- Introduction
- The arguments for taking corporate governance seriously
- Developments in corporate governance
- What have the developments in corporate governance achieved?
- International best practice standards
- Shareholder activism
- Governance and bribery and corruption
- Corporate manslaughter
- Reflections
- Summary

Case studies

- Case study 7.1 Women on boards of directors
- Case study 7.2 A law professor, as citizen, takes action
- Case study 7.3 A judge, as citizen, takes action
- Case study 7.4 The Herald of Free Enterprise

Activities and exercises

- Typical assignments
- Group activity 7.1
- Recommended further reading
- Useful websites

Learning outcomes

Having read this chapter and completed its associated activities, readers should be able to:

■ Debate the scope and appropriateness of developments in Anglo-American corporate governance since the early 1990s.

■ Discuss the challenges posed to Anglo-American development in corporate governance by the King Report.

■ Review international standards for corporate responsibility and accountability.

■ Discuss corporate accountability in relation to bribery and corruption, and corporate manslaughter as an indictable offence in the UK and USA.

Introduction

Corporate governance is a phrase with some longevity, although it has gained greater prominence since the early 1990s. A concern with corporate governance is a consequence of organisations being run by managers rather than the owners or the shareholders of the organisation. Managers may experience a conflict of interests. They may be tempted to manage an organisation for their own advantage rather than for the benefit of the owners and shareholders. Governance however reaches beyond the interests of the shareholders. It is also concerned with an organisation's obligation to be a good citizen. If corporations are seen as citizens then this status brings benefits but also duties. These include obeying the law as if they were real persons instead of legal fictions; an issue that will be considered in detail in relation to corporate manslaughter. A corporation's wider responsibilities as a citizen are discussed in Chapter 9.

Corporate governance encompasses the systems that are put in place to monitor, constrain and, if possible, prevent such distortions in the allocation of the benefits produced by an organisation and to ensure the duties of a citizen are met. In this chapter we will discuss the reason for requiring good corporate governance and consider the proposals for achieving it that have been published over time. Then we will look at some specific issues:

■ The governance arrangements required within corporations to ensure accountability to shareholders and, more generally, to the societies they operate within.

■ Corporate governance and the control of bribery and corruption.

■ Corporate manslaughter.

■ International standards for corporate behaviour.

Berle and Means' seminal publication in 1932 charted the history and implications of the decoupling of ownership (shareholders) from control (senior management) within the modern corporation. Niebuhr (1932) also wrote powerful critiques of corporate power and the exploitative and alienating tendencies of the capitalist system. Since the early 1990s there has been increasing attention to corporate governance as a result of major corporate scandals such as Maxwell Communications, BCCI and Polly Peck in the late 1980s and in the early 2000s Enron, WorldCom, Global Crossing and Parmalat.

Such problems are not only an issue in the private sector. In government and the public services there is a parallel concern that public officials and managers will use their power to build bureaucratic 'empires', which increase their status, and to promote their own careers, rather than seek to meet the needs of the public whom they nominally serve. This argument is put forward most strongly by the Public Choice Theorists, such as Buchanan and Tullock (1962), who argue that politicians and public officials are rent seekers who use their positions for their own benefit. Similar issues also arise in hybrid private and public sector firms, commonly referred to as SOEs (state owned enterprises). When government wholly owns a SOE there is a danger that politicians will interfere in the day-to-day management of the firm and distract it from its best strategic direction in order to obtain some short-term political advantage. Similarly, when a government is a major, or majority, shareholder in a SOE, it may use its dominant holding to ignore or override the wishes of the smaller shareholders. The OECD (2005) has published benchmark standards for how governance should operate in the case of SOEs. Corporate governance therefore is, in part, systems to limit the distortions caused by conflict of interest in the management of an organisation.

The arguments for taking corporate governance seriously

The desire to encourage, nay require, corporations to assume greater responsibility for their actions can be traced back over many decades, and reflects growing concerns regarding the power and influence of corporations over people's lives and even the independence and integrity of governments. For example, Oberman (2000) refers to academic debates over corporate social responsibilities taking place in the 1920s. As the power and influence of business corporations have assumed ever greater proportions, so too have the calls increased for mechanisms to be put in place that would make corporations more accountable as well as responsible to a wider constituency than merely their shareholders. The reasons for taking corporate governance seriously are discussed next.

Failure of large corporations damages societies

One reason why good corporate governance may be required by society more generally, and not just by owners and stakeholders, is that corporate collapses and failures, which can cause damage in society beyond the organisation itself, are often attributed to poor governance. A case can be made that the collapse of the Royal Bank of Scotland in the UK was due to poor corporate governance, which allowed too much power to accrue to the chief executive who remained unchallenged in his ambition to buy ABN Amro. The decision to purchase was a flawed one and its ripple effect could have caused the entire UK banking system to collapse. More recently poor governance was revealed in the case of the Japanese company Olympus. In 2011 an investigation revealed that the company had hidden business and investment losses of £1.09bn for nearly 20 years. The fraud only came to light when a new CEO began to ask questions about the accounts. He claimed that he was pressurised into resigning as CEO when he blew the whistle, but the company eventually admitted to the fraud. The independent investigation into the matter blamed the problem on poor corporate governance and the 'low esteem for transparency and governance' held by past presidents of the company. Michael Woodward, the whistleblowing CEO claimed that 'Japan has to change its corporate governance and have powerful non-executives' (BBC, 2011).

The dangers consequent on corporate failure are not new. For example, the 'Bubble Act' of 1719 came into being as the result of a corporate scandal, which, in relative terms, involved sums of money greater than the combined value of Enron and WorldCom. Lee (1984) and Edey (1984) referred to the manipulation of company accounting information by managers at the expense of the owners' interests during the early nineteenth century, while Carey (1984) referred to the contribution of William Z. Ripley, a Harvard professor, who, in the early 1920s wrote about the 'docility of corporate shareholders permitting themselves to be honeyfuggled'. In relation to the public utilities industries, Ridley referred to 'the hoodwinking of the shareholders', and of accountants Ripley observed, 'accountants are enabled to play ball with figures to an astounding degree' (Carey, 1984: 243).

It is clear from the very brief overview above that concerns over corporate governance are not new, but reactions to corporate scandals of the 1990s and early twenty-first century by organisations such as the major stock exchanges, professional accountancy bodies and governments appear to have been more obvious and public than before. Could this reflect a degree of vulnerability and sensitivity that was not felt in the past? It is difficult to say, although débacles such as Enron and WorldCom, Global Crossing and Parmalat pose fundamental problems for securities' markets. Investing in companies is a risky business and any investor must recognise and accept this fact. Thus, it is not the losing of money that is the problem. The problem is the failure of market mechanisms to provide the information and warning signals that the investing public has a right to expect. In all the corporate failures referred to in this chapter the most recent accounts of the corporations concerned gave little if any hint of the financial turmoil the corporations were experiencing.

In the cases of Enron and WorldCom the auditors appear to have been complicit in the deceit, whilst in the cases of Maxwell Communications and BCCI (financial scandals of the late 1980s and early 1990s) the causes of the auditors' performance are more opaque. Whatever the reasons, the important market mechanism that the role of audit is supposed to play (verifying the reliability of the financial information supplied to shareholders) failed. The accounting profession was seen to be, at best, an unreliable scrutineer of financial information. More significantly the independence and integrity of accountants and accounting firms were increasingly being called into question.

In addition to the failings of the audit function, market analysts were still recommending Enron and WorldCom stocks as 'buys' to the investing world until days before the companies crashed, although again the integrity of the market analysts concerned has subsequently been shown to have been heavily compromised. As a result of these failings of the securities' markets, confidence in their fairness, transparency and integrity was undermined, with the risk that investors might turn to other investment options, such as property, currencies, works of art, etc. Thus, while it might only be out of enlightened self-interest, the securities' markets cannot afford to tolerate unethical corporate behaviour. However, at the same time, the intensity of the demands of the securities' markets is unrelenting in terms of the enormous pressures placed upon company executives to deliver improved 'financials' (profits) year upon year, half-year upon half-year, quarter upon quarter.

It is not only organisational collapse that increases public demands for better corporate governance. Such demands can also be expressed when poor corporate governance triggers perceptions of fraternalistic relative deprivation in society. This occurs when one social group feels it is being treated unfairly relative to another social group. Such is the case with, what became known as, 'crony capitalism' in the UK. This is the belief that 'The City', the UK financial services industry, is thriving, while the rest of society faces austerity, because it is protected by its relationship with government; whilst proclaiming that it is being rewarded because of its free market enterprise. Attitudes such as this towards 'The City' creates calls for tougher corporate governance on, for example, the payment of bonuses.

Positive organisational ethics or corporate psychopaths

Certainly the most efficient and economic form of corporate governance is a relationship built upon trust, buttressed by the requisite levels of accountability and transparency. As soon as one begins to doubt a person's integrity and trustworthiness then monitoring and control processes come into play, but these are expensive and can themselves exacerbate a situation and breed an air of mistrust.

If an organisation wishes to develop a culture based upon virtues such as integrity, honesty, objectivity, justice and fairness, partly to reduce the costs of monitoring and control processes, then consistency in practices and the avoidance of double standards are essential. Virtuousness, also known as ethos, is defined as the ideal of moral excellence, and also as the internal values, of individuals and organisations, that lead to positive action for good. Positive organisational ethics scholars argue that by developing authentic leadership, an ethical organisational culture and operational processes that are aligned with those values, organisations can develop a 'living code of ethics' (Verbos et al., 2007). They argue that there is evidence that virtuous organisations can outperform less well-behaved organisations. They point to the amplifying and buffering effects of virtuousness. Amplifying happens when exhibiting virtue at works encourages others to respond in ways that creates a conducive atmosphere for work. This ethos also enables individuals and organisations to respond effectively, known as buffering, when things go wrong or bad actions are discovered.

Unfortunately virtuousness in organisations is too often not the case. As is indicated by Table 7.1, what is considered a virtue for some groups in organisations is seen as a vice in others.

Table 7.1   Organisational principles and human behaviour

Issue	General employees	Senior executives
Working for other organisations	Taking time off to do 'other' work would be described as moonlighting and subject to instant dismissal. Working for other organisations considered to be a vice.	Taking consulting or NED-type role with another organisation invariably seen as broadening for all concerned and a virtue.
Pay-motivation relationship	Paying people low wages incentivises employees to work hard. High wages merely breed sloth and inefficiency.	Senior executives need increasing levels of pay to incentivise them. The higher the pay, the higher the motivation.
Pensions	It is unreasonable to expect the state or organisations to provide for income after employment.	Generous pension packages are essential to entice the appropriate level of executive talent.
Working conditions	General working conditions should reflect basic functional requirements. To do more would reflect an unnecessary diversion of shareholder funds.	Require high-quality accommodation and to provide less will act as a disincentive to prospective appointees.
Perks	Very few and where they exist will need to reflect a close relationship between performance and perk. No such thing as a 'free lunch'.	Come in many forms from first-class travel to company cars (when little corporate travel is undertaken by road), to executive boxes at arts or sporting arenas, to company accommodation and company loans. Lunches may still not be free but are paid for by 'others'.

Some researchers argue that a characteristic of successful top managers is more often psychopathic rather than virtuous behaviour. Psychopaths have no conscience, empathy or concern for others. Boddy (2011) argues that corporate (as opposed to criminal) psychopaths combine these traits with charm and amiability, which increases their probability of achieving organisational success, and of becoming business leaders. Boddy used an inventory scale developed by Hare (1991) to propose an inventory for assessing psychopathic behaviours amongst managers. The characteristics include such things as accomplished lying, emotional shallowness and refusal to take responsibility for their own actions (Boddy, 2011: 14). The inventory was used to ask managers in organisations the degree to which they observed such behaviours in their own senior managers. This of course is a potential weakness in the researcher's methods because his claim that many top leaders are psychopaths is not based on a clinical assessment of such leaders but on the, possibly biased, opinions of those who work for them. Nevertheless Boddy's survey suggests that between 16 per cent and 28 per cent of respondents, varying according to industrial sector, claimed they had experienced working with corporate psychopaths. He further argues that, amongst other statistical correlations, corporate psychopathy is associated with increased bullying and conflict, and with a relatively low commitment to corporate social responsibility. Even if only a proportion of these findings are valid they would argue that corporate governance is needed to ensure that power does not become over concentrated in the hands of a few managers, especially if they might exhibit psychopathic behaviour. Corporate governance becomes important as a means of tilting the odds towards positive organisational ethics rather than corporate psychopathic behaviour in organisations. When put in this context the subject of corporate governance ceases to be (if it ever was) an arcane and dry technical subject. As we will see, different notions of corporate governance exist in different parts of the world, with some of the most enlightened thinking emanating from South Africa.

Does good corporate governance improve organisational performance?

As we have seen at various instances in this book, whenever there is a debate about whether organisations should adopt a particular approach or behaviour because they are good, moral or ethical there is always a debate about whether there is a 'business case' for doing so. Corporate governance is no different. Indeed if it could be shown that good governance equals good performance then little persuasion would be required to convince organisations to adopt it. There is a slew of research papers that analyse this relationship; and because the situation may be different in every country researchers have almost unlimited opportunities for publishing papers titled 'Corporate governance and corporate performance in [name a country or region]'. A sample of such papers is analysed in Table 7.2.

Table 7.2   A selection of studies analysing corporate governance and corporate performance

Country/ region	Authors	Remarks	Measures of performance	Measures of corporate governance (CG)	Associations & correlations with CG measures
Australia	Christensen et al. (2010)		Return on assets (ROA) Tobin's Q, which measures whether market valuation of a company is more or less than its book value	■ Board size ■ Increase frequency of board meetings ■ Proportion of independent directors ■ Dual CEO/ chair ■ Use of sub-committee (e.g. audit and remuneration sub-committees)	Negative with ROA but positive with Tobin's Q Negative with Tobin's Q Negative Negative with ROA positive with Tobin's Q Positive

▶

Table 7.2 Continued

Country/ region	Authors	Remarks	Measures of performance	Measures of corporate governance (CG)	Associations & correlations with CG measures
China	Shan and McIver (2011)	China has a two tier board structure – managing board & supervisory board. China also has a high degree of state ownership	Tobin's Q	■ Ratios of independent directors ■ Ownership concentration ■ Type of ownership (state ownership) ■ Expertise of supervisory board	Negative Negative Negative No relationship
Lebanon	Chalhoub (2009)	The study was restricted to banks in Lebanon. The CG data was obtained by a survey of bank managers	An aggregate measure of growth, profitability & customer rating	■ Embedding of GG into daily practice ■ CG experienced senior managers ■ Applying codes of ethics ■ Engaging shareholders in participation ■ Emphasising accountability	Positive Positive Positive Positive Positive
Germany	Stiglbauer (2010)	Germany has a two tier board structure – managing board & supervisory board	ROA Return on Equity (ROE) Tobin's Q	■ A rating scale of compliance with the German Code of Corporate Governance	No positive association between compliance and any performance measure A negative relationship with Tobin's Q
Brazil	Braga-Alves and Shastri (2011)	Corporate governance measures based on São Paulo Stock Exchange standards		■ One share one vote ■ Dispersed ownership ■ Mandatory bid on transfer of corporate control ■ Minimum five directors ■ Minimum term for directors ■ transparency	Overall positive relationship with Tobin's Q No relationship with operating performance

Table 7.2 Continued

Country/region	Authors	Remarks	Measures of performance	Measures of corporate governance (CG)	Associations & correlations with CG measures
Turkey	Osman Gürbüz (2010)	The index used is a Turkish one	Return on assets (ROA)	■ Inclusion on a corporate governance index	Firms listed on the corporate governance index outperform non-listed firms in some years but not in others
Malaysia	Ibrahim and Samad (2011)	The study compares family firms with non-family firms	Tobin's Q ROA	■ Board size ■ % independent directors ■ Dual CEO and chair of the board	Family firms show a negative relationship between independent directors and ROA. For non-family firms there is a positive relationship with Tobin's Q and ROA. Duality in family businesses is negatively related to Tobin's Q and ROA. In non-family firms is significantly related to ROA

A study by Kraus and Britzelmaier (2011) reviewed a number of empirical studies, including the one reviewed in Table 7.2, of the relationship between corporate governance and corporate performance in Germany. As is often the case when a simple relationship is sought between two variables, the results were inconsistent. It seems implausible that a company's financial performance would be determined by a single all-important factor. One might expect factors such as market conditions, quality of management, capability of staff and different approaches to corporate governance in different countries to have an influence as well. It is clear that there is no unambiguous evidence that good corporate governance is associated with improved corporate financial performance. Of course it is not necessary to be able to prove a business case for corporate governance to be regarded as worthwhile and important.

Developments in corporate governance

There has been a lot of activity with regard to corporate governance in the UK since the early 1990s and Figure 7.1 presents a schema of the various reports, with the addition of one notable reform in the USA, that of the Sarbanes-Oxley Act in

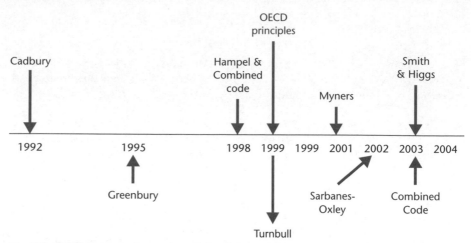

Fig. 7.1 Significant recent reports and developments in corporate governance

2002. A brief overview of these reports is provided so that the contestability of corporate responsibility and corporate governance can be discussed.

The **Cadbury Committee** was established as a response to some significant corporate collapses/scandals in the late 1980s and early 1990s, including BCCI, Polly Peck and Maxwell Communications. Given the comments made above regarding the questioning of the audit function performed by the large accounting firms and the resulting undermining of confidence in the London Stock Exchange, it will come as no surprise to learn that these were the two major sponsoring organisations of the Cadbury Committee. The major recommendations of the committee included the increased use of non-executive directors to counter what is referred to as the agency effect, and the splitting of the roles of chief executive and chairperson.

> The **agency effect** is derived from agency theory, which assumes **DEFINITION** that people are, at heart, untrustworthy. The directors of a company are the agents of the owners, the shareholders, and in law they have a duty to work for the owners' benefit. However, as a result of the privileged position that executive directors enjoy over shareholders with regard to the control of information, executive directors are deemed likely to exploit this power situation to their own advantage. This might manifest itself in 'managing' information (hence the importance of the audit function) and large remuneration packages.

The **Greenbury Committee** was set up to look into the issue of executive pay (Sir Richard Greenbury was at the time chief executive of Marks & Spencer and one of the highest paid directors in the UK). Even at this time the issue of executive pay, sometimes referred to as 'fat-cats pay', was a vexed issue but the work of the Greenbury Committee seems to have had little constraining effect, as indicated by Table 7.3. This table contrasts the movement in the FTSE 100 index with the average increase in the remuneration of the executive directors of the same top 100 UK corporations. If the movement in a company's market worth is

Table 7.3 Average increases in the remuneration of the directors of the FTSE 100 companies for 2000–2 compared with movements in the FTSE 100 share index over the same period

Year	Movement in directors' remuneration	Movements in FTSE 100 index
2000	+28%	–8%
2001	+17%	–15%
2002	+23%	–23%
Overall movements from Jan. 2000 to 31 Dec. 2002	**+84%**	**–40%**

a fair reflection of the performance of the company's senior management, then is it not reasonable to expect that there would be a close correlation between the change in corporate executives' remuneration and the change in market worth of the companies they manage, certainly over a reasonable period of time like three years?

A similar picture is evident in the USA. With the boundaries of self-control removed during the 1990s, but with the retention of the rhetoric of free markets, rapacious has been a frequently used adjective in discussions of corporate and executive behaviour. In both the USA and the UK stock options became a central part of executive remuneration packages during the 1990s, as attempts were made to tie the pay of senior executives to the performance of their companies, thereby trying to minimise the agency effect. The result was startling, although not necessarily in the way intended. Robert Monks (2003) commented upon the transfer of wealth reflected in the value of stock options held by a very small minority of senior executives in the USA.

The most important component of compensation was the grant of options that, according to the accounting rules after 1994, did not have to be accounted for as an expense by the issuing company. Typically, the top five executives in a company held 75% of the total options granted; the ratio of options to the total outstanding rose in the 1990s from 2% to 12%. This must be the greatest 'peaceful' transfer of wealth in recorded history.

(Monks, 2003: 165)

Two per cent, or one-fiftieth, of the value of the equity capital of corporate America is a huge figure. Twelve per cent, or nearly one-eighth, is a gargantuan number and this proportion of American equity capital is held by a relatively small number of senior executives.

Returning to reports on UK corporate governance, the **Hampel Committee** (1998) was formed to take stock of both the Cadbury and Greenbury reports and to suggest how best to implement their recommendations. Interestingly, the Hampel report, while recognising that boards of directors have a responsibility for *relations* with stakeholders, felt the need to emphasise that the *responsibility* of directors is to shareholders. Stakeholders are of concern to directors, but only in as far as they can contribute to the maximisation of shareholder wealth.

The Hampel Report led to the first '**Combined Code**', which was issued by the London Stock Exchange in 1998. The code specifies the corporate governance practices that quoted companies should follow if they wish to have a listing on the London Stock Exchange. The code is not backed by law and if a quoted company chooses not to follow it the company must explain the rationale for its different practice. For example, the supermarket chain, Morrisons, had, until it bought the Safeway group in 2004, combined the roles of chief executive and chairman, which was contrary to the 1998 Combined Code. Morrisons claimed that combining the two roles made sense for them and this was accepted by the London Stock Exchange. Investors became concerned when in 2008 the chief executive of Marks & Spencer took on both roles and became executive chairman (Wood, 2008). Marks & Spencer argued the move was to allow candidates eventually to replace Rose to develop. Some investors argued that such moves placed too much power in one person.

Case study 7.1	**Women on Boards of Directors**

Women on boards of directors is an interesting issue in corporate governance. The argument often presented is that there are too few women on boards of directors and that this is intrinsically inequitable and means that boards do not have the benefit of the contribution women could bring. It is certainly true that women are rare on boards. According to one survey (Terjesen et al., 2009) only one of the countries surveyed, Slovenia, had more than 20 per cent women directors. Many countries including Ireland, Japan, Italy, France and Switzerland had only 5 per cent or fewer women directors. In the UK in 2011 only 15 per cent of FTSE company directors were women, although the rate of appointment of women directors is speeding up. Over a quarter of directors appointed to the top 350 UK boards in 2011 were women.

Many boards only have a single woman on them and this is easily seen as tokenism. Token women tend to be ignored and stereotyped. One study (Torchia et al., 2011) has proposed that a critical mass of three women directors is needed before women can influence the board's decision-making processes. By conducting a correlation analysis of data from a Likert style survey of Norwegian companies, Torchia et al. concluded that the level of organisational innovation was higher in companies that had three or more women directors. The choice of Norway as the place to conduct the research was not accidental. It reflects the Norwegian government's decision in 2004 to require companies to have at least 40 per cent of women directors on their boards. Initially this requirement was covered by a voluntary code but, with a low rate of compliance by companies, the government instituted heavy sanctions for those companies that did not comply. After 10 years Norwegian companies have met the 40 per cent target; although the majority of board chairs are still men and only 2 per cent of the CEOs of companies listed on the Oslo Stock Exchange are women. The women directors are younger and better educated than their male counterparts (Storvik and Teigen, 2010). Attempts have been made to see if there is a correlation between the presence of women board member and the financial performance of companies. As it might be thought over-ambitious to expect that a single factor, such as the ratio of female directors, would have a discernible impact on financial results, it is not surprising that the results of research into the matter are mixed (Terjesen et al., 2009: 329). For example one study (Shrader et al., 1997) found a negative relationship between the proportion of women board members and various measures of financial performance amongst Fortune 500 firms. A study by Carter et al. (2003), however, found that firms with at least two women on the board performed better on two measures of financial performance than companies with all-male directors. The diversity of results from such studies probably reflects the impact of other, unmeasured factors, which may influence profitability.

The 'comply or explain' approach towards corporate governance developments in the UK is different from the approach of the USA, where changes are passed through the legislative processes and are thus legally binding. Such an example is the Sarbanes-Oxley Act of 2002. The latter was the result of two Congressmen formulating their response to a number of financial scandals, notably those of Enron, WorldCom and Global Crossing. The act places specific responsibilities upon chief executives and the chief financial officers (in UK terms, the finance directors) to personally sign off the accounts. In addition, certain accounting services that audit firms might wish to provide to their audit clients have been proscribed by the act. This reflects the concerns that have been expressed for many years that the level of non-audit fee income earned by accounting firms from their audit clients might compromise their independence and objectivity. The fact that Andersen's (Enron's auditors) generated around $25m of non-audit fee income from Enron, on top of the $25m audit income, was felt by many to have been an unhealthy situation, and it was not unique. Interestingly, Andersen's were also WorldCom's auditors.

The **Turnbull Report** of 1999 concerned itself with internal controls and internal audit, while the **Myners' Committee** was sponsored by the UK Treasury to look into the role of institutional investors in company affairs. With institutional investors (banks, pension funds, unit and investment trusts) such influential players on securities' markets, any hope of improved shareholder activism to challenge the power of directors would need to come from the institutional investors. In a nutshell, Myners recommended that institutional investors *should* be more active, but not a lot more.

The statements of corporate governance principles by the **OECD** (Organisation for Economic Co-operation and Development) in 1999 and 2005 represent a very Anglo-American view of the subject and bear a close resemblance to the 1998 and 2003 UK Combined Codes.

The reports of the **Higgs** and **Smith** Committees were published in 2003, the former being concerned with the roles of non-executive directors (NEDs) and the latter concerned with the work and roles of Audit Committees. Higgs recommended a scaling up of the importance of NEDs, such that the majority of main board directors should be NEDs, presumably to further minimise the agency effect. The report makes further recommendations with respect to how many NED appointments executive directors can hold etc., but these need not concern us. However, three questions remain unanswered by the Higgs Report and corporate governance developments in general.

1. The majority of directors on Enron's main board were NEDs, but this did not prevent the corruption that appears to have taken place at Enron. So why was the main recommendation of the Higgs Report that the majority of main board directors should be NEDs?

2. NEDs only attend the companies of which they are NEDs on one, possibly two, days each month. Does this not place even more power in the hands of the few remaining executive directors, who, agency theory claims, should not be trusted?

3. If minimising the agency effect is a key role of NEDs, why is it that the vast majority of NEDs are also executive directors in their primary employment? Why should person 'A', who is an executive director of company 'X' be subject to the agency effect and be untrustworthy in this role, but upon taking on the mantle of NED of company 'B' become a trustworthy individual whose role it is to ensure the integrity of company B's practices? What is the transformation process that turns A from untrustworthy to trustworthy?

As for the Smith Report on Audit Committees, it makes various recommendations, but it stops short of requiring accounting firms to stop providing any of their non-audit services to their audit clients. This is a far less prescriptive or punitive approach than that reflected in the Sarbanes-Oxley Act.

What have the developments in corporate governance achieved?

What do all these reports and recommendations say about corporate governance and ethics in business? For many they say very little and what they say is inadequate, given the scale of corporate governance issues. A more inclusive view of corporate governance sees the disregard for shareholder interests displayed by executives as but one of the corporate governance issues to be addressed. All the developments in corporate governance since 1992 amount to very little. An increase in NEDs here, some concerns expressed about accounting firms there, but really it is a 'steady-as-she-goes' approach, with only minor adjustments to the tiller.

Frustration with the myopia and impotence displayed by governments to correct what are seen as the inadequate responses to profound corporate governance issues such as child labour, forced labour, inhuman working conditions, despoliation of the environment, and the connivance and corrupt practices of governments (*see* the *Transparency International* website for an examination of the latter) with corporations has led to a series of other initiatives, which are highlighted in Figure 7.2.

The King Report on corporate governance

Before progressing to the issues reflected in the UN Global Compact, reference will be made to the second King Report, which was published in 2002 (the first having been published in 1994) and which relates to corporate governance in

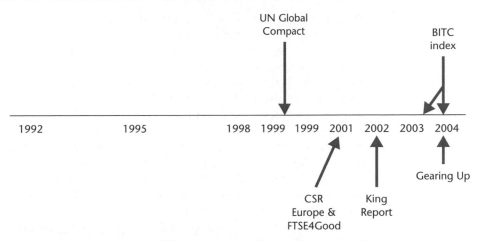

Fig. 7.2 Other interesting developments in corporate governance that have not impacted upon UK and USA stock exchange listing requirements.

South Africa. The opening of the report is interesting in that it refers to a statement made by Sir Adrian Cadbury (the same Cadbury who gave his name to the 1992 UK Cadbury report on corporate governance), but this time the statement was made by Cadbury in the World Bank's 1999 report on corporate governance.

> Corporate governance is concerned with holding the balance between economic and social goals and between individual and community goals. . . . The aim is to align as nearly as possible the interests of individuals, corporations and society.
>
> (King Committee on Corporate Governance, 2002: 6)

This is a much more expansive and inclusive view of corporate governance than that articulated in the 1992 UK Cadbury Report, or in any UK or US financial corporate governance reports since. There are further important features of the King Report that are highly relevant to the considerations of this chapter. The first is the continuation in the second (2002) King Report of the inclusive orientation of the first (1994) King Report. This orientation is reflected in the following extract.

> Unlike its counterparts in other countries at the time, the King Report 1994 went beyond the financial and regulatory aspects of corporate governance in advocating an integrated approach to good governance in the interests of a wide range of stakeholders having regard to the fundamental principles of good financial, social, ethical and environmental practice. In adopting a participative corporate governance system of enterprise with integrity, the King Committee in 1994 successfully formalised the need for companies to recognise that they no longer act independently from the societies and the environment in which they operate.
>
> (King Committee on Corporate Governance, 2002: 6)

In contrast, Anglo-American reforms to corporate governance have been allowed to concentrate exclusively upon corporations' responsibilities to shareholders. The King Committee took an explicitly inclusive view of a corporation's stakeholders, although it was not a naïve report that ignored or undervalued the economic imperatives faced by companies. It is a thoughtful, scholarly report, which distinguishes between accountability and responsibility, a distinction that UK reports on corporate governance have failed to make. The King Report was not a maverick study located at the margins of South Africa's economic interests. It was a study sponsored by the South Africa Institute of Directors, and whilst operating in the context of a market-based capitalist economy the King Report reflects a very different conception of the business-society debate. This is most intriguingly reflected in paragraph 38 and its subsections, where the report focuses upon the values that underpin South African society. This is a dimension to corporate governance that has not only been missed by UK and US corporate governance reports, it would currently not be countenanced as it reflects a profoundly different world view of the business–society relationship.

The very first of the values considered in the King Report is 'spiritual collectiveness'. Paragraph 38.1 reads as follows:

> Spiritual Collectiveness is prized over individualism. This determines the communal nature of life, where households live as an interdependent neighbourhood.

Other values considered include:

> Humility and helpfulness to others is more important than criticism of them.
>
> (paragraph 38.3)

> There is an inherent trust and belief in fairness of all human beings. This manifests itself in the predisposition towards universal brotherhood, even shared by African-Americans.
>
> (paragraph 38.6)

> High standards of morality are based on historical precedent. These are bolstered by the close kinship observed through totem or clan names and the extended family systems.
>
> (paragraph 38.7)

The above claims to community values and beliefs do not deny the historic tribalism that has seen African peoples at war with one another over centuries. However, it draws out the common values that unite rather than separate the tribes (which are effectively mini-nation states in western terms) and seeks to build notions of corporate governance that reflect cultural mores and values, rather than allow more recognisable business values and beliefs to migrate from the economic sphere, driving out the more inclusive, community-oriented values in the process.

Interestingly, paragraph 39 opens with the statement, 'Corporate governance is essentially about leadership', followed by the essential values that a leader should possess and display. The African 'great-soul-man' appears to being alluded to here, who is noticeable by his absence from Anglo-American debates.

The twentieth century was traumatic for South African society. The release of Nelson Mandela in 1990 heralded the ending of the brutal apartheid policies, and the King Report must be seen in this social and cultural context, but it should not be side-stepped or minimised as a result. It is a report that should demand our attention. It offers a very different perspective on corporate governance, arguing that business is a part of society rather than apart from society.

International best practice standards

The reports on corporate governance discussed have defined the structures and processes that companies should adopt. Organisations need to show their shareholders and the broader public that not only do they have effective corporate governance, but also that they behave in a corporately responsible way. They need mechanisms for expressing their accountability. In the past 20 years a number of standards for business ethics have been developed. Most multinational companies now devote much effort, and fees for the services of specialist consultancy firms, to report their progress such standards. These standards differ from codes of conduct and ethics in that they are meant to have a wide application, and are not written for particular organisations or professional groups. Standards set a minimum benchmark of behaviour against which organisations can be compared and judged. A standard often accredits, or gives a badge to, any organisation that meets the minimum standard. Membership-based organisations, often referred to as compacts, and international agreements concerned with improving the ethical standards of international business are discussed in Chapter 12.

Accountability 1000 (AA1000)

AA1000 is a quality assurance standard. That is to say it focuses, not on whether an organisation is acting ethically, but on whether it has good systems that will identify whether it is acting unethically and so enable it to put things right. It is like ISO 9000, which is also a process standard, but one concerned with quality assurance systems generally and not just those that focus on ethical matters. It was announced in 1999 by the Institute of Social and Ethical Accountability, which works under the name AccountAbility. It contains both principles and a set of standards against which an organisation can be assessed. The issue of accountability always raises the question of accountability to whom, and in this standard the answer is to stakeholders. The components required in a system that makes an organisation accountable to its stakeholders include:

- planning;
- accounting;
- auditing and reporting;
- embedding; and
- stakeholder engagement.

Embedding means ensuring that everyone in the organisation takes the meeting of ethical and social standards seriously and takes it into account in their daily work. This is contrary to the suspicion, about all standards, that organisations only pay attention to them when they are to be accredited or re-accredited and only then to the extent of making sure that the right boxes on the correct forms have been ticked. The standard is also concerned with materiality, that is to say whether the accountability systems include the entire range of topics, such as:

- environmental issues;
- workplace and employment issues;
- health and safety;
- behaviour of supply chain partners;
- employee involvement;
- training and people development;
- community involvement; and
- sustainable development.

In 2004 there were 22 companies using the standard, of which 16 were companies providing assurance services. This was a decrease from the 55 companies who were using the service in 2003 (AccountAbility, 2004). The International Organisation for Standardization (ISO) reported in 2004 that it was to prepare a set of standards for corporate social responsibility.

Global Reporting Initiative (GRI)

The GRI was initiated in New York and although originally directed at US businesses it is now based in Amsterdam. The original sponsor was CERES but the initiative was subsequently funded and supported by the UN. Its purpose is to propose guidelines for organisations to report on the economic, environmental and social implications of their business practices. The GRI provides a series of performance indicators that it recommends organisations should publish. Some of these are regarded as core and others as optional. But in either case they are divided between:

- *Economic*: monetary flows to stakeholders, e.g. donations to community, civil society or other groups.
- *Environmental*: e.g. in the area of biodiversity the impact of a company's activities on sensitive or protected land.
- *Social*: e.g. the composition of the senior management team, the number of men and women on it.

The performance indicators are either

■ descriptions of policy and procedures; or

■ numerical measures of impacts and outcomes.

The full list can be seen in the Sustainability Reporting Guidelines. In brief, the Guidelines can be seen as a crib for those who need to write triple-line (*see* p. 335) reporting documents.

Social Accountability 8000 (SA8000)

SA8000 is an international standard for corporate behaviour that identifies a range of criteria against which the activities and performance of organisations can be mapped and compared. The intention is that the standard (and the beliefs, values and ethics assumed within it) should be applicable throughout the world, with no exceptions. It is thus an attempt to specify a standard of employment conditions and practices with universal application.

The standard was developed by the Council on Economic Priorities Accreditation Agency (CEPAA). In 2000 it changed its name to Social Accountability International (SAI) and it keeps the standard under review, updates it from time to time and invites comments and advice. Indeed, once you have visited the website you may wish to pass on your own thoughts about the standard's comprehensiveness or robustness.

The standard has nine categories. These are:

■ Child Labour;

■ Forced Labour;

■ Health and Safety;

■ Freedom of Association and Right to Collective Bargaining;

■ Discrimination;

■ Disciplinary Practices;

■ Working Hours;

■ Remuneration; and

■ Management Systems.

Each of the categories has sub-headings. For example, 'Forced Labour' has only one, which effectively states, 'Thou shalt not be engaged in, or associated with, forced labour'. 'Management Systems', on the other hand, has 14 sub-headings. The standard is not enforced by any national law, but it is hoped that, as its use grows as a standard against which corporate practices and behaviours are judged, compliance will become the norm.

As the SA8000 standard is a recent development only a small number of companies have been accredited. Although a wide range of companies, governments and NGOs were consulted during the development of the standard some NGOs concerned with international labour standards criticise CEPAA for being too close to the views of industry. Nevertheless the standard is an attempt to formalise universal ethical standards for businesses and organisations.

The Ethics Compliance Management System Standard (ECS2000)

This standard was developed by the business ethics research project at the Rietaku Centre for Economic Research in Japan. This standard is fully committed to the business case for ethical behaviour in business and assumes that through a continuous improvement process unethical behaviour can be reduced, to the economic and financial benefit of the company. Not surprisingly, since Japan was the home of the Total Quality Management (TQM) movement and the commitment to *kaizen*, it is not unexpected that it would apply a similar approach to business ethics reporting. The standard proposes four stages in the creation of an ethical compliance system:

- Preparing a legal compliance manual and clarifying the organisation's ethical policy and values.
- Appointing an individual or group to oversee the implementation of the compliance manual.
- Carrying out an independent audit to check that the manual has been implemented.
- Identifying areas for development and improvement using the audit results.

This standard is a process-centred one. It cannot report on whether a company is acting ethically because each company will produce:

- a set of ethical standards, which the organisation will implement according to its own traditions and management beliefs [a code of ethics]; and
- a body of rules and regulations [a code of conduct] of specific relevance and importance to the organisation considering its work content, scale and the materials and services in which it deals.

(Reitaku Centre for Economic Studies, 1999: 8)

The standard can only report on whether the company is doing what it says it would do.

There are other standards, which have not been widely adopted. Q-Res is one such, it is an Italian initiative; the documents are available in English. The standard was published in draft form in 2001 and was piloted by seven companies. It aims to provide guidance on how to:

Activity 7.1	**Comparing and contrasting ethical best practice standards**

Compare and contrast the best practice standards just discussed. Identify the relevant strengths and weaknesses of each. Which would you recommend to a multinational company?

■ draw up codes of ethics and conduct;

■ improve training and communication on social responsibility matters; and

■ produce externally verified reports.

Shareholder activism

Corporate governance is, as we have seen, about creating structures, processes and benchmarks to make organisations accountable. But these are of no purpose if the opportunities they provide are not taken up. In other words if shareholders, and the public generally, do not care to act then corporate governance will be a façade only. If we begin by considering shareholders then corporate governance needs to be driven by active shareholders who bring the organisations they own to account. A public company may have many investors who each only hold a relatively small shareholding. Although these investors may enjoy the theatricality and hospitality of Annual General Meetings, they have little influence. Shareholder activism, targeting the most visible and the largest companies, has become popular in areas such as executive remuneration (M&S, Tesco, Shell, LloydsTSB, HSBC, RBS, GSK); board elections (Disney, Olympus, InterActiveCorp, News Corporation, HP, BSkyB); environmental issues (BP, Shell, Nestlé); generic drugs (GSK), and asbestos (Cape plc). This mode of action is normally conducted by groups of shareholders (typically religious and environmental groups, unions, or social investors) who file resolutions at general meetings to exert pressure on corporations to change their polices or their practices. Alternatively, shareholders may choose to express their quiet dissatisfaction to the media, or by opening voting against initiatives filed by the management.

Rehbein et al. (2004), after analysing 1,536 policy shareholder resolutions filed in the USA during 1991–8, found that 507 were employee-related resolutions (human rights, employment, and diversity); 105 were community-related resolutions (charitable contributions, banking/insurance, and domestic poverty); 341 were product-related resolutions (mainly tobacco, military contracting, animal rights, infant formula and alcohol), and 583 were environment related resolutions (environment and energy). In this context, a model of stakeholder group action was developed by Rowley and Moldoveanu (2003) combining an 'interest-based' dimension and a group 'identity-based' dimension. The combination of these two dimensions would inspire different type of actions, such as filing shareholder resolutions to change organisational polices and practices; filing resolutions aimed at increasing public awareness and general political debate by simultaneously targeting different organisations; contacting the media; and voting against management plans.

It is institutional investors, such as pension funds and insurance companies, which have long-term interests, that need to be proactive if companies are to be effectively controlled by their shareholders. However, in many countries, such as the UK, institutional investors hold less of a public company's stock than used to be the case as international investors and hedge funds hold greater proportions of a company's equity, and hold it on a more speculative basis. Nevertheless, institutional investors have tended to be more active in their engagement with the managements of companies and sometimes take an ethical perspective when choosing the companies they will invest in. One of the most active, and famous, pension funds in the field of ethical investing is "California Public Employees' Retirement System". (The California Public Employees Pension System).

In 2012 the British government proposed to utilise shareholder power to limit what was seen as the scandal of rapidly rising boardroom salaries at a time when the general population was facing austerity. It was proposed that shareholders should have the power to vote on top pay proposals and to reject them if necessary; at the time of writing shareholders could vote on executive pay but the decisions were not binding. Some commentators argued that it would be necessary for 75 per cent of such a vote to be in favour of a proposed pay increase for it to be approved. They thought this necessary because executives of institutional investor organisations were likely to be members of the same mutually supportive network of remuneration committees as the executives in public companies whose salaries they are supposed to constrain. Shareholder activism is not therefore necessarily an easy means for bringing companies to account.

Social contract, licence to practice and charter revocation

If corporate governance is about ensuring that a corporation works in the best interests of both its shareholders and society generally, should it be possible to close down a corporation that has seriously failed in its accountability to both groups? This is known as charter revocation in the USA. Such a possibility is based on the idea of a social contract. This is an interesting concept that can be traced back to Plato (Bosanquet, 1906) and Aristotle (Aristotle, 1976), and in western Europe in the seventeenth and eighteenth centuries to Hobbes (1968), Locke (1952) and Rousseau (1913). Lessnoff (1986) provides a good introduction to the history of social contract as an idea and as an argument.

A more recent articulation of the social contract is found in the argument that corporations have to earn and maintain a 'licence to operate'. The licence to operate reflects a commitment to more than economic imperatives, although the approach does not ignore economic issues. In other words corporations are given the right to exist as long as they operate within the norms and standards set by society. Two interesting writers working in this area are Thomas Donaldson and Thomas Dunfee. They have published in various forms over the past 20 years, for example, Donaldson (1982, 1989, 1990, 1996); Donaldson and Dunfee (1994, 1995, 1999); Dunfee (1991, 1996); and Dunfee and Donaldson (1995).

Companies are very rarely forced to close by governments, even when they have been found criminally negligent in their practices. Nevertheless corporations are increasingly using legal protection designed to protect individual citizens, such as the right to free speech provided by the American constitution, to make indirect contributions to the political campaigns of candidates they find sympathetic to their corporate needs. Such cases imply that corporations can claim the benefits of citizenship without accepting its burdens, such as facing a heavy sanction if their actions cause death or injury.

Case study 7.2	**A law professor, as citizen, takes action**

Robert Benson, a professor of law at Loyola University, petitioned the Californian state attorney to dissolve the Union Oil Company of California (Unocal) by revoking its charter. Bakan writes,

> Benson listed Unocal's transgressions in his 127 page application to the attorney general: the company had collaborated on a pipeline project with the outlaw Burmese military regime, which had allegedly used slave labor on the pipeline and forced whole villages to relocate: it had allegedly collaborated on projects with Afghanistan's former Taliban regime, which was notorious for its violations of human rights long before the United States waged war against it; it had, the application claimed, persistently violated California's environmental and employee safety regulations.
>
> (Bakan, 2004: 157)

Unsurprisingly, not least to Benson, the application was rejected by the attorney general, after only three working days, but Benson's objective was to gain public recognition that corporations are not above the law and are even subject to the corporate 'death penalty'.

> We're letting the people of California in on a well-kept secret, … the people mistakenly assume that we have to try to control these giant corporate repeat offenders one toxic spill at a time, one layoff at a time, one human rights violation at a time. But the law has always allowed the attorney general to go to court to simply dissolve a corporation for wrongdoing and sell its assets to others who will operate in the public interest.
>
> (Mokhiber, 1998)

Benson's action is an example of an individual taking action. In response to any thoughts that he might be naïve, Benson explained,

> We are not politically naïve. We don't think that this is going to get so far along the road that Unocal will actually be broken up anytime soon, although it should be. The petition was filed to change the legal and political culture. Our fundamental goal here is to change the public discourse and the media perception of the power of corporations versus people, to float the idea that people are sovereign over corporations.
>
> (Mokhiber, 1998)

Case study 7.3	**A judge, as citizen, takes action**

An Alabama Circuit Judge, William Wynn, took out an action to revoke the charters of America's five major cigarette companies. Wynn filed a complaint in a state court in Birmingham, Alabama, demanding that the corporate charters of Philip Morris, Brown & Williamson, R.J. Reynolds, The Liggett Group and Lorillard Corporation be revoked. Wynn was angry that Alabama had refused to join 22 states in suing the tobacco companies, and had spent the better part of a year researching the law, to find a way to force the state to act. He stumbled across a nineteenth-century statute giving any citizen the right to petition the state for a 'writ of quo warranto' – a Latin phrase

▶

meaning 'by what authority?' The writ of quo warranto allows a citizen to file a lawsuit against any corporation, posing the question: By what authority are you holding a corporate franchise to do business, when you are in fact breaking the law?

Judge Wynn uncovered a number of laws he believed the cigarette companies had violated, including contributing to the dependency of a minor, unlawful distribution of material harmful to a minor, endangering the welfare of a child, assault in the third degree, recklessly endangering another, deceptive business practice and causing the delinquency of a child. Though the companies have not been charged with these crimes in Alabama, Judge Wynn says that he is 'calling for the criminal enforcement of these misdemeanors.' And upon a finding that the companies have broken the law, he is then calling for charter revocation.

Perhaps the most surprising response to the lawsuit was that of the state's most influential paper, the *Birmingham News*. The paper not only ran a news story about the lawsuit, but published a very long opinion piece by Richard Grossman (a long-time advocate of using charter revocation laws), titled 'Slaying Big Tobacco.' Mainstream readers were thus exposed to the characteristically radical Grossman style, arguing that Judge Wynn is on 'solid legal ground when he demands the state of Alabama provide its sovereign people with a proper remedy to end the corporate usurpation of the people's authority'.

(Mokhiber, 1998)

Governance and bribery and corruption

So far in the chapter we have been discussing the structures, processes and standards necessary to achieve good corporate governance. In the next two sections we consider two particular areas, bribery and corruption and corporate manslaughter, in which achieving corporate accountability is both important and difficult.

One of the areas in which there is much concern about the quality of corporate governance is bribery and corruption. This is a major issue for multinational companies in particular because the circumstances in certain countries that make it very difficult to do business without paying bribes, especially where making such payments may not be seen as a big problem. At an international conference attended by top managers from multinationals and by academics the managers declared that although they did much business in China they did not pay bribes. The academics challenged them by claiming that bribes were paid, it was just that big companies could find ways of disguising the fact. This highlights the governance issue of the degree to which corporations, as good corporate citizens, should forego the possibility of using their clout to avoid some of the obligations of the common citizen to obey the law to the letter. Another example of the problem is the allegation that in the UK in 2011 a number of large corporations were able to influence the tax authorities to reduce their tax liabilities well below the amount that had been formally calculated. However, in this section the discussion will be restricted to the matter of bribery.

Bribes can take various forms. A suggested scale of impropriety for the payment of bribes is shown below.

A scale of bribery and corruption

■ Gifts – expressions of friendship and good faith, openly given, of low value and often reciprocated.

■ Tips – discretionary rewards for good service.

■ 'Grease' (sometimes known as facilitation payments) – small payments on a customary scale to encourage people to do what their job requires them to do. Not a payment to make them do what they should not do. Grease is often a recompense for the very low wages of those accepting the inducement. The Anti-terrorism, Crime and Security Act 2001 made it a crime in the UK for British firms to make such payments (or any other form of bribe) to officials overseas. The UK government did not anticipate that overseas officials extorting such payments in countries in which it was normal would lead to prosecutions in the UK.

■ Commissions – often large payments for acting as a go-between and facilitating deals. It could be a fair payment for professional services but if the payment is disproportionate it might be a way of delegating responsibility for paying bribes from the principal to an agent.

■ Bribes – payments to encourage people to do things that they should not.

The following factors should be considered when judging the badness of a bribe.

■ Whether it gives the bribe giver an unfair advantage or access to resources or benefits that would not otherwise be available to them.

■ Whether the amount of the bribe is greater than is customary.

■ Whether the opportunity to offer a bribe is not equally open to all and when different people or groups have to pay different amounts in bribes.

■ Whether it is illegal.

■ Whether its cultural impact is to undermine trust and probity in a society.

It can be argued that bribery of a government official is worse than bribery of a company official or a private individual. This is because a public body or official has a special obligation to the well-being of the population as a whole that cannot be discharged if that body or official responds to private and sectional interests through bribery. The OECD (2000) published a convention that outlawed the bribing of public officials in international business negotiations. A private individual or company in contrast might be thought to have a responsibility only to themselves, their close associates and their shareholders. In this case the damage caused by the giving or taking of bribes may be less.

Most organisations, and certainly all the big multinational corporations, formally eschew the payment of bribes; though their prohibition may not extend to all of its forms. A company may make a commission payment through a third-party agent in order to obtain a contract and therefore may claim that it did not pay a bribe; and that if a bribe had in fact been paid it was because the agent had acted without its knowledge or that managers within the company had acted on their own initiative against company policy and rules. Some argue that the money companies spend lobbying government in attempts to influence laws and policy in their favour is also a form of bribery. Table 7.4 illustrates the sort of evidence that gives rise to such concerns. The table reflects some of the donations made to the Republican Party during the 2000 American presidential campaign and the actions taken immediately following the inauguration of George W. Bush as President of the United States of America in 2001. All the actions were taken by the President during the first three months of his presidency.

Cross reference	A discussion of the extent to which bribery is accepted and necessary in different countries is discussed in Chapter 12, pp 419. There is also further discussion on pp 240 of how corporations try to influence the definition of bribery in ways that give them greater flexibility of action.

There is a debate about how best to try to reduce bribery and corruption. One side argues for a demand-side strategy others argue for a supply-side approach. The demand-side approach would try to change the climate and culture in bribery prone countries so that people do not demand bribes. The supply-side approach

Table 7.4 Actions taken by President G. W. Bush within three months of his inauguration in 2001

Industry	$m donated	Actions taken
Tobacco	7.0	Removal of federal lawsuits against cigarette manufacturers
Timber	3.2	Restrictions on logging roads scrapped
Oil and gas	24.4	Restrictions on CO_2 emissions abandoned; Kyoto agreement scrapped; moves to open Arctic refuge to drilling
Mining	2.6	Scrapping of environmental clean-up rules, e.g. arsenic limits in water supply
Banks & credit card companies	25.6	Bankruptcy bill making it easier for credit card companies to collect debts from bankrupt customers
Pharmaceuticals	17.8	Medicare (government-supported health insurance) reform removing price controls
Airlines	4.2	Federal barriers to strikes introduced; back-pedalling on antitrust (mergers and monopolies) legislation

Source: *The Guardian* G2, 27 April 2001, p. 2, Copyright Guardian News & Media Ltd. 2001.

tries to encourage companies to act with integrity and refuse to pay bribes, even if it means a loss of business; and to try to adapt their business models so that it is not necessary for them to pay bribes. Currently the supply-side approach is the dominant governance approach in attempts to diminish bribery and corruption (Calderón et al., 2009).

In the UK this trend is best illustrated by the Bribery Act of 2010, which came into force on 1 July 2011 (Great Britain, 2011a). The act is not new in making the payment of bribes by organisations illegal but it does add some novel features. UK companies that pay bribes in other countries, and non-UK companies that operate within the UK and pay bribes, even if those bribes have no connection with their UK business, are liable to prosecution under the act. As most multinational companies have businesses in the UK then the UK act has a near international jurisdiction as far as multinationals are concerned. This is a major change when it is considered that some countries, including France and Germany, used to make overseas bribes tax deductible. The act also makes it illegal to fail to prevent a person, including agents, from bribing on your behalf. In effect it means that top managers have to do all that is proportionate and reasonable to ensure that policies, rules, and indeed the right organisational culture, are in place, to minimise the possibility of bribe paying. Hospitality is not prohibited by the act, so managers can continue to invite their clients and customers to F1 Grand Prix and other such events. Facilitation payments, however, are prohibited, though the official guidelines say that, in the case of facilitation payments 'prosecutors will carefully consider all the facts and surrounding circumstances of cases which come to their attention to assess whether a payment amounts to a bribe and if so whether a prosecution is in the public interest' (Great Britain, 2011b: 7), which does not sound like a zealous interest to prosecute (*see also* p. 460).

A similar focus on the supply-side approach to dealing with bribery can also be seen in India. A report by KPMG (BBC, 2011) suggested that corruption in India had grown to such levels that it had become a threat to the country's continued economic growth. Most of the large-scale corruption in India flows from big businesses' relationships with government. One of the largest scandals concerned the sale of telecoms licences for mobile phone networks in which, it was alleged, a minister had undersold the licences in return for bribes, thereby depriving the government of billions of dollars. Kaushik Basu (2011), the chief economic advisor to the Indian ministry of finance proposed an interesting idea for limiting facilitation payments, or as he called them – harassment payments. At present under Indian law it is illegal to both give and receive a bribe; therefore it is in the interests of both parties to keep any bribe secret. But if making a facilitation payment was legalised and only the bribe receiver was to be punished by law, and even more so if a bribe taker was made, on being found guilty, to pay the bribe back to the bribe giver; then it would be in the bribe giver's interest to report the bribe to the authorities. Basu is not proposing that bribe paying to achieve an unfair or unjust advantage would be made legal. Many supply-side attempts to limit corruption rest on an attempt to manipulate behaviour by carrot or stick rather than to encourage honesty and good social behaviour. Basu does not entirely disagree with this (Basu, 2011: 10). His suggestion seeks to make it in the bribe payer's self-interest to report the bribe, if not to forgo making it in the first instance, but he also recognises the need for a long-term effort to improve cultural traits that will reduce the demand for bribes. The idea was not particularly well received (Sainath, 2011) and seems unlikely to be accepted into Indian law.

Corporate manslaughter

The concluding major topic in this chapter continues the theme of attempts to hold corporations to account for their roles in, or impacts upon, society. To do this, there is a need to consider both the legal position and the philosophical position of corporations with regard to this issue.

Until April 2008 the prosecution of corporations in the UK, as distinct from individual employees, for claimed acts of wilful neglect of a duty of care, has been difficult. However, in April 2008 the Corporate Manslaughter and Corporate Homicide Act (CMCHA) (2007) became law. Although actions through the civil courts against corporations had been possible prior to the act, the expense and the many years involved in prosecuting such cases made the civil law option one that was rarely taken up by members of the public and that continues to be the case today.

Tracing the history of the Corporate Manslaughter and Corporate Homicide Act (2007)

The next few pages trace the history of the CMCHA because this is instructive in understanding the forces of resistance that can frustrate what many might view as a perfectly reasonable development in the business-society relationship; a development that is in societal interests, but which some might regard as detrimental to business interests.

The incoming Labour Government of 1997 had made a manifesto pledge to introduce a bill on corporate manslaughter, but nothing of consequence transpired in the first administration of New Labour, which ended in it winning the general election of 2001. The manifesto of New Labour in that general election maintained a commitment to a bill on corporate manslaughter. The inclusion of a corporate manslaughter bill in the 2004 Queen's Speech (the mechanism that announces the proposed bills to be discussed in the forthcoming parliamentary session) was seen by many as a deceit, because it was generally believed that the prime minister would call a general election in May 2005, which proved to be correct, thereby confining all the proposed bills to the 'bills lost' bin.

Why this reticence to instigate a corporate manslaughter bill? For some, it is difficult to see beyond the power of the corporate lobby, persuading government that 'it would not be a good thing'. Yet in the USA it has been possible for many years, decades even, for corporations to be forced to stop trading because of corporate wrongdoings. Such acts, known as charter revocations acts, are very rarely used, but at least they exist. In the UK no such possibilities exist, other than for the Department of Trade and Industry in special situations and on behalf of creditors. But in the USA, a private citizen can instigate a winding-up procedure as a result of a corporate wrongdoing. In the USA the death penalty exists for corporate acts of murder as it does in some states for individuals. Notwithstanding that the death penalty for citizens has long been abolished in the UK, the possibilities of such a punishment in the corporate field raises very different issues and arguments.

The 'identification principle' and the 'guiding mind'

Prior to the CMCHA coming onto the statute books in 2008, if an employee lost his or her life as a result of negligence on the part of a corporation, it had been necessary to prove that a senior person in the organisation had failed in his/her corporate duties to show the required duty of care. If one could not identify that senior person and it be seen that s/he had failed in their duties, then a prosecution against the organisation would fail. Individual employees could be charged (and this is still the case) with manslaughter, e.g. a train driver involved in a rail crash, but charging the relevant rail company was far more difficult. Without being able to prove that an individual, who sat at the nerve centre of corporate decision making and who should have acted in ways that could have prevented the accident occurring, but had not, the organisation would escape prosecution. The requirement to point to a culpable senior executive who represented the failure of the corporation as a total entity was known as the *identification doctrine*.

In law, as in many other walks of life, one has to be clear about the precise meaning of words. So, when the phrase 'who sits at the nerve centre of corporate decision making' was used above, what would have been meant? For the corporation to be charged, the identified individual had to be shown to be the person with overall responsibility for this particular aspect of corporate activity, for example, health and safety matters, or rail track inspection. The need for this requirement was that because the law only viewed corporations as being answerable via its employees, the employee concerned had to be recognised as the person who was 'guiding' this aspect of corporate activity. This was the second legal requirement that operated prior to the CMCHA, i.e. to be able to prosecute a corporation for corporate manslaughter, the *guiding mind* of the organisation had to be identified and be shown to be implicated in the negligent act/s. Some real life examples of this principle will help to illustrate the issues involved.

Similar scenarios regarding the chasm that can appear to exist between a corporation's executive and operational management can be seen in other examples. A report in a safety journal during the inquiry into the disaster at *Piper Alpha* oil rig noted,

> The whole management evidence from Occidental [the owners of the oil rig] paints a picture of complete ignorance of the problems which existed. The senior management provided no support to the platform staff. They provided no training. They provided no guidance. The laid down no procedures. They did not participate in discussions with the operators. They did not seek the views of their employees.

(*Safety Management*, December, 1989, reported in Crainer, 1993: 116)

| Case study 7.4 | **The Herald of Free Enterprise** |

The case has already been mentioned in Chapter 6. It relates to the capsizing of the P&O ferry *Herald of Free Enterprise* outside Zeebrugge harbour in which 192 people lost their lives. It is possible that the captain of the ferry might have been able to be prosecuted for not fully checking that the bow doors were securely closed before the ferry set sail. However, the fact that crew members had, on five previous occasions, expressed concerns to their seniors about the lack of any warning lights on the bridge relating to the position of the bow doors was insufficient to bring a prosecution against the P&O Corporation. It was not possible to prove that these expressions of concern had reached the top echelons of the P&O corporation, the 'guiding mind'. Although comparative evidence was available concerning the (lack of) commitment that P&O was claimed to have towards safety issues, the prosecution lawyers were refused permission by the trial judge to call captains of the Sealink corporation (at the time of the trial Sealink was a rival ferry company), to contrast the safety practices of P&O ferries with those of other ferry operators. Four years after the capsizing of the *Herald of Free Enterprise*, safety issues at P&O were again raised when it was revealed that P&O crew members had to pay for their own basic safety training. One recruit recounted, 'I was sent to a college and given pages of information on things like where lifeboats are kept on a ferry, and how to evacuate in an emergency. But you don't get a chance to practise any of this on a ship. When I worked on a ferry for the first time it was up to me to find out where the evacuation points and passengers' lifejackets were' (Crainer, 1993: 67).

Even actions that might have appeared doubtful did not attract the judge's concerns. For example, while the inquests into the deaths of the 192 passengers and crew were still in progress, the *Herald of Free Enterprise*, which, unaccountably, had been renamed *Flushing Range* and with its bow doors welded together, was being towed to a scrap yard in Taiwan. Members of the Kent police had to fly to South Africa to intercept and inspect the renamed ship. As Crainer (1993) observes, for many concerned in the case, the vessel was 'regarded as an important piece of evidence in a criminal investigation'.

In terms of the 'guiding mind' P&O's marine superintendent admitted that he had misled the original inquiry into the disaster about when he had first heard of a proposal to fit warning lights on ferry bridges. It was also revealed that he discounted warnings from one of the company's senior masters about potential dangers because he thought the captains were exaggerating. Sheen (who chaired the initial enquiry) described Develin's [P&O's marine superintendent] responses to the legitimate concerns of the masters as 'flippant, facetious and fatuous' (Crainer, 1993). Yet Develin was not deemed sufficiently senior to equate with being (or being part of) P&O's 'guiding mind'.

Similarly, King (2001) remarked upon the actions of senior management at British Rail following the 1999 Paddington rail crash.

It should come as no surprise that soon after the UK suffered its second worse rail disaster of recent times – the 1999 Paddington crash – it was revealed that the rail companies had resisted calls to introduce a confidential reporting procedure, i.e. 'whistleblowing' procedure through which staff could report safety concerns without fear of recrimination.

(King, 2001: 152)

Of course, if a company has an internal grievance/concerns procedure, and issues are raised by employees within this process, senior management cannot later feign ignorance of any problems that subsequently result in injuries or death to consumers or general members of the public.

Twelve years after the *Herald of Free Enterprise* disaster, and following the high-profile rail crashes involving loss of life at Clapham and Southall, two trains collided just outside Paddington Station in 1999, killing 31 people and injuring over 400. In the report published in June 2001 into the causes of the crash, Lord Cullen, the enquiry chairman, condemned the entire rail industry for 'institutional paralysis'. He described the failure of the track operator, Railtrack, to act on previous reported incidents of train drivers passing through red signals as 'lamentable', He was extremely critical of one of the train companies involved, Thames Trains, (whose driver passed the red signal), and the company's safety culture, which he described as 'slack and less than adequate'. Lord Cullen also spoke of the 'significant failures of communication within the organisation'.

The driver of the Thames Train was inexperienced and had not been notified by the company of information that was in its possession that the signal just outside Paddington Station had been passed at danger (i.e. on red) eight times before. The problem appears to have been related to the signal being obscured at certain times of day due to the glare of the sun and/or overhanging foliage.

Lord Cullen was also critical of the quality of training given by Railtrack to its signallers, the 'slack and complacent regime at Slough' (the control centre for the signals in question). He was also extremely critical of the Railway Inspectorate, which he deemed 'lacked resources, acted without vigour and placed too much faith in *Railtrack*'. These words carry echoes of those used by Sheen, the chairman of the Department of Trade into the *Herald of Free Enterprise* disaster. Sheen spread the blame far more widely than those directly involved on the night of the disaster. Guilt lay with, 'all concerned in management. From top to bottom, the body corporate was infected with the disease of sloppiness.' No actions were ever brought against the corporations concerned!

However, the rail industry showed an incredible lack of learning capability when, in a little over 12 months after the Paddington rail crash, in October 2000, another serious incident occurred involving rail transport, when a train left the track at Hatfield due to faults in the track. This time four people lost their lives and many more were injured. Again management failures regarding reluctance to heed concerns about the quality of the track and its maintenance were suggested to be a significant feature of the case, but on 23 September 2004, a high court judge announced that no charges would be brought against either the company Railtrack (which was later renamed Network Rail) and three of its directors, including the former chief executive. The reason – lack of evidence, evidence that could be tied back to the guiding mind principle and the identification doctrine.

The issue of aggregation

Unlike the situation in the USA, UK courts will not accept the principle of *aggregation*. This relates back to the 'guiding mind' principle. In essence the refusal of UK courts to accept aggregation means that the guiding mind of an organisation was held within a tight area of the corporate structure, effectively the executive board, or person/s with delegated responsibility from the executive board. This was unlike the approach adopted in America as defined by the US Court of Appeal in 1987,

> corporations compartmentalise knowledge, subdividing the elements of specific duties and operations into small components. The aggregate of those components constitute the corporation's knowledge of a particular operation.

> (Crainer, 1993: 122)

The US Court of Appeal thus recognised the complexity of corporate structures and ruled that if responsibility for a particular facet of corporate activity, such as health and safety, was located in many different parts of a corporation, this was not a defence a corporation (as a totality) could employ to deny responsibility for a failure to adhere to acceptable safety practices. As a result of this approach, all the various parts of a corporation that are responsible for safety can be added together (aggregated) to produce the sum of the corporation's health and safety practices (or lack of). Until 2008, the UK steadfastly refused to adopt the US approach.

As the calls for a crime of corporate manslaughter to be formally recognised grew louder and more frequent in the UK, the UK Government, via the Home Office, published *Reforming the Law on Involuntary Manslaughter*, in 2000. However, no parliamentary time was found to debate the proposals. Four years later a bill on corporate manslaughter was included in the Queen's Speech, but, as mentioned earlier, this was frustrated by the general election of 2005. Thus, 18 years after the *Herald of Free Enterprise* disaster in which 192 people died, four serious rail crashes, the Kings Cross fire, the sinking of the pleasure craft *Marchioness*, and the Lime Bay canoeing tragedy, progress towards establishing a crime of corporate manslaughter continued to be frustrated.

It is important to recognise that the major accidents mentioned above were not the prime reason why there had been the drive to establish the crime of corporate manslaughter. They were headline examples of the need for legal recognition of corporate manslaughter, but every year the number of people in the UK who die as a result of injuries sustained whilst at work is considerably in excess of 200.

The three largest industries represented in these statistics are construction, agriculture and manufacturing, with construction the most risky of any industry by some margin. Most crucially, the Health and Safety Executive in the UK estimate that 70 per cent of deaths at work are potentially avoidable. This is what made the need for a crime of corporate manslaughter so urgent, but still progress was painfully slow.

Table 7.5 Fatalities as a result of injuries at work in the UK		
2005/6	**2006/7**	**2007/8**
241	247	228

The Corporate Manslaughter and Corporate Homicide Act (2007)

The catalysts for *Reforming the Law on Involuntary Manslaughter* had been the capsizing of the *Herald of Free Enterprise,* the Kings Cross fire and the many rail crashes, with the widely held belief that the law inhibited the successful prosecution of what appeared to be culpability within, and of, the organisations concerned. The identification doctrine was seen as the principal stumbling block to successful prosecution of companies.

The government's proposals were based upon the Law Commission Report No. 237, *Legislating the Criminal Code: Involuntary Manslaughters*. The principal proposals were:

1. There should be a special offence of corporate killing, broadly corresponding to the proposed offence of killing by gross carelessness.
2. The corporate offence should (like the individual offence) be prosecuted only where the corporation's conduct fell far below what could be reasonably expected.
3. The corporate offence should not (unlike the individual offence) require that the risk be obvious or that the defendant be capable of appreciating the risk.
4. A death should be regarded as having been caused by the conduct of the corporation if it is caused by a 'management failure', so that the way in which its activities are managed or organised fails to ensure the health and safety of persons employed in or affected by its activities.
5. Such a failure will be regarded as a cause of a person's death even if the immediate cause is the act or omission of an individual.
6. That individuals within a company could still be liable for the offences of reckless killing and killing by gross carelessness, as well as the company being liable for the offence of corporate killing.

When enacted in 2008, the CMCHA contained relatively few significant variations from the Law Commission Report, with the variations being as follows. Firstly the term 'management' was replaced by 'senior management'. This was to avoid the scenarios where middle and junior managers may act in ways that are negligent, but for reasons that are related to their own shoddy behaviour rather than being a reflection of a general lack of a duty of care by the organisation on matters such as health and safety issues.

The second difference was that the term 'gross' was now to be used before 'negligence' or 'breach'. Thus, to fall within the act, negligence on its own is insufficient. The behaviours or practices have to display gross negligence. The use of the term 'gross negligence' was largely a continuation of actual practice prior to 2008, rather than what was being proposed in debates leading up to the legislation. This was not an unreasonable qualification as it minimises the actions of litigious individuals and protects organisations from relatively minor lapses in standards of behaviour.

The effect of the above is that unlike point (3) above, the act does offer some narrowing of the liability of corporations. The offence (breach) has to be a 'gross breach', in that an organisation's conduct must have fallen *far* below what could have been reasonably expected.

Although at the time of writing this chapter the level of sanctions have yet to be defined, a commitment has been made that no upper financial limit will be set and the likely penalty levels are suggested to be five per cent of turnover, with the most grave of gross negligence cases likely to attract a fine of 10 per cent of turnover.

Switching the burden of proof to the corporation

A different approach to the CMCHA was proposed by the Council of Europe (European Union). This proposal would make companies responsible for all offences committed by their employees, but corporations would be allowed a due diligence defence, i.e. corporations would be exempted from liability if they could show that every precaution to avoid or minimise such an act occurring had been implemented. If adopted, this proposal would turn UK law on its head, i.e. in the UK the accused is presumed innocent until proven guilty. The EU proposal assumes guilt on the part of the accused, and it is then the responsibility of the accused (the corporation) to present evidence of its existing practices that would exempt it from liability. Clarkson (1998) expressed concern at the implications of this proposal in that (from a legal perspective) it would change the offence committed to one of a lesser order than criminal manslaughter. The new offence would be offset by a possible due diligence defence (as in the USA). The result would be the attribution of lesser sanctions than under a criminal prosecution for manslaughter.

The CMCHA does appear to make organisations that are guilty of gross negligence both culpable and accountable in law. It does not place any new standards of care upon organisations and it proposes no new regulations, but the act does appear to have addressed the profound criticisms aimed at organisations that show a disdain for human life and well-being. The Guiding Mind doctrine, the Identification principle and the Aggregation principle seem to have been addressed.

Is the corporate manslaughter debate now resolved?

In 1993, Crainer observed,

> Sadly the failure of the Zeebrugge corporate manslaughter trial seemed to condone an all-too-prevalent attitude among senior managers: 'Don't tell me what is going on because if I know, I might be held accountable'.

> (Crainer, 1993: 142)

Clarkson made a similar point when he observed,

> If the company's structures are impenetrable or if its policies are so 'sloppy' that no person has been made responsible for the relevant area of activity, a company can still shield itself from corporate criminal liability. In the *P&O* case,

where there was no safety manager or director, there would be no person whose acts and knowledge could be attributed to the company.

(Clarkson, 1998: 6)

Drawing upon the findings of the Sheen Report into the *Herald of Free Enterprise* disaster, in which the corporation was accused by Sheen of 'being infected with the disease of sloppiness' (Department of Transport, 1987), Clarkson observes, 'the worse the disease of sloppiness, the greater is the immunization against criminal liability'. These three quotes reflect the despair and frustration that many felt as corporate manslaughter remained off the statute books. Procrastination and prevarication seemed to be evident, as new discussion documents and initiatives from government sought more information on the likely impact of such an act on business, whilst high-profile tragedies occurred and many, many people continued to lose their lives as a result of injuries sustained at work.

Ultimately the acid test is, if the CMCHA had been on the statute books when the Herald of Free Enterprise disaster occurred; the Kings Cross fire occurred; when the Clapham rail crash; the Hatfield rail crash; the Southall rail crash and the Paddington rail crash, each occurred, could the organisations that were culpable have been able to be sued for corporate manslaughter? The answer appears to be 'Yes'.

The question that remains is, why did it take so long?

Criticisms of the principle of criminalising corporations

For some the criminalising of corporations is either conceptually flawed or wrong on consequential grounds. In terms of the conceptual issues, the arguments are familiar ones. They relate to the argument that a corporation is a legal fiction. In reality a corporation does not exist, and it cannot, literally, act – only humans can. However, a corporation is recognised at law as a juristic person; and, as evidenced earlier, corporations have not been slow in using the American Constitution to their advantage, a constitution that was designed solely for American citizens. Thus the criticisms based on conceptual arguments are weak and weakened by the actions of the very entities the critics seek to protect – corporations.

The consequentialist arguments are possibly weaker still. They relate to the claim that civil law settlements against corporations recognise the realities of situations and make awards that reflect the level of damage incurred (Fischel and Sykes, 1996). The empirical evidence to support this claim is debatable, but what is not debatable is that civil law has proved an unacceptable form of redress against corporations. The time and cost of taking a civil action against a corporation has proved too daunting for all but a few claimants and they speak despairingly of their experiences.

The CMCHA can withstand these criticisms. What will be of greater interest is the difference it might make on work-based fatalities. The UK Health and Safety Executive estimate that the act might increase the number of prosecutions by up to 13 in total per year in England, Wales, Scotland and Northern Ireland. The preferred outcome will be if the number of lawsuits falls, but so too do the number of work-based deaths.

Corporate *mens rea*

Clarkson offered a further variation on the quest to hold corporations to account, by the application of what he describes as 'corporate *mens rea*'. Clarkson offered his proposal because he feared that the doctrines of 'identification' and 'guiding mind' remained problematic within the then government's proposals, which have since formed the bedrock of the CMCHA.

DEFINITION

Mens rea is a legal term that means criminal intention, or knowledge that an act is wrong. Thus, corporate *mens rea* refers to an act or set of practices (or lack of) perpetrated in the name of a corporation that possess the essence of wrongdoing.

Clarkson argued,

> Doctrines – identification, aggregation, etc. – involve fictitious imputations of responsibility. The real question is not whether the question of corporate mens rea involves a fiction, but whether, of all the fictions, it is the one that most closely approximates modern-day corporate reality and perceptions . . . the important point about this approach is that it is not whether any individual within the company would have realised or foreseen the harm occurring but whether in a properly structured and organised, careful company, the risks would have been obvious.

(Clarkson, 1998: 10)

What this argument is saying is, 'Yes, corporate culpability is a fiction, or a problematic concept, but then so are many of the concepts that are involved in this debate'. Clarkson referred to legal concepts such as identification and aggregation as equivalent fictions/problematic concepts, but we could just as easily refer to concepts such as citizenship, democracy, property rights, free trade or a living wage. Property rights are an entirely socially constructed phenomenon, yet this has not prevented millions of lives being lost in its defence over the centuries. It is for societies to decide the laws that are appropriate for their own well-being and development. In many respects the fact that some of the laws relate to human beings, whilst others relate to socially constructed beings, is irrelevant.

Cross reference

In Chapter 9 we discuss one of Milton Friedman's main criticisms of corporations being required to be 'responsible' for their actions beyond the economic. The criticism in question was that as social constructs corporations could not have responsibilities; only people can. The reference, immediately above, to 'It is for societies to decide the laws that are appropriate for their own well-being and development. In many respects the fact that some of the laws relate to human beings, whilst others relate to socially constructed beings, is irrelevant', is extremely apposite in the context of Friedman's objections to calls for CSR.

This still leaves us with the issue of whether corporations can be construed or treated as corporate citizens. From the Heideggerian position (which we discuss in more detail in Chapter 10), corporations cannot be citizens, because the best that can be expected of corporations is that they view nature in exclusively instrumental ways. From a Heideggerian perspective, corporations have to be controlled in ways other than 'wishing' them to act in socially responsible ways. Windsor (2001) supported this view.

> The corporate citizenship notion conflates citizen (which a firm cannot be) and person (which a firm can be, but only as a legal fiction). The portrayal is fictional. . . . Fictional personhood is not a sound basis for artificial citizenship.
>
> (Windsor, 2001: 41)

The key proposal of the Law Commission report on involuntary manslaughter, was that management failure to introduce and ensure the application of reasonable safety practices is sufficient to justify the prosecution of corporate manslaughter. The philosophical arguments were kicked into touch. This was a fundamental change. The first prosecution and conviction under the 2007 act happened in February 2011. A geologist called Andrew Right worked for Cotswold Geotechnical Holdings; he died when an unsupported pit he was working in collapsed upon him. The company was found guilty of corporate manslaughter and was fined £385,000. The company was a small one with a sole director who was on the scene of the accident; so the case did not really test the issue of corporate responsibility within a large company. It was also a small company with financial problems, and the director was seriously ill. The judge took this into account when setting the level of the fine and the company was allowed to pay the fine over a 10-year period. He hoped that the company would survive and that the remaining four employees would keep their jobs. However, he said, if the company went into liquidation because of the fine it would be an unfortunate but unavoidable consequence of the company's breach of the 2007 act (The Telegraph, 2011).

Reflections

The focus of corporate governance is often very narrow and concerned only with the agency problem and relations between managers and owners. This is obviously important but it excludes organisations in the public sector and organisations that are state-owned enterprises for which governance is just as critical. Organisations exist in wider social and political structures and so governance is also a matter of organisations' accountability within these wider contexts. In this chapter this issue has been considered in relation to organisations' responsibility within the law. In the cases of both bribery and corporate manslaughter there have been moves to make organisations as much subject to the law as are individuals. The other main mechanism by which organisations may be made accountable is shareholder activism. It may be, however, that effective control over public companies lies not with shareholders but with the financial institutions that are companies' creditors. This reflects a general trend that, in times of economic stagnation, any conflict between tightening corporate governance and encouraging economic growth will be won by the latter.

Summary

In this chapter the following key points have been made:

- Corporate governance reforms in the UK and USA have retained an exclusive focus upon the interests of shareholders, unlike the King Report on corporate governance in South Africa.

- The King Report also raised the issue of values and beliefs as an explicit consideration of corporate governance, which in a South African context emphasised kinship, community and 'an inherent trust and belief in fairness of all human beings'. The issue of values within Anglo-American approaches towards corporate governance is not explicit, but implied. They are underpinned by ethical individualism and (from agency theory) a belief that individuals are self-serving and inherently untrustworthy.

- Large corporations express their commitment to accountability by formally committing to various international standards of good business conduct.

- Bribery and corruption is one area in which the law is increasingly being used to ensure good governance

- Corporate manslaughter is now a recognised crime. The consequences of its enactment will be observed with interest.

Typical assignments

1. The ethical principles that underpin official approaches towards corporate governance in South Africa (the King Report) and the UK (2003 Combined Code) both defend issues of rights, but the extent of those rights and to whom they relate varies significantly. Debate, using contrast and comparison, where you believe the weight of ethicality and pragmatics lies.

2. What impact has the UK Bribery Act had on organisations' internal governance policies and procedures designed to prevent bribe giving and receiving?

3. International codes of conduct reflect attempts to move a more socially oriented agenda into the boardrooms of corporations. Employing three different international codes,

   (a) compare and contrast the ethical principles upon which each is based; and

   (b) given the explicit or implicit objectives of the codes you have chosen, provide a reasoned analysis of their respective likely efficacy.

4. In addition to the Corporate Manslaughter and Corporate Homicide Act (2007), the EU has made some proposals and Clarkson (1998) has proposed the application of *mens rea.* Discuss and contrast where the conceptual and practical strengths and weaknesses of these different approaches lie.

Group activity 7.1

You are asked to work in groups of between three and six members and to assume the role of being the senior decision-making team of a leading institutional investor. Your tasks are as follows, with tasks A and B ideally completed before the commencement of the group session.

A   Define the principles that will guide your investment strategy. To do this you will need to consider, among other issues, the following:

   i   On whose behalf are you making decisions?

   ii   Are there any types of organisation in which you would not invest?

   iii   Are there any sectors in which you emphatically wish to invest?

   iv   What do you expect of the companies in which you invest in terms of communications and information updates?

   v   Are there any aspects of corporate governance that you would prioritise?

   vi   What will be your attitudes towards growth and risk?

   vii   What will be your expectations and attitude towards rates of return?An example of a leading institutional investor that has published its investment principles is the Hermes organisation. The following website will allow you to access the Hermes Principles, as well as a number of other important corporate governance publications: http://www.ecgi.org/codes/documents/hermes_principles.pdf.

B   Having established your investment principles, you must now select 10 quoted companies that will form your investment portfolio. You are not required to worry about how well these organisations have performed in the past year. For now, simply select 10 companies that you believe satisfy your investment principles.

C   You should prepare to discuss in open session the basis upon which you established your investment principles and the rationale for selecting the 10 companies in your investment portfolio.

Recommended further reading

You might find the following publications helpful.

Lindblom, C.E. (1977) *Politics and Markets: The World's Political-Economic Systems*, New York: Basic Books Inc.

Mallin, C. A. (2010) *Corporate Governance*, 3rd ed, Oxford: Oxford University Press.

Moon, J., Orlitzky, M. and Whelan, G. (eds) (2010) *Corporate Governance and Business Ethics*, in K. Keasey and M. Wright (Series editors) Corporate Governance in the New Global Economy, No. 10, Cheltenham: Edward Elgar. This is a collection of classic journal articles on corporate governance.

SustainAbility (2004) *Gearing Up: From Corporate Responsibility to Good Governance and Scalable Solutions*, New York: UN.

Useful websites

Topic	Website provider	URL
Corporate governance	European Corporate Governance Institute	http://www.ecgi.org/
International corporate governance	International Corporate Governance Network	http://www.icgn.org/
Corporate governance – The King Report		https://www.saica.co.za/TechnicalInformation/LegalandGovernance/King/tabid/626/language/en-ZA/Default.aspx
Gearing Up Report	SustainAbility	http://www.sustainability.com
Global Compact	United Nations	http://www.unglobalcompact.org
The AA1000 quality standard for corporate social responsibility	AccountAbility	http://www.accountability.org/aa1000/default.asp
The One World Trust website	One World Trust	http://www.oneworldtrust.org/
Transparency International website	Transparency International	http://www.transparency.org/
The Global Reporting Initiative web page	CERES/UN	http://www.globalreporting.org/
Social Accountability SA8000 web page	Social Accountability International	http://www.sa-intl.org

CHAPTER 8

Compliance and integrity: an organisation's internal accountability

Chapter at a glance

Chapter contents

- Learning outcomes
- Introduction
- An overview of the pressures upon organisations for ethical development
- Codes of conduct and codes of ethics
- Factors that will affect the impact of a code
- Writing a code of ethics
- Arguments against the employment of codes of conduct and ethics
- The difficulties of writing codes of conduct – the ethics of e-communication
- Ethical culture and ethos
- Reflections
- Summary

Activities and exercises

- Podcast 8.1 The ethical standards of BAE
- Activity 8.1 The negative consequences of developing codes of ethics
- Activity 8.2 Designing a code of conduct for e-mail and internet use at work
- Typical assignments
- Group activity 8.1
- Recommended further reading
- Useful websites

Having read this chapter and completed its associated activities, readers should be able to:

- Discuss the pressures upon organisations to employ codes of practice.

- Differentiate between various types of codes.

- Describe the practical problems faced when drafting codes.

- Understand the arguments for and against the employment of codes of practice within organisations.

- Show an awareness that codes of practice can sometimes conflict with one another, creating organisational tensions.

- Understand the significance and power of organisational culture and unwritten codes of conduct.

- Evaluate the role of ethical leadership.

- Evaluate the role of public pressure on maintaining organisational good behaviour.

Introduction

The previous chapter looked at an organisation's accountability to others outside of itself. This chapter looks inwards at how organisations seek to encourage, and ensure compliance with, good standards of behaviour and ethics. Initially codes are considered but then ethical leadership and ethical organisational cultures are discussed.

The International Labour Organisation (ILO) argued that worldwide interest in corporate codes of conduct was initially awakened in the 1980s by scandals in the US defence industry and the overt greed that was displayed on Wall Street. The ILO sees business ethics as a way for companies to promote self-regulation, thereby deterring government intervention and possible regulatory action.

Corporate interest quickly led to the institutionalisation of business ethics programmes, consisting largely of codes of conduct, ethics officers and ethics training. However, Brytting (1997) cited the Zeiss organisation as having a recognisable code of conduct for its employees in 1896, and Mill, writing in 1861, but cited by Warren (1993: 187), observed that 'it is the business of ethics to tell us what our duties are or by what test we may know them'. It has been argued that the more recent increase in the growth of corporate codes of conduct relates to the potential for such codes to reduce corporate exposure to punitive damages in claims of negligence. As Warren (1993: 109) observed in terms of the situation in the USA,

> The 1984 Sentencing Reform Act and the US Sentencing Commission's 1991 Federal Guidelines for Sentencing Organisations, allow for a fine on a corporation to be reduced by up to 95% if it can show that it has an effective program to prevent and detect violations of law.

Attempts to reduce negligence claims are not the only reason for organisations to be seen to be addressing the ethicality of their practices. Multinational corporations (MNCs) are not only increasingly powerful, but also open to critical scrutiny of any of their practices in all parts of the world. MNCs thus have a vested interest in harmonising and standardising practices throughout their respective organisations in order to minimise the risk of aberrant behaviour. We consider later in this chapter the initiatives being employed by MNCs to address concerns about their practices and those of their supplier networks.

An overview of the pressures upon organisations for ethical development

Figure 8.1 reflects the differing pressures on organisations to institute and formalise their ethical practices. Of all the connections depicted in Figure 8.1, the only unbroken line is that between 'Governments' and 'The organisation'. This reflects the mandatory nature of laws, as opposed to the other relationships that are characterised by frameworks, agreements, codes, understandings or memoranda, none of which is legally binding. The agreements, or framework documents, between governments and MNCs reflect the dilemma faced by many governments, particularly those of developing countries. The presence of MNCs within the host country can bring the prospect of accelerated economic development, but the

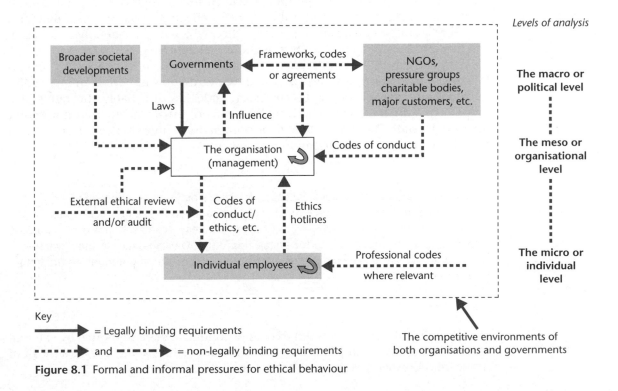

Figure 8.1 Formal and informal pressures for ethical behaviour

support, incentives and conditions that must be agreed to by the host government, in the face of alternative offers by other countries to the MNCs, can weaken the host government's bargaining powers. In such circumstances, legislation is unlikely to be deemed 'appropriate' to control the operations of the MNCs, and more adaptive, negotiable instruments such as framework agreements, or codes, become the norm. The non-legally binding agreements or codes of practice may be developed with or without the involvement of pressure groups and interested charitable bodies.

In turn, non-governmental bodies (NGOs), pressure groups and charitable bodies can exert pressure upon organisations independently of governments by developing their preferred codes of practice for business organisations and then contrasting these codes with the behaviour of specific organisations. These comparisons can reveal considerable discrepancies between espoused and actual behaviour and, given the glare of national and international publicity, can involve discussions about change. These relationships are reflected in the additional lines emanating from the 'NGOs, pressure groups' box and going towards the 'The organisation' box. Organisations such as Greenpeace, Friends of the Earth and the International Baby Food Action Network (IBFAN) are notable in this field.

Business organisations do not have to wait for external pressure before they act to enhance their own practices and behaviour. We illustrate below examples of ethical initiatives that appear to have come from within organisations, although the initiatives may have been in anticipation of government or pressure group involvement if the organisation did not respond in some way to an ethical issue.

There are examples of cooperation and collaboration between governments and pressure groups, between pressure groups and organisations/industries and between governments, pressure groups and business organisations, that appear to be addressing matters of ethical concern in effective ways. We also highlight, however, examples of apparent 'good' practice, which, when carefully scrutinised, are possibly less effective than they might at first appear.

Within Figure 8.1, the introduction of a corporate code of conduct by an employing organisation is shown by the downward-pointing arrow, aimed at 'Individual employees'. This is because such codes are invariably the result of a 'top-down initiative', with relatively little, or no, involvement from non-senior managerial staff. These codes tend to be statements of how employees are required to behave by the company/senior management.

Cross reference	However, companies can also incorporate 'ethics hotlines' to allow those employees with concerns about the ethicality of particular business practices to express their concerns, as we discussed in Chapter 6. These organisational vents can be both important mechanisms for concerned employees to express their worries, and effective early warning systems for organisations about potentially damaging practices and behaviour.

Both the ethics hotlines and the codes of conduct can be supported by external ethical review, for example, an annual or periodic ethics audit, but because all of these mechanisms are optional they are shown as broken lines.

An important point to emphasise is that the 'Codes of conduct, etc.' link between 'The organisation' and 'Individual employees' is not just about codes of conduct. The 'etc.' encompasses a range of other ways of communicating, inculcating and nurturing corporate values. McDonald and Nijhof (1999) cited:

■ training;

■ storytelling;

■ reward systems;

■ monitoring systems;

■ communication channels;

■ job design;

■ ethics officers;

■ information systems;

■ recruitment and selection policies and processes; and

■ organisational strategies

as further examples of ways in which organisations can influence the values and practices that become accepted as 'the ways things are done around here'. Many of these elements come within what is known as organisational culture. A consideration of some of the important issues of organisational culture for values and ethics, and vice versa, is undertaken towards the end of this chapter.

The arrows within 'The organisation' and 'Individual employees' boxes that appear to turn on themselves indicate that neither organisations, nor individuals, should expect or passively wait for developments on ethical behaviour to be externally imposed or influenced. If terms such as 'learning organisation' and 'reflective practitioner' are to mean anything, they will need to be evident in the critical reflection of both organisations and individuals on their respective practices. In many respects, the integrity with which organisations and individuals reflect upon notions of ethicality are fundamental elements of Figure 8.1. If change is only ever externally stimulated, rather than the result of internal reflection and action, then such change is subject to whims and pressures that will not necessarily be rooted in well-argued principles and values.

Podcast 8.1	**The ethical standards of BAE** Podcasts explaining how today's business news relates to the topics discussed here will be updated in an ongoing process. Podcast 8.1 discusses the report by Lord Woolf on the ethical standards of the major defence company BAE. To listen to this podcast, other archived podcasts or recent additions, please visit the companion website at www.pearsoned.co.uk/fisherlovellvalerosilva.

The arrow moving from the 'The organisation' to 'Governments' acknowledges that business organisations are not passive or disinterested bystanders in the development of laws affecting corporate practice. This arrow acknowledges the quite significant influence that specific organisations and industrial/commercial sectors can have on governments and the laws that are passed. Equally, it must be emphasised that the whole of Figure 8.1 sits within a commercial and competitive environment that bears upon the practices of individuals, organisations and governments.

Codes of conduct and codes of ethics

In market contexts where competitive forces are significant, consistency in all aspects of an organisation's operations is imperative. In order to stimulate, foster and maintain consistency in the behaviour of employees, consistency that also reflects the standards of behaviour that an organisation wishes its employees to adopt, organisations often develop codes of conduct and ethics. A distinction can be made between codes of ethics and codes of conduct that is helpful in examining the roles these types of statements perform. Although this distinction is not universally employed, indeed you may find some organisations employing codes of ethics that by our definition would be classed as codes of conduct, it offers some insight into the purpose of such codes. A study by Farrell and Cobbin (1996) discusses variations between codes of conduct and codes of ethics and the findings of this study add support to the distinction. A much higher level of prescription was found in the codes of conduct studied (average number of rules equalled 30.6), compared with the average number of rules contained in the codes of ethics (16.5).

DEFINITION

Codes of conduct tend to be instructions, or sets of rules, concerning behaviour. As a result they are likely to be reasonably prescriptive and proscriptive concerning particular aspects of employee behaviour. They identify specific acts that must be either adhered to (prescription), or avoided (proscription). However, the extent to which all possible situations can be addressed within a code of conduct is problematic.

Codes of ethics tend to be reasonably general in their tenor, encouraging employees to display particular characteristics such as loyalty, honesty, objectivity, probity and integrity. They do not normally address specific types of decisions; rather they encourage the application of what might be called 'virtues', although, as noted in Chapter 3, what are regarded as virtues can vary over time. While notions of honesty and integrity remain fairly constant over time, concepts such as justice and loyalty are more contentious.

The distinction between codes of ethics and conduct is similar to that used by Cadbury (2002: 17), in relation to corporate governance, when he distinguished principles and provisions. He explains:

> The question to ask of principles is how companies have applied them, while the equivalent question over provisions is how far they have been complied with.

From these definitions it is evident that, where all possible scenarios that an employee might face can be predicted with a high degree of confidence, as well all the circumstances relating to those scenarios, then a specific code of conduct might be possible, because ethical judgment becomes redundant. However, where the likely scenarios that an employee might face cannot be predicted in the requisite detail, then reference to general qualities and principles will be preferred, that is, codes of ethics become more appropriate.

The risk of confusing these two general positions is that, if a code of conduct fails to address a particular scenario that an employee actually faces, then the silence of the code on the matter in question might be interpreted by the employee as an indication that the employing organisation is at best indifferent to the ethics of the decision in hand. In this discussion, the employee might be said to be (or be treated as) morally immature, requiring a code of conduct or ethics to act as a reference point in times of need, but that is just what codes imply. By issuing such codes, a company is stating that it does not have sufficient confidence in all of its employees to be able to view a code of conduct or ethics as unnecessary. This is an implication that some, perhaps many, employees might find objectionable, but for an organisation that straddles many countries and cultures in its operations, the need for an articulation of expected behaviour and practices throughout its operations can be overwhelming.

The purposes of codes of conduct and ethics

At one level, codes of conduct and ethics can be seen as legitimate and necessary devices for senior management to develop in order to specify expected codes of behaviour of all employees. Each employee of an organisation will be seen as a representative of that organisation by others external to the organisation. Thus, it is important that employees reflect behaviour that is commensurate with the persona and reputation that the organisation wishes to project. In this context, some writers see codes of conduct as principally manipulative control devices to achieve managerial ends. Stevens (1994: 65) argued that 'some ethical codes are little more than legal barriers and self-defence mechanisms; others are intended to influence and shape employee behaviour'. These were observations that had been made earlier by, among others, Mathews (1988) and Warren (1993).

Developing and adding to the work of Bowie and Duska (1990), we have listed below eight roles for corporate codes. These are:

- *Damage limitation* – to reduce damages awarded by courts in the event of the company being sued for negligence by one of its employees.

- *Guidance* – the 'reference point' role, similar to what Passmore (1984) referred to as 'the reminding role'. An aide-memoire for employees when faced with an ethically complex situation.

- *Regulation* – this is the prescribing and proscribing role that will stipulate specific qualities that are essential, for example, independence, objectivity, etc., or acts that are prohibited.

- *Discipline and appeal* – this is the role of a code as a benchmark for an organisation or professional body to decide whether an employee/member has contravened required conduct and what form of punishment might ensue. In addition, the code can form the basis of an appeal by the accused.

■ *Information* – a code expresses to external audiences standards of behaviour that can be expected of employees/members.

■ *Proclamation* – this has echoes of 'information', but it relates more to the role of codes of conduct developed by professional bodies. To achieve 'professional' status, trade associations are normally required to assuage public concerns over the granting of monopoly rights to specific areas of commercial/social activity (e.g. auditing, doctoring, etc.). Ethical codes will attempt to reassure that these monopoly powers will not be abused.

■ *Negotiation* – this is not dissimilar to *guidance* in that codes can be used as a tool in negotiations and disputes with and between professionals, colleagues, employers, governments, etc.

■ *Stifling* – this is the creation of internal procedures for handling the ethical concerns of employees that are more concerned with management keeping a lid on internal dissent than acting as a conduit for internal debate and examination. Hunt's (1995 and 1998) work on whistleblowing in the health and social services reflects a number of examples of this use of codes of conduct and internal whistleblowing processes.

The attention paid to codes of conduct by both organisations and researchers does presume both that codes are a 'good' thing and that they do have a positive impact upon individual and corporate behaviour. With regard to the latter, Mathews (1988) was able to identify only a weak link between the existence of ethical codes and corporate behaviour. This latter point was taken up by Cassell et al. (1997: 1078), who argued that:

An important, if implicit, assumption of many writings on corporate codes . . . is that such codes do have a 'real' effect upon behaviour. This tends to be something that is taken for granted, but it is not empirically validated by subsequent investigation . . . recipients of the code: those who are required to make sense of it, and respond to it, often as one more instance of managerially-inspired change, amidst a plethora of pre-existing formal and informal control processes within which the impact of the code must be located. As with any example of formal organisational control, the actual, as opposed to the intended, effect may be subject to processes that entail negotiation and bargaining.

Stevens' (1994) observations were that codes were:

■ primarily concerned with employee conduct that might damage the firm, that is, they were thus skewed towards self-protection; and

■ preoccupied with the law.

The legalistic orientation of many codes has been noted by a number of writers, including Farrell and Cobbin (1996). The latter identified differences between American, Australian and UK corporate codes of conduct. They concluded that, of the codes they studied, the Australian codes tended to concentrate upon a reiteration of the legal environment within which individuals and organisations operate, emphasising the importance of not doing anything to harm the employing organisation's reputation. American codes included, but went beyond, this orientation, emphasising customers, equal opportunities and insider dealing, while the UK codes made more frequent reference to the community, customer welfare and the environment than the Australian or American codes. However, all of these are relative terms, 'the level of specific guidance on ethical content in each country's codes was very low' (1996: 54). As lawyers were identified as the most frequent developers of such codes (30 per cent), a legalistic orientation to the codes was not surprising.

Factors that will affect the impact of a code

Cassell et al. (1997), combining the work of Hopwood (1974) and Kelman (1961), identified three possible explanations why individuals might display behaviours that conform with desired organisational behaviours. These are:

1. *Internalisation*, in which the behaviours are accepted by the individual as their own, even though they are set externally. This does suggest, however, that the ethical values displayed will be subject to, and influenced by, further external forces, unless the organisational values are held by the individual at a profound and deep level.

2. *Compliance*, in which the displayed behaviour is associated with the desire to achieve some form of reward, or avoid an identifiable punishment. This form of behaviour will last as long as the punishment or reward is regarded as both significant and realisable by the individual/s concerned, but not beyond. This form of behaviour is thus not ethically based, but instrumental, calculating and unreliable.

3. *Identification*, in which behaviour is shaped by, and mirrors, the behaviours of significant others with whom the individual wishes to identify. Again because of the instrumental and externally located locus of a behaviour's rationale, the reliability of the behaviour in question is problematic.

Of these three possible explanations, only the first holds out the prospect of consistency for the organisations, the other two being unreliable due to external corruption. If this is so, then the individual must absorb the organisation's values in a conscious and knowing way because either:

■ The individual's existing values correspond closely with those espoused by the organisation and, thus, little change is required to the individual's own ethics; or

■ The individual recognises in the organisation's values a set of principles that transcend their own and to which they wish to aspire.

Alternatively the internalisation is not conscious, but unconscious, achieved by the constant drip-drip of organisational images and rhetoric. This might seem a very distant possibility in the current day and age, but one of the authors is reminded of an ethics workshop he held for a group of managers on a Master's programme. One of the managers worked for a well-known and respected retail organisation, respected among other things for the apparently strong employee benefits and care provided by the company. However, during the course of the workshop all the participants reviewed aspects of their organisation's practices, and this particular manager gradually shifted from a view of his employing organisation's paternalistic care as benign, to one that saw it as more oppressive and manipulative. This change in interpretation came not from questioning by the tutors, but from a series of interactive exercises with other members of the course. The manager in question had worked for the retail organisation for over 15 years and during that time had accepted the organisation's house journal, the management conferences he attended and other practices as evidence of his employer's good intent. His now more critical interpretation did not suddenly make his employers 'bad' employers, when for the previous 15 years they had been 'good' employers. What unsettled him was how uncritical he had been in accepting a particular interpretation of some of the organisation's actions and decisions over the years, some of which did not square with his original uncritical, 'rose-tinted' description of his organisation.

Using Goffman's (1959) dramaturgical metaphor, individuals can be said to 'act out' their preferred view of themselves on the stage of life. Information likely to enhance others' opinions of oneself is kept 'centre stage' rather than 'in the wings'. The concept of impression management pervades the literature on business ethics, and is particularly apparent in ethnographic accounts of how managers deal with ethical problems (e.g. Jackall, 1988; Toffler, 1991; Schein, 1992; Watson, 1994). Interestingly, the 'management' and 'organisational behaviour' literature is a much richer and a more academically robust source of material on this point than much of the business ethics literature.

Jackall (1988) argued that the unethical actions of managers do not result from the individual's moral deficiencies, but rather from the bureaucratic structures of modern organisations, which encourage managers to behave unethically. This view has been echoed by others within the literature. For example, Liedtka (1991) concluded that many of the managers in her study found themselves forced to choose between preserving their relationships within the firm (operating within the organisational political model) and following their own values (using a value-driven model). We will conclude our consideration of this issue with a quote from Cassell et al. (1997: 1088):

> It is our contention that although individual psychological and demographic factors play a role in influencing behaviour in relation to codes, that role is relatively minor given the significance of the organisational context and culture within which behaviour takes place.

Cassell et al. (1997) identified three factors they argued would determine the influence a code would have upon the behaviour of organisational members, namely:

1. The nature of the code, its content and the processes by which it has been designed, developed and implemented.

2. The organisational control mechanisms (both formal and informal). For example, will the employees see the introduction of a (new) code as just another mechanism by which the employing organisation wishes to determine individual behaviour, or a genuine attempt to help employees cope with complex ethical issues that they will face during their day-to-day practice?

3. Individual influences which focus upon perceptual and self-control processes.

Thus, if the individual employee acts in keeping with required organisational behaviour out of either compliance or identification motives, and is sceptical about factors (1) and (2) above, the prospects for a newly introduced code of conduct or practice are likely to be unpredictable and variable throughout an organisation, two outcomes the code was presumably intended to obviate.

Writing a code of ethics

The difficulty of writing a code of ethics is that, when such codes are completed they look banal and people comment, 'Well, that is all just common sense'. Their commonplaceness is intensified when they are reduced to their basic content and provided to all employees as laminated cards that can be stored alongside credit cards in wallets and purses. Commonplaces, of course, are mostly true and important statements about trust, integrity, honesty and fairness. The intention is clearly that employees should carry these cards around with them as reminders, thus implying that the staff need constant admonition to be honest and so on. In our research interviews, one respondent reported a debate in a focus group set up to discuss what should be included in the new code of ethics. One side of the argument was that 'Employees should act honestly' should be included. The contrary view was that this was such an obvious requirement that it did not need stating, and that if it was it implied that the management thought their employees potentially dishonest. It was decided not to include it.

Most organisations go to great trouble to ensure that their code of ethics is particular to them and their business and circumstances. Yet most codes of ethics look alike. It is unusual for codes to go against convention or the norms and institutions of the surrounding society. Table 8.1 attempts to illustrate this phenomenon by comparing elements from an ethical codes for the conduct of pharmaceutical medicine developed by Johnson and Johnson with that of the Covenant of the Goddess (Center for the Study of Ethics in the Professions, 2003), which is an association of white witches.

As there is much common ground between different organisations' codes of ethics, it is possible to identify the topics and themes most commonly mentioned. In the analysis in Table 8.2, the examples are taken from Johnson and Johnson's Credo, the UK Civil Service Code of Conduct (The Cabinet Office, 2004), BP's business policies and the statement of core values of Carbo Ceramics (2002) (this last example was more or less chosen at random from the many company statements available); note that none of these uses the term code of ethics, but nevertheless that is what they are.

Table 8.1 A comparison of elements from typical codes of ethics for the conduct of pharmaceutical medicine and of the Covenant of the Goddess Code of Ethics

Common theme	Ethical codes for the conduct of pharmaceutical medicine	Covenant of the Goddess ethical code
Credo based	The ethical codes of the pharmaceutical company Johnson and Johnson (n.d) are famously based on a Credo, which is a statement of basic values and principles to which everyone in the company must subscribe.	'Members of the covenant should ever keep in mind the underlying unity of our religion as well as the diversity of its manifestations.' 'These ethics shall be understood and interpreted in the light of one another, and especially in the light of the traditional laws of our religion.'
The credos are of similar antiquity	Credos, and similar statements, often date back to the origin of a company or to a founding father. The Johnson and Johnson Credo was first published in 1943	Modern witchcraft was probably invented as a religion in the 1920s and 1930s when there was a fashion for magic and druidism.
Do no harm	Most ethical codes in the fields of pharmacy and medicine include a classic command – above all do no harm, or something similar, which has its origins in the Hippocratic Oath, which in turn has its origins in ancient Greece	'An ye harm none, do as ye will.'
Respect the differences and autonomy of others	Most companies' codes have a statement that they respect the rights of individuals and recognise and value the diversity of their employees.	'Every person associated with the covenant shall respect the autonomy and sovereignty of each coven, as well as the right of each coven to oversee the spiritual, mental, emotional and physical development of its members and students in its own way, and shall exercise reasonable caution against infringing upon that right in any way.'
A position on openness and secrecy	At a time when governments are concerned with the cost effectiveness of drugs, pharmaceutical companies may commit to transparency or perhaps to a more limited commitment to providing fair, balanced accurate and comprehensive data.	'All persons associated with this covenant shall respect the traditional secrecy of our religion.' OK so the White Witches do not believe in transparency but they do have a principled position on the issue.
Right to a fair return	The belief that a fair return on investment is morally acceptable is core to the belief of commercial organisations.	'All persons have the right to charge reasonable fees for the services by which they earn their living, so long as our religion is not thereby exploited.'
Professional standards of those who practice the activity	Companies recognise the professional standards that apply to medicine and pharmacy and accept a responsibility to adhere to the principles of good clinical practice.	'Since our religion and the arts and practices peculiar to it are the gift of the Goddess, membership and training in a local coven or tradition are bestowed free, as gifts, and only on those persons who are deemed worthy to receive them.'

Source: The Covenant of the Goddess Code of Ethics and Johnson and Johnson Credo

Table 8.2 Common themes in codes of ethics

Theme	Example	Source of example
Integrity	The constitutional and practical role of the Civil Service is, with integrity, honesty, impartiality and objectivity, to assist the duly constituted Government [ ] whatever their political complexion, in formulating their policies, carrying out decisions and in administering public services for which they are responsible.	UK Civil Service Code
	We conduct our business with the highest ethical standards. We are truthful and honor our commitments and responsibilities.	Carbo Ceramics
Loyalty	Civil servants are servants of the Crown. Constitutionally, all the Administrations form part of the Crown and, subject to the provisions of this Code, civil servants owe their loyalty to the Administrations in which they serve.	UK Civil Service Code
No harm and risk management	We believe our first responsibility is to the doctors, nurses and patients, to mothers and fathers and all others who use our products and services. In meeting their needs, everything we do must be of high quality.	Johnson and Johnson
	We will regularly identify the hazards and assess the risks associated with our activities. We will take appropriate action to manage risks and hence prevent or reduce the impact of potential accidents or incidents.	BP
Respect for individual employees	We are responsible to our employees, the men and women who work with us throughout the world. Everyone must be considered as an individual. We must respect their dignity and recognize their merit. They must have a sense of security in their jobs. Compensation must be fair and adequate, and working conditions clean, orderly and safe. We must be mindful of ways to help our employees fulfil their family responsibilities. Employees must feel free to make suggestions and complaints. There must be equal opportunity for employment, development and advancement for those qualified. We must provide competent management, and their actions must be just and ethical.	Johnson and Johnson
Respect for the law	We will respect the law in the countries and communities in which we operate.	BP
Trust	Our commitment is to create mutual advantage in all our relationships so that people will trust us and want to do business with BP.	BP
Relationship with stakeholders	We will enable customers, governments, communities and our own people to participate in a new constructive dialogue. We aim for a radical openness – a new approach from a new company, transparent, questioning, flexible, restless and inclusive.	BP
	Our suppliers and distributors must have an opportunity to make a fair profit.	Johnson and Johnson

▶

Table 8.2 Continued

Theme	Example	Source of example
Developing communities	We are responsible to the communities in which we live and work and to the world community as well.	Johnson and Johnson
	We must be good citizens – support good works and charities and bear our fair share of taxes.	Johnson and Johnson
	We must encourage civic improvements and better health and education. We must maintain in good order the property we are privileged to use, protecting the environment and natural resources.	Johnson and Johnson
Goals and achievement	We set aggressive goals and strive to exceed them.	Carbo Ceramics
	We value and celebrate a high level of individual achievement and team performance.	
Return to shareholders	Our final responsibility is to our stockholders.	Johnson and Johnson
	Business must make a sound profit.	Johnson and Johnson
Environmental sustainability	We are committed to [ ] demonstrating respect for the natural environment and work towards our goals of no accidents, no harm to people and no damage to the environment.	BP
Political activity and contributions	BP will never make political contributions whether in cash or in kind anywhere in the world.	BP
Personal advantage	Civil servants should not misuse their official position or information acquired in the course of their official duties to further their private interests or those of others. They should not receive benefits of any kind from a third party which might reasonably be seen to compromise their personal integrity or judgment.	Civil Service Code
Commitment to external standards or assurance	BP supports the principles set forth in the UN Universal Declaration of Human Rights and will respect the 2000 International Labour Organisation, the 'Tripartite Declaration of Principles Concerning Multinational Enterprises and Social Policy' and the 2000 OECD 'Guidelines for Multinational Enterprises'.	BP

Sources: The Cabinet Office; Johnson & Johnson; BP plc; Carbo Ceramics

Activity 8.1	The negative consequences of developing codes of ethics

Although our consideration of codes of conduct and ethics has identified limitations in practice and referred to evidence that casts doubt upon the actual impact of codes 'on the ground', we have not suggested that the development and introduction of a code would be a negative development. There are, however, such arguments, and before discussing these we would like you to think through what these might be.

Identify as many negative aspects as possible associated with the development of a code of conduct or ethics.

Arguments against the employment of codes of conduct and ethics

While the employment of codes has an intuitive appeal, we can identify five possible objections to their development and employment.

1 Justification

This relates to the lack of any universally accepted set of common principles and ethics. If 'everything is relative' is taken to its logical conclusion and codes can only ever be culturally and socially specific, the notion of universal laws is rejected and with it the argument that a corporation can have a single code of conduct. If a multinational organisation produces a code of conduct that reflects a basic set of values, by definition this implies there are certain basic concepts that it wishes to universalise, at least within its own worldwide operations, but is this possible? The question might become one of distinguishing between negotiable and non-negotiable values – how and when does one balance local customs and traditions with one's own sense of values when the two are in conflict? For example, when is a gift a bribe?

Jensen et al. (2009) analysed codes of ethics using actor network theory, which amongst other things, considers the impact of non-human and virtual objects such as codes on human sense making. The writers of codes inscribe certain values and constraints into them; and they expect the code will be understood uniformly throughout the organisation. However, as the codes are received in different contexts (the authors say 'heterogenous materialities'), the codes of ethics 'oblige us humans to oblige them and as the chain of translation unfolds several versions of morality circulate in the organisation' (Jensen et al., 2009: 539). The case study the analysis was based on explored how a code of ethics in an American multinational company was re-interpreted within its Swedish subsidiary.

2 The inability of rules to govern actions

If codes cannot change behaviour for the better, and the empirical evidence for this is very limited, will the negative signals being sent out to employees, that the organisation does not trust them, be the abiding impact of the introduction of a code? If so, then the overall impact of a code is likely to be negative. This was a possible conclusion from a large-scale survey by Kaptein (2011) in which people were asked their opinions on various aspects of ethical codes in the organisations they worked in. The study looked at:

- whether a code of ethics was present or not;
- frequency of formal communication about the code;
- quality of communication about the code; and
- the embedding of the code by senior and local management.

The statistical analysis of the data suggested that in some circumstances the presence of a code was associated, counter-intuitively, with higher levels of unethical behaviour. It was also found that the simple presence of an ethical code was not associated with a lack of unethical behaviour. However, when some of the contextual factors just listed were in play, and added their influence to the simple presence of a code, the incidence of unethical behaviour was lower (Kaptein, 2011: 244–5).

3 Support structures

There is a need for, but a paucity of, support structures within organisations for employees to feel able to act in accordance with specified codes of behaviour. Where codes of conduct do exist, Warren (1993: 189) argued that:

> All too often ethical codes are handed down to employees from the executive above and the importance of trying to create a community or purpose within the company is ignored.

Warren (1993) referred to the field of industrial relations where evidence indicates that rules governing industrial relations need collective agreement if they are to be honoured in the observance as well as in the breach (e.g. Terry, 1975). This perspective is supported by Bird and Waters (1989: 83). They argued that just talking about ethical issues is unlikely to enhance the significance of the issues unless mechanisms are found for 'connecting this language with the experiences and expectations of people involved in business'. Taking this argument forward, Bird and Waters (1989: 84) argued that:

> Business people will continue to shun open discussions of actual moral issues unless means are provided to allow for legitimate dissent by managers who will not be personally blamed, criticised, ostracised, or punished for their views.

They found that talking to managers individually revealed that the managers had many concerns of an ethical nature. However, when asked if these issues were ever raised among managerial colleagues, either formally or informally, the managers replied that they were not. The managers identified a range of explanations for the collective managerial muteness on ethical issues. Such talk was perceived to be a threat to:

- efficiency (i.e. the imposition of rigid rules and regulations);
- the image of power and effectiveness (i.e. previous attempts had resulted in the dissenting manager being shown to be organisationally impotent); and

- organisational harmony (i.e. discussion of moral issues at work was perceived to be dysfunctional).

Thus, the introduction of a code of conduct requires an environment in which expressions of concern over particular practices are not perceived as simplistically 'anti-company' or 'wimpish'. Without such an environment, cynicism is likely to be fuelled, and the overall impact of the code will be negative.

4 The marginality of codes

Codes tend to be treated as 'add-ons', as constraints upon action, and thus act at the margins of corporate activity. To be effective, codes need to be at the centre of corporate beliefs. More particularly, a code becomes redundant if the corporate culture encapsulates those values and beliefs that would be reflected in a corporate code of conduct or ethics. If left at the margins, a code might be interpreted as a necessary accoutrement (garnish) to corporate activities, but one that can be circumvented, or 'negotiated' in certain circumstances. If so, then cynicism about corporate motives would be heightened and the overall effect of the code would be negative.

One particular way in which codes can become marginalised has been termed distancing. In a study by Helin and Sandstrom (2010: 594–6), it was noticed that when an American multinational forced upon its Swedish subsidiary an American code of ethics that had not been adapted to local law and norms, the staff all signed it even though they disagreed with it. This apparent paradox was explained by the staff distancing the code in how they made sense of their work and putting it to the edge of their daily practices. The organisation's staff thought that the code was so American, and so separate from their context, that there was no harm in signing it. A second distancing mechanism was to ignore the detailed content of the code by saying 'it's all common sense'; and thinking therefore that if you worked to that sense of local common sense, little engagement with the details of the code was necessary. A third distancing mechanism was to say that the code was unnecessary because the local systems were adequate and so, as the code would not come into play, it could be signed and ignored.

5 The diminution and ultimate invisibility of individual responsibility

Codes that specify behaviour in particular situations seek to take judgment out of ethically charged situations. Whilst this has the advantage of standardising behaviour throughout an organisation and potentially minimising the risk of behaviour that is unacceptable, there is also the risk of the individual using the 'I was only following orders' defence in the event of an enquiry into a dispute over a particular incident. This shifting of responsibility has been termed by Bauman (1994) as 'floating responsibility' and was discussed in Chapter 6. It becomes an organisational defence against individual conscience. The following of rules and adherence to the commands of superiors makes identification of responsibility difficult to isolate. Identification of responsibility for a particular action or inaction falls between the cracks of job descriptions and responsibilities, and codes of conduct. Morality (or the defining of it) thus becomes someone else's responsibility. The actions of individuals become automatic, with little thought or judgment on the part of the individual required. Whilst actual situations will often present complexities and nuances that take the individual into contexts not addressed adequately by a code, the existence and 'failings' of the code present the individual with an escape route from responsibility. To obey instructions is less demanding and far less risky than exercising moral judgment.

Bauman (1994) identified a second tendency, that of organisational actions being deemed amoral, that is neither good nor bad, only correct or incorrect. In this context codes of conduct can be used to make what could be transparent opaque. Codes might be expressed, not so much in moral terms, but in technical terms, implying a moral neutrality to the issues being addressed in the code.

The difficulties of writing codes of conduct – the ethics of e-communication

With the coming of new forms of electronic communication and diffusion of information, in particular e-mail and the Internet, new forms of ethical problems have appeared in organisations. As this has happened, organisations have tried to develop new codes of conduct governing e-communications, to minimise abuse. Their attempts to respond to new problems illustrate many of the problems and difficulties with codes of conduct discussed in the previous section. The matter is not an inconsequential one. In 1998, an IT manager was sacked from her job because she had booked her holiday on the Internet, using the company's computers, during work time (Wakefield, 1999). In 2003, four lawyers lost their jobs at a top London law firm after circulating an e-mail about oral sex among their colleagues; at some point it was e-mailed to a further 20 million people worldwide. A year later, 10 clerical workers at the Royal Sun Alliance in Liverpool were dismissed after e-mailing a risqué cartoon involving Bart Simpson and a donkey (Observer, 2004). People have no control over what they are sent by e-mail, and they may inadvertently, or so they will claim, download a pornographic image, for example. Even if they delete it immediately a record will remain, in this networked age, that they received the image. It might be difficult for them subsequently to disprove that they were simply an innocent dupe.

As access to e-mail and the Internet grows so the ethical issues become more important. The main problems are listed below.

1 Misuse by employers

■ Employers have the capacity, but not always the inclination, to monitor every action that employees take while using networked computers at work.

Employees' net surfing and e-mail correspondences are all logged. The question is the extent to which such surveillance is ethical and legitimate and when it could be claimed to break an employee's right to privacy. In 2003, the UK government passed the Regulation and Investigatory Powers Act, which made it illegal to monitor employees' e-mails without their consent. Guidelines issued by the Department of Trade and Industry, however, construed the act as allowing surveillance if contracts of employment included a clause that allowed employers to monitor e-mail and internet usage. The employers argued that they needed this right as all e-mails sent from their systems were their legal responsibility, which is why most e-mails now sent from organisational systems have a disclaimer (often longer than the message) denying any such responsibility.

■ Employers may assume that by e-mailing all staff they have exhausted their responsibility to communicate effectively with their staff.

2 Misuse by employees

■ Stealing employers' time by surfing the net when they should be working.

■ Using the e-mail and internet facilities for improper purposes, such as distributing racist messages or obscene materials.

■ Conducting a personal business using their employer's systems.

■ Harassing or stalking other employees by e-mail, a practice that has been recognised by Industrial Tribunals as illegal behaviour (Taylor, D., 2001).

■ Sending an internal e-mail communication to an external body. For example, an aggrieved employee who had taken Prince Charles to an Industrial Tribunal complaining of sex discrimination used an internal e-mail from the Prince's household as evidence in support of her case.

■ Misusing online selection and recruitment testing to misrepresent oneself to a potential employer. In 2003, 6 per cent of organisations were using some form of online testing for recruitment and selection purposes (Czerny, 2004).

3 Abuses of good communication

■ E-mail communication is anomalous; on the one hand it is seen as quick and informal yet on the other it is a recorded form of communication that can be used in a court of law. This leads people to show a lack of courtesy in their communications with others that they would not think of exhibiting on the telephone or in face-to-face communication (Taylor, D., 2001).

■ People often use e-mails to avoid giving news, often bad, that ought to be given personally. There was in 2004 a case of a large number of employees being informed by e-mail that they had been made redundant.

- The informality and distance of e-mails encourage people to be ruder, especially when they are angry, than they would be if addressing the subjects of their disgust directly. Reliance Industries (RIL) is a very large family firm in India. When the founder died there was a power struggle between his two sons, which was conducted almost entirely in e-mails and leaked to the media. The directors of the company thought the dispute would never be resolved by e-mails and said,

  [we do] not find the mode of e-mail suitable. Instead of e-mail it should be love mail. It is better to sit and talk.

  (*Hindustan Times*, 2004: 1)

- The extreme e-mail discourtesy is when someone writes an e-mail complaining about some hurt from another and then copies it to the entire company. Such a practice may have a beneficial aspect, such as when an e-mail that affects all staff, but which was intended to be confidential to a select group, is forwarded by one of that group to all employees. This can lead to a vigorous and democratic debate about the issue between all staff. E-mails can be an effective forum for rapid debate.

- Overusing mailing lists and the 'cc' function to flood people with e-mails that are of little interest to them.

One of the difficulties of writing a code of conduct to cover these issues is that most employers wish to draw a sensible balance between the employees' rights and those of the companies. Most organisations are happy to allow their employees to use e-mail and internet access for personal use, but, as one code expresses it,

  this should not interfere with or conflict with business use. Employees should exercise good judgement regarding the reasonableness of personal use.

This particular employer provided a junk mail group so that employees could post messages such as 'looking to rent' or 'something to sell'. Only a few organisations go to the extreme of prohibiting all personal use of the Internet and e-mail. One American University did, and incurred the wrath of its academic staff (Woodbury, 1998). One of the reasons for employers to exercise some discretion is that the custom and practice, the work culture, of many occupational groups does not see personal use of ICT as an ethical wrong. Stylianou et al. (2004) conducted research that shows that R&D staff think it is right to violate both intellectual property (IPR) and privacy rights (when using ICT) to favour open access to data and knowledge.

Programmers, more restrictively, think it acceptable to plagiarise (ignore IPR) but not to breach an employee's right to privacy. Some of the standard clauses in a code of conduct on the use of e-mail and the network might be as follows.

- No e-mail or communication should violate the law or company policy.

- Employees should take care to maintain the security of their passwords.

- Accessing and using copyright information in ways that break the law is a disciplinary offence.

- Confidential internal messages should not be posted outside the organisation.

- Chain messages should not be originated or passed on.

- E-mails should be brief, courteous and only sent to individuals with an interest in them, and not en bloc to groups.

- Employees should be informed of the level of monitoring of their e-mail and internet usage that will be carried out.

- The monitoring of an individual's private e-mails will not be routinely conducted unless it has been specifically authorised by a senior manager in support of a specific allegation of wrongdoing. (This is a particularly contentious clause.)

- Employers should give warnings to staff about misuse and make the penalties clear. Cronin (2004) has carried out some intriguing research on the efficacy of such warnings.

Of course, once someone starts to draft such regulations, the creation of a rule to prevent one problem, not using email to distribute political messages to staff for example, quickly creates another. Does this mean that Trade Union officials cannot use organisational email to send messages to its members? The other problem is the rate of innovation in e-communication. Each new development probably creates a new opportunity for misuse that had not been anticipated by the writers of codes (*see* the story of the Delhi schoolboy, p. 7).

Activity 8.2	Designing a code of conduct for e-mail and internet use at work

In what ways, if any, might a code of conduct designed to govern e-mail and internet use at work in:

- a research and consultancy company with a small staff of professional IT employees; and

- a large call centre dealing with service and other enquiries differ?

  If they do differ, why?

When codes of conduct collide

A fundamental problem within many types of organisation, but particularly those in the public and non-profit seeking sectors, is the issue of the codes of conduct of differing professional groupings and the potential conflicts that the respective codes can create. For example, the role of internal accounting information as a management information support system places the role of accountants within the managerial structures. This does not of itself set accountants and those professionals located within an organisation's managerial structures against those professionals who are outside those structures, but it creates the possibilities of conflict. One of the six principles upon which the International Federation of Accountants' Code of Ethics is based, and which is reflected in the codes of conduct of all the UK professional accountancy bodies, is that of confidentiality. The duty to protect the confidential nature of corporate information is underscored, even after a contract of employment is terminated.

A consideration of the codes of conduct or ethics within which other professionals must operate indicates the potential for conflict. For example, the United Kingdom Central Council for Nursing, Midwifery and Health Visiting (1996) states that 'each registered nurse, midwife and health visitor shall act, at all times, in such a manner as to safeguard and promote the interests of individual patients and clients'. In an environment that has seen health care subjected to considerable financial strictures over the past 20 years, a number of cases have highlighted the extremely difficult situations healthcare workers face in delivering effective and appropriate medical care 'that is in the interests of individual patients and clients'. The creation of managerial posts for medical staff such as nurses has only served to emphasise these tensions. Hunt (1995, 1998) recounted cases in healthcare and social services where individuals have tried to speak out about their concerns, but found their actions thwarted and future career progression blighted.

The very nature of the codes of conduct of nurses and accountants maps out the territory of potential conflict. While the nursing code requires patient advocacy, the accountants' code reflects an orientation of organisational loyalty. Indeed, in the cases of the codes of conduct developed by the American Institute of Internal Auditors and the (American) Government Finance Officers Association (Harris and Reynolds, 1993), explicit reference is made to loyalty to the employer. Even the HR managers interviewed in the Fisher and Lovell (2000) study displayed a greater organisational orientation than the stereotypical portrayal of HR managers might suggest.

The respective codes of conduct under which professional accountants and health-care workers must operate are both understandable and defensible when viewed separately. However, when placed within a single organisational context, the potential for conflict is evident.

Even within a code of conduct, tensions often exist. Proctor et al. (1993: 166) highlight the contradictory situation that confronts social workers:

> The preamble to the Code itself acknowledges that multiple principles could bear on any practice situation . . . thus, the potential for conflict is inherent in the profession's values and is reflected in its Code of Ethics.

At least the code of the social workers' professional body recognises these tensions. For accountants, the needs both to respect the confidentiality of corporate information and to respect the public interest are not usually formally recognised as posing any particular dilemma for accountants.

Interestingly, Article IV of the code of conduct of the Project Management Profession (1996: 2) contains the following clause:

Project management professionals shall protect the safety, health and welfare of the public and **speak out** against abuses in the areas affecting the public interest [emphasis added].

Some would argue that more than a pinch of salt needs to be on hand when considering the pronouncements of aspiring professional associations, but it is quite clear that this aspiring professional body expects its members to take public stands when appropriate. This is an unusually explicit statement from a trade association.

The above discussion has introduced an additional dimension, that of the ethics codes of professional associations. Much has been written on the rise of the professions (*see* Durkheim, 1992; Koehn, 1994; and Larson, 1977, for a discussion of these issues) and the roles of codes of ethics have been influential in this rise. Any trade association that gains the statutory right to control the membership of a particular aspect of human activity (e.g. the British Medical Association and doctoring; the Law Society and particular legal work; and certain professional accountancy bodies and auditing) will possess a code of ethics for its members to follow. The existence of a code of ethics will have been an essential element of the trade association's submission to control the membership of those who wish to practise as specific 'professionals', such as doctors, lawyers and auditors, etc. This is because the trade associations will need to assuage public concern that their state-granted monopolies will not be abused. The 'professional' bodies concerned will commit their members, above all else, to act 'in the public interest' whenever there is a clash of interest.

The 'public interest' is a very slippery concept. It refers to the interests of the public at large, not in a simplistic majority-type way, but rather in terms of what should be in the general interest of civic society if a rational, objective, long-term assessment of a situation is taken. Major scandals involving professional people cast very long shadows over the veracity and intentions of codes of conduct when employed by so-called professional bodies. Examples include the involvement of the international firm of accountants, Arthur Andersen, in the Enron affair. Shortly after Enron's collapse and the complicity of the auditing arm of Andersen's was revealed, this part of the company collapsed. Other examples are the failure of the accountancy profession to respond in any meaningful way to the travails of its senior members, or the way that doctors appear to have placed the interests of their profession and fellow colleagues' status above that of the public interest in cases such as the Bristol Heart Surgery Unit, or the body-parts shambles (*see* Case study 2.20, p. 87). Yet to stay within the membership of a 'profession', the individual member must attempt not to bring the profession into disrepute. As mentioned above, individual professional codes of ethics, while defensible when considered on their own, can present a conflict situation when juxtaposed in particular organisational contexts.

In the Fisher–Lovell (2000) study, few of the accountants and HR professionals had studied their respective professional bodies' code of ethics and little weight seemed to be placed on them. In some senses, the issue of the codes of ethics of professional associations has diminished in its relevance as an area of interest and study, as the mantle of professional bodies has slipped, and their claims to be acting in the public interest are seen as little more than façades behind which opaqueness is maintained and vested interests are concealed.

Given the arguments posed in this section against the use of codes, the question might be asked, 'So do codes have a future?' Judging by the increase in the number of organisational codes in evidence, codes certainly have a present. A survey conducted by Arthur Andersen and London Business School (1999) contrasted the prevalence of codes of conduct in 1996 and 1999. Whereas 59 per cent of companies surveyed in 1996 acknowledged the use of a code of conduct, the figure had grown to 78 per cent by 1999, and 81 per cent of companies surveyed in 1999 had values or mission statements. Thirteen years after the Andersen survey, it can be supposed that all large organisations will have a series of ethics codes and policies. The question is whether this recent upsurge in interest is anything more than a defensive reaction against potential legal claims, or, as in the case of public sector bodies, merely a necessary response to the outcome of the Nolan Committee reports. Does managerial attention to codes of conduct represent anything more than the latest management fad – after quality circles, business process re-engineering, the balanced scorecard, the learning organisation, etc.?

Cross reference	The Nolan principles, which were published in the First Nolan Committee Report on Standards in Public Life, can be read in Chapter 2, p. 72.

So far we have focused upon organisational responses to ethical issues by way of the development and employment of a range of different forms of codes of practice. We now move to a consideration of less overt, more subtle, but possibly more effective ways of shaping behaviour within organisations. This is the notion of corporate cultures, either singular or multiple. The development of a particular culture does not preclude the employment of a code of conduct; indeed the unwritten understandings that invariably comprise a particular culture often act as inviolate rules of conduct. All organisations will have 'ways of working', although those ways may be many and varied, with espoused behaviour sometimes deviating from actual behaviour.

Ethical culture and ethos

There are ethical issues about the propriety of using culture as a device for encouraging people to behave in one way rather than another. However, if we assume for the moment that it is acceptable for managers to foster a culture that encourages ethical behaviour, what would such a culture look like? Snell (1993, 2000) used the term moral ethos, rather than ethical culture, when he discussed this issue. He defined moral ethos as comprising a set of 'force-fields',

all of which impinge on members' understandings, judgements and decisions concerning good and bad, right and wrong.

(Snell, 2000: 267)

Snell argued that the moral ethos emerges from the interactions of such forces. For example, if the demand for loyalty is low, this may encourage openness within an organisation that supports criticism and acting with integrity. Contrarily, an organisation's demand for loyalty may inhibit the exercise of integrity. From an organisational perspective, loyalty is possibly the most important behaviour to cultivate among employees. Willmott (1998: 83) highlighted the contentious nature of codes of conduct and the implicit role of loyalty within them when he observed:

> the value ascribed to the adoption of codes is made conditional upon their contribution to business objectives. This implies that, in principle, the codes will be refined or discarded according to calculations about their continuing contribution to these objectives.

Integrity is less amenable to codes of conduct. For example, a code or rule to respect the confidentiality of corporate affairs in all circumstances might conflict with a broader social perspective of integrity.

Paralleling Kohlberg's stages of moral reasoning, Snell (1993: Chapter 6) identified six types of moral ethos that could arise within organisations. They are:

1. *Fear-ridden ethos.* Behaviour that is characterised by coercion, blind obedience and a myopic focus on organisational survival at any cost.

2. *Advantage-driven ethos.* Employees are rewarded for getting the best for the organisation even if this might involve deception, gamesmanship and exploitation of others if necessary. The ethos encourages private alliances, secrecy and personal advantage.

3. *Members-only ethos.* This ethos demands loyalty and a shared concern to present a good image to those outside the organisation. Clever upstarts are to be tamed and brought into the fold. Internally the focus on group membership can encourage paternalism, sexism and racism.

4. *Regulated ethos.* Regulation and accountability are typical of this ethos. Codes of conduct are written and employees are often expected to self-certify that they have obeyed the rules.

5. *Quality-seeking ethos.* This ethos seeks to encourage everyone to work to the highest ethical standards. Training and development encourages debate and argument about what those standards should be. The ethos can create a sense of arrogance and over-commitment.

6. *Soul-searching ethos.* The organisational ethos supports a spiritual learning community that emphasises integrity and an ongoing ethical dialogue.

Given that corporate cultures can be employed in manipulative ways, the issues of ethicality that pervade this area ultimately resolve themselves around

> the process of moral thought and self-scrutiny that precedes it. This understanding of ethics puts weight on the process of thought that precedes action, to qualify behaviour as ethical.

(Sinclair, 1993: 69)

Thus, the ethicality of a decision lies not in the behaviour displayed, or the decision taken, but in the forethought that preceded the behaviour or decision. This suggests that we need to think more critically about notions of culture. The 'forces' that Snell referred to can be seen at the visible level (e.g. the behaviour of individuals) or at more subtle, less visible levels (e.g. assumptions and beliefs that inform behaviour). Thus it is argued that culture operates at different levels, with important implications for business ethics.

Cross reference   Kohlberg's staged theory of moral development is discussed in detail in Chapter 5, p. 216, if you wish to confirm the parallels between his theory and Snell's stages of development of ethical ethos.

Levels of culture

Schein (1992) offered an analysis that reflects three levels of culture, each with a different level of visibility. The top or first level is the most visible level of culture. Within this category would be included evidence such as signs, symbols, written codes, forms of address (i.e. how seniors, peers and juniors are expected to be addressed), clothing (formal, informal), stories and myths (usually about past leaders), rituals, architecture and décor of the company's premises. These visible signs, practices and images are described as artefacts of culture. Schein argues that while these are the most visible evidence of culture, they are not always easy to decipher by the external observer. Forms of initiation and 'apprenticeship' are often required before the full significance of these artefacts is revealed.

The second level of culture is represented by the espoused values of a group. These are the beliefs that are articulated, that are audibly expressed. Sometimes these beliefs can be represented by a 'go-get-'em' philosophy, with staff encouraged to 'take the moment' or to 'go for it'. Whether these values are wholeheartedly believed is a matter of question, but if the stated values or beliefs tend to deliver the outcomes sought, then the credibility of the beliefs will grow and become accepted as 'the way things are done around here'. An interesting example of how language is used to create particular attitudes and cultures is reflected in the refusal of one leading security firm to allow its employees to use the term 'failure'. This reflects a refusal by the senior management to accept any level of underachievement by employees, or for the employees to see any demand as unattainable.

Schein referred to the third level as basic assumptions. These are the unspoken beliefs that exist within an organisation. They are the least visible, yet the most pervasive, form of culture because they represent deeply embedded ways of thinking about such questions as the nature of human nature, humanity's relationship with the environment, the nature of truth and of human activity. Basic assumptions are difficult to bring to the surface and challenge. Consequently they operate below the level of consciousness and can undermine the idea of moral agency, which requires conscious deliberation. If corporations are capable of subliminal influence on their employees' basic assumptions, then this would be a potent threat to moral agency. There is much debate (Smircich, 1983), however, about whether top managers do have this power or whether any attempts they make to guide cultures lead only to unanticipated changes. That corporations can shape employees' beliefs is not questioned; whether those influences can be controlled to the organisation's benefit is doubtful, at least in the short term.

How to develop the ethical ethos of organisations leads us to a consideration of ethical leadership.

Ethical leadership

In many large organisations, responsibility for ethical leadership is given to a new category of managers, which first emerged in the 1990s, called ethics & compliance (E&C) officers, although many other job titles are used for this role. They are often responsible for ethics education, ensuring compliance with codes and standards, advising top management and running corporate social responsibility programmes. As Adobor (2006) reported, the role is an ambiguous and contradictory one. He identified ten propositions about the skills and competencies that might make an E&C officer more effective. Some of these could be seen as undermining each other, such as the requirement to be morally developed but also to have good political influencing skills. Others could be tautological, such as the proposition that E&C officers are more effective in organisations with a good ethical climate, where presumably the demands upon them are smaller. One major problem is that an E&C officer may at times be required to challenge their top managers; an activity that would require them to be tolerated by their superiors in much the same way as fools and jesters would be allowed to challenge their sovereigns in medieval courts. This brings us to a consideration of the ethical leadership role of top managers.

The direction and example presented by senior management in terms of what is considered to be acceptable practice within an organisation must inform and shape the behaviour of others. Most textbooks argue that it is a leader's role to define the vision and core values of an organisation. The UK government, through an agency called the CSR Academy, has published a set of CSR competencies. These can be seen as a tool for establishing a set of behaviours and core values within organisations that would support the development of a CSR culture within an organisation. In Schein's terms, they would be cultural artefacts. The competencies are intended to make CSR an integral part of business practice not only in large companies but also in small ones. The competencies (CSR Academy, 2004):

- focus on the personal qualities, attitudes and mindsets that managers need to learn and which will in turn drive improvements in business performance;
- should become embedded into the education, training and development of managers and staff; and
- are a tool for assessing performance in all business functions.

The competencies are:

1. Understanding society and business's roles and obligations within it.
2. Building capacity within an organisation to work effectively in a responsible manner.

3. Questioning business as usual.

4. Stakeholder relations.

5. Strategic view and ensuring that social and environmental concerns are considered in broad decision making.

6. Harnessing diversity.

Alongside these competencies are a set of benchmark indicators that can be used to assess whether people in the company:

- are aware of CSR;

- understand the issues around CSR;

- apply the competencies at work;

- integrate the competencies into the culture of the company; and

- provide leadership on CSR across the organisation.

Competencies have normally been defined as an ability to do something. Distinctively, these CSR competencies are about understanding at the lower levels of attainment and only about action at the higher levels. As a cultural artefact, the extent to which the competencies will affect the levels of values and basic assumptions in organisations is limited. They are probably best seen as a way of raising the priority given to CSR in businesses, especially smaller ones, and of creating a market for training courses in CSR.

Kanungo and Mendonca (1996) pointed out that employees will not believe leaders who lack ethical integrity and the leaders' values will not be accepted. They suggested that ethical leadership has to be altruistic, putting the well-being of others in the organisation before self-interest. However, they noted that western culture was better known for its emphasis on egoism than on altruism. The HR management function has been identified (Connock and Johns, 1995: 159) as the natural repository of organisations' consciences, although a survey found that, in those companies that allocated business ethics to a particular department, responsibility was given to a range of departments (Arthur Andersen and London Business School, 1999: 19).

To suggest that where there is a virtuous set of senior managers all employees will automatically follow their examples of desired practice would be naïve. However, negative examples of immoral behaviour by senior executives can act like a cancer on ethical behaviour throughout an organisation, as the example provided in Case study 6.6 (*see* p. 240) illustrated. The organisation in question appeared to harbour unpalatable practices and beliefs at a senior level, which created moral indifference within the headquarters.

A significant problem for any organisation that publicises its commitment to high ethical standards in all its business dealings is that any one single departure from such standards is likely to attract considerable media attention and cast doubt upon the full range of the organisation's activities. If this does happen, the reaction could be both unreasonably harsh (depending of course upon the nature and scale of the alleged infraction), and also a somewhat disingenuous approach to the analysis and reporting of the incident. Even if the infraction in question is finally judged to be an intentional and knowingly unethical act on the part of the individual employee concerned (however senior), the individual transgression might be just that, an individual's error of judgment. It might not be a revelation of institutionally entrenched unethical practices. In such a situation, the more telling test of organisational commitment to a broadly accepted notion of corporate ethical behaviour would be how the organisation's senior management respond to the transgression and the steps it takes to remedy the problem. In short, no one is perfect, but when errors are made, or misjudgments are revealed, how do we as individuals and corporations react and respond? The openness of individuals and organisations to acknowledge an error or problem, and the learning that ensues from the incident in question, are more likely to reflect the depth of commitment to ethical practice than are pious claims to high ethical standards made in mission statements or corporate reports. It is at times of tension or challenge that ethical credentials are more likely to be revealed. Organisational learning is a much vaunted but also a most demanding and challenging notion. The processual model of managing is commensurate with such an approach, and Bucholz and Rosenthal (1998) adopt it to explain their view of moral development within organisations.

> The adjustment between the self and the other is neither assimilation of perspectives, one to the other, nor the fusion of perspectives into an indistinguishable oneness, but can best be understood as an 'accommodating participation' in which each creatively affects and is affected by the other through accepted means of adjudication . . . because of these dynamics, the leader does not 'stand apart' from a following group, nor is the leader an organizer of group ideas, but rather leadership is by its very nature in dynamic interaction with the group, and both are in a process of ongoing transformation because of this interaction.
>
> (Bucholz and Rosenthal, 1998: 418–19)

Such a processual and 'accommodating participatory' approach would represent a fundamental change of perspective for the type of managers represented in the studies reported by Bird and Waters (1989) and Lovell (2002). The processual perspective offers, on the one hand, the prospects for moral chaos, but, on the other, possibly the best hope for moral agency. The former because the type of leadership implied in the processual model requires a degree of maturity and humility, but also a strength of belief and conviction that might be beyond many managers and leaders. However, if some form of accommodation is achievable in ways that eschew indoctrination, the debates that would be evident might do much to address many of the concerns raised throughout this book.

An important caveat with respect to greater openness and transparency in corporate dealings is the issue of litigation. The greater demands made of public corporations in terms of their various impacts are in many respects a sign of a maturing society. However, there has been an attendant increase in the propensity of members of the public to take legal action against corporations when infractions occur. In such a context, it should not be surprising that corporations become very wary of revealing their 'failings' in public for fear of how such information might be employed. These complex issues can only be moved forward by debate and a developing sense of balance between:

- on the one hand, reparation for any 'injuries' experienced as a result of sub-standard performance by an individual or organisation, where culpability is evident; and

- on the other, a recognition that 'things' will and do go less than satisfactorily on occasions and that if the 'failing' was innocent, and all reasonable measures had been taken to avoid its occurrence in the first place, then retribution should be avoided, to encourage and foster learning from the experience.

These words are easy to say and write, but much more difficult to put into practice. Yet this is the challenge facing organisations. No easy compromise or solution is on offer, only the prospect of continued action and attention to the levels of behaviour deemed acceptable within our societies.

Reflections

Thomas Hobbes, a seventeenth-century philosopher, took a pessimistic view of humanity. From the Hobbesian view of human behaviour, that people will not behave morally without the fear of retribution, flows the necessity for rules, of which codes of conduct are an obvious example. Bauman saw rules and codes, based upon reason, as leading to a morality associated with law – the laws of business and bureaucracy. This adherence to procedural rationality requires that

> all other emotions must be toned down or chased out of court . . . the most prominent of the exiled emotions are moral sentiments; that resilient and unruly 'voice of conscience'.

> (Bauman, 1994: 8)

Interestingly, Bauman argued that when the term ethics appears in the vocabulary of bureaucracy, it is invariably in connection with 'professional ethics'. The latter term is considered to be breached when a member shows disloyalty either to the organisation or to (organisational) colleagues. A qualified notion of honesty thus becomes of critical importance, that is, the keeping of promises and contractual obligations. This leads to predictability and consistency in organisations, an extremely important managerial need. When this is coupled with the notion of 'floating responsibility', an escape route is provided for those seeking a quiet life in the face of an awkward organisational issue.

People's instrumentalism is seen as something to be encouraged by Clutterbuck (1992: 100–1) as he exhorted organisations to reward exemplary behaviour, possibly with cash payments, and to 'punish breaches of the code publicly; use the key motivators of influence, promotion and access to resources'. This simplistic view of human nature and notions of managing assumes that instrumentalism is the only determinant, or at least the dominant explanation, of human behaviour. From a purely instrumental perspective, it is also an expensive option. In the governing of human relationships, trust is a far less expensive option than contractualism or financial incentives. But the problem remains of whether trust can be relied upon. When associated with notions of loyalty, it becomes increasingly problematic. For example, in a situation where it has become known to you that a product of your employing organisation poses health risks to consumers, which is paramount, your loyalty to:

- your work colleagues;

- your employing organisation;

- your family (who depend on your income);

- the consumer; or

- the general public?

The converse of the loyalty question is which of these groups has the right to trust you and your actions in such a situation.

Maybe the least that can be said for codes of ethics is that they give the principled employee a reference point should times become ethically challenged and certain organisational practices give rise to serious cause for concern. At its best, a code can reflect an honestly expressed expectation about moral conduct within an organisation, with the code probably written in terms of principles rather than in a prescriptive or proscriptive fashion. Employees would be encouraged to act with moral agency and the codes would be supported by mechanisms that would allow concerned employees to raise concerns in a neutral and anonymous forum, preferably using external counsellors.

Within the complex arenas that are modern business corporations, codes of conduct, codes of ethics and the prevailing culture/s will be important reference points for many of the players involved with, or affected by, the activities of the corporation. At different times, the eight roles of codes discussed in this chapter will be seen in operation. Yet if ethics is at the heart of an organisation's practices and its *raison d'être*, embedded within its culture/s, written codes become less important. They become less defensive in terms of their tenor, being essentially codes of ethics.

Summary

In this chapter, the following key points have been made:

- While not universally or uniformly recognised, distinctions between codes of conduct and codes of ethics help crystallise the intended purpose of a code.

- Codes of practice can be important mechanisms that allow business corporations to negotiate their position in a society.

- Codes of practice have multiple roles within organisations, which will not necessarily be mutually exclusive.

- The development of a code of practice is, at one and the same time, an understandable development by a corporation, but also a reflection of a lack of trust in the integrity and reliability of its employees.

- There are arguments against developing codes of practice that require ethical practice to be at the heart of an organisation's activities and 'ways of working'.

- Organisational cultures and leadership are critical to understanding an organisation's actual (as distinct from espoused) values.

Typical assignments

1. Why have codes of ethics become so commonplace in corporations and how useful are they?

2. Draft a code of conduct to cover e-communications (e-mail, web use and so on). Explain and justify your proposed code.

3. What are the drawbacks and problems associated with codes of ethics?

4. Discuss the role of leadership and organisational culture in developing a socially responsible company.

Group activity 8.1

Search the World Wide Web to find a code of ethics that you can download. The easiest way might be to think of a company you have heard of and track down its code. Analyse it by answering the following questions.

- Is it a code of ethics, a code of conduct or both?

- Does it look like a standard code, the same as everyone else's, or does it look as if it has been tailored to that organisation?

- Is it a code that recognises that some things within it are likely to be aspirations?

- Is it clear and unambiguous or does it leave lots of 'wriggle room'? If it does, is such a 'fudge factor' necessary?

- Does it look like a PR document or one that will be helpful to employees?

- If you were an employee of the organisation what would you think the code implied about the organisation's view of its staff?

Recommended further reading

A useful text is R.A. Buchholz and S.B. Rosenthal (1998) *Business Ethics: The Pragmatic Path Beyond Principles to Process*, London: Prentice Hall. Deborah Smith's pamphlet, *Demonstrating Corporate Values – Which Standard for Your Company?*, published by the Institute of Business Ethics in 2002 is an excellent comparative guide to the various codes and standards of ethical business available to organisations. The following articles will be of interest to those who wish to study the topic further: C. Cassell, P. Johnson and K. Smith (1997) 'Opening the black box: Corporate codes of ethics in their organisational context', *Journal of Business Ethics*, 16, 1077–93; G. McDonald and A. Nijhof (1999) 'Beyond codes of ethics: An integrated framework for stimulating morally responsible behaviour in organisations', *Leadership & Organisation Development Journal*, 20(3), 133–46; R.C. Warren (1993) 'Codes of ethics: Bricks without straw', *Business Ethics: A European Review*, 2(4), 185–91. See also S. Srivastva and D.L. Cooperrider (1988) *Executive Integrity: The Search for High Human Values in Organisational Life*, San Francisco: Jossey-Bass Inc., pp. 1–28.

Useful websites

Topic	Website provider	URL
The CSR Competency framework	Business in the Community (BITC)	http://www.bitc.org.uk/cr_academy/cr_practitioner_competency_map/
This is a good place to find copies of professional, governmental and organisational codes of ethics. Particularly fun is the code of ethics for witches (the Covenant of the Goddess). Most of the codes on this site are utterly serious	Centre for the Study of Ethics in Professions, University of Illinois	http://ethics.iit.edu/research/codes-ethics-collection
This link takes you to the quick test but TI's whole ethics website is an interesting corporate ethics website	Texas Instruments	http://www.ti.com/corp/docs/company/citizen/ethics/benchmark.shtml
A useful website on a wide range of business ethics issues.	Business for Social Responsibility	https://www.bsr.org/en/tag/governance-accountability
Home page of the professional association for Ethics & Compliance officers	ECOA	http://www.theecoa.org/imis15/ECOAPublic/
Shell's corporate principles, but you can Google most large organisations for their statements of values and principles	Shell	http://www.shell.com/home/content/aboutshell/who_we_are/our_values/sgbp/

CHAPTER 9

Corporate social responsibility

Chapter at a glance

Chapter contents

- Learning outcomes
- Introduction
- The early calls for social responsibility (SR)
- The emergence of corporate social responsibility (CSR)
- Corporate citizenship, political donations and lobbying
- Corporate social responsibility: shareholder and stakeholder approaches
- Contemporary issues in CSR
- The future of CSR
- Summary
- Typical assignments

Case studies

- Case study 9.1 The tobacco industry
- Case study 9.2 When can genetically modified crops be grown?
- Case study 9.3 Markets, prices and need
- Case study 9.4 An economically successful corporation with a view of its social position
- Case study 9.5 The U'wa and Oil Exploration

Activities and exercises

- Activity 9.1 Voting habits
- Activity 9.2 An important question
- Activity 9.3 Questions for further critique
- Activity 9.4 Challenging Friedman
- Activity 9.5 Stakeholder and shareholder approaches to host communities
- Activity 9.6 CSR Reporting
- Typical assignments
- Recommended further reading
- Useful websites

Having read this chapter and completed its associated activities, readers should be able to:

- Discuss the development of corporate social responsibility (CSR) and, in more recent times, the business world's allegiance to the notion of corporate responsibility.

- Critically evaluate the counter-arguments to CSR.

- Critically assess the appropriateness of following a shareholder or a stakeholder approach to the management of organisations.

- Discuss the challenges and opportunities that notions such as fair trade; greenwashing; ethical consumerism; and diversity and equality bring to CSR.

- Critically assess the emergence of CSR reporting.

Introduction

This chapter explores some of the basic elements of a *genre* of approaches aimed at describing and addressing the relationship between business organisations, society and the environment, under the banner of corporate social responsibility (CSR). The interest in this relationship is not new: it long precedes the creation of the modern corporation, as exemplified by the Quaker boycott of slave-grown sugar and rum in the UK in the 1700s; the publication of Eduard Dekker's novel *Max Havelaar* on the coffee trade in 1860, and countless campaigns and political reforms to improve working conditions and human rights in the eighteenth and nineteenth centuries. However, various factors have contributed to the analysis from different perspectives of this dynamic relationship. These include the emergence of the corporation (with its separation of management control from ownership), the development of the social sciences and their application to business, the widespread popularity of management education, and the development of new legal frameworks, together with the increase in awareness of the impact of corporations on society and on the environment.

In this context, CSR does not constitute a body of knowledge defined *a priori*; it is, rather, a complex grouping of ideas and practices aimed at expressing the changing interests and the concerns felt by individuals and groups within and outside corporations. These are reflected, for example, in the recent preoccupations with waste, pollution, recycling and the environment. In this context, Benn and Bolton (2011) reviewed 50 different and interconnected concepts that could be directly related to CSR. Some examples are: corporate responsibility (CR); stakeholder responsibility; corporate citizenship; sustainable development; fair trade; ethical consumerism; green marketing; intra-/inter-generational equity and socially responsible investment. These concepts are used interchangeably by different stakeholders, including political parties and the media, to praise organisations or to condemn their actions. Alongside its theoretical formulations, CSR is also very difficult to assess in practice. For example, many CSR experts were praising Enron and BP as examples of best practice on social and environmental responsibility not long ago, as they were savings and investment banks, and mortgage lenders. Some even dismiss CSR completely as a management fad, or a new, cynical way to make money from people's genuine concerns and from environmental issues. The reality, as Clark (2007) pointed out, is that the amounts wasted on the losses due to financial fraud and the increases in executive compensation in corporations in the recent period far exceed any resources companies have devoted to CSR, not to mention the sums invested in advertising corporate commitment to CSR.

The early calls for social responsibility (SR)

Long before the modern corporation was developed, or talked about in its current form, serious concerns were expressed regarding the welfare of workers to make them more productive, to compensate for labour shortages during wars, for social or religious reasons, or for a combination of these and other factors. Examples include the welfare of women and children working in factories in the UK and the USA; the fitness of the men who worked in factories and who could be asked to serve in the armed forces, and the appalling housing conditions endured by workers and their families. The corresponding initiatives, which contained a mixture of humanitarianism, paternalism, philanthropy, business interests and religious fervour, ranged through the building of hospitals, bathhouses, lunch-rooms and entire factory villages with schools and churches. They also adopted political campaigning and even boycotts, such as against the use of very small children to clean chimneys, the banning of alcohol near factories and in factory towns and, finally, important reflections on the use of money and 'ethical investment', as promoted by the Methodists (Kurtz, 2009).

It was also very common for wealthy industrialists to make donations and endowments to community, arts and educational projects. In this sense, there is a long list of individuals and their organisations (including Rockefeller and Carnegie in the USA, and the Cadburys, Hanburys and Rowntrees in the UK), which actively engaged in some kind of SR, even though some of them were also criticised for other business practices. In this sense, the distinction between business interests and personal, religious and social concerns is sometimes very difficult to establish.

The emergence of corporate social responsibility (CSR)

The desire to encourage – nay, require – corporations to assume greater responsibility for their actions can be traced back over many decades, following the development of large corporations and the separation of corporate control from ownership. It also reflects growing concerns regarding the power and influence of corporations over people's lives and even the independence and integrity of governments. In this sense, academic debates over corporate social responsibilities were already taking place in the first half of the twentieth century, including Clark

(1916); Berle (1932, 1965); Berle and Means (1932); Dodd (1932); and Bowen's highly influential book, *Social Responsibility of the Businessman*, published in 1953.

Despite the very large number of publications that seem to address the concept of CSR, its definition remains elusive. Attempts to revise and classify different approaches have been provided by many authors including Heal (1970); Klonoski (1991); Carroll (1999); and Windsor (2006). Definitions range from Elkington's (2006) 'Triple Bottom Line' (TBL) concept, which 'expresses the fact' that companies and other organisations simultaneously create or destroy economic, social and environmental value; *The Economist* (2005) highlights the integration of stakeholders' social, environmental and other concerns into the company's business operations; *SustainAbility* (2005) defines CSR as a business approach with open and transparent business practices, ethical behaviour, respect for stakeholders and a commitment to add economic, social and environmental value; the UK's Department for Business Innovation and Skills (BIS) stated in 2009 that:

> The Government sees [corporate responsibility] CR as the business contribution to our sustainable development goals. Essentially it is about how business takes account of its economic, social and environmental impacts in the way it operates – maximising the benefits and minimising the downsides. Specifically, we see CR as the voluntary actions that business can take, over and above compliance with minimum legal requirements, to address both its own competitive interests and the interests of wider society.

Finally, the UN stated, in its *Sustainable Development Innovation Briefs* (2007), that:

> At its broadest, CSR can be defined as the overall contribution of business to sustainable development... Defining corporate social responsibility in more detail than this remains a vexed issue. In practice views differ based on two factors. First, the extent to which importance is placed on the centrality of the 'financial business case' for responsible business behaviour in defining the scope of CSR practices – i.e. the extent to which tangible benefits to companies must be demonstrable. Secondly, the extent to which government is seen to have a role in framing the agenda – and how.

(2007: 1)

Followed by a definition of a minimum, median and maximum standards for CSR:

> A *minimum* standard for CSR might be that businesses fulfil their legal obligations or, if laws or enforcement are lacking, that they 'do no harm'. A *median* approach goes beyond compliance, calling for businesses to do their best, where a 'business case' can be made, to contribute positively to sustainable development by addressing their social and environmental impacts, and potentially also through social or community investments. A *maximum* standard points toward the active alignment of internal business goals with externally set societal goals (those that support sustainable development).

(2007: 1, emphasis added)

In this context, the key drivers of CSR theory and practice can be identified as top managers; investors; consumer and shareholder activism; academics and management consultants; governments; and civil society. In this chapter we have chosen to explore the concepts of corporate citizenship; shareholder value; and stakeholder approaches, followed by certain initiatives and consumer reactions such as fair trade, green-washing, and ethical consumerism and boycotts. Finally, we will consider CSR reporting, and the relationship between CSR and diversity and equality. The next chapter will focus on sustainability. Corporate governance has been discussed in Chapter 7.

Corporate citizenship, political donations and lobbying

Corporate citizenship

The development of the argument from one of requiring corporations to act in socially responsible ways to more recent calls for corporations to be seen as corporate citizens, reflects a desire to lock corporations, both formally and possibly legally, into the responsibilities that this status would confer. With corporations playing an increasingly influential role over very many aspects of social and political life, the demand for greater accountability and responsibility on the part of corporations is unlikely to diminish.

> **DEFINITION**
>
> The term **citizen** normally relates to the relationship between an individual and the political state in which the individual lives.
> It carries with it notions of rights and responsibilities on the part of the individual and the state. However, this reciprocity (i.e. two-way relationship) is unlikely to be an equal one. Within democratic theories of the state, citizens have ultimate sovereignty over the state, or at least sovereignty over those who represent the citizenry within government. Practice, however, usually reflects a quite different balance of power.

Being described as a 'citizen' does not of itself imply much about morality. It is a noun in need of an adjective, such as 'good' or 'moral', before it can confer a positive societal influence. Wood and Logsdon (2001) referred to this issue when they observed, in the context of the corporate citizen debate,

> One important debate distinguishes the concept of citizenship-as-legal-status from the concept of citizen-as-desirable-activity. The minimum requirements to be called a citizen are very different from the requirement to be called a 'good citizen.'
>
> (Logsdon, 2001: 88)

The role of the citizen can vary from the active notion of citizenship evident in ancient Greece (for those conferred as free men) to a passive acceptance of governance from a sovereign body or from the bureaucratic state. Within the corporate citizen debate, the demands made of corporations vary from a minimalist and societally neutral influence to a proactive role. The societally neutral arguments do not, however, reflect a status quo, or even a single understanding of what might be meant by societally neutral. For example, would being societally neutral mean that:

Negative and positive effects of corporate activities could be balanced out (possibly involving an international perspective), or would a corporation's impacts need to harm no one or nothing at any time?

There is a general acceptance that corporations do have social responsibilities?

Acting within legal constraints would be acceptable, even if the law were judged by many to be inadequate (as a result of the political lobbying by corporations)?

These debates are still developing and represent just some of the issues that make the general area of business and values both dynamic and vital.

Hobbes, a seventeenth-century philosopher mentioned in Chapter 3, held a pessimistic view of human nature, seeing people as essentially selfish and untrustworthy (*see* Pojman, 1998). Thus, Hobbes deemed that a sovereign power to which the people would owe allegiance was necessary. The relationship between the sovereign power and the citizen is, in a Hobbesian world, one of subjugation. Thus, being a citizen within a Hobbesian state is a quite different circumstance from that which would be acceptable in the twenty-first century. If the notion of conferring citizenship status upon corporations is one that concerns people, with their misgivings whether corporations do act in socially beneficial ways, then a Hobbesian notion of citizenship has some appeal. Much, though, depends upon the constitution and constituent parts of the sovereign power.

As societies have developed and the scope of governments has increased, the lack of possibilities for the active participation of citizens has come to be viewed as a weakness of modern conceptions of democratic states. In contemporary societies political citizenship is increasingly limited to periodic elections of political representatives, and even the relevance of these is being questioned. For example, according to Henn and Foard (2011), at the UK General Election in 2010 only 44 per cent of 18- to 21-year-olds participated. Furthermore, fewer than one in five young people (17 per cent) have a positive view of political parties and MPs, while over two-thirds (85 per cent) see governments as dishonest and untrustworthy; more than half (57 per cent) said that, although elections allowed voters to express their opinions, they do not achieve meaningful change. In the UK, local elections and those for the European Union achieve even lower levels of elector participation: approximately two out of three eligible people do not vote. These findings, and similar low numbers of voters in the elections that took place in 2001 and in 2005, reinforce the concern of policy makers and political parties regarding the lack of engagement of the people in the formal political process. However, Henn and Foard (2011) also found that most young people in the UK have a marked interest in politics, and would consider voting in future elections. In this context, some interesting questions to explore could include the extent to which individuals are choosing to engage in political, social and environmental issues through large companies and their products, and supporting NGOs (i.e. either as consumers and/or activists), rather than campaigning for political parties or going to the polls. Thus, when we, or others, use the term 'citizen', we need to be clear about the form of citizenship under discussion.

Activity 9.1	Voting habits

The next time you are in a group – in a seminar room, pub or other social gathering – try to establish how many people voted at the last general election, and if you think the conversation will stand the enquiry, how many people voted at the last local election when it was held independently of a general election. Do you think the percentages you establish sit comfortably in a democratic state?

One of the most widely expressed concerns about modern corporations is that they have relatively unfettered authority, with only limited responsibilities (basically to keep within the laws of the land), yet there is a need to be more specific about the form and level of participation in the operations of the state that are being suggested when the phrase 'corporate citizenship' is employed. Given the significance of business organisations within democratic (as well as undemocratic) states, the presumption must be that the notion of corporate citizenship assumed by its advocates would reflect the acceptance of certain societal responsibilities, although whether there is envisaged to be an equal bestowing of citizens' rights on corporations is far from clear.

Before progressing any further, it is worth reflecting upon the observations of Charles Lindblom, a former Professor of Economics and Political Science at Yale University. In his book *Politics and Markets* (1977), Lindblom concluded his analysis of the relationships between large corporations and political systems (and the book itself) with the following paragraph:

> It has been a curious feature of democratic thought that it has not faced up to the private corporation in an ostensible democracy. Enormously large, rich in resources . . . they can insist that government meet their demands, even if these demands run counter to . . . citizens . . . Moreover they do not disqualify themselves from playing the role of citizen . . . they exercise unusual veto powers . . . The large private corporation fits oddly into democratic theory and vision. Indeed it does not fit.
>
> (Lindblom, 1977: 356)

The final five-word sentence is the last in the book and is particularly piercing. Lindblom was bringing into sharp focus the lack of compatibility between democratic aspirations for political systems and the autocratic, sometimes feudal, systems that operate in many, if not the majority of, corporations, and it is the latter in which most people spend most of their waking lives. Large corporations have influence in and upon even the most significant of political powers, also through political donations and lobbying.

Political donations

In June 1971, President Richard Nixon was recorded as saying to his Chief of Staff regarding political donations:

> My point is that anybody who wants to be an ambassador must at least give $250,000 . . . from now on, the contributors have got to be, I mean, a big thing, and I'm not gonna do it for political friends and all that crap.

More recently, concerns regarding Barack Obama's presidential campaign accepting untraceable donations in the form of prepaid credit cards were also expressed by *The Washington Post* in 2008. Additionally, contributions from BP-related individuals and groups to US politicians were under the spotlight after the Gulf of Mexico oil spill (Thomson Reuters News, 05/05/2010).

In the UK the relationship between political donations and government decisions has also long been under public scrutiny: from the days of the Liberal-Conservative coalition in the 1930s when Arthur Maundy Gregory became the only person jailed for selling peerages, to the government of Margaret Thatcher in the 1980s and her fundraiser Alistair McAlpine, later Lord McAlpine. More recent cases include the donation by the disgraced entrepreneur Michael Brown to the Liberal Democrats in 2005, and the 'loans-for-honours' scandal that involved the Labour party under Tony Blair – although other parties engaged in similar practices.

Following the 'loans-for-honours' scandal in 2006–7, the rules on political donations in the UK are now closely regulated by The Political Parties and Elections Act 2009 (PPEA). Political parties must declare to the electoral commission all permissible donations of above £7,500 from individuals, trade unions or British-based companies every three months. The list is then published for the public to scrutinise. Currently, consensus is being sought by the independent Committee on Standards in Public Life, following an inquiry chaired by Christopher Kelly, on further reform of party funding and political donations.

Political lobbying

The multinational influence of large corporations also became apparent after the collapse of Enron, when it was established that it had generously given money to the election campaigns of several US politicians and to both the Conservative and the Labour parties in the UK (before new rules were introduced in 2001). In return, Enron executives were able to meet UK ministers, civil servants and MPs and to lobby for the overturning of the UK government's block on building new gas-fuelled power stations. This and similar events highlight the relationship between donations to political parties for electoral campaigns, and the lobbying of serving ministers and civil servants.

Furthermore, the current UK Conservative-Liberal Democrat government coalition has been heavily criticised for the privileged access to government information, and the perceived influence on government policy, enjoyed by lobbying companies and individuals representing large businesses. Examples include the former UK Defence Secretary Liam Fox (BBC News, 18/10/2011) and the Bell Pottinger 'access to Downing Street', scandals in 2011 (BBC News, 06/12/2011).

The above examples are not cited in support of a claim that all businesses are corrupt or corrupting. However, just as a few examples of negative or unethical business practices should not tar all businesses with these behaviours, nor should a few examples of positive business behaviour suggest that all is right in the corporate and political worlds. For our purposes the point illustrated by these cases is the way in which the business lobby groups have successfully influenced legislative matters. It is important to highlight that lobbying is not only legitimate, given how individuals and organisations want to influence decisions that may affect their interests, their social and political lives, and their environment; it is also necessary, as a government needs access to the knowledge and the opinions of different stakeholders (including companies) to enrich its policy-making process. However, the term 'lobbying' has become synonymous with buying influence over the government – and with, at the very least the potential for, corruption.

The UK House of Commons asked the Public Administration Select Committee to conduct a parliamentary inquiry into lobbying in 2008. The results were published in the *Lobbying: Access and Influence in Whitehall* report in January 2009. In the report's summary, the Committee stated that although lobbying should be – and often is – a force for good, there were at the time three specific areas of public concern: the perceived existence of an 'inside track' that gives privileged access and disproportionate influence to commercial organisations; the transfer of staff in both directions between Government and (predominantly) business, a practice known as the 'revolving door'; and the activities of the 'lobbyist for hire' industry made famous by the former trade and transport secretary Stephen Byers, who in 2010 described himself as 'a cab for hire'.

After their inquiry, the Committee concluded that 'in this country, public affairs consultancies and in-house lobbyists are subject to virtually no regulation and, as we have found, very little self-regulation of any substance'. The Committee also warned against new regulations and controls for professional lobbyists that could make it more difficult for individuals and small organisations to contact ministers, MPs and civil servants 'stifling input into the policy-making process'. In this context, the report proposed a Register of Lobbying Activity provided in statute, independently managed and enforced, to include information provided by both lobbyists and those being lobbied. Such a register has not yet been implemented.

In other countries, too, lobbying has been scrutinised. In Canada, the Commissioner of Lobbying was been created to enforce lobbying legislation following the Lobbying Act 2008. Canada's approach is coming closer to the heavily state-regulated USA, where the Lobbying Disclosures Act 1995 was developed following certain lobbying scandals. In Australia, there was no lobbying regulation until 2008, and discussions are taking place on whether recent legislation (Lobbying Code of Conduct) has been successful. The German Bundestag is the only European house of parliament with specific regulation of lobbying, while the EU Parliament has attempted to regulate lobbying in a piecemeal fashion with calls for a common register for all lobbyists and a monitoring body.

Corporate social responsibility

As corporate citizens corporations have the right to engage in political debate and to enjoy freedom of speech but their wealth and power can give them disproportionate influence when compared with individual citizens. A 2010 Supreme Court judgement in the USA allowed corporations to exercise their right to freedom of speech by paying for political advertising as long as they did not pay the money directly to candidates or political parties. Such privilege might be thought to imply correspondingly weighty responsibilities towards the societies of which they claim citizenship. These responsibilities will be discussed next.

Activity 9.2	An important question

Is it fair, sensible and/or ethical to ask, let alone expect, business organisations (or company executives) to take on the role of correcting the world's ills? How can organisations, established to fulfil a highly specific economic role, adopt the responsibility for enacting or at least contributing to roles that might be expected to be the responsibility of political parties and governments?

Activity 9.2 raises fundamental questions for organisations, their owners (shareholders) and their top management. To explore both the implications of these questions and how one might respond to them, let us examine the shareholder approach championed by, among others, Milton Friedman.

Milton Friedman's shareholder approach

Milton Friedman (1912–2006) was a Nobel prize-winning economist associated with the Chicago School of Economics. His ideas became strongly influential in the US and the UK from the 1960s, especially after the publication of his book *Capitalism and Freedom* (1962). His approach to the role of business in society must be read in the context of the Cold War and the political struggle between capitalism and communism – he was a powerful economic adviser to the then US president Ronald Reagan. Finally, he also influenced the thinking of some of the economic advisers of Prime Minister Margaret Thatcher in the UK.

Friedman is also widely known for an article he wrote for *The New York Times Magazine* in 1970 titled 'The social responsibility of business is to increase its profits'. In this article, he tried to address the growing calls for business to become more socially responsible, reflecting on the role of the corporate executive as 'an employee of the owner of the business'. In Friedman's view corporate executives are hired to follow the desire of the shareholders to maximise their profits, legally and according to ethical custom. He did not oppose the giving by company executives, or any other employee, of their own money and time to charity or philanthropy, while acknowledging the importance in society of organisations created for a charitable or philanthropic purpose. However, he strongly questions any discretional use by company executives of other people's money (here, the shareholders') for purposes other than that of maximising profits.

In this context, Friedman is not opposed to the use of company funds in charity/philanthropy if the purpose were, for example, to increase the company's profile and therefore its share value. Indeed, many companies are engaged in charity and philanthropy as a marketing (or as a public relations) strategy, based on a commercial cost/benefit analysis, that is to say, as a 'commercial investment'. Porter and Kramer (2002) make a similar point yet refer to such acts as 'strategic philanthropy'. Windsor (2001) reinforced the philanthropy argument with the demand that all business activities, including 'good deeds', should 'add-value', or more precisely 'add-shareholder-value'. This is most emphatically a Friedmanite position.

Activity 9.3	Questions for further critique

Can we consider the instrumental association with charity or philanthropy ethical? What is wrong with this approach if the donations benefit people in need, or the environment? Isn't this a classical win-win situation? How much discretion should a company executive have when allocating funds to non-core activities? Conversely, are these strategies not part of what is often called 'green-washing'?

Friedman also challenges the notion that companies could divert their funds to causes that should be supported by the State through the taxation of the whole population; otherwise, any such donation would be made only at the expense of lower dividends, higher prices or lower wages (or a combination of all three). Friedman asked, 'How can it be ethical that a corporation should act first as unpaid tax collector (i.e. levying a tax on the shareholders, customers and/or employees) and then as unaccountable benefactor?' It is either for publicly elected representatives of the people (i.e. national or local politicians) to provide financial support to public services or charities from public funds, or for individuals to decide to which charities they wish to make private donations.

This second point is very interesting, as we can reasonably wonder whether these sometimes very large charitable company donations (and international aid) actually mask:

- weak government planning in the cases of disasters or infrastructure projects, such as in the Katrina disaster in the USA;

- the embezzlement of taxes and international aid by government officials in certain 'failed states'; and

- the creation of a 'dependency culture', which relieves governments from responsibility to deal with problems because they know that private organisations or rich countries will eventually 'come to the rescue' after a well-publicised appeal.

Do we expect organisations to have the knowledge and expertise to decide how best to help? Should companies have a say in how governments spend their taxes or allot the funds they donate to foreign aid?

Finally, Friedman also states that organisations cannot have ethical responsibilities, as they are mere social and legal constructs. They have no separate moral existence. In Freidman's view only individuals have responsibilities. Following this line of argument, it could even be argued that through awarding organisations a separate existence, corporate executives become anonymous and less accountable, adopting less responsibility for the consequences of their actions, since corporations as 'new accountable citizens' could take the blame.

Activity 9.4	Challenging Friedman

Taking the criticisms raised by Friedman, try to develop arguments that challenge his claims. It is important that you think through the arguments Friedman is making, so take your time.

Responding to Friedman's arguments

Friedman's ideas were very persuasive. He was also a great communicator, as shown in the many interview clips that can be found on the Internet. However, in order fully to understand the consequences of his approach, we need to explore the context in which the notions were developed.

Freidman was a *neo-liberal* and a *libertarian*. From these perspectives society is best served by policies that allow the individuals to pursue their own interests with the minimum of government interference, provided that they do not limit the freedom of others. In Friedman's view the role of government should be limited to the areas of defence, justice and legislating rules to resolve conflicts. Any other activities should be left to the enterprise of individuals in a private competitive market. However, we could reasonably argue that these principles would assume that all individuals had the same level of access to knowledge and resources, the same political clout, and that they all enjoyed (or could afford) the same start – if all other factors are left to merit and hard work.

Cross reference	The neo-liberal approach is described in more detail in Chapter 1, p. 25.

Friedman's views, superficially at least, seem more appropriate for small owner-managed organisations with very little interdependence, and with a limited local impact; and to a period of time before the internet revolution. Since the 1970s many organisations have become larger, richer and more powerful than many national governments. For example, in July 2011, Apple was reported as holding more cash than the US government, having at its disposal over $75bn. British Petroleum (BP), another example, was able to put aside $41bn to cover the Gulf of Mexico clean-up costs in 2010, an amount equivalent to only two-and-half times its profits for the previous year. A symbiotic relationship has developed between large corporations, politicians and governments. Political parties now need corporate donations to pay for their basic expenses, let alone to fight elections; news organisations have become so large, powerful and international that they can even influence elections, such as Fox News in the US, News International in the UK or 'RedeGlobo' in Brazil – the richest country in South America. Finally, national governments have become dependent on the taxes paid by certain corporations, and are constantly courting top executives in the hope that the companies they represent neither relocate their headquarters to tax havens nor outsource thousands of jobs overseas at short notice in a bid to reduce labour costs.

The ownership of organisations has also radically changed. For example, shareholders with and without voting rights, who used to share a domicile with the companies they invested in, now live all over the world. In some cases, shares were bought in now collapsed financial institutions on behalf of pension groups, small investors and private savers, without a full disclosure of the risks involved and sometimes even without the knowledge of those affected.

Simultaneously, in the decades after Friedman's article was written, the supporters of *neo-liberalism* worked hard in private organisations, and in government and international institutions, to align their policies to private economic interests. For example, powerful individuals working for private financial institutions seamlessly moved to jobs as government advisers on economic policy only to return, a couple of years later, to the same private financial institutions. This 'revolving door' phenomenon, illustrated in many recent Hollywood films (e.g. Ferguson's *Inside Job*), on the current financial crisis, has eroded even the basic roles of regulation and control that governments should hold if Friedman's ideas were to be implemented.

In a similar attack on *neo-liberal* ideology, this time aimed at the IMF and World Bank, Burgo and Stewart (2002) used Malawi as an illustration of enforced privatisation policies to have created a food crisis. The case is explained in greater detail in Chapter 13 (*see* Case study 13.1 on p. 507). In summary, in the mid-1990s, the IMF insisted on the deregulation of the grain and foodstuffs agency before any further loans and aid finance were to be granted. The result, which Burgo and Stewart attribute principally to the deregulation policy, was a collapse in grain supplies and widespread famine in 2002. Interestingly, the Commerce and Industry Minister of Malawi, Mr Mpasu, was asked by the UK Government to speak to a meeting of G7 ministers in Cancun of the benefits of liberalising the Malawi economy. He stood up and said, 'We have opened our economy. That's why we are flat on our backs' (Elliott, 2003).

Finally, it is important to revisit Friedman's argument that corporations 'as social and political constructs', as opposed to individuals, do not have ethical responsibilities. In the case of organisations owned-managed by a single individual/family, or by a very small group of long-term investors, it could be argued that the decisions taken by these organisations represent the views and interests of their owners, who could subsequently be held to account for their respective company's actions. Recent scandals could give the impression that this is also the case for large corporations. For example, Rupert Murdoch and his son James were summoned by the House of Commons in the UK to answer questions regarding their newspaper's involvement in the phone hacking scandal in 2011, just as the former Sir Fred Goodwin from the failed RBS bank and other bankers were called to account in 2009; Tony Hayward from BP was also summoned by the House of Representatives in the US in 2010. However, what became obvious in these exchanges, and in other similar cases, was that the operations of these corporations were so vast and complex that top executives, and their auditors, have become no more than figureheads; they have very little knowledge of what was or is actually going on in their organisations, and only a vague understanding of the implications of the policies they have suggested and/or approved – assuming that incompetence, conflict of interests and collusion are left out of the equation. For example, the Chair of the UK High Pay Commission stated in October 2011 that executive remuneration 'packages have become so complex that executives don't even understand it themselves' – although they managed to increase their pay by 43 per cent over the year, as opposed to 2.6 per cent for the average UK worker.

Despite this lack of connection between individual managers and the actions of their organisations, corporations in America claimed the same rights as individuals under the American Constitution. For example, in 1996 the US Supreme Court unanimously overturned a Rhode Island law that had stood for 40 years. This law had prohibited businesses advertising the prices of beers and spirits. Referring to the First Amendment the Supreme Court ruled that corporations could claim the same rights of protection as individuals. In 1998 in the case of *First National Bank of Boston v. Bellotti* the American Supreme Court again ruled that the First Amendment protects corporations in the same way as it protects individuals in terms of freedom of speech. Thus, notwithstanding their being social constructs, the corporations involved in these cases were granted the same rights under the American Constitution as those available to individual American citizens.

In the introduction of the South African 'King II Report on Corporate Governance' (2002), published in Johannesburg at the time of the Earth Summit, a further and critical legal point is highlighted. The conventional rhetoric is that corporate executives are required to run corporations in the interests of shareholders. However, the report challenges this claim by referring to some jurisdictions in which, upon incorporation,

> [T]he company becomes a separate persona in law and no person whether natural or juristic can be owned. Courts have also held that shareowners have no direct interests in the property, business or assets owned by the company, their only rights being a right to vote and a right to dividends. Shareowners also change from time to time while, as the owner, the company remains constant. Consequently, directors, in exercising their fiduciary duties, must act in the interest of the company as a separate person.
>
> (King II Report, Paragraph 17.3)

Following the logic of this separation, the corporate executives are committed to acting in the interests of the company, which would suggest that, if they deem it appropriate, this could include acting in ways that could be labelled 'corporately socially responsible'. Such an approach places the company's long-term economic survival above all others. The interests of shareholders and those of the company would coincide *via* the process known as 'the correspondence principle', in which investors select companies to invest in on the basis of each company's known objectives and performance. Thus corporate executives do not have to worry about acting in the ways shareholders would prefer. If the actions of corporate executives are consistent with past decisions and rationale then their actions will correspond with the interests of the shareowners, because the shareowners would have decided to invest in the company on this very basis. As a recognisable legal entity, it might also be argued: if corporations can be assigned the rights of citizenship, why should they not be assigned equivalent levels of responsibilities? If this argument is accepted, it raises questions about how one renders operational a broader view of a corporation's responsibilities.

In sum, the effect wielded by contemporary organisations (large and small) on individuals and groups is so dramatic and can take place on such a large scale that when things go wrong, either by mismanagement, corruption, unexpected events, or by genuine accidents, the damage caused is almost irreversible and can affect people all over the world. The impact and the speed of these effects are also greatly amplified by globalisation and by the Internet, electronic communications and international banking. For instance, the migration of capital from one region to another, from one country to another, as it seeks out the most advantageous investment opportunities, can have destabilising impacts upon those areas affected by the capital flows. The political influence of corporations and their lobbying and influencing of governments has eroded meaningful legal and regulatory mechanisms. Finally, if organisations are exclusively bound by the minimum required by the law and local custom, how can they respond meaningfully to the challenges from climate change, deforestation and the deterioration of the natural habitat due to the relentless (although legal) exploitation of natural resources across national and legal boundaries? The following case studies are illustrations of the type of problems that can emerge from a neo-liberal approach that does not accept that corporations have a social responsibility.

Case study 9.1	The tobacco industry

For many years, medical research had indicated a clear link between the use of tobacco products and various forms of cancer, although these findings had always been contested vigorously by the tobacco industry. Yet, in 2000, the tobacco company Reynolds broke ranks and announced in court that it was accepting liability for certain smokers' ill-health. There is evidence to suggest that the tobacco companies had confirmed the link between their products and cancer-based illnesses many years previously but concealed the evidence. Since sales of tobacco products in most western countries have been either stagnant or in decline since the early 1990s, the tobacco companies had targeted developing countries (and particularly young people) as growth markets for their products.

Notwithstanding the many previous denials of the tobacco companies of the link between cigarettes and cancer, it is now clear that such a link is accepted. This is exemplified by the use made of a study commissioned by the multinational tobacco company, Philip Morris. In 2001 the tobacco firm, one of the world's leading producers of tobacco products, and responsible for 80 per cent of the cigarettes sold in the Czech Republic, felt the need to respond to claims that cigarette smoking was costing the Czech economy significant sums by virtue of high levels of hospitalisation, absenteeism from work and thus lower tax collection levels caused by smoking-related illnesses. The study commissioned by the tobacco company concluded that, rather than impose costs on the Czech economy, cigarettes saved the Czech government over £100m each year. The basis for this assessment was that, because cigarette smokers would be dying earlier than non-smokers, due to smoking-related illnesses, this would save the government hospitalisation costs associated with old age, as well as lower pension costs and lower housing costs.

Case study 9.2	When can genetically modified crops be grown?

In many western countries, including the UK, the planting of genetically modified (GM) crops is limited and tightly controlled by governments. Following a series of trials the UK government announced that only one genetically modified crop had passed its tests. The principal companies concerned had accepted the need to monitor the trials and to develop a thorough body of evidence before large-scale commercial planting could be considered. Yet, at the very time the UK government was proclaiming a moratorium in the UK, in the Indian state of Andhra Pradesh, a 384 square mile area known as Genome Valley, was being developed for GM crop production, funded by overseas aid from the UK government. In excess of £50m was allocated to this project by the UK government in 2001. Monsanto, the principal company involved in the controlled trials in the UK, was among the companies invited to participate in the development in Andhra Pradesh. Farmers in Andhra Pradesh expressed concerns that development of prairie-style fields would result in the mass migration of millions of small farmers and labourers to the cities in search of work. The Andhra Pradesh project (known as Vision 2020) was the result of a study undertaken by a large American consulting firm, which, critics argue, gave little, if any, consideration to alternative forms of raising agricultural efficiency that utilised local resources more effectively and sensitively. Local farmers in Andhra Pradesh wished to control their own destinies, but the fear was that this scheme, with such influential corporate involvement, involvement that will have secured governmental support before it was officially announced, would lead to a social disaster in the region.

Case study 9.3	Markets, prices and need

The pharmaceutical industry tends to be the target of a lot of angst when it comes to illustrating the problems/issues raised by global markets and global corporations. Among other things, the pharmaceutical corporations are often criticised for concentrating the overwhelming proportion of their research and development budgets on diseases of the rich. For example, there are new products continually coming to the market, which claim to address issues of impotence, hair loss, wrinkles, obesity, etc., whereas diseases such as malaria, Ebola and HIV-AIDS either remain under-investigated or the drugs available are too expensive for millions of people experiencing the diseases. However, the drugs companies point out that they are commercial corporations, subject to the disciplines of financial markets. If governments wish them to channel/divert research and development budgets into specific areas

▶

of medical treatment, then the pharmaceutical companies need to be compensated for the opportunity cost of this activity. One of the responses to these claims is that generic producers can manufacture HIV-AIDS drugs, for example, for a fraction of the price charged by the global pharmaceutical companies (around one-eighth of the price). The pharmaceutical companies respond by arguing that they need to recover the research and developments costs of those drugs that never reach their intended markets, costs that the generic producers do not incur.

Whilst the ethical weight of the above arguments is not suggested to be equal, we will sidestep offering a view on where the balance lies, but consider one of the ways the pharmaceutical companies (Big Pharma) responded to criticisms of their policies with regard to HIV-AIDS.

In 2001 the South African Government took Big Pharma to court over the pricing of retroviral drugs (the drugs used to treat HIV-AIDS). The day before the judicial decision was to be given, the pharmaceutical companies, realising that they were going to 'lose' the decision, effectively began to discuss an 'out-of-court settlement'. This took the form of initially a 50-word statement, which, after many months of 'debate', became a massive obfuscating document. Many felt the pharmaceutical companies had pulled victory from the jaws of defeat. This feeling was reinforced when in October 2003 the US Senate announced the name of the person who was to head the American AIDS Initiative. It was Randall Tobias, a former head of Eli Lilly, one of the world's big pharmaceutical companies. He was not required to sell his shareholding in pharmaceutical companies, meaning that, if Mr Tobias took any decisions that harmed the interests of Big Pharma, he would also be negatively affecting his own wealth position. The question of a conflict of interest was raised by many but never adequately responded to.

It is therefore clear that regardless of the appeal of the arguments presented by Friedman and other 'radical' neo-liberals and libertarians, and in view of the events and developments that have taken place since, to focus exclusively on shareholder value is at best naïve and ill-informed, and at worst dangerous and irresponsible. As the failure of this approach has been painfully demonstrated in the current economic crisis, a more inclusive and systemic approach, one that is also more culturally, socially and environmentally sensitive, is required. This in turn heralds the stakeholder approach.

Edward Freeman's stakeholders approach

The stakeholder theory for the analysis of social phenomena, briefly mentioned in Chapters 1 and 3, is a powerful heuristic device applied since the 1930s in many areas such as law, strategic planning, project management, marketing and systems thinking. In this sense, Preston and Sapienza (1990) traced the stakeholder 'concept' to the article *For Whom are Corporate Managers Trustees?* published by E. Merrick Dodd in the Harvard Law Review in May 1932, and to policies developed by General Electric during the Depression, Johnson and Johnson in the 1940s, Sears in the early 1950s, and finally, to the research conducted in Scandinavia by William Dill in the late 1950s. The correspondent variety in the way the concept is defined and applied allows us to understand stakeholder theory as a *genre*, rather than as a single set of principles or a formula to be applied mechanistically in all situations.

In the area of strategic management, Edward Freeman's 1984 book *Strategic Management: A Stakeholder Approach* is considered inspirational for the countless books and articles in the areas of business ethics, CSR and sustainability that address the stakeholder theory. Freeman acknowledged that the term *stakeholder* was first used in an internal memorandum at the Stanford Research Institute (SRI) in 1963, as referring to 'those groups without whose support the organization would cease to exist', including shareowners, employees, customers, suppliers, lenders and society (Freeman and Reed, 1983). Other influential publications in the years that followed worth mentioning are Ackoff's *Redesigning the Future* (1974); Churchman's *The Systems Approach* (1968), and Checkland's *Systems Thinking, Systems Practice* (1981) in the area of systems thinking. Finally, highly publicised research projects established stakeholder analysis at the heart of business schools such as the Harvard Business School project on 'Corporate Social Responsibility'; the Wharton School's 'Stakeholder Project', and the University of Toronto's 10-year research project on 'Corporate Social Performance' (Clarkson, 1995).

Freeman's definition of stakeholder as 'any group or individual who can affect or is affected by the achievement of the firm's objectives' (1984: 46) was aimed at developing a 'wider definition' than that of the SRI by including public interest groups, protest groups, government agencies, trade associations, and unions, as well as employees, customer segments, shareowners, the media, and even competitors and other 'adversary groups'. In this sense, he concludes that

> Semantics aside, if corporations are to formulate and implement strategies in turbulent environments, theories of strategy must have concepts, such as the wide sense of stakeholder, which allows the analysis of all external forces and pressures whether they are friendly or hostile.
>
> (Freeman, 1983: 92)

The issue of stakeholder identification, the interplay between the different stakeholders, and the dynamic relationship between specific stakeholders and particular areas of the corporation, are of paramount importance for the application of the stakeholder approach to business. Furthermore, one issue that has not yet been sufficiently deeply explored is whether managers and/or top executives should, distinct from the rest of the employees, be considered as stakeholders; executives may engage in opportunistic and self-serving behaviours at the expense of other stakeholders in areas such as executive pay, bonuses, executive pensions and the so-called 'golden handshake' agreements prior to leaving for other executive posts.

Clarkson (1995), based on a 10-year research programme at the University of Toronto involving 70 large corporations, highlights the importance of identifying and focusing on 'stakeholder issues' as opposed to 'social issues', as an initial stage in analysing and evaluating the social performance of both the organisation and its managers. Clarkson (1995) also classified stakeholders into the categories of primary stakeholders, those 'without whose continuing participation the corporation cannot survive as a going concern', and secondary stakeholders, those 'who influence or affect, or are influenced or affected by, the corporation, but are not engaged in transactions with the corporation and are not essential for its survival' (1995: 107). Mitchell et al. (1997), on

Figure 9.1 Examples of organisational stakeholders

the other hand, provided a typology to contribute to a theory of stakeholder identification in terms of three attributes: 'power', 'legitimacy' and 'urgency'. These attributes are dynamic and socially constructed (not objective), and stakeholders 'may not be conscious of possessing the attribute or, if conscious of possession, may not choose to enact any implied behaviours' (1997: 868). Their central argument is that as well as legitimacy, 'power and urgency must be attended to if managers are to serve the legal and moral interests of legiti-mate stakeholders' (1997: 882). Following their typology, a stakeholder holds a 'definitive' stakeholder status if it possesses these three attributes. Stakeholders

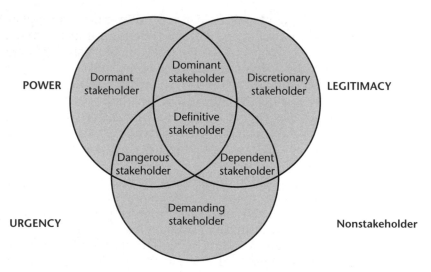

Figure 9.2 Stakeholder typology: one, two, or three attributes present

Source: From Mitchell et al. (1977) 'Toward a theory of stakeholder identification and salience: defining the principle of Who and What Really Counts', *The Academy of Management Review*, 22 (4), 874.

possessing a single attribute, or a combination of any other two attributes, are awarded a different status, ranging from dormant or discretionary to dominant or dangerous.

In general, as noted by Agle and Mitchell (2008), when reviewing the stakeholder debate certain strands can be identified: firstly, research aimed at measuring whether the instrumental use of the stakeholder approach provides competitive advantage and/or shareholder value; secondly, the normative justification of stakeholder theory, as illustrated by Donaldson and Preston (1995), and finally, the shareholder-stakeholder debate, also known as the 'Friedman-Freeman' debate.

The instrumental use of stakeholder theory

The debate on whether stakeholder theory provides an organisation with some competitive advantage, or whether it provides improved shareholder value, is also known as its 'business case'. The main areas usually explored include cost and risk reduction, competitive advantage, reputation and legitimacy, and synergistic value creation (Kurucz et al., 2009). For example, when evaluating the impact of CSR, McWilliams and Siegel (2001) asked whether socially responsible firms out-perform or underperform other organisations that do not meet the same social criteria – an approach that could also be seen as covertly Friedmanite. However, a clear answer to this and other similar questions has not yet been found. Whether a company will financially perform either better, worse, or the same, depends on the authors considered, as Margolis and Walsh (2003) found when they analysed the results of 127 studies examining this issue published between 1972 and 2002.

An initial consideration could be that, if one assumes that companies perform the same under either a shareholder or a stakeholder approach, then it follows that a stakeholder approach is not detrimental to shareholders but also that it could benefit a wider group of stakeholders. However, as previously highlighted, the central problem of whom to include as a legitimate stakeholder, and how to balance the interests of different stakeholders, seems to be of paramount importance in arriving at such a neutral result.

A more nuanced answer is provided, for example, by Hillman and Keim (2001): they found that if a CSR strategy is tied directly to primary stakeholders, the investment may also benefit the shareholders; however, participating in social issues beyond direct stakeholders may adversely affect a firm's ability to create shareholder wealth. An equally interesting conclusion was reached by McWilliams and Siegel (2001), who stated, from a 'supply and demand' theory perspective, that 'there is a level of CSR investment that maximizes profit, while also satisfying stakeholder demand for CSR'. Finally, we also need to highlight the difficulties that may arise from considering the applicability of these findings to organisations that operate within multiple countries and legal systems, that have employees who routinely work in more than one country, or that have multiple headquarters. A very clear example would be the differences in relationships between companies and unions observed in countries such as the UK, the US, France, Germany and Japan.

Case study 9.4	An economically successful corporation with a view of its social position

Capital One is a credit card company that chooses not to publicise its social projects because it is uneasy that it might be accused of only undertaking its social activities in order to gain publicity. Most of its social engagements go unreported and thus unrecognised, but the following example did attract media attention and the company acknowledged its role in the programme.

The projects in question related to the development of sophisticated software to facilitate the interrogation of differing national databases by a local police force in the pursuit of suspected paedophiles. The company supported a number of its programmers in working with the local police force over many months in developing the software, which has subsequently proved to be an important advance in police work and adopted by other police forces. The programmers also committed a lot of their own free time to the project. When talking with people at the company, one of the authors was left in no doubt that everyone was extremely supportive of the project and that its effect upon staff morale had been both positive and significant, manifesting itself in enhanced levels of efficiency and innovation in all areas of the programming division's work.

The Friedmanite response might be that such an example is fine, as long as it is undertaken in the belief that it will positively affect shareholder interests. If this is thought unlikely then such activities should not be undertaken. Interestingly, the senior management argued strenuously that the decision to support the project was not taken for Friedmanite reasons. The senior executives argued that decisions relating to their 'social projects' were taken on non-consequentialist grounds. The senior management review projects that have been identified by the 'Social-Resonsibility Team' (which comprises four full-time staff). There also appeared to be some consultation with all the employees to help shape the 'social projects' agenda for the coming year.

The senior management argued that they saw their company as part of the local community and wanted to be regarded as a part of that community. They wanted to be regarded as a good employer, thereby attracting not just 'good' employees, but employees coming with the right approach and commitment. Such a policy did enhance organisational efficiency, but the senior management regarded the policy decision as reflecting more of a principled than an instrumental stance. At its root, the senior management philosophy was an inclusive approach to organisational 'Being'.

A final aspect often overlooked, as Blowfield (2007) highlights, is the emphasis placed upon the economic impact of CSR on the firm – as opposed to the impact on the assumed beneficiaries. In this context Margolis and Walsh argued that

> [I]f corporate responses to social misery are evaluated only in terms of their instrumental benefits for the firm and its shareholders, we never learn about their impact on society, most notably on the intended beneficiaries of these initiatives. Nor do we investigate the conditions under which it is permissible to act on stakeholder interests that are inconsistent with shareholder interests.

(Margolis and Walsh, 2003: 282)

Regardless of whether the business case and/or the impact on society of a CSR strategy can be proved, it is clear that many companies have embraced this approach, as Agle and Mitchell (2008) reported; they had randomly examined the websites of 100 companies drawn from the Fortune 500 list and found that 64 of these embraced approaches to 'maximise the well-being of all stakeholders' – what this commitment means in practice, and why each of these companies have embraced this stakeholder approach, is open to discussion. In this sense, Clarkson concluded that

> The existence of a corporate code of conduct, practice, or ethics is certainly evidence that a company is aware of some responsibilities but does not tell the researcher how the code [or mission statement], is being implemented or whether it is simply window dressing. Many company codes were primarily defensive, aimed at protecting the company and its property from its employees

> (Clarkson, 1995: 95)

Perhaps some of the urgency to adopt a CSR strategy is driven by what Porter and Kramer referred to as 'the rating game' although, as they pointed out,

> [M]easuring and publicizing social performance is a potentially powerful way to influence corporate behaviours – assuming that the ratings are consistently measured and accurately reflect corporate social impact. Unfortunately, neither condition holds true in the current profusion of CSR checklists.

> (Porter and Kramer, 2006: 81)

Blowfield (2007) also addressed the problems with ratings by distinguishing those that are economically oriented from those that are normatively (ethically) oriented, agreeing with Schafer (2005) that economic rating systems are clearly dominant.

In sum, when designing a stakeholder strategy, or when deciding how much to spend on CSR by allocating some of the profits to environmental causes, by supporting a particular philanthropic initiative or a charity, or by investing in a new and expensive 'green roof', there seems to be no clear explanation of how certain companies made their choices. Perhaps some answers can be found by looking at the top executives' backgrounds, hobbies, personal interests and previous associations – or by examining adverse publicity aimed specifically at their company or at their competitors. Some companies merely pick a means of proving their social credentials.

The normative justification of stakeholder theory

Following the discussion on the instrumental use of stakeholder theory, which demonstrated serious difficulties and dilemmas when designing, costing, implementing and comparing different CSR strategies, it is possible to wonder if there indeed exists any qualitative difference between a cost-benefit analysis based exclusively on shareholders' interests, and a similar analysis that includes other stakeholders – however many. In other words, if the main objective were to be to choose between a shareholder and a stakeholder approach based on competitive advantage and financial performance, then the stakeholder approach would simply become an extended shareholder approach. At this point, a crucial question arises: Where are the ethics? This question points towards the 'normative' justification of stakeholder analysis.

Part of the main problem seems to arise from the separation between economics and ethics, as often expressed in statements such as 'corporations must satisfy their business responsibilities *as well as* their social responsibilities'. This separation is vehemently attacked by Freeman, who calls it the 'separation thesis' (Freeman and Liedtka, 1991; Freeman et al., 2004; Freeman, 2008). Donaldson and Preston (1995) also acknowledged the separation while arguing that the anomaly could be resolved by assuming that the 'normative validity' of stakeholder theory should underpin its 'instrumental power'. Freeman et al. (2004) went further by commenting that 'maximising shareholder value' was not a neutral statement, as it held 'vast ideological content'. Along similar lines, Kurucz et al. (2009) suggested that in this 'schism', the economic proof of CSR is perceived as somehow non-normative (i.e. value free), while adding that the instrumental and normative justifications for CSR represent a debate between two fundamental conceptions of what is a corporation: it could be either a disconnected simple entity with stable interests, or an interconnected complex entity with multidimensional, dynamic interests. Driver (2006), from a psychoanalytical perspective, argues that the reason why economic models of CSR seem to dominate is related to their ability to reflect a 'more common and illusory concept of the organizational self' (autonomous and one-dimensional), as opposed to normative models that seem to reflect a 'more accurate, if less common, concept of the organizational self' (interdependent and multidimensional). In other words, instead of representing two separate and opposite paradigms, they are situated along a continuum from illusion and dysfunction to truth and functionality, or from pathology to health. (Driver, 2006: 352).

In this context, Donaldson and Preston (1995) concluded that the separation between economics and ethics should disappear if managers and other agents acted as if all stakeholders' interests had *intrinsic* value. Furthermore, Donaldson (2008) also suggested that corporations are on the verge of a 'normative revolution' that calls for a revisit to the questions: 'Why does the corporation exist?' and 'What are these institutions for?' He then asks managers to

[A]scribe some intrinsic worth to stakeholders. That is to say, a stakeholder, such as an employee, must be granted intrinsic worth that is not derivative from the worth they create for others. Human beings have value in themselves. Their rights stand on their own. These rights themselves are morally and logically prior to the way in which respecting their rights may generate more productivity for others or the corporation.

(Donaldson, 2008: 175–6)

Finally, Freeman concluded that organisations should avoid the 'separation thesis', embracing the variety of shareholders as part of a stakeholder map, ultimately to prevent managers rationalising and justifying risky, unethical and/or illegal behaviour.

Our claim is that a view that places morality largely out of the conversation, and that reduces managerial responsibility to making money is more likely to foster unethical behaviour.

(Freeman et al., 2004: 367).

These last statements lead us to revisit the discussion of the 'shareholder versus stakeholder' debate.

The shareholder versus stakeholder debate revisited

Following on from the issues discussed earlier in the chapter, it is clear that most commentators would not dismiss the concept of shareholders as being important stakeholders in any organisation – although the notion that shareholders can be grouped into a single entity, with the same interests, needs to be revised. Furthermore, the recent fragmentation of ownership into smallholdings makes it possible that some shareholders would see themselves as primarily or simultaneously belonging to other stakeholder groups.

Freeman is keen to end the shareholder-stakeholder debate by confirming that 'as a capitalist and a diehard libertarian who believes in human freedom and hope, and community and solidarity, as two sides of the same coin, I tire of these debates that don't do much to create value' (2008: 163); he also acknowledges Friedman's contribution in many areas of knowledge and policy:

> One can only stand in awe of Friedman's substantial contribution to our understanding of markets, monetary policy, international trade, and the role of freedom in democratic, market societies
>
> (Freeman, 2008: 162)

Finally, in a recent interview for the Business Roundtable Institute for Corporate Ethics, he suggested that if Friedman were alive today he would also be a stakeholder theorist, viewing it as the best way to achieve long-term shareholder value. He also shared Friedman's argument against social responsibility as a separate activity from running a business. Freeman has also called for the demise of the idea of CSR, stating that

> We have to confess that after years of trying to make sense of this idea we have come full circle to agree with Milton Friedman that the concept of corporate social responsibility is a dangerous idea. We have slightly different reasons for our conclusions.
>
> (Freeman and Liedtka, 1991: 92)

In this critical analysis of the concept, Freeman and Liedtka (1991) propose seven reasons for abandoning the concept of CSR, including that it promotes incompetence 'by leading managers to involve themselves in areas beyond their expertise – that is, repairing society's ills', and that it accepts the separation between business and ethics. They promote instead a new dialogue based on three propositions, as follows:

> Corporations are connected networks of stakeholder interests. Corporations are places in which both individual human beings and human communities engage in caring activities that are aimed at mutual support and unparalleled human achievement. Corporations are mere means through which human beings are able to create and re-create, describe and re-describe, their visions for self and community.
>
> (Freeman and Liedtka, 1991: 96)

In this sense, he advocates the replacement of Corporate *Social* Responsibility by Corporate *Stakeholder* Responsibility as an integrated business/ethics model, with a central focus on creating value for all stakeholders (Freeman and Velamuri, 2005). The idea of *creating shared value* for stakeholders has also been explored from different angles by Noland and Phillips (2010) and, more recently, by Porter and Kramer (2011), who focus on the connections between societal and economic progress. Porter and Kramer believe that the practice of *shared value* can unleash the next wave of global growth by 'reconceiving' products and markets; redefining productivity in the value chain, and by enabling local cluster development (2011: 65).

The tension between stakeholder and shareholder perspectives can also be seen in the development of UK company law. The Labour Party's 1997 manifesto included a commitment to reform company law by recognising a stakeholder perspective (as opposed to an exclusively shareholder responsibility). Upon election the Labour government established a committee to consider how the stakeholder commitment could be operationalised. The committee deliberated for nearly two years. An interim report was published after the first year, which retained an attachment to the notion of pluralism in corporate decision making, although the wording can be seen to be becoming a little ambiguous:

> The principal arguments are that the present scheme of law fails adequately to recognise that businesses best generate wealth where participants operate harmoniously as teams and that managers should recognise the wider interests of the community.

One year later the committee published its final report, but by then the term pluralism had been lost and in its place appeared the term 'enlightened shareholder value'. The removal of the commitment to pluralism led to the resignation from the committee of the finance director of The Body Shop. He described himself as an advocate of social and environmental responsibility and was not prepared to remain a member of the committee once the commitment to enlightened shareholder value had replaced pluralism. Newspaper reports on the outcome of the committee's work talked of frantic lobbying by business interests, which ultimately led not only to the retention of the shareholders' interests being the only one formally recognised in UK law, but also to the conversion of the committee's proposals for compulsory statements on corporate issues into proposals that would only be voluntary, that is, at the discretion of directors.

When the new Companies Act was passed in 2006 it adopted the enlightened shareholder value approach. This maintains profit maximisation as the objective of a company but subjects it to developing relationships of trust with stakeholders as the best way of achieving this aim. Such a mild constraint is similar to Sternberg's (2000) idea of 'decency' as the only limitation on shareholder value creation. She attributes two qualities to decency: the first is acting in a legal manner; and the second is acting in a way that establishes and maintains trust between the company and its customers, suppliers, distributors and all the others it comes into contact with. Decency is the honesty, fairness, and the avoidance of coercion or threat, that are necessary for an organisation to succeed, over the long term.

Case study 9.5	**The U'wa and oil exploration**

The U'wa are an indigenous people that live in a remote area in Colombia, South America. Traditionally, their land extended across the Colombian-Venezuelan border. However, as a result of the international border demarcation imposed on their land in the nineteenth century, their estimated 10,000 population now lives in Colombia. As has been the case for other indigenous tribes in the Americas they have lost most of their land to descendants of European colonisers, through processes of land titulation, forced eviction and violence. However, recent constitutional changes in Colombia have, at least on paper, helped them to recover some of their traditional land. Their language is part of the Chibcha family. They have no written tradition, using song to pass their knowledge and customs to new generations.

In 1992, the oil multinational Occidental ('Oxy') was granted a licence by the Colombian government to drill oil in the U'wa land. This event caused a major upheaval in the tribe, as they had always considered oil to be the blood of *Mother Earth*. Drilling would be similar to wounding her. The U'wa even threatened mass suicide (a practice they have, sadly, used in the past instead of surrendering to the European colonisers and their Christian beliefs) if drilling and oil exploitation took take place on their land.

As the Colombian government needed the possible oil revenues to boost the economy, it initially sent the army to clear the drilling site, assuming that the U'wa would leave behind their customs, embrace 'progress' and receive some generous royalties. Most Colombians, although empathising with the U'wa, did not understand why they would not take the opportunity to make some money, build schools, roads, brick houses, and become 'civilised'.

After a successful international campaign, Occidental, and later Shell and Repsol YPF withdrew from the project. However, the Colombian government oil company 'Ecopetrol' still remains interested, even though the drilling licence was revoked by the Colombian Supreme Court.

The U'wa still remain on their ancestral land; oil drilling and exploration has not taken place. Since 1992, oil has become an even more important commodity; its price has increased from $17 a barrel in 1992 to over $100 a barrel today. As the Colombian government looks for oil fields to replace imports, and oil companies are also desperately looking for new areas of exploration, the U'wa remain in a fragile situation. Please visit Case study 10.1 '*Herbal remedy from the Amazon rain forest*', presented in the next chapter.

Activity 9.5	**Stakeholder and shareholder approaches to host communities**

Groups such as the U'wa, whose land includes oil reserves, are known as host communities. Critically explore this real-life case study using shareholder and stakeholder approaches. What strategic approach would a company take towards the U'wa as a host community if it adopted a shareholder or a stakeholder position? Additional information about the case can be found online at: http://www.goldmanprize.org/1998/southcentralamerica.

Contemporary issues in CSR

A multitude of theoretical frameworks and practical initiatives related to the social responsibility of business have been created in the previous decades addressing the perceived needs of different stakeholders within and outside the organisation. Some examples include: traditional philanthropy and charity; strategic philanthropy; fair trade; business at the bottom of the pyramid (BoP); sustainability and sustainable development; TBL; cradle-to-cradle (C2C); life-cycle analysis and product stewardship; green marketing; ethical consumerism; corporate citizenship and accountability; inter-/intra-generational equity; organisational diversity; and socially responsible investment.

While some highlight general guidelines or normative frameworks for stakeholder management, others constitute a more detailed programme for action and accreditation sometimes backed by NGOs or government agencies. The costs involved in obtaining and maintaining an accreditation vary considerably: from a single donation or sponsorship deal, a small percentage of annual profits, to a large-scale organisational redesign. Furthermore, as certain initiatives have evolved into accrediting organisations and/or NGOs in their own right, they now seem to compete for the limited attention and financial resources from companies, consumers and governments alike. For instance, coffee-trading companies can opt for a Fairtrade or a Rainforest Alliance certification, each with its respective logo and accreditation process. In the following sections we shall briefly discuss a few of these ideas.

From fair trade to 'Fairtrade'

The power imbalances between producers from less developed countries and traders from more developed countries seem to be an inherent feature of trans-national trade. This has resulted in the accumulation of wealth in rich countries to the detriment of producers who lack the same negotiating power or the same level of state subsidies. The Organisation of Petroleum Exporting Countries (OPEC) is one of the few examples where producing countries have successfully gathered to influence the global price and the availability of a single raw commodity. In other areas, such as in the production of food and perishable products, crafts and other semi-processed goods, direct access to markets has proved particularly difficult for small producers.

Furthermore, market price fluctuations have created 'boom or bust' situations that sometimes threaten the livelihood of small farmers and the viability of entire regional economies. Other factors that adversely affect small producers also include unseasonable weather patterns; the 'dumping' practices by developed countries; overproduction that follows 'low production high price' periods, sometimes promoted by development agencies (Booth and Whetstone, 2007); and even badly managed 'food aid' programmes.

The disproportionate impact of international trade on small producers and rural communities has not passed unnoticed. For example, Eduard Dekker's novel *Max Havelaar* already highlighted this issue in the 1860s, within the context of Dutch-Indonesia. More recently, and especially since the 1940s, certain initiatives and organisations have been created to help small producers in less developed countries to improve their access to markets and to enjoy more stable and predictable market conditions. Examples include The Ten Thousand Villages in 1946; SERRV International in 1949; the creation of Oxfam's 'worldshops' in 1959; the UN's 'Trade not Aid' in 1960s; and Oxfam's 'Helping by Selling' in 1965. It is important to highlight that some of these small and medium-scale initiatives were presented as alternatives or challenges to the capitalist market economy, and others were supported by religious and charitable organisations, such as the Quakers' 'Economic Justice' campaign. As registered charities, most of these organisations are accustomed to external monitoring and auditing.

The notion of fair trade started to become mainstream with the introduction of the first Fairtrade label 'Max Havelaar' in 1988. It was given to coffee from the Union of Indigenous Communities of the Isthmus Region (UICIR) in Mexico and was sold in supermarkets across the Netherlands. This initiative was replicated in different developed countries in Europe and in the US, followed by the creation of the Fairtrade Labelling Organisations International (FLO) in 1997 to agree on standards and individual product certification. Finally, the World Fair Trade Organisation (WFTO) launched a parallel process of certification aimed at fair trade organisations. There are also many independent Alternative Trading Organisations (ATO), usually not-for-profit and value-based NGOs, aimed at 'humanising the trade process' following similar fair trade guidelines, sometimes also inspired by religious or ideological principles.

The basic idea behind the Fairtrade scheme is to pay small producers in less developed countries a guaranteed minimum price for their crops, one that will cover the cost of production. This is supplemented by minimum standards for workers (following local legislation) and discretionary additional payments for communal projects. The Fairtrade scheme is worth over £1.1bn per year in the UK, with more than 2,500 products marked with the Fairtrade logo. Individual organisations and even entire towns in the UK have achieved Fairtrade certification if these products, especially coffee and tea, are widely sold and consumed. The scheme does not, though, benefit small farmers and producers (including small grocers) in developed countries who could also be at the mercy of market forces and multinational power, as UK farmers highlighted in the ongoing dispute over the profits from milk and other farm products (BBC News Online, 2012c).

As traders could argue that if market prices fall below the cost of production their profits would be hurt, and to provide cover for any additional expenses, a premium is added to the final consumer price. In the case of coffee, the second-largest export commodity after petroleum (Levi and Linton, 2003) and the biggest UK Fairtrade product, a BBC *Money Programme: How fair is Fairtrade?* (10/03/2006) investigation demonstrated that using 2005 market prices, Fairtrade coffee farmers were paid 4–12 pence per pack of coffee, while the Fairtrade premium was in the region of 50 pence per pack; this was equivalent to a 30 per cent increase in the retail price. No explanation could be found for the 38–46 pence increase per pack as supermarkets are very secretive with their data. In this context, some researchers have argued that most of the money goes into certifications costs and other business expenses (Griffith, 2011), while others argue that the scheme is so inefficient that only 10 per cent of the Fairtrade premium trickles down to the farmer (Harford, 2007). Furthermore, the same BBC programme also highlighted that under those market conditions Fairtrade prices paid to small farmers were very similar to market prices.

One of the main problems with the scheme is that consumers may seem to expect that most, if not all, of the Fairtrade premium they pay at the till should go to the farmers – which is not part of the 'Fairtrade Guarantee'. Other issues, such as,

- the lack of transparency from large UK supermarkets about the price they pay to Fairtrade and non-Fairtrade farmers;

- the knowledge that, in the case of coffee, most of the value-added processes, such as roasting and packaging, take place in the UK;

- and the fact that the Fairtrade premium could have an effect on the level of donations that consumers give to fully-audited charitable causes (Fairtrade is often perceived as a charity donation)

could make others uneasy about the scheme's impact. The role of supermarkets and large traders as recipients and administrators of charitable donations has also been questioned (Blythman, 2007).

Furthermore, the British government aid organisation (DfID) stated, after a Freedom of Information request, that despite all the millions given to Fairtrade, it holds no evaluations of its impact (Griffith, 2011). Other questionable practices include simultaneously selling Fairtrade bananas loose, and in sealed plastic bags at an even higher price, stating that they are two different Fairtrade products, although they may have the same origin – not to mention the impact of the unnecessary extra packaging on waste and on the environment. Finally, the inconsistencies in the certification process have also been widely acknowledged; the difficulties and the costs involved in certifying and monitoring a large number of small farmers in remote areas that often use migrant workers, and the packaging at source of non-Fairtrade products as Fairtrade to satisfy the growing demand (Weitzman, 2006).

Through selecting small independent farmers, or small cooperatives, traders bypass larger and well-managed associations of producers with a stronger price negotiating power. Examples include the Colombian Coffee Growers Federation, one of the largest rural NGOs in the world: it gathers from over 50,000 small family-owned farms, and similar medium- and large-sized associations in other countries. Choosing very small interventions also provides strong positive images for packaging and marketing. Doing so does not undermine the positive impact on the selected farms; however, it fails to provide a true picture of the realities of coffee harvesting, worldwide overproduction and pricing. By determining and fixing low prices, traders could also become involved in illegal price-fixing activities aimed at protecting their own profits, thus undermining the negotiating power of existing federations of small growers.

The fact that most Fairtrade coffee campaigns seem to involve certain of the features just discussed highlights how these campaigns can be perceived as marketing driven. There are carefully choreographed photographs of mothers with smiling children, new schools, happy farmers with moustaches and white hats in the manner of Juan Valdéz – a fictional character created to promote Colombian coffee in the US, and the production of blogs about lone businessmen travelling to inaccessible areas to help farmers. Booth and Weston (2007) also mention that most of the Fairtrade Foundation's net income is spent on promoting its own brand. Finally, some traders also benefit from the positive PR without acknowledging the scale of their Fairtrade commitment in terms of their overall purchase, using the scheme to 'green-wash' their image by associating their name with a good cause. Once more, supermarkets and other food multinationals are reluctant to show data to compare Fairtrade and non-Fairtrade purchases (e.g. price paid and quantities involved); the way in which the premium paid by consumers is included in their accounts; how these monies are managed and spent; and the details of the contracts farmers need to accept in order for them to gain access to the supermarkets' shelves.

The immediate PR impact and additional profits seem to be attractive to the supermarkets and traders. However, it is possible that, as Fairtrade becomes mainstream, the lack of transparency and proper auditing from traders and supermarkets could have unintended consequences: consumers could become 'Fairtrade fatigued', or equate the measure to a PR or marketing gimmick. Finally, the Fairtrade certification process could give the wrong impression, that is, that non-Fairtrade certified products and companies are necessarily exploitative of farmers and consumers, or that they condone or engage in unethical business practices – the opposite could also be the case in the guise of a charitable endeavour.

The disproportionate power to provide access to markets, acting as a gatekeeper through its own certification process, could also 'persuade' companies and farmers to join the organisation, undermining the basic idea of free and fair trade. Furthermore, it is very difficult to compare the impact of Fairtrade on such a diverse range of products, coming from countries with very different socio-economic and political circumstances. Fairtrade illustrates the issues that could arise from a very good idea, one focusing on traditional issues of inequality (Wilkinson, 2007), yet becoming a mainstream corporate, marketing and profit-making phenomenon.

Green-washing

Green-washing was first used by Jay Westerveld, a biologist and environmental activist, in 1986 when attacking the practices of certain hotels that place green cards in rooms cynically asking customers to re-use towels to save the planet. It generally applies to individuals, products, companies and NGOs that try to link themselves to ethical causes or policies in order to improve their image. It may also be part of a campaign to reduce costs, to increase profit margins, to improve marketing positioning, or to compensate for other questionable activities or products. Green-washing is clearly linked to marketing and the use of the media.

One of the most corrosive aspects of green-washing comes from campaigns aimed at stalling progressive legislation on environmental, human rights, equality and diversity issues. Examples include the discredited Global Climate Coalition, an organisation composed of companies in the energy, car and fossil fuel production industries. In the 1990s, they campaigned against agreement on the relationship between human activity and climate change, thus against the ratification of the Kyoto protocol. Multinationals often take over companies and brands with a good green record to enhance their image or to attract new consumers (Ben & Jerry's by Unilever in 2000; PJ Smoothies by Pepsi in 2005; The Body Shop by L'Oréal in 2006; Innocent by Coca-Cola in 2010). Similar examples include replacing natural rainforests with 'sustainable plantations' of palm oil, timber, monocrops for biofuels or hunting whales for dubious 'new' research.

Political parties also embark on green-washing when adopting environmental or socially progressive campaign pledges, while nevertheless courting or accepting funds from companies and wealthy individuals with a history of opposing these or similar issues.

TerraChoice International, an environmental consultancy group based in Canada, has since 2007 published their Green-washing Reports aimed at helping consumers to identify what they call the 'seven sins' of green-washing:

- 'hidden trade-offs', which involve selecting a certain eco-friendly attribute over other or more significant concerns (e.g. fossil fuel and nuclear industries);

- claims that cannot be verified (no proof) or are extrapolated out of context;

- using vague language such as 'all natural', 'chemical free' or 'non-toxic' – which is not necessarily 'green', as certain pollutants or toxins are found in nature;

- using self-created labels, stamps or images to mislead consumers, including re-designing company logos to include green colours;

- making irrelevant claims such as being free from internationally or industry-wide banned substances, or free from irrelevant product testing;

- creating compound words to soften the nature of the product such as 'green-herbicides', 'organic-cigarettes', 'fuel-efficient 4x4 for the school run' or 'eco-friendly'; and

- lying by claiming or implying company-wide certifications when these have been awarded only to individual or niche products.

More recently, government agencies have also reacted against green-washing in advertising. For example, in 2007 the Norwegian Consumer Ombudsman stated that cars 'are neither green nor clean, and cannot do anything good for the environment except less damage than others'. The Ombudsman, after consulting relevant stakeholders, examined the following statements used in advertisements by certain car manufacturers:

- Toyota Prius: 'The world's most environmentally friendly car';

- Opel: 'Environmentally friendly engines';

- Peugeot: '. . . the powerful and environmentally friendly Hdi turbodiesel engine...';

- Suzuki: 'The sales and environmental winner';

- Smart: 'Try out the world's most environmentally friendly and fun city car...';

- Toyota: 'The world's cleanest diesel engines';

- Saab: '. . . environmentally friendly turbodiesel . . .';

- Mitsubishi: '. . . environmentally friendly turbodiesel with particle filter';

- Citroën: 'Environmentally friendly diesel engine with particle filter'; and

- Fiat: 'Environmentally friendly technology'.

The Ombudsman then issued a briefing letter stating that:

> [I]t is impossible to show that a vehicle causes substantially less pressure on the environment than all other vehicles. On the basis of this we ask that expressions like "environmentally friendly", "green", "clean", "environment car", "natural" or similar are not used in the marketing of vehicles. This applies regardless of whether the environmental claims are used separately or with more detailed explanations in the marketing. In our assessment marketing of the "environmentally friendly because . . . " or "green because . . . " type would also give a misleading and incorrect picture of the vehicle's environmental properties and its effect on the environment.

> (Forbrukerombudet, Case No. 06/2449–6, Date: 03.09.07: 3)

Other groups such as Greenpeace have developed campaigns such as 'StopGreenwash', providing information for consumers and asking companies to 'clean up your act, not your image'. It focuses predominantly on the oil, automotive, electricity, coal, nuclear and foresting industries. It also provides examples and useful criteria for consumers to identify green-washing, and for companies to avoid making 'unintentional' claims that could be considered green-washing.

Ethical consumerism and consumer boycotts

Consumers are often assumed to be rational, autonomous individuals, continuously making ethically informed decisions about brands and products. This basic approach also assumes that companies can be easily associated with single brands and products, produced in-house, or in a single country. However, it is very common to see examples of companies that purposely advertise their own products as different brands, in competition with each other, or companies that take over rival products and brands through friendly or hostile acquisitions; these products are often manufactured and assembled in different countries, reaching consumers through official and grey market distribution channels.

Furthermore, it is very difficult to determine consumers' values (as opposed to how they respond to surveys and in focus groups); how these values are ranked; how these values influence their buying intentions; and how they interact at the moment of making a purchase. Consumers' future loyalty to brands and products is also far from assured, as consumers' values change over time. They are also subject to: demographic changes; marketing; their ability to find and process complex information about competing products and services; product availability; and disposable income at the moment of purchase. All of these issues play a part when considering the complex relationship between consumers and companies, their brands and products, in relation to CSR policies (or lack of them) and business practices.

In this context, the interest of consumers in the values and actions of the companies (and their brands and products) has been articulated in many different concepts. Examples include: fair trade, ethical consumerism, green consumerism, conscience consumerism, environmental consumerism and sustainable consumerism. These concepts not only ask individuals to consume in a particular manner, but also to refrain from purchasing certain products.

Boycotts, described as the organised abstaining from purchase in order to exert influence (Smith, 1990; Friedman, 1985), have probably been the most visible and effective form of rejection of certain products and companies, of particular CSR policies (or lack of them), or of discrepancies between CSR polices and business practices. Although the term 'boycott' was first used in 1880, the practice of boycotting products has a very long history. For example, in the 1700s Quaker abolitionists established a connection between the demand for sugar in Britain and the use of slave labour in the West Indies, promoting a boycott of slave-grown sugar and rum. It is said that by 1792, almost 400,000 Britons (about 7 per cent of the population) were boycotting slave-grown sugar; American colonialists also boycotted British goods until the repeal of the Stamp Act in 1766; Latin American societies boycotted Spanish and Portuguese products during their campaigns for independence in the 1800s; Gandhi successfully organised boycotts of British salt and cloth until independence was achieved in India in 1947; the Montgomery bus boycott of 1955 was an important contribution to the modern civil rights movement in the USA. Boycotts and other corporate social monitoring systems (Paul and Lydenberg, 1992) usually use social pressure and not legal obligation to encourage individual participation (Garrett, 1987).

More recently, Garrett (1987) posed the following question: 'What do American Broadcasting Company, Anheuser-Busch, Burger King, Coca-Cola, Coors Brewing, Dow Chemical, General Electric, General Foods, Hasbro, Marriott, McDonald's, Scott Paper, SmithKline Beckman, and Union Carbide have in common?', replying that all of these companies had been the targets of boycotts. We could easily update this list to include several multinationals such as Nike, Mitsubishi, Pepsi, Nestlé, Target, Best Buy, Gap, Heinz, BP and Shell. The reasons for the boycotts were related to environmental, employment or social issues, or a combination of these. One of the most successful and notorious boycotts in recent times was faced by Shell, following Greenpeace's campaign against the disposal of the Brent Spar oil storage facility in the North Sea (Grolin, 1998). Other recent examples include: Nestlé (chocolate and palm oil); Nike and Gap (sweatshops); and VW (environment). As the list grows longer and boycotts more common, many multinationals are starting to assume that preparations for the possibility of a boycott are a sensible precaution, as its impact could be felt on product sales, brand reputation due to negative press or TV coverage, and share value.

Boycotts are often organised by NGOs following a particular political, social or environmental agenda, and could represent a form of social control (Klein et al., 2002). Some of the reasons why boycotts have become more popular could be related to a perceived lack of consumer protection from government agencies and a marked disengagement with traditional politics, reactions that prompt individuals to respond to alternative means of protecting and promoting their interests and rights. In an analysis of a sample of 90 consumer boycotts in the USA in the 1970–80 period, Friedman (1985) noted that almost half of the groups involved included racial minorities and labour organisations, while the others involved religious, women's rights, consumer, anti-war, environmental and gay rights groups. In this context, Garrett (1987) concludes, after analysing from a marketing perspective the effects of 30 publicly announced boycotts in the media, that marketing managers and protest group leaders could benefit from understanding the determinants of the effectiveness of boycotts, commenting that boycotts could also be supplemented by legal action, ownership control, rumour generation and sabotage.

Using social dilemma and reference group theory, Sen et al. (2001) concluded that consumer participation in a boycott was related to a combination of the perceived possibility of success (in terms of overall participation, boycott efficacy and the communications strategy), the consumer's susceptibility to normative social influences (reference group) and the associated costs (including access to product substitutes and product need).

However, how influential any boycott call will be is unpredictable. Its success could be measured, for example, in terms of its media exposure and PR, loss of sales, customers and share value, or in terms of whether it changed the organisation's behaviour. In 1990, *The Economist* reported: 'Pressure groups are besieging American companies, politicizing business, and often presenting executives with impossible choices. Consumer boycotts are becoming an epidemic for one simple reason: they work' (Smith, 2003). However, it has also been reported that consumers are prepared to ignore boycotts that involve their favourite brands (*The Guardian*, 22 November 2002). Finally, there is also the possibility that as simultaneous calls for boycotts related to economic, social and environmental issues are constantly promoted, consumers have become desensitised and have thus stopped responding.

Other forms of activism, possibly inspired by ethical concerns regarding organisational values and perceived gaps between organisational CSR policies (or lack of them) and actions, include: 'vendettas' (Corlette, 1989); 'letter writing campaigns' (Smith and Cooper-Martin, 1997), and electronic-/internet-supported campaigns. Furthermore, a specific form of boycott called 'disinvestment' (Davidson et al., 1995) has also been used against industries such as tobacco, alcohol, nuclear, gambling and arms production, and even against entire countries such as South Africa, Iran, Israel, Burma and Cuba to exert pressure for social and political change (sometimes supplemented by legally enforceable government embargoes).

CSR, diversity and equality

The concepts of diversity and equality have as a result of globalisation become central to organisations. There is fierce international competition to attract and retain talented employees in developed economies, while promoting the movement of capital to areas of the world with cheaper production and labour costs. Governments in less developed countries, on the other hand, have adopted neo-liberal policies in order to attract foreign investment, such as facilitating the free flow of capital and providing competitive taxation (for companies and expatriate workers) and labour legislation. Furthermore, with the development of the Internet, the 24-hour news culture, the growth of investigative journalism and affordable foreign travel, individuals in developed countries have become interested, better informed and sensitised with respect to the working conditions of the workers who produce the cheaper goods they have become accustomed to consume and the impact of multinational operations on non-western cultures and communities (see previous section on fair trade). As a consequence of these factors organisations have become, or need to become, more diverse; and more diversity raises issues of equality.

The interest in diversity and equality is further supported by developments in legislation, especially in western Europe and the USA. Declining birth rates, an aging workforce, the increased participation and the success of women in the workplace, gay and lesbian movements, recent professional and non-skilled migration, refugees, and government policies that encouraged migration in the previous century, have made important changes to the population make-up of many developed societies. For example, the UK Government actively encouraged migration from the Caribbean and other Commonwealth countries to recruit workers for ammunition factories during the wars, and to compensate for acute labour shortages in the NHS, public transport and in infrastructure projects in the 1940s and 1950s. Canada and Australia, particularly in the 1960s, have also encouraged the immigration of workers to boost their economies.

More recently, the recruitment of South African health workers for the NHS in the 1990s proved controversial as Nelson Mandela accused Britain of poaching vital workers – a controversial practice found in most rich countries. Furthermore, although workers from less developed countries should have the same right to migrate as workers from developed countries in order to improve their economic and social prospects, the net migration of skilled workers overwhelmingly favours rich countries.

In the midst of these important changes, the UK Government has developed legislation to protect certain groups in society and to promote their contribution to the economy. Examples include: the Equal Pay Act (1970); Sex Discrimination Act (1975 and 1986); Race Relations Act (1976); Disability Discrimination Act (1995); Civil Partnership Act (2004); and the Employment Equality (Religion or Belief and Sexual Orientation) Regulations in 2003.

Most recently, the Equality Act 2010 was introduced to respond to the diverse nature of British society, the individual's right to self-determination, and different stages in a person's life. The act is based on the identification of nine protected characteristics: age; disability; gender reassignment; marriage and civil partnership; pregnancy and maternity; race; religion and belief; sex; and sexual orientation. In this sense, the act is intended to cover all individuals in society rather than focusing on certain minorities exclusively (e.g. sexual orientation includes gays and lesbians, heterosexuals and bisexuals). The same individual may also possess several protected characteristics.

Individuals may invoke the act when witnessing others being discriminated against or when an individual is harassed for a protected characteristic he or she does not possess; it also prohibits discrimination by association (e.g. when a heterosexual is discriminated against because of his or her friendship with a gay man or a lesbian). Despite the importance of this legislation to continue the protection of 'established' minority groups, it is important to highlight that discrimination can originate from any sector of society, as individuals from traditionally minority groups have been accused of discrimination and violence against individuals from other minority groups (e.g. the Birmingham race riots in the UK in 2005 in which there was conflict between British Asians and British Afro-Caribbeans). In this sense, the courts will need to provide guidance on how to balance the possibly competing claims of different individuals in situations such as the provision of products and services.

Legislation to protect individuals against discrimination and to promote diversity in society and in organisations is very similar across the EU. Differences start to emerge when comparisons are made within legislation in the USA, where the laws of each State can differ noticeably. However, the main challenge for western multinationals emerges when they operate in countries that follow strict codes of conduct where individual, social and religious difference is not tolerated, and where individual self-determination and equality are considered a threat to the perceived order, punishable in certain instances with the death penalty. Taking these issues seriously requires companies to develop suitable policies and management systems.

Companies need, for example, to have robust HR systems in place to avoid sending employees to assignments in countries where they may be imprisoned or worse for behaviours, beliefs and personal characteristics considered acceptable 'back home'. Family life may also be seriously disrupted when unmarried partners, partners from different religions or those holding different nationalities cannot travel together for long-term assignments, requiring alternative career and development paths if a long-term overseas assignment is required.

Multinational executives face serious dilemmas when confronted by discriminatory behaviours and practices that are tolerated in a host country, as rejecting or punishing these practices could be seen as 'cultural imperialism' or as acting against local laws and customs. Examples include health and safety, child labour, the treatment of female employees, and working hours and overtime. Furthermore, some practices such as child labour are not only widespread, but also necessary for the survival of many poor families where parents find it impossible to feed several children on their small or casual incomes. To deny children the possibility of work would therefore diminish their possibilities for survival or destine them to unseen exploitation and trafficking. Levi Strauss set an interesting policy of offering free schooling, books and uniforms to children under 14 years old who were discovered working in their factories (Varley, 1998). Finally, having the same salaries and benefits all over the world may become problematic, as these pockets of wealth in otherwise poor countries could cause high rates of local inflation, which distort food and housing prices for others, and promote uncontrolled internal migration. However, paying local wages could amount to accusations of sweatshop exploitation – although the difference between a low salary and exploitation is a subject of heated debate (Fukuyama, 1999; Arnold, 2003; Arnold and Hartman, 2005; Zwolinski, 2007).

CSR reporting

Many companies have started to include a CR/CSR report in their websites and printed information. These voluntary reports provide well-rehearsed statements, facts and pledges in order to demonstrate the organisation's CSR credentials. They are also intended to attract potential investors and employees, or to support the organisation's PR and marketing strategies. As with CSR more generally, there is no clear evidence that CSR reporting enhances financial value. However, it may be appropriate to suggest that an organisation could give the *wrong* impression, that of being dismissive of CSR issues (or be less transparent than its competitors), if it does not board the CSR reporting wagon. Furthermore, as these reports are mainly self-congratulatory, the emergence of CSR reporting could correspond to what Roberts (2003) has termed 'the ethics of narcissus':

> Stimulated by new forms of negative external visibility, the corporate response has been to seek to manufacture the appearance of its own goodness through the production of corporate ethical codes and new forms of social and environmental reports.

> (Roberts, 2003: 263).

The reporting guidelines of the Global Reporting Initiative (GRI) have become widely used, although certain multinational consultancy companies heavily promote their own methodologies. Owen and O'Dwyer (2009) provide an interest summary of the history of CSR reporting, and of the emergence of sustainability reporting and assurance practice. More recently, KPMG analysed the CSR reports of more than 3,400 companies globally (including the world's 250 largest companies) for its *Survey of Corporate Responsibility Reporting 2011*. The survey concluded that companies in the majority of European countries could be considered as 'leading the pack' in terms of the quality of their data and systems, and their communication strategies. These companies have also included external assurance – which in itself has become a multi-million pound consultancy and endorsement service. Anecdotally, companies in the USA were considered as part of the 'scratching the surface' group as, according to KPMG, companies in this country seem to focus 'on communication rather than on CR processes'.

Cross reference	The Global Reporting Initiative is discussed in detail in Chapter 7, p. 276.

In terms of the level of reporting, KPMG found 100 per cent reporting in the UK; Japan (99 per cent); South Africa (97 per cent); USA (83 per cent); Nigeria (68 per cent); Mexico (66 per cent); Switzerland (64 per cent); Germany (62 per cent); Russia (58 per cent) and Australia (57 per cent). However, it would be difficult to demonstrate whether these levels of (positive) reporting correspond to the same level of good corporate behaviour in the respective countries, or whether comparisons can indeed meaningfully be established within these high levels of reporting. These and other issues were not part of the remit of this survey.

An ongoing study by the Sustainability Research Institute (SRI) at Leeds University (UK) and the Euromed Management School (France) is currently analysing 4,000 CSR reports, rankings and surveys published by companies all over the world in the past decade. The preliminary findings have highlighted the low quality of the data submitted in many reports, and how certain reports omit from the calculations parts of the information on the company.

The researchers have found that, for example, the energy company ENEL (Italy) reported annual carbon emissions equivalent to four times the emissions of the entire planet; Volkswagen and E.ON failed to report the emissions of a huge coal power plant in Germany as each thought it was the other's reporting responsibility; oil and tobacco companies do not assume that the impact of their products in the environment and on public health is their responsibility to report (allowing them to claim impeccable CSR credentials); Ford reported more mineral waste in North America than worldwide (i.e. including North America); British Telecom (BT), several times reporting award winner, stated that 99.8 per cent of its international waste is produced by just a handful of office workers in Belgium, while employees of its SE Asian and Australian operations travelled only by air and consumed no water! The publication of these data also calls into question the value of external assurance consultancy and certification services. Furthermore, there is no clear evidence of the contribution of CSR reporting towards the integration of CSR issues into organisational strategy, that is, beyond concerns for legal responsibilities and liabilities.

In this context, the difficult decisions and dilemmas faced by managers when considering the production of CSR reports cannot be underestimated. Issues include, for example, what data to report; how to report the data; and what type of external assurance, if any, would be advisable. There could also be enormous costs and consultancy fees associated with the production and updating of these reports. Furthermore, the reports must satisfy the expectations of a very diverse audience, and face close examination by NGOs, pressure groups and the media. In this sense, an organisation could find that the information provided is extracted from within very different cultural and political contexts worldwide, producing unexpected and sometimes contradictory responses. In this sense, what starts as a very interesting and safe initiative to promote the company's CSR credentials could become a PR and marketing disaster, or the basis for a shares and/or a product boycott. As Cohen (1963) pointed out when referring to the printed media, these CSR reports cannot tell people what to think, yet the information provided may be very successful in telling readers what to think about, and what to check in the future.

Activity 9.6	CSR Reporting

Find the CSR reports (or CSR webpages) of two of your favourite companies, and of their main competitor. Contrast their CSR policies and other CSR credentials. What do these reports say to you as: (1) a current and prospective shareholder; (2) an employee; (3) a graduate in search for a job; (4) a consumer; (5) a pressure group or an NGO. Discuss.

The future of CSR

The challenges and difficulties discussed in the previous sections do not justify turning a blind eye to the exploitation of small farmers in far-away countries, nor to the exploitation of workers (including women, children, and those belonging to minority groups), as recent sweatshop scandals have demonstrated. Companies such as Nestlé, Nike and Gap have learned the hard way that in their legitimate search for cheaper sites, suppliers and profits, their social responsibilities extend not only to their own factories overseas, but also to the practices of their suppliers and distributors. Commercial secrecy is no longer an option; companies are 'encouraged' by shareholders and activists to disclose the lists of their suppliers, and to report their CSR policies and practices regularly. Finally, companies also need to make sure their reports are not considered a cynical attempt to greenwash their image. For example, Apple's recently released list of suppliers included Foxxconn, a production facility in China with 230,000 employees, most of whom live in site barracks, work long shifts, and earn less than $17 a day. Foxxconn has a very high rate of worker suicide and claims of unpaid overtime (*The Economist*, 23 January 2012). The fact that Foxxconn also produces for Amazon, Dell, IBM, Hewlett-Packard, Motorola, Nintendo, Nokia, Samsung, Sony and others has not made a large difference to Apple, as different companies face different levels of scrutiny and expectation by shareholders, the media, consumers and other stakeholders. An investigative report on Foxxconn published in *The New York Times* (25 January 2012) titled 'In China, Human Costs Are Built into an iPad', illustrates this final point.

Regardless of whether CSR is a 'force for good', a management fad, or a marketing gimmick, and even though most experts agree that 'unfortunately, there is no evidence that behaving more virtuously makes firms more profitable' (Vogel, 2005), having a CSR strategy has become a central part of the managing of modern organisations. As discussed in the context of ethical consumerism, companies and individuals do not always have a consistent attitude towards their favourite companies and products.

The rhetorical commitment to CSR has its contradictions. Western consumers see no contradiction in their insatiable appetite for the 4x4 cars and SUVs used to bring their Fairtrade and other environmentally friendly products home; they also demand their standard of consumption to be protected by their governments while assuming that (undefined) others must make the behavioural changes required. Companies behave differently in different countries, depending on their social policies and on how badly local governments need their investment in infrastructure and in jobs. The role of the media in highlighting corporate corruption, social exploitation and environmental degradation is also compromised by its dependence on multinational advertising for it to stay in business. The role of international institutions and governments in transforming voluntary codes of conduct, such as the UN's Global Compact, into enforceable and verifiable laws is still in its infancy in many areas – including business-led initiatives such as the Dow Jones Sustainability Indexes (US) and the FTSE4Good (UK). This plethora of initiatives, certifications, NGOs, and voluntary regulations and monitoring systems has made progress more piecemeal and confusing.

Furthermore, Doane (2005) argues against the widespread perception that companies can 'do well' and 'do good' at the same time, highlighting what she calls the four myths of CSR:

■ the market can deliver both short-term financial returns and long-term social benefits;

■ the ethical consumer will drive change;

■ there will be a competitive 'race to the top' over ethics among businesses; and

■ that in the global economy, countries will compete to have the best ethical practices.

In this context, she argues for the implementation of other strategies, such as direct (mandatory) regulation of corporate behaviour and changes in the legal structure of the corporation to deliver ethically responsible corporations, rather than relying on these four CSR mantras. Furthermore, she highlights the efforts of the Corporate Responsibility Coalition (CORE) to promote innovative legislation in the UK, and of the Corporation 20/20 to enshrine CSR within the foundations of new and existing corporations in the US. In this sense, Vogel (2005) also concludes that:

> Precisely because CSR is voluntary and market-driven, companies will engage in CSR only to the extent that it makes business sense for them to do so. Civil regulation has proven capable of forcing *some* companies to internalize *some* of the negative externalities associated with *some* of their economic activities. But CSR can reduce only some market failures. It often cannot effectively address the opportunistic behaviors such as free riding that can undermine the effectiveness of private or self-regulation. Unlike government regulation, it cannot force companies to make unprofitable but socially beneficial decisions.

(Vogel, 2005: 4)

Despite the impact of CSR at a global level – or lack of it – it is possible to find countless examples of genuine best practice regarding the design and implementation of CSR policies. As the twenty-first century advances, great improvements in product design and recycling; the banning of harmful substances and pollutants; an interest in ethical sourcing; and the increasing provision of jobs with better working conditions in third-world factories give hope for the future.

There is also an interest in stressing the importance of CSR in business schools. It comes after an examination of the curricula vitae of many disgraced executives and politicians involved in the current financial and political crisis revealed that they held MBA degrees from the most prestigious universities in the US, the UK and Europe. The inclusion of business ethics modules in the core syllabus of business programmes, and student-led initiatives such as the 'MBA Oath' at prestigious universities, provide evidence at least of awareness of, and intent for, the future.

Summary

In this chapter the following key points have been made:

■ CSR constitutes a *genre* of approaches developed over time rather than a body of knowledge defined *a priori*. Interest in the impact of business in society can be traced back many centuries. Furthermore, different CSR approaches and theoretical frameworks must be related to specific historical and cultural circumstances. In this context, a single definition of CSR will remain elusive.

- The debate between Milton Friedman's shareholder approach and Edward Freeman's stakeholder approach has been central to discussions on CSR since the 1970s. Other related issues have been highlighted such as the possibility of establishing a 'business case' for CSR, as well as a normative justification for the stakeholder approach.

- There is also an important debate currently taking place in terms of whether it makes sense to treat corporations as if they were citizens. In this context, it is worth examining the role of corporate political donations and corporate lobbying in modern society.

- Other topics that have become relevant include the development of fair trade; the use of CSR as a marketing tool to green-wash corporations; the emergence of the 'ethical consumer' and the role of boycotts; the production of CSR reports; and finally, the relationship between CSR, diversity and equality.

Typical assignments

1. When, and why, did corporate social responsibility (CSR) become an important issue for organisations?

2. If corporations are corporate citizens to what extent should their rights and duties as citizens match those of individual citizens?

3. To what degree is it right and practical for the expectations of stakeholders to be taken into account by boards of directors?

4. How fair is 'Fairtrade'?

5. Of what value, and to whom, is most of the CSR that emerges from multinational corporations?

Recommended further reading

Crane, A., McWilliams, A., Matten, D., Moon, J., Siegel, D.S., (eds) *The Oxford Handbook of Corporate Social Responsibility*, OUP is a good starting point for your reading on this topic. Donaldson, T. and Dunfee, T. W. (1999) *Ties That Bind: A Social Contracts Approach to Business Ethics*, Harvard Business School Press is a seminal book. Other books worth looking at are:

Andriof, J. and McIntosh, M. (eds) *Perspectives on Corporate Citizenship*, Sheffield: Greenleaf Publishing.
Crane, A., Matten, D. and Spence, L. J. (2008) *Corporate Social Responsibility, Readings and Cases in a Global Context*, London: Routledge.
Benn, S., and Bolton, D. (2011) *Key Concepts in Corporate Social Responsibility*, UK: Sage.
SustainAbility (2005) *The Changing landscape of Liability: A Director's Guide to Trends in Corporate, Environmental, Social and Economic Liability*, London.

Useful websites

Topic	Website provider	URL
Business Roundtable Institute for Corporate Ethics	Institute for Corporate Ethics	http://www.corporate-ethics.org
Corporate Responsibility: the corporate responsibility coalition	CORE Coalition	http://corporate-responsibility.org/
Danish Government CSR	Danish Government	http://www.csrgov.dk/
Fairtrade	Fairtrade Foundation	http://www.fairtrade.org.uk/
Green-washing	Greenpeace	http://stopgreenwash.org/
Consumerism	Norwegian Consumer Ombudsman	http://www.forbrukerombudet.no/id/490
Rainforest depletion	Rainforest Alliance	http://www.rainforest-alliance.org/
Sustainability Research Institute	Leeds University	http://www.see.leeds.ac.uk/research/sri
The Sustainability standard	SustainAbility	http://www.sustainability.com/
Diversity and equality	The Chartered Institute for Personnel and Development	www.cipd.co.uk
Carbon emissions	UK Department for Business Innovation and Skills (BIS)	http://www.bis.gov.uk/policies/business-sectors/low-carbon-business-opportunities/sustainable-development/corporate-responsibility
Human Rights	UK Equality and Human Rights Commission	http://www.equalityhumanrights.com/
UN Global Compact	The United Nations	http://www.unglobalcompact.org/
The MBA oath	Class of 2009 MBA Graduates of Harvard Business School	http://mbaoath.org/

CHAPTER 10

Sustainability

Chapter at a glance

Chapter contents

- Learning outcomes
- Introduction
- Sustainability discourses and drivers
- Carbon market mechanisms
- Sustainable development (SD)
- The instrumental use of nature
- The future of sustainability
- Summary

Case studies

- Case study 10.1 Herbal remedy from the Amazon rain forest

Activities and exercises

- Group Activity 10.1
- Typical assignments
- Recommended further reading
- Useful websites

Learning outcomes

Having read this chapter and completed its associated activities, readers should be able to:

- Discuss the importance of sustainability as a concept in relation to certain discourses and practices.

- Critically evaluate the possibility of sustainability in the current capitalist (consumerist) economy.

- Critically assess the relationship between Corporate Social Responsibility and Sustainability.

- Discuss the relationship between institutions (such as the UN), corporations, governments and individuals, regarding sustainability issues.

- Participate in debates concerning various initiatives regarding sustainability.

- Debate the 'enframing of technology' mindset that represents one of the major obstacles to moving towards more sustainable activities, practices and processes.

Introduction

This chapter explores what constitutes another *genre* of approaches aimed at describing and addressing the concept of sustainability, a concept closely linked to that of CSR as discussed in the previous chapter. In fact, sustainability and CSR are terms often used interchangeably by governments and NGOs, companies, and management consultants. As in the case of other management concepts, fashion has also dictated which wording is *en vogue*, as political parties develop their new campaign slogans, companies co-opt the language used by their critics in concerns over their image and share price, and consultants try to reinvigorate their businesses. Some practitioners would argue that sustainability already includes CSR; others state the opposite. Furthermore, as discussed in the previous chapter, Freeman and Velamuri (2005) recently argued for the new overarching concept of Corporate *Stakeholder* Responsibility to be used instead, while Porter and Kramer (2011) proposed the notion of 'shared value'.

We could suggest, as a starting point, and from the stakeholder perspective presented in the previous chapter, that the concept of sustainability lays emphasis on the relationship between, on the one hand, consumers and organisations, and on the other, contemporary conceptions of 'nature'. However, other discourses related to sustainability that feature prominently include: population growth; consumerism; recycling and waste; the role of the media; climate change; carbon markets; the promise and failure of Third World development, and the rights of non-industrial indigenous populations; environmentalism; sustainable development (SD); and the questioning of the 'neutrality' and 'benignity' of science and technology.

More recently, debates related to issues within the biotechnology and biodiversity industries, such as genetically modified (GM) foods, food additives, endocrine disruptors, and the attempts to patent genes and other biological materials found in the Third World by western multinationals, have been of great concern. Furthermore, the 'free trade agreements' and other international treaties signed between developed and developing countries, frequently used to support those patenting attempts as extensions to interpretations of copyright and intellectual property, have also been in the spotlight.

| Case study 10.1 | Herbal remedy from the Amazon rain forest |

A medical anthropologist at Cambridge University brought to the UK a plant she had been offered by an indigenous tribe to cure a toothache from which she suffered while she was conducting her PhD research in Peru, more than 20 years ago.

This plant is now the main ingredient for a new and potent anaesthetic to be used in routine dental treatment. As the new product can be used as a gel, it could supersede the need to use needles to deliver anaesthetics.

The new product has been developed and will be sold worldwide by a pharmaceutical company mostly owned by the University of Cambridge. A 'model' was developed to give the community that had discovered the medicinal use of this plant some royalties. Details of the royalties 'model' are not known. Although 'education and conservation projects' were mentioned to the BBC, we could nevertheless use this real life example to reflect some related topics. Please revisit 'the U'wa and oil exploration' case study presented in the previous chapter:

- Who should be the main beneficiary of the profits from the selling of the new product? Should a patent be created? If so, what is to be patented, the plant ingredient, the gel? Who should be the owner of the patent?

- Why is it important to consider who designed the 'royalties model', and how it will be administered and managed in the future?

- Who decides how the royalties will be used?

- Has the researcher profited from the free care given by the tribe when she was in pain? Would this be ethical?

- Is it ethical for students and professional researchers to travel to developing countries to extract knowledge developed by indigenous tribes, then profit from this knowledge?

- How should the relationship between pharmaceuticals and indigenous populations be regulated? By whom? What criteria should a 'good practice' framework contain?

- Is knowledge treated and protected differently when produced by a company/university in a developed country than when an indigenous tribe produces it? Is this ethical?

- Is this a new form of colonialism and exploitation?

More information: http://news.bbc.co.uk/today/hi/today/newsid_9705000/9705853.stm

From this complex and evolving list of discourses and 'world issues', it may be appreciated why it would be impossible to develop a single definition of 'sustainability'. Some of these topics remain highly contentious in terms of world politics and economic interests, and even in terms of the scientific proof; examples include rising world temperatures, GM foods, and methane emissions. Several authors, such as Gladwin et al. (1995), have attempted to classify and analyse several versions. However, it is the definitions from the UN summits that have become the most widely cited, especially in the context of 'sustainable development', as will be discussed at the end of the chapter.

Finally, as our appreciation of 'nature' and the impact of human activity are framed within specific cultural, ethical, economic, and political contexts, it can be expected that the very notion of sustainability (i.e. what needs to be sustained; what is worth sustaining; and who decides) will be interpreted differently in different regions of the world.

In the years preceding the economic crisis that started in 2007, the issue of climate change and carbon emissions became the main subject of attention in the developed world, boosted by the western media, the film industry, politicians and NGOs – including the UN. The vast amounts of resources invested by western governments and multinationals in shaping the UN's agenda and in promoting their own sustainability credentials, and the subsequent creation of a multibillion-dollar trade mechanism in carbon emissions, will ensure that climate change and carbon emissions will remain centre stage in the years to come.

In the following section examples of the most salient 'sustainability discourses and drivers' will be explored. Please note that some of these are closely related to topics discussed in the previous chapter.

Sustainability discourses and drivers

The perception of danger

Serious concerns about the effects of industrialisation, urban living and the environment have long been expressed. Examples include the cholera epidemics in London linked to drinking water contaminated with human sewage in the 1850s, and the effects of the widespread use of coal as fuel, which culminated in the severe smog episodes that affected St Louis (US) in 1939, Donora (US) in 1948, London in 1952 and New York in 1953. These events were linked to thousands of premature deaths and serious illnesses. The power of science in explaining the causes of these problems, the contribution of industry in providing new products (e.g. 'cleaner' varieties of coal), and of engineering by improving civil works, were perceived as the undisputed tools necessary to achieving development and health.

More recently, the chemical and pharmaceutical industries, together with decisive international action led by the UN and the World Health Organization (WHO), were also seen as a powerful combination to address certain world problems. Examples include the fight against smallpox that began in 1958, which culminated in its eradication in 1979; the development and widespread use of high-yielding varieties of cereals and grains that, with the use of pesticides and improved irrigation techniques, have since the 1940s saved millions from starvation in the Third World – an initiative called the Green Revolution. Finally, the promise of unlimited clean energy provided by nuclear fusion, and the development of the consumer society, gave the impression to individuals in developed countries that a new era of prosperity and wealth was within reach. As a consequence, the model of development heralded by the industrialised nations of the West was perceived as a template for Third World countries to follow. Science and technology would allow humans to 'master' and to 'control' nature, in order to exploit its almost infinite resources. In this context, the UN reported in 1951 that

> [P]rogress occurs where people believe that man can, by conscious effort, master nature. This is a lesson which the human mind has been a long time learning.
>
> (UN, 1951:13)

However, events such as the publication of Rachel Carson's *Silent Spring* in 1962 highlighting the negative effects of the indiscriminate use of pesticides on the environment; the powerful images broadcast by the media of the devastation caused by the use of chemical weapons during the Vietnam War, including the photographs of the conflict taken by Nick Ut; the threat of nuclear war; the youth and social movements in the US and in Europe; and the creation of Greenpeace in 1971, contributed to challenges to the supremacy of the chemical and nuclear industries. These factors highlighted the dangers potentially posed by science, technology and industry when left both unchecked and at the mercy of political and economic interests. A new era of 'environmentalism' was beginning, questioning the image of humans as the 'masters' of nature.

Events such as the Three Mile Island nuclear disaster in the US in 1979, the Bhopal gas tragedy in India that killed thousands in 1984, the Chernobyl nuclear disaster in 1986, and countless oil spillages that have damaged otherwise pristine natural areas all over the world – including the recent BP oil spill in the Gulf of Mexico – have reinforced this perception of danger. However, whether environmentalism represents a real rupture with previous conceptions of the 'man-nature' relationship, or merely provides a new re-interpretation of western anxieties and culture, a view to be 'packaged and sold' to the rest of the world, is still the subject of heated debate (Argyrou, 2005). Furthermore, the issue of how we view nature, and how we view ourselves with respect to nature, will later be explored in relation to the concept of phenomenology.

Systems thinking

Systems thinking has played a very important role in the initial attempts to understand the interconnectedness found between the natural and social worlds, and in challenging the view that humans were intrinsically superior to other biological entities and were thus the 'masters' of nature. Paradoxically, systems thinking came to prominence during the Second World War, playing an important role in the development of the post-war chemical and nuclear industries and economies. However, it was the biologists L. von Bertalanffy, H. Maturana, F. Varela and the philosopher C. West Churchman who used concepts such as 'feedback', 'self-regulation' and 'emerging properties' in understanding the complexity of social systems. Their ideas allowed new generations of social and natural scientists to frame the relationship between humans and the natural world as being based on 'co-dependency' and 'co-evolution' rather than on a narrow understanding of the Darwinian concepts of 'competition' and the 'survival of the fittest'.

The publication of Ray Bradbury's short story *A Sound of Thunder* in 1952; the work of the meteorologist Edward Lorenz, who coined the term 'The Butterfly Effect' in the early 1960s; Fritjof Capra's books *The Turning Point* (1982) – film adaptation: *MindWalk* – and *The Web of Life* (1997), helped to popularise systemic thinking. These views have also informed ethical debates on the exploitation of natural resources, biodiversity and the possibility of animal rights, and have contributed to the exploration of ethical frameworks found in Asian, African, Latin American and ancient cultures. The notion of 'systems thinking' will be revisited later on, in the context of consumerism.

Population growth and poverty

The exponential growth of the world's population constitutes another sustainability driver that is worth exploring. The UN has estimated that it took about 127 years for the world population to increase from one billion to the two billion inhabitants present in 1927. However, it took the world only another 32 years to reach three billion inhabitants in 1959, 15 years to reach four billion in 1974, and 12 years to reach six billion in 1999. The seven-billionth inhabitant was born 11 years later in 2011. Although birth rates are declining overall thanks to government policy and the availability of contraceptives, it is still estimated that the world population will reach eight billion by 2025.

Beyond this date, the UN has offered different world population projections for the year 2100. The lower estimate, if birth rates continue to decline, will account for a decrease in world population to a total of six billion; the medium prediction accounts for ten billion, and the higher prediction provides the possibility of 16 billion inhabitants.

Regardless of which projection becomes a reality, the new inhabitants will face a dire situation as the majority will be born in poor countries, already struggling to provide the basic needs to their current populations. For example, although the current populations of Germany and Ethiopia are very similar at 81–82 million, the population of Germany is estimated to decrease to 75 million by 2040, while the population of Ethiopia could increase to 145 million in the same period. Currently, there are three billion people in the world with incomes below $2.50 a day; one billion with no access to clean water; and 1.2 billion suffering from chronic hunger. In China, and thanks to the deeply controversial 'one child policy' that drove fertility rates down to 1.7, the total population will start dropping by the year 2030 – the fertility rate for a stable population is estimated at 2.1

The opposite will be the case in India, even though fertility rates have dropped dramatically, due in part to the now infamous 'sterilisation programme' of the 1970s, with India becoming the most densely populated country before the year 2030 with a current fertility rate of about 2.8.

The number of new arrivals, and the respective locations of those births, are not the only issues of concern: an ageing population will pose new challenges to already stretched pension and health systems, as fewer economically active individuals will bear the burden of contributing to the care of the elderly, of those in need, and of the very young.

The cultural and political issues surrounding population growth are very important to consider. The availability of contraceptives and sex education, which remain the most effective ways to reduce population growth, is most controversial in certain religious systems and cultures. The need for condoms to reduce sexually transmitted diseases within the economically active, who support children, the elderly and local economies, has also been questioned in certain countries as constituting western imperialism. Finally, the impact of birth control and of 'gender selective' abortion procedures, as performed mainly on women in cultures that still prefer the birth of male offspring, need to be examined with insights from feminism and critical development approaches.

DEFINITION

Eco-feminism assumes that there is a connection between processes of subjugation, exploitation and the destruction of nature, and similar processes targeting women all over the world. The concept can also be extended to other areas such as racism, ageism and heterosexism. These processes can occur with the participation of those affected (who have internalised their 'given role' in society) and/or through psychological, religious, economic and physical violence. Eco-feminism is not a movement against men, as men are also subjected to and could become victims of the same processes, while some women could also personally benefit. Instead, it challenges the common assumptions and beliefs that promote these destructive and oppressive practices, such as patriarchy; hierarchy; competition for domination; religious dogma; discrimination; exploitation; suppression of emotion and empathy; unacceptable levels of risk; and war. Some of these assumptions also lie at the core of certain management structures and practices.

The currently impossible task of providing people from poor countries with the same standard of living enjoyed by those born in developed countries has other and serious ethical implications. We need to consider, for example, that the living standards enjoyed in developed nations (and wealthy élites elsewhere) are heavily supported by raw materials imported from poor countries, and by the cheap labour they provide to manufacture the products we buy, use and discard every single day. The ethical behaviour of companies that outsource manufacturing and other low-paid, low-skilled jobs to poor countries cannot be ignored either, as discussed in the previous chapter.

Finally, the lack of food, clean water, or education; civil unrest and war; and the effects of the desperate migration to wealthier countries (or regions) that will certainly follow, will create new challenges that will affect us all. A recent study by the UN reported that people living in North America, Europe, and high-income Asia-Pacific countries collectively hold almost 90 per cent of total world wealth (UNU-WIDER, 2006).

However, the image of 'developed vs. developing' countries masks increasing differences in education, wealth, health, and life expectancy found within most countries. In the UK, for example, according to a report on 'fuel poverty' commissioned in 2011 by the Tory-Liberal Democrat coalition government,

7.8 million people could not afford their energy bills in 2009, a number projected to rise to 8.5 million by 2016 . . . fuel poverty exacerbates other hardship faced by those on low incomes, has serious health effects (including contributing to extra deaths every winter), and acts as a block to efforts to cut carbon emissions.

(Hills, 2012)

The Office for National Statistics recorded in October 2011 that life expectancy was highest in Kensington and Chelsea (London) and lowest in Glasgow City; the gap at birth has in the previous seven years increased from 12.5 to 13.5 years for males, and from 10.1 to 11.8 years for females. Unemployment has risen to almost three million in 2012 (over 8.4 per cent of the total population) with a disproportionate effect on the young. Hirsch and Beckhelling (2011) also reported that 3.5 million children lived in poverty in 2011. Finally, statistics in many countries in the Euro region (Greece; Italy; Spain; Portugal) have been dramatically worse than in the UK since the current recession started. A brief analysis of the levels of poverty, health unemployment, and the distribution of wealth in the USA are also alarming. The situation for the millions who have immigrated into developed countries (especially refugees; non-legal residents; and those who are victims of human trafficking) is also a reason for serious concern as the recession takes away low-paid, low-skilled jobs.

In the Third World, the situation is also complex. A country such as Brazil, whose economy is larger than that of the UK, still endures levels of poverty and destitution similar to those found at the beginning of the last century; a similar situation is found in Venezuela (a country with the second-largest oil reserves in the world) after almost two decades of socialist government, and in the rest of Latin America.

In most developing countries, certain groups enjoy a standard of living and consumption far superior to that of the average European or North American. These élites either control or disproportionately benefit from their countries' natural resources while most of their populations struggle to earn a wage that keeps them just above misery levels. The situation is similar in Africa and in emerging countries such as China, South Africa and Russia. The élites also consume luxury exports from developed countries contributing to their Gross Domestic Product (GDP). Furthermore, universities and other higher education systems in developed countries derive an increasingly larger percentage of their income from the tuition fees paid by wealthy students travelling from those developing countries.

Consumerism

Consumerism, and its related term *affluenza*, has been widely discussed in the context of sustainability. It is broadly applied to the compulsive acquisition of products and services not needed to satisfy basic human needs, and to the disposal of still functioning products to acquire new ones that offer the same or a very similar function. These behaviours are supported by an addiction to economic growth; the availability of cheaper products; marketing; and credit. In this sense, the term 'conspicuous consumption' was firstly used by the economist Thorstein Veblen in his 1899 book *The Theory of the Leisure Class*, referring to the behaviours and attitudes to wealth of the *nouveau riche*. Thus, products are bought, for example, to satisfy hedonistic values such as fantasies and fun (Holbrook and Hirschman, 1982); status and wealth display; as a proof of success; and as a transfer mechanism to compensate for a variety of mild and serious psychological disorders.

Other areas of exploration regarding consumerism include: the relationship between consumerism and identity, as explored by Williamson (1978), who states that 'the conscious chosen meaning in most people's lives comes from what they consume'; the relationship between advertising and desire/satisfaction as highlighted by Taylor and Saarinen (1994), who argued that 'desire does not desire satisfaction. To the contrary desire desires desire. The reason images are so desirable is that they never satisfy'; and, finally, the understanding of the consumer as an active agent in the construction of meaning (Elliott, 1997).

However, consumerism has also been promoted as an important element in the development of western capitalist societies. For example, Paul M. Mazur, an investment banker and partner at the now bankrupt Lehman Brothers, introduced the concept of 'obsolescence' to the Advertising Club of New York in 1928 as 'wear alone' was too slow for the needs of the American industry:

> [I]f what had filled the consumer market yesterday could only be made obsolete today, that whole market would be again available tomorrow.
>
> (Slade, 2007:60)

In the same year, Justus George, then editor, introduced the concept of 'progressive obsolescence' in the Trade Journal *Advertising and Selling*:

> [W]e must introduce people to buy a greater variety of goods on the same principle that they now buy automobiles, radios, clothes, namely: buying goods not to wear out, but to trade in or discard after a short time . . . buying for up-to-dateness, efficiency, and style, buying for the sense of modernness rather than simply for the last ounce of use.
>
> (Slade, 2007:58)

During the recession that followed, even 'planned obsolescence' dictated by government was suggested as a way to reactivate the economy (London, 1932) as

> People everywhere are today disobeying the law of obsolescence. They are using their old cars, their old tyres, their old radios and their old clothing much longer than statisticians had expected on the basis of earlier experience . . . Wouldn't it be profitable to spend a sum of - say - two billion dollars to buy up, immediately, obsolete and useless buildings, machinery, automobiles and other outworn junk, and in their place create from twenty to thirty billion dollars' worth of work in the construction field and in the factory? Such a process would put the entire country on the road to recovery and eventually would restore normal employment and business prosperity.
>
> (London, 1932)

Finally, Brooks Stevens, founding member of the Industrial Designers Society of America, described in the 1950s the concept of 'psychological obsolescence' as

[I]nstilling in the buyer the desire to own something a little newer, a little better, a little sooner than is necessary.

(Slade, 2007: 153)

These concepts, and especially the idea of government intervention, were recently implemented when the current recession began in 2007. Governments in countries such as Germany, Spain, France, Italy and the UK offered 'car scrap schemes', which involved financial incentives to encourage people to buy new cars to help the car manufacturing industry. However, the scheme was abandoned in the UK as it became clear that overall car sales had not increased: rather, that people used the scheme to make already planned purchases cheaper. An alternative scheme attempted in the Isle of Wight (UK) by the bus company Southern Vectis in 2009 offered residents the opportunity to scrap their old cars for a £720 bus pass, encouraging people to use public transport.

More recently, 'consumer confidence', an economic indicator that translates into spending habits, individuals' feelings about the state of the economy in general and their own financial situations, became a topic central to government policy. The idea that consumers would 'spend our way out of the recession' has been heralded as the answer to the current crisis, regardless of alarming levels of personal debt in the developed world. For instance, personal debt in the UK was estimated at £1.5tn in 2009, equivalent to each person owing over £25,000. Excluding mortgages and insecure loans, in 2011 the average household owed nearly £9,000 (Citizens Advice Bureau). Furthermore, according to the UK's Office of Budget Responsibility, UK personal debt will grow by nearly 50 per cent before 2015, when it is forecast to reach £2.12tn. In certain Euro-zone countries and in the US the situation is even more worrying still. Nevertheless, governments all over the world look desperately to the latest retail reports in search of an increase in retail activity demonstrating that 'consumer confidence' has returned.

When a draft of a speech by David Cameron in 2011 advising people in the UK to get their finances in order by paying off their credit and store cards circulated, the comment was criticised by retailers and economists. The British Retail Consortium warned that urging people to 'retrench' was 'at odds with promoting growth', and the Institute for Public Policy Research stated that if consumers took the PM at his word, the UK economy would be 'in real trouble', shrinking significantly over the years to come (*The Telegraph*, 2011). The speech was later modified.

According to Cooper (2010), this emphasis on obsolescence and consumption in order to sustain increasing levels of economic growth follows a linear economic model

[W]hich assumes at the outset of any production process that the Earth has an unlimited supply of raw materials and energy and, at the end, an infinite capacity to absorb pollution and waste.

(Cooper, 2010:12)

Recent initiatives to improve the manufacturing of products and the use of natural resources will not have a long-term impact if consumption continues to increase. Furthermore, new product features could even cancel any 'environmental savings' from previous versions of the same product; that is to say, 'green shopping', 'green consumerism' and 'sustainable consumerism' still constitute shopping and consumerism. However, our economic system is so dependent on consumerism that a sudden slowdown of production processes could cause high levels of unemployment and other social problems.

In this context, Cooper (2010) advocates instead a circular 'systems thinking' economic model, which

> [R]equires that the throughput of materials and energy be minimized by optimising product longevity, reusing or reconditioning products and their components, and recycling – alongside other measures such as energy efficiency.
>
> (Cooper 2010: 12)

It would be combined with the concept of 'slow consumption' (Cooper, 2005; 2010). This approach is supported by increasing 'product life-span', which involves improving production processes, creating skilled jobs in repair and maintenance work, consumer satisfaction, and second-hand markets. In sum, Cooper believes that the combination of 'longer life-spans' and 'slow consumption' (within a 'systems thinking' economic model) would provide an antidote to the notion of 'obsolescence' and would allow the economy to absorb lower levels of production.

Fashion students at New York University (US) started a project called 'Sloth' in 2012 following this 'slow consumption' idea. This could be an interesting experiment, as Joergens (2006) found, on the other hand,

> [L]ittle evidence that ethical issues have any effect on consumers' fashion purchase behaviour. When it comes to fashion purchase, the majority of consumers are more interested in their own personal fashion needs than the needs of others involved in the apparel supply chain.
>
> (Joergens, 2006: 369)

These contrasting statements, introduce the exploration of the possible reasons why consumers in the developed world continue to consume at increasing levels.

One possible approach is that people are unaware and need to be educated. Following this belief countless initiatives to inform and educate individuals have been incorporated into schools, universities, development agencies, governments, the media and NGOs; these include, for example, handbooks of sustainability literacy (Stibbe, 2011; Benn and Bolton, 2011); sustainability games (Truscheit and Otte, 2004), and sustainability books for managers (Barrow, 2006; Epstein, 2008; Weybrecht, 2011).

In this context, even though many people recognise the significance of the 'environmental crisis', relatively few individuals do anything 'significant' about this recognition in their personal lives. Grove-White (2005), for example, blames an emphasis on scientific facts and 'scientism' that has failed to engage people at an emotional level. Argyrou (2005), on the other hand, suggests that facts become visible, relevant and meaningful under certain cultural conditions:

It is the wider historical and cultural context we must sketch if we are not to remain hopelessly caught up in it, innocently attached – which is not to say innocuously – to the untenable positions, whether environmentalist or counter-environmentalist.

(Argyrou, 2005: 39)

Another possibility for increased consumerism in the developed world comes from the mixed messages sent by government and the media, and produced in the workplace. Since the current recession began, governments routinely ask people to increase consuming (shopping) as a contribution to keeping the economy moving. The positive impact on the environment of household and office recycling, as well as buying new and 'more energy efficient appliances', has, although significant, nevertheless been exaggerated.

Companies distance themselves from the true costs of their emissions by outsourcing production and carbon-trading schemes; they also introduce a 'green logo' and add a few well-chosen words to advertising and packaging; finally, companies commission a 'sustainability report' from a consultancy company in order to reassure employees and customers that they have become 'carbon neutral' almost overnight, as they try to keep up with similar claims from competitors – as discussed in the previous chapter in the context of 'green-washing'.

Finally, over-optimistic targets agreed at UN summits, such as the Kyoto protocol and the Millennium Goals, encourage governments and companies to 'find ways' to show they have complied with them, and/or contribute to the general feeling that nothing can be done, while the unrealistic (although desirable) targets are nevertheless not met.

This cocktail of claims and counter-claims, statistics, bad news, business practices and 'guilt messages' makes individuals feel powerless, switch off from environmental messages and, in extreme cases, completely disengage from consumerism, then join radical environmental groups to take direct action.

Recycling and waste

The idea of recycling has also been presented as part of the solution to issues such as the overexploitation of natural resources, consumerism, pollution and waste. However, the practicalities of recycling and waste disposal remain controversial on several grounds.

For example, recycling could boost consumption if individuals *wrongly* believed that recycling offsets the use of all of the resources involved in the production, transport and distribution of products. The cost of recycling may be very high as it involves the collection, transport, separation/sorting, distribution and re-use of these materials. Furthermore, the number and the location of recycling facilities in Europe are insufficient and inadequate. Many city councils use recycling processes that mainly involve shipping waste to a foreign country for processing and/or dumping in landfill sites. In March 2012, the Indonesian government asked the UK to take back 1,800 tonnes of suspected contaminated waste labelled as 'scrap metal' (BBC News Online, 2012). Furthermore, although electronics need to be recycled in the EU, Greenpeace and the BBC have tracked unbroken electronic equipment to

Ghana and Nigeria (BBC-*Panorama*, 2011); even the EU admitted in 2012 that at the moment only one-third of electronic waste (e-waste) is dealt with appropriately. Finally, recently updated European regulations such as the Waste Electrical and Electronic Equipment (WEEE) Directive will still allow many states until 2021 to reach minimum, not maximum, targets. The situation in one of the largest e-waste landfill sites in the world located in Guiyu, China, shows a new trend: half of the e-waste currently being processed in China is generated in China (Moskvitch, 2012). This trend is likely to continue as EU and US regulations regarding e-waste improve.

The introduction of digital and high definition television in Europe and in the US boosted the replacement of many millions of the previous yet functioning cathode ray tube (CRT) sets for LCD and plasma sets in a very short period of time. This example of planned obsolescence was exacerbated by the fact that most homes had more than one CRT TV set. The development of 3-D transmissions and internet television will probably create another wave of replacements. Similar examples occurred with the arrival of DVD, followed by Blue-Ray technology and Digital (DAB) radio – while superior quality FM transmissions continue.

Another area of concern is the number of mobile phones, especially in the developing world. According to the Cisco Visual Networking Index, it is estimated that by the end of 2012 there will be more than seven billion mobile phones active, reaching ten billion by 2016 (Cisco, 2012), excluding the increased number of new and similar devices. Most of these handsets use minerals extracted from areas suffering from slavery and civil war in the Eastern Democratic Republic of the Congo, as highlighted in the Frank P. Poulsen's (2010) documentary *Blood in the Mobile*; the devices will also expose children and other vulnerable individuals to toxic material, who work in rudimentary recycling facilities and landfill sites in the developing world. In this sense,

> All of the discarded components in this growing mountain of e-waste contain high levels of permanent biological toxins (PBTs), ranging from arsenic, antimony, beryllium, and cadmium to lead, nickel, and zinc. When e-waste is burned anywhere in the world, dioxins, furans, and other pollutants are release into the air, with potentially disastrous health consequences around the globe. When e-waste is buried in a land-fill, PBTs eventually seep into the groundwater, poisoning it.

> (Slade, 2007: 261)

Finally, consumers also find it difficult to contribute to recycling when certain products contain a mixture of recyclable and non-recyclable materials, and when some products that may look easily recyclable are in fact not so. The most notorious example of the latter is food cartons made of tetra-pack style packaging, which are far more difficult to recycle than are glass or plastic, and require specific recycling facilities as they contain a combination of plastic, aluminium and paper.

In this context, alternatives such as the 'cradle to cradle' model proposed by McDonough and Braungart (2009) contributes to efforts to find novel ways of designing, producing and recycling products; for example, by replacing more highly polluting raw materials with less damaging alternatives, and by using organic materials that are biodegradable and improve the soil. The fact that in the future most of the waste from developed countries (including e-waste) will be more difficult to export (due to awareness in developing countries of pollution, and increasingly stricter legislation) will, it is hoped, compel every individual to consider alternatives to current patterns of consuming, discharging and recycling.

The role of the media

The mass media (printed and broadcast) represent very important players in framing and presenting sustainability issues to individuals and communities. The power of the editors of newspapers, magazines, and TV channels (as well as of certain marketing and public relations companies) is immense as they decide which issues will be reported, how to frame them in relation to other pieces of news, when to move on to more 'important/pressing' items, and even 'when is a good day to bury bad news'. Most individuals' view of the world is created through their daily interaction with mass media, either with news channels, newspapers or through advertising. The independence and credibility of certain news corporations have been heavily questioned in the UK, leading to the inquiry into the 'culture, practices and ethics of the press' chaired by Lord Justice Leveson in 2012. The Internet has also created a new dimension threatening the supremacy of established media, as highlighted in Andrew Rossi's recent documentary *Page One: Inside the New York Times* (2011). However, the existence of small internet video-clips with unidentified authorship and editing, unverifiable locations or dates, and the sometimes-questionable research and lack of context that accompany them, raise many new ethical issues for the whole of the media and the news industry.

In this complex context, SustainAbility conducted a very interesting mapping exercise as part of a report prepared in partnership with the United Nations Environment Programme (UNEP) and Ketchum, 'in order to make sense of the evolution of the environmental, CSR and SD agendas' (SustainAbility, et al., 2002: 6). The exercise plotted three main waves (*see* Figure 10.1): the initial wave of media interest around the world (called 'Limits') began with the publication of Carson's book in 1962 and peaked in 1969–73; a second wave ('Green') started in 1984 with the Bhopal disaster, and peaked in 1989–91; finally, a third wave ('Globalisation') began in 1999 with the riots at the World Trade Organization's (WTO) meeting in Seattle (the US) - this is still ongoing.

This report is very comprehensive not only as it gathers media activity in Europe, the US, Latin America and Asia, but also as it charts how often issues such as climate change, recycling, urban air quality, globalisation and green politics were mentioned. Finally, the report highlights the importance given in the media in terms of time or column inches to the different UN reports and World Summits, and to recent environmental and social disasters. The report concludes that even though the media are considered among the least trusted and least accountable of modern institutions, they still have a vital role to play in shaping the urgency and relevance of CSR and SD issues given their power, reach, and financial resources.

Even in cases where corporations try to take into account the environmental impact of their decisions, there is a fine balance that needs to be achieved among the corporate response, the interest of pressure groups, public preconceptions of corporate behaviour and the media. The case of the dumping of the Brent Spar oil storage platform in the North Sea by Shell in 1995 highlights the fact that even sound environmental decisions cannot be taken in isolation (Grolin, 1998).

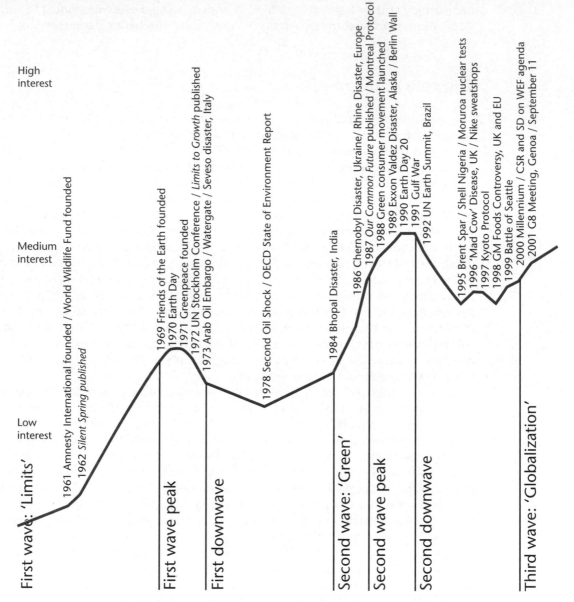

Figure 10.1 Waves and Downwaves (1961–2001).

Source: *Good News & Bad: The Media, Corporate Social Responsibility and Sustainable Development*, The Beacon Press, UK, p. 7. (SustainAbility, Ketchum, United Nations Environment Programme, 2002). Copyright © SustainAbility 2002. http://www.grainesdechangement.com/docs/medias/Good-News-and-Bad.pdf

Climate change

Climate change, including global warming, is perhaps one of the most powerful drivers of sustainability. Although greenhouse gases occur naturally, there is an established link between the increased concentration of greenhouse gases as a result of human activity and a corresponding, although not linear, increase in long-term global temperatures (IPCC, 2007). In this context, *Carbon Dioxide* (CO_2) accounts for about 75 per cent of human activity emissions (burning fossil fuels such as petroleum, coal, wood and natural gas contributes 55 per cent, and deforestation 20 per cent); *Methane* contributes 15 per cent (mainly from agricultural activity), and *Nitrous Oxides* account for most of the remaining 10 per cent – generated by industrial and agricultural activities including nitrogen-based fertilizers. However, it is important to highlight that there are many other gases produced that, although not linked to the greenhouse effect, are also very dangerous to human health and pollute the environment.

Awareness of climate change started in 1971 when Stephen Schneider, then a NASA scientist, published a paper claiming that the cooling effect of dirt, aerosols and other particles in the air could outweigh the warming effect of CO_2. The article made headlines in the *New York Times* and several other media organisations, and the story of a future '*mini ice-age*' began. Schneider revised his findings in 1974 and became instead, until his death in 2010, one of the most important advocates of '*long-term global warming*' – although he always stated that science can only offer probabilities and plausible scenarios rather than provide accurate predictions. This is specially the case when considering, for example, the impossibility of creating a computer model able to include all environmental factors, and the complexity of the judgments and assumptions needed for such a modelling exercise to take place.

However, the Intergovernmental Panel on Climate Change – IPCC (2007) projected that if we continue 'business as usual' the global mean temperature will increase over the next century by 2.8°C, with a three per cent chance of rising 6°C or more, in relation to average temperatures recorded between 1980–99. These estimates do not take into account new emissions generated by other sustainability drivers such as population growth, the possible development of certain areas in the Third World and unexpected natural events, which could release additional greenhouse gases.

Although precise future temperatures can only be estimated, the latest computer models illustrate the devastating effects that even small long-term temperature increases could produce in currently warm and hot countries; on sea levels worldwide; on the spread of disease; on droughts; and on the availability of drinking water. This is especially alarming for the billions who live in coastal areas, and those who are already malnourished or on the brink of famine due to unstable crops. Countless films, such as Davis Guggenheim's documentary *An Inconvenient Truth* (2006), highlight the urgency and seriousness of this issue.

Furthermore, according to the World Wildlife Fund (WWF)'s One Planet Living initiative, we would currently need three planet Earths if everyone enjoyed the same standard of living as the average European, and five planets if living as the average North American – this is also known as the 'ecological footprint'.

Individuals will interpret and respond to these projections and plausible scenarios according to their own psychology and personal ethics. Communities and countries will also devise policies and actions from within their cultural and political frameworks, and in accordance with their economic circumstances. That is to say, global warming is ultimately a cultural, political and an ethical issue.

For example, in the developed world, individuals may find comfort in their daily lives from those who reject the reliability of the data, trust that science will somehow find the answer and 'save the day', or adopt a 'wait and see' attitude. Politicians and political parties (such as the Tea Party in the US) may worry that new legislation curbing emissions could threaten manufacturing- and oil-related jobs in their constituencies and their corporate supporters. The current financial crisis has demonstrated how economies in the developed world are still heavily dependent on car manufacturing jobs and other similar industries for both internal markets and for export all over the world. Presidents and prime ministers rally around the inauguration of the latest car manufacturing facility and offer tax breaks to attract further foreign investment and future jobs. The cost of new energy-efficient technologies (e.g. electric/bio-fuel-based cars) is still beyond the pocket of the average consumer in developed nations. Furthermore, it is important to point out how although cars that run on certain bio-fuels produce less than 10 per cent of several exhaust pollutants, they nevertheless produce 80 per cent of the greenhouse emissions of petrol-consuming vehicles when their impact on land cultivation, electricity production, manufacturing and disposal is included (BBC New Online, 2012d). In this sense, the current growth in car ownership all over the world (mostly petrol-run vehicles) will not compensate for these future reductions. Finally, the impossible costs of building, maintaining and subsidising new mass transport systems in the major cities of the world, as opposed to building new roads for vehicles, must be taken into account – projects of this scale are also vulnerable to wide-spread corruption and bribes in the Third World; they are frequently completed late and over budget, and do not adequately consider future needs.

The aviation needed for business trips, cargo and holidays has recently again attracted attention. Even though new aircraft are becoming more fuel efficient, the astonishing growth of this industry worldwide will dwarf any design improvements. More recently, China, India, Russia, the US and 26 other countries threatened court action and trade sanctions against the EU as a response to a 'carbon tax' on airlines agreed as part of an Emissions Trading Scheme (ETS) intended to start in 2012. They claim that this 'imposition' from Europe will damage their economies and will hurt the profits of their national airlines. Countries dependent on long-haul tourism could be especially affected if the new charges are passed on to passengers (the new charge is based on flight duration and distance), if airlines went bankrupt, or if the price of aviation fuel (currently tax free) were to increase.

Finally, reducing emissions will also be very challenging as, for example, most of the housing stock (which accounts for about 27 per cent of total emissions in the UK) and other infrastructure will still be in use for many decades. Energy improvements can only partially reduce carbon emissions, and will certainly not compensate for the continuing demand for more new housing and infrastructure in developed countries alone. For example, housing emissions in the UK have already increased by five per cent in the period 1997–2011, despite major improvement initiatives such as the Decent Homes Programme, which targeted social housing.

In the developing world, questions have been asked about how the necessary reductions in carbon emissions could be met without compromising their legitimate desire to improve their living conditions. As Argyrou (2005) and Escobar (2011) argue, the Third World has been told for decades that it could 'leap the centuries' from colonial domination to the 'western present' by using science and technology, by agreeing to implement an economic model that promised jobs and the prospect of becoming consumers. Now, these same countries have been asked to 'stop in mid-air' while the West figures out what to do, and is being 'gently asked' to share the blame for climate change. Nothing is said about the polluting technologies and factories that have been exported from developed nations, and the fact that these factories' emissions are linked to the manufacturing of affordable products needed to satisfy western consumerism. At the moment China is allocated most of these products' emissions within a model that emphasises *who produces* as opposed to *who consumes*. In this sense, China accounts for 75 per cent of the developed world's offshore emissions. If imports and exports were taken into account, China would be the second-largest world greenhouse gas emitter after the US (Peters et al., 2011).

Furthermore, although the UK's carbon emissions seemed to have decreased by six per cent in 1990–2004, the truth is that they instead increased by 11 per cent in that period – if emissions from the manufacturing of imports were included (Jackson, 2009). While it has been recognised that emissions continue to rise in the developed world, estimates would be dramatically higher if their consumption were also taken into account.

Meanwhile, cities such as Shanghai and Beijing; Delhi and Mumbai; Mexico City and Bogotá struggle to control the smog generated by the new cars exported by developed nations, and those produced locally with foreign-financed facilities and state subsidies. In India, Tata Motors and Bajaj Auto are currently competing for the country's appetite for the world's cheapest car. Paradoxically, the BBC reported in 2012 that recent census data in India revealed that while nearly half (48 per cent) of India's 1.2 billion people had no toilet at home, 53 per cent owned a mobile phone.

DEFINITION

The **Carbon Footprint** is the total amount of greenhouse emissions (CO_2 and methane) caused by a company, event, process or even a person's daily activities. Although these measurements are not precise, they are intended to encourage individuals and organisations to make changes that cause fewer emissions, such as using public transport instead of driving. Berners-Lee's (2010) *How Bad Are Bananas?* provides a useful guide of the carbon footprint of 'everything'. Other responses, which remain ethically controversial, include off-setting emissions and carbon trading, as described later in this chapter.

Finally, a main challenge to global warming could perhaps come from an unexpected source: methane (CH_4). This gas produced naturally in wetlands and as a by-product of agriculture is also found frozen in the permafrost regions in Siberia, the Arctic and in deep oceanic sediment. Methane has around 25 times the warming potential of CO_2 (UN-EP, 2008). The UN calls methane 'a global warming wildcard'. The danger comes from the fact that in recent years the permafrost (which also stores enormous amounts of carbon) has started to melt due to rising temperatures. In this sense, Bloom et al. (2010) reported that:

> [T]ropical wetlands contribute 52 to 58% of global emissions, with the remainder coming from the extra-tropics, 2% of which is from Arctic latitudes. We estimate a 7% rise in wetland CH_4 emissions over 2003-2007, due to warming of mid-latitude and Arctic wetland regions, which we find is consistent with recent changes in atmospheric CH_4.
>
> (Bloom et al., 2010: 322).

As *Time* reported in March 2010, much research is needed to understand this unprecedented finding. When considering this phenomenon in isolation, the good news, according to the National Snow and Ice Date Centre (US) and the UN-EP (2008), is that we have not, as yet, reached the tipping point for an uncontrollable cycle of permafrost melting and methane release to take place. Paradoxically, the melting of the permafrost and of Arctic ice has also opened the door for new oil drilling and mining in those areas.

In response to climate change, and specifically to greenhouse emissions, the UN called for a world summit in Kyoto (Japan) in 1997 to agree and take action on this urgent problem. The Kyoto protocol – linked to the UN's Framework Convention on Climate Change (UN-FCCC) – sets targets on the reduction of greenhouse gas emissions. It was adopted in December 1997, pending ratification by individual governments; the details for its implementation were agreed in Marrakesh in 2001 and the treaty entered into force in 2005. The core of Kyoto was the commitment to reduce by 2012 the emission of greenhouse gases to a level five per cent lower than those of 1990.

The treaty was designed and agreed by 37 industrialised countries. Other countries later joined, allowing them to participate in the carbon trading market mechanisms, which started in 2005. A total of 191 governments had signed and ratified the agreement by 2011.

Choosing 1990 as a baseline proved controversial, as certain countries had recently reduced their emissions by, for example, replacing coal with natural gas for electricity generation (UK), and by the collapse of old heavy industry in the ex-Soviet countries in the early 1990s (Germany). Perhaps this uneven starting point was a sign of things to come.

The US government did not ratify the signed agreement; Australia did not ratify it until 2008, and Canada abandoned it in 2011 after admitting that its emissions had risen by 30 per cent (*The Guardian*, 2011). Even though the agreement has not produced the expected results, the importance of working towards a world consensus on the link between greenhouse gases and climate change as emissions worldwide continue to rise cannot be underestimated.

After several failed attempts to improve and to enforce the agreement, and as the world awaits the results of the Rio de Janeiro Conference on Sustainable Development in June 2012 (also called 'Rio+20' as it commemorates the 'Earth Summit' held in the city in 1992), Kyoto still represents the best point of reference for governments and NGOs to discuss greenhouse gas emissions and global warming. Perhaps another very important and equally controversial legacy of Kyoto also relevant to business is the creation of the Carbon Market Mechanisms.

Table 10.1   The carbon footprint of everyday activities

Activity	Options	CO_2 – Carbon Footprint
E-mail	**Spam e-mail**	**0.3 g**
	Standard e-mail	4 g
	E-mail with attachment	50 g
	One year of e-mails (per person)	135 kg
Hand drying	**Letting them drip**	**Zero**
	Dyson Airblade	3 g
	One paper towel	10 g
	Standard electric dryer	20 g
Water	**Tap water (500 ml)**	**0.4 g**
	Bottle of local water	110 g
	Bottle water average	160 g
	Bottle travelling 600 miles (road)	215 g
Pint of beer	**Local brewed cask (pub)**	**300 g**
	Bottled (shop), foreign pint (pub)	500 g
	Bottled (shop) heavily transported	900 g
Shower	**3 min – efficient gas boiler**	**90 g**
	6 min – average electric	500 g
	15 min – power shower	1.7 kg
Electricity	**Icelandic grid**	**60 g**
	UK grid	600 g
	US grid	660 g
	Chinese grid	900 g
	Australian grid	1 kg
Driving	**200 miles (average car)**	**135 kg**

Source: Data from Berners-Lee, 2010.

Carbon market mechanisms

The carbon market mechanisms are based on the concept developed by the British economist Arthur C. Pigou, who in 1920 stated that companies should be charged a price equivalent to the cost of the social damage they create – also known as 'negative externalities'. In theory, companies would find it advantageous to restrict the output of the most socially damaging products and activities to a level that would still allow them to make a profit after paying the new charge; they could also work towards developing new products/activities that cause less social damage to avoid completely paying the new charge, making even greater profits. If the charge were to increase over time, giving companies the opportunity to adapt and innovate, it is theoretically possible that these damaging products/activities could be completely abandoned as they would be considered unprofitable. In relation to carbon emissions the IMF explained:

> The classic prescription for externality problems – facing polluters with a price for their emissions equal to the marginal social damage they cause – implies charging a price for emitting CO_2 equal to the present value of the social damage it causes. Faced with such a "carbon price" – an addition to the price paid for the underlying resource itself (such as coal) – they will not emit beyond the point at which the marginal cost of reducing ('abating' or 'mitigating') their emissions is less than that price. In this way, the marginal social cost of abatement is equated to its marginal social benefit – from reduced damage.
>
> (IMF, 2008: 9)

However, this process could provide a disproportionate advantage to companies that can afford the research and development (R&D) costs of these new, less damaging products/activities without dramatically increasing consumer prices; certain companies could also be able to outsource 'undesirable' production processes/practices to other companies operating in areas where such a charge does not exist. Finally, this charge could also disproportionately affect those with lower incomes if the R&D costs translate to higher consumer prices, or if there were a lack of alternative and cheaper products.

In this context, and as it became clear that the signatory countries would not achieve the agreed reductions, Kyoto established three market-based mechanisms: *Emissions Trading* (also known as the Carbon Market); the *Clean Development Mechanism* (CDM); and the *Joint Implementation*.

These market-based mechanisms are based on the Assigned Amount Units (AAU) awarded by Kyoto to each country according to their 1990s allowed emissions (UN-FCCC, 2006: 3). Each unit was equal to one metric tonne of carbon dioxide equivalent, calculated using its global warming potential. Some of these units were later assigned to particular companies by governments and institutions such as the European Union. The arrangement gave the countries producing the highest greenhouse gas emissions in 1990 the largest number of units. The units could be then transferred and traded as 'spare units' in the form of:

- Certified Emission Reduction (CER) generated from a CDM project activity;
- Removal Unit (RMU) on the basis of land use, land-use change and forestry (LULUCF) activities such as reforestation; and
- Emission Reduction Unit (ERU) generated by a joint implementation project.

Carbon emissions trading

As any *Monopoly* player would know, a trading system requires that each participant has some (but not too many) surplus units in order to begin trading, and an initial price for each unit to be realistically set. However, as pricing is a subjective process that requires experience in dealing with that particular 'currency', mistakes could easily follow. Many analysts think that Kyoto gave too many spare units to certain countries due to the chosen base year and to over-estimates found in 1990s emissions data; the initial given price of each unit was also later found to be too high. In this sense, Russia alone is alleged to have the potential to sell over four billion spare units (Ramming et al., 2008).

According to the UN, carbon trading was worth over $30bn in 2006, and some analysts expected it to become a $1tn global market in the next 10 years. Barclay's believed, before the current financial crisis started, that 'Carbon will be the world's biggest commodity market, and it could become the world's biggest market overall'. (Kanter, 2007). However, international transfers of ownership need to be validated by the UN-FCCC and each transfer within the European Union is, additionally, validated by the European Commission.

At present, the European Union Emission Trading Scheme (EU-ETS) is the largest greenhouse gas emissions trading scheme. The programme is intended to cap emissions from large installations within the EU by, at least initially, giving them free 'European allowances' for their emissions (EUA).

According to Davies (2007), the carbon market's leading analysts, Point Carbon, calculated that the EU scheme also handed out too many free emission units, with an estimated price of €30/tonne later found to be over optimistic. The same paper also reported that once certain companies realised that they had millions of units they did not need, they sold them at a great profit. These included six UK electricity generators, which earned some £800m in each of the three years of the scheme, as well as major oil companies such as Esso, BP and Shell.

Some of the money many companies 'found' by virtue of participating in the scheme, before they achieved any emissions reductions, was paid by organisations in need of units to compensate for their lack of progress in reducing their own emissions, or even to improve their 'green' credentials. These included hospitals and 18 UK universities. As the carbon price collapsed near the end of the first phase of Kyoto in 2007, and when the lack of actual emissions reductions became apparent, many companies lost large amounts of money that could otherwise have been invested in actual emission reduction initiatives. For example, Davies (2007) reported that the £92,500 investment made by the University of Manchester (UK) in EUA, was worth less than £1,000.

The focus on greenhouse emissions could also become counter-productive in the long term, as it could mask other dangerous pollutants simultaneously produced; companies would be able mask their true environmental impact and find a 'cheaper' way out. Emissions from aviation fuel, for example, which produces many pollutants as well as greenhouse gases, could be reduced artificially by buying cheaper/easier CO_2 emissions elsewhere.

A major investigation conducted by *The Guardian* in 2007 concluded that the underlying idea supporting these schemes comes from politicians and business executives trying to meet the demands for action while preserving the commercial status quo. In this context, the Sussex University's Energy Group concluded, as cited in a comprehensive report of carbon trading published by the Swedish *Dag Hammarskjöld Foundation* in 2009, that a market price for carbon:

[I]s a very poor weapon in what is supposed to be a war to save humanity. In the 1970s, high price rises did little to wean industrial societies off oil – and there is little reason to believe that a carbon price can do so either.

(Cited in Gilbertson and Reyes, 2009: 12)

Furthermore, as the EU-ETS starts its third phase, which runs from 2013–20, Gilbertson and Reyes (2009) also conclude that while the scheme may have learned from some of its mistakes and 'although some of these loopholes may be closed, the increasing complexity and international linking of the European with other carbon markets means that others will be opened – allowing emissions 'reduction' permits to continue circulating without a significant need actually to reduce emissions domestically' (Gilbertson and Reyes, 2009: 51).

In the US, the MIT Energy Initiative, in the context of the relationship between national governments and individual states, concluded in 2008 that the key achievement so far of the EU-ETS has been its ability to balance centralised EU control and a great degree of freedom at the national level, which could sound attractive in the future to US politicians, adding: 'We may be talking 20, 30 years down the road, but that's the sort of basic architecture towards which some sort of global climate regime would tend. . . . Looking beyond the US, I think the EU-ETS has a lot to tell us about how a global system might actually work.' (Stauffer, 2008). This comment was made before the current financial crisis caused by similar 'hot air' financial products, began.

More recently, many news agencies reported that the UBS bank had stated in a research report in November 2011 that the EU-ETS had cost European consumers $287bn, in return for almost zero impact on carbon reduction. According to this bank, carbon prices could go as low as €3/tonne – although other banks involved in carbon trading disagree.

The Clean Development Mechanism

The Clean Development Mechanism (CDM) is the second market-based scheme, this time administered exclusively by the UN. It is aimed at facilitating organisations in developed nations to earn saleable CER credits, which can be counted towards meeting Kyoto targets, by investing in '*real and additional*' emission-reduction projects in developing nations. Furthermore, it was assumed that organisations would opt for this *offsetting mechanism* only to supplement their emission reductions.

The scheme has raised many criticisms. Firstly, it soon transpired that although projects were expected to provide '*real and additional*' greenhouse emission savings, many were already completed by the time an application was submitted, or approval and funding had already been provided, i.e. the project would have become a reality irrespective of its participation in the scheme. In this sense, the scheme would become a very expensive subsidy without any *real* greenhouse emissions savings actually taking place.

Secondly, although some projects provided greenhouse emission reductions, such as destroying certain greenhouse emissions by incineration, other dangerous pollutants were also produced. Furthermore, the payments provided under the scheme could in some cases become the *raison d'être* for the company in the developing country. That is to say, projects would be created to attract payments instead of serving a market or social need. According to Davies (2007), 53 per cent of the existing CERs come from just six vast projects in India, China and South Korea, involving companies that manufacture refrigerant products. A gas produced as a side effect of this manufacturing process is HFC-23, which is 11,700 times more likely than CO_2 to encourage global warming. In order for the companies to convert this gas into highly profitable certified units, all they need to do is to build a cheap incinerator to burn the gas. The end result has been the building of new refrigerant facilities that now earn millions of euros from these credits – more than from selling their refrigerant products !

The complexity of the process does not help either; each project has to complete a highly technical Project Design Document (according to one of the approved 124 methodologies), usually with the help of an external Project Design Consultant. It then seeks approval from the host country's Designated National Authority (usually an environment minister), and later is presented to an external validator or Designated Operational Entity (another consultancy firm). Once the project has been validated, a request for registration can be made. The fact that some of the external advisers in the submission process are also carbon traders raises further ethical questions.

The project is next submitted to a three-stage approval process (CDM secretariat; the UN-FCCC Registration and Issuance, and the CDM Executive Board). As Lambert Schneider from the German Öko-Institut stated at a conference on EU-ETS:

> If you are a good storyteller you get your project approved. If you are not a good storyteller you don't get your project through.

> (Cited in Gilbertson and Reyes, 2009: 64)

Finally, monitoring reports need to be submitted and approved before the CERs are issued – although many CERs could have been traded in advance on a futures market.

The process raises many questions regarding possibilities for unethical behaviour, conflicts of interests, collusion, and lack of oversight.

Similarly, Ball (2008) highlighted that the project design, approval, and monitoring systems challenge the capacity of the already stretched UN regulators to monitor these projects on the ground, then to take corrective action when needed. The article showed how evaluating whether a project would have been built without carbon-credit revenue is a highly complex judgment call.

Another concern is that not all regions in the world are benefiting in equal proportions. According to a report by HSBC, India's share of the $2.2tn market for low carbon goods and services in 2020 could be as much as $135bn. However, if current trends continue, African projects would receive only a fraction of this sum. The BBC reported that of the 3,511 projects registered with the UN by October 2011, just 72 were in Africa. The expense involved in all of the paperwork and the necessary networking and technical knowledge required 'is an expense that many African companies and governments simply cannot afford' (Duke, 2011).

Joint implementation

Joint implementation is another UN-administered *offsetting* scheme, similar to the CDM involving countries that already have binding targets. Most projects are in countries considered 'economies in transition' such as Russia (65–70 per cent), Ukraine, and Central and Eastern Europe – as costs there are lower. As the UN states:

> Joint implementation offers Parties a flexible and cost-efficient means of fulfilling a part of their Kyoto commitments, while the host Party benefits from foreign investment and technology transfer. A JI project must provide a reduction in emissions by sources, or an enhancement of removals by sinks, that is *additional* to what would otherwise have occurred. Projects must have the approval of the host Party and participants have to be authorised to participate by a Party involved in the project.
>
> (Website of UN-FCCC; italics added).

This scheme has not been criticised as heavily as have the other two mechanisms; however, as with the CDM scheme, the interpretation of *additional* reductions is still controversial, given the discussion of whether this is only a very expensive means of subsidy and lacks real reductions in emissions. The fact that certain countries could simultaneously benefit from selling spare units (carbon trading) and from being the recipients of funds in joint implementation initiatives raises further questions.

Implementation of some energy reduction/emissions initiatives, combined with the participation in carbon trading and offsetting schemes has allowed organisations to claim that they are 'carbon neutral'. This is a very interesting exercise, which allows organisations to improve their green credentials. It does not mean that the organisation has stopped emitting greenhouse gases and other pollutants; indeed, the opposite could be the case depending on the organisations' financial 'ingenuity' and muscle. This is shockingly the case when companies with the highest emissions levels, and manufacturers and traders of dangerous pollutants, suddenly become carbon neutral. Participating in these schemes, together with pledges to support other UN initiatives such as the Millennium Goals, has also been called *"Blue-washing"*, making reference to the colour of the UN flag.

Carbon market mechanisms – an afterthought

We have already indicated the central role of ethical, cultural and political frameworks used when collecting, interpreting, and responding to information. Even specific economic situations influence our appreciation of the world around us.

Scientists need to use their judgment when deciding what data to collect and consider, and what parameters to apply when designing their modelling systems. Furthermore, for climate data to be useful they must cover many centuries, gaps in historical information, and unreliable measurements taken long ago, making the task of predicting future weather patterns even more difficult. The recent *'Climategate'* scandal in 2009, when extracts of emails between scientists, hacked from the University of East Anglia's Climatic Research Unit (UK), were leaked as proof that global warming was a scientific conspiracy, highlighted these issues. Professor Phil Jones, director of the research unit, was by several inquiries later cleared of any wrongdoing. The research unit's *interpretation* of the weather data available has been found similar to interpretations made by other world-famous research centres. However, there were also calls for data and interpretations to be more open and transparent.

In this context, the carbon market mechanisms could be seen as a product of the business culture that characterised the 1990–2007 period of economic growth, based on market speculation, which subsequently gave rise to the current world crisis. The production of very complex financial products endlessly bought and sold (individually or as part of very complex packages), future betting, and other similar speculative behaviours earned enormous commissions for traders and hedge funds. Such financial products created neither social wealth nor prosperity, and almost bankrupted the wealthiest economies and societies of the planet. The price fluctuations observed regarding carbon trading mirror those of other financial instruments. From the tulip mania in the Netherlands in the seventeenth century to the recent internet and housing bubbles, society has experienced the dark side of the 'invisible hand' of the market. Following Gilbertson and Reyes (2009):

> Carbon trading is aimed at the wrong target. It is not directed at reorganising industrial societies' energy, transport and housing systems – starting today – so that they don't need coal, oil and gas. It is not contributing to the de-industrialisation of agriculture or the protection of forests . . . Instead, it is organised around keeping the wheels on the fossil fuel industry for as long as possible.
>
> (Gilbertson and Reyes, 2009: 15)

In this sense, as greenhouse emissions continue dramatically to rise in the developed world, private and public organisations engaging in the available carbon market mechanisms must reflect on the ethics of distancing themselves from the emissions they produce, and of paying someone else to 'clean up' their continuing environmental pollution. Organisations should not be able to trade their right to pollute (Banerjee, 2012) or to treat pollution as another commodity that can be 'off-shored' to become someone else's problem. As moral corruption in the 'market of indulgencies' contributed to the Protestant Reformation in the sixteenth century, it is possible that the ethical shortcomings identified at the heart of the carbon market mechanisms will challenge the way the UN and other international organisations engage with corporate wealth and power.

Sustainable development (SD)

The notion of sustainable development (SD) has taken centre stage in the relationship between humans and the environment. This notion has become the formal response by business and policy makers to most of the issues and problems discussed above. On the one hand, it encapsulates the developed world's anxieties that emerged from the failed project of development 'designed for' the Third World (Escobar, 2011), and the realisation that current levels of growth and consumerism cannot be maintained indefinitely. On the other hand, SD is also informed by evolving discourses regarding notions such as nature, the environment, (which now include non-industrial indigenous populations), and the over-exploitation of natural resources. The state of play between these genuine concerns has been crystallised in the different UN resolutions, from the 1951 report on *Measures for the Economic Development of Under-Developed Countries* to the 2010 *Summit on the Millennium Development Goals*. These resolutions illustrate how developed countries have a difficult and delicate balance to strike:

> Although it was the 'developed' world that had discovered the environment in its complexity and fragility, at the level of national governments and bureaucracies, they remained as mindful as ever of their status as 'developed' and the imperative of retaining their pre-eminence' in the community of nations.
>
> (Argyrou, 2005: 165)

In this context, we can introduce what has become the most frequently cited definition of sustainable development, produced by the United Nations World Commission on Environment and Development in 1987, also known as the Brundtland Commission Report:

> Sustainable development is development that meets the needs of the present without compromising the ability of future generations to meet their own needs.

The importance of this definition is not that it contains the unified agreement of the world; rather, that its simplicity resonates in so many different contexts, dissolving otherwise uncompromising positions and shocking realities. It legitimises the trader who profits from carbon trade transactions; the organisations that buy pollution permits to become 'carbon neutral', as well as those organisations that issue these permits in the developing world; the consumer who takes a recently replaced electronic gadget to the recycling facility and the plastic bottle to the recycling bin after drinking its contents of imported 'designer' water; the tourist who flies across the globe to spend some spare cash in a brand-new sustainable resort, and the middle-class person who owns a seldom occupied (although 'environmentally friendly') second home. All of these activities, once morally problematic, are now seen as contributing to that universal goal.

In sum, by emphasising care for future generations, the Brundtland definition masks the asymmetrical power relations between consumers in the developed world, and the poor and destitute everywhere. Furthermore, even though 'developed (wo)man' is now the custodian of nature for future generations, s/he still holds the power, and now the 'moral duty', to decide what resources can be used, to what extent, for what purpose, as well as how to make them a commodity and benefit from their trade.

As carbon emissions have increased well beyond those agreed at Kyoto (once the impact of imports and other factors are taken into account), and the worldwide indicators that measure other sustainability drivers illustrate lack of improvement, wealthy individuals all over the world are using 'sustainability' and 'sustainable development' as by-words for consumerism in the new millennium.

Finally, the impact of the SD discourse in the management of organisations may be observed in the annual sustainability reports and in the ubiquitous sustainability website sections prepared by consultancy firms. This phenomenon, closely linked to CSR reporting, was discussed in the previous chapter. An important element here is that the SD discourse is embedded within contradictory organisational discourses: some emphasise profit making and growth, and others promote unlimited consumerism. This is not to be considered an anomaly. On the contrary, as SD business initiatives and reporting are now considered an adequate response to the challenges of sustainability, it helps organisations morally to justify businesses growth and profit, under the banner of the 'business case' for sustainability. Examples include Elkington's (1994; 1997) *'Triple Bottom Line'* and *'People, Planet, Profits'* frameworks. The role of institutions such as the UN in this process cannot be underestimated.

North (1990), from an institutional economist's point of view, described the relationship between institutions and organisations using a game analogy: institutions design and provide the rules of the game, and organisations act as the players. In the case of SD, the 'rule setting' role is provided by the UN, the WTO, the EU, and other major NGOs. These institutions are perceived as being guided by extremely high ethical values, as arbitrators *par excellence,* and as representing the will and the needs of all peoples – and now of the planet. However, as we highlighted in the context of carbon trading, the UN suffers at a basic level from enormous constraints in terms of human and financial resources; these are made more acute by, for example, the continuous refusal of certain countries to pay their agreed contributions (e.g. the US government's refusal fully to pay over $1.3bn it has owed the UN in arrears since the mid-1990s), and by powerful political and economic interests. Furthermore, the involvement of big multinationals in the development of frameworks, international agreements and regulations is another area of concern.

For example, Banerjee (2003) highlighted that the controversial *Trade-Related Aspects of Intellectual Property Rights* (TRIPS) international agreement was developed 'in large part' by a group of multinational firms that included Bristol Myers, Merck, DuPont, Pfizer and Monsanto, as members of the Intellectual Property Committee (IPC).

The TRIPS agreement was negotiated in 1994 with the blessing of the UN through the General Agreement on Tariffs and Trade (GATT; later replaced by the WTO). These negotiations took place before the full impact of commerce on the biotech/genetic industries became clear, and at a time when the internet information revolution was still in its infancy. In this context, Banerjee cites Rifkin (1999), who described how the Monsanto's representative summarised their TRIPS strategy:

[We were able to] distil from the laws of the most advanced countries the fundamental principles for protecting all forms of intellectual property. . . Besides selling our concept at home, we went to Geneva where we presented our document to the staff of the GATT Secretariat . . . What I have described to you is absolutely unprecedented in GATT. Industry identified a major problem for international trade. It crafted a solution, reduced it to a concrete proposal, and sold it to our own and other governments . . . the [multinational] *industries and traders of the world have played simultaneously the role of patients, the diagnosticians and the prescribing physicians.*

(Banerjee, 2003:167 italics added)

This example not only undermines the neutral role of the UN and other NGOs; it also supports Argyrou's comment mentioned at the start of this section.

From the organisational perspective, institutional economists have observed that certain processes (which could include technologies and methodologies) develop in such a way that, over time, it becomes almost impossible to consider alternatives, even if these could provide superior solutions. Such phenomenon can be explained by the systems notion of 'positive feedback'.

Arthur (1994) described some of the conditions necessary for this process to occur: the presence of high set-up costs, which could make the implementation of further initiatives even more expensive; the development of specialised knowledge and expertise, which makes organisations reluctant to invest further time and resources in learning, testing and adapting further models; and finally, the advantages of using methodologies successfully implemented by competitors.

Other possible factors include: the reassuring feeling of knowing 'we are following' what the leading and 'SD award-winning' organisations in the field are doing, or are adhering to the UN's guidelines – as is the case of the Global Reporting Initiative (GRI) – and the fact that these technologies/methodologies become cheaper to implement over time. This 'positive feedback' mechanism could in part explain the production of countless SD books, 'Do-It-Yourself' kits and reporting manuals. Finally, the tempting effects of following a 'carefully-worded' PR and marketing campaigns; *'free-riding'*; *'green-washing'* and *'blue-washing'* need to be taken into account – even though companies will always give explicit assurances that they are not engaging in these types of behaviour.

The instrumental use of nature

In the opening chapters of this book, three of the 'theories of the firm' were presented: *Classical liberal economic, Pluralist (A and B),* and *Corporatist.* Each of the theories locates the business corporation within a capitalist-driven, market-based economy. Each accepts the need for corporations legitimately to seek out new ways to generate profits on behalf of shareholders, yet with other interest groups (employees, customers and suppliers) benefiting in differing ways as a result of these corporate activities. Within these perspectives nature, in all of its various forms, is seen as a resource at the disposal of certain societies and corporations.

This chapter has also illustrated that most of the sustainability drivers and discourses assume humans as being separate from nature. Furthermore, certain powerful groups believe that the understanding that humans could have descended from apes through evolutionary processes, or the knowledge that humans and chimpanzees share 96 per cent of DNA, constitute an attack on the 'intrinsic superiority' and the 'divine origin' of humans. For these groups, nature also seems to 'fulfil its destiny' when it is transformed into profit or employed to facilitate economic activity, within certain legal and social frameworks.

In this context, specific cultural systems have produced the technologies and knowledge systems needed to identify, classify, control and manipulate nature, as well as the economic arrangements that seem obsessively to compel individuals and organisations to transform nature into profit. Such technologies and knowledge systems in turn contribute to the continuation and reification of the social arrangements that made them possible.

An important element at the core of this process, for example, is the law of property rights regulating the ownership of areas of land and sea, such as the Arctic and Antarctic regions, including their mineral deposits and other financially valued resources. Even the moon is subject to property rights claims on its mineral deposits. Currently, companies are trying to benefit from recently decoded human and non-human DNA by patenting certain sequences and biological processes, thus attempting to 'own' them. The ability of humanity to benefit from such 'code-breaking' research would be subject to commercial exploitation of these medical understandings – as the recent US Supreme Court ruling, *Mayo vs. Prometheus*, on patenting biology demonstrates (*The Economist*, 2012).

In this sense, deeper philosophical issues can be identified when one considers new scientific knowledge that could possibly alleviate great human suffering, such as developments in the areas of genetically inherited diseases and disabilities. The relationship between humans and nature, and how nature is conceptualised, are at the centre of important debates in philosophy, theology, and in the social sciences (Argyrou, 2005; Banerjee, 2003; Escobar, 2011).

Martin Heidegger (1959) is the person most closely identified with the perspective we are about to discuss. It is known as Phenomenology.

DEFINITION

Phenomenology is the belief that the world around us can be understood only through our lived experiences. The world does not exist outside of those experiences. We impose understandings and interpretations on that world, or worlds, based upon the values, perspectives and beliefs we hold. Our relationship with nature is therefore symbiotic, i.e. mutually dependent.

While Heidegger was not the first to challenge the notion that subjects and objects are distinct and separate entities, his analysis was more radical than those exposed by other important philosophers such as Edmund Husserl (1931; 1965).

As the definition above indicates, Heidegger's principal argument was that we cannot understand nature other than how we experience it. Nature does not exist outside of our experiences of it, and what we experience is mediated by our respective cultures (including our political and religious beliefs). This is to say: nature is created and re-created through cultural understandings and assessments that change over time, and under different circumstances and needs.

For example, it would be possible to illustrate how our experience of nuclear energy has changed in relation to political needs and social changes. Firstly, it was developed as a weapon during the Second World War, then considered a necessary deterrent towards guaranteeing peace during the Cold War. It has also been presented as the panacea for energy shortages, with the construction of over 400 reactors all over the world. More recently, most nuclear reactors in the US, Europe and Japan are to be decommissioned due to unsustainably high running costs, following nuclear accidents (such as the Fukushima disaster in 2011), and adverse public opinion. Nuclear energy is now perceived, at least in the West and in Japan, as dangerous.

At the same time, in other parts of the world, countries argue that they have the 'right' – and almost the moral duty – to develop nuclear energy, despite the known risks posed by these facilities, the cost of decommissioning a reactor at the end of its useful life, and the problems of storing the waste they produce, which will remain radioactive for several millennia, while not being able to afford to feed their populations.

Heidegger offers no magic formula to solve the issues that arise from different cultural frameworks, but he does offer a way of thinking, a way of seeing, that could prove helpful.

Heidegger's concern was with what he described as the 'enframing of technology', or what we might call a technology mentality, i.e. the seeing of nature as purely instrumental (as a standing reserve and a stockpile of resources), as simply a means to an end. If nature represents merely the opportunity to make money, if that is all nature means to us, then, from a Heideggerian perspective, society has become emotionally and spiritually bankrupt.

> If an object is viewed in purely **instrumental** terms it possesses **DEFINITION**
> no worth beyond its functional use, that is, what might be obtained for it by either selling it as it is, or converting it into another form of tradable object. It is purely a means to an end. The end in this case is to make money, although this is not the only 'end' that can be considered.

Heidegger was not anti-technology. He recognised the contributions that technological advancements made and continue to make to people's lives. Improvements in sanitation, health care and education can be seen as benefiting either directly or indirectly from technology. In Heidegger's view, we have a symbiotic relationship with nature, i.e., the relationship between humans and nature is one of mutual dependency. As we exploit nature, we cannot avoid, to a greater or lesser extent, having an impact upon ourselves. In this context 'ourselves' is used in a very broad sense, reflecting impacts not necessarily only upon our own generation, but also those that are yet to come – as in the case of the storage of nuclear waste from the generation of electricity and nuclear weapons.

The treatment of nature in purely instrumental ways is not limited to profit-seeking organisations, nor is the 'enframing of technology' limited to capitalist systems. Examples of the destruction of the environment in the name of 'progress' can be seen in many different political and economic contexts. Examples include the disastrous policies of China's Great Leap Forward period, the construction of the Three Gorges Dam project, and the destruction of complete rainforests to collect valuable wood and minerals. A similar example is the destruction of ancient woodlands and rain forests to plant a monoculture for biofuels, reducing biodiversity yet leading to good financial returns and 'excellent carbon trading' credentials.

Is it possible for corporations to view nature in anything other than an instrumental fashion? In addition, if we cannot expect everyone to see nature in the same manner:

■ How can a corporation place a value upon any object, other than in terms of its instrumental worth to the corporation?

■ How can objects have meaning for a corporation beyond their functional or instrumental worth?

■ Where is a corporation's memory that might allow it to attach feelings to objects that transcend their instrumental worth?

■ What is the market value of the site of the Parthenon of ancient Greece, or of the Great Wall of China, to a property developer? What is the market value of a rainforest, which contains valuable mineral deposits?

We are approaching a possibly critical point in our consideration of sustainability, corporate social responsibility and corporate citizenship, certainly in terms of Heidegger's view of a 'technology mentality'. Asking where a corporation's memory might lie, or whether a corporation can indeed possess feelings towards objects, is attributing to business enterprises human characteristics, falling into what is known as *anthropomorphism*.

When we use the term 'corporation' in the sense being discussed here, we are referring to the senior decision makers. A corporation's 'memory' will reside with individuals, or possibly in the form of company stories and myths. The use of 'corporation' is, in fact, a shorthand version.

If corporations can only ever view objects in instrumental ways, then perhaps society cannot expect corporations to appreciate the complexity of our views regarding nature, or meaningfully to engage in debates regarding disagreements and dilemmas.

Following Heidegger, the fundamental objection is that corporations *cannot* fully act in socially responsible ways because they possess on nature a perspective that is extremely limited. A societal perspective on nature compatible with a Heideggerian perspective is denied to a corporation, as long as corporations are constituted in their current form.

Corporations cannot be citizens because their value systems are highly constrained and unable to handle concepts of value beyond instrumentality. A corporation's perspective is 'enframed by technology'. However, this does not dismiss corporations as irrelevancies to modern life. Clearly, business, in its many forms, is fundamental to modern life. In many respects it is the dominant force in most societies.

The future of sustainability

Having becoming aware of the complexity of the issues surrounding the concept of sustainability, a word so commonly used that it often seems unproblematic, it is possible that executives and individuals find themselves facing a unsolvable dilemma: how to address meaningfully the complexity of sustainability issues, if current organisational and business structures are the main contributor to, while affected by, the ongoing environmental crisis.

Firstly, organisations and individuals must avoid the '*sustainability blackmail*', which argues that they should either uncritically follow what is prescribed by 'sustainability-award winning' organisations, NGOs and by leading consultancy firms, or else become labelled as uncaring of or anti-sustainability.

Secondly, although the short-term task involves promoting initiatives that, for example, reduce packaging, transport, the use of energy and waste, the long-term goal should be to devise *alternatives* to business structures and practices that are currently based on unlimited consumerism, unlimited growth and that promote an instrumental use of nature – including humans, other biological beings and mineral resources. However, achievements in the short-term should not be used to give the *wrong* impression that current business structures and practices can become sustainable with some adjustments – this strategy will only briefly delay a chaotic future.

In this context, an important task would be to redefine the roles of business, government and of civil society in order to reclaim nature (with its mineral, its biological resources and processes, and its genetic diversity), for humanity and away from private commercial interests. The *flag planting* ceremonies that characterised colonialism, and even the Apollo mission to the moon, should become a warning of a dangerous and unsustainable past, and not part of the corporate future.

Assuming that the facts, stories and myths that underline the notion of sustainability (as well as those that support its critics) are culturally and historically produced and organised, it is possible to understand why it is so difficult for corporations and individuals to imagine a radically different way of living and doing business. This would presuppose the possibility of standing outside of our present. The predicament does not mean that we have to accept uncritically what is presented to us. Our cultural and historical conditions do not mean that we are destined to follow a predetermined path either; rather, that we cannot anticipate what that path will be. In this sense, although there is neither 'light at the end of the tunnel' nor easy answers, we should leave no room for despair.

> Wayfarer, the only way
> is your footsteps, there is no other.
>
> Wayfarer, there is no way,
> you make the way as you go.
> As you go, you make the way
> and stopping to look behind,
> you see the path that your feet
> will never travel again.
>
> Wayfarer, there is no way -
> only foam trails in the sea.
>
> Antonio Machado, Selected Poems (1988), translated by A.S. Trueblood, Cambridge: Harvard University Press.

Summary

In this chapter the following key points have been made:

- Sustainability is a concept related to several social, economic and environmental discourses, such as population growth and poverty; systems thinking;

consumerism; recycling and waste; climate change; and sustainable develop-ment. These discourses are not neutral, i.e., they reflect cultural, political and economic interests.

■ Recently, climate change and global warming have been seen as the major sus-tainability issues, driven by the UN (Kyoto Agreement) and governments all over the world.

■ Kyoto created 'carbon trading mechanisms' to complement emissions reduc-tion efforts. However, these remain ethically controversial. Their long-term im-pact on the environment is also unclear.

■ The relationship between CSR and sustainability is also contested, as some be-lieve that one concept is merely a dimension of the other.

■ 'Blue-washing', a concept similar to 'green-washing', is applied to companies that subscribe to unenforceable UN principles and protocols (e.g. Millennium Goals; Global Compact) to boost their image yet without fundamentally chang-ing business structures or products.

■ Although in the short term companies should be encouraged to adopt carbon reduction and other environmental measures, in the long term a more radi-cal economic and social transformation is required. This is especially urgent as consumerism, environmental destruction and carbon emissions increase worldwide.

Typical assignments

1. In the context of global warming, debate the appropriateness of the price mecha-nism as the primary democratic tool of resource allocation.

2. Critically evaluate Heidegger's notion of the 'enframing of technology' in terms of its contribution to debates concerning global economic growth rate forecasts.

3. Discuss the motion that 'consumer social responsibility is as important as corporate social responsibility'.

4. How effective are market mechanisms such as carbon trading in contributing to sustainability goals?

Group activity 10.1

1. You are asked to work in groups of between three and six members and to as-sume the role of being the senior decision-making team of a leading institu-tional investor. Your tasks are as follows, with tasks A and B ideally completed before the commencement of the group session.

▶

a. Define the principles that will guide your investment strategy. To do this you will need to consider, among other issues, the following:

(i) On whose behalf are you making decisions?

(ii) Are there any types of organisation in which you would not invest?

(iii) Are there any sectors in which you emphatically wish to invest?

(iv) What do you expect of the companies in which you invest in terms of communications and information updates?

(v) Are there any aspects of corporate governance that you would prioritise?

(vi) What will be your attitudes towards growth and risk?

(vii) What will be your expectations and attitudes towards rates of return?

b. Having established your investment principles, you must now select 10 quoted companies that will form your investment portfolio. You are not required to worry about how well these organizations have performed in the past year. For now, simply select 10 companies that you believe satisfy your investment principles.

2. During the group session you will be provided with two sets of information of the share prices of quoted companies, taken from the financial pages of daily newspapers. One set will be dated within seven days of the group session, whilst the other will be 12 months old. From these two sets of information you will identify how the share prices of the companies in your portfolio have moved during the past 12 months, both absolutely and in terms of the sector index. You can include the dividend return in your calculations if this information is available, but for the purposes of the exercise it is not crucial.

3. You should consider (with complete honesty and openness) how the issues of sustainability and social practices weighed

■ in your initial portfolio selection; and

■ in your considerations about possible changes your team might make in the light of the first year's financial performance.

Recommended further reading

Argyrou, V. (2005) *The Logic of Environmentalism: Anthropology, Ecology and Postcolonialism,* Oxford: Berghahn Books.

Bansal. P. and Hoffman, A.J. (eds) (2012) *The Oxford Handbook of Business and the Natural Environment,* Oxford: Oxford University Press.

Barrow, C.J. (2006) *Environmental Management for Sustainable Development,* Oxon, UK: Routledge.

Berners-Lee, M. (2010) *How Bad are Bananas? The Carbon Footprint of Everything,* London: Profile Books.

Cooper, T. (2010) *Longer Lasting Products: Alternatives to the Throwaway Society*, Surrey, England: Gower Publishing Limited.

Escobar, A. (2011) *Encountering Development: The Making and Unmaking of the Third World*, 2nd Edition, NY: Princeton University Press.

Slade, G. (2007) *Made to Break: Technology and Obsolescence in America*, Cambridge, MA: Harvard University Press.

Stibbe, A. (2011) *The Handbook of Sustainability Literacy: Skills for a Changing World*, Devon, UK: Green Books.

Useful websites

Topic	Website	URL
Critiques of capitalism	RSA Animate – Crisis of Capitalism	http://www.youtube.com/watch?v=qOP2V_np2c0
Sustainability	SustainAbility	http://www.sustainability.com/
Global development	Dag Hammarskjöld Foundation	http://www.dhf.uu.se/
Environmental issues	UN – Environment Programme	http://www.unep.org/
Climate change	UN – Framework Convention on Climate Change	http://unfccc.int/2860.php
Climate change	UN – Rio+20, Conference on SD	http://www.uncsd2012.org/rio20/index.html
Climate change	UN – Kyoto Protocol	http://unfccc.int/kyoto_protocol/items/2830.php
An international standard for corporate responsibility	UN – Global Compact	http://www.unglobalcompact.org/
Environmental activism	Greenpeace	http://www.greenpeace.org.uk/
Environmental activism	Rainforest Alliance	http://www.rainforest-alliance.org/
Sustainability	Sustainability Research Institute (Leeds University)	http://www.see.leeds.ac.uk/research/sri
Low carbon initiative for business	UK Department for Business Innovation and Skills (BIS)	http://www.bis.gov.uk/policies/business-sectors/low-carbon-business-opportunities/sustainable-development

Please also see the useful website section in Chapter 9.

PART D

The international context

CHAPTER 11

Global and local values – and international business

Chapter at a glance

Chapter contents

- Learning outcomes
- Introduction
- Business and managerial values in different countries and societies
- The normative debate about ethical universalism and relativism in the business context
- When different sets of organisational and managerial values meet
- Reflections
- Summary

Case studies

- Case study 11.1 The college principal's new car
- Case study 11.2 Testing Maori employees for drugs in a New Zealand company

Activities and exercises

- Podcast 11.1 Gift giving and politeness
- Video clip 11.1 Impact of culture on business
- Activity 11.1 Bases of trust
- Activity 11.2 Improving communications within teams of people of different cultural backgrounds
- Activity 11.3 The public good versus religious or cultural demands
- Typical assignments
- Group activity 11.1
- Recommended further reading
- Useful websites

Having read the chapter and completed its associated activities, readers should be able to:

■ Describe how the ethical and business values of countries and societies differ.

■ Argue about the validity of particular values and ethical standards of different countries.

■ Evaluate the options for responding to the ethical issues and dilemmas that arise from international business and globalisation.

■ Relate these issues to the debates about ethical universalism and ethical relativism.

■ Understand the processes of learning that occur when people with partly overlapping but partly distinct values interact.

Introduction

Societies and countries may differ in their business ethics and values. Any differences or similarities may be internal to societies or countries or between them.

■ Different countries may have, in the high ethics established within their religion, philosophical traditions and literature, different ideals about the conduct of business and organisational life. Cultural tradition in one place might see business growth and profitability as an end in itself; in other places economic ends might be seen as subordinate to other goals.

■ Within a country or society there may be competing sets of values concerning business and management. Within Muslim countries, for example, there may be differences between modernizers, who want to work to the values of global business, and traditionalists, who may wish to apply Islamic values to business practices.

■ Even if countries and societies share the same values they may vary in the degree to which they practise them. While two countries might, at a formal level, regard bribery as immoral, one country might conduct its business in line with this standard but the second country might not.

■ There may be differences within a country and society between the values embodied in its high traditions and those values adopted in everyday life.

Cross reference	In Chapter 4, pp. 153–61, it was argued that people will have different ideas about whether values are unified in a seamless whole or whether they are fragmented, in the modern world. Those who see values as fragmented do not necessarily believe this to be a problem.

Such differences, between and within countries, raise questions that are the subject of this chapter.

1. The first question asks about the similarities and differences between different countries' and societies' ethical principles and practices concerning business.

2. The second question is whether such differences can ever be justified. In ethical terms this question is a particular example of the general debate between ethical relativism and ethical universalism. Ethical universalism, in brief, is the argument that there can only be one set of true ethical principles that must apply everywhere in the world; ethical relativism is the argument that different places can have different values and principles that are valid to that particular locality.

3. The third question is whether diversity of values between societies and communities can be of advantage to international businesses as a source of organisational learning.

Essentialism
DEFINITIONS

Before we go any further with this chapter we must consider an
ethical question that arises from the assumption that has been made that countries and societies have distinctive values and ethical standards that are generally shared by all those within the country or society. This assumption is known as essentialism. According to essentialist theory, a society, or even a nation state, has a set of stable, internally consistent values that change only slowly. Essentialists therefore tend to emphasise the differences between the values of different societies and underplay the differences within the society (Holden, 2002: 27). At one level, this is just a consequence of the simplification needed to discuss matters of inter-cultural values at a high level of generalisation. Critics argue, however, that such generalisation about different societies' values can have a more pernicious effect. By reducing complex societies to simple labels such as Islamic or African, and defining them by a few core ideas, which are often the opposite of those claimed by western business people, the task of managing businesses and organisations in Islamic or African countries is simplified and stereotyped for the western manager. These managers then do not have to deal with the complexity, merely respond to the stereotypes.

The alternative view is to stress the differences of values within societies by focusing on the processes by which individuals make sense of the many influences that bear on their sense of values and of right and wrong. These influences will not only include the influences from the family and community but also from the international media.

This chapter can be accused of essentialism. However, it is not naïve essentialism. Some research, for example, shows that being evasive and not providing all the information you have on a matter is not seen as wrong in Hong Kong (Yeung et al., 1999), but in the USA it is (McCornack et al., 1992). However, it would be silly to say that no one in Hong Kong felt it was wrong to tell less than the whole truth or that no American ever bluffed or spoke the truth only selectively.

▶

> A non-naïve view of essentialism depends upon a sensible understanding of the idea of the average. Individual diversity can form a pattern in the aggregate. A statement such as 'people in Hong Kong do not think withholding information is lying' is a statement of that group's average view. Within an average there can be a range of actual views. Many people in Hong Kong will think it a terrible thing to hold back the full truth. Just as likely is that individual people in Hong Kong may take different positions on the matter at different times and in different circumstances. It is also, of course, important to recognise that when one generalises about large entities, such as India, there will be much regional and local diversity in values and principles. The essentialist statements made in this chapter, indeed in this book, should be taken for what they are, a statement that the view or principle attributed to a group has the highest probability of being taken by individuals within that group at any one time. A belief that individuals construct and adapt their own stories about right and wrong does not preclude generalisations about whole populations. A determined anti-essentialist, however, would most likely find this argument unacceptable because it does not concede the whole ground to individuality.

The case studies provided in Chapter 2 illustrate many ethical issues that may arise from an international diversity of ethical values. The issue is whether universal codes of conduct should be established which carry moral authority, or the sanctions of international law, to prevent companies acting badly in the world market place. Such universal provisions could be seen as ethically necessary but can also be seen as a form of ethical colonialism in which western multinational companies, and even NGOs, use their strength to force societies to accept values that are not their own. Apart from any moral objection to such processes, Jaeger and Kanungo (1990: 1) expressed a practical criticism:

> uncritical transfer of management theories and techniques based on Western ideologies and value systems has in many ways contributed to organisational inefficiency and ineffectiveness in the developing country context.

Western organisations' concern for equal opportunities in staff selection processes, for example, might contradict local obligations to support friends, family and relations. Such situations can lead to employees experiencing psychological conflicts between the values of their society and those imposed on them by their western employers (Tripathi, 1990; Viswesvaran and Deshpande, 1996). These issues have not arisen only recently, with the expansion of multinational organisations in the world. The dominance of western values has long been recognised and disputed. Vivekenanda, a nineteenth-century Indian nationalist and religious leader, argued:

> I will tell you something for your guidance in life. Everything that comes from India take as true, until you find cogent reasons for disbelieving it. Everything that comes from Europe take as false, until you find cogent reasons for believing it.

(Quoted in Chakraborty, 1999: 4)

The chapter is divided into three sections that deal with each of the questions raised in the introduction.

- The first section describes the extent to which ethical standards, values and practices of business differ between and within countries. It also discusses attempts to produce universal standards for business ethics.

- The second section offers a normative discussion of whether it matters if different countries have different ethical systems. It raises the philosophical debate between universalists, who believe there can only be one true ethical system, and relativists, who believe that cultural ethical difference is justifiable. It is argued that relativism does not mean that 'anything goes' because there are ways of judging between valid differences in business ethics and invalid ones.

- The third section deals with the question of how people should behave in a world in which a universal business ethic is not established and in which countries may have valid differences in their business ethics.

Business and managerial values in different countries and societies

This section of the chapter assesses the extent to which values and ethics are universal in the business and organisational arenas and the extent to which they differ between countries and societies.

Universal values?

There are ethical norms and values that are transnational, shared by many countries. Sometimes these reflect common cultures, as in the Islamic countries. Sometimes they are the result of coincidence or a reflection of the commonalities of human nature and condition (Wines and Napier, 1992). There have been attempts to identify such standards, to codify them and publish them as a universal guide.

One important example is the Declaration of Human Rights, which was published by the United Nations in 1948 and subsequently, in 1966, divided into two separate codes, one covering civil and political rights and one, more relevant to our field, covering economic, cultural and social rights.

The Universal Declaration of Human Rights

This includes, inter alia, the rights:

- not to be held in slavery;
- not to be subjected to torture or degrading treatment;
- to equality before the law;

▶

- to a standard of living adequate for the well-being of self and family;
- to work and to just and favourable conditions of work;
- to equal pay for equal work; and
- to rest and leisure and periodic holidays with pay.

(*Source*: The United Nations, 1948)

Other attempts have focused on standards for international business. Sometimes companies and industries publish codes that they believe should govern their business operations worldwide. This sort of standard has been particularly common in relation to the employment practices used by companies' partners in their international supply chains. There are arguments for saying that the World Trade Organization (WTO), which was set up in 1995 as a successor to the General Agreement on Tariffs and Trade (GATT), should be the body to take on this ethical responsibility as it is the regulatory body for world trade. In particular Tsogas (1999) argued that it should publish and regulate labour standards across the world. The WTO has not taken on this role.

The Caux Round Table is an international body that, with the involvement of the Minnesota Center for Corporate Responsibility, developed a set of ethical principles for international business. It was founded in 1986 by Olivier Giscard D'Estaing of INSEAD, a French business school, and Frederick Philips, chairman of Philips Electronics. They accepted that law and markets provided insufficient guides for conduct. They therefore defined ethical principles based on the Japanese concept of *kyosei* – cooperating to achieve a mutual common prosperity – and human dignity (Caux Round Table, 2001).

Implicit agreement on transnational standards, or even formal agreement about universal ethical standards, does not, of course, mean that those standards are implemented. The gap between espoused values and values in practice has been conceptualised by Hofstede (1991: 9) as the difference between the desirable and the desired. The desirable is an ethical norm that states what is right and good; the desired is a description of what people actually seek to achieve. Bribery and corruption is a case in point. Most societies in the world see it as undesirable, but that does not prevent large numbers of people in many societies desiring the benefits it can bring them.

Most countries formally proscribe the giving and taking of bribes for the reasons outlined above. Yet in many countries corruption is endemic. Transparency International is an NGO that researches the level of perceived bribery and corruption, in terms of both offering and receiving bribes, in a wide range of countries. They produce two indices based on surveys of informed persons. The indices do not measure the actual frequency of corruption but people's opinion of its frequency.

Selections from the 2011 Corruption Perceptions Index are shown in Table 11.1. Some 183 countries were analysed for the index but they are not all shown in the table for reasons of space. The complete results can be seen on Transparency International's website. The index uses a 0–10 scale in which 0 means highly corrupt and 10 means very honest.

Table 11.1   The Transparency International Corruption Perceptions Index (CPI) 2011 –perceptions of public sector corruption

Country	Rank	CPI score	Country	Rank	CPI score
New Zealand	1	9.5	Italy	69	3.9
Finland	2	9.4	China	75	3.6
Singapore	5	9.2	India	95	3.1
Hong Kong	12	8.4	Russia	143	2.3
United Kingdom	16	7.8	Indonesia	143	3.0
USA	24	7.1	Kenya	154	2.2
South Africa	64	4.1	Somalia	182	1.0

Source: Adapted from Transparency International, 2011

The second index produced by Transparency International (2011), the Bribe Payers Index (BPI), is based on a survey of 21 countries. The respondents were asked how likely it was that companies from named countries would pay bribes to win or retain business. The results are shown in Table 11.2. Again an index number of 10 represents a perceived low level of bribery and 0 a high level. It is worth noting that the BPI scores for most countries had improved since the previous survey in 2006. Two sectors dominated the bribery table when it came to identifying those sectors in which bribes were most likely to be paid, principally because they would be demanded or expected. These were public works and construction (first), followed by utilities. Third and fourth were real estate, and oil and gas. In 2011, arms and defence were no longer in the top four sectors for corruption.

Table 11.2   The Transparency International Bribe Payers Index (BPI) 2011

Country	Rank	BPI score	Country	Rank	BPI score
Switzerland	1	8.8	Spain	11	8.0
Netherlands	1	8.8	France	11	8.0
Australia	3	8.5	South Korea	13	7.9
Belgium	3	8.7	Malaysia	15	7.6
Germany	4	8.6	South Africa	15	7.6
Japan	4	8.6	Taiwan	19	7.5
Canada	6	8.5	India	19	7.5
United Kingdom	8	8.3	Argentina	23	7.3
Singapore	8	8.3	China	27	6.5
USA	10	8.1	Russia	28	6.1

Source: Adapted from Transparency International, 2011, *Bribe Payers Index (BPI)*

Table 11.3 relates to developing countries' experiences of donor countries applying pressure other than bribery, for example, diplomatic pressure, financial pressure, tied foreign aid, threat of reduced foreign aid, and tied arms deals. In practically all cases countries receiving the aid reported significant increases in these forms of pressure. All respondents taking part in the survey were asked to identify the three governments they would principally associate with the type of practices mentioned above. In all, there were 567 responses to the survey and 22 countries were identified as employing some or all of these unfair practices. The percentage figures in Table 11.3 indicate the frequency with which the countries were mentioned.

Table 11.3 The Transparency International table of 'Countries using other unfair means to gain or retain business', 2002

Country	Rank	%	Country	Rank	%
USA	1	58	Russia	6	13
France	2	26	Italy	10	5
United Kingdom	3	19	Canada	15	3
Japan	4	18	Australia	19	1
China	5	16	Sweden	22	<1

Source: Adapted from Transparency International, 2002, *Bribe Payers Index (BPI)*

Cross reference	Bribery and corruption are discussed in more detail in Chapter 7.

More attempts are being made to produce universal ethical codes for international business. But there is still much work to be done. Even if the difficulties of promulgating codes are overcome, the problem of differing degrees of conformance to the codes remains. The gap between intention and implementation connects to a final observation on the search for a universal code. It is that such codes mostly deal with terminal values; that is to say, values about what the end purposes of human life and activity are. The discussion of corruption suggests that in business ethics the emphasis is on instrumental values, which deal with how we should behave with each other. It is in the matter of instrumental values that most cultural differences in business values lie, as we shall see in the next section.

Cross reference	The terms 'terminal' and 'instrumental' values were coined by Rokeach, whose work on values is discussed in Chapter 4, p. 151-52.

Relative values?

This section explores the extent to which different societies and cultures have different values and ethical standards in the fields of business and organisational life. Geert Hofstede (1991 and 2001) carried out the seminal empirical work on national value differences in organisations. He conducted a questionnaire survey of employees in the national subsidiaries of IBM. Responses were obtained from 72 national subsidiaries in 1968 and 1972. The results from the smaller subsidiaries were ignored and so the analysis finally enabled a comparison between the personal values of employees in 53 countries. He identified four dimensions along which the values of employees in different countries varied.

■ *Power distance* – the extent to which the less powerful members of organisations expect and accept that power is distributed unequally.

■ *Individualism* – high in countries in which the ties between individuals are loose and everyone is expected to look out for themselves. It is low in collectivist countries where people are integrated into strong, cohesive groups and are expected to give loyalty to these groups in return for their protection.

■ *Masculinity* – high in those countries in which gender roles are distinct and in which men are expected to be assertive, tough and focused on material success and women are supposed to be more modest, tender and concerned with the quality of life. In societies in which masculinity is low the gender roles overlap and both men and women are supposed to be modest, tender and concerned with the quality of life.

■ *Uncertainty avoidance* – the extent to which society members feel threatened by uncertain or unknown situations. Societies in which there is low uncertainty avoidance are comfortable with ambiguity; those in which there is high uncertainty avoidance seek to finesse ambiguity away.

Table 11.4 shows the relative positions of the USA, Great Britain and India, and the highest and lowest scoring countries on each index.

Table 11.4   Values and rank score for selected countries on four indices of national value differences

Country	Power distance index	Individualism index	Masculinity index	Uncertainty avoidance index
Highest scoring country	Malaysia (104)	USA (91)	Japan (95)	Greece (112)
USA	38/53 (40)	–	15 (62)	43/53 (46)
Great Britain	42/53 (35)	3/53 (89)	9 (66)	47/53 (35)
India	10/53 (77)	21/53 (48)	20 (54)	40/53 (40)
Lowest scoring country	Austria (11)	Guatemala (6)	Sweden (5)	Singapore (8)

Figures in brackets are the countries' scores on the scales.
Source: Based on Hofstede, 1991: 26, 53, 84, 113

Differences in values need not cause ethical difficulties. For example, differences in values about uncertainty avoidance or perceptions of time may not raise major ethical problems, but differences in other values do. The identification by Trompenaars and Hampden-Turner (1993: 144–5) of national differences in attitudes towards nature, for example, affects ethical matters such as humanity's use or abuse of the physical world. North American culture, which rose historically from a small society that found itself in a huge continent, developed values that emphasised control over one's environment and destiny as the key to success. In a post-Kyoto world these values appear to be a threat to environmental sustainability. Among the value dimensions identified by Hofstede, power distance, masculinity and individualism all raise ethical questions about the nature of good and moral relationships between people.

The various approaches to leadership in different countries may be related to their values. Hofstede looked at two dimensions in particular to map these differences, and the analysis is shown in Figure 11.1. This shows how four national cultures might be expected to handle conflicts between people in business and organisations. In France, where large power distances are accepted and people are ill-disposed towards uncertainty, it would be done through the chain of command. Those higher in the hierarchy would be expected to resolve disputes between their subordinates. German values also favour order and predictability but have a lower acceptance of large power distances. The German approach to conflict would be to improve procedures that would remove the causes of the conflicts. The British, with their tolerance of ambiguity, but not of big power distances, would prefer to tackle the problems through informal negotiations between the opponents. People would negotiate with each other as if they were farmers haggling in the village marketplace. Other countries, and India is an example, see relationships in a holistic rather than a functional manner. This can

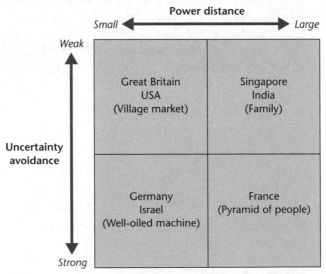

Figure 11.1 The relationship between Hofstede's cultural dimension and national leadership styles
Source: Hofstede, 2001: 377

be explained by considering attitudes to friendship. Dewey (1993), who studied British civil servants in India, and their relationship with Indians, in the early twentieth century, discovered they had contradictory views of friendship. The British took their idea of friendship from Oxbridge common rooms and gentlemen's clubs and saw it as a relationship that carried little obligation beyond that of good conversation. The Indians, however, saw friendship as a fundamental bond that carried obligations to sacrifice oneself, if necessary, to support a friend in all their endeavours. Unsurprisingly, Dewey found that British officials' attempts to befriend Indians often collapsed in recriminations of faithlessness. The importance Indians place on personal obligations is reflected in Hofstede's suggestion about how managers, in countries like India, might handle conflicts. He argued they would use a metaphor of the family in which problems were resolved by deference to the head of the family or by accepting the demands imposed by a friend.

Video clip 11.1	**Impact of culture on business** The clip deals with cultural values in Latin America and their impact on business practices. To view the video clip from the interview please visit this book's companion website at www.pearsoned.co.uk/fisherlovellvalerosilva.

Hofstede (1991) was concerned that his original IBM survey was conducted using a research questionnaire written from a western cultural perspective. A new survey based on Chinese perspectives was prepared and administered to respondents in 23 countries around the world. The results from the Chinese Values Survey supported the identification of three of Hofstede's value dimensions. The fourth one, however, uncertainty avoidance, could not be statistically identified in the raw results from the survey. Uncertainty is avoided, Hofstede argued, by establishing the truth. If the Chinese survey did not register this concern then it might be explained by the emphasis in Chinese values on virtue rather than truth. He proposed a fifth value dimension, which he labelled Confucian dynamism. Confucianism, the traditional philosophy of China, is not concerned with establishing religious Truths. Like Hinduism it is more concerned with practice than belief. To follow Confucianism or Hinduism it is not necessary to believe a creed, but it is required to behave in a particular way. This differentiates these religions from Christianity and Islam, which, while providing rules for daily life, require commitment to a creed. Confucianism stresses the importance of subordination in five key relationships (ruler-subject, father-son, older brother-younger brother, husband-wife, senior friend-junior friend), virtuous behaviour towards others and the adoption of key virtues such as thrift, hard work and study. Table 11.5 sets outs the Confucian values.

Table 11.5 Confucian values

Long-term Confucian values	Short-term Confucian values
■ Persistence and perseverance	■ Personal steadiness and stability
■ Ordering relationships by status	■ Protecting your 'face'
■ Thrift	■ Respect for tradition, reciprocation of greetings, favour and gifts
■ Having a sense of shame	

Source: Based on Hofstede, 1991: 165–6

The Confucian dynamism scale effectively measures the extent to which a society values a long-term rather than a short-term orientation. But the acceptance of the whole set of Confucian values marks, according to Hofstede (2001: 363), a major divide between western and eastern ethical approaches. Western ethical approaches are focused on identifying the moral truth, either by deontological or consequentialist means. The eastern traditions are more concerned with virtuous behaviour, which calls for the development of personal insight and judgment rather than knowledge. As pointed out in Chapter 3, many writers are arguing that a virtue ethics approach would be better suited to western businesses and organisations than that of western moral philosophy.

Moveable values

The argument so far has been based on the assumption that countries and societies have definable and discrete ethical beliefs and values. It would be wrong, however, to interpret this as meaning that they have fixed and monolithic ethical systems. Within societies and countries there will be competing interpretations of the shared values, and arguments about how they should change and develop. It is always dangerous therefore to talk about American values, British values or Indian values as if they could be authoritatively and definitively defined.

The development of thinking about management values in India can provide an example of how such debates progress. Much business and management education in India is based on American models. It is unsurprising that Indian managers have often acquired through their training an American set of business values. Many Indian academics and business people have seen this as demeaning to an ancient civilisation such as India's. Indeed they want to reverse the situation and emphasise the benefits that companies could achieve by learning from Indian traditions. A conference was held in Kozhikode, India in 2012, which explored the importance of Indian spiritual traditions for business (EABIS, 2012). Indian management thinkers have begun to develop an indigenous approach to management that is based in Indian thought and traditions (Gopinath, 1998). This, of course, is difficult because India has a rich and varied religious and philosophical history from which values might be drawn. Hinduism is the main strand but Islam,

Sikhism, Jainism, Zoroastrianism and others share a significant presence in Indian thought. Zoroastrianism is a particularly important element because it is the religion of the Parsi community from which many important Indian entrepreneurs come. We will concentrate on attempts to build modern business values from Hindu philosophy.

In Hindu thought there are four aims for humanity, *dharma* (righteousness), *artha* (wealth creation), *kama* (pleasure or material needs) and *moksha* (salvation from the transient to the eternal and the infinite). This philosophy is normally interpreted as making business and wealth creation an ethical imperative as long as it is circumscribed by a sense of duty and ethics. It is therefore opposed to the Friedmanite version of business ethics, which imposes no duty on businesses other than making profits for the shareholders. Chakraborty (1993, 1999) has developed a detailed system of business ethics and values based on the Vedanta and Yoga schools of Hindu philosophy. He has used it as a basis for consultancy and management development in Indian companies. Vedanta is based upon the *Upanishads*, which are sacred Hindu scriptures written between the fifth and eighth centuries BC. It is based on the existence of a supreme being or absolute called the Brahman. Surprisingly, for those who see Hinduism as a religion with many gods, Vedanta emphasises a monist belief in a single supreme being. The Brahman is the only reality. The world we perceive through our senses is, more or less depending upon which branch of Vedanta is followed, an illusion. The individual soul, through ignorance of the Brahman, believes in its own independent existence and importance. This sense of ego is the cause of all troubles in life. The end of religious striving is liberation from this false sense of individualism and a practical awareness of oneness with the absolute, with the Brahman. In Yoga this oneness can be expressed by the *purusha–prakriti* pairing. *Purusha* is the worldly and active term and *prakriti* is the still and contemplative term. The aim, according to Aurobindo Ghose, is to create a dual consciousness in which there is 'the one engaged in surface-level activity, caught in obscurity and struggle; the other, behind, remaining calm and strong with effortless insight' (Chakraborty, 1999: 6). It is this sense of oneness that, once achieved, leads to a life of unselfish service, which is the basis of Chakraborty's criticism of western management values and ethics. He argued that management development should not emphasise techniques and calculation but should encourage the spiritual development of managers and employees. Only when people have made a personal psychological journey will they be able to make ethical decisions in their jobs. This is an important theme in much Indian management literature. Mahesh (1995) and Diwedi (in Saini and Khan, 2000) stress the importance of ethical leadership and leaders with 'oriental soul'. Chakraborty argued, to take one specific example, that people who have achieved *moksha* would take a different view of change in business from that advocated by western textbooks. He criticised the fashion for constant change in business, in the name of economic growth, that has only led to disharmony between nations and between individuals. He proposed (Chakraborty, 1999: 24) some Vedantic principles that might be applied to organisational change:

■ Natural change, that is the cycle of birth, growth and death, is good but manmade change often goes against natural change and leads to irreparable harm to the environment and to relations between people.

■ For people to develop dual consciousness it is necessary for structures and institutions that have been developed from tradition to remain constant. Constant change of organisational structures and processes distracts people from their psychological development.

■ Change in organisation and business often implies exchanging a condition closer to the eternal for a position that is more ephemeral and transient. In particular the tendency for organisations to focus on the measurable, at the expense of that which is not, ethically weakens organisations.

Chakraborty's work is a complex attempt to produce business values that are specific to India and which provide a critique of western and American values. It will be subject to debate and challenge within India if for no other reason than that it is based on only one of India's religions, and indeed on a particular strand of Hinduism.

Other writers have drawn on different sources in Indian classical literature and identified other schemes of business ethics. One common source is the *Arthashastra* of Kautilya (Rangarajan, 1992), sometimes known as Chanakya. This is a vast treatise on statecraft, probably written in the third century BC and designed as a manual for the guidance of kings. Little is known of the author although there are many legends, and it is not even certain that a single person produced the work. This is a practical rather than a scriptural work and it is often compared with Machiavelli's *The Prince* (*see* p. 217). Most commentators on the work recognise that, like Machiavelli, Kautilya accepts that evil things sometimes have to be done in the best interests of the state. Several writers have argued that the lessons from the *Arthashastra* fit well with the values of modern western strategic thinking. Starzl and Dhir (1986) argued that the modern business world resembles the competing feudal states of India in the third century BC and that there is potential for Kautilya's principles to be applied to strategic planning. Kumar and Rao (1996) interpreted the *Arthashastra* as a recipe for modern value-based management. By this they meant the style of management, advocated by Peters and Waterman (1982), that involves defining corporate values and ensuring that staff are committed to them. They did not see Kautilya as being Machiavellian but instead saw his work as a source of 'ethical, moral and value based guidelines . . . which will be useful for present day management and organisations'.

Whether Kautilya, as some argue, is seen as providing unethical but practical advice on statecraft or, as others argue, is a source of value-based managerial prescriptions, he is still the source of a set of values that are held to be close to those of western management thought. This indigenous approach to management therefore is contrary to Chakraborty's approach, based on Vedanta, which is highly critical of western business values. This contradiction illustrates why it should not be assumed that countries or societies have simple, clear and consensual business ethics.

The two Indian perspectives discussed are themselves just particular views from within the Indian managerial and academic community. The bulk of management books published in India take a mainstream approach to management based on, and contributing to, a worldwide general consensus about the matter of management. Indeed Indian managerial technocrats have faced the ethical charge, also levelled at management generally, of being instrumentally rational, that it is to say they too focused on means and are not concerned with the proper ends of those means. A study by Sahay and Walsham (1997: 432) of a GIS and satellite imaging system that was designed to benefit Indian farmers identified the scientists' lack of interest in anything beyond the working of the new technology. They did not see the exploitation of the technology to ensure the agricultural benefits as their concern. India's pre-eminence in IT and software has brought it much benefit but it also produces a view that the setting up of a software package, such as a customer relations marketing (CRM) system, is the whole solution to the problem of establishing relationships with customers and certainly does not question what the nature of that relationship should be.

Of course, Indian management writers do not simply accept the prescriptions and techniques of western management writers. An example is the Indian response to the American notion of human resource management (HRM), which has almost exclusively replaced the old personnel management in industrialised countries. The key theme of HRM is that it is not simply a necessary administrative function, which was how its predecessor personnel management was seen, but it is a strategically central function that makes a direct contribution to organisations' financial and other success. This idea is new in India where the emphasis has been on personnel management, industrial relations and human resource development (Saini and Khan, 2000). Rao (2000) pointed out some ethical problems with the fashion for the adoption of HRM. HRM ignores context, in particular the tradition of strong unions in India and the illegality of retrenchment, which means that voluntary retirement is the most common method of downsizing in India. To replace this approach with HRM's distrust of unions and with a strategic approach to downsizing (as recommended by the Federation of Indian Chambers of Commerce and Industry) on the basis of hunches as to what works in the USA would be unwise. He also points out the ethical hypocrisy of HRM.

> Employees may be told that they are the organisations's most valued resource, and soon after they find themselves in a redundancy programme. They may be exposed to various participative management styles, teamwork, cellular working etc., and simultaneously exposed to aggressive anti-union policies.

> (Rao, 2000: 116)

Rao (2000: 133) accuses American concepts of HRM of being 'pseudospiritual' (because they are based on American values rather than on scientific research); an ironic charge because in the world of national stereotypes India, not the USA, is the place of spirituality and ashrams. He argues that adopting American practices will lead India to long-term disaster. Other Indian commentators on HRM (Dwivedi, 2000) contrarily seek to take aspects of HRM, such as empowerment, and to root them in classical Indian philosophy by seeing the implementation of the concept developing through four stages of *kali*, *dvaper*, *tretya* and *satya* (in Hindi thought these are the four *yuga* or ages that make up a historical aeon and they each have their own spiritual characteristics. We are currently in the *kali-yuga*). The manner of India's adoption of HRM exemplifies the complex relationships between different sets of management values and ethical positions. It is not a simple matter of there being an outright acceptance of American ideas of HRM, or a simple rejection of it and its replacement by an entirely Indian view, rather it is a process of interactive sense-making in which something distinct, but not separate from what preceded it, emerges.

The discussion so far in this section has focused on the formal and normative literature about what Indian business ethics should be. The business values actually adopted in India can be seen in the broad sweep of Indian history in the second half of the twentieth century. From Indian independence in 1947 until 1991 public policy focused on economic isolationism and self-sufficiency. As Nehru, the first prime minister of independent India, said, 'It is better to have a second-rate thing made in one's own country than a first-rate thing one has to import'. The socialism that predominated in these years also led to the development of a Licence Raj in which there were many bureaucratic controls on business. This approach to economic development also reflected Mahatma Gandhi's moral preference for self-sufficiency. At this period policy reflected Hindu values that refused pre-eminence to economic growth.

In 1991, the government of India changed its policy and started a process of economic liberalisation. The licensing system was abolished, trade barriers were lowered and foreign investment was made easier. The amount of direct foreign investment rose from virtually nothing to $2bn a year. Liberalisation encouraged Indian companies to adopt western business values and Indians working for western multinationals in India exhibited western business values (Singh, 1990: 92). The change in India's business policies provides the context in which, as we have seen, Indian managers have begun to adopt HRM. The change may also encourage Kautilya's ethics rather than those of Vedanta.

Although there are attempts at producing universal ethical standards they have not yet had a major impact on international business. There is evidence that people in different countries have different values that they apply to business. In broad terms there is a dialogue, a process of sense-making, between the predominant values of western businesses and cultures and the desire of many in developing countries who wish to see business ethics that reflect their indigenous ethical and religious traditions.

The normative debate about ethical universalism and relativism in the business context

The normative implications and arguments

The existence of different ethical standards and values in different societies and countries raises difficulties for normative and philosophical thinking about ethics. If different countries have different customary values that each regards as valid then philosophers' attempts to define what is good and right are undermined. All that a multinational company has to do is follow the maxim, 'When in Rome do as the Romans do'. But what if we feel that what is allowed in some countries is wrong? Does a relativist position mean that any practice or value in a society has to be accepted as long as it has a patina of tradition? A number of arguments can be put forward that constrain the apparent arbitrariness of relativist ethics.

The need for standards is universal

Although societies may have different ethical practices and values they all have a universal requirement to have such norms (Blackburn, 2001: 22). Societies may treat their children differently when they come of age. Some buy them cars and send them as far away as possible to universities, some send them out to find their fortune, some require them to join the family firm and some require them to get married as soon as possible. But all these societies share a need to have some ethical standards about how they treat their new adults. It is a similar situation in organisations. They all need, for example, ethical standards for the treatment of family members working in an organisation. In some cultures they would be seen as an embarrassment and people would feel guilty that they might be seen to be favouring their relatives. In other cultures it would be expected that family members would be favoured. Family members might be less favourably treated in cultures where they are seen as a threat to the status of other family members in the organisation. Yet, in all this variety there is an acceptance that there need to be some standards to help people cope with this particular situation. This allows a universal imperative to underlie ethical diversity.

In some cases it really does not matter what the rule is as long as there is one. It is important that all the drivers in a country drive on the right or on the left, but which they choose is of little consequence. Many differences in business and managerial values fall into this category in which value diversity causes no ethical problems. Attitudes to working hours and holidays are an example. Americans generally put more hours into their job than Europeans, and the gap between the two is increasing. Americans also have less entitlement to holidays. The Spanish in contrast to the Americans take two-hour lunch breaks, eat late at night, go to bed late, have lots of public holidays and take extended vacations in July or August (*Director*, 2001: 32). This is often explained by the different cultural values of the Americans and the Europeans. The former value increasing their income over leisure and there is some evidence that the Americans are correct in thinking that extra effort leads to higher income. One study showed that extra effort does result in promotions and pay increases (Koretz, 2001). The Europeans place a premium on leisure. These differences in values may have good and bad economic consequences – the Europeans are poorer than they might be if they had adopted American values – but the differences are ethically neutral. As long as most Europeans are happy with their values, and most Americans happy with theirs, it does not matter ethically which values they choose. It is possible that there is a loss of happiness caused by Americans spending less time with their families but it is by no means certain that the detriment is not counterbalanced by some families being happier when one of their number is at work and by the pleasure they gain from spending the extra money that is earned.

Some value differences between countries do raise ethical problems, however. Attitudes towards discrimination at work against certain population groups often differ and they can become points of inter-cultural conflict. For example, the degree to which discrimination against women is accepted varies between countries. It would be helpful to find ways of distinguishing between important and inconsequential differences in ethical norms. Donaldson and Dunfee have attempted to do this by using the idea of a social contract and to develop a distinctive approach, which they call *Integrative Social Contract Theory* (ISCT). At the core of the theory

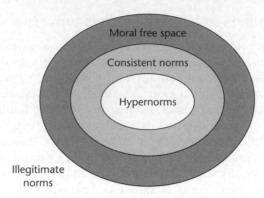

Figure 11.2 Integrated social contract theory

are four norms or categories of values. One way to visualise ISCT is in the form of concentric circles, with the core foundational values at the centre (Figure 11.2).

The norms are described as follows.

Hypernorms. These are argued to be fundamental human rights or basic pre-scriptions common to most religions. The values they represent are by definition acceptable to all cultures and all organisations. These have the characteristics of universal norms and in order to be workable will be few in number. What is and what is not a hypernorm would be agreed by rational debate and any contender for 'hypernorm' status would fail if it could be shown not to be universalisable. The issue of universal norms raises all the problems that Kantian ethics encounter, but rather than turning to something akin to Ross's (1930) *prima facie obligations*, Donaldson and Dunfee introduce two 'lower level' norms that allow for 'local' variations to be possible. The first of these is *consistent norms*.

Consistent norms. These values are more culturally specific than hypernorms, but they will be consistent with hypernorms and other legitimate norms, the latter being defined as a norm that does not contradict the hypernorm test (Donaldson and Dunfee, 1999: 46). Donaldson and Dunfee cite corporate mission statements as examples of 'consistent norms'.

Moral free space. This notion accepts that hypothetically people would allow that, in particular and different places, is acceptable for local norms to be established. An example could be norms about the use of child labour, which might be seen as acceptable as long as minimum conditions, such as providing education to child employees, are met. Moral free space means that conflicting norms may exist within, say, a multinational company. This is contentious, and this interpretation does not meet with universal agreement, but it does show the flexibility that would be essential for such a framework to be useful for a multinational corporation endeavouring to make sense of developing an ethi-cal framework where certain practices, for example nepotism, might be unac-ceptable in most western cultures, but acceptable and important in others, for example Indian society.

Illegitimate norms. These norms are irreconcilable with *hypernorms*. For some this might be the case with regard to the treatment of women and children in some societ-ies, but for others some of these 'problems' might fit within a 'moral free space' that would allow some development of understanding on all sides to see if a longer-term relationship might be possible with some modification to the 'problems' in question.

As a result of the above type of example, ISCT has been criticised for being relativist. Donaldson and Dunfee refute this, arguing that ISCT is pluralist, combining the notion of universal norms of behaviour (hypernorms) with the recognition of important cultural differences (consistent norms and moral free space). The authors also recognise that, within the theory, individuals, corporations and communities have to work out for themselves what are their respective 'norms', at all levels.

> Business ethics should be viewed more as a story in the process of being written than as a moral code like the Ten Commandments. It can, and should . . . adjust over time – to evolving technology, and to the cultural or religious attitudes of particular economic conditions.

> (Donaldson and Dunfee, 1999: viii)

Donaldson and Dunfee go on to say,

> At the heart of social contract effort is a simple assumption, namely that we can understand better the obligations of key social institutions, such as business or government, by attempting to understand what is entailed in a fair agreement or 'contract' between those institutions and society and also in the implicit contracts that exist among the different communities and institutions within society.

> (Donaldson and Dunfee, 1999: 16–7)

In order to provide a mechanism that might help operationalise ISCT, Donaldson and Dunfee employ a modified form of Rawls' veil of ignorance. Unlike Rawls' conception of the veil of ignorance, in which those (metaphorically) placed behind the veil have no knowledge of any aspect of their status, ethnic origin, physical abilities, gender, geographic location, political and economic system, etc., in Donaldson and Dunfee's conception only those aspects of a person's identity that are economic in nature, e.g. level of personal skill, nature of economic system, type of employing organisation, employment position held, etc. are concealed. It is hoped that this modified Rawlsian artifice may facilitate reflection and debate about an 'objective' fairness that should be inherent within an economic system, and the ethical and moral base of that system.

ISCT attempts to hold on to both the integrity of universalisable norms (minimum accepted standards of behaviour irrespective of where in the world the norms are being considered), but avoiding the inflexibility of non-consequentialist stances. This is addressed by the introduction of the consistent norms and the moral free space. It is an interesting development, providing as it does a schema or framework that business people can employ to interrogate the ethical and moral issues that might be at stake in a particular situation. Donaldson and Dunfee are emphatic that ISCT is not a framework, let alone an approach, that can be employed unthinkingly. By its very nature it is a framework for facilitating discussion, debate and argument. It is not a decision-making tool for the type of ethically charged situations that corporations are often faced with, as these are invariably too complex and multi-faceted to lend themselves to easy formulation and calculation. However, the ideas and categories within ISCT do provide a language and a set of concepts that may help parties to a decision to think constructively about the different issues and dimensions inherent within a complex business scenario.

A contingency approach

So far it has been argued that the need for some values and standards may be universally present in all societies but that the particular values adopted by different societies may, in practice, vary. In terms of the ISCT theory just discussed there may be some moral free space. This does not mean that anything goes: that because there is no one best scheme of values all contenders may be equally valid. If a system of values is relative it must be relative to something; and if this is so then it must be possible to argue that some sets of ethics are more relevant to the 'thing' than other sets. The difficult question, of course, is 'what is the thing' to which ethics can be judged relevant. There are several answers. According to situational ethics, which developed from Anglican theology (Fletcher, 1966), that thing is love, the obligation to act lovingly towards others. Another possible answer, which may be of particular use in a business and management context, is the economic and social context people find themselves in. Although it may be possible to argue that a set of ethical standards is more or less suited to particular circumstances, the naturalistic fallacy prevents us from claiming that such standards are true, in the same way that true standards could be derived from the notion of love. This is because it is not possible to derive an 'ought' statement from an 'is' statement. A social and economic account of a society is a descriptive statement and so moral imperatives cannot be derived from it. Love, however, is a normative, moral concept and can be the basis for a definition of universal values. Nevertheless a contingency approach rescues relativist ethics from being undiscriminating; it does allow some ethical schemes to be judged as better than others.

DEFINITION

The **naturalistic fallacy** was defined by philosopher G.E. Moore (1873–1958). Naturalism is the belief that the criterion of right action is some feature of the world that can be described, such as the happiness of people. Moore argued that this was wrong and took an intuitionist view that fundamental moral truths are directly understood by a special faculty of moral knowledge or thinking. Moral thinking, just as mathematical thinking, is *a priori* and exists independently of our perceptions of the world. The knowledge that one plus one equals two is not based upon experimentation. The good can be explained but it is too simple to be defined. The good can no more be defined than can the colour yellow. In general terms the naturalistic fallacy is taken to mean that a moral statement about what is good or right (i.e. what ought to be) cannot be inferred from any description of how things in the world are. To say, for example, that a particular ethical code adopted in one country makes its citizens prosperous and happy does not imply that those values and standards are moral.

The contingency idea is a common one in management theory. It is the idea that there is no one best way of doing something, no universal answer, but that there will be different best ways for different circumstances. Styles of leadership, organisational structures and cultures and strategic choices may all be contingent upon particular aspects of an organisation's nature and circumstances. This idea might be applied to business ethics.

All societies need a system of ethical values and standards that, with more or less effectiveness, creates circumstances in which people feel safe to do business. These values and standards should encourage the trust necessary for people and organisations to work with others, or at least provide remedies and sanctions if trust is broken. But insurance against untrustworthy business contacts can be achieved by various sets of values and norms. In different places at different times this end might be achieved by:

■ reliance on contracts and the rule of law;

■ relying on family and friendship and only doing business with those from whom trust can be taken for granted. In China, this is known as *guanxi*, the network of personal and family connections that cement business relationships;

■ developing personal and individual relationships with those with whom business is done; and

■ deal making so that it is in the mutual self-interest of both parties to show trust.

The ethical end of all of these means is the same, but it could be that each would be effective in particular circumstances. The contingency idea provides a possible yardstick against which the relative merit of a set of ethical standards might be judged. So while it might not be possible to say that a particular set of values is true and definitive and allows room for no other, it could be argued that one set of values is better suited to the contingent circumstances than another. As Umberto Eco (1992: 52) wrote when discussing the wide range of interpretations one can put on a particular text, 'If there are no rules that help ascertain which interpretations are the "best" ones there is at least a rule for ascertaining which ones are "bad"'.

This idea can be explored by looking at Indian and Chinese overseas businesses operating in the Asian arena. A particular feature of businesses in South-east Asia (Hong Kong, Indonesia, Malaysia, Thailand and the Philippines) is the presence of networks of Chinese and Indian family-based firms. The family businesses that make up these networks are often large conglomerates. Haley and Haley (1998) argued that these networks exist in a different strategic environment from that of most large western companies.

■ The Chinese and Indians are mostly ethnically separate from the populations of the countries in which their companies do business. They have the uncertainty of being alien, and in the case of the Indian networks the memory of their community's expulsion from Uganda in 1972 provides a reminder of the risks borne by aliens.

■ Governments in the region are often whole or part owners of major companies and this increases the importance to strategic success of contacts with, and access to, ministers and public servants.

- There is in South-east Asia an 'informational void'. Relative to the western economies there is a shortage of objective, statistical, research-based market and business information.

- There are doubts about the extent of the rule of law and, in some cases, about the adequacy of the 'background institutions' that support trust in business transactions.

These features make the strategic environment uncertain and difficult for overseas entrepreneurs. In South-east Asia contract and law were thought to provide a poor source of security for the Indian and Chinese networks. Instead they created the trust they needed by working within their family- or community-based networks, where trust is ensured by traditional community values and/or by family relationships. Both the Chinese and Indian networks share a belief in filial loyalty to fathers. Chinese Confucianism identifies this as one of the five relationships that are an ethical duty. The intensity of familial loyalty is as strong among the Indian networks. The concept of *dharma* imposes the need to achieve financial success as a duty to the family (Gidoomal and Porter, 1997; Haley and Haley, 1998: 310). Hayley and Hayley also pointed out, though, that in their dealings with large western corporations, which generate less uncertainty, the overseas Indian networks do view their contractual obligations as ethically binding. The Chinese networks also place importance on developing personal relationships with individuals outside the family.

The existence of the Chinese and Indian networks allows the businesses within them to operate differently from western corporations. They are secretive and keep low public profiles. They use their family-based networks for support, finance and advice. Rather than base decisions on objective research, network members often use the subjective judgments and experience of trusted members of the network. The Indian overseas businesses often use their own networks to finance their ventures, thus avoiding the conventional banking system. This is a development of a traditional Indian financial instrument known as the *hoondie*. A *hoondie* is a bill of exchange issued within a network and the system is based upon the honour and reputation of those within it. The reliance on internal network resources, including trusted contacts within regional governments, and on qualitative judgments that can be rapidly collated, allows overseas Indian and Chinese businesses to take decisions and actions very rapidly. Haley and Haley (1998: 314) argued that these Indian and Chinese entrepreneurs take an emergent approach to strategy, which responds to knowledge of changes in the business environment that are detected and disseminated by the network. Through their webs of contacts these businesses also seek to influence the regional governments so as to acquire and maintain a favourable business environment and government contracts. The choice of the Indian and Chinese networks to give ethical priority to family and personal relationships rather than to legal or corporate relationships is arguably appropriate for their circumstances.

As shown in Table 11.6, Japanese business values are different from those of the overseas Indian and Chinese business networks. Japanese society values traders whereas the status of merchants in Chinese and Indian cultures is questionable. The importance of primogeniture in Japan means that Japanese family businesses outlive Chinese ones. In Japan's business culture trust is built upon contractual

Table 11.6   Value attributes of overseas business networks in South-east Asia

Attributes	Chinese	Indian	Japanese
Firm			
Merchants	Reviled	Specialised	Exalted
Primogeniture	None	Very strong	Strong
Firm's lifespan	Short	Medium	Long
Loyalty			
Family definition	Blood	Blood	Role
Focus	Individual	Group	Institution
Intensity	Low	High	High
Filial piety v. patriotism	Opposed	No relationship	Equivalent
Commercial trust			
Ethical foundation	Five relationships and social harmony	Dharma	Mutual self-interest
Ethical focus	The Way	Family	Service to father figure
Expectations of benefits	Immediate and up-front	Immediate and up-front	Delayed

Source: From Boxing with shadows: competing effectively with the overseas Chinese and overseas Indian business networks in the Asian Arena, *Journal of Organisational Change Management*, Vol. 11, No. 4, Fig. III, p. 308 (Haley, G. T. and Haley, U. C. V. 1998), © Emerald Group Publishing Limited. All rights reserved.

obligations and personal and corporate self-interest, whereas the obligations of personal relations are more important in the Chinese and Indian environments. Japanese business people are more likely to take a long-term view, whereas the overseas Indian and Chinese business networks expect more immediate returns. Haley and Haley (1998: 307) argued that Japan's different business values were appropriate to their different strategic environments compared to the Chinese and Indian overseas business networks. While the latter, as has already been argued, worked in an informational void and were operating in regional markets in South-east Asia, the Japanese companies aimed their exports at North American and European markets. They have not operated in the informational void experienced by the overseas business networks and their emphasis on contractual obligations and mutual self-interest is arguably well suited to dealings with western economies.

This is not to imply that there may not be cultural clashes between Europe and North America on the one hand and Japan on the other. Trompenaars and Hampden-Turner (1993: 196–7) gave an example of how an American's neglect of role and ritual in his dealings with a Japanese company president caused problems in a negotiation. The American was trying to nail down the specifics of a deal and ignored the largely ceremonial role of presidents of Japanese firms. In his frustration at the evasive answers he was receiving in response to detailed questions he absent-mindedly rolled up the president's business card, which had been formally presented to him, and scraped his fingernails clean with it. The Japanese president was apparently displeased. Nevertheless, the common emphasis of Americans and Japanese on contractual obligations and corporate mutual self-interest as an ethical basis for trust would generally be of benefit to the business relations between the two countries.

Activity 11.1	Bases of trust

The discussion above has identified a number of different bases upon which trust in others, in business dealings and negotiations, can be developed.

■ Contracts and mutual self-interest

■ Family and clan relationships

■ Personal relationships (as in *guanxi*).

What problems or benefits might emerge if business people from different social and cultural backgrounds were to find themselves in a business negotiation in which they based their trust in others on different factors?

1. Contracts and mutual self-interest .... Family and clan relationships

2. Contracts and mutual self-interest .... Personal relationships

3. Family and clan relationships .... Personal relationships

4. Family and clan relationships .... Family and clan relationships

(but both are from different family networks)

A contingent approach to ethics does not mean that circumstances cause the acceptance of particular values or ethical norms. The business conditions found in South-east Asia did not cause the overseas Indian and Chinese business networks to adopt their particular values. These came, as much as from anywhere, from the traditional values of their communities. The fit between their values and the strategic environment did, however, create an 'evolutionary' pressure that maintained them.

The relationship between situational factors and a society's ethical norms is mediated by people's thinking, debating and power game. People will only begin to change their values if they think there is a misfit between their values and their circumstances. Such awareness does not come easily for an individual and may only have an impact through generational changes. The direction of the influence between situation and ethical norms may also alternate. The situation might influence changes in norms, or norms may encourage changes in the situation. These processes tend to operate over long periods of time. They can be illustrated by the history of Christian and Islamic attitudes towards the payment of interest on loans.

Interest is the money paid for the use of money. It is an essential feature of modern financial systems. The Bible, however, clearly states that taking interest on a loan is wrong. Usury is the formal term for charging any interest on a loan, although it is now only used for extortionate rates of interest. The Old Testament forbade the Israelites to charge each other usury but they were allowed to levy usury on 'foreigners' (Deuteronomy 23: 20). The logic appears to be that in ancient societies most loans were for consumption, to help people survive hard times, rather than to finance entrepreneurial activities. In this circumstance it was wrong to charge interest. The New Testament also finds usury wrong. It is implied that even charging usury to 'foreigners' is wrong. As part of loving one's enemy interest-free loans should be made to any who needed them. In medieval times these Biblical injunctions were taken very seriously. Interest was seen as unjust because it meant charging a continuing rent for the use of money that could only be spent once (Buckley, 1998).

Such an ethical position was not helpful to the growing number of merchants and entrepreneurs who emerged in Europe during the Reformation. Slowly the official position on usury began to change to one that was more conducive to business enterprise. It was recognised that there was a legitimate difference between loans for consumption and loans for investment. The idea developed, for example, that a creditor could receive compensatory payments for the loss of use of their money from the start of the loan and not simply, as was traditional, for failure to pay off the loan at the agreed date. But it was not accepted that the creditor who loaned for entrepreneurial purposes should have a risk-free entitlement to interest whilst the merchant bore all the commercial risk of the enterprise. It was felt that the financier should share the risk in a partnership agreement.

Jean Calvin, who lived in the highly commercial city of Geneva in the sixteenth century, triggered a change in the Christian view of interest, although his writings were not a great change on the traditional position. He argued that the poor should still be given loans without interest but that otherwise it was acceptable to charge interest on a loan as long as the rate was reasonable and the security taken was not excessive. He dismissed the Biblical strictures against interest because they were designed for a society very different from the mercantile one in which he lived (Tawney, 1966: 115–16). Although Calvin's ethical adjustment was small it led to a widespread acceptance of the justness of interest as long as the rate was fair. The issue moved from the ethics of interest to the ethics of the rate of interest. This example illustrates how ethical norms might change under the influence of new circumstances.

Such changes, however, are not inevitable. Islam, for example, has the same view of interest as that expressed in the Bible. But in Islam, unlike in Christianity, the injunction has survived into modern times so that practising Muslims have developed financial techniques that work without the concept of interest. Interest (*riba*), defined as any risk-free or guaranteed rate of return on a loan or investment, is prohibited. Loans must be made without interest according to Islamic law (*sharia*) (Failaka International, 2001). Islam defines money as a means of exchange that has no intrinsic value. Value is only generated by the human effort behind exchanges and transactions. It follows that money should not be made from money, because that is the same as receiving something for nothing. Islam is not against entrepreneurial activity but it should properly be conducted through partnership financing (*mudaraba*) in which the entrepreneur and the financier share profits or losses according to a pre-agreed ratio.

The prohibition against *riba* makes contact with western banks and financial instruments, based as they are on the idea of interest, improper for practising Muslims. Credit cards are a particular problem. Some scholars argue that Muslims can open credit card accounts as long as they always pay off the debt each month and so avoid incurring interest charges. Others (Al Andalusia, 2001) argue that when a credit card account is opened a contract is signed which commits the cardholder to paying interest in certain circumstances. Muslims should not sign such a contract in which they agree, in principle, to sin. However, financial techniques can be developed that avoid *riba*. For example, the *Bai Muajjal* form of contract is permissible. The bank or provider of capital buys goods or assets on behalf of a business owner. They then sell the goods to the client at an agreed price that involves a percentage for profit. This is proper because, as in Christian thought, it is acceptable to charge a higher price if the payment is to be deferred. At least one bank provides an Islamic credit card based on this form of contract (Failaka International, 2001). Many banks now offer personal and business financing that avoids *riba* (Arif, 1988; Lariba.com, 2001). According to some reports (Anon., 1995), the deposit assets held by Islamic banks increased from $5bn in 1985 to over $60bn in 1994. The development of Islamic financial instruments is an example of how situations and circumstances can be adapted contingently to a set of ethical principles.

A stakeholder approach

In addition to the contingency principle, there is another criterion that can be used to judge the relative merits of a system of business ethics and values. It is the question of who benefits from a particular scheme of ethics. This criterion depends upon drawing a stakeholder map of all the groups and constituencies who may be affected by, or have a concern with, an ethical proposition. Identifying who benefits and who suffers from its application can test the validity of the proposition. This can be explained by reference to a Rawlsian perspective, as discussed in Chapter 3. One of the principles Rawls proposed was that social and economic inequalities are to be arranged so that they are both (a) reasonably expected to be to everyone's advantage, and (b) attached to positions and offices open to all. Rawls calls the first part of this statement the difference principle. Different systems of business ethics could be tested against the difference principle and if they do not benefit all the stakeholders involved then they could be judged invalid.

An example can be taken from current Indian recruitment practice. Traditional Indian society was divided into *jati* or castes. These were extended kinship groups that could be classified under four main *varna* – the priestly castes, the warrior castes, the merchants and the farmers. A person's caste no longer determines their occupation but it still carries social and status significance in India. This is particularly so for the groups who are excluded from the caste categories. These are the *dalits*, in traditional terms the untouchables, and people from the tribal areas of India. These groups are normally the most economically and socially excluded groups in India (Dhesi, 1998). Caste discrimination is illegal in India. The government operates a system of positive discrimination in which quotas of jobs in public organisations and nationalised industries and places in colleges and universities are reserved for *dalits* and tribals. How would this policy stand against the difference principle? It clearly benefits a group of people, the *dalits* and the tribals, who would be disadvantaged if the policy were not in place. It could be argued that it is to the advantage of all to overcome discrimination against the worst off in society if for no other reason than to prevent the civil unrest that such discrimination might lead to. However, the policy might contravene Rawls' second principle, that positions should be open to all. Blackburn (2001: 27) suggests that when judging whether a local ethical standard is acceptable it is not enough simply to consider the views of the 'Brahmins, mullahs, priests and elders who hold themselves to be spokesmen for *their* culture'. A wider group of stakeholders needs to be considered, especially those who are oppressed or disadvantaged by that ethical standard. A stakeholder analysis based on Rawls' difference principle provides a mechanism for judging the validity of a particular ethical position in business.

The diversity of business values and ethics in different societies and countries does not mean that any ethical position can be justified. An acceptance of an ethical relativist position does not imply that any value or practice has to be accepted as long as it can be shown to be indigenous or traditional. In this section a number of tests have been suggested which could be used by managers to decide whether a particular local ethical stance should be regarded as valid or not. It has to be accepted, of course, that this might not be enough for a convinced ethical universalist, who would want to argue that there can only be one true ethical system, and that everyone ought to adopt it.

When different sets of organisational and managerial values meet

Introduction

The normal view of the different values and standards in different countries is that at a time of increasing world trade it is a problem. The experience of coming from one country and suddenly working in a different culture is described as culture shock. For multinational companies and organisations therefore the existence of different national values is a management problem to be overcome.

Holden (2002: 284–5) points out that this traditional view is unhelpful and unnecessarily negative. He argues that the old view was based on an over-simple idea that national cultures and sets of values were entirely distinct from each other and were separate objects that bumped and scraped against each other. He illustrates in his book that different cultures are best understood as overlapping networks of ideas and values both within and between countries. Indeed many individuals will have an accumulation of sets of values that may not necessarily fit together neatly in their own minds. A manager in a western-owned company operating in India may have been born in India but brought up and educated in the USA, have worked for a time in the UK and Azerbaijan and holiday frequently in Spain. Such a person's values will form a complex network. They will have some values based on their upbringing in a Hindu family of a particular caste. Their education and admiration for the USA will probably reinforce some aspects of their values at the expense of others. Their work experience in Azerbaijan may have highlighted their dislike of some traditional aspects of Soviet and Hindu values, such as automatic respect for those grown old. Experiences while a junior would have similarly buttressed these views but their more recent jobs as a senior manager may have modified the value they attach to experience. For such a person this interlocking set of values can only be an asset when they find themselves confronting the task of managing their new team in the company in India. Their cultural awareness would help make them skilled at negotiating a range of issues from the role of bribery to the appropriate leadership style. The point that Holden (2002: 284) makes is that a cultural mix should be seen as an organisational resource. For him cross-cultural management in MNCs should be seen as an aspect of knowledge management that enables people to learn from the surrounding diversity of cultures.

In the next section an attempt is made to analyse the process of learning that takes place when people have sets of values that partly overlap but are in part distinct.

A dialectical analysis

Since the disintegration of the Soviet Union into many smaller independent states the attempts by western trainers to inculcate western business values into managers in the new countries have provided many case studies of what happens when competing sets of values clash. In this section it is argued that the process, seen in a case study from Azerbaijan, can best be understood as an aspect of Hegel's dialectic (Fisher et al, 2008).

DEFINITION

Dialectics of self-consciousness, Lord and bondsman and of the unhappy consciousness

The basic structure of the dialectic is explained on p. 195. In this definition box we will describe a particular sequence of dialectics, part of a wider set of dialectics described in the *Phenomenology of Spirit* (Hegel, 2003: 104–30). The three dialectic processes are:

1. the dialectic of self-consciousness;

2. the dialectic of master and slave; and

3. the dialectic of unhappy consciousness.

The first dialectic, of self-consciousness, begins when the idea of consciousness 'as pure abstraction of self-consciousness' is challenged 'by the particularity everywhere characteristic of existence as such' (Hegel, 2003: 107). This duality brings self-consciousnesses into a life and death conflict (as Hegel expresses it, hyperbolically, for our purposes). The presence of various others contradicts each self-consciousness' sense of its own absolute existence and so it must cancel out the other. This dialectic will be used to explore the initial relationships between western experts and the trainees they appointed to the new college, and between the intermediaries and the local managers they sought to influence.

This first duality is overcome by one self-consciousness cancelling the other by gaining power and control over it. This then begins the dialectic of the master and the slave, or Lord and bondsman in some translations.

> They stand as two opposed forms or modes of consciousness. The one is independent, and its essential nature is to be for itself: the other is dependent, and its essence is life or existence for another. The former is the master, or Lord, the latter the bondsman.
>
> (Hegel, 2003: 108)

In such a hierarchical relationship the dominant party confirms its superiority by comparing its high status to the subordinate partner's low status. Contradictorily this makes the dominant party dependent on the subordinate. This mirror imaging, in which the greater is reflected in the lesser and vice versa, contradicts the master's formal superiority by revealing its dependence on the slave for practicalities and for confirmation of its status. As the slave becomes aware of its importance to the master through its practical labour the dualism is resolved thus:

> In labour where there seemed to be merely some outsider's [the master's] mind and ideas involved, the bondsman becomes aware, through this re-discovery of himself by himself, of having and being a 'mind of his own'.
>
> (Hegel, 2003: 111)

This dialectic will be used to analyse the stage in the relationship when the western experts discover themselves dependent on the Azerbaijani trainees, in their role as intermediaries; and the trainees find themselves dependent on the Azerbaijani managers they are training and developing.

In the dialectic of the unhappy consciousness the newly self-aware consciousness experiences, within itself (and not between itself and others as was the case in the preceding dialectic), a conflict between stoicism and scepticism that resolves itself as an acceptance of a thing for lack of something better. The conflict between stoicism and scepticism is again one between empty form and chaotic particularity.

> Scepticism is the realisation of that of which stoicism is merely the notion, and is the actual experience of what freedom of thought is . . .

> This consciousness [ ] is here neither more nor less than an absolutely fortuitous embroglio, the giddy whirl of a perpetually self-creating disorder.
>
> (Hegel, 2003: 118, 119–120)

The mutual learning that happened when imported western experts met the Azerbaijanis who were to be trained as the new academic faculty of the School of Public Administration will be explored using a case study of a project to set up a new School for Public Administration in Azerbaijan. The project was one of many, begun after the collapse of the Soviet Union, that were designed to modernise the new post-Soviet republics by replacing their institutions with western, democratic and free-market ones. The School for Public Administration was to deliver a range of programmes to government officials, including a master's degree, that was intended to create western-style public service organisations. It was to be a new faculty within the rump of a former Soviet institute that had retained its rector, who had been appointed in Soviet times, its administrative and technical staff, but not its academic staff. A number of local trainees were recruited, whom the western experts would train to become the academic faculty of the new school.

The project was based on a cascade model that was analogous to, but not knowingly based upon, a process that had its classical formulation in Macaulay's minute on education in India. The intention in India was to use an English education to form

> a class of persons, Indian in colour and blood, but English in tastes, opinions, in morals and in intellect . . . who may be interpreters between us and the millions we govern.

(Keay, 2000: 431)

This model necessarily implies three main stakeholders, the western experts (as the European Union officials insisted they be called), the Azerbaijanis who were recruited to the college and who were to be trained to become its academic faculty (and who would be the intermediaries) and the managers in Azerbaijani organisations who would be trained by the new staff of the new school. As these managers were mostly appointed in the Soviet period they fell under the two categories of the *nomenklatura* (privileged elite who held their posts through Communist party patronage) and the *apparatchiks* (party functionaries who implemented policy). However, in this section only the relationship between the western experts and the Azerbaijani trainees will be considered.

The manner in which this relationship develops is outlined in Table 11.7.

The dialectic of self-consciousness

In the Azerbaijan project the relationship between the western experts and local trainees (the change agents to be) was intended to be equal and open. In the early days this ideal relationship was contradicted by both parties' perception of the other as separate and distinct from themselves. There was a mutual suspicion and lack of empathy as in the dialectic of self-consciousness (Mabbott, 1967: 38). The dialectic begins with the abstract, undiscriminating philanthropy of the western experts. In formal terms they saw their role as bringing the benefits of democracy, public service and markets to the former Soviet state. They expressed a formal and universal benevolence but their ignorance of the local context made their efforts unfocused. The impossibility of direct transplantation of western ideals into

Table 11.7   The dialectic of western experts and local change agents

The dialectic of self-consciousness		
Thesis	**Antithesis**	**Synthesis**
The western experts express an undiscriminating and universalised philanthropy, which assumes that the local and western parties can have an equal and mutually beneficial partnership.	In practice both the local and western parties are self-conscious and wary of the other. They accuse each other of individualism, each party seeking to fulfil its own selfish ambitions. This leads to a lack of trust.	The lack of trust is overcome by the development of a hierarchical relationship between the two parties. The western experts are seen as dominant.
The dialectic of master and slave		
Thesis	**Antithesis**	**Synthesis**
The western experts are seen as high-status individuals whose role is to introduce locals to new western values and techniques.	Although formally superior the western experts are practically dependent upon the local trainees' cooperation. Socially the locals' demands upon the westerners were greater than the westerners' demands of friendship.	The western experts and local change agents recognise their mutual dependence and develop a more equal working relationship based upon the assumption of shared western values.
The dialectic of unhappy consciousness		
Thesis	**Antithesis**	**Synthesis**
Both western experts and local change agents stoically accept that it is necessary to bring Azerbaijani organisations into line with a western free-market model.	But sceptically both now doubt whether a simple transfer of western values and practices into Azerbaijan is feasible or workable. They struggle over how the two institutional templates should be meshed.	A reasoned concatenation of the two templates based upon some concept of unity-in-diversity; however this process was still ongoing, and might last for some time.

post-Soviet soil, combined with their ignorance of local conditions, meant that the western experts found it easier to proselytise than to generate practical proposals. As Mabbott (1967: 38–39) noted of the consequences of this contradiction, if such people do good (as opposed to talking about it), it is only by chance.

The western experts, made self-conscious by the combination of universal benevolence and practical impotence, externalised their frustration and thought their good intentions were undermined by the self-interestedness of the local agents. They believed that the trainees were only involving themselves with the project so that they could gain access to resources (dollars, cars and computers) or a job with a western organisation in Azerbaijan or, even better, employment in Europe or the USA. It was the local staff's enthusiasm for trips to the UK and Europe and for developing marketable skills in IT and English language that encouraged the western experts' suspicions of the trainees' private motives. Others involved in similar projects however have pointed to the importance of visits to western countries. Bedward et al., (2003) saw them as a means of allowing people from the former command economies to learn from the west without having the lessons imposed upon them. The private interests of the local trainees can be seen in the career paths they followed during and after the project. Of the 23 local trainees recruited to the new school, six left Azerbaijan to work or study in the West and nine obtained jobs with western organisations based in Baku within the time span of the project.

The western experts' suspicions of the trainees were mirrored by the trainees' doubts about the experts. The local agents noted the contradiction between the western experts' professed intentions and their suspicious attitude towards them. They concluded that the western experts were not in their country out of altruism. They believed the western experts were there for the benefits of expatriate employment and to improve their personal circumstances. This was not an isolated phenomenon of this particular project. As Lenke and Davies (1995: 23) reported about a western-led management development programme in Hungary, the locals commented on the western experts' superior, colonialist and expatriate attitudes, their ignorance of the Hungarian context and their social segregation.

This suspicion can be illustrated by another incident. Two of the western experts had boasted, while working in Azerbaijan, that they were having an affair and that they had only agreed to work on the project because it gave them a holiday overseas and a chance to be together away from their respective spouses. Two other team members complained about the couple. As a matter of principle, they objected to the way the couple's freeloading was disrespectful of other team members' efforts. They also expressed a more important concern that our Azerbaijani partners, who had learnt of the affair, were asking questions about the pair's lack of commitment, and this was threatening the credibility of the project.

The cumulative effect of such mutual suspicions, developed out of a self-conscious suspicion each of the other, led to mistrust between the two groups. Abramson (1999) identified a similar dialectic, of acceptance and subversion, in his analysis of western-funded attempts to build institutions of civil society in Uzbekistan. He argued that western agencies, by creating NGOs (which would provide an alternative to the state as the focus of social action), formed new elites. These new elites retained the tendency, developed during Soviet rule, to subvert systems to their personal advantage. Consequently, the formal 'concept of civil society loses any universally understood meaning and value' (Abramson, 1999: 241) as the new elites, in their concrete implementation of the ideal of civil society, merely saw western programmes as a means to benefit themselves, as indeed do the 'young Americans with fat pay-checks and [western corporations] with fat contracts'. The many individual acts of self-interest negated the formal intentions of the development projects.

The synthesis of the contradictions was an acceptance of a hierarchical relationship between western experts and local change agents in which the experts were dominant (they after all controlled the flow of resources from the funding body) and the local agents were dependent. Lack of trust is one such absence. The removal of self-consciousness, which constrained the formation of any relationship between western experts and local agents, allowed the emergence of a hierarchical relationship between them. The absence of trust was replaced by a mutual and conscious commitment between the two parties, albeit an unequal one. This synthesis becomes the starting point, the thesis, of the next dialectic.

The dialectic of master and slave

In this second dialectic, in the development of the relationship between western experts and trainees, the formal term, the thesis, was that the experts were dominant over the locals because they were the source of the new ideas and values that were required to modernise Azerbaijani public services. The antithesis was that, in practice, the experts were dependent upon the trainees because they could not work without their cooperation, or indeed without their presence. This latter point became a major cause of conflict. The local trainees were paid only a small salary by the Azerbaijan government and they needed time to earn extra money to support themselves and their families. The westerners, however, needed them to attend the classes and seminars and to turn up on time. The project team was constantly trying to find ways to improve the local trainees' attendance record, always with limited success. The formal dominance of the western experts was negated by their practical dependence upon the local agents, who displayed a disregard for punctuality.

Tensions could be seen in the relationship between the western experts and the local trainees. The Middle Eastern courtesies and respect given by the locals to the western experts gave the latter a sense of status that they would not have received from others in their own culture. This led to an asymmetry in the social relations between the western experts and local agents. As discussed earlier, Dewey (1993) identified different notions of friendship in western and eastern societies. The western, and middle class, notion saw friendship as a limited relationship, which required little more than mutual entertainment and polite, constrained civilities. This was the view of most of the western experts. The eastern view, one that was shared by the Azerbaijanis, was that the expectations of friendship were almost without limit. They saw friendship as creating personal obligations such that the western friend would be obliged to help them find jobs in western companies or places to study in overseas universities. The local staff saw the experts as potential patrons and so offered them deference. However, in return for deference the Azerbaijanis anticipated a large and bankable return. The westerners were formally dominant but were under heavier demands of friendship. This inversion in the social relationships is another version of the master/slave dialectic because the Azerbaijanis' expectations of the western experts outweighed the social obligations that the westerners put on their Azerbaijani friends.

The contradiction between western expert as 'master' and the local trainer as 'slave' diminished as the latter came to realise that the experts depended on them. As the experts' superiority diminished the two were brought nearer to equality. Master and slave recognised that they would each benefit from mutual cooperation. As Jankowicz and Dobosz-Bourne (2003) reported, in their study of modernising projects in the countries of the former Warsaw Pact, effective cross-cultural transfer of knowledge can only occur when there is a negotiation of mutual meanings between the western experts and the local learners. Several local participants in the project moved from being trainees to becoming academic colleagues over the three and a half years of the project, replacing the hierarchical relationship of patron and client. The western experts' developing respect for some of the local trainees led to an attempt by the western project team to shift power from the institution's rector, who had held this post since Soviet times, to one of the younger local staff. It was necessary to appoint a director of the School of Public Administration. The person appointed was a young woman selected from among the local staff. It was recognised that she would have difficulties dealing with the older, and male, culture of top government officialdom. It was also a recognition by the western project team that some of the local trainees were capable of taking on such a job. The new director was seen as someone with whom the experts could work as a partner.

The dialectic of unhappy consciousness

The last observed stage of the relationship between the western experts and the local trainers may be viewed as a dialectic of unhappy consciousness. The newly independent trainees, who should now be called trainers, stoically accepted that there could be no mean between vice and virtue, and accepted the western institutional template, but their scepticism about the application of this template to Azerbaijan led them to a state of unhappy consciousness, a form of melancholic acceptance. The contradiction was not then between experts and local colleagues but within the minds of both. They were struggling with the ethical question of relativism and universalism: Is the western business and managerial template applicable everywhere or should each society develop its own business values and institutions? Holden (2002) would see this situation as a helpful one because it has moved away from insisting on a single universal set of values that must be true everywhere and has moved to a situation that requires mutual learning. As the dialectical analysis suggests, however, this process of learning is not straightforward; rather it proceeds by working through a series of contradictions and misunderstanding. This requires both good manners and the ability to participate with others' values and ethical principles.

Activity 11.2	**Improving communications within teams of people of different cultural backgrounds**

If you were a human resource manager responsible for improving cooperation and communication between employees (who come from different cultural backgrounds but who work together in teams in your transnational company), what practical recommendations would you make for training or development activities that would help them move smoothly through the difficulties of developing a mutual understanding and appreciation of each other's values?

Good manners and participative competence

How should managers cope with the kinds of tensions described in the previous section? How should the manager, and corporately the organisation they work for, respond to this complexity? One possible response is that managers working with, or in, other countries should show good manners by accepting others' cultures. This does not mean that managers should become promiscuous in the manner in which they take up and put down values. Indeed, Hofstede argued (1991: 237), a person cannot show tolerance of others' values unless they are secure in their own values. Tolerance is necessary, the more so when differences in priorities and practice do not raise serious ethical difficulties. Good manners imply trying to see situations from other people's perspective, empathising with their anxieties and taking what actions you can to put them at ease. A more formal term for good manners might be participative competence (Holden, 2002: 273–4). He defines this as:

> the ability to interact on equal terms in multicultural environments in such a way that knowledge is shared and that the learning experience is professionally enhancing.

The ability to participate competently in different countries calls for different skills and sensitivities. In India, a happy receipt of compliments given, without taking them too seriously, and in France a glad acceptance that the lunch break is more important than the meeting that was abruptly stopped for it, add to participative competence. However, there are common understandings that are vital to such competence. They are that, despite apparent problems of mutual understandings, the others with whom you are dealing share with you the basic structures of communication and the ability to infer not just from the spoken language but from the interaction of voice, expression, stance and actions. Both people in a multicultural encounter are seeking to make sense of the encounter and are using a wide range of cues to make a common understanding

Podcast 11.1

Gift giving and politeness

Podcasts explaining how today's business news relates to the topics discussed here will be updated in an ongoing process. Podcast 11.1 looks at the impact of different traditions of gift giving in different cultures. To listen to this podcast, other archived podcasts or recent additions, please visit the companion website at www.pearsoned.co.uk/fisherlovellvalerosilva.

The following suggestions for helping to develop participative competence, largely based on those developed by De George (1999), are all variations on a famous ethical precept – first, do no harm.

> **First, do no harm** is an ancient moral precept. It is often claimed **DEFINITION** to be taken from the Hippocratic oath, which doctors in classical times were required to take. This is not so. The nearest the oath gets to it is in the following statement, 'I will follow that system of regimen which, according to my ability and judgement, I consider for the benefit of my patients, and abstain from all that is deleterious and mischievous'. Today few doctors are required to take the oath.

There are various disciplines that can be learned for acquiring good manners. One is to recognise that we all possess a wide range of values that we can use to understand others' positions. For example, fear of losing 'face' is often cited as a matter of great importance to the Chinese. But there cannot be a western manager who has not also felt shame when they made a fool of themselves in front of colleagues or bosses. Recognising the humour in a conflict of values can also aid their reconciliation.

Case study 11.1   **The college principal's new car**

This case was part of the experience of the project to set up a new college of public administration in Azerbaijan (*see* p. 457). It concerns the rector, who had built his career in the old Soviet regime but was now to be rector of the new college. He was in his late sixties and was, every inch of his substantial frame, a Soviet *apparatchik*. As part of the package the project delivered two brand-new western-built vehicles to the college. One was a minibus, the other was a good quality car. Both vehicles were, according to the project specification, for the use of the western project team. In practice the minibus was the more useful vehicle because it coped well with the difficult road conditions and could be used to move all the team around, complete with their equipment. The principal began to use the car more and more as if it were his personal vehicle. It was easy for him to do this because both of the drivers were on his staff and took their orders from him. This became an issue because the principal clearly saw the car as his 'commission' for facilitating the project. If the western funding body were to discover this, it would think it a misuse of project funds. The issue became a matter of dispute between the principal and the project team. Then one day the team saw that some cowboy builders had been brought in and were rapidly constructing a ramshackle garage in the college grounds. The strongest part of the garage was the padlocked steel doors to which only the principal held the key. The project team saw the funny side and could remember occasions when they had tried to guard hard-won privileges and perks that they had won from their organisations. Humour discharged the project team's anger and a compromise deal was made about the use of the car.

Responding to the particularness of host countries' ethical standards and values

This guideline goes a little beyond good manners. It suggests that, unless there are good ethical reasons for not doing so, organisations should learn and respect the values and ethical practices of the host country. This is not an easy thing to achieve. Expatriate staff are often criticised because they try to recreate their pattern of life from their own country rather than learn about and come to terms with the culture of their host country. This has been recognised as a problem for international non-governmental organisations. Lewis (2001: 105) has raised the question of defining the management challenges that arise from employing expatriate non-governmental organisation staff from the northern world to work in partnership with southern-world non-governmental organisation partners. He asks, but does not answer, the question of whether such staff should be driven by their own values or by the values of their partner organisations.

Cross reference	The argument about the importance of the particulars of individual cases when deciding how to respond to an ethical issue is related to the discussion of casuistry in Chapter 13.

Case study 11.2	**Testing Maori employees for drugs in a New Zealand company**

A company that employed Maoris and non-Maoris decided that they wanted to start a programme of testing employees for drug abuse. Their reasons were to improve the safety record at their plant and to fulfil their obligations under New Zealand's health and safety laws. Carrying out drugs testing on employees, however, raised ethical questions about employees' rights to privacy, and the question of the legality of such testing under New Zealand law was uncertain. The Maori employees appeared to be more critical of the proposal than the other staff. A particular point of conflict, however, was that the company tried to negotiate with employees separately to gain their consent to the testing. Maori culture is collectivist and the staff demanded that the issue between them and the company should be negotiated collectively.

(*Source*: Blackburn, 2000)

Activity 11.3

When should the demands, expectations or values of the state outweigh the values and social expectations of religious, national or ethnic groups? Consider the following examples.

- When the state's health and safety laws imply that the wearing of a certain national dress in a production plant would be a health and safety hazard.

- When the state's belief in secularism is challenged by Muslim women's insistence on wearing the *hijab* (head scarf). This issue was highlighted in 2004 when France passed a law that prohibited Muslim schoolgirls wearing the *hijab* in schools.

Reflections

The international work of companies and organisations involves an engagement with different values and ethical standards. This chapter has concerned the ethical validity of such diversity and the question of how people in organisations should respond to it. There are two processes in operation. One is an attempt to universalise, to create core principles that can be accepted worldwide. The other is localisation in which values, which some think are universal, are adapted and modified to meet particular circumstances. Both processes, however, involve judgment and choice. They do not represent an uncritical acceptance that all values and principles that exist must be of equal worth and must be protected. What managers are involved in is a process termed 'sense-making' by Weick (1995 and 2001). According to Weick, sense-making is a retrospective activity triggered by actions and influenced by cues and heuristics. If these processes are to be seen, as Holden suggests, as an organisational resource then it is necessary for organisations to bring the process of learning, which is open to multicultural interaction, to the surface. It is worth considering some aspects of developing participative competence in terms of Weickian sense-making.

Cross reference	Weick's theory of the process of sense-making is also discussed in Chapter 4, p. 155.

- **Action and social context.** People only make sense of situations when their circumstances force them to. Putting people in multicultural forums requires them to interact and reform their views.

- **Identity formation.** Historically, people from particular communities have defined their identities in contrast to an assumed and poorly understood 'other' (*see* the definition of orientalism on p. 481). Denying people access to stereotypes by confronting them with real people will ease the learning resulting from the coming together of different value sets.

- **Cues.** The way that people make sense of value differences is by observing the cues created by the ways in which others deal with them, and by noting the results. If those who take a traditional 'expat' view of other countries gain promotion then the cues will be readily read.

- **Plausibility.** The sense that people may make of their experiences must be plausible to them. The sense they make of others' cultures and values may be wrong but seem plausible unless they have had to work with those from other communities and societies.

Managers who make sense of the world's diversity of values only from the cues and circumstances provided by their own organisational, group or national cultures may simply develop stereotypes rather than acquire participative competence.

Summary

In this chapter the following key points have been made:

- Universal standards for international business have been written but they are not universally accepted; nor do they cover all the issues relevant to business.

- Different countries and societies have some ethical standards and values concerning business in common, but they differ on others.

- In countries outside the western industrialised zone there is a process of dialogue in which, predominantly, American business values are integrated and challenged in a process of sense-making.

- An acceptance of ethical plurality does not mean that any value has to be accepted as long as it can be shown to be authentically indigenous to a place.

- Although extreme universalists and relativists might reject the idea, it is arguable that a contingency approach or, alternatively a stakeholder and Rawlsian approach, can be used to distinguish appropriate from inappropriate local ethical standards.

- If this is so, then transnational and multinational companies have to make moral judgments about whether they should adopt or challenge the business standards of the countries they are working in. In this process it is helpful if managers in such companies see the value diversity they face as an asset and an opportunity for organisational learning rather than as a culture shock problem that has to be overcome.

- This process of mutual learning from different values in different places and among different groups can be understood as a dialectical process.

- In dealing with these matters transnational and multinational organisations need to show:

  – good manners; and

  – a willingness to respond to the particularness of the host countries' ethical standards and values.

Typical assignments

1. In what circumstances should a company accept local values and practices that differ from its own core values and when should it not? Illustrate your answer with particular examples.

2. How useful and valid is it to argue that countries can be classified by the different managerial and organisational values they exhibit?

3. What is likely to happen when managers from different societies with different values come into contact? How should this process be managed?

4. Are there some areas of business and management where universal standards and principles apply to all? What are they?

Group activity 11.1

If you have a group of students who have different ethnic backgrounds, or have lived in different countries, choose two of those countries to concentrate on. Discuss and compare the views of:

- teenagers and young adults in each country; and
- their parents' generation in each country

on

- McDonald's and other fast food outlets;
- multinational companies as employers;
- credit cards;
- reserving quotas of jobs for people of a particular social or ethnic category in universities, government agencies and state-owned enterprises; and
- the importance of personal relationships in the conduct of business.

Recommended further reading

F. Trompenaars and C. Hampden-Turner (1993) *Riding the Waves of Culture*, 2nd edn, London: Nicholes Brealey, is good on the problems of managing intercultural misunderstandings. Nigel Holden (2002) *Cross Cultural Management. A Knowledge Management Perspective*, Harlow: Pearson Education, provides an interesting perspective based on the principles of knowledge management. He challenges the common assumption that cultural differences are simply a cause of problems.

Useful websites

Topic	Website provider	URL
Transparency International home page	Transparency International	http://www.transparency.org/
The Universal Declaration of Human rights	United Nations	http://www.un.org/en/documents/udhr/
Islamic Finance	Sala@m	http://www.salaam.co.uk/themeofthemonth/november02_index.php

Topic	Website provider	URL
Islamic Finance	Bloomberg	http://topics.bloomberg.com/islamic-finance/
A web page concerned with the work of Geert Hofstede	The International Business Centre	http://geert-hofstede.international-business-center.com/index.shtml
A web page for a major company working on international business cultures	Trompenaars Hampden-Turner, Consultants	http://www.thtconsulting.com/Website/index.asp
Caux Round Table	Caux Round Table	http://www.cauxroundtable.org/

CHAPTER 12

Globalisation and international business

Chapter at a glance

Chapter contents

- Learning outcomes
- Introduction
- Trickle down or just trickery?
- Developing institutions or taking advantage?
- Creating political tensions between and within states
- Staying put or getting out?
- Cultural diversity or cultural homogenisation?
- Global governance
- Reflections
- Summary

Case studies

- Case study 12.1 Anita Roddick's views on globalisation
- Case study 12.2 The Bhopal disaster
- Case study 12.3 Indonesia
- Case study 12.4 The oil industry and the Niger Delta
- Case study 12.5 The Baku-Tblisi-Ceyhan (BTC) oil pipeline
- Case study 12.6 Businesses and South Africa in the apartheid era
- Case study 12.7 McDonald's fries
- Case study 12.8 The International Code of Marketing of Breastmilk Substitutes
- Case study 12.9 Breastmilk substitutes in Malawi

Activities and exercises

- Video clip 12.1 The debates on globalisation
- Video clip 12.2 *American Apparel: Social responsibility*
- Discussion activity 12.1 Compensation and the Bhopal case
- Discussion activity 12.2 Halliburton and Iraq
- Discussion activity 12.3 The impact of corporations operating in areas of conflict
- Discussion activity 12.4 Sovereignty and the BTC pipeline
- Discussion activity 12.5 When should a company withdraw from a country?
- Discussion activity 12.6 Problems of implementing voluntary codes
- Typical assignments

■ Group activity 12.1
■ Recommended further reading
■ Useful websites

Learning outcomes

Having read the chapter and completed its associated activities, readers should be able to:

■ Define globalisation and the ethical issues that it raises.

■ Evaluate the evidence and arguments concerning the fairness of the economic impact of world trade liberalisation.

■ Evaluate the roles of multinational enterprises in relation to developing the institutions of ethical business practice.

■ Identify the potential for close relationships between multinational enterprises and governments to damage ethically responsible business practices.

■ Identify the risks to peace and stability that multinational enterprises may cause by their operations in politically and militarily unstable regions.

■ Judge the arguments for multinational enterprises remaining within ethically dubious countries, and trying to change things from the inside, or for withdrawing.

■ Rehearse the argument about the social and cultural impact of globalisation.

■ Identify the strengths and weaknesses of various approaches to developing codes and compacts for the conduct of international business.

Introduction

The ethics of globalisation, for most, rests on a fine point of utilitarianism. Does globalisation result in more harm than good? If it creates both harm and good in large measures, but the harm and the good are felt by different groups of people, how should the benefits experienced by some be weighed against the disadvantages heaped on others? It would probably not be sufficient to quieten the disadvantaged to simply point out that in aggregate the good outweighs the bad.

Cross reference	Utilitarianism is one of the major ethical theories. It is discussed in detail in Chapter 3, p. 117. Those who take a human rights perspective, which is also discussed in Chapter 3, do not approach the ethical issues of globalisation from a utilitarian perspective but simply argue that companies operating in the global marketplace should take care to respect human rights.

A consideration of the ethics of globalisation, and of the role of multinational enterprises (MNEs) within it must therefore include an analysis of its impact. The likely areas of impact can be deduced from the definition of globalisation.

DEFINITION

Globalisation is a process that is bringing societies that were previously economically, politically and culturally diverse into convergence. This is being achieved by a combination of the success of capitalism, the growth of a common mass culture (McLuhan and Powers' (1989) 'global village') and the wish of people in all societies, through their rational choices, to choose the same goals. It is a process that affects three domains: the political, the economic and the cultural and social.

The World Commission on the Social Dimension of Globalization (WCSDG, 2004: §132–5) identified the following characteristics of globalisation.

- Liberalisation of international trade.
- Growth of foreign direct investment (FDI) and massive cross-border financial flows.
- Growth of the new technology of IT and communications, which makes communication between countries easier.
- The greater ease of transporting goods and people around the world, which makes it possible for markets to be global in scope.

This last characteristic gives rise to a different definition of globalisation, which sees it not as a description of a process but as a strategy that a company can choose to adopt. Companies may decide to produce and market their goods and services for a global market (Holden, 2002: 44).

In this chapter the impacts and ethical considerations of globalisation will be reviewed under the following headings.

- Trickle down or just trickery? Does the opening of national markets to world trade and an increase in international trade benefit all countries?

- Developing institutions or taking advantage? Do multinational companies seek to improve the institutional arrangements (by advocating and practising good employment practices and operating to high standards of business) in host countries or do they seek to benefit from the weak institutional and legal frameworks governing business in many developing countries?

- Creating political tensions between and within states. Does the involvement of multinational companies, many of which have a higher turnover than developing countries have gross domestic product (GDP), exacerbate regional political instabilities and create political disturbances and unrest?

- Staying put or getting out? Multinational enterprises may find themselves operating in countries where they become complicit with intolerable unfairness and abuses of human rights, and they have to decide whether to remain or withdraw.

- Cultural diversity or cultural homogenisation? Does the global reach of multinational companies threaten indigenous cultures and values and lead all societies to a standardised culture that diminishes the variety of human cultures?

The remainder of the chapter will consider the various attempts to create a worldwide framework of global governance to guide and police the propriety and fairness of international trade and its globalising consequences.

However, the ethical issues of globalisation are not new. They could be found in the actions of colonial companies, such as the Dutch and English East India Companies, which were as powerful and globally dominating in the eighteenth and nineteenth centuries as multinationals are today. The modern themes listed above for this chapter had their equivalents in the eighteenth- and early nineteenth-century history of the British East India Company in particular.

- **The charge that the East India Company impoverished India.** In the eighteenth century it was a common charge that the company was draining India of its wealth and transferring it to Britain. It was accused of enriching new elites, both Indian and British (called nabobs), while the mass of the Indian population suffered intermittent famines. The charges were crystallised when Warren Hastings, the governor-general, was impeached by Parliament in 1786 over issues that would today be termed corporate governance. He was found not guilty in 1795.

- **Exploiting weak institutions in host countries.** When the East India Company was establishing itself in India in the eighteenth century the nominal sovereign power was the Moghul Empire, which by that time was in decline. The company was able to exploit the empire's institutional weaknesses to its own commercial advantage by acquiring formal government roles, such as the tax-collecting function of the *diwani* of Bengal.

- **Increasing political tensions in a region.** The decline of the Moghul Empire created military and political tensions as different groups sought to fill the political vacuum. The East India Company was one of these and it developed its own armies and spent much of the eighteenth century fighting wars in India.

- **Staying in or withdrawing decision.** The company's business stretched as far as China, from where it imported tea to Britain. The tea had to be paid for and conveniently the company had a monopoly of opium production in India. It was convenient to ship the opium to China, where there was a good market, and use the proceeds to buy the tea. Unfortunately the Chinese government banned the sale of opium in 1729 because of its damaging effects on the users. The company formally withdrew from the illegal trade, but it would sell the opium to private traders in Calcutta and then turn a blind eye when they exported it at their own risk to China. However, by the 1830s the revenues from the opium trade, which in the eighteenth century had been only about 5 per cent of the company's turnover, had become much more important and Britain engaged in gunboat diplomacy in China, not just to protect the opium trade but to protect its much more important general monopoly of trade with China.

■ **Cultural diversity or cultural globalisation?** William Dalrymple's (2002) book on the interaction between the company's officials and the Mughal elite in India in the eighteenth century tells an intriguing history of how originally many of the British in India were fascinated by the culture of the Mughal courts, adopted their customs, married Mughal women and became 'white Mughals'. But in the late eighteenth century, and certainly during the Victorian era, the British came to despise Indian culture and kept aloof from it so that those Indians who wished to benefit from the opportunities that the company offered had to adapt to British ideas, values and customs.

The World Commission on the Social Dimension of Globalization (WCSDG) (2004: §134) has pointed out that one difference between the eighteenth- and nineteenth-century globalisation and that of today is that the earlier period involved large migrations of people – Africans to the Americas, Indians to East and South Africa, the Welsh to Patagonia and so on. Many of these movements themselves raised moral questions because the migrations were enforced by the slave trade. In the current phase of globalisation money and goods are free to cross borders but, in general, people are not. However, this is not to say that globalisation does not still create some problems associated with migration. The ethical charge is still that people are moved to the advantage of the First World and the disadvantage of the Third World. One particular instance concerns the National Health Service (NHS) in the UK. The NHS is short of doctors and it will be several years before the expansion of medical education delivers the needed fully qualified doctors. To fill the immediate gap the NHS has recruited doctors from other countries, from Africa in particular. In 2004, two-thirds of newly registered doctors in the UK came from abroad. Many African countries desperately need the doctors they train to remain, not least to help deal with the AIDS epidemic they face. Yet in Zambia, to take one example, only 50 of the 600 doctors trained there since independence are still practising in the country. This migration also has the advantage for the UK that it does not have to bear the cost of training many of the doctors it employs. This movement of doctors is seen by both the British government and the British Medical Association as an ethical problem. In this case, however, the migration is not an enforced one. Doctors trained in Africa are inevitably attracted by the better salaries and working conditions that they would experience in the UK (BBC News Online, 2005b).

Although the claims that globalisation has brought new ethical problems need to be seen in historical context, globalisation has increased the velocity and awareness of the ethical problems of worldwide economic integration. As Petrick (2000: 1) expressed it, the 'high velocity global market place is complex and challenging'. The international marketplace can now operate in real time – as do the world's stock exchanges as trading moves through time zones from one exchange to another – and not have to deal with the time lags in communication that characterised earlier times. This is the other main difference between the current and the historical periods of globalisation.

The networks of global, multinational and transnational companies and organisations and NGOs form the arenas in which such problems may arise and the business cultures of different societies and countries may come into contact with each other. It will be useful to define the differences between them.

> **DEFINITION**
>
> **Multinational enterprises** (MNEs) have been divided into three types (Harzing, 2000):
>
> - **Multi-domestic companies** are federations of autonomous subsidiaries that operate in different countries.
> - **Global companies**, by comparison, view themselves as operating in a world market and their products and services make relatively little concession to the particularities of different national markets.
> - **Transnational companies** are networks and tend to have little specific national identification or base, although they do have a legal base in a particular country. Worldwide consultancy and accountancy firms are a good example of this type of organisation. They are run by international managements and are willing to move their capital and operations to any favourable location (Hirst and Thompson, 1996: 11).

Now that the key terms have been defined we can consider the ethical issues of globalisation in turn.

Trickle down or just trickery?

Does the evidence we have of the effects of globalisation and trade deregulation on world markets display an improvement of people's well-being? The available evidence is at best mixed. At worst we are experiencing even greater concentrations of power within corporations over resources that lie outside the political arena, with fundamental questions regarding authority, responsibility and accountability remaining unanswered. The observations of late Anita Roddick, founder of the Body Shop organisation, are interesting in this context. She was responding to an article by Philippe Legrain that had appeared in the *Guardian* (on the day before the publication of her letter). The latter had made the case that the deregulation of world markets, in line with the actions of the WTO, should be welcomed by all, as ultimately all would benefit. Case study 12.1 presents the views of Ms Roddick.

Case study 12.1	Anita Roddick's views on globalisation

Anita Roddick is famous for championing responsible retailing through the *Body Shop* chain of shops. In 1999 she went to a meeting of the WTO in Seattle. Unlike most retailers who were participants and lobbyists within the conference' Ms Roddick had gone to join the protestors. The experience became an unusual one for an entrepreneur as she was baton-charged and tear-gassed

▶

by riot police. She admitted that this may have prejudiced her against the views of Mr Legrain that free trade made the poor better off. She mocked his claim that seamstresses in Bangladesh are not exploited because 'they earn more than they would as farmers'. Ms Roddick attributed this short-sighted view to the fact that people like Legrain never left the international conference centres in which they discussed these issues. She on the other hand had travelled to places such as Nicaragua. Nicaragua was one of those countries that had been forced by the World Trade Organization (WTO) and the International Monetary Fund (IMF) to adopt free market and free trade economic policies. The consequence, she reported, was workers in the free trade zone being paid $5 a day making jeans that were then retailed in the USA with a large profit margin. These workers could not live a decent life on such a salary and lived in shanty accommodation without adequate water supply or sanitation. Her own experience, however, suggested things need not be so. In 1993 the world price for sesame seed grown by Nicaraguan farmers had collapsed. In partnership with Christian Aid, *The Body Shop* had helped set up fair trade schemes with cooperatives of small farmers in Nicaragua. Such schemes did not make the farmers rich but gave them some stability on which a decent life could be built.

The two sides of this debate are:

1. The trickle-down case – that freeing international trade from restrictions increases the total wealth of the world and that, while this will inevitably reward the elites, the benefits will also trickle down to everyone. This argument is based on standard economic theory, which proposes that free international trade encourages countries to specialise in exporting those services and products in which they have a competitive advantage and not to produce those that other countries can produce more efficiently. This leads to a situation in which all countries are producing the most added value they can and are not wasting resources on producing things inefficiently that could better be imported from elsewhere. This maximises the world's wealth and all benefit.

2. The contrary case argues that, whilst the trickle-down case may be logical, the international trade market has a number of imperfections, which can prevent the anticipated benefits for all emerging. The first is that large companies from the industrialised countries have greater bargaining power than the small-scale companies and traders in the developing world from whom they buy goods. The former therefore gain the most advantage from international trade. The second imperfection is that the industrialised countries demand that the developing countries place no barriers on international trade but do not return the favour. The most obvious example is that the European Union's Common Agricultural Policy subsidises food production in Europe and so makes it difficult for food producers in the developing world to export their produce to Europe. The third imperfection is that the global institutions set up to regulate international trade, notably the WTO, do not fairly represent the interests of the many parties to them. The institutions respond more to the needs of the industrialised countries, which have their own global institutions such as the Group of Eight (G8) and less to the voices of the countries of the developing world. The consequence of these imperfections

is that international trade does not necessarily deliver what it promises, and that its promises are sleight of hand and trickery to disguise the fact that the poor in the poorest countries do not benefit from the liberalisation of foreign trade. Even if international trade does make some poor countries better off there is no guarantee that those benefits will be fairly enjoyed by the whole population. Most of the oil exported from Nigeria comes from the Niger delta region. The major oil companies are inevitably active in the region and the government of Nigeria receives most of its revenues from the oil industry, but the population of the delta has not benefited economically. Indeed the environmental damage to agricultural land caused by the oil operations has worsened even that poor standard of living it used to have.

Video clip 12.1

The debates on globalisation

The clip rehearses the arguments for and against globalisation.

To view the video clip from the interview please visit this book's companion website at www.pearsoned.co.uk/fisherlovell valerosilva.

It is necessary to consider the evidence relating to this debate. Some researchers have focused on identifying whether there is a statistical correlation between growth in world trade and changes in the level of income inequality between countries. As is often the case, research studies do not agree. Lundberg and Squire (2003) found that increasing the openness of international trade makes for greater income inequality between countries. Dollar and Kraay (2002 and 2004), however, found that increasing international trade had little or no impact on income inequality. The figures for countries' poverty levels (percentage of people living on less than $1.08 a day at 1993 purchasing levels) and countries' growth in international trade (measured by exports as a percentage of GDP) was studied by Ravallion (2004). He found a negative correlation between the two, namely as a country's trade increases the amount of poverty decreases, but the correlation was too weak to carry conviction.

China has often been cited as a case where the expansion of its international trade, following the start of its 'Open Door' policy in the early 1980s, was a major factor in its success against poverty (World Bank, 2002). An analysis of the statistics by Ravallion and Chen (2004) gives a negative correlation of –0.75 between trade increases and decreases in poverty. As always with correlations, however, it may be dangerous to assume that statistical association implies a cause and effect relationship. The greatest decrease in poverty in China occurred in the early 1980s when trade was liberalised. The poverty rate fell from 76 per cent in 1980 to 23 per cent in 1985 (Ravallion, 2004: 9). However, this was also a period of great increases in agricultural production following the de-collectivisation of agriculture. Conversely the greatest changes in China's openness to international trade occurred after 1985 when poverty had already fallen. It is at least arguable that the reduction in poverty was more to do with agrarian reform than with trade liberalisation. Ravallion also studied the differential impact of China's accession to the WTO in 2001, which involved massive reductions in China's tariff barriers to trade. His analysis suggests that between 2001 and 2007:

- 75 per cent of rural households are predicted to lose income but only 10 per cent of urban households would suffer similarly.

- Some areas of China will lose income while other areas will gain.

- In rural areas larger households will benefit more from trade liberalisation than small ones.

- In urban areas smaller households will benefit more than larger ones.

Similar patterns can be found in other countries. In India, some states have benefited massively from trade liberalisation and the growth of the IT industry. Other states, notably Bihar on the Gangetic plain, continue with a subsistence economy with increasing levels of poverty. Equally it is the urban areas that benefit from increasing international trade and the rural populations that mostly suffer. The World Bank completed a study of the likely impact of a decrease in the tariffs protecting cereal production in Morocco. The impact of a 30 per cent reduction in tariffs would have been to increase rural poverty while improving the lot of urban households.

The general conclusion concerning the relationship between the opening up of countries to international trade and the level of poverty is that trade openness may not be the key issue in decreasing poverty but that its impact within a particular country is likely to be variable between regions and groups within the country.

It seems unlikely therefore that world trade liberalisation can be morally justified by its impact on reducing poverty. Rather, the consequence of world trade liberalisation for developing countries may be to create a two-track economic and social system, sometimes known as dualism and sometimes as the informal economy.

Dualism or the informal economy

Dualism was first observed in the British and Dutch empires in South Asia, the British in India and the Dutch in what is now Indonesia. The term means that two economic systems exist in one place in parallel with one another but with little connection or interaction between them. In the nineteenth-century Asian empires there would typically be a capitalist plantation economy, which was integrated into international trade by exporting raw material to the West and which used hired labour. Alongside it would be a subsistence agricultural sector, which ate what it produced and participated very little in markets. An argument was often made that the plantation managers acted in an economically rational way while the peasant producers exhibited a backward sloping supply curve for labour; in other words the more they earned the less inclined they were to work. However, subsequently it was recognised that this phenomenon was explained by structural barriers that made it too difficult for subsistence producers to put effort into the production of risky cash crops, which they would not be able to eat if the market failed to offer them a worthwhile price, quite a likely consequence as they were forced to sell to monopsonistic middlemen. The modern equivalent of this situation is known as the informal economy, which exists in many countries. It consists of small-scale manufacturing, service provision and agricultural work. It is characterised by:

- A lack of recognition and formality: these enterprises do not submit accounts or have legal recognition, they do not recognise laws and regulations and, in many countries, will obtain their electricity by tapping into the grid illegally. The informal market will often specialise in pirated goods, such as tapes and CDs. They are a tolerated, but therefore fragile, form of enterprise.

- No access to the formal sources of credit.

- They do not have access to wider regional, national and international markets.

- A lack of rights and legal protections for the people within it.

- Women forming a large proportion of the informal workforce.

- Wages and income being at or close to poverty levels.

- An entrepreneurial creativity and energy that helps respond very quickly to market demand.

The WCSDG (2004) reported that globalisation had a great potential for good but that this potential was not yet being fulfilled. Its vision was a moral one.

> We have come to an agreement on a common goal: a fair globalisation which creates opportunities for all. We wish to make globalisation a means to expand human well-being and freedom, and to bring democracy and development to local communities where people live. Our primary concerns are that globalisation should benefit all countries and should raise the welfare of all people throughout the world.
>
> (WCSDG, 2004: §3 and 171)

It is clear that the liberalisation of international trade will not automatically meet that vision through a trickle-down process.

- Between 1985 and 2000, 16 developing countries had a per capita income growth of more than 3 per cent, 32 developing countries grew at less than 2 per cent, 23 countries showed negative growth. China and India were transitional countries with high growth rates.

- The gap between GDP per capita in the poorest and richest countries has increased. In the early 1960s per capita income was 50 times higher in the 20 richest countries than in the 20 poorest. By the new millennium this figure had increased to 110.

- In the developed countries, particularly in the UK and the USA, the ratio between the top 10 per cent highest earners and the lowest 10 per cent earners has increased between the mid-1980s and the mid-1990s by 35.1 per cent in the UK and 36.8 per cent in the USA.

■ In the developing countries the volatility of flows of foreign direct investment has brought new jobs to countries, most obviously in the movement of call centres from the West to South Asia, but has also decreased the security of jobs in these mobile industries. (WCSDG, 2004: §210)

If there is no global action to help spread the undoubted benefits of increasing trade then unfairness will result.

Developing institutions or taking advantage?

Many of the ethical criticisms of multinationals and transnationals arise from their tendency to exploit local conditions for commercial advantage. In practice, developing countries may have lower expectations, and weaker laws, concerning acceptable conditions of employment, minimum wage rates, pollution control, health and safety, and many other factors concerning management and business. The problem is to determine to what extent it is right and proper to exploit these circumstances to gain a commercial advantage. There will be extreme cases when it would be uncontroversial to say that such exploitation is bad. A company dumping in Third World markets a product that has been declared unfit for use or consumption in the country of origin is such as case. It is perhaps a little more difficult when we consider companies that move their manufacturing operations to new countries where the cost of labour is much lower. It would be clear that they are taking advantage of the lower wages; the question is whether this is simply the market working effectively or an unethical taking of advantage. The typical corporate response to this charge is that inward investment gives jobs to those who would not otherwise have them. The company is thus doing good by giving people jobs and ought not to be expected to pay them wages above the going rates. Local employers would also object and claim they were being harmed if a multinational started to pay its staff above the labour market rate. Often, however, a form of dual economy emerges in which the multinational companies in a developing country exist in parallel with the local companies but occupy a separate economic 'world', paying higher wages and granting better employment conditions than companies in the local economy. Such a development seems to have happened with the development of the IT industry in India. As the *Economist* (2001) reported, most of India's new economy holds aloof from the old Indian economy. Software engineers in Bengaluru, the capital of India's IT industry, work in good conditions in state-of-the-art corporate campuses, whereas the rest of the economy operates in poor to bad conditions. Such dual economies produce their own ethical problems and critics demand to know why the benefits of inward investment are not being spread more widely in society. Chakraborty (1999: 20) laments the impact of western companies employing Indian MBAs at a salary three times that which an Indian company would pay, but still lower than an equivalent person would be paid in the USA, because of the disaffection produced among those not lucky enough to be employed by a multinational.

Case study 12.2

The Bhopal disaster

This episode is a tragic and classic case study in business ethics. Union Carbide, an American-owned company, owned 50.9 per cent of a pesticide plant in Bhopal, central India. The government of India had apparently been so keen to receive this inward investment that it had found a way around its own legislation, which at that time allowed overseas companies to own not more than 40 per cent of any Indian company in which they invested. On the night of the 2–3 December 1984, 40 tonnes of poisonous gases were thrown into the air over Bhopal from the plant. The gases burned the eyes and lungs of people on whom it settled and, when it crossed into their blood stream, it damaged many physiological systems. Over 3,000 people died and 20,000 were injured. At least that was one estimate; the death and morbidity rates of the accident are still the subject of controversy. Campaigners claim that the accident has caused 20,000 deaths in the past 20 years since the accident and that half a million have become chronically ill (Ramesh, 2004).

There appear to have been a number of contributory factors that led to the leakage. They mostly related to a cost-cutting culture in a factory that at that time was making a loss and only working at a third of its capacity. On the night of the disaster six safety measures designed to prevent a leak were inadequate, malfunctioning or switched off. Safety audits had been done that had revealed major safety concerns but no action had been taken. These all raise the question of the extent to which Union Carbide had taken advantage of low levels of safety monitoring and expectations to save costs.

It can be argued that a concern to save costs characterised the company's behaviour during the aftermath of the disaster. On one account the company's legal team arrived in Bhopal days before their medical team (Bhopal.net, 2001). One of the issues after the accident was whether the case should be settled in an American court, as the government of India wanted, or in an Indian court, as the company wished, and as was in fact the case. The company fought liability for the accident and agreed an out-of-court settlement five years later with the government of India for $470m. The families of those who died received an interim payment of $550 per fatality. Had the deaths occurred in the USA the families might have received a hundred times that amount (De George, 1999: 511). Associations of the injured are still fighting for further compensation (Corpwatch, 2001). The Bhopal.com website (2001), owned by the Union Carbide Corporation, argues that the 1989 settlement has provided sufficient money from its investment to provide the compensation, and that the compensation was much higher than any settlement that would have been payable under Indian law. The company saw this settlement as complete and final.

It was the twentieth anniversary of the incident in 2004 and this became a time for taking stock. The site of the plant in 2004 belonged to the government of India. The site had not been cleared and there were reports that it still contained potentially damaging chemicals. Dow Chemicals, which had taken over Union Carbide, claimed that it had no further responsibilities in India while the government of India was still pursuing its demand, that Dow Chemicals should clean up the site, through the Indian courts.

There is an outstanding criminal case against Warren Anderson, the former chief executive of Union Carbide. The Indian CBI (Central Bureau of Investigation) had sought Anderson's extradition from his retirement in the USA to stand trial in India. However, the American government had not responded, pointing to technical difficulties in the claim. In 2011 the CBI was still pursuing the case.

The poor of Bhopal, who had borne the brunt of the toxic effects of the discharge, were often still living close to the plant. Only part of Union Carbide's payment had been distributed to the

▶

victims. By 2004 there was a balance of £174m (the compensation fund had been swelled by interest over 15 years). The problems of identifying the victims and deciding what proportion of the compensation sum each should receive had brought the payments to a standstill. In 2004, however, the Supreme Court of India demanded that the government should pay the money out on a per capita basis (Brown, 2004); which would mean that each victim would receive about $300. There was some scepticism among the activists in Bhopal as to whether the money would appear in the victims' hands.

A group of activists, the 'Yes Men Group', arranged an elaborate hoax so that when BBC producers arranged an interview with a representative of Dow Chemicals (the successor company to Union Carbide) they were actually talking to one of the hoaxers who stated, when interviewed on radio, that Dow Chemicals was accepting full responsibility for the Bhopal disaster. He later said that he was 'speaking on behalf of Dow in a certain way. I was expressing what they should express' (Wells and Ramesh, 2004). Residents of Bhopal had broken down in tears when they heard that Dow had finally accepted their responsibilities, a collapse that was no doubt repeated when they learnt it was not true.

In 2012 the question of whether Dow was liable for the ongoing consequences of the disaster was still a live one. Dow was one of the official sponsors of the London Olympic Games. The Indian Olympic Committee threatened to boycott the games if Dow was not dropped as a sponsor. The International Olympic Committee replied that it had sympathy for the victims of Bhopal but that, as Dow had no ownership stake in Union Carbide until 2000, it had no connection with, or responsibility for the disaster.

Discussion activity 12.1   Compensation and the Bhopal case

The harm caused by an event such as the Bhopal gas leak can have consequences for many years; yet the corporations, who may be liable for the harm through their negligence, cannot, as commercial organisations, tolerate having long-term, open-ended liabilities on their balance sheets. Discuss whether the belief that responsibility can be ended by a one-off payment in final settlement can be sustained when the harm may be so extensive and widespread?

The Bhopal case illustrates the ability of MNEs to exercise some choice over which legal jurisdiction they choose to submit to, as a way of taking advantage of the different institutional contexts of different countries. Sometimes organisations attempt to do this but fail to achieve the hoped for advantage. An example is the giant Russian oil company Yukos. Yukos was accused by the Russian government of having evaded the payment of taxes. The government enforced the sale of Yukos's largest asset, a company called Yuganskneftegaz that produced two-thirds of Yukos's oil production. It was likely that Gazprom, the Russian state-owned oil company, would become the purchaser and it had arranged financial backing for the deal from Deutsche Bank. It so happens that the US courts claim worldwide bankruptcy jurisdiction for companies that operate in the USA. Consequently Yukos opened an office in Dallas and put $2m into its American bank account. It then applied to the courts in Dallas for temporary bankruptcy protection. This was granted and a restraining order was issued to stop the sale of Yugansk. The sale went ahead but the displeasure of the US legal system was enough to frighten away Gazprom's western financial backers, and Deutsche Bank withdrew its financial support. The restraining order made it illegal for any company to work with Gazprom, and Deutsche Bank has a large American operation. The bank has applied to the American courts to have the restraining order removed (Mortished, 2004).

There have been cases where MNEs have avoided the institutional arrangements of industrialised countries. One such case is McDonald's operations in Europe. Most European countries have legislation on worker participation that is designed to give employees some influence on company decision-making. This is known as co-determination and in Germany the legislation allows for both supervisory boards and works councils. Supervisory boards are strategic bodies within a company, and companies with more than 2,000 employees should have employee representatives on the supervisory board. If McDonald's operations in Germany were registered in Germany it would have to have a supervisory board; however, it is a fully owned subsidiary of the American parent company and so has avoided the necessity (Royle, 2000: 124). McDonald's are, however, obliged to allow, and meet with, a plant level Works Council if the employees request it. The company had 350 fully owned restaurants in Germany and 650 franchises and each one was entitled to have a Works Council as well as a company level and a group level Works Council. In practice, in 1999, there was no group or company council and there were only between 40 and 50 plant level councils in the 1,000 restaurants. McDonald's management had used a number of tactics to discourage its employees setting up Works Councils. The simplest was sending flying squads of managers to restaurants to dissuade staff from setting up a Works Councils and to use McDonald's own systems of communication and feedback. On occasion the company would transfer the ownership of a company between holding companies, an action that had the effect of delaying the election of a Works Council. Most commonly they would 'buy out' Works Council representatives with cash and then nominate their own candidates to capture the Council and keep it compliant with management's wishes (Royle, 2000: 126–127). It was reported in 1995 that McDonald's spent £250,000 buying out 46 works councillors and their supporters. US companies, used to unregulated labour markets, would inevitably find continental European labour markets uncongenial, sufficiently so for them on occasion to seek to avoid the legal and institutional requirements.

However, most examples of MNEs taking advantage of easier institutional conditions refer to developing countries that have a strong desire for FDI. It is arguable that the exploitation of institutional weaknesses is an unsatisfactory form of advantage. The problems of investing and operating in a country that has weak institutions and poor governance outweigh, in the long term, the advantages. As the Report of the Commission for Africa (Commission for Africa, 2005: 24–5) points out, both MNEs and developing countries would benefit if those countries could develop an effective form of governance that encourages investment. By effective governance is meant:

■ security and peace;

■ sound economic policies under the law;

- collecting taxes and providing adequate public services;

- adequate physical infrastructure such as transport and telecommunications;

- effective legal systems and respect for contracts and property rights;

- maintenance of human rights; and

- appropriate constitutional checks on the actions of government.

Video clip 12.2

American Apparel: Social responsibility

The clip deals with a company that chose not to outsource its manufacturing to a developing country. Was it acting as a good citizen?

To view the video clip from the interview please visit this book's companion website at **www.pearsoned.co.uk/fisherlovellvalerosilva**.

Multinational and transnational countries should act as good corporate citizens in the host countries in which they operate. They should play a part in developing the ethical codes, norms and practices of business. This may be particularly important in developing countries which, through lack of resources or of opportunity, have poorly developed legal and voluntary frameworks intended to encourage ethical business behaviour.

Collusion between governments and corporations

Since Eisenhower invented the term 'military-industrial complex' in 1961 there have been concerns that the American government and large American companies, especially those involved in strategic industries, have become mutually dependent in a way that damages the government's ability to ensure that the marketplace operates fairly and ethically. Governments anywhere may use their discretion to take decisions that unfairly advantage companies based in their countries. Very often the criticisms concern the actions of government to support domestic companies' export sales.

An example occurred in the UK in 2005 when the government was found to have been publicly supporting moves to prevent UK companies paying facilitation payments overseas while, at the same time, supporting the business lobby's opposition to the controls (Eaglesham and Tait, 2005). In May 2004 the government's Export Credits Guarantee Department (which underwrites British companies' export deals) introduced tough anti-corruption rules. Among other provisions these would have forced companies to guarantee that their joint venture partners would not act corruptly and to disclose commissions paid to agents. A number of British companies, including Airbus, Rolls Royce and BAE Systems, lobbied against the rules. They argued that if these rules stood major contracts would be lost. The Secretary of State for Trade and Industry relented and agreed to a new set of rules in which these requirements were dropped, even though her civil servants had advised that any changes should have been put out for public consultation. However, the Corner House, an anti-corruption group, threatened to go to court to have the old rules reinstated because the anti-corruption groups had not been consulted. On this occasion the Secretary of State relented to the demands of the anti-corruption lobby and a process of public consultation was agreed. If it had not been for some leaked documents, however, the regulations would have been quietly changed in order to protect the interests of some major companies, and consequently, as some would argue, the interests of the UK. The price would have been tacit collusion with bribery in the world marketplace.

Another example of government acting to protect the interest of corporations rather than the broader interest of good corporate governance may be the decision by the director of the Serious Fraud Office in 2006 to cease its investigation into BAE's arms deal with Saudi Arabia because to continue it would have posed a threat to UK national security. It was suggested that Saudi Arabia would cease its anti-terrorist intelligence cooperation with the UK if the investigation continued. In 2008 the High Court ruled it had been unlawful to stop the investigation because the administration of justice should not respond to threats.

Cross reference	The nature of bribery and of grease payments in particular is discussed in Chapter 7, p. 283. This particular case is also raised in Chapter 6, p. 240.

Case study 12.3	**Indonesia**

The situation regarding the fate of Indonesia since 1965/66, as documented by Pilger (2001), is one of the most troublesome examples of corporate capital and western governments working in tandem, first to engineer a change in political leadership, and then to dictate both economic policy and the way ownership and control of a nation state's natural resources would be allowed to develop. It involves the overthrow of the then leader President Sukarno in 1965/66 by General Suharto, with significant western support. The prize in ousting Sukarno was great. Of Indonesia, Richard Nixon, a former President of the United States, said, 'With its 100 million people, and its 300-mile arc of islands containing the region's richest hoard of natural resources, Indonesia is the greatest prize in southeast Asia.'

The UK also had a vested interest in seeing a regime in power that was friendlier to the West than Sukarno and his ruling Communist party. In 1964 the UK Foreign Office produced an analysis of the region and 'called for the "defence" of western interests in southeast Asia, a major producer of essential commodities. The region produces nearly 85% of the world's natural rubber, over 45% of the tin, 65% of the copra and 23% of the chromium ore' (Pilger, 2001: 26).

The complicity of the US and the UK in the bloody aftermath of the Suharto take over (it is claimed that as many as one million have been murdered) appears to have been considerable

▶

and is documented by Pilger (2001). The American Central Intelligence Agency (CIA) reported that, 'in terms of the numbers killed the massacres rank as one of the worst mass murders of the 20th century' (Pilger, 2001: 24).

With Suharto in power, a conference took place between corporations, predominantly American, but also including some UK and other European corporations, and the Indonesian government. In Pilger's words, 'the Indonesian economy was carved up, sector by sector. In one room, forests; in another minerals. The Freeport Company got a mountain of copper in West Papua. A US/European consortium got West Papua's nickel. The giant Alcoa company got the biggest slice of Indonesia's bauxite. A group of the US, Japanese and French got the tropical forests of Sumatra, West Papua and Kalimantan. In addition a foreign investment law was hurried on to the statute books by Suharto, allowing all profits made by foreign companies to be tax-free for at least the first five years of operations'.

Over the next 30 years the World Bank provided loan finance amounting to £30bn to Indonesia. Of this, it is estimated by the World Bank itself that up to £10bn went into Suharto's own pockets, or those of his family and associates.

'In 1997 an internal World Bank report confirmed that at least 20–30% of the bank's loans [to Indonesia] are diverted through informal payments to GOI [Government of Indonesia] staff and politicians' (Pilger, 2001: 22).

In recent years attention has been drawn to the working conditions (e.g. up to 36-hour shifts) and pay (equivalent to 72p per hour) of factory workers in Indonesia making products for major companies such as Nike, Adidas, Reebok and GAP, and the squalor of the living conditions they endure in the camps located next to the 'economic processing zones' (i.e. the factories). In 1998, following mounting demonstrations in the Indonesian capital of Jakarta by large crowds protesting at their poverty and their desperate living conditions, Suharto left office, taking with him many billions of pounds sterling provided for his country over the years by the World Bank. These are monies that the country is obliged to keep paying the interest on, before it can even start repaying the capital.

The fall of Suharto might have marked the end of Indonesia's plight, but it may not have done. In 2000 the IMF offered the post-Suharto government a 'rescue package' of multi-million-dollar loans. However, there were conditions. These included the elimination of tariffs on staple foods. 'Trade in all qualities of rice has been opened to general importers and exporters' (Pilger, 2001: 24), decreed the IMF's letter of intent. Fertilisers and pesticides lost their 70 per cent subsidy, thereby ending for many farmers the prospect of staying on their land. They too will be forced to try to find work in the cities, which are already overburdened with unemployed 'citizens' looking for work. However, 'it gives the green light to the giant food grains corporations to move into Indonesia' (Pilger, 2001: 24).

Discussion activity 12.2	Halliburton and Iraq

Use a World Wide Web search engine to find material on the relationships between the American oil company Halliburton and the American administration of President Bush concerning the re-building of Iraq after the defeat of Saddam Hussein. Discuss the issues the case raises about close connections between governments and global businesses.

Creating political tensions between and within states

As MNEs are often bigger than many states they frequently begin to act as sovereign bodies and players in international power politics or realpolitik.

The term **realpolitik** originated in Germany in 1853 to describe   **DEFINITION**
an approach to relations with other countries. It does not mean
a naked self-interest or use of power but it does imply that ethical considerations
have to be balanced against what is possible, where the balance of power lies, and
self-interest. The idea of course is an ancient one. It can be found in the Arthrashastra of Kautilya.

A King whose territory has a common boundary with that of an antagonist is an ally.

(Rangarajan, 1992: 555)

In other words, my enemy's enemy is my friend. This is the principle that MNEs may
have to follow. It would explain why the oil companies in the following case study
found themselves in alliance with the federal Nigerian government, which was then
a military dictatorship.

The natural aim of trading companies is to achieve political stability so that their trading plans are not inconvenienced. However, since the days of the European colonial trading companies – the Dutch East India Company, the English East India Company, the Hudson Bay Company and many others – international trading companies have been drawn into regional power struggles between and within states. Their ambition may be profit but the pursuit of that goal often requires them to act as political entities and, in some cases, to take on aspects of sovereignty. Inasmuch as they become additional factors in regional conflicts they have the opportunity to act to diminish or inflame these disputes. When companies intervene in local and regional politics and conflict in support of their commercial objectives they cannot be certain that the outcomes will be the ones they wished for. Companies may have good intentions but their actions may make matters worse. Consequently, serious ethical implications attach to companies' decisions to act politically; they may seriously disturb the peace and prosperity of communities and societies.

Case study 12.4	**The oil industry and the Niger Delta**

The Nigerian oil fields are in the Niger Delta in the south-eastern part of the country, and this has been a politically troubled area for many years. Since 2001 there has been ethnic violence in the area between Muslims and Christians with 5,000 people killed in four years. ▶

There is conflict between tribes indigenous to the area and the Nigerian government and, consequently, a large military presence in the region. Much of the political instability, however, is a consequence of the presence of the international oil industry in the region. The people of the delta feel that they have not benefited from, and in fact have been damaged by, the presence of the oil industry. A sense of deprivation is often expressed as resentment against other groups who, it is felt, have fared better. Link this relative sense of deprivation to the tribal diversity of the delta and the probability of civil unrest is much increased. This of course is the opposite of what the oil companies wanted and they allied themselves with the Nigerian government, then a military dictatorship, by supporting a military crack down against what they saw as greed by the communities in the delta who were prepared to foment unrest to extract the maximum benefits from and damage an oil industry that was necessary to the economic well-being of the whole of Nigeria.

Two of the major ethnic groups in the delta are the Ogoni and the Ijaw. The Ogoni started a campaign against the environmental damage, social exclusion and poverty caused by the oil industry. These troubles came to the world's notice in 1995 when activists linked Shell to the military government's trial and execution of the Ogoni activist Ken Saro-Wiwa (Planet Ark, 2004). It was also argued that the government encouraged violent conflicts between the Ogoni and neighbouring communities – the Andoni, the Okrika and the Ndoki. This violence then gave the government an excuse to use the security forces against the Ogoni, whose uprising ended when the Ogoni leadership split amidst mutual accusations that competing leaders were only interested in furthering their own financial and political ambitions. By the late 1990s the struggle against the petro-business had been taken up by a youth movement among the Ijaw. This developed into what became known as the first and second Egbusu wars.

The presence of the international oil industry was the focus of violent conflicts between sections of the Nigerian population and its government and between Nigerian communities. It is not claimed that there would have been only peace if there had been no oil industry. But it can be claimed that by allying themselves to the government, rather than responding to the concerns of the communities, the presence of the oil industry made the problems worse. A class action being prepared against Shell will accuse the company directors of supporting military operations by Nigeria's former government against Ogoni land separatists in the Niger Delta in the 1990s.

In 2003 Shell commissioned a conflict resolution consultancy based in Lagos to prepare a report on its troubles in the Niger River Delta. The 93-page report was published in 2004. In that year's annual sustainability report the community development manager, Emmanuel Etomi, wrote that he accepted that the oil industry was 'inadvertently contributing' to conflict in the country; and

> How we sometimes feed conflict by the way we award contracts, gain access to land and deal with community representatives; how ill-equipped our security is to reduce conflict; and how drastically conflict reduces the effect of our community development programmes.

The consultants' report argued that ethnic violence would cause Shell to withdraw from the area by 2009 (Hope, 2004).

(*Source*: Ibeanu (2000); Ojefia (n.d.))

| Discussion activity 12.3 | The impact of corporations operating in areas of conflict |

Corporations working in politically troubled areas will often need the support of the local government. This might lead such corporations to assume that their ally's enemy is also their enemy, and cause them to come into conflict with local communities, who are antagonistic towards the government, but whose support they also need to conduct their business. Discuss how corporations might avoid this dilemma.

The oil industry is the natural one to consider in this section because it deals with the most strategically important product in the world. Oil has become the driving force of much international politics as the USA seeks to protect its sources of oil from the inconvenient fact that much of the oil comes from countries with which it is out of sympathy, Russia seeks to maintain its control over central Asian oil fields, and China desperately seeks the oil it needs to finance its rapid industrialisation. Whereas the previous case study dealt with the impact of the oil industry on the internal politics of a country, Case study 12.5 deals with its impact on the relationships between states.

| Case study 12.5 | The Baku–Tblisi–Ceyhan (BTC) oil pipeline |

The Caucasus region, like the Balkans, has long been an area of nationalist, ethnic and religious rivalries. When the region was part of the Soviet Union these tensions were held in check. Now that each of the groups within the region has its own sovereign territory, and the few who do not, the South Ossetians and the Chechens for example, are seeking it, the conflicts between them have again become palpable. If to this mixture is added the internationally strategic significance of the new oil fields discovered under the Caspian Sea then the industrialised countries, which need the oil, and the multinational oil companies, which need the business, also become involved in what has become called the New Great Game, in homage to the strategic conflict between Britain and Russia in the nineteenth century over which was to control the region (Kleveman, 2003).

Azerbaijan is a central player in this game. The modern oil industry had its origin in the Azerbaijani capital Baku in the 1880s and the city experienced an oil boom that lasted until 1905. The industry revived after the Second World War when Azerbaijan was an important component of the Soviet Union's oil industry. When Azerbaijan gained independence in 1991 it wished to assert its actual as well as legal independence from Russia. Its only asset for achieving this was the state-owned oil company SOCAR. The new state went into partnership with BP and Amoco by forming the Azerbaijan International Operating Company (AIOC). BP later took over Amoco and so became the major western oil company operating in Azerbaijan.

▶

If Azerbaijan were more conveniently located, so that oil could be easily taken to the West, there would be few problems. However, the country is landlocked and a long pipeline was needed. There were several possible routes.

- To a port on Turkey's Black Sea coast; but Turkey rejected this option because it would have involved oil tankers going through the narrow Bosporus, which links the Black Sea to the Mediterranean and the danger of pollution was unacceptable.

- Through Armenia to either the Black Sea or Mediterranean coast; but Azerbaijan and Armenia had fought a war over, and Armenia still occupies, the Azerbaijani province of Nagorno-Karabakh. Although hostilities have ceased peace talks between the two countries make little progress. Georgia's volnerability became patent in 2008.

- Through Russia; but Azerbaijan is trying to assert its independence from its former masters.

- Through Iran; but the United States would not wish to entrust the security of a pipeline from which it drew oil to a fundamentalist Shiite state with which it is already in diplomatic dispute.

- Through Georgia; but Georgia is politically unstable with intrusions from Chechen rebels in the north and its own internal separatist movements among the Abkhazians and the South Ossetians. Georgia's vulnerability became patent in 2008.

The route finally chosen was from Baku, through Georgia and then through Turkey to the Mediterranean coast. BP and the other oil companies grumbled about the cost of the pipeline, which was inevitably taking a circuitous route. The additional costs also made the oil companies feel more anxious about the potential political problems of building and operating the pipeline.

This insecurity was perhaps what led the oil companies to insist on international treaties, rather than commercial contracts, to govern the pipeline. Consequently an inter-governmental agreement and three host government agreements (HGAs) were drafted, largely by BP's lawyers, and signed by the governments. Pressure groups such as the Corner House (2003) have argued that these agreements give the oil companies virtual sovereign powers over the territory that the pipeline traverses in its long journey through Turkey, Georgia and Azerbaijan. They effectively exempt BP and its partners from any laws in the three countries, present or future, that would conflict with the pipeline project. The governments have to compensate BP if any law or tax damages the financial viability of the pipeline. The consortium is also given the right to prevent building development in the pipeline zone and to restrict the movement of livestock. Amnesty International (2003) argued that the HGA signed by Turkey creates a disincentive for Turkey to improve its human rights record. Turkey has to pay the consortium compensation if there is any economic disruption to the project. Such disruption might take the form of local protests against the pipeline, especially as 30,000 people will have to give up their property rights to make way for the pipeline. The government of Turkey might be prepared to sacrifice the human rights of any protestors to avoid paying compensation. The agreements were a revival of the OECD proposals for a Multilateral Agreement on Investment, which was dropped in 1998 because of the public outcry it caused (Friends of the Earth, 1997).

Despite these treaty provisions some of the Caucasian states are flexing their muscles against the oil companies. In 2003 Edward Shevardnadze was forced out of government by popular pressure. In 2004 the new government ordered BP to stop work on the pipeline in Borjormi, an area of Georgia that is classified as an area of natural beauty and in which are located mineral water springs that provide a good proportion of Georgia's exports. The government argued that BP had not provided a full environmental assessment (Malhiason, 2004).

There is a danger that the presence of the pipeline will exacerbate the political and military tensions in the areas it traverses. The pipeline passes near to Nagorno-Karabakh, near to South Ossetia and near to the Kurdish area of Turkey where there is a conflict between the PKP and the Turkish military. All the countries in the region are also the seats of conflict between Russia and western nations as to who can include the region in its sphere of influence. The pipeline could become a focal point for military or terrorist attack, and to protect from this possibility it is likely that western troops will be posted to protect it and create a militarised strip running through the region. The oil companies could only be grateful for the support even if they knew that the military presence might increase the probability of an attack on the pipeline.

There is a dilemma for companies pursuing projects in politically unstable areas. Their presence makes them an object of contention between competing political factions and interests. This causes them to seek means of protecting their investment. But the means they use, presence of foreign troops, HGAs, creates local objections and protests making them even more the focus of political and, possibly military, conflict.

(*Additional sources*: baku-ceyhan campaign, 2003a, 2003b and n.d.)

Discussion activity 12.4	Sovereignty and the BTC pipeline

In the past western governments have sometimes assumed sovereign powers in other countries to secure vital trade links. Two examples are the US government and the Panama Canal, and the British and French governments which had control over the Suez Canal. Use a World Wide Web search engine to discover what the historical outcomes were in these two cases. Then discuss what lessons, if any, can be drawn from these examples for projects such as the BTC pipeline.

Staying put or getting out?

The issue facing multinational companies, however, may not just be that the norms of business behaviour in the countries they operate in are undeveloped. Companies may find themselves in countries where the regimes are commonly regarded as oppressive and human rights are being denied. This situation raises the question of what obligations private companies might have to challenge unethical behaviour by states. Murphy (2001) proposed a theory of benevolence in which people (he was not discussing companies) are not morally obliged to do more to solve the world's problems than would be their portion if everyone else were doing their share. In other words, people (and companies?) should only do their portion even if others are not doing theirs and so there remains much that the individual or company could do.

Unethical states may, however, seek to influence how international companies conduct their business. If such regimes demand that companies use unacceptable employment practices, for example, or direct their investments in ways that reward their political supporters, then companies may be forced to consider whether it is ethical to remain in that country

Lord Browne (Browne of Madingley, 2004), group chief executive of BP, put forward an unambiguous principle.

> Companies must obey the law in every jurisdiction in which we operate and if we find the law unacceptable and at odds with our own values we shouldn't be operating in that jurisdiction.

Withdrawing from a failed or oppressive state may meet ethical requirements because the organisation would cease to be complicit in wrongdoing, but such a move may make the situation of the population in the state worse. Talisman is a Canadian oil company, which was active in Sudan, a country that has been suffering a civil war between its Muslim north and its Christian and Animist south for two decades. Talisman was charged by human rights groups that its presence exacerbated the civil war, that the money it paid for the oil was used to buy arms and that its oil development had displaced thousands of people. In 2003 Talisman withdrew from the Nile Petroleum Operation Company (NPOC), which it owned in partnership with the China National Petroleum Corporation, Petronas the Malaysian oil company and the Sudanese state-owned oil company. Talisman sold its share of NPOC to an arm of India's Oil and Natural Gas Corporation. The organisations that now own NPOC are all state owned. They do not raise their capital on the international markets nor are they accountable to shareholders. Seymour (2003) argued that these organisations benefited from the political turmoil in Sudan, which acted to keep their western competitors out. (Since a peace deal brought the civil war to an end in 2005 western oil companies have shown a renewed interest in Sudan.) He also argued that because they are companies owned by governments, which were often intolerant of critical voices within their own countries, these corporations are immune from the demands of human rights groups such as had encouraged Talisman to quit Sudan.

> [ ] with the sale of Talisman's share, a company that its critics had ensured had an interest in attempting to moderate the government of Sudan's policies has left. What remains are companies that actively support the government of Sudan and its war against southerners, with all its attendant human rights abuses. The moral calculus is thus vastly more complex, and our celebration of Talisman's departure utterly displaced.

(Seymour, 2003: 5)

Case study 12.6	**Businesses and South Africa in the apartheid era**

In the 1950s the apartheid regime in South Africa was created by a series of laws that enforced racial segregation by restricting the areas in which blacks and coloureds could live and by limiting the jobs they could apply for. There were many foreign-owned companies that had long been present in South Africa. These companies had to obey the apartheid laws. As, by common consensus in the world beyond South Africa, apartheid was evil, and the foreign-owned companies were not in a position to change it, the question arose as to whether in conscience they should disinvest from South Africa. In 1977 Leon Sullivan, a director of General Motors, a company that had a subsidiary in South Africa, proposed a set of principles to govern its business in South Africa (Minnesota Center for Corporate Responsibility, 2001). They amounted to a refusal to obey the apartheid laws. Segregation was not to be practised in its plants and staff were to be paid and promoted according to merit not race. They also imposed an obligation to improve the quality of life in those communities in which companies did business. Many American companies trading in South Africa signed up to the principles. It was hoped that such large numbers would discourage the South African government from prosecuting the companies for breaking the apartheid laws and that their efforts might lead to the collapse of apartheid.

However, in 1987 Sullivan declared that the experiment was showing no sign of undermining apartheid. He claimed that American companies should withdraw from their South African operations. In that year General Motors sold its holdings in South Africa. In 1991 the South African government began to repeal the apartheid regime. Nelson Mandela was elected President of South Africa in 1994.

The issue of the moral, and perhaps legal, responsibility of MNEs for the apartheid era has remained. The issue came into prominence in 2004, as in the Yukos case (*see* p. 480), because the US judiciary was claiming a worldwide jurisdiction in certain circumstance. The American Alien Tort Claims Act of 1789 allows American companies to be sued in the American courts for certain classes of wrong that were committed in other countries. The validity of this law was confirmed by a Supreme Court ruling in 2004. An American law firm proposed to start a case on behalf of the Khulumani Support Group of South Africa against IBM. The allegation is that IBM supplied the then South African government with the computers that enabled them to put the pass laws, which allocated individuals to a racial category that determined where they might go and what they might do, into effect. The passed laws were at the heart of the apartheid system. In case it be argued that in supplying the hardware IBM cannot be liable because they could not determine the use to which the computers might be put, the allegation also argues that IBM supplied the software (Robins, 2004).

The South African government is opposed to the case although many human rights groups are supporting it. They point out that the MNEs are fully cooperating in rehabilitating the lives of those damaged by apartheid. It is also no doubt seen to be in the country's national interest to keep the MNEs engaged with South Africa's economic growth.

Discussion activity 12.5	When should a company withdraw from a country?

Draw up and discuss guidelines that could be used to help a company decide whether a country it was working in had such a corrupt government and institutions that they should withdraw from it.

Cultural diversity or cultural homogenisation?

The World Commission on the Social Dimension of Globalization (WCSDG, 2004) identified a number of broadly cultural aspects of globalisation. The major impact concerns what it terms interconnectivity (WCSDG, 2004: §218). The rapid spread of telecommunications and the Internet, and in particular of television and the global entertainment industry, has made people everywhere more conscious of each other's ambitions, expectations and circumstances. For the relatively poor this process creates a sense of missing out that they would not have if their horizons were more local and circumscribed. For the relatively rich it increases their sense of privilege, which may create a feeling of obligation to those less fortunate. This may well explain the growth of NGOs and international charities and indeed the increase in anti-globalisation activisms. Travel is an aspect of this increasing interconnectivity and the fact that many Europeans had travelled to Thailand, in particular, explains both the high loss of life of European tourists in the 2004 Asian tsunami and the huge and sympathetic response from the western world.

A common cliché is that travel broadens the mind. However, ironically, as we travel more, taking advantage of the spread of budget airlines, our ethical horizons can become narrower. If we visit the places much frequented we may only see a Disney-fied version of the local culture – folkloric evenings in Greece, having lunch with the inhabitants of the floating islands on Lake Titicaca – and mistakenly think it true. Julian Barnes' (1999) comic novel *England, England* explores the idea of a replica England built on the Isle of Wight to attract the tourists. Merely flying to broaden our minds may show a lack of awareness of sustainability issues. Aviation fuel is untaxed, which makes flying cheaper than if it were taxed as are other forms of transport. Therefore as the demand for air travel, especially for holidays, increases aeroplanes become a major source of the greenhouse gases that may contribute to global warming. Therefore our desire to travel may be harming us all.

A particular criticism of globalisation is the tendency of powerful countries and companies to impose their values on weaker societies. This is sometimes called McDonaldisation, a process by which western brands and organisational methods and structures replace local products and thereby reduce choice and variety.

The charges of McDonaldisation and Logo-isation define the ethical questions surrounding the cultural and social aspects of globalisation. Do these processes destroy local cultures and replace them with North American values, and if they do is this a bad thing?

DEFINITION

Ritzer (1993) in his book *The McDonaldization of Society* took the global success of McDonald's as an example of the growth of a common, worldwide, mass culture. Ritzer argued that the process of **McDonaldisation** represents the expansion of instrumental rationality – a drive for efficiency, predictability, calculability and control – with no questioning of the ends being sought. The criticism of mass culture, of which McDonaldisation is a modern example, is that it causes people to be satisfied with a 'vulgar simplicity' (Harrington, 1965: 188). Advertising and sound-bite communications, it is alleged, diminish the masses' ability to exercise moral agency. They lose the ability to distinguish the good from the bad, gourmet cooking from burgers, the noble life from consumerism.

This criticism was taken up and popularised by Naomi Klein (2000) in her book *No Logo*. She argues that globalisation, and in particular the branding of consumer goods, has limited people's choices throughout the world. This has been done by:

■ Replacing culture and education with marketing. Brands divert people from the product or service they are buying and focus them on purchasing the perceived status and values that are associated with the brand. People buy coffee from Star-bucks, she argues (Klein, 2000: 21), for the sense of being a member of a warm, bookish, jazz listening, armchair lounging community; and not for the coffee. The purchase of coffee therefore ceases to be a rational expression of personal values but an entrapment by emotional lures. It may of course have always been so. If one replaces jazz and armchairs with tobacco fug, cosy booths and clubbable warmth one has a description of the original coffee shops in eighteenth-century London.

■ Creating less secure, less fulfilling and poorly paid jobs for people, not just in the developing world but in the industrialised worlds as well. This has been achieved by the casualisation of labour through outsourcing, flexible work and part-time employment. Interestingly, again, a return to the nature of the work force in eighteenth-century England.

Klein, however, is not simply an observer; her intention is to report on and encourage the forces of anti-globalisation and the activities of anti-brand warriors.

Cross reference	The discussion of McDonaldisation and Logo-isation is a particular aspect of a more general issue that is discussed in Chapter 11, namely the extent to which different countries or cultural groups wish to develop or maintain their own values and priorities in relation to business and management.

Does globalisation damage indigenous and local cultures?

The first of these questions is slightly easier to address because it is a practical matter. MNEs may take a range of actions concerning the introduction of their international brands into new countries.

■ Introduce the brand and product in its traditional form. Such is the case with Coca Cola, which is marketed as a global product.

■ Introduce the brand but adapt the product to local tastes and preferences. In Greece, for example, McDonald's burgers are mostly lamb, in recognition of local tastes; in India they sell no beef or pork patties at all in response to religious prohibitions.

■ Decide not to enter the market but wait to see if local demand develops. No major western coffee chain has yet opened in India to sell espressos and lattes.

However, in Delhi and other metropolitan areas local chains such as Barista are expanding.

■ In some cases an MNE may prevent the importation of a western product or service into a country. China has opened its market but its government is concerned that this should not present any threat to its ideology and policies. MNEs therefore will take care not to offend the Chinese government lest they experience some problems with their licences to operate in China. The country is a vast potential market for satellite television and other services and News Corporation International is a major provider through its Star TV service. News Corporation International dropped the BBC World Service from the range of channels it provided to China because the government objected to a documentary that the BBC had broadcast on Mao Tse-tung (Klein, 2000: 171).

■ The case of what the WCSDG calls indigenous and tribal peoples (WCSDG, 2004: §311) is a particularly difficult one. There are a few communities remaining that are totally separated from life in the rest of the world. The question is whether these societies should be protected not only from intrusion by companies but also from all other forms of contact including tourism. The question of the appropriateness of tourism was highlighted in 2012 by the case of the Jarawa tribe who live in the Andaman & Nicobar Islands. Tour companies were accused of encouraging tourists to interact with Jarawa people, even though it is illegal under Indian law, and of treating the community as a 'human safari park'.

Case study 12.7	McDonald's fries

The original McDonald's fries were cooked in beef fat. This of course made them objectionable to vegetarians and to Hindus for whom the cow is sacred. In 1990 McDonald's announced that in future all its fries would be cooked in vegetable oil. It emerged in 2001, however, that this was only part of the story. In North America the fries were first cooked in centralised plants using beef fat. They were then frozen and transported to the restaurants for further frying in vegetable oil. McDonald's announced that it was 'not too big to apologise' and that it had given incomplete information to its customers. American Hindus have started seeking damages. Other customers have no problem with the use of beef fat and may even think that it improves the taste of the fries. McDonald's has nearly 30 restaurants in India, where its burgers are made from lamb rather than beef. It assured its Indian customers that its cooking methods were strictly vegetarian.

(*Source*: Evans, 2001)

The situation is not a simple one, therefore, of the imposition of western brands and products, and by implication western consumer values, on local cultures. Such an argument in any case implies a naïve and orientalist distinction between the spiritual east and the materialist west, and presumes a story in which the simple and non-materialist lives of the east are destroyed by crass western commercial values. Social and economic histories point out that people and communities in the East are as concerned with material things and profits as those in the West. For a detailed and very local account of the importance of the market – the bazaar – in the lives of local people in the Gangetic plain of India in the nineteenth and twentieth centuries, read Yang (1998).

Orientalism

DEFINITION

This term was coined by Edward Said (1978) to explain the stereotyped view that the western imperial powers had of the eastern societies they were colonising.

> This is the apogee of Orientalist confidence. No merely asserted generality is denied the dignity of truth; no theoretical list of oriental attributes is without application to the behaviour of orientals in the real world. On the one hand there are Westerners, and on the other there are Arab-orientals; the former are (in no particular order) rational, peaceful, liberal, logical, capable of holding real values, without natural suspicion; the latter are none of these things.
>
> (Said, 1978: 49)

Said argued that such stereotyping was an ideological device to support colonialist exploitation of the east.

Cross reference

The concept of orientalism is closely associated with that of essentialism, which is discussed in Chapter 11, p. 415.

Globalisation and consumer choice

Let us assume, and it is a big assumption, that western brands and products are changing the local and family values of developing countries. Is this a bad thing? We will not answer the question but we will try to lay out the form that an argument about the matter might take. The process would be bad

- if it were accepted unwittingly by those affected, who were unaware of the changes and their significance; or
- if it broke some generally accepted ethical principle.

The main commentators on these questions take different positions.

- Klein argues that branding and marketing are devices to circumvent people's tendency to make rational choices by appealing to them through symbolism and emotion. She would also argue that this effect is just as strong, and perhaps stronger, in the industrialised West than it might be in developing countries. Branding is therefore to be regarded as a bad thing because people are unconscious of the changes they were experiencing. This argument is a version of the Marxist concept of false consciousness (Sklair, 1995). This states that in capitalist societies the masses are exploited but are lured into believing that they are living in the best of all possible worlds. They are not able to recognise their own oppression.

- The Ritzer argument in McDonaldisation (*see* p. 491) is not that people do not make rational choices in a consumer society, simply that they use the wrong sort of rationality. Instrumental rationality, which is what it is argued consumers use, is conscious and calculated but it is focused on achieving the wrong ends. Instead of seeking the good life, as Aristotle demanded in the West and as is required by many other philosophies and religions, modern consumers satisfy themselves with designer labels and the newest gadgets. This is essentially a Weberian analysis in which the day-to-day operations of modern organisations constrain people's actions to implementing means, and mistakenly assuming them to be ends. On this basis consumerism can be seen as breaking an important ethical principle and thus is to be seen as a bad thing.

- The third position believes that in the new global village people in different societies choose freely to enjoy the benefits and comforts provided by iPods, computer games, Internet access and coffee lattes. This view was taken by Kerr et al., (1960). On this argument globalisation, and the standardisation of tastes it brings, are to be thought a good thing.

DEFINITIONS

Weberian is the adjectival form of the name of the sociologist Max Weber. He defined bureaucracy (the following definition is heavily dependent on Watson (2002: 240–2)) as a distinctive form of organisation and decision-making that had replaced traditional methods. In bureaucracies decisions are made using instrumental or formal rationality that involves a calculation as to which option would best meet the desired objectives. This approach has many benefits; it enables, for example, doctors to develop ever more complex means of assisting human conception. However, Weber also noted that a fixation on techniques would lead to a neglect of discussion of the value of the ends being sought. This was his idea of the *stalhartesGehäuse* (meaning steel-hard house but often translated as iron cage). In the example given instrumental rationality could mean that if the technology to clone human beings is developed it would be used without considering whether it was right to do so.

The net effect of globalisation would seem to be one in which the populations of the developing and the transitional countries are increasingly sharing common expectations and demands for services and products. The expansion of international trade and FDI that fuels globalisation has increased the wealth of the world. However, the distribution of these beneficial impacts has been skewed. Some areas, notably Asia and Latin America and the Caribbean, have received much larger inflows of FDI than other areas such as Africa and Eastern Europe

(International Labour Organization, ILO 2004: 28). Within the developing countries the elite have benefited more than the bulk of the populations, which in some cases have become worse off. At an ethical level these outcomes offend against Rawls' fairness principle (*see* p. 116); in practice it creates a destabilising situation in which many people's expectations are increasing while their conditions are worsening. There is recognition among international institutions, such as the United Nations, the Group of Eight (G8) and many others, that this situation is unfair and potentially a source of conflict within the world. There is consequently much discussion about the governance of international businesses, and it is to this topic that we now turn.

Global governance

At the close of the Second World War a series of international conferences set up the basic institutions of global governance, namely the United Nations, the World Bank, the International Monetary Fund and the General Agreement on Tariffs and Trade (GATT). There have been changes since; GATT was replaced in 1995 by the WTO for example. Although the number of sovereign states has increased, from about 50 after 1945 to 190 now, the system of global governance has remained much the same. A number of deficiencies in this system of governance have been recognised by the WCSDG (ILO, 2004: §340–52).

■ The western industrialised companies have an excessive influence in the formal bodies of global governance. The emergent industrialised countries such as China, India and Brazil can exert influence in such bodies when they act in concert, but the western countries still have the greatest influence and the developing countries have little. This is so even in organisations like the WTO, where the developing countries have a formal equality with the industrialised ones.

■ The developing countries often cannot afford to attend the many international conferences that influence global governance and do not have the technical expertise necessary to make their cases as strong as they might be.

■ An international civil society has emerged since the end of the Second World War formed of NGOs such as international charities and lobby organisations such as Greenpeace. These organisations have no formal role in the institutions of governance.

■ The MNEs have become much more significant in the world. They have become bigger and more globally extensive. They have great influence on global governance through private lobbying and public relations activities. They are not, however, formally involved in the institutions and do not carry the accountability that formal membership would imply.

■ Many decisions that affect global governance are made by exclusive bodies, such as the G8 and the Organisation for Economic Cooperation and Development (OECD).

- The system of global governance is disjointed and unconnected. There are many bodies operating separately – and often doing much good, such as the development of international accountancy standards. However, these initiatives are often unconnected and carry differing levels of authority. Some aspects of global governance have the status of international law and treaty obligations: there are voluntary agreements backed by public bodies such as the United Nations and voluntary agreements between any permutation of private companies, NGOs and governments.

Global governance is the set of rules set up by the international community of governments, companies and NGOs and formal bodies to govern political, economic and social affairs. Some of these are discussed in the next section of the chapter.

Cross reference	There is a general discussion of ethical codes in Chapters 7 and 8. In this chapter we concentrate on those standards and codes that are concerned with the consequences of international trade.

Voluntary codes

Mention was made earlier in the chapter of the dilemma that national governments, particularly those of developing countries, sometimes face when wishing to encourage inward investment by MNEs, but also wishing to maintain some form of influence, if not control, over the activities of the MNEs in the host country. Some form of middle ground is often required between the polar extremes of legislation governing particular aspects of economic or corporate activity on the one hand, and a totally laissez-faire approach on the other. Codes of conduct, agreements and framework documents are examples of such 'middle ground'.

If a code of conduct for MNEs has the support of sovereign states, this does not mean the issues encompassed by the code have become international law. Until they do the codes are not legally binding on MNEs. Thus, the obligations cited by a code will be moral, but not legal.

An example of such a code of practice that has received much publicity concerns the selling of breastmilk substitutes in developing countries.

Case study 12.8	**The International Code of Marketing of Breastmilk Substitutes**

The International Code of Marketing of Breastmilk Substitutes, the first international code of its kind, was adopted by the World Health Organization (WHO) in 1981 and by the World Health Assembly (WHA) in 1984. The code was intended to control the practices of those producing and selling breastmilk substitutes and related products (e.g. feeding bottles), particularly in developing countries. These countries tend to have relatively high birth rates but weak economies. It can be argued that expenditure on breastmilk substitutes is a misuse of a nation's resources, when the natural alternative is cost free and more nutritious for the child. However, to the large corporations producing these products the markets of the developing world represent significant profit opportunities. The problem had become so acute in certain African countries that breastfeeding had become almost eradicated. The international code bans free supplies of breastmilk substitutes in hospitals, because once mothers leave hospital the breastmilk substitutes are no longer free. Yet in 1996 Nestlé, a significant producer of breastmilk substitutes, was reported to be providing free and low-cost supplies of infant formula to hospitals in Kunming Province in China. Save the Children reported:

> Nestlé has made Lactogen widely available in six hospitals in Kunming, where it has targeted health professionals with both free and discounted supplies of the formula. This helps to create an incentive for the health workers, not only to use the formula within the hospitals, but also actively to encourage its use among mothers of newborn children. Lactogen has been displayed in some of the hospitals for sale. The report prepared by our China staff and local health workers alleged that there had been an increase in the consumption of Lactogen and that breastfeeding rates had fallen.

> Despite getting companies to sign up to the International Association of Infant Food Manufacturers (IFM) and in 1991 pledging to eradicate the supply of free and discounted supplies, a monitoring report entitled 'Breaking the Rules, Stretching the Rules' found that in 19 of 31 countries surveyed contraventions of the pledge were evident. In addition, a study in Pakistan in 1998 found widespread use and distribution of free supplies, with doctors being 'purchased by the companies'.

(*Source*: IBFAN, n.d.)

Even when codes of practice are established, compliance by MNEs is not necessarily automatic, and enforcement can be difficult, as evidenced by the selling of breastmilk substitutes in Malawi.

Case study 12.9	**Breastmilk substitutes in Malawi**

In 1994 the Health Ministry of Malawi had discussed with Nestlé the need to have the instructions on their products written in Chichewa, the national language of Malawi, a requirement that was in compliance with Article 9.2 of the International Code of Marketing of Breastmilk Substitutes. Despite these discussions, Nestlé did not respond positively and the instructions remained in English. The level of literacy is not high in Malawi and, of those women who could read at the time, it was estimated that only a little over one-half could read English.

Under Article 9.1 of the Code, labels on breastmilk substitutes should not discourage breastfeeding. However, on its Bona infant formula, Nestlé continued to assert in a section headed 'Important Notice', 'Infant formula can be used from birth onwards when breastfeeding is not possible, or as a supplement to breastfeeding'. This statement was retained on the packaging despite there being general recognition that supplementing breastfeeding with breastmilk substitutes brings forward the time when a mother's natural milk dries up, thereby bringing forward the time when breastmilk substitutes will be required as the sole source of infant nutrition.

| Discussion activity 12.6 | Problems of implementing voluntary codes |

Should the response to the difficulties in implementing voluntary codes illustrated in Case studies 12.8 and 12.9 be:

■ to work harder at convincing companies to adhere to the codes; or

■ to pass legislation in the companies' base countries that make it illegal not to adhere to the codes?

Humanitarian aid provides another opportunity for breastmilk substitute products to be introduced into vulnerable, but lucrative, markets. The International Baby Food Action Network (IBFAN) claims that:

> The baby food industry has used emergencies generally to promote its products and used 'humanitarian aid' as a way of entering into the emerging markets of Europe and the former Soviet Union.
>
> (IBFAN, n.d.)

These cases illustrate some of the problems inherent within a 'pledge', 'code' or 'framework agreement' that is not supported by legal or meaningful sanctions.

Another area of contention relates to the use of child labour. Corporate policy statements of MNEs on the use of child labour within its supplier networks tend to reflect one of four options:

1. stipulate a minimum age for employment by their suppliers;

2. refer to national laws of the host country regarding minimum age of working;

3. refer to international standards; or

4. a combination of some or all of the above.

However, some company policy statements that prohibit the use of child labour in the production of their products do not define what they mean by child labour, thus leaving discretion and judgment to local suppliers. This takes us to the issue of the rigour with which codes of practice are implemented and monitored, particularly those relating to overseas suppliers.

Putting MNE codes of practice into effect

Codes of conduct for MNEs can take various forms and the ILO cites three factors that tend to determine the credibility with which codes for MNEs are regarded.

1. The specific governments that have adopted and support the codes, and the particular MNEs that have 'signed up' to the codes.

2. Whether a code actually addresses the critical issues of the business activity being considered.

3. The effectiveness of the monitoring mechanisms employed and the sanctions available.

The International Chamber of Commerce (ICC) is active in pursuing a self-regulatory framework for business operations on the world stage. It sets standards that recognise the tensions inherent within any competitive market setting. The following statement is drawn from one of its publications:

> The globalisation of the world's economies, and the intense competition which ensues there from, require the international business community to adopt standard rules. The adoption of these self-disciplinary rules is the best way that business leaders have of demonstrating that they are motivated by a sense of social responsibility, particularly in light of the increased liberalization of markets.
>
> (International Chamber of Commerce, 1997)

A number of initiatives and codes have been developed to address specific global business issues. Examples include the following:

- The 1990s saw the scope of some agreements expand to take in broader social issues. An example is the Japan Federation of Economic Organizations. Established in 1996, it covered a number of issues including philanthropic activities, resistance against organisations that undermine social cohesion, policies to enrich the lives of employees, safe and comfortable work environments, a respect for individual dignity and 'specialness' and corporate transparency.

- In 1996 the British Toy and Hobby Association developed a code of practice that forbids the use of forced, indentured or under-age labour in the production of toys. The agreement also speaks to the working and living conditions of employees. An amended form of this code was adopted by the International Council of Toy Industries later in 1996.

- In February 1997, the ILO, the Sialkot Chamber of Commerce (SCCI) in Pakistan and UNICEF formed an agreement to eliminate child labour in the production of footballs by 1999. This specific initiative was the result of worldwide publicity of the use of child labour in the production of footballs, although no other products or industries were specifically targeted. It appears that this initiative has been largely, if not completely, successful. It does appear that high-profile media coverage is conducive to, and possibly necessary for, change to be levered and achieved.

- In the USA similar codes have been developed in relation to other industries, e.g. the Apparel Partnership on Sweatshops and Child Labor, which was adopted in 1997.

- The OECD has also produced guidelines for MNEs covering labour relations.

- A variety of organisations have sponsored the Sweatshop and Clean Clothes Codes, which cover labour relations, health and safety issues, freedom of association, wages and benefits and hours of work.

- The Declaration of Principles concerning Multinational Enterprises, developed in 1997 and involving the ILO, is a code that addresses issues such as freedom of association, terms and conditions of work.

At first sight the existence of such codes presents a preferable state of affairs to that of no codes at all. However, a closer inspection of such codes poses some uncomfortable challenges to this assumption. For example, within the Sweatshop Code, the wording relating to 'wages and benefits' specifies:

> Employers shall pay employees, as a floor, at least the minimum wage required by local law or the prevailing industry wage, whichever is the higher, and shall provide legally mandated benefits.

This leaves much responsibility with governments to institute laws that enhance working and employment conditions. The lobbying of governments by business organisations, including MNEs, will clearly be listened to in government circles. Those employed in sweatshop conditions are not often well represented at the political negotiating table. In the meantime global organisations and western customers of the manufacturing output of developing countries remain free to exploit the cost differentials of sourcing their production capacity overseas. Indeed, the very reason why many western apparel companies have closed their western production capability and transferred production to locations in the Philippines, India, Honduras, etc. has been to exploit the cost advantages of the developing world, cost advantages that have often involved sweatshop conditions and child labour.

With regard to 'hours of work' the Sweatshop Code states:

> Except in extraordinary business circumstances, employees shall (i) not be required to work more than the lesser of (a) 48 hours per week and 12 hours overtime or (b) the limits on regular and overtime hours allowed by the law of the country of manufacture or, where the laws of such country do not limit the hours of work, the regular work week in such country plus 12 hours overtime and (ii) be entitled to at least one day off in every seven day period.

Thus, unless local laws state otherwise, an employer can require their workers to work 60 hours per week, and stay within the obligations of the code. Employees might be entitled to one day off per week, but whether they will get this is another matter. In addition, when demand is high, the working week can extend beyond the 60 hours. This should be constrained to 'extraordinary business circumstances', but the latter is not defined and less than scrupulous employers will use this as a loophole to work employees for all seven days of the week and exceed the 60 hours per employee. The code could be far more stringent in its demands on behalf of the employees (the majority of whom tend to be women), but of course, the closer wage rates and working conditions are pushed towards western levels, the less the original decision to source production to the developing country makes economic sense.

There are examples of organisations appearing to make serious efforts to put their codes into practice. The ILO reported that Levi-Strauss, for example, conducts annual global training programmes to ensure its audit managers are familiar with their internal code, and has conducted five-day training programmes in the Dominican Republic for 'terms of engagement' auditors. Liz Claiborne (an American retail organisation of women's fashion clothes) has also reported that it had intensified its efforts to identify and remove labour abuses.

An example is provided by McDonald and Nijhof (1999: 140) of an organisation that employed 6,000 people, and whose CEO sought to roll out an ethics awareness-raising programme across the whole organisation. This involved writing the associated code of conduct in both English and Chinese and then training a series of trainers to deliver the associated workshops. The latter included a video message from the CEO, in which he stated that he would rather the organisation lose a contract than undermine the code. The programme was delivered throughout the company. For the CEO, 'the code needs to come off the pages and into people's lives'. As McDonald and Nijhof report, elements that were not included in the initiative were an annual ethics audit and an ethics hotline. Whether these have since been instituted is unknown.

The rigour with which MNEs police their own codes of conduct (particularly those they apply to their suppliers) does appear to vary. Of the organisation Liz Claiborne, the plant manager of Primo Industries, an apparel contractor based in El Salvador, stated, 'they are the toughest on child labour'. The plant manager told US Department of Labor officials that inspectors from Liz Claiborne visited the plant 'approximately twice a month to check on quality control and see whether rules and regulations are being implemented'. Such vigilance by the Claiborne organisation must involve costs that some other organisations (maybe its competitors) do not appear to incur, at least not to the same extent. A manager with the Indian company, Zoro Garments, 75 per cent of whose output goes to US markets, is quoted as saying that:

> Representatives of US customers have visited Zoro's factory occasionally for quality control inspections, [but] most of the visits were walk-throughs with some general questions raised about the use of child labour, but no check-list of requirements was administered.

> (ILO, 2004)

A complicating issue occurs where the MNE sources products from a variety of overseas suppliers, with some of these suppliers being in monopsony relationships with the MNE, while for other suppliers the MNE in question might be only one among a range of customers. Thus, can an MNE be held responsible for the work conditions and labour practices of a supplier from which it sources relatively few orders? Whatever one's position on this question, it has to be taken for granted that, for production costs of suppliers in developing countries to be so much lower than those of their western competitors, wage rates and employment conditions cannot be equal. Thus, for MNEs, or any other form of organisation, to feign ignorance of the working conditions of some of its suppliers ignores the logic of the situations. Rather than assuming that all is satisfactory, they must know that the cost differentials between suppliers in developing and developed countries would suggest a default position that all is not satisfactory, and that evidence is required to disprove this assumption.

Establishing a corporate code of conduct is one thing; making it a part of everyday practice is another. Of the 42 apparel companies surveyed by the US Department of Labor in 1996, to establish how many of them had endeavoured to ensure that workers in their overseas suppliers were aware of their code of conduct, 'very few respondents indicated that they had tried'. Only three companies insisted on their codes being posted on their suppliers' notice boards. In a further study reported by the ILO, of 70 supplier companies, 23 (33 per cent) indicated that they were not aware of corporate codes of conduct issued by their US customers.

The US Department of Labor also undertakes company visits and the ILO website gives information on ILO visits to a variety of countries including El Salvador, the Dominican Republic, Honduras, India and the Philippines. In a study of 70 companies, managers at only 47 of these stated an awareness of such codes, and of these only 34 could produce a copy of a code. Thus, less than half of the sites visited could produce a principal customer's code, yet the US retailers refer to their supplier codes as evidence of their (the apparel retailers') commitment to ethical practices at their overseas suppliers.

Awareness of such codes was highest in El Salvador, where managers at six out of the nine companies visited were aware of such codes, whereas in India managers at only two of the seven producer sites visited were aware. Even where awareness was acknowledged, awareness was not the same as accepting the codes and adhering to them. As the ILO observed,

> Although a significant number of suppliers knew about the US corporate codes of conduct, meetings with workers and their representatives in the countries visited suggested that relatively few workers were aware of the existence of codes of conduct, and even fewer understood their implications.

The UN Global Compact

This international standard is worth separate consideration because it was initiated by the UN Secretary-General at the Davos World Economic Forum in 1999. This is an informal conference at which politicians, MNE chief executives, NGO representatives and high-profile lobbyists meet. The compact is supported by the ILO, The Office of the UN Commissioner for Human Rights (OHCHR), the United Nations Environment Programme (UNEP), the UN Industrial Development Organization (UNIDO) and others.

The compact was, and remains, a voluntary code, which is intended to influence corporate practices by:

1. gaining the support and membership of leading organisations, and then

2. increasing the acceptance and take up of corporate responsibility by disseminating examples of good practice that hopefully other organisations will adopt.

The compact focuses upon nine key principles of corporate activity, which are grouped into three categories.

Human rights

Principle 1 – Businesses are asked to support the protection of international human rights within their sphere of influence; and

Principle 2 – To ensure their own corporations are not complicit in human rights abuses.

Labour

Principle 3 – Businesses are asked to uphold the freedom of association and the effective recognition of the rights to collective bargaining;

Principle 4 – To eliminate all forms of forced and compulsory labour;

Principle 5 – To abolish child labour; and

Principle 6 – To help eliminate discrimination in respect of employment and occupation.

Environment

Principle 7 – Businesses are asked to support a precautionary approach to environmental challenges;

Principle 8 – To undertake initiatives to promote greater environmental responsibility;

Principle 9 – To encourage the development and diffusion of environmentally friendly technologies

In 1999 those responsible for the compact saw the future for social change to be through international corporations, hence the focus on working with significant organisations to both gain their support (patronage) and stimulate corporate responsibility (CR) by highlighting examples of good practice that 'work' and that could be seen to be compatible with being a successful company.

The foreword to the 2004 report *Gearing Up*, which was commissioned by the executive of Global Compact, reflected a development in this thinking and strategy. There now appears to be a recognition that it was unrealistic to expect corporations to respond to initiatives such as the Global Compact independent of governments. While the original Global Compact may have been a response to political failings, a voluntary initiative that appears to ask businesses to make good the failings of governments, ironically, needs the commitment and positive engagement of governments to help it develop. For this reason *Gearing Up* argues for a greater level of dialogue, collaboration and partnership between businesses and governments for the future development of corporate responsibility.

The Global Compact, however, is developing in a different form from that of other ethical and CSR standards, which take an assurance based ('ticking the box') approach. The compact is more like a learning network in which understanding and learning about the problems of behaving in a socially and environmentally responsible way are discussed and explored. Those who have signed up to the compact are encouraged to take part in seminars, act as mentors, join networks and enter into partnerships to carry out projects. Many of the world's well-known companies have signed up including BT, BMW, Standard Chartered Bank, Nike, Novartis, Shell, Warburg and Unilever.

In 2001 the theme of the Global Compact policy dialogue was 'the role of the public sector in zones of conflict'. So, despite the criticism often made of it, it does address the issues of globalisation and conflict. The participants were from businesses, NGOs, trade unions and the UN. Tools and techniques for ameliorating conflict, such as risk assessment and multi-stakeholder processes of community development (see the Shell case study on p. 000). It was also agreed that partnership projects would be set up to try to make practical changes in selected regions (McIntosh et al., 2003: 182). The Global Compact also undertakes outreach activities and tries to involve small and medium-sized companies as well as city governments.

A more critical voice is that of Christian Aid. In its 2004 report, *Behind the Mask*, Christian Aid dismissed the UN Global Compact as having had 'almost no impact' (p.16). The lack of transparency associated with the Global Compact and its lack of monitoring and verification are other failings in the initiative's credibility. For Christian Aid it would seem that the Global Compact is an example of the worst sort of CSR initiative, that is one that enjoys a lot of publicity and hype, but is in fact a toothless tiger, with few if any monitoring or verification powers or resources. For some it is a sham and governments are complicit, instrumental even, in this charade.

The Global Compact contains the sorts of commitments and aspirations that many supporters and advocates of CSR or CR would welcome, as well as displaying many of the limitations of a number of CR initiatives. Thus, with the important caveat from Christian Aid expressed in the above paragraph, were turn to a key aim of the *Gearing Up* report, which is stated as making 'the link between corporate responsibility . . . initiatives and wider sustainable development challenges', with the report linked to the Millennium Development Goals (MDGs) (Table 12.1).

The *Gearing Up* report moves on, via a discussion of its findings and case studies, to identify six possible ways (or, probably more accurately, rates of change) that CR could have an impact. The six possibilities reflect different levels of engagement by 'business' in economic and non economic development, including one option (termed 'reverse') which reflects the possibility that businesses might publicly articulate a commitment to being catalysts for change, while, behind the scenes, doing all they can to frustrate and hinder developments.

Table 12.1 The Millennium Development Goals

1. Eradicate extreme poverty and hunger

2. Achieve universal primary education

3. Promote gender equality and empower women

4. Reduce child mortality

5. Improve maternal health

6. Combat HIV/AIDS, malaria and other diseases

7. Ensure environmental sustainability, and

8. Develop a global partnership for development (this relates to trade issues, but also debt relief and access to affordable, essential drugs in developing countries).

Reflections

Individual MNEs have, in many cases, become so large that as individual corporations they can have a major impact on the prosperity and the peacefulness of the communities, countries and regions they work within. This gives them a power equivalent to that of governments. If they have the influence of governments then they ought also to have the accountability that goes with it. Historically large corporations have become governments. The British East India Company, for example, formed in the seventeenth century as a company of merchants, became by degrees the government of India in the nineteenth century. The task for the development of global governance is to find the institutions and mechanisms by which large corporations can be brought to account for their global impacts.

Corporations may have an ethical responsibility to behave well in their international dealings but it is the individual managers in multinationals, transnationals and international NGOs who exercise that responsibility. In Case study 12.6 it was an individual, Leon Sullivan, who drove forward the response to apartheid.

Summary

In this chapter the following key points have been made:

- Globalisation concerns the economic, political and cultural impact of the expansion of international trade and international interconnectivity.

- The ethical issues surrounding globalisation include whether MNEs do or do not offend against human rights and/or benefit themselves and certain others and only at the cost of making others worse off in their pursuit of global business.

- The standard argument in favour of the liberalisation of world trade is that it increases the total sum of wealth in the world, which through a 'trickle-down' effect benefits all. The evidence suggests that the benefits of increasing world trade are patchily distributed. Some countries, notably China, Brazil and India, have benefited but others have experienced a worsening of their relative economic performance. Within developing and transitional countries some sections of the population have paid a price for trade liberalisation while other groups have benefited.

- MNEs are tempted to choose the location of their operations to gain the benefits of institutions and legal jurisdictions that will give them better financial returns.

- The foreign and domestic policies of the governments of countries can be distorted by the needs and demands of MNEs that are based in those countries in ways that diminish the public good.

- The operations of MNEs in developing countries can make internal political and ethnic tensions worse. When their operations stretch over several mutually antagonistic countries in a region the presence of the MNEs can either make the tensions worse or, at the least, act as a focus of discontent for the disaffected.

■ MNEs may find themselves operating in countries whose governments are thought to be tyrannical and dismissive of human rights. This raises the ethical question of when the situation is so bad that the company should withdraw from that country.

■ Globalisation is in part a diminution of cultural diversity across the world and the growth of a worldwide consumerist and brand-led culture. The ethical issue is whether this change is one that people have entered into freely and in full knowledge or whether they have been manipulated into acceptance because it suits the purposes of the MNEs.

■ Cultural change is an unpredictable process, however, and it is likely that different cultures will absorb western consumerist values and adapt and change them in unexpected ways.

■ There has been much development of voluntary codes that are intended to provide a framework for the global governance of MNEs and world trade. Although this is a good development the implementation of such standards and codes is a difficult one when the demands conflict with commercial imperatives.

■ The Global Compact is a development that promises a new type of approach to global governance, one based on networks of learning rather than the assurance of adherence to bureaucratic standards.

Typical assignments

1. In what circumstances should an MNE withdraw from a country for ethical reasons? Illustrate your argument with examples.

2. To what extent does the UN Global Compact represent an innovative and effective approach to the governance of MNEs?

3. What responsibilities, if any, do MNEs have in helping countries develop fair and effective systems of governance?

4. Does the expansion of international trade benefit everybody? Does it matter if it does not?

Group activity 12.1

For the purposes of this activity, you should assume that most desktop computers are made in a variety of Asian countries. Three parties are in discussions over the development of a code of practice that might cover the activities of the local suppliers to the multinational corporate purchasers of the computers.

The code of practice would cover the operations of the MNEs in **one** of the countries concerned. The three parties are a spokesperson for the Society of Computer Manufacturers and Assemblers, a representative from the host country's ministry for trade and industry and a representative from the pressure group Workers in the Manufacture and Assembly of Computers (WMAC), who is also a local trade union representative.

Divide the seminar group into three sub-groups (one for each of the parties involved). Each sub-group should decide its position, in terms of what is:

(a) morally justifiable, and

(b) likely to be achieved,

on the following issues:

- standard hours of work;

- acceptable overtime working;

- pension rights;

- accident and injury protection and benefits for dependants;

- number of continuous working days in normal and abnormal circumstances;

- health and safety standards (equivalent to western standards);

- employment rights (e.g. period of notice required by both employer and employee);

- minimum employment age;

- social infrastructure support (e.g. support for local schools, sports clubs, youth clubs, medical facilities); and

- grievance procedures.

Then, as a complete group, debate the contrasts between the three perspectives.

Recommended further reading

Jan Aart Scholte's book *Globalisation: A Critical Introduction* (2000) provides a good introduction to the topic, as does Held and McGrew (2000) *The Global Transformations Reader*. Another very popular book is *Globalisation and its Discontents* by Joseph Stiglitz (2004). *Living Corporate Citizenship* by McIntosh, Thomas, Leipziger and Coleman (2003) is a good read and describes most of the main standards for international business but it also has a particularly extensive discussion of the Global Compact and lots of case studies of projects undertaken by companies. Unusually, two semi-official publications make good introductions to the topic of globalisation. The first is the World Commission on the Social Dimension of Globalization (2004) *A Fair Globalization: Creating Opportunities for All* and the second is the *Report of the Commission for Africa* (2005), which was instigated by the British government.

Useful websites

Topic	Website provider	URL
A very useful site providing links to materials on businesses and human rights. The materials are classified by topicality, regions, sectors, individual companies, laws and principles	Business & Human Rights Resource Centre	http://www.business-humanrights.org/Home
International poverty measures	The World Bank	http://iresearch.worldbank.org/povcalnet
The Corner House anti-corruption organisation	The Corner House	http://www.thecornerhouse.org.uk/
The Global Compact	The Global Compact Secretariat	www.unglobalcompact.org
Businesses and human rights	Amnesty International Business group	www.amnesty.org.uk/business
World Trade Organization	World Trade Organization	http://www.wto.org/
Globalisation	International Forum on Globalization	http://www.ifg.org/
A vast list of resources on globalisation	The Róbinson Rojas Archive	http://www.rrojasda\tabank.org/dev3000.htm

CHAPTER 13

Moral agency at work and a modest proposal for affecting ethics in business

Chapter at a glance

Chapter contents

- Learning outcomes
- Introduction
- Challenges to moral agency in modern organisations
- The corporation and democratic ideals
- Sustainability
- Business sustainability
- Challenging central assumptions of economics, politics and human behaviour
- A modest proposal for affecting ethics in business
- The processes of moral agency
- Thinking through the issues and deciding on the best action
- Summary

Case studies

- Case Study 13.1 Malawi and the consequences of deregulating and privatising the grain market

Activities and exercises

- Video clip 13.1 Interview with the canon precentor of St Paul's Cathedral, London. St Pauls and Canary Wharf
- Video clip 13.2 Interview with the canon precentor of St. Paul's Cathedral, London. Decision making and debate in cathedral management
- Podcast 13.1 The prime minister: practices and institutions
- Activity 13.1 A case loosely based on the MG Rover story
- Typical assignments
- Group activity 13.1
- Recommended further reading
- Useful websites

Having read this chapter and completed its associated activities, readers should be able to:

■ Identify the main challenges and issues concerning the place and role of business ethics in management and business.

■ Consider a number of proposals that are designed to confront these challenges and issues.

■ Evaluate the ways in which a willingness to look at the particularities of cases and to apply moral imagination can lead to a more ethical position than responding to all ethical problems on a routine basis.

■ Identify some of the barriers that prevent people having the will to act according to their conscience.

■ Identify ways in which habits and cultures could be developed in an organisation that encourages people to act as moral agents.

Introduction

The title of this chapter, 'moral agency at work', has a deliberate ambiguity. It can refer to the role and importance of moral agency in organisations and work. Alternatively, it might mean how moral agency works, the processes that moral agency involves. We are concerned with both aspects in this chapter. The two levels of analysis, the individual and the corporate, that have been shuttled between throughout this book are brought together in this chapter. Both perspectives must be addressed if organisations in business and management are to operate socially, ethically and environmentally responsibly. We want to make a case, and a series of proposals, for taking moral agency seriously at a corporate level, and also to suggest some ways in which individuals might approach choosing and taking the ethical action on difficult moral issues at work. Our modest proposal addresses both.

Challenges to moral agency in modern organisations

Throughout the book we have endeavoured to present the full range of perspectives on each of the critical issues raised. This has not meant that we have given each perspective equal weight, because each perspective may not have warranted such attention, either because of the weight of evidence or arguments relating to competing perspectives or because of the complexities involved.

What must be clear from the issues and arguments we have examined is that there are a number of challenges that have to be adequately handled if already significant problems are not to become overpowering and out of control, assuming they are not already. We would identify the following as matters of significant import, although not in any order of rank.

- The relationship between corporations and democratic ideals, and the relationships between business, society and the state.

- The sustainability of business practices and business organisations with regard to.
  - global warming and its implications; and
  - the raising to a public level, once again, of debates concerning the defensibility and wisdom of preferencing economic growth above all other considerations.

- Challenging narrow conceptions of the self, in particular:
  - the enframing of the technological mind-set;
  - the myopic fixation upon the self, a form of 'Cult of the Self', with little if any regard for others; and
  - the defining of individuality within notions of consumerism, but little else.

- Underpinning all the above, the ability of individuals to exercise moral agency within organisations without fear of retribution or recrimination.

It has been a theme of this book that in business organisations there can be great tensions between how an ethical theory says people should behave and how their social values and a specific organisational culture can incline them to behave. All the issues we raise in this final chapter, whether set at an individualistic, organisational, national or international level, will ultimately be addressed, or not, by the actions of individuals, acting independently, or collectively in groups of varying sizes. This does not deny the significance of structures such as ideology, discourses, group values and, most critically, issues of power. We tend towards Giddens' (1984) notion of structuration, that is, while recognising the dominance of structures, we would argue that agency can effect change, particularly at moments of crisis, but also at other times. By recognising the significance of agency in change processes we thereby recognise and bring into sharp focus the issue of moral agency.

The structure/agency debate

DEFINITION

This question is of concern to social sciences, philosophy and history as well as to business ethics, which draws from all these disciplines. When people act, which has the greater influence on their actions:

- things (broadly called structures) that are external to them such as social and cultural norms, economic structure and circumstances, and historical forces and trends; or
- their own will and powers of detached analysis (broadly termed agency).

In terms of historical study the question refers to whether only certain people – who used to be called great men, a category that extends now to include great women – act as agents and others simply follow the flow of long-term historical movements. As in most such debates, and as Giddens intimates, the answer is that there is a complex interaction between agency and structures. Structuration is the idea that there is a duality to human action. It can be seen as guided by rules, resources and social relationships, but from the second perspective it can be seen that human actions can both define and change those structures.

We have also argued that, whilst there are competing positions on practically any point of issue within business ethics, the arguments supporting each position are unlikely to be equally robust, defensible or contain the same quality of ethical argument. Our stance has been to explore the different ethical positions to allow you to make informed judgments. We do not seek or offer a Holy Grail of business ethics, but we have outlined some modest proposals for business ethics that we would like you to consider. However, before doing so, we will consider the broad issues raised here.

The corporation and democratic ideals

You will recall that a key criticism, made by Milton Friedman, against calls for corporate social responsibility beyond profit making was that to encourage and support such developments would undermine democratic ideals. We would agree that in this respect Friedman has a 'justice' argument on his side with respect to this particular criticism. Indeed, one of the central arguments of neo-liberal economics is its integrity in sustaining democratic ideals, most notably individual freedoms. Yet, paradoxically, and leaving the CSR argument to one side, the role and place of the corporation in modern society raises profound and disturbing questions regarding democratic ideals. The democratic pretensions of neo-liberal economics are, for others, its great deceit.

Charles Lindblom argues that:

> It has been a curious feature of democratic thought that it has not faced up to the private corporation in an ostensible democracy. Enormously large, rich in resources . . . they can insist that government meet their demands, even if these demands run counter to . . . citizens . . . Moreover they do not disqualify themselves from playing the role of citizen . . . they exercise unusual veto powers. . . . The large private corporation fits oddly into democratic theory and vision. Indeed it does not fit.
>
> (Lindblom, 1977: 356)

Bakan (2004), in an acclaimed book that was the basis of the film *The Corporation* (Achbar el al., 2003), went further, likening the corporation to a monster that has become uncontrollable.

> Governments create corporations, much like Dr. Frankenstein created his monster, yet once they exist, corporations, like the monster, threaten to overpower their creator.
>
> (Bakan, 2004: 149)

This level of hyperbole can cause a contrary reaction of disdain and dismissal by being seen as empty rhetoric, although Bakan cites evidence to support his description. Bakan argued that if the corporation was to take human form it would be a psychopath – cheating, lying, even killing to serve the interests of its shareholders. An example of the unattractiveness of some corporations is the British MG

Rover volume car producer. The company had been owned by BMW, which had decided that Rover's Longbridge plant did not have the capacity to produce cars at the volume necessary to achieve the economies of scale enjoyed by other volume car makers. BMW sold the company to Phoenix for £10. In addition to gaining the company, Phoenix also received a large amount of cash and assets from the former owner. The four partners of Phoenix did not use this money to introduce new models and so keep the marque competitive, nor did they fill the hole in the employees' pension fund. Instead, the partners ensured they were personally well remunerated, awarded themselves a £10m loan note, set up a £12m pension fund for themselves, gained personal control of a lucrative financing business, and asset stripped the company by selling off its land and intellectual property rights. As the *Financial Times* pointed out,

> **FT** This is capitalism at its ugliest. There is no suggestion that the Phoenix team broke any laws. They did what any ruthless entrepreneur would have done in their situation: incentivise, strip assets, take cash out early.
> But they betrayed the trust placed in them by their workers, the government and the public. Yes they kept the business afloat for five years. But they did so by burning through someone else's money and without delivering the new generation of models that might have given Rover a slim chance.

> (Leading article: A tale of greed and gullibility, *The Financial Times*, 9 April 2005, p. 10, Copyright © The Financial Times Ltd.)

Using less emotive language Basu et al. (2002) wrote an open letter to CEOs arguing that capitalism is facing a crisis and that simply repeating the mantra 'shareholder interests and only shareholder interests' (which for too many might more accurately be 'executives' interests and only executives' interests') is not acceptable. For Basu et al. (2002), change has to take place and it has to be fundamental.

For J.K. Galbraith (2004), one of the leading economists of the twentieth century, neo-liberal economics has been fraudulent in the naïveté of its assumptions and the camouflage it has provided for individual greed. For Galbraith, the initial deceit was evident as early as the late nineteenth century and the early twentieth century, when the search took place for an alternative phrase for capitalism, following the problems of corporate collapses and fraud during this period.

> Because of the problems with 'capitalism' the search was underway for a new term. 'Free Enterprise' had a trial in the United States. It did not take. In Europe, there was 'Social Democracy' – capitalism and socialism in a companionate mix. In the United States, however, socialism was (as it remains) unacceptable. In the next years reference was to the New Deal; this however, was too clearly identified with Franklin D. Roosevelt and his cohorts. So in reasonably learned expression there came 'the market system'. There was no adverse history here, in fact no history at all. It would have been hard, indeed, to find a more meaningless designation – this a reason for the choice.

> (Galbraith, 2004: 18)

Galbraith continued,

> Reference to the market system as a benign alternative to capitalism is a bland, meaningless disguise of the deeper corporate reality – of producer power extending to influence over, even control of, consumer demand. This, however, cannot be said. It is without emphasis in contemporary economic discussion and instruction … But no one can doubt that the renaming of the system, the escape from the unacceptable term 'capitalism', has been somewhat successful … Reference to a market system is, to repeat, without meaning, erroneous, bland, design….No individual firm, no individual capitalist, is now thought to have power; that the market is subject to skilled and comprehensive management is unmentioned even in most economic teaching. Here is fraud. Sensitive friends and beneficiaries of the system do not wish to assign definitive authority to the corporation. Better the benign reference to the market.
>
> (Galbraith, 2004: 19–20)

A further subtle change in language is commented upon by Galbraith, indicative of the way public discourses are shifted/manipulated.

> The phrase 'monopoly capitalism' once in common use, has been dropped from the academic and political lexicon. The consumer is no longer subordinate to monopoly power; he or she is now sovereign or is so described. . . . As the ballot gives authority to the citizen, so in economic life the demand curve accords authority to the consumer. In both instances there is a significant measure of fraud. With both ballot and buyer, there is a formidable, well-financed management of the public response. And so especially in the age of the advertising and modern sales promotion. Here an accepted fraud, not least in academic instruction.
>
> (Galbraith, 2004: 24)

If democratic ideals and aspirations are important and to be taken seriously, then, like Bakan, Basu et al. and Galbraith, we would argue that changes have to be debated, and then acted upon, although the prospects for such open, balanced and informed debates are not propitious. For example, in 2003, when a female grocers' cooperative in the State of Oregon, USA, sought to gain sufficient names on a petition at a federal election that would have allowed a vote to have been taken on food products in the state having to have upgraded labelling to bring them in line with the labelling requirements that exist in the European Union (EU) (revealing, for example, the proportion of genetically modified elements in the products), the multinational GM food corporations mounted a $5m advertising campaign against the proposal, claiming the labelling would cost jobs. The proposal never received the required number of signatures and the 'debate' was stillborn.

Globalisation is invariably portrayed as an inevitable consequence of technological developments, an unavoidable reality. What are more contestable are the ramifications of the developments. The problem of externalities has long been an issue concerning business-society relationships. Deregulation can be seen as a way of transferring even more corporate costs to society. Externalities are those costs caused as a result of corporate activity, but which are not borne by the corporation. They are paid for by individuals and broader societal groups. Examples of externalised costs are the effect of air and noise pollution caused by corporations involved in transport services. Unhealthy and unsafe corporate practices are usually paid for by employee or consumer injuries, unless adequate compensation can be obtained, although whether the loss of a loved one can be adequately compensated is a moot point. Despoliation of water courses, forests and environmental habitats is controlled to a certain extent in developing economies, although not always adequately, as is illustrated below with regard to waste disposal. The situation in many developing economies is far less regulated, so the costs of the despoliation are carried by the indigenous people and their descendents. As a consequence of all the above examples and the many, many more that exist, corporate profits are overstated and shareholders receive inflated returns because 'Others' are bearing some of the corporate costs.

Sustainability

We will now move to a consideration of the issues loosely coupled under the broad banner of sustainability, and in particular environmental sustainability. We referred in Chapter 10 to the ideas and arguments of Martin Heidegger in exploring the notion of 'Being-in-the-world', which means that our consciousness of the world is always mediated through a 'mood' or feeling. Moods are the value, the importance, the meaning that something has for those who aware of that thing; these moods can change. 'Being' is very much a social construct, a sense of intrinsic value; if values are socially constructed then our environmental resources can be valued in different ways. A piece of urban scrubland, such as the site of a demolished gas works near a city centre, for example can be valued for its economic potential as a place to build luxury flats or it can be valued because it is the habitat of a rare species of flower. In modern societies the natural world is often valued as property to be used or exploited. If people feel they own something then they feel free to dispose of it in whatever way suits them. It is seeing things as property that has led to the problem of the over-production of waste. We can use the subject of waste to highlight the importance of sustainability.

The issue of waste generation and disposal may not sound like an obvious candidate for inclusion in a book on business ethics, but as one studies the subject it reveals itself as a series of major ethical issues. The vast majority of the waste generated is the result of individual consumption that is associated with lifestyle choices. For example, a high proportion of purchases are made, not because existing possessions are exhausted or inoperable, but because of the desire to own the latest model or gadget (e.g. motor cars or mobile phones). Lives are so busy and/or allocation of time is so skewed that we find it more convenient to purchase ready-cooked meals with all the associated processing costs than to prepare meals ourselves. Vegetables and fruits, capable of being grown locally, are sourced from across the world, with the associated impact upon global warming of long-haul transportation. Yet to buy locally may, in turn, deny farmers in developing economies the markets they so desperately need. The ethical choices are not always harmonious and the ethical implications of our actions not always palatable.

In 2004 German citizens recycled 40 per cent of their waste. The equivalent percentage in the UK in 2004 was 17 per cent, explaining why the UK is still described as 'the dirty man of Europe'. However, by elevating the analysis to the 'UK' somehow absolves individuals from their culpability. That is why we referred to German citizens recycling 40 per cent of their waste, rather than Germany recycling 40 per cent of its waste. A nation state does not act as such, but its individual citizens do.

The disposal of plastic wrappings and containers remains a major problem. Landfill sites are becoming exhausted and new ones difficult to obtain because of planning permission problems. If incineration is used to dispose of waste, harmful dioxins are released into the air, particularly as a result of incinerating chemically based products like plastic bottles and other plastic packaging. Dioxins are hazardous, carcinogenic agents – they cause cancers.

To try to control the disposal of hazardous waste, the UK government has employed a twin strategy, the first element being a concentration of the disposal of toxic waste into a few highly controlled sites, the second element being the price mechanism. The cost of disposing of all waste, but particularly toxic waste, has risen sharply since 2000, presumably to try to temper the use of chemical-based products, but the result has been an example of an unintended consequence, although not a particularly difficult one to predict. With legal disposal becoming specialised and localised (there is no official toxic waste disposal site for London) and increasingly expensive, illegal disposal has proliferated and on a grand scale. The companies operating the illegal disposal of waste, both toxic and non-toxic, are referred to as the eco-mafia. They operate fleets of lorries and look to all intents and purposes like bona fide operators. They obtain contracts by bidding at below market rates, but having collected the waste they then dump it on open land, in rivers, or anywhere that is accessible, pocketing the disposal fee they would otherwise have had to pay to the official disposal site. They are ruthless and shameless.

Toxic waste is disposed of into river courses and streams and thus enters the water table and ultimately our drinking water. Solid waste (including the ash from incinerators which contains dioxins) is dumped brazenly on open land, but with no record of the waste's contents or from where the waste was acquired. Waste management and disposal is the most unregulated of industries. On a BBC television programme in 2005 – *If… the toxic timebomb goes off*, the value of illegal waste disposal, in the UK alone, between 1994 and 2004 was estimated at £90bn! The stakes are high, the profits huge, the ramifications horrific. In Italy it was estimated that 30 per cent of all waste disposal is done illegally.

In Ireland supermarkets are required to charge customers 10c per plastic bag used. As a result the usage of plastic bags has dropped remarkably and the acquisitions of 'bags-for-life' have increased dramatically. In this case the price mechanism has affected behaviour in the desired way because there was no alternative, the costs and profits are small, and the effects upon lifestyles minuscule. However, in the case of the disposal of industrial waste the eco-mafia has entrenched itself in a profound way.

Part of the 'solution' has to involve a re-think of disposal methods, locations and price, but more significantly attention has to be concentrated upon the generation of waste and this includes and involves the individual citizen. They, we, have to accept our part in shaping solutions to these profound problems. Just as we can express our 'voice' via our purchasing choices, these 'conversations' need to include the packaging choices that companies make. Thus, the second standard that we raise is the role of the individual, as employer, as employee, as consumer, as citizen.

Business sustainability

Any discussion of business sustainability would include the issues raised above, but it would also bring into focus two other sets of relationships. The first is the set of relationships between the corporation and its external contexts. These would include the notion of stakeholding interests, but, as discussed above, the way a corporation conducts its affairs with regard to political processes and politicians, and its treatment of environmental resources may have an increasing bearing upon the way it is perceived and respected by important groups. The second is the set of relationships between the corporation and its internal contexts. These would include the employees of the corporation and, where they were applicable, supervisory boards.

As discussed in Chapters 6 and 12, corporations are increasingly subject to scrutiny via international codes of conduct, such as the UN Global Compact, the OECD's Guidelines for Multinational Enterprises, the Ethical Trading Initiative as well as various industry-specific or issue-specific codes, such as the Sweatshop Code and the Breastmilk Substitutes Code. However, while the number of codes increases, concerns regarding the efficacy of such codes also grows.

Christian Aid (2004) provided three case studies of alleged double standards, hypocrisy and/or duplicity by, respectively, (Shell and the continuing problems of the people of the Niger delta from Shell's oil exploration there); BAT and the medical ailments of the tobacco pickers of Kenya and Brazil; and Coca-Cola and its alleged (mis)use of a village water source in Plachimada, India.

Cross reference	The case of Shell and its oil operations in the Niger delta is described in more detail in Chapter 12, p. 471.

Each of these companies claims high ethical standards. They each produce a social accountability report and BAT and Shell have been recognised as in the van of social reporting. However, the form of voluntary reporting and accountability argued for in the Global Compact has been criticised by Christian Aid as, at best, of little significance, but, at worst, providing a façade of social responsibility for its members, while behind the façade little appears to change. The comments of David Millar, of the Stirling Media Research Institute, provide evidence for the lack of faith in CSR articulated by Christian Aid.

One of the key functions of CSR is to enable further deregulation by pointing to the involvement of business in ethical and sustainable activities and to indicate that 'multi-stakeholder dialogue' with civil society obviates the need for binding regulation.

(Christian Aid, 2004: 15)

In a similar fashion, but this time in response to the CSR initiatives emanating from the European Union, the personnel director of BT (the UK's largest telecoms corporation) observed,

> It [CSR] is about doing business in a way that persuades our customers to buy from us, our employees to work hard for us and our communities to accept us.
>
> (Cowe, 2001)

Thus, at its most cynical, CSR and voluntary social reporting requirements provide the façade that allows statutory regulation to be held at bay and politicians to claim that positive developments are taking place, while the operational activities of the corporations are left to get on with their *raison d'être*, the business of business.

There are notable exceptions to this pessimistic view of developments but the concern is that the evidence revealed by studies such as those reported by Christian Aid (2004) are possibly more reflective of general practices and attitudes. What fuels these concerns is that companies such as Shell, BAT and Coca-Cola are high-profile, multinational corporations, with the resources to undertake the type of social and environmental engagements that the so-called socially responsible corporation is being 'encouraged' to undertake. They are also corporations with much to lose should they alienate their public by revelations of the kind of evidence revealed by Christian Aid. In this context, what price the activities of corporations that are less high-profile and with less public scrutiny than these three MNCs?

Business sustainability has to relate to a state of affairs that has at its centre a notion of symbiosis. This refers to a mutual dependency between the social (including the company's relationships with its employees); the environmental; the political (and here the 'mutual dependency' needs to be more circumspect and distant than it sometimes is); and the undoubted competitive nature of business. Because there are in-built tensions within these sets of relationships, tensions that sometimes may become very troublesome, there is required a binding agent, or series of binding agents, that can hold the relationships together when the tensions are at their most profound and destabilising. These 'glues' will have to be multifaceted, being comprised of processes, rules, laws, voluntary initiatives and far greater accountability, with that accountability possessing adequate penalties for individuals and corporations who fail or choose not to comply.

Possibly the most significant element of the binding agents, we would argue, has to be the ethics and morals that inform individual, social and corporate behaviour. The ethics and morals will invariably be articulated via, and filtered through, an individual's values and beliefs, as we discussed in Chapters 4–6. We have also recognised that the organisational contexts in which an individual is located will undoubtedly shape the extent to which a person's values are ultimately able to be reflected in their decisions and actions. The Public Interest Disclosure Act (1998) has gone some way to providing protection for those employees who speak out about organisational malpractices, but the act may need strengthening, as it has been since it entered the statute books with the removal of the ceiling on awards that can be made. More significantly, however, the act will need protection from those who may endeavour to weaken its scope and protection.

Challenging central assumptions of economics, politics and human behaviour

The matters under this heading refer to profound issues, which if not addressed adequately will make irrelevant many of the other issues/concerns. Neo-liberal economics informs the actions of significant world institutions, notably the IMF, the WTO and the World Bank. Under the guise of 'free trade and markets' to benefit everyone via the trickle-down effect, the ideology overrides social and political objections. By encouraging everyone to focus upon themselves, neo-liberalism argues, the broad economy will benefit and flourish. Selfishness is not the devil it is made out to be. It leads to an overall benefit, or that is the mantra.

Cross reference	The trickle-down arguments are discussed in detail in Chapter 12, p. 459.

Some anomalies might be explained as the result of unintended consequences. For example, EU farm subsidies (and those paid by other governments to their landowners) can be explained as 'transition payments', moving farming practices into a more efficient, modern era, while minimising social disruption in the farming communities. However, the distinction between 'transition payments' and trade barriers or anti-free-trade subsidies is not always clear. The waters of this particular issue are further muddied when one considers the strictures the western-funded institutions, the World Bank, the IMF and the WTO, place upon less developed economies and their exported food produce. With regard to the latter, a fundamental element of many, if not most, loans is that the loans are subject to local subsidies being removed and the local markets opened up to worldwide competition. Deregulation of local markets is imposed, as is privatisation.

Case study 13.1	**Malawi and the consequences of deregulating and privatising the grain market**

In 2002 Malawi experienced its worst famine since 1949. The primary reason for the famine was laid at the feet of the IMF (and to a lesser extent the World Bank) in a report published by the World Development Movement in 2002. The Malawi Agricultural Development and Marketing Corporation had been state owned and maintained a central stock of grain and regulated the prices of the grain. The report's authors (Owusu and Ng'ambi, 2002) accepted that the corporation was ripe for reform, but argued that the IMF ignored the need to protect the social aims of the corporation. Since 1996 the IMF, World Bank and other donors had pursued a programme of austerity, deregulation and privatisation in Malawi, but without the attendant infrastructure of accountability and good governance. In 2002 Malawi spent $70m servicing its debt, which represented 20 per cent of the national budget, more than the combined spend of the government on education, health and agriculture. The harvests failed (not for the first time), but the grain stocks were totally inadequate to cope with the needs of the people. The donors washed their hands of responsibility, claiming that 'the causes of the food shortages are complex, including lapses in the government's early warning systems, distortions in domestic markets, and mismanagement of food reserves'. What was not acknowledged was that the enforced privatisation and deregulation were not accompanied by a grain market that bore any resemblance to the conditions normally required for a market to operate effectively. There was asymmetry of information, exploitation of a lack of multiple buyers and sellers, a lack of product substitution, a lack of an effective mechanism to establish a market clearing price, and no contingency planning to cope with market failure for such an essential human right, i.e. food to eat.

Without any form of market regulation, other forms of regulation should have been insisted upon by the donor institutions, but they were not. A regulator was required to stand in the place of inadequate market dynamics, as is the case with the regulators of gas, water and electricity supply in the UK. Transparent accountability and effective governance regimes neither existed, nor were demanded. These forms of regulation should have been insisted upon by the donor institutions, but such action went against neo-liberal ideology.

The Commerce and Industry Minister of Malawi, Mr Mpasu, who, when asked by the UK government to speak to a meeting of the Group of Seven (G7) ministers in Cancun of the benefits of liberalising the Malawi economy, stood up and said, 'We have opened our economy. That's why we are flat on our backs'. However, Elliot (2003: 25) went further when he asked,

> How is it that the G7 can export neo-liberal policies to Africa yet the United States would not dream of accepting 'structural adjustments' for its own malfunctioning economy? Isn't it strange that if a country like Zambia deviates from its IMF-imposed programme it gets punished, but if France thumbs its nose at the stability and growth pact (like Germany), nothing happens? ... The language of globalisation is all about democracy, free trade and the sharing of technological advances. The reality is about rule by elites, mercantilism and selfishness.

In addition to the lack of justice inherent in the above example, with the commitment to place neo-liberal ideology above democratic principles, there is a second important democratic consideration.

In the developed economies, particularly the UK and the USA, it is common for financial institutions (e.g. banks and pension funds) to own substantial tracts of land, with the result that the majority of farm subsidies paid out by the European Union and other western governments go not to individual farmers, but to the financial institutions. Although it is the lone farmer that is invariably depicted as being in receipt of the subsidies, protecting the rural idyll as they till the soil, the reality is different. Eighty per cent of farm subsidies paid out in America are paid to corporations. In the UK and the USA, the ubiquitous taxpayer pays money to various national and supranational governments, which in turn distribute a significant proportion of these taxes in the form of farm subsidies to the large corporate landowners. Thus, the claimed protection of local farmers, via the transition payments and against imported food produce, in fact primarily benefits large corporate interests. The commitment of the corporations to their estates is, however, purely instrumental. Their commitment is not to the land but to the pound, the euro or the dollar. Where is the democratic integrity or vision in so much of the assets of modern societies being beyond the control of the various polities or their elected representatives? One must ask whether the power of large corporations, their sweep of influence, or the extent of corporate, not public or private individual, ownership of societies' assets and levers of power is acceptable.

A modest proposal for affecting ethics in business

The following draws upon the work of Bakan (2004), and also reflects our suggestions for addressing the anti-democratic nature of current business-society relationships. The proposals are presented in four parts.

1 The need to strengthen the regulatory systems

In line with Bakan (2004) and Galbraith (2004) we cannot see any significant improvements to the issues raised above without more robust regulatory frameworks. As Galbraith (2004: 67) observed, 'No one should suppose that supervisory participation by directors and shareholders is sufficient. Remedy and safeguard must have the force of law'. To this end we argue for:

- strengthened government regulations on corporate governance, reflecting a more inclusive approach to defining corporate obligations in line with the King Report (*see* p. 272);

- an elevation of the primary rights of citizens over corporations;

- regulatory agencies to be resourced appropriately, for example, but not confined to, the health and safety inspectorates;

- regulatory agencies being held to more effective public account, possibly via parliamentary scrutiny;

- fines for corporate non-compliance with penalties being set at punitive levels;

- repeat offending corporations being subject to the equivalent of charter revocation legislation, with directors barred from obtaining future directorships;

- environmental and health and safety laws being based upon the precautionary principle, making legislation anticipatory, rather than reactive;

- where appropriate, regulatory systems being more decentralised to minimise regulatory capture and over-bureaucracy; and

- the monitoring roles of workers' associations and trade unions, consumer groups being enhanced.

2 The need to strengthen political infrastructures

■ All political elections must be publicly funded. The financial support given to political parties by corporations and the involvement of corporations in political processes (and vice versa) is more of an issue in America than Europe but it is becoming an issue in Europe, particularly Italy.

■ A comprehensive review of the lobbying system, with much heightened levels of transparency, must take place.

■ 'New voices' should be encouraged to participate into parliamentary and/or public scrutiny of corporate affairs.

3 The need to create a robust public sphere

■ A public debate is required regarding the sphere of human activity and development that should not be subject to corporate exploitation. Although this does not exclude private provision of public services, it does envisage a greater public involvement in determining the quality and levels of those services and assessing their actual delivery. Areas such as health, education, power and water, genes and other biological materials fall into this category.

The caveat of the requirement for a public debate is central to our argument. We do not claim to have a monopoly on knowing the 'right' system or where the boundaries should be unequivocally drawn. The growing national debate in 2005 over the very poor quality of school meals in the UK, as a result of school dinner services being privatised and deregulated during the early 1980s and 1990s, is an example of the type of debate we would hope to see.

4 The need to challenge international neo-liberalism

■ Nations should work together to shift the ideologies and practices of international institutions such as the WTO, IMF and World Bank away from market fundamentalism and its facilitation of deregulation and privatisation, in the interests of western corporations, but against the interests of less developed economies. Such developments are unlikely to happen without the significant involvement of pressure groups, including consumer rights perspectives, but also NGOs such as Christian Aid, the Red Cross, World Wildlife Fund, Greenpeace, Friends of the Earth, Oxfam and World Vision.

■ Of course, those NGOs that seek to challenge the neo-liberal consensus should also be accountable. There is a danger that as people become less trusting of governments and international institutions the NGOs will compete with each other to have their alternative view become the consensus. In competing with each other the NGOs may seek to discredit other's views and present their own with a greater rhetorical certainty than is justified. As Beck (1999: 137) puts it,

the more threatening the shadows that fall on the present day from a terrible future looming in the distance, the more compelling the shock that can be provoked by dramatizing risk today.

(Beck, 1999: 137)

In view of this danger NGOs need to be accountable for their claims and the unintended consequences these may have.

■ The last proposal is to some extent an observation of what might actually be happening, although to suggest that it become accepted theory would be considered a heresy by many. It is that the shareholder be seen as a first-order preference shareholder, as a constraint rather than the dominant or sole corporate objective. As discussed earlier, a constraint is in many respects more demanding than an objective. In mathematical speak, a constraint is an independent variable, say a 12 per cent return on capital employed, whereas an objective is a dependent variable, the latter only being able to be achieved within constraints laid down, such as return on capital employed. So at one level the shareholders remain important business considerations and the market for capital is recognised as an important business issue/constraint. However, the proposal moves us from the sterile debate that companies cannot do X or Y because they (the senior executives) have to act solely in the interests of shareholders. What at one level might seem a small change in perspective offered by this proposal in fact moves us to begin discussing business possibilities and options that are currently not allowed on to (official) boardroom agendas.

The processes of moral agency

Throughout the book we have often returned to the question of whether the business system – the free market, capitalist system – is in itself moral. Some argue that free markets, which are based on the exercise of individual choice, are intrinsically good. Some argue the opposite while others yet believe markets are not inevitably immoral but that they need to be regulated. Some argue that no answer to the question of the morality of business is possible. They claim that business ethics is an impossibility (Parker, 1998b: 294) because every attempt to define what ethical business means draws us into an agony of philosophical debate or creative accounting.

If we were to assume pessimistically that the market system were immoral, or that it is impossible to define how it should behave to be moral, does that mean it is impossible to behave ethically within it? Can good deeds be done in a bad world or does accepting one's existence within a bad world taint everything? Such pessimism denies the potential of agency, that is the ability of individuals (and collectives of individuals) to effect change by way of direct action or indirect action, such as the lobbying of governments to effect greater legal controls over business activity.

Although the focus of this chapter has so far been upon the large corporation, and so much of business ethics literature is focused on corporate social responsibility, no discernible changes will take place as long as the individual can be counted upon to be a passive, detached, disconnected bystander to the contests that take place on a regular basis that shape our social, environmental, economic and political lives. This is why we have devoted a large part of our attention in this book to the issues of business ethics as they affect and are affected by individuals. Developments will take place, for the better or for the worse, and they will be shaped by, instigated by and ultimately implemented by many individuals. Some will act in groups, some individually and alone. Some will argue for one outcome, others for other outcomes. The issues will often be complex, multifaceted, conflicting and not easily resolved. A unique solution will not always be an option, but rather a compromise may need to be sought. This prospect may be unattractive to some, requiring as it does a more active engagement with different decision-making processes and issues than might be appealing. However, the more that individuals opt out of decision-making processes, including those within business organisations, the more the democratic ideal is sacrificed and ultimately lost.

Active engagement with ethical issues at work has three component parts:

1. Taking a broad ethical perspective.

2. Thinking through the issues and deciding whether something is sufficiently bad that something should be done, and deciding what exactly one should do.

3. Summoning up the will to take the action that should be done.

We want to make some proposals on all of these matters.

Taking a broad ethical perspective

When working in an organisation or when practising a profession, as has been noted several times in this book, it is easy to take a narrow perspective on moral and ethical matters. People may, to say the same thing in different ways:

■ bracket their personal moral values and beliefs and decide that these should be laid aside whilst at work; or

■ reduce their ethical horizons so that the field in which they seek to behave ethically is restricted to friends and family;

■ assume that, at work, the utilitarian wish to maximise happiness is the same thing as maximising the financial returns to the organisation they work for;

■ fall prey to 'floating responsibility' and assume that others should and will take action against bad things being done;

■ assume that their happiness can best be measured in terms of their wealth and income.

The practice of moral agency requires that people take a broader perspective by recognising that their own moral development means aiming for more than financial success and accepting their commitment to improving society at large. This acceptance is what Aristotle meant by the word *eudemonia*. The canon precentor of St Paul's Cathedral, London, in a videoed interview on this book's website argues that even the financial dealers and bankers of Canary Wharf, London's financial centre, recognise that making money is not the totality of human endeavour. As she says in another part of the interview not included in the video clip:

> We're saying that to live well as a human being, part of that living well and flourishing as a human being, is recognising your connection to the rest of the created order, then we have to do something about that and not waste the energy we use.

The energy she mentions is the energy we use to heat and run our buildings; but her statement can also be taken as a wider belief about how we should seek to flourish as human beings.

Video clip 13.1

Interview with the canon precentor of St Paul's Cathedral, London. St Pauls and Canary Wharf

The canon precentor discusses how, even in the financial centre of Canary Wharf in London, there are concerns about what constitutes the good life. To view the video clip from the interview, please visit this book's companion website at www.pearsoned.co.uk/fisherlovellvalerosilva.

Economics has been accused of being a dismal science because it focuses only on things that can be measured in money. But even economists, such as Richard Layard (2006), have recognised that their analysis should be concerned with maximising happiness rather than money; although other economists (Johns and Ormerod, 2007) believe that it is conceptually impossible to measure happiness. Whilst happiness, through the treatment of depression, for example, is not the same as moral development; moral development just as certainly must be part of happiness.

Embarrassment may be the result for anyone who, in discussions on management decisions at work, brought to the table the concept of human flourishing or happiness. Yet this may be the foundation of moral agency.

Thinking through the issues and deciding on the best action

Most people, in their working lives, do not consciously apply ethical theories and philosophical arguments. Values provide the means for thinking about ethical issues. Values are the common sense reflections of ethical theories that we accept without argument and use heuristically in our thinking. Plato used the metaphor of the cave to explain how our perceptions are inadequate representations of the true world. Imagine people who live in a cave that they never leave. They are constrained to look only at the back wall of the cave on to which the sun projects the silhouettes of the world beyond the cave. They believe what they see to be the world. The metaphor identifies values as dim reflections of the ethical theories debated in Chapter 3. Inasmuch as people use intuitive values to make decisions it implies that people muddle through ethical issues at work. Though this may not be a bad thing. Intriguingly it seems that computer software based on Artificial Intelligence (AI), which uses neural nets to make decisions, is also muddled, inefficient yet effective. Neural nets have a capacity for induction. That is to say, they can learn. They evolve as they process many particular cases and their consequences. Two neural nets developed from the same case material will not necessarily be the same but they will share the characteristics of being 'wastefully redundant and strangely ordered' (6, P., 2001: 410). They will also do the job. Neural nets work by enriching systems of classification; they begin by trying to fit situations into pre-existing categories but then, as they note distinguishing peculiarities, they create new categories. Something similar to this process will form the basis of our proposal.

The alternative to 'muddling through' would be choosing what to do, when faced with difficult moral issues, on the basis of a mechanical application of pre-determined rules or principles. There are, no doubt, some ethical issues in business and organisational life that are clear-cut and what it is right to do is unambiguous. Our discussions of cases in this book, and our interviews with managers and employees, indicate that in many matters there are, at the least, contrary views on what is right and wrong. Often, in the perceptions of those involved, the issues are seen as dilemmas. The particulars of a case often defy our values and ethical principles. As Oscar Wilde (1996) quipped, 'generalities in morals mean absolutely nothing'.

Our contention is that a better understanding of theories of ethics and moral behaviour, and an encouragement to think more critically about the values that inform our behaviour, will find a middle way between muddling through and unthinking application of general precepts. Such an approach will provide each of us with a greater opportunity for reducing the intractability of complex ethical situations.

We propose that a good approach to thinking about ethical issues can be constructed from the following three elements.

1. Moral imagination – which challenges the tendency to fit new problems into old categories of problems we have dealt with in the past (known as paradigm cases) and that provide us with tried and tested solutions.

2. Casuistry – which requires that each ethical issue be treated as a separate case and the particularities and peculiarities of each be understood.

3. Dialogue and debate – with all the various interest groups who may have different perspectives on the issues.

Moral imagination is a term developed by Werhane (1999) to describe a way of thinking about messy moral matters that uses creativity to avoid moral morasses. Her argument starts from the position that we all view the world through socially constructed mind-sets or schemas. When we come across a problem we unconsciously associate it with similar problems that we have experienced in the past. If we can conveniently categorise the problem as the same as those of the past it is easy to draw the conclusion that what worked in the past will work for the current problem. Werhane points out that every situation will differ from others in some particulars and that those differences may be more important in determining what should be done than the similarities with past cases. Moral imagination is the process of looking for new ways of thinking about the current problems that enable new solutions and options for action to emerge. William Hazlitt (2004: 84–5) expressed this point with insightful imagery in an essay he wrote in 1826. People without imagination

> stick to the table of contents and never open the volume of the mind. They are for having maps, not pictures of the world we live in: as much as to say that a bird's-eye view of things contains the truth, the whole truth, and nothing but the truth.

Moral imagination requires pictures and passion, not maps alone.

Cross reference	The importance of mind-sets and schemas in thinking about ethical issues has been treated extensively in Chapter 4, which deals with heuristics. Heuristics are a form of schema, derived from past experiences, that provides an efficient way of deciding what should be done. It is argued in that chapter that heuristics can be both efficient and effective as decision-making devices, but in difficult moral dilemmas it may be that they are more prone to be counter-productive. In Chapter 5 the same concerns are explored through the notions of categorisation and particularisation.

Bowie with Werhane (2005: 120–1) include the following in their definition of moral imagination:

- Perceiving the ethical nuances of the case.
- Disengaging from the immediate issue and understanding the mental models (to use Senge's term) that limit one's understanding of the issues.
- Fantasising about new possibilities.
- Evaluating the new possibilities from a moral perspective.

Casuistry, in its everyday sense, is something to be avoided. It means twisting and distorting arguments to support a conclusion that has been previously agreed for other, and often ignoble, reasons. Casuistry does have a more formal and less pejorative meaning. According to Jonsen and Toulmin (1988: 341), casuistry is a method of moral reasoning that is based on consideration of particular cases and not on the application of general ethical theories or principles. As they express it,

> A morality built from general rules and universal principles alone too easily becomes a tyrannical disproportioned thing, and . . . only those people who have learned to 'make equitable allowances' for the subtle individual differences among otherwise similar circumstances have developed a true feeling for the deepest demand of ethics.

Cross reference	There are many similarities between the notion of casuistical thinking and the highest level of moral development described in Kohlberg's theory of moral development discussed on p. 217.

There are significant points of connection between the ideas of moral imagination and casuistry. The key points are:

■ moral issues should be considered on a case by case basis;

■ an emphasis on the subtle difference between apparently similar cases;

■ particularities can be identified by making case by case comparisons; and

■ the differences between cases can be used as the basis for moral double-loop learning. This is a concept developed by Argyris (1993) to define the kind of learning that challenges our customary mental models. Double-loop learning occurs when we challenge the assumptions, goals and rules that contributed to the emergence of a problem; and we do not simply find an operational way of overcoming the problem, which is called single-loop learning.

All of the themes raised so far suggest that questions of business ethics cannot be resolved by a rigid application of rules and codes. This makes dialogue and debate about business ethics necessary, but here we have a paradox. While the importance of dialogue and debate has been stressed throughout the book, we have also referred to research studies that indicate that moral behaviour is not, in practice, something managers discuss much. The continuing moral muteness of managers is a cause for concern and a significant impediment to enhancing the prospects for moral agency within business organisations.

Video clip 13.2	**Interview with the canon precentor of St Paul's Cathedral, London. Decision making and debate in cathedral management**
	An account of the importance of debate and discussion, rather than voting as a process of decision making. To view the video clip from the interview, please visit this book's companion website at www.pearsoned.co.uk/fisherlovellvalerosilva.

With whom should this dialogue take place? The answer is: with the stakeholders. The dialogue should not be restricted to only those stakeholders who have property rights in the matter. Nor should the dialogue simply be bilateral, between the central organisation involved and the various interested parties. The central organisation in the stakeholder map should also enable discussions to take place between the various stakeholder groups. Bowie and Werhane (2005: 117, 131–3) give an interesting example related to ExxonMobil's project, in conjunction with other oil companies, to drill for oil in the African country of Chad and transport it through a pipeline that passes through neighbouring Cameroon. Within these countries there are tensions between the Bantu and the Bakula Pygmy tribes over whose territory is affected by the drilling and the pipeline, and who should be compensated by the oil companies and to what degree. These tribes have fought each other in the past. In such a situation it would be important to encourage dialogue between the two tribes and, because there are weak legal and institutional infrastructures in the two countries, there may be a need for ExxonMobil to support dialogue between the two African governments and between the governments and international NGOs, which may be able to help the countries develop institutional arrangements that could monitor and sustain any agreements reached between the governments and between the tribes.

Cross reference	Stakeholder theory has been a recurrent theme in this book. It is discussed in chapters 1 & 9.

Dialogue and debate are, on their own, insufficient to enhance moral agency. They require support structures such as formal mechanisms to raise ethical concerns at work, as well as organisational cultures that are conducive to well-intentioned expressions of concern and the fostering of ethical behaviour. Without these support structures, debate and dialogue become merely additional justifications for cynicism, suspicion and pessimism.

Figure 13.1 is an attempt to integrate the three themes of:

■ moral imagination,

■ casuistry,

■ dialogue and debate among stakeholders

into a series of questions that could be used to guide the consideration of tricky moral issues at work according to the processes of principled judgment.

Activity 13.1   A case loosely based on the MG Rover story

What follows is a case loosely based on the MG Rover story described earlier in this chapter (p. 500–501). The details however are largely invented.

You are the board of China Xian Automotive Company (CXAC), a very large, state-owned, Chinese car manufacturer. You have been involved for nearly a year in negotiations with the owners of Anglian Lanchester, the last remaining British-owned volume car manufacturer. Five years ago Anglian Lanchester had belonged to Deutsche Vehicles who had decided the company was not viable as a volume car producer. Deutsche Vehicles wanted to turn it into a niche producer of sports cars. This would have lost many jobs in the Middle England region and, with the encouragement of the government, Anglian Lanchester was sold instead to the Raven Consortium for a nominal sum. The new owners did not manage in the subsequent

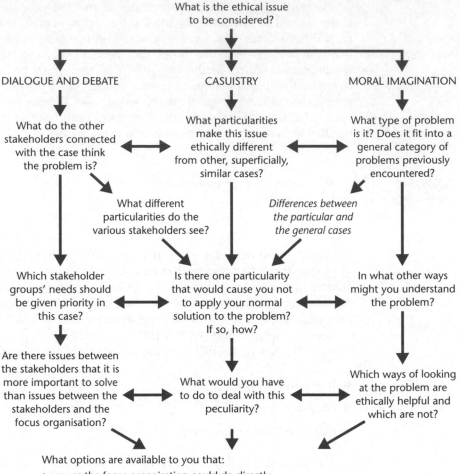

Figure 13.1 A sequence of questions for guiding principled judgment

five years to develop the new range of models that were the only chance for the company to regain viability. The talks between Raven and CXAC explored the possibility that in return for investment to develop new models the Chinese would acquire the brands and technology of Anglian Lanchester's range, which they would produce in China.

CXAC, however, were not really interested in acquiring a marginal car plant in England. They wanted the brand, models and production technology to produce cars in China to meet a rapidly expanding domestic market. During the negotiations they did purchase from Raven the intellectual property rights associated with Anglian Lanchester's range of cars. CXAC were not unaware of the fact that if they withdrew from the deal Anglian Lanchester would most likely go into liquidation and they would then be able to buy what they needed at knock-down prices from the administrator. However, if the deal goes through the British government would provide some substantial soft loans to ease the survival of Anglian Lanchester.

▶

The question is whether you should:

- complete the deal, and so keep Anglian Lanchester afloat and protect the jobs of the many who work for it; or
- withdraw from the deal.

Now consider the following sets of particular circumstances. How would any of the following particulars affect your decision? Decide whether it would make any difference to your view of what it would be right to do in the case, if one or another of the following pairs of particulars were true.

Assumption	Contra-assumption
There is a large population of people of Chinese origin living in Middle England, who migrated to the UK when the Chinese population of an Indian Ocean country that was once part of the British Empire were thrown out by the majority indigenous population. Many of these people work for Anglian Lanchester.	There are no great ethnic or cultural connections between Middle England and China.
Britain is a richer country than China and so might be expected to take responsibility for the well-being of its own citizens.	Imagine that, instead, China was the rich industrialised country and Britain was a developing country for whom the loss of the Anglian Lanchester jobs would be a major blow.
The intellectual property rights had been bought by CXAC as a confidence-building measure, as a mark of good faith that it intended to complete the deal.	CXAC had bought the intellectual property rights because the owners of Anglian Lanchester had lobbied hard for the sale in order to keep the company solvent.
The owners of Anglian Lanchester, the four partners in the Raven Consortium, had made substantial fortunes from Anglian Lanchester even while the company had been failing.	The owners of the Raven Consortium had heavily invested their personal money in Anglian Lanchester in order to keep it going.
There are adequate funds in the employees' pension fund that will provide the employees with better pensions than your Chinese employees might expect.	The pension fund will be insolvent if the company ceases trading. The staff of Anglian Lanchester will lose their pensions if you withdraw from the deal.

We have placed considerable emphasis upon the notion of moral agency because without this the individual is diminished. Organisations represent the places that the majority of people inhabit for most of their waking lives. If they are unable to exercise moral agency, to follow their consciences, and are required to do things they believe are wrong for fear of reprisals if they do not, then we have created, at best, amoral communities, and at worst immoral communities.

Employing Aristotle's use of the mean to identify a balance of behaviour that avoids the extremes of indulgence or neglect with respect to moral agency we argue for a form of moral agency that recognises and avoids the excesses of priggishness or self-righteousness. We call this mean 'principled judgment'. To see the correction of a 'wrong' as justifiable because it assuages the moralist's conscience, irrespective of the harm that might be caused by righting the wrong, would be an example of moral agency transgressing into the indulgence of self-righteousness.

Principled judgment is the mean, or balance, between moral impotence and self-righteousness.

Self-righteousness demands a reflexive wrestling with one's conscience that implies a greater concern for the state of one's soul than for the state of the world. It seems imbalanced to others because

> . . . we feel so extremely uncomfortable in the presence of people who are noted for their special virtuousness, for they radiate an atmosphere of the torture to which they subject themselves.

(Jung, 1953)

Moral impotence, on the other hand, implies a failing that is not necessarily the fault of the individual. While feelings of impotency can be the result of individual failing, it can also be the consequence of factors beyond the control of the individual. In the latter case, an authoritarian regime, coupled with an unsupportive organisational culture, may render the individual employee seemingly helpless in the face of practices with which they are uncomfortable. However, much will depend upon the circumstances of individual cases before one can make judgments about the sources of the moral impotency.

Summoning up the will to take the action that should be done

Knowing what should be done is one thing. Doing it is something else again. The problem to be faced in business ethics is that people often do not do what they know they ought to do. The Kew Gardens case, which was mentioned in Chapter 5, p. 215, provides a classic formulation of the problem. In 1984 in Kew Gardens in New York Kitty Genovese was murdered in full view of 38 onlookers in the nearby apartment block. None of the observers took any action. They did not go to Genovese's aid nor did they phone the police. Was this because people were callous and unconcerned or was it perhaps because they were afraid for their own safety if they became involved? One interesting interpretation of the onlookers' lack of action involves the idea of social proof (Silk, 1999). In a situation where something bad is apparently happening people assume that it cannot be so and look for a more benign interpretation. Perhaps it is not a murder being witnessed but a scene being shot for a film and there is surely a camera crew just out of sight. Before they accept the worst-case interpretation people look for social evidence or proof that it is in fact a murder. As Silk points out, if the fire alarm sounds at work we all look around us to see if others are taking it seriously before we decide there really might be some danger and evacuate the building. In the Kew Gardens case perhaps all the observers were waiting for someone else to start the hue and cry before they could feel sure that they were in fact witnessing a murder. A related aspect of social proof is that, if there are a number of witnesses who are aware of each other, but not in direct communication with each other, as was the case with the Kew Gardens observers who were each looking out of their separate apartment windows, people tend to assume that others will take action and so they do not.

Cross reference	The notion of social proof or social evidence is very close to Bauman's concept of *floating responsibility*, which is discussed in Chapter 6, p. 428.

A Cambridge academic published in 1908 a tongue-in-cheek guide to university politics. He also attributed people's inclination to act against their natural preference, to be honest and good, to their anticipation of the actions or inactions of others.

> The number of rogues is about equal to the number of men who always act honestly; and it is very small. The majority would sooner behave honestly than not. The reason why they do not give way to this natural preference of humanity is that they are afraid that others will not; and the others do not because they are afraid that they will not. Thus, it comes about that, while behaviour that looks dishonest is fairly common, sincere dishonesty is about as rare as the courage to evoke good faith in your neighbours by shewing that you trust them.

Source: Cornford in Johnson (1994: 103)

If it is true that people's tendency not to see the bad behaviour under their noses is a consequence of their perception of the social situation then they may be encouraged to take ethical responsibility by creating organisational and institutional contexts that reinforce individual responsibility. From this perspective, as an aside, the current focus on teams as the basic units of organisations may contribute to the failure of employees to recognise and respond to the ethical problems because the responsibility to do so is diffused throughout the team.

This idea can be theorised using Alistair MacIntyre's distinction between practices and institutions (Moore, 2003). A practice is a cooperative activity and when people strive to perform the activity well it gives them all kinds of personal, inner satisfactions and rewards, such as the pleasure of becoming better and more skilful and the pleasure of forming relationships with other people. Practices are about the joys of becoming a better human being. On the other hand an institution is an organised arena in which people can undertake their practices. Institutions unlike practices, are concerned with external things like

- money;
- resources of all kinds;
- power; and
- status.

Institutions are about competing with other organisations to grab these things so that they can then use them to build the arenas in which people can develop their practices.

Let us take playing chess as a small example. Developing skill at chess is a practice and it brings its own pleasures and satisfactions. But to play chess you need an institution – a chess club – complete with rules, competitions prizes, elections and officers. Practices can only exist within institutions. But there is a tension between them. Practices are focused on internal rewards and cooperation between people. Institutions are concerned with external rewards and on competition. Institutions can call for pragmatic behaviour, they do what they need to do to survive. You may have joined the chess club for the pure joy of playing the game; but to be able to play the game you may have to indulge in some low electioneering to prevent an idiot being elected chair of the club and leading the club into decline. Put brutally, the collaborative virtues of practices can be corrupted by institutions. What is needed is personal courage to resist the pressures from institutions to behave badly.

Podcast 13.1

The Prime Minister: practices and institutions

Podcasts explaining how today's business news relates to the topics discussed here will be updated in an ongoing process. Podcast 13.1 uses the theory of practices and institutions to explain an example of political behaviour. To listen to this podcast, other archived podcasts or recent additions, please visit the companion website at www.pearsoned.co.uk/fisherlovellvalerosilva.

Of course, it may be necessary to try to amend institutions so that it makes it easier for people to behave courageously. An example of how institutional changes might encourage individual responsibility can be illustrated by the story of Bernie Ebbers. He was the CEO of Worldcom. He had built it up from a small telecoms company to the second largest long-distance phone company in the USA. Following the dotcom crash the business came under pressure and it coped in part by fraud. It exaggerated its revenue and misreported its expenses in an effort to maintain its share price. When it collapsed it was the largest bankruptcy in American history. In 2005 Bernie Ebbers was found guilty of conspiracy and fraud, in particular of filing false documents (BBC News Online, 2005a). He had used the 'Aw Shucks' defence, unsuccessfully, during his trial (Evans, 2005). Ebbers had portrayed himself as a chief executive who did not know the details of his company's accounts. He was just a simple salesman who knew how to cut costs but he was not clever enough to understand the complexities of corporate finance and accounts. That sort of thing he left to his finance director who must be the person who was guilty of fraud, whereas – "Aw shucks" – Ebbers was not sophisticated enough to have committed the fraud. The prosecution in his trial thought it beyond belief that Ebbers could have built up the company from nothing and yet have been ignorant of finance. The defence can be interpreted as an example of the social-proof theory. Ebbers would have looked at his senior finance managers and, if they were acting as if nothing was wrong, then there was nothing wrong. Although Ebbers appealed against his conviction, he started his prison sentence in July 2006. The success of the prosecution sent out an institutional message to other CEOs that the 'Aw shucks' defence will not work. This may incline them to recognise and react to ethical issues because they know that they cannot use the lack of actions from others to excuse their own inactivity. At both an institutional level and an organisational level, we should be setting up structures and establishing norms that make it less easy for managers to evade their moral obligations.

Summary

In this chapter the following key points have been made:

- There are strong arguments that corporations represent a brake on the achievement of democratic aspirations and that they should be made more accountable within democratic processes.

- A response to the problems of sustainability needs the privileges accruing to property rights to be reviewed and market mechanisms to be designed so that they discourage corporations from unsustainable practices.

- There is a need to raise public debate worldwide about the ideological assumptions and preferences that are built into the international organisations that oversee the world's trade and economic development.

- In ethical matters 'the devil is in the detail' and issues should be tackled on a case-by-case basis and their particularities and peculiarities attended to.

- Decision makers in organisations should be encouraged to adopt a 'moral imagination' approach when they review issues that have ethical dimensions, as most managerial decisions do.

- At both societal and organisational levels institutions and structures should be developed that overcome the natural human tendency to underrate or fail to respond to ethical problems.

Typical assignments

1. Are NGOs who work to improve the social and environmental responsibility of corporations more ethical, and less in need of being brought to account, than the corporations they criticise?

2. Should the law make it easier for corporations to be wound up if they are found to have acted unethically and caused great harm?

3. What is moral imagination and how might it be applied in corporate decision making?

4. In what ways, at both the institutional and the organisational levels, might changes be made that would encourage managers to recognise and respond to ethical issue in organisations?

Group activity 13.1

Watch a video or DVD of the feature film documentary *The Corporation* based on Bakan's book of the same name (see Useful websites section below). Discuss, as suggested on the film's website, whether the approach to corporations should be:

■   to rewrite – change the legal form and privileges of corporations;

■   to regulate – create more methods and bodies to monitor and regulate corporations; or

■   to reform – encourage organisations to manage themselves better and more ethically; perhaps (returning to the introductory theme of this book) corporations could be so encouraged by disseminating good and heroic stories of organisations and CEOs who chose to act ethically.

Recommended further reading

The two key books for this chapter are Bakan, J. (2004) *The Corporation: The Pathological Pursuit of Profit and Power*, London: Constable, and Patricia Werhane (1999) *Moral Imagination and Management Decision-making*, New York: Oxford University Press. If you do not read Bakan, watch the film *The Corporation*.

Useful websites

Topic	Website provider	URL
A page that provides web links to a wide range of resources related to business ethics	European Business Ethics Network (EBEN)	http://eben-net.org/page.php?LAN=0&FILE=resources
The web page for scholars and practitioners trying to foster positive organisational ethics	Centre for Positive Organisational Scholarship	http://www.centerforpos.org/the-center/about/center-its-mission/
The murder of Kitty Genovese in Kew Gardens in 1964 triggered much ethical debate. An Objectivist account of the Kew gardens Case	Christine Silk	http://www.atlassociety.org/kitty-genovese
A more general account of the case	Wikipedia	http://en.wikipedia.org/wiki/Kitty_Genovese

CHAPTER 14

Concluding integrative case studies

Introduction

In this final chapter, two case studies are presented which integrate ideas and issues that have been discussed throughout this book and provide an opportunity to explore how different perspectives and multiple problems interconnect in real life. Nevertheless we think it is useful to distinguish between the broad fields of corporate responsibility and corporate governance, and we have provided an integrative case study for each of these areas. The first case study focuses on corporate responsibility in relation to the problem of excessive alcohol consumption and its social and health consequences in the UK. The second integrative case study explores the issues of corporate governance by identifying the concerns that emerge when a large, privately owned, multinational company becomes a publicly quoted company through an initial public offering (IPO). Private companies are legally only required to be accountable to their owners (though socially and morally it can be argued they have broader obligations). In the case of public companies the notion of ownership becomes diluted to that of shareholding, being a shareholder is not quite the same thing as being a proprietor, and requires more transparency and wider accountability.

Integrative case study 1	Binge drinking and corporate social responsibility Written 2008, minor additions 2012

Introduction

In the 2000s the British media became more and more exercised by, what was termed, binge drinking. The middle classes were accused of becoming over-dependent on their evening bottle of chardonnay, as a distraction from work pressures; young people in their twenties were seen as indulging in excessive drinking on Friday and Saturday nights; and, most worryingly, children under the legal age for drinking were also forming a drink habit at an early age. One consequence of binge drinking, it was claimed, was accidents and illness, ranging from being drunk to the point of unconsciousness, to liver damage and other serious diseases. The other major consequence was antisocial and criminal behaviour. This might just be loutish behaviour but could also be fights and knifings.

Source: The Art Archive

Source: © Ace Stock Limited/Alamy

There is a debate about whether binge drinking is a serious social problem or just a moral panic maintained for the purpose of selling newspapers (Borsay, 2007). Hogarth's picture of eighteenth-century Gin Lane suggests binge drinking may not be a new problem. Whether real or not the issue has caused a debate about what should be done, and more particularly whose responsibility it is to do something. This is the connection with corporate social responsibility. To what extent are:

- the brewers and distillers who manufacture alcoholic beverages,
- the advertising agencies and media companies that advertise alcohol,
- the alcoholic beverage retailers, the owners of pubs, bars and clubs, and
- the owners and staff of off-licences and supermarkets

responsible for the problem and what, if anything, should they be doing to minimise it? Or to what extent is the solution of the problem the responsibility of:

- the government,
- parents, or
- consumers.

The case study will provide some basic information on the issue and then discuss the issues and debates over where responsibility for dealing with the problem lies.

Background information

The British are not the greatest drinkers of alcohol in Europe. Consumption in Portugal, France, Germany, Spain and Luxembourg is slightly higher than that of the UK. However, it is often claimed that the pattern of drinking in the UK is different from that in Europe. In Europe people more often drink when eating a meal. In the UK, drinking is commonly a singular activity that is more often practised intensively at the weekends rather than paced out during the week. It is only necessary to listen to people's conversations to suspect that this is true. Some people talk about a deliberate intention to get 'hammered' or 'blasted' when they go out on Friday and Saturday nights. There is also statistical evidence to support this conclusion. According to an IAS/EU survey (reported by the BBC, n.d.),

- in Italy, Portugal and Spain 30–50 per cent of drinking was associated only with eating a meal,
- in France and Germany about 30 per cent of drinking was only associated with eating.
- In the UK, Ireland and Finland 70 per cent or more of drinking is not associated with eating.
- In contrast, in Italy, the European country in which drinking is most closely associated with eating, 80 per cent of respondents said that drinking was 'only' or 'mainly' associated with eating.

In the UK, approximately 40 per cent of men and 15 per cent of women said they binge drank on at least one day per week. In Ireland this figure was higher at 50 per cent for men; but in most of Europe only about 10 per cent of males binge drank.

Alcohol consumption by men and women in excess of the recommended guidelines diminishes with age; women's drinking decreasing at a faster rate than men's. According to National Office of Statistics findings (reported by the BBC, n.d.):

- among the 16–24 age group 50 per cent of men exceeded the alcoholic drinks guidelines at least once a week whilst the equivalent figure for women was 40 per cent.
- Amongst the 40–64 age group the figure for men had decreased to 40 per cent but had diminished to 20 per cent for women; still a high enough figure.
- Older people are more moderate. Just under 20 per cent of men of the over-65 age group drank in excess of the guidelines and fewer than 5 per cent of women.

Men drink more than women but women, especially young women are increasing their consumption at a fast rate. In 1992 girls aged 14 in England drank on average of 3.8 units a week; by 2004 that had risen to 9.7 units (Campbell, 2008).

The effects of alcohol on public health are becoming more obvious. Hospital admissions in England where alcohol was diagnosed as a cause increased from 147,659 in 2003–4 to 193,637 in 2006–7. It was claimed that between 2001 and 2007 the number of admissions of children for alcohol-related causes had increased by 37 per cent. There is a statistical association between alcohol consumption and sexual risk. People who attended a genito-urinary clinic (according to one study; Standerwick et al., 2007) binged heavily. They drank on average 13 units of alcohol on a normal night and 26 on a 'heavy' night. In total 86 per cent of those attending the clinic drank more than the Government's binge drinking level of six units; and 32 per cent of them thought alcohol played a part in their clinic attendance.

Intuitively it seems that there must be a connection between alcohol consumption and antisocial behaviour. Some research studies of children between the ages of 11 and 15 suggest that there is; but that it is early antisocial behaviour that is a predictor of alcohol consumption and not the other way around (Young et al., 2007). The susceptibility effect, in which antisocial behaviour leads to drinking, is more important than the disinhibition effect, in which drinking increases the likelihood of antisocial behaviour. Young people who had been given alcohol by their parents were less likely to behave antisocially and to increase their alcohol consumption than were those who had obtained their drink from shops, bars, clubs, friends or siblings.

The Cabinet Office (2003) published a report on the costs of alcohol misuse. Other studies have been done and there is a wide range in results, the estimated costs of misuse range from 2 per cent to 5 per cent of gross national product (GNP). Nevertheless the study is useful in both identifying the range of consequences of alcohol misuse and the costs to individuals, organisations and society at large. It identified the following costs:

1. health-care costs,
2. costs of alcohol-related crime,
3. workplace and lost production costs,
4. human costs such as pain and suffering.

The private costs of drinkers' pain and suffering were excluded from the analysis but those of people such as the victims of alcohol-related crime were included. The total cost in 2001, the year studied, was between £18bn and £20bn. Of this total about £4bn was attributable to workplace and wider economy costs, £12bn to crime (including drink driving) with the balance being health-care costs.

Alcohol can be beneficial as well as the cause of social and health problems. Medical advice is constantly changing with new research but there does seem to be a recognition that moderate drinking can have positive health effects. It is more certainly the case that alcohol generates much pleasure and eases social relationships. It also, of course, generates much wealth and employment in the economy and large export earnings.

The corporate CSR policies

The big companies in the drinks manufacturing and retailing industry all have corporate social responsibility policies that can be accessed on their websites. They mostly state their commitment to social responsibility under a number of heads. Punch Taverns provides an example.

> Punch Taverns is committed to a progressive approach to corporate responsibility. We have grouped our activities into four areas which we believe are core to our strategy – Commitment to the Community, Marketplace Leadership, Employer of Choice and Commitment to the Environment.
>
> With 75 per cent of our 8400 plus leased, tenanted and managed estate being community pubs, they form an integral part of local life and we support this through the 'Pub is the Hub' scheme. We also have a policy for fundraising and charitable donations and support active involvement with local groups, schools and charities.
>
> (*Source*: Punch Taverns at http://www.punchtaverns.com/Punch/Corporate/
> Social+responsibility/Our+communities/)

J.D. Wetherspoon realises that in relation to responsible drinking it has to prove its good endeavours. It says on its website:

> At Wetherspoon, we understand that we are in the business of selling alcohol and cannot take the moral high ground, but we have tried to create a **convivial environment** which encourages people, within reason, to behave well.
>
> In many licensing applications around the UK, trade competitors, over the years, have tried to say that Wetherspoon 'causes trouble' in the areas where our pubs are located. However, when the issue has been examined in court, the evidence strongly indicates that there is **no increase in crime or disorder** in the locality of our pubs, as a result of our openings. In a planning application in South Shields, the local inspector

telephoned all of the licensing districts in which we traded and indicated that Wetherspoon had an **extremely good reputation**.

(Source: http://www.jdwetherspoon.co.uk/
social-responsibility/drinks.php#section-header)
J.D. Wetherspoon identify a number of steps they have taken such as:

- selling soft drinks and coffee at a low price,
- installing CCTV systems,
- encouraging food sales,
- trying to attract a wide range of age groups and not just young people; for at least some of the time, and
- trying to attract more women customers.

There are often tensions, however. Throughout the industry the margins in food are lower than those on alcoholic drinks, which makes focusing on food a commercial risk. It can also be difficult to create a demographic mix amongst the clientele when some bars are particularly branded to appeal to younger people.

Corporate performance and reputation in the sector and the effect of the smoking ban

Table 14.1 gives information on the financial performances of some of the biggest companies that run bars, pubs and clubs. They are all making similar returns on their capital investment. These companies have not performed particularly well in the stock markets

Table 14.1 Financial performances of key companies in the leisure/drinks retailing industry

PunchTaverns From Mergent (GBP, thousands)	2006	2005	2004	2003	2002
Turnover	1 546 100	782 900	637 600	429 000	634 700
PBIT	552 000	397 200	303 000	229 900	258 200
Capital employed	7 513 300	4 701 200	3 662 100	2 161 400	2 051 700
No. of employees	23 399	Aug-06			
Ratios					
Profit margin (PBIT/turnover)	36%	51%	48%	54%	41%
ROI (PBIT/capital employed)	7%	8%	8%	11%	13%
Profit per employee (GBP per person)	23 591				
Greene King From Mergent (GBP, thousands)	2005	2004	2003	2002	2001
Turnover	732 600	552 700	535 600	494 500	431 700
PBIT	148 700	102 900	97 900	86 400	84 000
Capital employed	1 758 100	1 139 400	935 800	862 700	744 000

Table 14.1 Continued

No. of employees	16 023	Jan-05			
Ratios					
Profit margin (PBIT/turnover)	20%	19%	18%	17%	19%
ROI (PBIT/capital employed)	8%	9%	10%	10%	11%
Profit per employee (GBP per person)	9 280				

J.D. Wetherspoon From Mergent (GBP, thousands)	2007	2006	2005	2004	2003
Turnover	888 473	847 516	809 861	787 126	790 913
PBIT	91 113	83 616	64 126	77 628	74 983
Capital employed	714 764	674 987	664 222	677 710	680 989
No. of employees	11 893	Jul-07			
Ratios					
Profit margin (PBIT/turnover)	10%	10%	8%	10%	9%
ROI (PBIT/capital employed)	13%	12%	10%	11%	11%
Profit per employee (GBP per person)	7 661				

Marstons From Mergent (GBP, thousands)	2006	2005	2004	2003	2002
Turnover	595 500	556 100	513 700	490 500	505 600
PBIT	152 300	134 800	105 400	94 700	93 800
Capital employed	1 812 600	1 755 700	1 248 600	904 100	932 600
No. of employees	5 021	Sep-06			
Ratios					
Profit margin (PBIT/turnover)	26%	24%	21%	19%	19%
ROI (PBIT/capital employed)	8%	8%	8%	10%	10%
Profit per employee (GBP per person)	30 333				

Share price performance over approx. 12 months

FTSE 250	Lower by 5%
Sector (Travel & Leisure)	Lower by 17%
Punch Taverns	Lower by 35.5%
Greene King	Lower by 25.3%
Wetherspoon JD	Lower by 44.2%
Marston's	Lower by 21.2%

Source: Data complied by S. Malde from Mergent Online, http://www.mergentonline.com

over the period 2002–06. Their share prices have performed less well than the average for the FTSE 250 and not as well as the average for companies in the travel and leisure sector.

Acting in a corporately responsible manner can be costly. J.D. Wetherspoon had planned to convert all its pubs to non-smoking in 2006 in advance of it becoming a legal requirement. But after it had converted 49 of its 654 pubs, sales in the converted pubs dropped 7 per cent and the company put the conversion programme on hold (Blitz, 2006). The Republic of Ireland was one of the first countries to introduce a smoking ban in pubs and bars. There was a significant debate about the economic costs of the action. The Vintners Association of Ireland claimed that the ban led to the closure of 400–500 pubs. Statistics for employment in the hotels and restaurants sector (including pubs) in Ireland showed a fall after the start of the ban in 2004, although by 2007 the employment levels had grown again (Central Statistics Office: Ireland, n.d.). Nevertheless an argument can be made that acting responsibly can cost jobs as well as profits.

Three of the companies in Table 14.1 made it into the top five of 'Britain's Most Admired Companies' survey for 2007. This is a survey of the reputation of companies in the eyes of senior business people. Reputation is assessed against several criteria but Table 14.2 shows only the overall score and the scores for community and environmental responsibility.

Corporate reputation, together with brands and intellectual property, is increasingly viewed as one of the intangibles that make up a large proportion of a company's stock market valuation.

Licensing laws and enforcement

The 2003 Licensing Act allowed pubs and supermarket to apply for 24-hour opening for selling alcoholic drinks. Only a small minority, 1.5 per cent of the 200,000 licences granted, was for 24 hours, and a quarter of these licences were for supermarkets rather than for pubs and bars. Fifty per cent of the licences were for closing by midnight. Companies have

Table 14.2 Britain's most admired companies: Restaurants, pubs and breweries sector 2007

Company	Overall score	Score on community and company environmental responsibility
Diageo	66.5	7.0
Enterprise Inns	53.6	5.6
Greene King	57.0	5.9
Marston's	54.2	5.5
Mitchells & Butlers	60.6	5.9
Punch Taverns	52.9	5.3
Restaurant Group (The)	52.0	5.1
SABMiller	60.5	6.2
Scottish & Newcastle	54.8	6.0
Wetherspoon (J.D.)	57.7	6.1
The highest scoring company in the survey was Marks & Spencer	76.33	8.0

Source: D.M. Brown, Nottingham Business School

to apply for the licence and it can be denied if the licensing authority does not consider the applicants to be fit or if the application is inappropriate for the area in which the bar is situated. Local authorities, for example, can declare saturation zones in areas in which they think there are too many bars and clubs. This gives them grounds for refusing new licences. Once granted, of course, licences can be revoked. A 'three strikes and you are out' rule has been proposed for bars and pubs that serve under-age customers; get caught three times and the licence is rescinded.

The law also stipulates the ages at which people can drink legally in the UK. Children can drink alcohol at home from the age of five. Outside the home the legal age is 18, except that a teenager older than 16, eating a meal with an adult, can have a drink of beer, cider or wine. Some claims have been made that underage drinkers get half of their drink from home or from their parents. Sir Terry Leahy, Chief executive of Tesco proposed that the legal age for drinking at home should be increased (Carlin, 2007).

Enforcement of the licensing laws has been tightened up over recent years. If bars and pubs sell drinks to children or to drunks not only can the licensee be fined but so can the individual member of staff who served them. Traditionally the employer took vicarious responsibility for the employees' actions. There are on-the-spot fines of £50 for selling to young people aged between 16 and 18 and £80 for selling to children younger than 16. Trading Standards officers were also given the power to carry out test purchases (mystery shopper exercises). Policing powers have also increased; with such abilities as being able to seize alcohol from children. An important question is who should pay for the costs of this additional policing. The government was interested in making the pub companies pay, a move that was condemned by Tim Martin, the chief executive of J.D. Wetherspoon, who claimed that ministers were 'morons' for making such a claim (Press Association, 2005).

Product advertising and design

Alcohol, like cigarettes, is addictive and cause health problems. Unlike cigarettes it exacerbates, if not causes, violence and antisocial behaviour. Advertising tobacco is banned but advertising of alcoholic drinks is not. This contrast raises the question of whether it should be. In the UK currently adverts for alcoholic drinks carry a small strap line recommending that people drink sensibly.

The alcohol manufactures and retailer, including the pub companies, set up the Portman Group (www.portman-group.org.uk) in 1989 to encourage sensible drinking. This group runs the Drinkaware website (www.drinkawaretrust.org.uk). It also publishes and oversees the voluntary code of practice on the naming, packaging and promotion of alcoholic drinks, the fourth edition of which came into effect in 2008 (Portman Group, 2008). This code prohibits the following in advertising and merchandising material:

- particular appeal to under 18s;
- confusion as to the product's alcoholic nature;
- emphasis of its alcoholic strength;
- association with bravado, or with dangerous or antisocial behaviour;
- association with sexual success;
- any link to illegal, irresponsible or immoderate consumption;
- urging consumers to drink rapidly or 'down' their drinks in one;
- suggestion that drinking can lead to social success or popularity; and
- claims that the product can enhance mental or physical capabilities.

The code of practice has more of the features of a code of ethics rather than of a code of conduct. Its appeal for companies to follow the spirit as well as the letter of the code suggests that it is a set of principles that have to be interpreted. A code of conduct in contrast would emphasise specific instructions, perhaps even to the point of stating the font size and type that are used in warnings and product information. If a company refuses to change a product or sales material that has been found in breach of the code the only sanction the group has is to expel the company from membership of the group. The reputational damage of such an action would be quite serious for a company. Some organisations, such as the Church of England, have a policy of not investing in the drinks industry. The church does not have a temperance policy; it is not in principle opposed to alcohol but argues that it is not ethical to invest in an industry whose activities can encourage excessive drinking. The church did modify its stance a little in 2004 and was prepared to invest in those companies in the industry that were diversifying away from a reliance on alcohol sales.

The Advertising Standards Authority (ASA) is the UK's industry body set up to self-regulate advertising. Ofcom, the government body that regulates the communication industries, has delegated the responsibility for monitoring broadcast advertising codes to the ASA. The ASA is particularly concerned with television advertising for alcoholic drinks and in 2005 it published new rules for alcohol advertising. Two years later, in 2007, Ofcom commissioned research into the impact of this new code on young people. It found that:

- The proportion of 11–13 year olds who claim never to have drunk increased from 31 per cent to 46 per cent.
- The popularity of alcopops has reduced amongst this age group; but that of cider has increased.
- Television is the main adverting channel for alcoholic drinks, although there has been a fall in expenditure on television advertising and a shift towards outdoor and radio expenditure.
- In volume terms (the number of commercial slots) the volume of alcohol advertisng on television has increased, largely accounted for by an increase in cider advertising.
- With the exception of vodka there has been a drop in advertising recall that parallels the decrease in expenditure on TV advertising; however, the increase of expenditure on cider advertising is matched by an increase in recall.
- There was no change in how much the respondents said they liked the adverts; there was an increase in the number of those who thought the adverts made alcohol look cool but a drop in those who thought the adverts were aimed directly at young people.

(Ofcom, 2007)

Alcohol labelling is not compulsory in the UK, but as part of a public health responsibility deal in 2011 the industry made a voluntary agreement on labelling of alcohol. The information given includes:

- the number of units in the bottle;
- the recommended daily units for women; and
- a recommendation to seek advice concerning alcohol and pregnancy.

Of course, alcohol labelling only works on bottles sold in shops; it is more of a practical problem in relation to drinks served in pubs and bars. The British Medical Association lobbies for compulsory alcohol labelling.

Apart from the issue of advertising, there is the question of whether there are some products the industry should not be manufacturing or selling. It used to be illegal to sell absinthe; so, as this has recently been legalised, there is a precedent for prohibiting some alcoholic drinks although, of course, the American experience of total prohibition was not a good one. There has been a decline in the consumption of the industry's staple, beer. Beer drinking peaked in 1979 but between then and 2007 consumption has dropped 22 per cent. This led to a search for new products, one of the outcomes of which were alcopops. These are attractively bottled drinks that taste sweet and are very palatable. Traditionally, acquiring a taste for alcohol has been a rite of passage in which getting used to the tastes of beer and spirits was a struggle. Alcopops made the transition to alcohol easy. In the late 1990s there were many calls for alcopops to be banned. Most supermarkets and Bass, the major manufacturer, objected, taking the line that it was not their job to make moral decisions for their customers and that banning the products would not limit under-age drinking. Tesco, however, did ban alcoholic milkshakes, the Co-op and J.D. Wetherspoon also stopped selling alcopops as did Iceland, whose chairman said.

> While commercially this decision will hurt, as a family company we must act responsibly and reflect the views of customers. There is definite evidence that these drinks are encouraging under-age drinking – this cannot be tolerated. We very much hope that our action will motivate other retailers to do likewise and would ask manufacturers of these products to consider their community obligations.

(Institute of Alcohol Studies, 1997)

In 2008 there was disquiet in the media because strong lager was being sold more cheaply than water (although the price of designer bottled waters may not be a sensible yardstick). Tesco experimented with withdrawing strong lagers from its stores in parts of Westminster (McGuiness, 2008). According to the article, the police claimed that the confiscation of alcohol from people on the street had halved after the withdrawl. Asda also announced that it would stop selling 'shooters' – single shot, sweet, fruit flavoured drinks that contain over 15 per cent alcohol. Such drinks were particularly attractive and accessible to under-age drinkers. The Asda chief executive said (Smithers, 2008) that the company was against across the board price rises on alcohol, which would, 'disproportionately hit the vast majority of people who drink sensibly and in moderation'.

The ban on shooters might be seen as a pre-emptive move to limit the justification for the government seeking to increase the price of alcoholic drinks in general. The industry argues there is no simple correlation between the price of alcohol and the rate of its consumption. It can be argued that if the low price of alcohol were the cause of binge drinking then drunkenness might be expected to be a bigger problem in continental Europe where, mostly, alcohol is cheaper; but it is not.

Prices, promotions and taxes

This brings us on to the question of pricing and the extent to which it should be used as a means of discouraging excessive drinking. The government seems to have a taste for using price to lessen poor behaviour; whether it is congestion charges to reduce the volume of cars on the road, bin taxes to encourage recycling or duties on alcohol to reduce drinking. That such charges increase the government's revenue may be a helpful side effect. The issue looks different from the point of view of the drinks industry. It is a competitive market and margins are reducing; and so moving volume of the product becomes important. Much of the industry used promotions such as happy hours, two for the price of one and so on to increase sales. In 2003, J.D. Wetherspoon admitted that their staff were required to ask customers if they wanted a double of low-price spirits when they asked for a single; a practice known as upselling. Some licensing authorities made objections but Wetherspoon claimed they were simply giving the customer a choice, which they could refuse if they wished (McCauley 2003).

However, such policies make pub companies fair game for any newspaper that mounts a sting operation to get a story. In 2005, for example, the *Daily Mail* sent a reporter to work undercover in a pub. The reporter's experience allowed the paper to publish a 'shock, horror' headline and story that suggested that the pub company was not interested in promoting sensible drinking but just wanted to boost its profits as much as possible by encouraging its customers to keep on drinking (Thompson, 2005). Corporations are protective of their reputations. Subsequently many companies, including J.D. Wetherspoon, stopped all such promotions. Upselling and promotions are still common in the industry, however.

The pub and bar companies point out that they are often criticised for encouraging under-age drinking by selling drink cheaply but that most youngsters get their drink from the supermarkets or from their parents, who would have bought it from the supermarket. It is the supermarkets' pricing polices that are the problem they claim. As Punch Taverns point out on its website.

> But responsible retailing isn't a challenge that solely affects the on-trade, it applies to anyone selling alcohol including the supermarkets and off licences. We believe the time has come for the off-trade to take similar steps and stop using low cost pricing to attract and retain customers. We therefore welcome the government's early day motion 495 'Price of Alcohol in Supermarkets and Off Licences' for restricting promotions on alcohol in supermarkets.
>
> A typical pint of beer now costs 3.4 times as much in a pub as it does in a supermarket. Pubs and clubs provides a controlled environment in which alcohol is served but the same cannot be said for the off-trade where you cannot monitor who consumes the alcohol once it has been purchased.

> (Source: Punch Taverns at
> http://www.punchtaverns.com/Punch/Corporate/Social+
> responsibility/The+Punch+position/Responsible+retail/)

The supermarkets have come under pressure to increase the price of alcohol. They reply that they exist in a competitive environment and that if an individual supermarket raises its prices then customers will go to other supermarkets. If, however, they were to get together with each other to agree to raise prices they would be acting as a cartel and breaking competition law. Tesco have said that they are willing to work with the government on possible legislation that would limit supermarkets' ability to sell alcohol cheaply (BBC News Online, 2008).

People in Scotland drink more alcohol than those in the rest of the UK. It is estimated that the costs of dealing with the social and health consequences of excessive drinking in the country is £900 for every citizen. So it is not surprising that the Scottish government has been at the forefront of moves to put a minimum price on alcohol, with the intention of reducing consumption. In 2011 legislation was passed, prohibiting discounted sales of multiple volumes of alcohol, in an attempt to reduce promotions such as two-for-one deals. Some supermarkets, however, managed to find loopholes in the law, which they could use to continue discounting (BBC, 2012a). In 2012 it is anticipated that the Scottish parliament will pass a bill that will set a minimum price for alcohol; though at the time of writing the minimum price has not been set and there are claims that such a law would contravene European Union law (BBC, 2012b)

A significant proportion of the price of alcoholic drinks is the excise charged by governments. Government can therefore influence the price of drinks through its fiscal policies. In 2008 there was a consensus between all the political parties that the excise on alcoholic drinks favoured by young drinkers should be increased.

Employment practices

The employees of pubs and clubs are often young. In one company 68 per cent of its employees are under 26 years. This makes sense when most of the customers are of a similar age. It does perhaps create some problems in relation to the recent law on age discrimination in employment. Having a young staff, with a lack of experience, might also create problems especially now that bar staff can be personally fined for selling alcohol to young or drunk customers. Stories told by some pub managers suggest that a young staff can occasionally indulge in inappropriate behaviour when they close the bar at night and have a quick drink to unwind. That working at a bar is a taxing job, which might lead to a need to let one's hair down is suggested by an item in the 'Shooters Arms Pub Blog' at http://shooters-arms. co.uk/2006/04/23/top-ten-ways-to-piss-off-bar-staff/.

Some chains have decided to widen the age range of their employees. This may change the expectations of both employer and employees. Most bar staff only remain with an employer for a short time. They do not see it as a long-term career and many are students paying their way through university. In return many of the companies in the industry have little concern for, and commitment to, their employees. Cost reduction is often the only strategy available to a company. The figures on 'profit per employee' in Table 14.1 suggest how companies might see maximising the value obtained from staff as a key issue. Head and Lucas (2004) in their study of employment practices in the non-unionised hotel industry found that many 'peripheral' staff were subject to tough human resource management practices, which occasionally ignore the employees' legal rights. One example was the use of zero hours contracts that require staff to be available for duty but only count the hours when there is work for them to do. Employees are not paid for those hours when there are no customers or no work to do. Such practices do not apply to all businesses in the leisure industry but neither are they simply restricted to the small companies. Such an attitude to human resource management does contradict another trend in the industry, which is to require training and assessment standards for staff. Bouncers, as they used to be called, now have to be trained and accredited and to wear badges that display their accreditation when at work.

The role of community and government

What are the roles of communities and government in trying to reduce the problems associated with alcohol? Government has a duty to secure the safety of its citizens and in enabling them to live better lives. The government has given local authorities the power to promote or improve the economic, social and environmental well-being of their areas. One county council (Nottinghamshire County Council) is intent on improving Nottinghamshire as a place to live and work in over the next five years.

If such aims are to be achieved, especially in relation to the problem of binge drinking, then the various levels and agencies of government need to work in partnership. Local government bodies such as the police authorities and local councils have specific responsibilities and so does central government. The government, for example, runs advertising campaigns on alcohol misuse and, in particular, drink driving. It also sets the strategic framework for local alcohol related services. It is often argued that dealing with alcohol misuse requires a cultural change; and the plans and strategies of government presupposes that government has a role in, and is indeed capable of, bringing about large scale cultural changes. The evidence on whether these assumptions are true is mixed. The government's anti-smoking and anti-drink driving campaigns do appear to have had some success in the long run. Attempts to change other cultural patterns, such as encouraging people to switch to public transport and leave their cars at home, have been less successful. It can be argued that even if governments can manipulate social and cultural attitudes they have no right to do so. A communitarian approach would emphasise internal cultural change within communities as they organise their own resources to deal with social problems. Many of the pub companies provide support for such community developments through their corporate social responsibility activities. J.D. Wetherspoon, for example, support, as do other companies, sports teams in the locality of their pubs as well as joining or starting Pubwatch schemes. Pubwatches (http://www.nationalpubwatch.org.uk/index.php) are groups of licensees who band together to identify and take action against people who cause or threaten damage, disorder or violence, or use or deal in drugs in their premises or are a general nuisance. They normally use a communication system to keep each other informed, so that a person who is ejected from one pub cannot simply go to the pub next door and get served. Government, of course, can and does also support community initiatives. The issue for government is how much direct action it should take. Should it act as a nanny state, should it support communities in tackling their own problems or should it merely set a minimal legislative framework and then leave well alone?

Conclusions

Alcohol offers both gains and problems for societies. Where the balance between the two settles depends upon the interplay between many complex factors. This case study raises questions about the responsibilities that companies, government, communities and individuals have in achieving an ethical and sensible balance.

Discussion issues

1. How should the industry decide which alcoholic drinks it is socially responsible to manufacture and sell?

2. To what extent should the owners of pubs, clubs and bars be responsible for any alcohol-related antisocial behaviour that happens in their locality? Should they be responsible for the consequent policing costs?

3. What are the arguments for and against alcohol labelling and health warnings on alcoholic beverages? What positions do you think the different stakeholders of the industry would take?

4. Ayn Rand, in her novels, stresses her admiration for individual strength, will power and self-responsibility. If these things are important (and you may disagree) does it follow that there should be little legal or self-regulatory constraint on the advertising and promotion of alcoholic beverages?

5. In utilitarian terms, do the pleasures experienced by the many who drink responsibly outweigh the pains caused by the minority who do not? If they do does it matter?

6. Does the pub and bar industry do enough to promote a continental style drinking culture in the UK? Would it be in their financial interests to do so?

7. What are the arguments for and against 24-hour licensing from the viewpoints of different stakeholders?

8. How important is corporate reputation to companies in the industry; and if it is important, does this create a business case for companies to take corporate social responsibility seriously?

9. If it is true that working as a waiter or bar staff in continental Europe is seen as a respectable job that people of many ages do, in contrast with the UK where such work is seen as of little worth, to what extent have companies in the UK industry fostered this attitude; and what impact does it have on staff's attitudes to doing their jobs well and responsibly?

10. Which is more appropriate for the alcoholic drinks industry:

    ■ self-regulation or legislative and governmental control?

    ■ codes of ethics or codes of conduct?

11. Is investment in alcoholic drinks manufacturing and retailing companies an ethical investment?

12. What should be the relative roles of the government, companies, communities and individuals in dealing with alcohol-related social and health problems?

Integrative case study 2	Accountability issues of the Glencore IPO

Written by Shishir Malde

Introduction

In western culture great importance has always been given to an individual's right to privacy; including the right to keep their private business matters secret. However, good corporate governance requires openness, transparency and accountability. The issues arising from this tension can be very real when a private company seeks to become a publicly quoted one. Very different levels of openness are required of private and public companies. This case study explores the governance debates that are involved with the movement of a very large private company into a public one quoted on the London Stock Exchange (LSE).

On 24 May 2011, the LSE announced the flotation of Glencore International Plc (Glencore) through an IPO. Glencore was immediately quoted on the FTSE 100 share index, which consists of the top 100 listed companies in terms of their market value. Glencore was only the third such company to get an immediate listing on the FTSE 100 share index in the LSE's history and the first in the last 25 years; the previous two were the newly privatised publicly-owned companies: British Telecom and British Gas. Normally companies have to wait for 30 to 45 days after being listed before they can enter the index.

At launch Glencore's market capitalisation (market value of equity) was estimated at over $59bn or around £37bn. It was initially reported that the company would sell between 15 per cent and 20 per cent of its share capital at the IPO and raise funds of between $10bn and $11bn (around £6.2bn–£6.8bn), making it the largest IPO in the LSE's history (*Daily Telegraph*, 2011). It would appear that over 80 per cent of Glencore's shares remained in the hands of its management and employees. Although the main listing took place in London, a smaller listing was also made on the Hong Kong stock exchange.

As a private company, Glencore faced less media scrutiny and did not need to publicise its levels of accountability and corporate governance in detail or widely. Media reports suggested that relatively little was known of Glencore as a private company and it was thought that Glencore maintained high levels of secrecy in order to gain substantial competitive advantage over its rivals (see for example Robertson et al., 2011). However, on flotation, as a public company, with a diverse range of shareholders, it would have had to become less secretive and more open.

On announcing its intention to go public through its pre-launch prospectus, given the scale of the launch and its prominence, Glencore was subject to increasing levels of scrutiny in the media from the time of the announcement to after it floated publicly. Concerns were raised about a number of alleged accountability issues and the processes it undertook to meet its corporate governance obligations in preparation for its launch as a publicly listed company.

This case study examines possible reasons for Glencore's desire to become a publicly listed company even though this would lead to increased levels of attention and scrutiny. It then considers the media reports of alleged accountability issues that the company faced and its response to the allegations.

Company background and the Glencore IPO

Company background

Glencore was originally founded as Marc Rich & Co by commodities trader Marc Rich in 1974. Mark Rich had a controversial business career. In 1983 he and his business partner were accused of tax evasion and defrauding the US treasury; and of trading with Iran, during the American hostage crisis. It was reported that on hearing about their imminent prosecution, they fled to Switzerland. President Clinton then controversially pardoned Marc Rich on the last day of his presidency amid protests from the entire American political spectrum. Subsequent investigations found nothing wrong with the manner in which the pardon had been granted (Robertson, 2011a).

Marc Rich sold his shares and the present management team (known as partners) became the owners of the company, which was renamed as Glencore in 1994. The company employs over 50,000 people around the world and operates in more than 40 countries. The BBC reported that before the IPO, Glencore was owned by 485 partners (BBC, 2011a). Willy Strothotte became Glencore's CEO in 1993, and also took over the role of chairman in 1994. The two roles were split in 2002, when Ivan Glasenberg became the CEO and Willy Strothotte continued as chairman (Kumar, 2011a). Before the IPO in 2011, in order to comply with corporate governance, Willy Strothotte stood down as chairman and was replaced by Simon Murray as the independent, non-executive chairman (Terazono, 2011).

Glencore is thought to be one of the largest natural resources companies in the world, with profit before tax of $4.3bn on revenues of $145bn in 2010 (Glencore, 2011a: 30), having increased significantly from previous years. In particular, the company has benefited from the high demand for commodities from countries in Asia, especially China. Glencore's successful trading continued in 2011, with strong demand for grain and oil. In the first three months of 2011, just prior to the IPO, sales revenue grew by 39 per cent and net profit by 47 per cent, compared to the same period in 2010 (Glencore, 2011b: 1).

Glencore has large market shares in metals and minerals, in energy products such as oil and coal, and in agricultural products. It trades and transports its products around the world. According to the *Independent* newspaper, it owned more ships than the Royal Navy (Kumar, 2011b). Glencore's value is split in three roughly equal proportions between the mines and the property it owns; the trading and transporting of its products; and the investment it has in other companies (Reece, 2011). For example, the 2010 annual report provides a list of the companies in which Glencore had a stake and included a 34.5 per cent stake in Xstrata, a FTSE 100 mining company. It also had significant stakes in many diverse companies around the world such as Century Aluminium in the USA; Minara Resources, a world top-10 nickel producer based in Australia; and Katanga Mining, a large scale copper-cobalt producer in DR Congo (Glencore, 2011a: 74).

According to *The Times* newspaper (Robertson et al., 2011), Glencore's competitive advantage is based on gathering market intelligence, identifying sources for the lowest price and moving them to buyers willing to pay the highest price, quickly. Glencore is prepared to go to the more risky areas of the world to source the products it needs and is reputed to have a highly regarded management group in control of the business. However, Glencore's traders have guarded their intelligence sources vigilantly, thus creating a competitive and secretive culture.

The Glencore IPO

A number of reasons were put forward to explain why the IPO listing was beneficial for Glencore. Perhaps the most important reason was to enable Glencore to get access to investor funds available on the LSE. According to the BBC (2011a), Ivan Glasenberg, Glencore's CEO, stated that the IPO would provide Glencore with the financial flexibility to pursue sustainable long-term growth opportunities. It is thought that the IPO funds and future share issues would be used to pay for acquisitions of companies in the future, undertake new projects and to repay debt. As stated earlier, the key source of Glencore's competitive advantage was in purchasing its own assets of property and mines to ensure speedy fulfilment of resource requirements. However, since the costs of acquiring these assets were increasing rapidly, it is thought that Glencore needed a range of funds for its expansion plans. For example, prior to the IPO, there was speculation in the media of a possible merger with Xstrata (*The Times*, 2011), in which Glencore already had a stake of 34.5 per cent. Glencore and Xstrata announced their intention to merge in February 2012.

Determining a value for Glencore in preparation for the IPO provided Glencore's partners, its owners, with a value of their personal wealth in the company. Reports in the media suggested that the estimated average worth of each of the 485 Glencore partners would be £103m after the IPO (Cave, 2011). It was also reported that five senior managers and directors, including the chief executive, would each have shares worth over $1bn (White, 2011b).

A listing on a well-regarded stock exchange enhances the reputation and public image of the company. The City of London in general and the LSE in particular would certainly be regarded as having high reputation. In addition Glencore was only the third company to gain an immediate listing on the FTSE 100 index. It was the largest IPO in the LSE's history. In a statement to the LSE, Ivan Glasenberg said that 'Glencore's offer has seen substantial interest from investors from around the world and was significantly oversubscribed throughout the price range providing Glencore with a high-quality, diverse and geographically spread investor base' (BBC, 2011b). A listing on the FTSE 100 index would have ensured that the demand for shares would be high because most institutions and funds managers would hold shares in the large companies to balance their investment portfolios. For example, it is likely that most pension funds in the UK would have Glencore shares in their portfolios.

Reputation is also increased by having a diverse range of large, well-known shareholders, known as cornerstone investors, who are willing to buy the shares issued at the IPO and agree to hold the shares for a period of time. This is used to signal to the market that the shares are well regarded. It was reported before the IPO that Glencore had a number of cornerstone investors, who had agreed to buy about a third of the shares sold and to hold them for a period of six months. They included fund managers such as Abu Dhabi Sovereign Wealth Fund, Black Rock and Fidelity; the Government of Singapore Investment Corporation and the Swiss banks: UBS, Pictet and Credit Suisse (White, 2011a). However, Low (2009) commented that cornerstone investors were needed by companies facing corporate governance issues to shore up their reputation and cast doubt on the beneficial impact of such investors on IPOs.

In addition to providing future source of finance, the Glencore IPO could be considered to offer a way for the initial partners to realise the reward of their success, as they would be able to sell some of their equity more easily. However, it was reported in the media that Glencore's partners were subject to a lock-in period of five years during which time they could not sell their shares (*Daily Telegraph*, 2011). Lock-in periods are normally used to ensure that the management continue to operate the company in the best interests of all the shareholders.

At the IPO Glencore shares were issued at a price of 530p/share, which was mid-way between the price-range of 480p to 580p suggested initially. In the stabilisation period, when the underwriters control the share price to avoid large fluctuations, immediately following the IPO, the share price fluctuated within a small price range of 559p to 508p (Goodley, 2011). However, after this period ended around mid-June 2011 the share price fell as low as 350p in August 2011 before recovering to around 425p in January 2012. Analysts had predicted this greater volatility in the share price after the stabilisation period probably due to the small free float.

It is likely that as a company Glencore benefited from the IPO for the reasons given above and has continued to perform successfully in terms of revenue and profit growth. However, it is less certain to what extent the investors have benefitted due to the lower share price subsequent to the IPO. In addition the IPO increased the level of scrutiny on Glencore's accountability and governance. This scrutiny, in the lead up to the IPO and subsequently, raised a number of issues. The following section considers these issues and Glencore's response to them.

Accountability Issues

In the run up to the IPO and subsequently, six accountability issues concerning Glencore and its listing were debated in the media. This section discusses these issues and Glencore's response to them.

Ethical and legal issues

Prior to the IPO, Glencore faced allegations of corruption, tax avoidance and causing environmental damage. There were also suggestions that it was excessively secretive about its operations. The manner in which it attempted to maintain its competitive advantage resulted in the allegations of breaches in ethical behaviour and legality. For example, by having interests in countries with weaker political and governance systems, Glencore may have formed relationships with individuals and organisations engaged in questionable practices; it has been suggested that Glencore sweats its assets excessively to minimise costs and maximise output resulting in controversies, and leading to less focus on environmental protection and employee safety. The IPO prospectus gave some details of Glencore's activities where it faced such controversies. However, it was reported that perhaps the information provided in the prospectus was not as detailed as could be. This led to suggestions that Glencore would find it difficult to change its secretive nature in spite of becoming a publicly listed company (see for example: Robertson et al, 2011; *The Times*, 2011; BBC, 2011b; BBC, 2011c; Sibun & Ebrahimi, 2011).

Allegations of corruption included receiving market sensitive information, where current and former employees allegedly leaked details of secret European quotas, which allowed Glencore to earn money from the Euro budget. An OECD report alleged that Mopani Copper Mines, a Glencore subsidiary, had avoided paying tax in Zambia. Furthermore, it was suggested that in two metal plants in Zambia the legal emission limits of sulphur dioxide were exceeded and could have caused respiratory problems amongst the local population. In Colombia, it was alleged that a Glencore subsidiary was operating on government-owned land, but that this land had been forcibly taken from previous residents (Robertson et al, 2011).

The allegations of lack of proper accountability and corporate governance concerned the European Investment Bank (EIB), the European Union's lending institution, to such an extent that it decided to freeze further lending to Glencore or its subsidiaries. In 2005 it had lent $50m to Mopani Copper Mines. In a statement the EIB said that it had 'serious concerns' about Glencore's governance and that these went 'beyond the Mopani investment'. Therefore, the decision was taken not to provide Glencore or its subsidiaries with additional finance (BBC, 2011c).

In response, Glencore said that it took good corporate governance very seriously. It denied any wrong doing, including in the case of tax avoidance in Zambia and was of the opinion that it would be exonerated. On the issue raised by the EIB, Glencore said that it welcomed the fact that the EIB was looking at the issue closely, however the company was of the opinion that the allegations were based on an incomplete study and that the company had refuted the draft conclusions made in the document (BBC, 2011c).

Members of the board of directors

BOA Merrill Lynch, a large investment bank, issued principles for market flotations and with regard to the make-up of the board of directors (BoD), it recommended that independent directors should be appointed, and the board's structure determined well before the intention to float (Dunkley, 2011). However, with regard to Glencore, in a Reuters survey, some City observers and analysts felt that the BoD had been put together hurriedly and there was concern that some of the non-executive directors were too close to Ivan Glasenberg, the CEO, and therefore the BoD was not sufficiently independent (Cave, 2011).

The non-executive directors on Glencore's BoD at the time of the IPO, and currently, are as follows (Glencore, 2012): Simon Murray, the independent non-executive chairman; Tony Hayward (the former chief of BP), the senior non-executive director; Peter Coates; Leonhard Fischer; William Macaulay; and Li Ning.

Two articles in *The Times* newspaper (Robertson, 2011b and Robertson, 2011c) reported the following associations between Glencore's directors that might be considered to diminish their independence. There were close connections between Glencore board members and two business associates: Oleg Deripaska and Nat Rothschild. Glencore had a small stake in Mr Deripaska's company, United Company Rusal and Mr Glasenberg sat on Rusal's BoD. Nat Rothschild was a co-chairman in Mr Deripaska's En+ holding company and was Mr Deripaska's friend. But Mr Rothschild also owned convertible bonds in Glencore and he was friends with Simon Murray and Tony Hayward. In addition to this Mr Rothschild and Mr Hayward had business links and were partners in a joint venture called Vallares. It was reported that Mr Rothschild acted as a go-between in putting Mr Hayward and Mr Glasenberg together. William Macaulay was CEO and chairman of First Reserve Bank, which was involved in Glencore's $2.2bn convertible bond launch. When the IPO took place, both Mr Rothschild and First Reserve Bank were set to profit from the convertible bonds they held.In a separate report, Mr Murray suggested that Mr Rothschild had played a role in his appointment as chairman (Ahmed, 2011a).

Peter Coates was a former employee of Glencore and was the head of Xstrata's coal business until 2007. He was the chairman of Minara Resources, a Glencore subsidiary, until he resigned just over a month before the IPO. Credit Suisse, where Leonhard Fischer was a director, had a significant involvement with Glencore's IPO flotation and in Mr Rothschild's Vallares investment. Li Ning graduated from University of Southern California with Mr Glasenberg.

In response Glencore said that the members of the BoD were some of best and most experienced people in business and industry, and that it was a strong board. For example, Li Ning was recommended to Glencore by the head of the Hong Kong stock exchange. The head-hunter firm, Egon Zehnder, had been asked to launch a search for an appropriate chairman some six months prior to the IPO. It was also reported that Mr Hayward had said that he would remove himself from any discussion where there was any conflict of interest (Ahmed, 2011b).

Appointment of the independent chairman

Concerns were raised about the appointment of the independent non-executive chairman at Glencore before the IPO. Good succession planning is very important with respect to following good practice in corporate governance and accountability, however in a survey conducted by Reuters, a significant number of potential investors felt that the process of the appointment of the chairman at Glencore was not done as well as should have been (Cave, 2011).

Robert Peston, a well-known BBC business editor, said in a blog (Peston, 2011a) that he had been informed that Lord Browne, a former head of BP (*see* Case study 2.15 on p. 78), had been approached to take over as chairman of Glencore and had accepted. This was reported in the media but subsequently Robert Peston wrote that the talks between Lord Browne and Glencore had broken down due to questions on corporate governance being raised by Lord Browne. He went on write that he was of the opinion that Glencore were not comfortable with supplying the detail Lord Browne was asking for, and therefore Lord Browne would not be taking over as chairman. Furthermore, he stated in his blog that Glencore may go back to Simon Murray, whose name had been mentioned before the approach to Lord Browne had been made. In a later blog on the same day, Robert Peston reported that Simon Murray had been appointed as chairman.

Although Lord Browne did not make any comment, it was reported that he did not take the role of chairman for two reasons; firstly because he was asking for greater degree of transparency than Glencore were comfortable with providing, and the company felt that he would not be suitable in the role; and secondly because he was not comfortable with the news leaking out to the media before the formal appointment and felt that he was being forced into accepting the role (Waller, 2011).

The question arises whether Glencore did not follow the accepted due process or whether it was merely rushing into making an appointment too quickly and perhaps a little naively. Willy Strothotte, who was the chairman of both Glencore and Xstrata prior to the IPO, had stepped down as chairman of both companies, and Glencore and Xstrata were going to have separate chairmen. Therefore, Glencore was ensuring that it complied with the Combined Code on UK corporate governance in ensuring that a chairman was in place prior to the launch. Furthermore, as stated in the previous section, the search for the chairman had commenced six months prior to the IPO and Simon Murray had been mooted as the possible chairman before Lord Browne was approached. Glencore might have felt that Lord Browne would have been a more high-profile appointment and would have been helpful for the IPO, but, perhaps, it had not prepared for his appointment adequately, and therefore had to go back to its original choice. As Robert Peston went on to say it was all a bit confusing and confused, and not how the company would have wanted the launch to be perceived (Peston, 2011a).

Gender quotas on UK company boards

In an interview reported in *The Sunday Telegraph*, Simon Murray, Glencore's chairman, expressed strong views on the proposal to have more female representation on the boards of directors in UK companies (Cave, 2011). He said that although he would always welcome women on corporate boards, he did not want it to be mandatory or a policy to have quotas. However, he then went on to question women's commitment because he thought that they had a variety of interests outside the business environment. He gave the example of women wanting to have and raise children. He said that because women were entitled to, and took, long maternity leave during and after pregnancy, it would be difficult to see how they could participate effectively on a BoD.

Mr Murray made his comments in response to a report published in early 2011 by Lord Davies for the Department of Business, Innovation and Skills urging all FTSE 100 companies to have at least 25 per cent women on their boards of directors by 2015. Although not mandatory in the UK, in a number of European countries it is a requirement to have a proportion of women on boards. Therefore this report could be seen as an attempt to set the UK on a common path with other forward-looking European countries.

Mr Murray's comments were widely condemned, by among others, Vince Cable (the Secretary of State for Business, Innovation and Skills), Lord Davies and Sir Roger Carr (the chairman of Centrica), who described the comments as ill judged and disappointing (Ebrahimi and Mason, 2011). At the time of writing this case study, Glencore had no women on its board of directors, as was the case for most of the overseas mining companies listed on the FTSE 100.

Following the remarks made and the condemnation they received, Mr Murray apologised for the offence his remarks may have caused. He said he was fully in favour of equal opportunities both in the boardroom and the rest of the company. He went on to say that businesses were in danger of putting themselves at a competitive disadvantage if they did not have adequate representation by women. Glencore said that it and Mr Murray were both committed to equal opportunities (Ebrahimi and Mason, 2011).

It was suggested that because Glencore had no women on its BoD and the board was small at the time of the IPO, it may consider adding one or two members to it. A woman representative like Lady Judge, the chairman of UK Atomic Agency was mooted (Ahmed, 2011b).

Top management remuneration

In 2012 the remuneration of top managers was a matter of public concern in the UK. There was a populist anger that, in times when most people were experiencing a cut in their pay in real terms, managers of large corporation were increasing their incomes substantially. Institutional shareholders became more active in trying to control top executive pay. In one high-profile case the chief executive of the Royal Bank of Scotland was forced by public pressure to waive his performance-related bonus. Ivan Glasenberg in 2012 owned a 15.8 per cent stake in Glencore. As chief executive he was contractually entitled to a £1.85m performance-related bonus but he waived it saying it was unnecessary. He made the argument that he should receive any bonus for performance as a shareholder rather than through his executive pay. Indeed he had received good returns as a shareholder. He received an interim dividend of £34m in 2011–12 and it was reported that his final dividend would be £69m. He said he would reinvest the earnings in the company's shares. Mick Davis, the CEO of Xstrata also turned down a £11m 'retention' bonus should the merger of Xstrata and Glencore go ahead (Webb and Thompson, 2012).

Share issue

At the IPO Glencore initially offered between 15 per cent and 20 per cent of its total shares for public sale (*Daily Telegraph*, 2011), while the directors and partners retained over 80 per cent of the ownership of the company. The LSE and the UK Listing Authority (UKLA) rules stipulate that normally companies should float at least 25 per cent of the share capital into public hands but that Glencore had been allowed an additional year after flotation to ensure that it complied with this requirement (Waller, 2011).

The concern raised about small floats was that they effectively made public shareholders equivalent to minority or non-voting shareholders. Companies with a diverse range of shareholders would need to ensure that they acted in the best interests of all their shareholders and if they do not then shareholders, as a group or bloc, can influence the decision-making processes in those companies. However, in the case of minority shareholders, the ability to influence the decision-making process is severely limited because even if all the public shareholders acted together, their total shares would not be enough to veto board decisions.

Some investors and analysts suggested that because of the small proportion of Glencore shares being listed, they should have been offered for sale at a discount of 20 per cent (Ebrahimi, 2011), which is the norm for minority or non-voting shares.

In the case of Glencore, this may have been less of a concern, since the partners (owners) were tied to the company for a period of time, reportedly five years, and the company had promised to increase dividends every year (*Daily Telegraph*, 2011). Glencore suggested that during the five years the partners could not sell their shares and therefore they would automatically be acting in the best interests of all the shareholders, including the minority shareholders (Ahmed, 2011a).

Monitoring role of the LSA and UKLA

The final issue does not relate directly to Glencore but to the role of the LSE and UKLA in monitoring the accountability and corporate governance of companies wishing to obtain a listing on the stock exchange. One of the attributes often cited is the high regard in which the LSE is held and this reputation is related to the high-corporate standards that it maintains. These standards are related to the regulatory environment it expects from corporations listed on it. Concerns were raised that in an effort to attract new business, the LSE and the UKLA were relaxing their strict listing rules, and that this may harm the LSE's reputation in the future (Fortson, 2011).

The main competitors to the LSE are the New York and Frankfurt stock exchanges, and it is expected that the City of London and the UK would benefit if companies are attracted to list on the LSE and away from its competitors. The USA, for example, has imposed new disclosure and regulatory burdens on companies in its Sarbanes-Oxley legislation, therefore making it less attractive for companies to list. Several questions arise as a result of this. First, could the LSE and UKLA be aiming to attract companies away from New York and Frankfurt by offering them less regulatory burden and less need to demonstrate accountability and governance? Indications are that London is getting more companies to list compared to Frankfurt and New York, but there is no conclusive evidence to suggest that this is because of lower accountability and governance (Peston, 2011b). Second, could less regulation and supervision be beneficial to the UK if it results in falling reputation? Although it is difficult to assess this, early indications seem to indicate that LSE's reputation has not been damaged (Peston, 2011b). Finally, should the LSE and UKLA play a more active and sustained role in ensuring higher levels of accountability in companies and ensuring that sufficient shares are offered to the public with new issues, to ensure that shareholders do hold sufficient power to monitor and act on corporate decisions? Marc Teasdale, the head of the UKLA, suggested that it was not UKLA's role to ensure the highest standards in relation to corporate governance, and in any case it cannot ensure that because it does not have the power to do so. Instead the UKLA's role is to ensure that enough shares are available for trade to ensure that a proper secondary market for shares exists (Fortson, 2011).

Discussion issues

1. Why do you think it is important for companies in public ownership to demonstrate their compliance with good corporate governance of openness, transparency and accountability when compared to private companies? And why do you think the media were of the opinion that Glencore would find that transition difficult?

2. The case study presents a number of possible reasons for Glencore undertaking an IPO and going into public ownership. Rank these reasons in an order of importance to Glencore and explain your reasoning behind your ranking.

3. The case study identifies that a key source of Glencore's competitive advantage is to be the first to know and the first to act. Speed, efficiency and effectiveness are the key factors here. On the other hand undertaking due diligence of suppliers to ensure their ethical compliance takes time and money, and could compromise Glencore's competitive advantage. Assess the ethical and legal issues identified in the case study and discuss whether Glencore would sacrifice competitive advantage if it increased its due diligence of ethical compliance. Where do you think the balance should lie?

4. Assess the associations between the non-executive directors and Glencore's senior executives. Do you think close associations as described in the case study are inevitable in the commercial world in order to ensure the highest levels of experience and expertise? Or do you think the relationships are too close? How can a company ensure that it selects independent directors on its board, while at the same time ensuring their quality?

5. Do you think the non-selection of Lord Browne as chairman of the BoD was damaging to Glencore or was too much made of it by the media? You may wish to read Robert Peston's BBC blog at http://www.bbc.co.uk/blogs/thereporters/robertpeston/2011/04/browne_not_going_to_glencore.html)

6. Why do you think there is a lower female representation on UK company boards compared to male representation? Do you think formal policy is needed in this area or do you think Simon Murray's concerns were justified to some extent? You may wish to read Lord Davies' report which can be obtained from http://www.bis.gov.uk/news/topstories/2011/Feb/women-on-boards.

7. Discuss whether you think it makes a difference how the reward, salary, bonuses or dividends, for Glencore's success is received. Consider aspects such as who makes the decisions on executive remuneration, bonuses and dividends. When does such reward become excessive?

8. Were investors right to be concerned about the small proportion of shares offered for public sale by Glencore? How do you think the interests of such shareholders are affected negatively? To what extent do you think the tie-in period of five years will reduce this issue?

9. Comment on the LSE's and UKLA's apparent strategy of attracting new companies to list in London. How would you respond to the comments made in the case study on the UKLA's role? Who should monitor corporate governance compliance by UK companies?

Filmography

Introduction and Acknowledgments

Teaching business ethics with the use of films has become very popular in recent years.

We have prepared a list of films that could help lecturers and students find examples for discussion and analysis. We would like to express our gratitude to the *Broadway Cinema*, Nottingham, UK, for supporting our research by letting us consult its archives, and for allowing us to use the film synopses from its programme brochures.

- **A Crude Awakening: The Oil Crash**, Basil Gelpke and Ray McCormack, Switzerland 2006 (1hr 23 min). The beautifully photographed film shows how our exploitation of oil has led not only to fabulous lifestyles our ancestors could never have imagined, but also ongoing political and economic instability worldwide.

- **A Nous La Liberté**, René Clair, France 1932 (1hr 27 min). The story of an escaped convict who becomes a wealthy industrialist but whose past returns to upset his carefully laid plans. A Nous La Liberté is both a powerful critique of industrialised society and a comic delight.

- **Aaltra**, Benoit Delepine, Belgium 2004 (1hr 33 min). A wheelchair-bound duo embark on an epic journey across Europe in an attempt to track down and claim compensation from Aaltra, the manufacturer of the faulty tractor that caused their injuries.

- **After the Apocalypse**, Antony Butts, UK 2010 (1hr 4min). During the Soviet era, the people of Semipalatinsk in Kazakhstan were used as human guinea pigs in the testing of nuclear weapons. Today they live with the consequences.

- **An Inconvenient Truth**, Davis Guggenheim, US 2006 (1hr 37 min). An eloquent multi-media lecture by eco-warrior and former presidential nominee Al Gore, this informative documentary provides a harrowing affirmation of the dangers of global warming. Taut, intelligent and darkly humorous, the film is a stern warning and a call to arms. A must-see for anyone who hopes to save the world from ignorance and inaction.

- **Bamako**, Abderrahmane Sissako, Mali/France 2006 (1hr 57min). In the courtyard of a communal dwelling in Mali, a remarkable tribunal has been convened.

The people of Africa are putting on trial officials from the International Monetary Fund and other international institutions, charging them with promoting policies that have increased the continent's deprivation. The accused and their attorneys defend their record and seek to shift the blame.

- **Black Gold,** Marc and Nick Francis, UK 2006 (1hr 17min). Your coffee will never taste the same again. This is a timely documentary about our obsession with coffee and the consequences this demand has on coffee farmers. While we pay premium prices for the lattes and cappuccinos we consume, the low price paid to Ethiopian coffee farmers in the birthplace of coffee has forced many to abandon their fields. Takes on not just the coffee industry, but the world trading system, revealing the dark side of the WTO and the so-called Fairtrade.

- **Blood Diamond**, Edward Zwick, US/Germany 2006 (2hr 23min). Compelling action-adventure set in Sierra Leone as a mercenary, a crusading reporter and an African fisherman join forces against a backdrop of bloody civil war and the plundering of the country's natural resources.

- **Blood in the Mobile**, Frank Piasecki Poulsen, Denmark 2010 (1hr 25 min). We can't live without our mobile phones, but their production has a dark and bloody side. Minerals used to make our mobiles come from mines in the Eastern DR Congo, funding a brutal civil war responsible for around 5 million deaths, atrocious child labour and some 300,000 rapes in the last 15 years. It is a war that will continue as long as armed groups can trade the minerals. Director Frank Poulsen travels to Congo and gets access to its largest illegal tin mine, where enslaved children dig for days in narrow tunnels. He then tries to confront Nokia, the world's largest phone company. Are they implicated in trading 'conflict minerals'?

- **Blue Vinyl,** Judith Helfand and Daniel Gold, US 2002 (1hr 37 min). With humour, chutzpah and a piece of vinyl siding firmly in hand, filmmaker Judith Helfand set out in search of the truth about polyvinyl chloride (PVC), America's most popular plastic. A detective story, an eco-activism doc, and a comedy, Blue Vinyl puts a human face on the dangers posed by PVC at every stage of its life cycle.

- **Bread and Roses**, Ken Loach, US 2000 (1hr 50 min). After surviving a perilous journey from Mexico to the US, Maya secures a job among other immigrant cleaners with a non-union cleaning agency. A meeting with Sam, a committed activist, leads to a guerrilla-style manoeuvre against their employers for standard union benefits. But it is a fight that carries serious risks for Maya. Based on the real life Justice For Janitors campaign in 1990, Bread and Roses is a politically and socially aware film about human dignity in the face of corporate might and indifference.

- **Capitalism: A Love Story**, Michael Moore, US 2009 (2hr 7min). Intelligent, controversial and entertaining, this is the latest rallying cry from Michael Moore. Targeting Wall Street and the White House through the Bush years, he reveals the hypocrisies, inequalities and injustices of the corporate and political superstructure in the USA at a time of financial crisis.

- **Chain,** Jem Cohen, US 2004 (1hr 39 min). As regional character disappears and corporate culture homogenises our surroundings, it is increasingly hard to tell where you are. In Chain, malls, theme parks, hotels and corporate centres worldwide are joined into one monolithic contemporary super landscape that shapes the live of two women caught in it. Cohen contrives to turn the entire planet into a stretch of New Jersey commercial property; a universe that feels entirely real yet has the distinct smack of JG Ballard 'otherness'.

- **Citizen Kane**, Orson Welles, US 1941 (1hr 59min). The newspaper tycoon Charles Foster Kane, one of the most powerful men in America dies, muttering a mysterious last word: 'Rosebud'. A curious reporter begins to delve into Kane's past in order to solve the riddle of his dying breath. A landmark in cinema history.

- **Cold Souls,** Sophie Barthes, US/France 2009 (1hr 49min). Paul Giamatti is consumed by anxiety. He stumbles upon a solution in an advert in the New Yorker about a high-tech company promising to alleviate suffering by extracting souls. Giamatti takes up the offer only to discover that his soul is the shape and size of a chickpea. Complications ensue. A surreal, metaphysical comedy, which satirises tempting, bigger, better and soulless American consumerism.

- **Countdown to Zero,** Lucy Walker, UK 2010 (1hr 31min). This film traces the history of the atomic bomb from its origins to the present state of global affairs. Nine nations possess nuclear capability, with others racing to join them. The fate of the world is held in a delicate balance that could be shattered by an act of terrorism, failed diplomacy or a simple accident.

- **Crash**, Paul Haggis, US 2004 (1hr 52 min). The film gets under the skin of racial intolerance in the racial melting pot of LA.

- **Creation**, Jon Amiel, UK 2009 (1hr 48 min). An intimate biographical drama about naturalist Charles Darwin, which follows his struggle to reconcile the views of his deeply religious wife with his world-changing theories.

- **Czech Dream**, Vit Klusak, Czech Republic 2004 (1hr 30 min). Follows two students who used a state grant to promote the opening of an entirely fictitious big-box mega-market in a Prague field. The resulting scandal, alternately hilarious and discomfiting, illuminates the waking nightmare of consumerism in a country still adjusting to the strengths and pitfalls of the concept.

- **Darwin's Nightmare**, Hubert Sauper, France/Belgium/Austria 2004 (1hr 47 min). Darwin's Nightmare is a much acclaimed film about the sweeping consequences of the introduction of an invasive species of perch into Lake Victoria – the world's largest tropical lake. It details with devastating lucidity how the Nile perch is good for European consumers but bad for Lake Victoria's environment and the area's fishermen. Biting, passionate and utterly fascinating in the questions it raises about globalisation and its beneficiaries.

- **Dirty Oil**, Leslie Iwerks, US 2009 (1hr 25min). This documentary goes deep into the strip-mined world of Northern Alberta, Canada. Here, vast and toxic soils supply the US with the majority of its oil. Told through the eyes of scientists, politicians, and environmentalists, the filmmakers journey to both sides of the border to uncover the toll this 'black gold rush' is taking on our planet.

- **Disclosure**, Barry Levinson, US 1994 (2hr 9min). This film invites a critical examination of the implications of allegations of sexual harassment levied by men or women in the context of office politics. It also can be viewed as another representation of how working women and their sexuality could be a threat to the position of males in modern organisations, therefore reinforcing common stereotypes.

- **District 9**, Neill Blomkamp, South Africa 2009 (1hr 52min). Alien beings have come to Earth. The Earthlings couldn't think of what else to do with them – so why not have a corporation encamp them in a slum and attempt to squeeze all of the bio-tech and weapons knowledge they can out of them? The sociological undertones here are fascinating too.

- **Drowned Out**, Franny Armstrong, UK 2002 (1hr 15min). The people of Jalsindhi in Central India must make a decision fast. In the next few weeks, their village will disappear under water as the giant Namada Dam fills. Their choices are: move to the slums in the city, accept a place at a resettlement site or stay at home and drown. Drowned Out follows the villagers through their protests, hunger strikes and rallies, as well as police brutality and a six-year Supreme Court case. It stays with them as the dam fills and the river starts to rise....

- **Enron: The Smartest Guys in the Room**, Alex Gibney, US 2005 (1hr 49min). The unacceptable face of capitalism is not so much exposed as torn to shreds in this riveting documentary about the collapse of power giant Enron. The company, which had links to the Bush family, was one of the biggest corporations in the US before its sudden bankruptcy in 2001 in which thousands of workers were left without jobs or pensions. The best two hours you will ever spend learning about accountancy!

- **Erasing David**, David Bond, UK 2010 (1hr 20min). Director David Bond finds out how much private companies and government know about him by attempting to disappear. Tracked by two ruthless private investigators, his chilling journey forces him to contemplate the loss of privacy.

- **Erin Brockovich**, Steven Soderbergh, US 2000 (2hr 10min). Based on Erin Brockovich's investigation and legal fight against the Pacific Gas and Electric Company (PG&E). The case relates to the systematic cover-up of the industrial poisoning of the water supply of an entire community. The film highlights the fact that the company knew the water was contaminated, did nothing about it and tried to keep the facts secret from the community directly affected.

- **Everyone Their Grain of Sand**, Beth Bird, US/Mexico 2005 (1hr 27min). Chronicles the struggles of the fiercely determined citizens of Maclovio Rojas, Tijuana, Mexico, as they battle the state government's attempts to evict them from their land to make way for corporate development. The film provides a rare glimpse of the human cost of economic globalisation in a part of the world where working people are valued only as cheap labour to fuel the profits of multinational corporations.

- **Farewell**, Elem Klimov, USSR 1983 (1hr 48min). The aptly named Farewell concerns the Siberian peasant community, which is displaced when its village is destroyed and relocated in a development of faceless apartment blocks. Many of the villagers resist, such as the elderly Darya who prefers to die rather than acquiesce although her son works as a foreman of the operation. A beautifully composed drama.

- **Fast Food Nation**, Richard Linklater, US 2006 (1hr 53 min). A fast-food company's advertising man learns that there is something very unsavoury in the burgers he sells. To find out why, he takes a journey into the dark side of the All-American meal, to the immigrant-staffed slaughterhouses, teeming feedlots and the cookie-cutter strip malls of Middle America.

- **Fight Club**, David Fincher, US 1999 (2hr 19min). An anti-consumerist rant, a critique of machismo and men's movements, or a satire of cultism – you decide...

- **Gasland**, Josh Fox, US 2010 (1hr 47min). When filmmaker Josh Fox discovers that Natural Gas drilling is coming to his area, he sets off on a journey to uncover the consequences of the US natural gas drilling boom.

- **Germinal**, Claude Berri, France 1993 (2hr 38 min). Germinal, based on the landmark novel by Emile Zola, presents a startlingly authentic and powerful look into the tumultuous, tragedy riddled lives of 19th-century French coal miners. A grandiose slab of French history that resonates as powerfully today as it did when Zola wrote it.

- **Glengarry Glen Ross**, James Foley, US 1992 (1hr 40 min). Scripted by Davind Mamet, and featuring an all-star ensemble cast, this classic film focuses on a competitive group of real estate salesmen who've gone from feast to famine in a market gone cold. When an executive 'motivator' demands a sales contest among the agents in the cramped office, the stakes are critically high; any agent who fails to meet his quota of sales will lose his job. So just how far will the desperate salesmen go to meet their quota, and who will be the winners and losers in the battle to close the leads?

- **Global Haywire**, Bruce Petty, Australia 2006 (1hr 22min). This film is a truly unique semi-animated documentary questioning whether and why we have reached such a drastic stage in the relationship between East and West. Tariq Ali, Noam Chomsky, Gore Vidal, Arundhati Roy and Robert Fisk mix with students, experts and even cartoon characters in this illuminating debate on terrorism, oil crises and globalisation.

- **Good Night, and Good Luck**, George Clooney, US 2005 (1hr 33 min). Stylish black-and-white recreation of 1950s television era as crusading broadcast journalist Edward R. Murrow and his colleagues take on Sen. Joseph McCarthy in his crusade against communism, under the watchful eye of CBS President William Paley. George Clooney directed this timely tribute to a television golden-age legend, dramatising the facts as known, and skilfully interweaving the footage with actual TV programmes and commercials of the time. A great discussion point for the ethics of journalism and the media.

- **Green Zone**, Paul Greengrass, France/US 2010 (1 hr 55 min). Matt Damon stars in a story about the hunt for WMDs in Iraq during the post-invasion days.

- **I.O.U.S.A.**, Patrick Creadon, US 2008 (1hr 25 min). I.O.U.S.A. unflinchingly examines America's rapidly growing national debt and its consequences for the country and its citizens. The film follows US Comptroller General David Walker as he criss-crosses the country outlining potential financial scenarios and proposing solutions to American citizens about how they can collectively recreate a fiscally sound nation for future generations.

- **In This World**, Michael Winterbottom, UK 2002 (1hr 30 min). An amazing story, which acts as an effective rebuttal to all the media's fear mongering about refugees. Enayat and Jamal are Afghan refugees who live in a camp in Peshawar and attempt to escape to Britain. Their dangerous journey leads them along the 'silk road' through Pakistan, Iran and Turkey towards London.

- **Incendies**, Denis Villeneuve, Canada 2010 (2hr 10min). This masterful, operatic opus (scaled to the epic sounds of Radiohead), based on the acclaimed play by Wajdi Mouawad, gives a very intelligent reflection on personal ethics and agency, identity, interconnectedness and conflict.

- **Inside Job**, Charles Ferguson, US 2010 (1hr 48min). A film about how unchecked deregulation and speculation on Wall Street has corrupted the world economy. Matt Damon narrates this tour through a tangled forest of derivatives, credit default swaps and subprime mortgages, revealing exactly why the meltdowns of Lehman Brothers and Merrill Lynch were no accident.

- **Invictus**, Clint Eastwood, US 2009 (2hr 13min). This is a stirring drama about South African leader Nelson Mandela who used the 1995 Rugby World Cup to unite his people and heal the rifts of an apartheid-torn country. Blending entertainment, social message and history, it is a rousing and inspiring film packed with humour and humanity.

- **Iraq for Sale: The War Profiteers**, Robert Greenwald, USA 2009 (1hr 15min). This film takes us inside the lives of the soldiers. widows and children who have been changed forever as a result of profiteering in the reconstruction of Iraq. Who are these private corporations and who is allowing them to do so? An insightful documentary.

- **It's a Free World**, Ken Loach, UK 2007 (2hr 7min). After being sacked by her sexist bosses, Angie sets up her own recruitment agency, but she becomes gradually embroiled in the world of illegal migrant labour. In some ways, It's a Free World serves as a sequel to Loach's union organising drama Bread and Roses, examining how globalisation and trade liberalisation have transformed the lives of working people.

- **Made in Dagenham**, Nigel Cole, UK 2010 (1hr 52min). In 1968, women machinists at Ford's Dagenham plant downed tools in protest against sexual discrimination. With humour, common sense and courage, they took on their corporate paymasters, an increasingly belligerent local community and finally the government itself.

- **Manderlay**, Lars Von Trier, Denmark 2005 (2hr 18 min). Grace and her gangster father have arrived in the Deep South at the decaying plantation of Manderlay, where people are living as if slavery had never been abolished. Grace tries to end what she sees as a corrupt remnant of the past – but it soon emerges that both victims and victimisers have interests in the status quo. An interesting take on notions of power relations and identity – perhaps from a poststructuralist perspective.

- **McLibel: Two Worlds Collide**, Franny Armstrong, UK 1997 (53 min). Filmed over three years, McLibel: Two Worlds Collide follows Helen Steel and Dave Morris as the campaigners turn into unlikely global heroes during their record-breaking court battle against the giant fast food multinational

McDonalds. Using interviews with witnesses and reconstructions of key moments in court, the film examines the main issues in the trial – nutrition, animals, advertising, employment, the environment – and the implications the whole episode has for freedom of speech and anti-corporate protest.

- **Metropolis**, Fritz Lang, Germany 1927 (153 min). The most expensive silent movie ever made, and recently included in UNESCO's Memory of the World Register, Metropolis highlights the differences between the 'managers', who live in luxury, and the 'workers', who live and work underground. References to the Tower of Babel and Frankenstein can be found. A critique of the treatment of workers as production robots. Visually stunning. Rereleased in 2010.

- **Michael Clayton**, Tony Gilroy, US 2007 (1hr 59 min). Michael Clayton is a jaded fixer for a large corporate law firm, divorced and in dire financial straits. A colleague, Arthur, who has been leading a chemical giant's defence against litigation by farm workers who claim to have been poisoned by toxic waste, joins the farmers' side and suffers a breakdown. Clayton is sent to bring Arthur back to New York, but events draw him into ever murkier – and more dangerous – waters. A gripping conspiracy thriller. Think Erin Brockovich meets The Insider.

- **Milk**, Gus Van Sant, US 2008 (2hr 8 min). Sean Penn takes the title role in this superbly crafted biopic tracing the last eight years in the life of Harvey Milk, the political and gay activist. From senior citizens to union workers, he changed the very nature of what it means to be a fighter for human rights and became, before his untimely death, a genuine hero.

- **Mindwalk**, Bernt Capra, US 1990 (1hr 52min). Based on the book *The Turning Point* (Fritjof Capra), the film provides a comprehensive view of systems (holistic) thinking. Practical problems related to the relationship between nature, science, technology, politics, business ethics, and society are debated by a poet, a nuclear scientist, and a politician. Music by Philip Glass. Sadly, only available on VHS.

- **Modern Times,** Charlie Chaplin, US 1936 (1hr 27min). Chaplin's first overtly political-theme film. An unflattering portrayal of industrial society and production lines worldwide in times of economic depression.

- **Mondays in the Sun,** Fernando Leon de Aranoa, Spain 2002 (1hr 53 min). Drama about the residents of a coastal town in the north of Spain who are dealt a heavy blow when the shipyard shuts down. Most compelling is the group's angry, socialist conscience, played with ferocious energy by Javier Bardem.

- **Mondovino,** Jonathan Nossiter, France 2004 (2hr 17 min). Over the last three years, Nossiter has travelled the globe to examine the changes faced by the wine industry and the outrages perpetuated on what traditional growers reverently call 'el terroir'. His dogged (and weirdly dog-filled) encounters with wine's biggest planters in Burgundy, Tuscany and the Napa Valley add up to a pointed study of the effects of American capitalism on a centuries-old business. Nossiter's spirited attack on the forces of globalisation confirms that we are what we drink.

- **Mr Smith Goes to Washington**, Frank Capra, US 1939 (2hr 9min). A film about a senator trying to be honest in a world where integrity takes a back seat to money and power. This story of corruption in politics and the greatness of the men who resist it would not be lost in today's political and corporate world.

- **Murderball**, Henry A Rubin, Dana A Shapiro, US 2005 (1hr 25 min). Murderball is the original name for the full-contact sport now known as quad rugby and is played by quadriplegics in armoured wheelchairs. Watching the competitors in action – both on court and off – smashes every stereotype there is about disability.

- **Northfork**, Michael Polish, US 2003 (1hr 43 min). A beautiful and engaging magic-realist fairy tale set in 50s Montana in which a small town faces evacuation for a new dam: but some folk are reluctant to leave, and the government sends agents to deal with them.

- **Of Gods and Men**, Xavier Beauvois, France 2010 (2hr 1min). The harrowing true story of a brotherhood of French monks in the highlands of North Africa who find themselves threatened during the Algerian civil war of the 1990s. When insurgents arrive, they find themselves faced with an impossible decision: to flee, or to stand their ground and fulfil their spiritual mission. A poetic, austerely beautiful triumph.

- **Our Daily Bread**, Nikolaus Geyrhalter, Austria 2005 (1hr 32 min). Precisely how the food we eat is harvested, slaughtered, quartered and packaged is the subject of this brilliant poetic documentary. The film is less an outraged exposé than a bemused meditation on the surreality of modern life, crammed with spellbinding images that hover between the monumental and the quietly sinister. It forces us to face the reality of our human practices. If you want to eat, this is what it takes to eat the food on the table.

- **Outfoxed: Rupert Murdoch's War on Journalism**, Robert Greenwald, US 2004 (1hr 15 min). This documentary provides an in-depth look at Fox News and the dangers of corporations taking control of the public's right to know. Identifying Fox as the home of biased journalism and insidious propaganda, Outfoxed will have you questioning the validity of an organisation whose motto is 'fair and balanced'.

- **Philadelphia**, Jonathan Demme, US 1993 (2hr 5min). An acclaimed film on the impact of discrimination and homophobia in organisations. The film is based on the story of Geoffrey Bowers, a lawyer who in 1987 sued the firm Baker & McKenzie for unfair dismissal in one of the first AIDS discrimination cases. The film could, on the other hand, be criticised for its unrealistic portrait of the main characters' loving relationship, its 'straight-acting' only characters, and a paternalistic attitude towards AIDS sufferers who happen to be gay. The film has been also acclaimed for using a black man to personify 'America'.

- **Pierrepoint**, Adrian Shergold, UK 2005 (1hr 35min). Following the footsteps of his father and uncle before him, Albert Pierrepoint joins the 'family business' in 1934, rising through the ranks to become the most feared and respected hangman in the land. Concerned not with the morality of execution but with ensuring a quick and humane death, Pierrepoint became something of a celebrity in his day and was personally summoned to dispatch the Nuremberg criminals. With its fine acting, realistic sets and confident direction, Pierrepoint perfectly captures a forgotten time and place in history and is a fascinating examination of the moral and personal demons that plagued England's last public executioner.

- **Power & Terror: Noam Chomsky in Our Times,** John Junkerman, Japan 2002 (1hr 24min). Without a doubt, Noam Chomsky is one of the most straight-talking and committed dissidents of our time. A steadfast critic of US foreign policy, in the aftermath of the terrorist attacks of September 11, he provided analysis and historical perspective through a series of public lectures, interviews, and his best selling book *9-11: Was There an Alternative?*

- **Roger and Me,** Michael Moore, US 1989 (1hr 30 min). Roger & Me chronicles the efforts of the world's largest corporation General Motors, as its relocation decisions turn its hometown of Flint, Michigan, into a ghost town. In his quest to discover why GM would want to do such a thing, Flint native and Oscar-winning writer and documentary maker Michael Moore attempts to meet the chairman, Roger Smith, and invite him to 'talk things over'.

- **Sicko,** Michael Moore, US 2007 (2hr 3min). America is the richest country on earth and yet its global position in health care puts it at number 38 on the list. Moore examines the divide between rich and poor, and the state of health care in America with a unique and thoroughly entertaining perspective.

- **Slavery: A Global Investigation**, Kate Blewett and Brian Woods, US 2002 (1hr 20min). Slavery is officially banned by all countries, yet despite this there are an estimated 27 million slaves – people paid no money, locked away and controlled by violence – in the world today. This powerful and revealing film examines three separate industries where slaves are still to be found: the cocoa industry in the Ivory Coast, domestic slavery in Britain and the USA, and the carpet industry in northern India.

- **Starsuckers**, Chris Atkins, UK 2009 (1hr 43 min). A fascinating journey into the dark underbelly of modern media, uncovering the real reasons for our addiction to fame and blowing the lid on the corporations and individuals who profit from it.

- **Super-Size Me,** Morgan Spurlock, US 2004 (1hr 40 min). Director Morgan Spurlock gave himself a month-long challenge: for 30 days he could only eat items on the McDonald's menu. He must eat three meals a day, he must eat everything on the menu at least once, and he must supersize if asked.

- **Syriana**, Stephen Gaghan, US 2005 (2hr 7 min). Syriana is an espionage thriller set in the Middle East. Clooney stars as Bob Barnes, a long-time CIA agent whose last mission turns out to be more complicated then he imagined, placing him in the middle of a dangerous conspiracy involving government corruption, oil, and international terrorism. A gripping geopolitical thriller and wake-up call to the complacent.

- **Taking Down Fences, Global Economics, & Responding to Crises,** Naomi Klein, US 2002 (1hr). Filmed at the World Social Forum in Porto Alegre in 2002, Naomi Klein talks about the anti-capitalist globalisation movement and its many courageous acts of resistance around the world; Walden Bello presents his principles for a 'de-globalisation' movement based on decentralisation; and Susan George urges that we jumpstart an economy of renewability.

- **Thank You for Smoking**, Jasson Reitman, US 2005 (1hr 32 min). Nick Naylor is the best PR guy that money can buy, gleefully spreading the word about the joys of smoking. But the master of spin is faced with his biggest challenge yet; an opportunistic senator wants to put poison labels on cigarette packs; a former Marlboro Man is stricken with cancer and, on top of this, Nick has to show his son what Dad does for a living... Writer/Director Jason Reitman's highly amusing and well-acted adaptation of Christopher Buckley's novel stays true to the source material, while showing a real flair for visual gags.

- **The Aerial**, Esteban Sapir, Argentina 2007 (1hr 30min). As 'Mr TV' has stolen the citizen's voices, a fractured family must come together to stop him from stealing their words as well. Mixing live action and animation, this film offers an intelligent meditation on the power of the media to hypnotise and oppress the masses.

- **The Age of Stupid**, Franny Armstrong, UK 2009 (1hr 33 min). It's the year 2055 and runaway climate change has ravaged the planet. An old man living in the devastated world watches archive footage form 2008 and asks: Why didn't we stop climate change when we had the chance? This films pulls together clips of archive news and documentary from 1950–2008 to build a message showing what went wrong and why.

- **The Apprenticeship of Duddy Kravitz**, Ted Kotcheff, Canada 1974 (2hr 1min). A sad, funny, memorable satire, based on a novel by Mordecai Richler, which points out the potential emotional loss that arises from the pressure to succeed put on the young by families. Richard Dreyfus turns in an early memorable performance as the zealous Jewish boy determined to become rich at all costs, losing all personal contact with women, friends and family in his desperate business transactions.

- **The Company Men**, John Wells, US 2010 (1hr 44min). Bobby Walker is living the American dream: great job, beautiful family, shiny Porsche in the garage. When corporate downsizing leaves him and co-workers jobless, the men are forced to re-define their lives as men, husbands and fathers. This film introduces us to the new realities of American life.

- **The Constant Gardener**, Fernando Meirelles, US 2005 (2hr 9min). A captivating and intelligent political thriller with a strong social conscience. Ralph Fiennes plays a mild-mannered British diplomat whose investigation into the death of his activist wife uncovers a trail of conspiracy, corporate greed and government complicity.

- **The Corporation**, Jennifer Abbott and Mark Achbar, US 2003 (2hr 24 min). 'One hundred and fifty years ago the corporation was a relatively insignificant entity. Today, it is a vivid, dramatic and pervasive presence in all our lives. Like the Church, the Monarchy and the Communist Party in other times and places, the corporation is today's dominant institution...' This acute, epic documentary tracks the history and modern day ascendancy of corporations using a vast archive of found footage and newly found interviews with CEOs, university professors, and radical activists. Everything you need to know about your new global overlords but were afraid to ask!

- **The Devil Wears Prada**, David Frankel, US 2006 (1hr 49min). Funny and vibrant adaptation of Lauren Weisberger's best-seller about the fashion business. Different work ethics are contrasted in the context of consumerism and the luxury business.

- **The End of Poverty**, Philippe Diaz, US 2008 (1hr 46min). A phenomenal documentary on why poverty exists when there is so much wealth in the world. A must-see for anyone wanting to understand not only the US economic system but the foundations of today's global economy.

- **The End of the Line**, Rupert Murray, UK 2009 (1hr 26 min). Artfully photographed and narrated, it tells the riveting story of the effects of our global love affair with fish and food. Multinational corporations, major retailers and celebrity restaurateurs are supplying ever-increasing amounts of fish and food, with little regard for the damage they are doing to their oceans. A must-see for anyone who loves fish.

- **The Event**, Tom Fitzgerald, Canada 2003 (1hr 52 min). The Event raises the morally challenging question: should you have the right to choose the time and place of your death?

- **The Fight for True Farming**, Eve Lamont, Canada 2005 (1hr 30 min). In this documentary, crop and animal farmers in Quebec, the Canadian West, the US Northeast and France offer solutions to the social and environmental scrooges of factory farming. Driven by forces of globalisation, rampant agribusiness is harming the environment and threatening the survival of farms. The proliferation of GM crops is a further threat to biodiversity as well as to farmer's autonomy. This is a film of grim lucidity and irrepressible hope.

- **The First Grader**, Justin Chadwick, UK 2010 (1hr 42min). Based on the true story of Maruge, an 84-year-old villager who takes the Kenyan government's declaration of 'free education for all' at face value and enrols in his town's small children's school. His decision causes turmoil among teachers, students, their parents and even the government, but he remains steadfast in his commitment to get an education. A truly inspiring look at age and how the old are 'supposed' to live.

- **The Great Warming**, Michael Taylor, US 2006 (1hr 22 min). Narrated by Alanis Morissette and Keanu Reeves, this is a detailed look at the effects of global warming in an informative documentary crafted to highlight the damaging effects of the industrial revolution on the global ecosystem. This wide-ranging, compelling film taps into the growing groundswell of public concern about climate change to present an emotional, accurate picture of our children's planet.

- **The Greatest Movie Ever Sold**, Morgan Spurlock, US 2011(1hr 27min). Morgan Spurlock, the provocateur behind Super Size Me and Where in the World is Osama Bin Laden?, wanted to make a documentary about product placement. In fact, given its prevalence, he decided he could probably raise the $1.5 million himself – via product placement. The result is a madcap journey through the increasingly parodic halls of America's marketing departments. Great viewing.

- **The Informant**, Steven Soderbergh, US 2009 (1hr 48min). Mark is a top-level executive at an agriculture giant, who turns whistleblower to the FBI over a global embezzlement scam. Mark imagines himself a celebrated hero and has his sights set on a massive promotion, so he eagerly agrees to wear a wire and to carry a hidden tape recorder in his briefcase. This film tells the true story of Mark Whitacre, a tale almost too crazy to be believed.

- **The Insider**, Michael Mann, US 1999 (2hr 30min). The true story of Dr Jeffrey Wigand (Russell Crowe), a disillusioned tobacco industry scientist who is courted by the 60 minutes news programme to lift the lid on the secrets and lies of big tobacco. The interests of money rule the action as writer/director Michael Mann weaves a story of personal conscience and the pervasive influence of corporate power to portray a subtly telling picture of corporate America.

- **The Invention of Lying**, Ricky Gervais & Matthew Robinson, UK 2009 (1hr 39min). The story takes place in an alternate reality in which lying does not even exist. Everyone – from politicians to advertisers to the man and woman on the street – speaks the truth and nothing but the truth. But, when a down-on-his-luck writer suddenly develops the ability to lie, he finds that dishonesty has its rewards.

- **The Maid**, Sebastian Silva, Chile 2009 (1hr 36min). This Chilean hit combines family drama with a metaphorical analysis of Latin American society. Raquel has been the maid for a Santiago family for 20 years, enjoying and suffering all the intimacies and antagonisms her role brings. But change is on its way.

- **The Navigators**, Ken Loach, UK 2001 (1hr 36min). The Navigators is the powerful story of a group of South Yorkshire railway track workers at the time of the privatisation of British Rail. As the profound effects of privatisation and the grave repercussions for the safety of the rail system become apparent, the solidarity of the men, previously unified by a sense of community and pride in a working tradition, begins to crumble.

- **The Social Network**, David Fincher, US 2010. This film is a scintillating look at the meteoric rise and acrimonious fall of the founders of Facebook – Harvard undergraduates who develop their zeitgeist-altering phenomenon out of their dorm rooms. A timeless study of unchecked ambition, status and privilege in modern western society.

- **The Take**, Avi Lewis, Canada 2004 (1hr 27 min). Written by 'No Logo' superstar Naomi Klein, the film deals with the most positive outcome of Argentina's recent economic crisis – workers who 'expropriate' unused factories and run them co-operatively. This doesn't go down well with the factories' owners, who sniff profits from their once defunct businesses and there are moves to evict the new 'bosses'. A film that bravely challenges accepted wisdom about the inevitability of capitalism.

- **The World According to Monsanto**, Marie-Monique Robin, France 2008 (1hr 48min). Founded in 1901 Monsanto has become the world leader in genetically modified organisms, as well as the creator of some of the most environmentally damaging products ever made, including the herbicide Agent Orange. Using unpublished documents and first-hand accounts by victims, scientists and politicians, director Marie-Monique Robin pieces together the story of an industrial giant that, thanks in part to lies, pressure tactics and attempted corruption, has spread GM crops worldwide with no real monitoring of their effects on nature or human health.

- **The Yes Men**, Chris Smith, Dan Ollman and Sarah Price, US 2004 (1hr 23min). A comedic documentary which follows 'The Yes Men', a small group of prankster activists, as they gain worldwide notoriety for impersonating members of the World Trade Organisation. The film begins when Andy and Mike set up a website that mimics the WTO's, and it is mistaken for the real thing. They play along with the ruse and soon find themselves invited to important functions as WTO representatives. So Andy and Mike don suits and set out to shock unwitting audiences into reassessing their opinions about corporate globalisation.

- **The Yes Men Fix the World**, Andy Bichlbaum and Mike Bonanno, US 2009 (1hr 27 min). Andy and Mike take on Dow Chemical, Exxon Mobil, Halliburton and the US government's response to hurricane Katrina. While the absurdity of their actions will amuse, the Yes Men also have a serious point to make: business as usual is no longer acceptable.

- **The Zone,** Rodrigo Plá, Spain/Mexico 2007. A taut social thriller that brutally reveals the dangers of growing polarisation between have and have-nots. The Zone is a wealthy guarded and gated estate in Mexico City. Privilege equals power and the inhabitants of The Zone only uphold its own laws as a parallel morality develops.

- **There Will Be Blood**, Paul Thomas Anderson, US 2007 (2hr 38 min). This enthralling and powerfully eccentric American epic, written and directed by Paul Thomas Anderson (adapting Upton Sinclair's 1927 novel 'Oil!'), covers a thirty-year span in the life of Daniel Plainview (Daniel Day-Lewis), who begins as a lonely silver miner in 1898 and winds up as one of the richest, and craziest, tycoons in the early twentieth-century California.

- **Total Denial**, Milena Kaneva, US 2006 (1hr 32 min). Human Rights activist Ka Hsaw Wa spent over a decade in the jungles of Burma and Thailand gathering evidence from thousands of victims of human rights and environmental abuses that arose from the construction of the Yadana oil pipeline. Milena Kaneva's undeniably inspiring documentary tells the story of the historic lawsuit brought against UNOCAL/TOTAL, owners of the pipeline, by just 15 Karen villagers.

- **Up in the Air**, Jason Reitman, US 2009 (1hr 49min). George Clooney stars as a corporate downsizing expert whose cherished life on the road is threatened as he is on the cusp of reaching 10 million frequent flyer miles. The film wittily tackles the harsh reality of credit crunch America's shrinking economy and the consequences of widespread corporate layoffs.

- **Up the Yangtze**, Yung Chang, China 2007 (1hr 33min). China is building the largest hydroelectric dam in the world, entire cities are being submerged, two million people displaced. Meanwhile, luxury cruise ships take tourists on 'farewell' tours to see the legendary landscape before it is flooded. Set on board, the film cuts between the well-intentioned but naïve western passengers and two young Chinese crew members, one of whom is from a family whose home will disappear. Through their stories we see the contradictions of modern China.

- **Wal-Mart: The High Cost of Low Price**, Robert Greenwald, US 2005 (1hr 38 min). An engrossing documentary about the Wal-Mart (owners of ASDA), the retail giant that has been called 'the world's largest, richest and probably meanest corporation'. Activist and filmmaker Robert Greenwald (Uncovered: The War on Iraq, Outfoxed) ?exposes Wal-Mart's unsavoury business practices, much as Morgan Spurlock did to McDonald's in Super-Size Me.

- **White Material**, Claire Denis, France 2009 (1hr 45min). This film is about a female, French, plantation owner, in a country that is increasingly torn apart by a violent civil war. The headstrong Maria ignores warnings about an approaching rebel army with child soldiers and wants to keep the coffee plantation going at any cost, even when the workers flee the plantation. It is the story of a woman who thinks that she is where she belongs, while many Africans regard her as an outsider, an unwanted reminder of European colonialism.

- **Who Killed the Electric Car?**, Chris Paine, US 2006 (1hr 32 min). A lively, informative whodunit about an energy-efficient vehicle that debuted with fanfare and went out with a whimper. A sleek two-seater whose batteries could be charged overnight at home, the EV1 earned loyal drivers including Tom Hanks, Ted Danson and Mel Gibson, who provide some hilarious interview segments. GM eventually yanked the cars off the road, saying demand was insufficient. But Paine builds an impressive case against business interests potentially fretting over lost profits that could result from the fuel-efficient, low-maintenance cars.

- **Work Hard, Play Hard**, Jean-Marc Moutout, France 2003 (1hr 35 mins). Phillipe is a young business graduate who starts work at a management consultancy firm. Assigned to audit a company on the verge of a takeover, his task is to survey the staff and decide on imminent redundancies. Initially he is reluctant to get involved and his principles and the influence of his girlfriend Eva threaten to stand in the way of him having to make difficult decisions. Eventually, though, he begins to realise that the hard-headed approach of his supervisor and mentor, Hugo is the best way to achieve results, and adopts the mantra of the company 'work hard, play hard'.

- **You & Me**, Larissa Shepitko, USSR 1971 (1hr 37 min). Shepitko's third feature evidenced her sincere and subtle directional skills and consolidated her reputation as a world-class filmmaker. The film tells the tale of two surgeons who betray an early promise, to pursue conforming lives and false values in later life. The film transcends its simple storyline to explore personal moral choices and critiques the shallow pursuit of consumerism.

References

6, P. (2001) 'Ethics, regulation and the new artificial intelligence, part II', *Information, Communication & Society*, 4 (3), 406–34.

ABC News Online (2005a) *Shareholders' group opposes tsunami donations*, World Wide Web, http://www.abc.nrt.au/news/newsitems/200501/s1278005.html . Site visited 17 January 2005.

ABC News Online (2005b) Shareholders' groups oppose tsumani donations, World Wide web:// www.abc.nrt.au/news/newsitems/200501/s1278362.html . Site visited 17 January 2005

Abramson, D.M. (1999) 'A critical look at NGOs and civil society as a means to an end in Uzbekistan', *Human Organisation*, 58 (3), Fall, 240–50.

AccountAbility (2004) *AA1000 series*, World Wide Web, http://www.accountability.org.uk/aa1000/default.asp. Site visited 19 September 2004.

Achbar, M., Abbott, J. and Bakan, M. (Directors) (2003) *The Corporation*, a film, New York: Zeitgeist Films.

Ackoff, R. L. (1974) *Redesigning the Future: A Systems Approach for Societal Problems*, UK: John Wiley and Sons.

Adair, J. (1980) *Management and Morality. The Problems and Opportunities of Social Capitalism*, Farnborough: Gower.

Adobor, H. (2006) 'Exploring the role performance of Corporate Ethics Officers', *Journal of Business Ethics*, 69, 57–75.

Agle, B.R. and Mitchell, R.K. (2008) 'Introduction: Recent research and new questions', in Dialogue: toward superior stakeholder theory, *Business Ethics Quarterly*, 18 (2), 153–9.

Ahmed, K. (2011a) 'Glencore's chief seeks to reassure over governance', Business, *The Sunday Telegraph*, 1 May: 1

Ahmed, K. (2011b) 'Glencore's Struggle, In: The FSA's Silence on RBS is now untenable', Business, *The Sunday Telegraph,* 1 May: 4

Al Andalusia, S.C. (2001) *Credit cards*, World Wide Web, http://www.islamzine .com/carlo/shari33.html. Site visited 20 August 2001.

Alden, E. (2001) 'Brands feel the impact as activists target customers', *Financial Times*, 18 July: 11.

Allhoff, F. and Vaidya, A. (2008) (eds) *Business in Ethical Focus: An Anthology*, Ontario: Broadview Press.

Al-Rashed, W.E. (2010) 'Corporate performance under Corporate Governance in the GCC Countries', *Malaysian Accounting Review*, Special edition, 9 (2), 139–63.

Alvesson, M. and Willmott, H. (1996) *Making Sense of Management. A Critical Introduction*, London: Sage.

Amnesty International (1997) *The 'Enron project' in Maharashtra – protest suppressed in the name of development*, World Wide Web, http://web.amnesty.org/802568F7005C4453/0/73E2D8C20C9F126F8025690000693183?Open&Highlight=2,enron. Site visited 22 January 2002.

Amnesty International UK (2003) *Baku-Tbilisi-Ceyhan Pipeline Project Puts Human Rights on the Line*, World Wide Web, http://www.amnesty.org.uk/business/btc/press.shtml. Site visited 12 March 2005.

Anon. (1995) *Principles of Islamic Banking*, World Wide Web, http://cwis.usc.edu/deptMSA/economics/nbank1.html. Site visited 20 August 2001.

Anon. (1997) 'Branson to tell EU of "illegal" BA practices', *Financial Times*, 11 November.

Anon. (1999a) 'Brussels gets tough with British Airways', *Financial Times*, 15 July.

Anon. (1999b) 'US judge throws out last Virgin complaint against BA', *Financial Times*, 26 October.

Anon. (2001) 'Cancer research hampered after Alder Hey', *Guardian Unlimited*, 22 May, World Wide Web, http://www.societyguardian.co.uk/alderhey/story/0,7999,494612,00hl. Site visited 12 March 2003.

Argyris, C. (1993) *Knowledge for Action. A Guide to Overcoming Barriers to Organizational Change*, San Francisco: Jossey-Bass.

Argyrou, V. (2005) *The Logic of Environmentalism: Anthropology, Ecology and Postcolonialism*, Oxford: Berghahn Books.

Arif, M. (1988) 'Islamic Banking', *Asian-Pacific Economic Literature*, 2(2), September: 46–62.

Aristotle (1976) *The Ethics of Aristotle*, trans. J.A.K. Thompson, Harmondsworth: Penguin.

Arjoon, S. (2007) 'Ethical decision-making: A case for the Triple Font Theory', *Journal of Business Ethics*, 71, 395–410

Armstrong, M. (1998) *Performance Management*, London: Kogan Page.

Arnold, D.G. (2003) 'Exploitation and the sweatshop quandary', *Business Ethics Quarterly*, 13 (2), 243–56.

Arnold, D.G. and Hartman, L. (2005) 'Beyond Sweatshops; Positive Deviancy and Global Labour Practices', *Business Ethics: A European Review*, 14: 206–22.

Arthur Andersen and London Business School (1999) *Ethical Concerns and Reputation Risk Management. A Study of Leading UK Companies*, London: Arthur Andersen.

Arthur, W.B. (1994) *Increasing Returns and Path Dependence in the Economy*, Ann Arbor: University of Michigan Press.

Badaracco, J.L. Jr (1997) *Defining Moments: When Managers Must Choose Between Right and Right*, Boston: Harvard Business School Press.

Bakan, J. (2004) *The Corporation: The Pathological Pursuit of Profit and Power*, London: Constable.

baku-ceyhan campaign (2003a) *Conflict, Militarization, Human Rights and the Baku-Ceyhan Pipeline*, World Wide Web, http://www.bakuceyhan.org.uk/more_info/humanrights.htm. Site visited 24 January 2005.

baku-ceyhan campaign (2003b) *Environmental Risks in the BTC*, World Wide Web, http://www.bakuceyhan.org.uk/more_info/impacts.htm. Site visited 24 January 2005.

baku-ceyhan campaign (n.d.) *Colonialism and the Baku-Ceyhan Pipeline*, World Wide Web, http://www.bakuceyhan.org.uk/more_info/colonialism.htm. Site visited 24 January 2005.

Baldwin, S., Godfrey, C. and Propper, C. (eds) (1990) *Quality of Life: Perspectives and Policies*, London: Routledge.

Ball, J. (2008) *U.N. Effort To Curtail Emissions In Turmoil*, Wall Street Journal, 12 April, World Wide Web, http://online.wsj.com/article/SB120796372237309757.html. Site visited 19 April 2012.

Banerjee, S.B. (2003) 'Who sustains whose development? Sustainable development and the reinvention of nature', *Organization Studies,* 24 (1), 143–80.

Banerjee, S.B. (2012) 'Critical perspective on business and the natural environment', in Bansal, P. and Hoffman, A.J., (eds), *The Oxford Handbook of Business and the Natural Environmen*t, Oxford, UK: Oxford University Press.

Barber, T. and Parker, A. (2004) 'Parmalat suspects deny fraud role', *Financial Times*, 5 January: 1.

Barlow, T. (2001) 'Body and mind: Treatments that cost an arm and a leg', *Financial Times*, 7 April.

Barnes, J. (1999) *England, England*, London: Picador.

Barr, N. (1985) 'Economic welfare and social justice', *Journal of Society and Politics*, 14 (2), 175–87.

Barrow, C.J. (2006) *Environmental Management for Sustainable Development,* Oxon, UK: Routledge.

Barry, B. (1989) *Theories of Justice: A Treatise on Social Justice*, Hemel-Hempstead: Harvester-Wheatsheaf.

Bartlett, R. (2000) *England under the Norman and Angevin Kings, 1075–1225*, Oxford: The Clarendon Press.

Basu, K. (2011) *Why, for a Class of Bribes, the Act of Giving a Bribe Should Be Treated as Legal?* Ministry of Finance, Government of India. Available on the World Wide Web, http://finmin.nic.in/WorkingPaper/Act_Giving_Bribe_Legal.pdf. Site visited 12 September 2011.

Basu, N., Mintzberg, H. and Simons, R. (2002) 'Memo to: CEOs'. Reprinted in *Fast Company*, 59, April: 117.

Bauman, Z. (1993) *Postmodern Ethics*, Oxford: Blackwell.

Bauman, Z. (1994) *Alone Again: Ethics After Certainty*, London: Demos.

Bauman, Z. (1995) *Life in Fragments: Essays in Postmodern Moralities*, Oxford: Blackwell.

BBC (2011) '"The Sun did not do it", an interview with Trevor Kavanagh', *Today*, BBC Radio 4, 20 July 2011, 8.10am. Available on the World Wide Web, http://news.bbc.co.uk/today/hi/today/newsid_9543000/9543338.stm. Site visited 1 September 2011.

BBC News Online (2004a) *Dizaei to face a police tribunal*, 30 March, World Wide Web, http://www.bbc.co.uk/1/hi/England/London/3583107. Site visited 10 February 2005.

BBC News Online (2004b) *Cleared officer returns to work*, 30 October, World Wide Web, http://www.bbc.co.uk/1/hi/England/London/3226687. Site visited 8 February 2005.

BBC News Online (2005a) *Ebbers guilty of Worldcom fraud*, 15 March, World Wide Web, http://news.bbc.co.uk/1/hi/business/4351975.stm. Site visited 17 March 2005.

BBC News Online (2005b) *NHS 'taking away Africa's medics*, 15 March, World Wide Web, http://www.bbc.co.uk/go/pr/fr/-/1/hi/health/4349545. Site visited 16 February 2005.

BBC News Online (2006a) *Farepak bosses branded 'villains'*, 22 November, World Wide Web, http://news.bbc.co.uk/1/hi/scotland/6171050.stm. Site visited 17 March 2008.

BBC News Online (2006b) *Africa rises to HIV drugs challenge*, World Wide Web, http://news.bbc.co.uk/go/pr/fr/-/hi/business/5027532.stm. Site visited 26 March 2008.

BBC News Online (2007a) *Gap pulls 'child labour' clothing*, World Wide Web, http://news.bbc.co.uk/go/pr/fr/-/hi/world/south_asia/7066019.stm. Site visited 17 March 2008.

BBC News Online (2007b) *BA gets £121.5m price-fixing fine*, World Wide Web, http://news.bbc.co.uk/go/pr/fr/-/hi/business/6925397.stm. Site visited 1 August 2007.

BBC News Online (2007c) *Southern water facing a £20.3m fine*, World Wide Web, http://news.bbc.co.uk/go/pr/fr/-/hi/business/7093924.stm. Site visited 15 November 2007.

BBC News Online (2008a) *Tesco backs cheap alcohol limits*, World Wide Web, http://newsvote.bbc.co.uk/mpapps/pagetools/print/news.bbc.co.uk/1/hi/uk/7256036.stm. Site visited 21 February 2008.

BBC News Online (2008c) *UK House Prices,* World Wide Web, http://news.bbc.co.uk/1/Shared/spl/hi/uk_house_prices/html/house.stm. Site visited 3 March 2008.

BBC News Online (2010) 'Network rail bonuses approved despite controversy',

BBC News Online (2011)'Olympus investigation panel finds 'rotten management' World Wide Web http://www.bbc.co.uk/news/business-16044943. Site visited 12 January 2012

BBC News Online (2011a) *Glencore flotation to raise upto $11bn*, BBC Business News, 14 April, World Wide Web, http://www.bbc.co.uk/news/business-13077187, site visited 12 February 2012.

BBC News Online (2011b) *Glencore's shares flat on first conditional trading day*, BBC Business News, 19 May, World Wide Web, http://www.bbc.co.uk/news/business-13451081, site visited 12 February 2012.

BBC News Online, (2011c) *EIB freezes Glencore lending on governance concerns*, BBC Business News, 1 June, World Wide Web, http://www.bbc.co.uk/news/business-13620185, site visited 12 February 2012.

BBC News Online (2012) *Indonesia presses UK to take back 'contaminated' scrap*, 16 March, World Wide Web, http://www.bbc.co.uk/news/uk-17392981 Site visited 19 April 2012.

BBC News Online (2012a) *EC deny backing for Scotland's minimum alcohol price plan*, World Wide Web, http://bbc.co.uk/news/uk-scotland-politics=16601003?print=true, Site visited 28 February 2012.

BBC News Online (2012b) *MSPs say supermarkets 'undermining spirit' of alcohol laws*, World Wide Web, http://bbc.co.uk/news/uk-scotland-politics=16941681?print=true, Site visited 28 February 2012.

BBC News Online (2012c) *Farmers hold protest over money received for products,* 26 July, World Wide Web, http://www.bbc.co.uk/news/uk-northern-ireland-18988770. Site visited 30 July 2012.

BBC News Online (2012d) *Electric cars 'pose environmental threat'*, 05 October, World Wide Web, http://www.bbc.co.uk/news/business-19830232. Site visited 07 October 2012.

BBC-Panorama (2011) *E-waste from the UK illegally dumped in Ghana*, 16 May, World Wide Web, http://news.bbc.co.uk/panorama/hi/front_page/ newsid_9481000/9481923.stm. Site visited 19 April 2012.

Beardshaw, V. (1981) *Conscientious Objectors at Work*, London: Social Audit.

Beck, L.W. (1959) *Immanuel Kant: Foundations of the Metaphysics of Morals*, Indianapolis: Bobbs-Merrill Educational Publishing.

Beck, U. (1999) *World Risk Society*, Cambridge: Polity Press.

Bedward, D., Jankowicz, A.D. and Rexworthy, C. (2003) 'East meets West: a case example of knowledge transfer', *Human Resource Development International*, 6 (4), 527–46.

Belbin, R.M. (1981) *Management Teams: Why they Succeed or Fail*, London: Heinemann.

Benn, S. and Bolton, D. (2011) *Key Concepts in Corporate Social Responsibility*, London: Sage.

Bennett, C. (2005) 'Where's the fair trade in £3 jeans?', G2, *Guardian*, 31 March: 5.

Bennett, R. and Voyle, S. (2001) 'Supermarkets facing more scrutiny after election: The relationship between food suppliers and retailers is likely to be probed', *Financial Times*, 11 April.

Bentham, J. (1982) *An Introduction to the Principles of Morals and Legislation*, eds J.H. Burns and H.L.A. Hart, London: Methuen. Original edition 1781.

Bentham, J. (1994) 'The Commonplace Book', in Bowring, J. (ed.), *The Works of Jeremy Bentham*, Vol. X, Bristol: Thoemnes Press. Original edition (1843), Edinburgh: Tait.

Berle, A.A. (1932) 'For whom corporate managers are trustees: a note', *Harvard Law Review*, 45, (8) 1365–72.

Berle, A.A. (1965) 'The impact of the corporation on classical economic theory', *Quarterly Journal of Economics*, 79 (1), 25–40.

Berle, A. and Means, G. (1932) *The Modern Corporation and Private Property*, New York: Macmillan.

Berners-Lee, M. (2010) *How Bad are Bananas? The Carbon Footprint of Everything*, London: Profile Books.

Bhopal.com (2001) *Bhopal incident review and the settlement*, World Wide Web, http://www.bhopal.com. Site visited 15 October 2001.

Bhopal.net (2001) *The Union Carbide Disaster. Quick Fact Tour*, World Wide Web, http://www.bhopal.net/intro2.html. Site visited 25 October 2001.

Billig, M. (1996) *Arguing and Thinking: A Rhetorical Approach to Social Psychology*, 2nd edn, Cambridge: Cambridge University Press.

Birch, D. (2001) 'Corporate Citizenship: Rethinking Business beyond Corporate Social Responsibility', in Andriof, J. and McIntosh, M. (eds), *Perspectives on Corporate Citizenship*, 53–65, Sheffield: Greenleaf Publishing.

Birchall, J. and Braithwaite, T. (2008) 'Tesco denies claims of US troubles', *Financial Times*, 27 February, Companies section: 22.

Bird, F.B. and Waters, J.A. (1989) 'The Moral Muteness of Managers', *California Management Review*, Fall: 73–88.

Birmingham City Council (n.d.) *Sustainable Strategy and Action Plan 2002–2005*, World Wide Web, http://www.birmingham.gov.uk? Generate Contebnt? CONTENT_ITEM=ID2708&CO. Site visited 12 May 2008.

Blackburn, M. (2000) 'Managing the cross-cultural aspect of workplace privacy', paper presented at *Cross-cultural Business Ethics*, 2nd International Conference, 17–19 April, University of Westminster, London.

Blackburn, S. (2001) *Being Good. A Short Introduction to Ethics*, Oxford: Oxford University Press.

Blanchard, K. and Peale, N. (1988) *The Power of Ethical Management*, New York: Fawcett Crest.

Blitz, R. (2006) 'Wetherspoon halts plan to curb smoking', *Financial Times*, 4 March, Companies section, 16.

Bloom, A.A., Palmer, P.I., Fraser, A., Reay, D.S. and Frankenberg, C. (2010) 'Large-scale controls of methanogenesis inferred from methane and gravity space-borne data', *Science*, 327 (5963), 322–25.

Blowfield, M. (2007) 'Reasons to be cheerful? what we know about CSR's impact', *Third World Quarterly*, 28 (4), 683–95.

Blythman, J. (2007) *Shopped: The Shocking Power of British Supermarkets*, UK: Harper.

Boddy, C. (2011) *Corporate Psychopaths: Organisational Destroyers*, Basingstoke: Palgrave MacMillan.

Boffey, D. and Townsend, M. (2011) 'Scotland yard's finest called to account over 'culture of collusion' with the press', *The Observer*, 17 july: 30.

Bolger, A. (2006) 'Farepak fund collects enough to pay 15p in the pound' *Financial Times*, 30 November, National News, 2.

Booth, P. and Whetstone, L. (2007) 'Half a cheer for fair trade', *Economic Affairs*, June: 29–36.

Borrie, G. (1996) 'Business ethics and accountability', in Brindle, M. and Dehn, G. (eds), *Four Windows on Whistleblowing*, 1–23, London: Public Concern at Work.

Borrie, G. and Dehn, G. (2002) *Whistleblowing: The New Perspective*, London: Public Concern at Work, World Wide Web, http://www.pcaw.co.uk/policy_pub/newperspective.html.

Borsay, P. (2007) 'Binge drinking and moral panics: historical parallels?' *History and Policy*, World Wide Web, http://www.historyandpolicy.org/papers/policy-paper-62.html. Site visited 25 February 2008.

Bosanquet, B. (1906) *A Companion to Plato's Republic*, London: Rivingtons.

Boseley, S. (2001a) 'Arrogance of doctors led to organ scandal', *Guardian*, 11 January: 3. *Guardian* and *Observer* on CD-ROM.

Boseley, S. (2001b) '50,0000 organs secretly stored in hospitals', *Guardian*, 11 January: 1. *Guardian* and *Observer* on CD-ROM.

Bowe, C. (2001) 'Firestone cuts ties with Ford over tyre recall', *Financial Times*, 22 May: 36.

Bowen, H.R. (1953) *Social Responsibilities of the Businessman*, USA: Harper & Brothers.

Bowie, N.E. (1999) *Business Ethics: A Kantian Perspective*, Oxford: Blackwell Publishers.

Bowie, N.E. and Duska, R. (1990) *Business Ethics*, Englewood Cliffs, NJ: Prentice Hall.

Bowie, N.E. and Werhane, P.H. (2005) *Management Ethics*, Oxford: Blackwell.

BP (2001) *BP's 2001 Environmental and Social Report*, World Wide Web, http://www.bp.com/environ_social/review_2001/index.asp. Site visited 28 March 2002.

Bradbury, R. (2005) *A Sound of Thunder and Other Stories*, New York: Harper Perennial.

Bradley, S. (2000) 'Villagers not sweet on 7-day sugar plan', *Bury Free Press*, 30 June.

Braga-Alves, M.V. and Shastri, K. (2011) 'Corprate governance, valuation and performance: evidence from a voluntary market reform in Brazil', *Financial Management*, Spring, 139–57.

Braungart, M. and McDonough, W. (2009) *Cradle to Cradle: Re-Making the Way We Make Things*, London: Vintage Books.

Bridges, J. (Director) (1979) *The China Syndrome* (DVD), UCA.

Brigley, S. and Vass, P. (1997) *Privatised Ethics. The Case of the Regulated Industries*, in Davies, P.W.F. (ed.), *Current Issues in Business Ethics*, London: Routledge.

Brindle, M. and Dehn, G. (1996) *Four Windows on Whistleblowing*, London: Public Concern at Work.

British Airways (2000) *British Airways Social and Environmental Report 2000*, London: British Airways.

Brooke Hamilton, J.S., Knousse, B. and Hill, V. (2009), 'Google in China: A manager-friendly heuristic model for resolving cross-cultural ethical conflicts', *Journal of Business Ethics*, 86, 143–57.

Brown, C. (2008) 'MPs blame regulator's failures for the run on the Northern Rock bank', *The Independent*, 26 January: 26.

Brown, J.M. (1972) *Gandhi's Rise to Power: Indian Politics 1915–1922*, Cambridge: Cambridge University Press.

Brown, M. (2001) 'Capitalism: Reconstruction theory', *Financial Management*, 20 November.

Brown, P. (2004) 'India ordered to pay out Bhopal fund', *Guardian*, 20 July: 11.

Browne of Madingley (2004) *The Ethics of Business – The Botwinick Lecture*, Columbia Business School, 19 November 2004, World Wide Web, http://www.bp.com/genericarticle.do?categoryId=98*contended-7002497. Site visited 2 December 2004.

Brunsson, N. (1986) 'Organising for inconsistencies: On organisational conflict, depression and hypocrisy as substitutes for action', *Scandinavian Journal of Management Studies*, May: 165–85.

Brunsson, N. (1989) *The Organisation of Hypocrisy: Talk, Decisions and Actions in Organisations*, Chichester: John Wiley & Sons.

Bruntland, G. (ed.) (1987) *Our common future: The World Commission on Environment and Development*, Oxford: Oxford University Press.

Brytting, T. (1997) 'Moral support structures in private industry – The Swedish case', *Journal of Business Ethics*, 16, 663–97.

Buchanan, J. and Tullock, G. (1962) The Calculus of Consent: Logical Foundations of Constitutional Democracy, Ann Arbor: University of Michigan Press.

Bucholz, R.A. and Rosenthal, S.B. (1998) *Business Ethics: The Pragmatic Path Beyond Principles to Process*, London: Prentice Hall.

Buckley, S.L. (1998) *Usury Friendly? The Ethics of Moneylending – a Biblical Interpretation*, Cambridge: Grove Books.

Burgo, E. and Stewart, H. (2002) 'IMF policies led to Malawi famine', *Guardian*, 29 October.

Burns, J. and Shrimsley, R. (2000) 'Racism "remains rife" in the Met: Complaints of discrimination at all levels add to ethnic recruitment crisis says report', *Financial Times*, 14 December.

Burrell, G. (1997) *Pandemonium: Towards a Retro-organizational Theory*, London: Sage.

Burt, T. (2004) 'Breeden report opens the floodgates: Hollinger Chronicles', *Financial Times*, 4 September: 11.

Cabinet Office (2003) *Alcohol Misuses: How much does it cost?* Cabinet Office: London, World Wide Web, http://www.cabinetoffice.gov.uk/upload/assets/ www.cabinetoffice.gov.uk/strategy/econ.pdf. Site visited 3 March 2008.

Cabinet Office (2004) *The Civil Service Code*, World Wide Web, http://www .cabinet-office.gov.uk/central/1999/cscode.htm. Site visited 13 March 2002.

Cadbury Schweppes (2004) *Cocoa procurement: Free Trade*, World Wide Web, http://www.cadburyschweppes.com/EN/EnvironmentSociety/EthicalTrading/ CocoaProcurement/fair_trade.htm. Site visited 22 December 2004.

Cadbury, A. (2002) *Corporate Governance and Chairmanship: A Personal View*, Oxford: Oxford University Press.

Calderón, R. Alvarez-Arce, J. and Mayoral, S. (2009) 'Corporation as a crucial ally against corruption', *Journal of Business Ethics*, 87 (3), 19–332.

Campbell, D. (2008) 'The hidden risks of drinking for women', *The Observer*, 24 February, News section: 8.

Cantor, N., Mischel, W. and Schwartz, J. (1982) 'Social knowledge: Structure, content, use and abuse', in Hastorf, A.H. and Isen, A.M. (eds), *Cognitive Social Psychology*, New York: Elsevier.

Capra, F. (1982) *The Turning Point*, Flamingo, HarperCollins.

Capra, F. (1997) *The Web of Life: A New Synthesis of Mind and Matter*, Flamingo, HarperCollins.

Carbo Ceramics (2002) *Mission Statement*, World Wide Web, http://www.carboce- ramics.com/1024/company/mission.html. Site visited 10 December 2004.

Carey, J.L. (1984) 'The origins of financial reporting' in Lee, T.A. and Parker, R.H. (eds), *The Evolution of Corporate Financial Reporting*, 241–64, New York & London: Garland Publishing Inc.

Carlin, B. (2007) 'Raise home drinking age limit, says boss,' *Telegraph.co.uk.*, World Wide Web, http://www.telegraph.co.uk/news/main/jhtml?xml+/ news/2007/11/22/ntesco122xml. Site visited 25 February 2008.

Carr, A.Z. (1968) 'Is business bluffing ethical?', *Business and Society Review*, 100 (1), 1–7.

Carroll, A. and Buchholtz, A. (2000) *Business and Society: Ethics and Stakeholder Management*, 4th edn, Cincinnati, OH: Thomson Southwestern College Publishing.

Carroll, A.B. (1990) 'Principles of business ethics: Their role in decision making and an initial consensus', *Management Decision*, 28 (8), 20–4.

Carroll, A.B. (1999) 'Corporate social responsibility: Evolution of a definitional construct', *Business and Society*, 38 (3), 268–95.

Carson, R. (1962) *Silent Spring*, Boston, US: Houghton Mifflin.

Carter, C. (2004) 'Parmalat subsidy superior to CAP', *Financial Times*, 25 February, Letters to the Editor: 18.

Carter, D., Simkins, B. and Simpson. G. (2003) 'Corporate governance, board diversity and firm value', *Financial Review*, 38, 33–53.

Cassell, C., Johnson, P. and Smith, K. (1997) 'Opening the black box: Corporate codes of ethics in their organisational context', *Journal of Business Ethics*, 16, 1077–93.

Casson, M. (1991) *The Economics of Business Culture: Games Theory, Transaction Costs and Economic Performance*, Oxford: Oxford University Press, Clarendon Paperbacks.

Caulkin, S. (2004) 'Money for less than nothing', *The Observer, Business*, 12 December: 10.

Caux Round Table (2001) *Caux Round Table Principles for Business*, World Wide Web, http://www.cauxroundtable.org/ENGLISH.HTM. Site visited 26 October 2001.

Cavanagh, G.F., Moberg, D.J. and Velasquez, M. (1981) 'The ethics of organizational politics', *The Academy of Management Review*, 6 (3), 363–74.

Cavanagh, G. F., Moberg, D.J. and Velasquez, M. (1995), 'Making business ethics practical', *Business Ethics Quarterly*, 5 (3) 399–418.

Cave, A. (2011) 'The Sunday Interview with Simon Murray', Business, The *Sunday Telegraph*, 24 April: 9.

CEBR (2009) *City bonuses have bounced back by 50% but still are far lower than the 2007/8 peaks*. Press release, Centre for Economic and Business Research, 21 October 2009.

Center for Public Enquiry (2000) *The Public I: Major tobacco multinational implicated in cigarette smuggling, tax evasion, documents show*, World Wide Web, http://www.public-i.org/story_01_013100.htm. Site visited 3 June 2000.

Center for the Study of Ethics in the Professions (2003) *Covenant of the Goddess Code of Ethics*, World Wide Web, http://www.iit.edu/departments/csep/codes/coe/COG-CoE.html. Site visited 2 December 2004.

Central Statistics Office: Ireland, (n.d.). *Labour market: principal statistics,* World Wide Web, http://www.cso.ie/statistics/empandunempilo.htm. Site visited 3 March 2008.

CEPAA (1997) *Guidance Document for Social Accountability 8000*, London: CEPAA.

Chakraborty, S.K. (1993) *Managerial Transformations by Values*, New Delhi: Sage.

Chakraborty, S.K. (1999) *Values and Ethics for Organisations. Theory and Practice*, New Delhi: Oxford University Press.

Chalhoub, M.S. (2009) 'Relations between dimensions of corporate governance and corporate performance: San Empirical Study among Banks in the Lebanon', *International Journal of Management*, 26 (3), 476–85.

Chandler, D. (2001) *Semiotics: The Basics*, London: Routledge.

Chang, H.-J. (2002) *Kicking away the Ladder*, London: Anthem Press.

Checkland, P. (1981) *Systems Thinking: Systems Practice,* UK: Wiley and Sons.

Christensen, J., Kent, P. and Stewart, J. (2010) 'Corporate governance and company performance in Australia', *Australian Accounting Review*, No. 55, 20 (4), 372–86.

Christian Aid (2004) *Behind the Mask: The Real Face of Corporate Social Responsibility*, London: Christian Aid.

Churchman, C.W. (1968) *The Systems Approach*, New York: Delacorte Press.

CIMA (Chartered Institute of Management Accountants) (2008) *Managing Responsible Business*, London: CIMA.

Cisco (2012) *Cisco Visual Networking Index: Global Mobile Data Traffic Forecast Update, 2011–2016*, World Wide Web, http://www.cisco.com/en/US/solutions/collateral/ns341/ns525/ns537/ns705/ns827/white_paper_c11-520862.html. Site visited 19 April 2012.

Clark, A. and Borger, J. (2001) 'Cheaper drugs for Africa: Manufacturer to relax its patent on two Aids remedies', *Guardian*, 15 March: 3. *Guardian* and *Observer* on CD-ROM.

Clark, D. (2004) *The Rough Guide to Ethical Shopping*, London: Rough Guides.

Clark, J.M. (1916) 'The changing basis of economic responsibility', *Journal of Political Economy*, 24 (3), 209–29.

Clark, T. (2007) 'The materiality of sustainability: Corporate social and environmental responsibility as instruments of strategic change?' in Dunphy, D. and Benn, S. (eds), *Corporate Governance and Sustainability: Challenges for Theory and Practice*, 219–51, New York: Routledge.

Clarke, K. (2000) 'Dilemma of a cigarette exporter', *Guardian Unlimited*, 3 February, World Wide Web, http://www.newsunlimited.co.uk/bat/0,2763,131913,00.html. Site visited 12 August 2001.

Clarkson, C.M.V. (1998) 'Corporate culpability', *Web Journal of Legal Issues*, Blackstone Press Ltd, World Wide Web, http://webjcli.ncl.uk/1998/issue2/clarkson2.html. Site visited 19 March 2009.

Clarkson, M.B.E. (1995) 'A stakeholder framework for analyzing and evaluating corporate social performance', *The Academy of Management Review,* 20 (1), 92–117.

Clean Clothes Campaign (n.d.) World Wide Web, http://www.cleanclothes.org/companies/levi5-5-98.htm. Site visited 23 June 2007.

Clutterbuck, D. (1992) *The Role of the Chief Executive in Maintaining an Ethical Climate*, London: Clutterbuck Associates.

CNN International (2003) *Parmalat to Decide on Bankruptcy*, World Wide Web, http://editioncnn.com/2003/BUSINESS/italy.parmalat/index.html. Site visited 8 February 2005.

Cohen B. (1963) *The Press and Foreign Policy*. Princeton: Princeton University Press.

Commission for Africa (2005) *Our Common Interest. Report of the Commission for Africa*, World Wide Web, http://news.bbc.co.uk/1/shared/bsp/hi/pdfs/11_03_05africa.pdf. Site visited 2 April 2005.

Competition Commission (2007) *Market investigation into the supply of groceries in the UK: Provisional findings report*, World Wide Web, http://www.competitioncommission.gov.uk/inquiries/ref2006/grocery/prov_find_report.pdf. Site visited 12 November 2007.

Connock, S. and Johns, T. (1995) *Ethical Leadership*, London: Institute of Personnel Development.

Cooper, T. (2005) 'Slower consumption: Reflections on product life cycles and the "Throwaway Society"', *Journal of Industrial Ecology*, 9 (1/2), 51–67.

Cooper, T. (2010) *Longer Lasting Products: Alternatives to the Throwaway Society*, Surrey, England: Gower Publishing Limited.

Corlette, J.A. (1989) 'The 'modified vendetta sanction' as method of corporate collective punishment', *Journal of Business Ethics*, 8 (12), 937–42.

Corporate Manslaughter and Corporate Homicide Act (2007), http://www.justice.gov.uk/publications/corporatemanslaughter2007.htm. Site visited 4 February 2008.

Corpwatch (2001) *Personal Appeal from Bhopal to Shareholders of Union Carbide: You Can Still End the Disaster in Bhopal*, World Wide Web, http://www.corpwatc.org/trac/bhopal/shareholder.html. Site visited 25 October 2001.

Covey, S.R. (1991) *Principle-centred Leadership*, New York: Summit Books.

Covey, S.R. (1992) *The Seven Habits of Highly Effective People: Powerful Lessons in Personal Change*, London: Simon and Schuster.

Cowe, R. (2001) 'Europe rises to social challenge: Corporate citizenship', *Financial Times*, 19 July.

Crainer, S. (1993) *Zeebrugge: Learning from Disaster*, London: Herald Charitable Trust.

Crees, M. (2007) 'The company of stone', *Times Literary Supplement*, 27 July, 17.

Crichton, M. (2004) *State of Fear*, New York: HarperCollins.

Cronin, J. (2004) *DBA dissertation*, Nottingham Business School, Nottingham Trent University.

Crooks, E. (2007) 'A shabby end to a brilliant career', *Financial Times*, 2 May, Companies UK section: 21.

Crouch, C. and Marquand, D. (eds) (1993) *Ethics and Markets: Co-operation and Competition Within Capitalist Economies*, Oxford: Blackwell Publishers.

CSR Academy (2004) *The CSR Competency Framework*, London: CSR Academy, World Wide Web, http://www.csracademy.org.uk/competency.htm. Site visited 28 February 2005.

Cyert, R.M. and March, J.G. (1992) *A Behavioral Theory of the Firm*, 2nd edn, New Jersey: Blackwell.

Czarniawska, B. (2004) *Narratives in Social Science Research*, London: Sage.

Czerny, A. (2004) 'Support for "ethical" testing', *People Management*, 11 March: 10.

D'Entreves, A.P. (1965) *Aquinas. Selected Political Writings*, trans. J.G. Dawson, Oxford: Basil Blackwell.

Daily Telegraph, The (2011) 'Should investors dig deep for glencore float?', Business, 15 April: 14

Dallas, M. (1996) 'Accountability for performance – Does audit have a role?' in *Adding Value? Audit and Accountability in the Public Services*, Public Finance Foundation and Chartered Institute of Public Finance and Accountancy (CIPFA): London.

Dalrymple, W. (1999) *The Age of Kali. Travels and Encounters In India*, London: Flamingo Press.

Dalrymple, W. (2002) *The White Mughals*, London: Flamingo.

Davidson, W.N., Worrell, D.L. and El-Jelly, A. (1995) 'Influencing managers to change unpopular corporate behavior through boycotts and divestitures: a stock market test', *Business & Society*, 34 (2), 171–96.

Davies, N. (2007) *Truth about Kyoto: huge profits, little carbon saved*, The Guardian, 2 June, World Wide Web, http://www.guardian.co.uk/environment/2007/jun/02/india.greenpolitics?INTCMP=SRCH Site visited 19 April 2012.

Davies, P.W.F. (ed.) (1997) *Current Issues in Business Ethics*, London: Routledge.

De George, R.T. (1999) *Business Ethics*, 5th edn, New Jersey: Prentice Hall.

De Pelsmacker, P., Driesen, L. and Rayp, G. (2003) *Are Fair Trade Labels Good Business? Ethics and Coffee Buying Intentions*, University of Ghent, Faculty of Economics and Business Administration, Working Paper, World Wide Web, http://www.feb.ugent.be/fac/research/WP/Papers/wp_03_165.pdf. Site visited 22 December 2004.

DegliInnocenti, N. and Reed, J. (2004) 'Anger at delay to AIDS drugs in South Africa', *Financial Times*, 21 January: 9.

Department for Business, Innovation & Skills (2002) *Corporate Social Responsibility Report*, London: The National Archives.

Department of Transport (1987) *MV Herald of Free Enterprise, Formal Investigation by Hon. Mr Justice Sheen, Wreck Commissioner, Court Report 8074* (The Sheen Report), London: HMSO.

Derrida, J. with Bennington, G. (1985) 'On colleges and philosophy', in Appignanesi, L. (ed.), *Postmodernism. ICA Documents*, London: Free Associates Books.

Dewey, C. (1993) *Anglo-Indian Attitudes: the Mind of the Indian Civil Service*, London: The Hambledon Press.

Dhesi, A.S. (1998) 'Caste, class synergies and discrimination in India', *International Journal of Social Economics*, 25 (6, 7, 8), 1030–48.

Dickson, D. (1974) *Alternative Technology and the Politics of Technical Change*, London: Fontana/Collins.

Director (2001) 'Spanish shuffle', *Director*, February: 29.

Doane, D. (2005) *The Myth of CSR: The problem with assuming that companies can do well while also doing good is that markets don't really work that way*, USA: Stanford Social Innovation Review, Stanford Graduate School of Business.

Dodd, E.M. (1932) 'For whom are corporate managers trustees?', *Harvard Law Review*, 45 (7), 1145–63.

Dodd, V. (2011a) 'Yard chiefs told Guardian: you've got it wrong', *The Guardian*, 16 July 2011, 8.

Dodd, V. (2011b) 'Home secretary adds to pressure on Met chief over decision to appoint Coulson's deputy', *The Guardian*, 16 July 2011, 8.

Dollar, D. and Kraay, A. (2002) 'Growth is Good for the Poor', *Journal of Economic Growth*, 7 (3), 195–225.

Dollar, D. and Kraay, A. (2004) 'Trade, growth and poverty', *Economic Journal*, 114 (493), F22–49.

Donald Hirsch D. and Beckhelling J. (2011) *Child Poverty Map*, London: Centre for Research in Social Policy, Loughborough University & End Child Poverty Action Group.

Donaldson, T. (1982) *Corporations and Morality*, Englewood Cliffs, NJ: Prentice Hall.

Donaldson, T. (1989) *The Ethics of International Business*, New York: Oxford University Press.

Donaldson, T. (1990) 'Morally privileged relationships', *Journal of Value Enquiry*, 24, 1–15.

Donaldson, T. (1996) 'Values in tension: Ethics away from home', *Harvard Business Review*, 74 (5), 48–56.

Donaldson, T. (2008) 'Two stories', in Dialogue: toward superior stakeholder theory, *Business Ethics Quarterly*, 18 (2), 172–6.

Donaldson, T. and Dunfee, T.W. (1994) 'Toward a unified conception of business ethics: Integrative social contracts theory', *Academy of Management Review*, 19 (2), 252–84.

Donaldson, T. and Dunfee, T.W. (1995) 'Integrative social contracts theory: A communitarian conception of economic ethics', *Economics and Philosophy*, 11 (1), 85–112.

Donaldson, T. and Dunfee, T.W. (1999) *Ties That Bind: A Social Contracts Approach to Business Ethics*, Boston, MA: Harvard Business School Press.

Donaldson, T. and Preston, L.E. (1995) 'The stakeholder theory of the corporation; concepts, evidence and implications', *Academy of Management Review*, 20 (1), 65–91.

Donaldson, T. and Werhane, P.H. (1979) *Ethical Issues in Business: A Philosophical Approach*, New Jersey: Prentice Hall.

Done, K. (2003) 'Branson's Concorde bid grounded by Airbus Chief', *Financial Times*, 30 April: 3.

Done, K. (2004) 'Airlines battle for profitable Indian routes', *Financial Times*, 11 November: 6.

Donkin, R. (2007) 'Executives should pay the price of failure', *Financial Times*, 15 November, FT report – recruitment; 7.

Donner, W. (1991) *The Liberal Self: John Stuart Mill's Moral and Political Philosophy*, New York: Cornell University Press.

Doran, J. (2004) 'The bank in American backwaters that has the answers to your prayers', *The Times*, Business section, 11 December: 70.

Doran, J. and Mansell, I. (2004) 'Shell settlements "bolster" billion-dollar class actions', *The Times*, 26 August: 50.

Dorff, E.N. (1997) 'The implications of Judaism for business and privacy', *Business Ethics Quarterly*, 7 (2), 31–44.

Driver, M. (2006) 'Beyond the stalemate of economics versus ethics: corporate social responsibility and the discourse of the organizational self', *Journal of Business Ethics,* 66 (4), 337–56

Dugatkin, L. (2000) *Cheating Monkeys and Citizen Bees*, Cambridge, MA: Harvard University Press.

Duke, S. (2011) *Has the Kyoto protocol failed Africa?*, BBC, 2 December, World Wide Web, http://www.bbc.co.uk/news/world-africa-15989873. Site visited 19 April 2012.

Dunfee, T.W. (1991) 'Business ethics and extant social contracts', *Business Ethics Quarterly*, 1 (1), 23–51.

Dunfee, T.W. (1996) *Ethical challenges of managing across cultures*, Invited plenary paper presented at the Ninth Annual European Business Ethics Networks Conference, Seeheim, Germany.

Dunfee, T.W. and Donaldson, T. (1995) 'Contractarian business ethics: Current status and next steps', *Business Ethics Quarterly*, 5 (2), 173–86.

Dunkley, J. (2011) 'Credit runs low at BoA Merrill Lynch', Business, *The Daily Telegraph*, 13 July: 8

Durkheim, E. (1992) *Professional Ethics and Civic Morals*, trans. C. Brookfield, London: Routledge.

Dwivedi, R.S. (2000) 'The paradox of employee empowerment: Illusion or reality?' in Saini, D.S. and Khan, S.A. (eds), *Human Resource Management. Perspectives for a New Era*, New Delhi: Response Books, Sage.

Dworkin, R. (1977) *Taking Rights Seriously*, London: Duckworth.

Dyer, G. (2003a) 'Taking action to head off its critics', *Financial Times*, 28 November, FT Report, Business and AIDS section: 18.

Dyer, G. (2003b) 'South Africa revives patent drugs issue', *Financial Times*, 17 October, International economy section: 12.

EABIS (The Academy of Business in Society) (2012) *Practical wisdom from the Indian traditions*, conference held at the Indian Institute of Management, Kozhikode, India. 12–13 January 2012.

Eaglesham, J. and Tait, N. (2005) 'DTI backs down on bribery rules', *Financial Times*, 14 January: 1.

Eagleton, T. (1996) *The Illusions of Postmodernism*, Oxford: Blackwell.

Eastwood, A. and Maynard, A. (1990) 'Treating Aids. Is it Ethical to be Efficient', in Baldwin, S., Godfrey, C. and Propper, C. (eds), *Quality of Life: Perspectives and Policies*, London: Routledge.

Ebrahimi, H. (2011) 'Glencore governance fears could cut IPO price by 20pc', *The Daily Telegraph*, Business, 22 April: 1.

Ebrahimi, H. and Mason, R. (2011) 'Glencore chairman criticised for sexism', *The Daily Telegraph*, Business, 25 April: 1

Eco, U. (1985) *Reflections on the Name of the Rose*, London: Secker and Warburg.

Eco, U. (with Richard Rorty, Johnathan Culler and Christine Brooke-Rose, ed. Stefan Collini) (1992) *Interpretation and Overinterpretation*, Cambridge: Cambridge University Press.

Economist (2001) *The Plot Thickens: A Survey of India's Economy*, 2 June.

Economist (2012) *Apple and the American Economy*, 23 January.

Economist Intelligence Unit (2005) *The Importance of Corporate Responsibility*, London: *The Economist*.

Economist Intelligence Unit, (2008), 'Risk 2018: Planning for an unpredictable decade', *The Economist*.

Eden, C., Jones, S. and Sims, D. (1979) *Thinking in Organisations*, London: Macmillan Press.

Edey, H.C. (1984) 'Company accounting in the nineteenth and twentieth centuries' in Lee, T.A. and Parker, R.H. (eds), *The Evolution of Corporate Financial Reporting*, New York and London: Garland Publishing Inc., 225–30.

Edmond, D. (2010) 'Matters of life and death', *Prospect*, 7 October issue no. 175, World Wide Web, http://www.prospectmagazine.co.uk/2010/10/ethics-trolley-problem/. Site visited 23 January 2012.

Elkington, J. (1994) `Towards the Sustainable Corporation: Win-Win-Win Business Strategies for Sustainable Development', California Management Review, 36(2), 90–100.

Elkington, J. (1997) Cannibals with Forks: Triple Bottom Line of 21st Century Business, Oxford: Capstone.

Elkington, J. (1999) 'Triple bottom line reporting: Looking for balance', *Australian CPA*, March, World Wide Web, http://www.cpaonline.com.au/03_publications/02_aust_cpa_magazine/1999/03_mar/3_2_3_31_reporting.asp. Site visited 12 June 2001.

Elkington, J. (2006) 'Governance for sustainability', *Corporate Governance,* 14 (6), 522–29.

Elliott, L. (2003) 'Policy made on the road to perdition', *Guardian*, 13 October: 25.

Elliott, L. (2005) 'Oil firms fund campaign to deny climate change', *Guardian*, 27 January: 1.

Elliott, L. (2007) 'Climate change cannot be bargained with', *Guardian,* 29 October.

Elliott, R. (1997) 'Existential consumption and irrational desire', *European Journal of Marketing*, 31(3/4) 285–96.

Elshtain, J.B., Aird, E., Etzioni, A., Galston, W., Glendon, M.A., Minow, M. and Rossi, A. (n.d.) *The Communitarian Network. A Communitarian Position Paper on the Family*, World Wide Web, http://www.gwu.edu/~ccps/pop_fam.html. Site visited 15 November 2001.

Epstein, M.J. (2008) *Making Sustainability Work,* Sheffield, UK: Greenleaf Publishing Limited.

Erturk, J., Froud, J., Sukhdev, J. and Williams, C. (2004) *Pay for Corporate Performance or Pay as Social Division: Re-thinking the Problem of Top Management Pay in Giant Corporations*, University of Manchester and Royal Holloway College, London University.

Escobar, A. (2011) *Encountering Development: The Making and Unmaking of the Third World*, 2nd edn, New York: Princeton University Press.

Etzioni, A. (1988) *The Moral Dimension: Towards a New Economics*, New York: The Free Press.

Etzioni, A. (1993) *The Spirit of Community*, New York: Crown.

Evans, R. (2004) 'Hewitt weakened rules against corporate graft', *Guardian*, 23 December: 8.

Evans, S. (2001) 'McDonald's grilled over "veggie" fries', *BBC News Online*, World Wide Web, http://news.bbc.co.uk. Site visited 24 May 2001.

Evans, S. (2005) 'Blow dealt to the "Aw Shucks!" defence', *BBC News Online*, 16 March, World Wide Web, http://news.bbc.co.uk/1/hi/business/4337543 .stm. Site visited 17 March 2005.

ExecutiveCaliber (2004) *Parmalat*, World Wide Web, http://executivecaliber.ws/ sys-tmp/parmalat/. Site visited 8 February 2005.

Failaka International Inc. (2001) *Glossary of Islamic Financial Terms*, World Wide Web, http://www.failaka.com/Glossary.html. Site visited 20 August 2001.

Farrell, B.J. and Cobbin, D.M. (1996) 'A content analysis of codes of ethics in Australian enterprises', *Journal of Managerial Psychology*, 11(1), 37–55.

Ferguson, C. (Director) (2010) *Inside Job*, a film, US: Sony Pictures Classics.

Festinger, L. (1957) *A Theory of Cognitive Dissonance*, New York: Row Peterson.

Financial Times (2000) 'Leading article: Spy trap', 22 August.

Financial Times (2001) 'Leading article: Changing Track', 9 May.

Financial Times (2004) 'A hole dug over 30 years', 20 February.

Financial Times (2005) 'Leading article: A tale of greed and gullibility', 9 April: 10.

Fineman, S. and Gabriel, Y. (1996) *Experiencing Organisations*, London: Sage.

Firestone Tire Resource Center (n.d.), World Wide Web, http://www.citizen.org/ fireuf/index7.htm. Site visited 22 May 2001.

Fischel, D.R. and Sykes, A.O. (1996) 'Corporate crime', *Journal of Legal Studies* 25: 319. *doi:10.1086/467980.*

Fischer, F. (1983) 'Ethical Discourse in Public Administration', *Administration and Society*, 15 (1), 5–42.

Fischoff, B., Slovic, P. and Lichtenstein, S. (1977) 'Knowing with certainty: the appropriateness of extreme confidence', *Journal of Experimental Psychology*, 3 (4), 552–64.

Fisher, C. and Lovell, A.T.A. (2000) *Accountant's Responses to Ethical Issues at Work*, London: CIMA Publishing.

Fisher, C.M. (1998) *Resource Allocation in the Public Sector: Values, Priorities, and Markets in the Management of Public Services*, London: Routledge.

Fisher, C.M. (1999) 'Ethical stances: The perceptions of accountants and HR specialists of ethical conundrums at work', *Business Ethics: A European Review*, 18 (4), 236–48.

Fisher, C.M. (2000) 'The ethics of inactivity: human resource managers and Quietism', *Business and Professional Ethics Journal*, 19, 55–72.

Fisher, C.M. (2001) 'Managers' perceptions of ethical codes: Dialectics and dynamics', *Business Ethics: A European Review*, 10 (2), 145–57.

Fisher, C.M. and Rice, C. (1999) 'Managing messy moral matters', in Leopold, J., Harris, L. and Watson, T.J. (1999) *Strategic Human Resources. Principles, Perspectives and Practices*, London: Pearson Education.

Fisher, C.M., Doughty, D. and Mussayeva, S. (2008) 'Learning and tensions in managerial intercultural encounters: a dialectical interpretation', *Management Learning*, July, 39 (3) 311–27.

Fletcher, J. (1966) *Situation Ethics*, London: SCM Press.

Forster, E.M. (1975) *Two Cheers for Democracy*, New York: Holmes & Meier.

Fortson, D. (2011) 'City relaxes its rules to attract mega deals', Business, *The Sunday Times*, 30 October: 8

Foster, N. (2001) *The Foster Catalogue 2001*, London: Prestel.

Francis, D. and Young, D. (1979) *Improving Work Groups: A Practical Manual for Team Building*, La Jolla, CA: University Associates.

Freeman, R.E. (1984) *Strategic Management: A Stakeholder Approach,* US: HarperCollins.

Freeman, R.E. and Liedtka, J. (1991) 'Corporate social responsibility: a critical approach', *Business Horizons,* July-August: 92–8.

Freeman, R.E. and Reed, D.L. (1983) 'Stockholders and stakeholders: a new perspective on corporate governance', *California Management Review,* 23 (3) 88–106.

Freeman, R.E. and Velamuri, S.R. (2005) 'A new approach to CSR: Corporate stakeholder responsibility', World Wide web, http://consciouscapitalism.org/library/pdf/resources_company.pdf. Site visited 4 may 2008.

Freeman, R.E., Wicks, A.C. and Parmar, B. (2004) 'Stakeholder theory and the corporate objective revisited', *Organization Science,* 15 (3), 364–9.

Freeman, R.E. (2008) 'Ending the so-called 'Friedman-Freeman' debate', *in* Dialogue: toward superior stakeholder theory, *Business Ethics Quarterly*, 18 (2) 162–6.

Friedman, J. (1994) *Cultural Identity and Global Process*, London: Sage.

Friedman, M. (1962) *Capitalism and Freedom,* US: University of Chicago Press.

Friedman, M. (1970) 'The social responsibility of business is to increase its profits', *New York Times Magazine,* 13 September, 33, 122–6.

Friedman, M. (1985) *Consumer Boycotts*, NY: Routledge.

Friends of the Earth – US (1997) *OECD Multilateral Agreement on Investment: Fact Sheet*, World Wide Web, http://www.globalpolicy.org/socecon/bwi-wto/oecd-mai.htm. Site visited 25 January 2005.

Fukuyama, F. (1993) *The End of History and the Last Man*, Harmondsworth: Penguin.

Fukuyama, F. (1999) 'The left should love globalization', *The Wall Street Journal,* 1 December.

Gabriel, Y., Fineman, S. and Sims, D. (2000) *Organizing & Organizations*, 2nd edn, London: Sage.

Galbraith, J.K. (2004) *The Economics of Innocent Fraud: Truth for Our Time*, Allen Lane: Penguin Books.

Galton, M. and Delafield, A. (1981) 'Expectancy effects in primary classrooms', in Simons, B. and Willcocks, J. (eds) (1981) *Research and Practice in the Primary Classroom*, London: Routledge, Kegan and Paul.

Gap Inc. (2007) *Gap Inc. Code of Vendor Conduct*, World Wide Web, www.gapinc.com/public/documents/code_vendor_conduct.pdf. Site visited 12 January 2008.

Garrett, D. E. (1987) 'The effectiveness of marketing policy boycotts: environmental opposition to marketing', *Journal of Marketing,* 51 (2), 46–57.

Giddens, A. (1984) *The Constitution of Society*, Cambridge: Polity Press.

Giddens, A. (1985) 'Reason without revolution? Habermas's Theorie des Kommunikativen Handelns', in Bernstein, R.J. (ed.), *Habermas and Modernity*, Cambridge: Polity Press in association with Oxford: Blackwells.

Gidoomal, R. and Porter, D. (1997) *The UK Maharajahs: Inside the South Asian Success Story*, London: Nicholas Brealey.

Gigerenzer, G., Todd, P. and the ABC Research Group (1999) *Simple Heuristics that Make us Smart*, Oxford: Oxford University Press.

Gilbertson T. and Reyes O. (2009) *Carbon Trading: How it Works and Why it Fails,* Critical Currents Series, No.7. Dag Hammarskjöld Foundation. Uppsala, Sweden. World Wide Web, http://www.dhf.uu.se/publications/critical-currents/carbon-trading-%e2%80%93-how-it-works-and-why-it-fails/. Site visited 19 April 2012.

Gilligan, C. (1982) *In a Different Voice: Psychological Theory and Women's Development*, Cambridge, MA: Harvard University Press.

Gladwin, T.N., Kennelly, J.J. and Krause, T-S. (1995) 'Shifting paradigms for sustainable development: Implications for management theory and research', *Academy of Management Review*, 20 (4) 874–907.

Glencore (2011a) *Annual Report 2010*.

Glencore (2011b) *First Quarter 2011 Interim Management Statement*.

Glencore (2012) *Board of Directors*, World Wide Web, http://www.glencore.com/board-of-directors.php, site visited 12 February 2012.

Global Compact Office and Sustainability (2004) *Gearing Up from Corporate Responsibility and Good Governance to Scalable Solutions*, The Global Compact Office: New York.

Goffman, E. (1959) *The Presentation of the Self in Everyday Life*, New York: Doubleday Anchor Books.

Gompers, P., Ishii, J. and Metrick, A. (2004) *Incentives vs. Control: An Analysis of U.S. Dual-Class Companies*, NBER Working papers no. 10240, Cambridge, MA: National Bureau of Economic Research.

Gonella, C., Pilling, A. and Zadek, S. (1998) *Making Values Count*, Research Report No. 57 of the Association of Chartered Certified Accountants, London: Certified Accountants Educational Trust.

Goodley, S. (2011) 'Financial: Glencore faces crunch week for shares', Financial Pages, *The Guardian*, 13 June: 20.

Goodwin, R.N. (1974) *The American Condition*, New York: Doubleday.

Gopinath, C. (1998) 'Alternative approaches to indigenous management in India', *Management International Review*, 38 (3), 257–75.

Gosling, P. (2004) *Accountability in the Public Services*, London: ACCA.

Grant, J., Kirchgaessner, S. and McNulty, S. (2007) 'BP hopes $370m settlement will draw a line under US scandals', *Financial Times*, 26 October: 1.

Great Britain (2011a) *Bribery Act 2010 Chapter 23*, London: HMSO.

Great Britain (2011b) Ministry of Justice (2011) *The Bribery Act: Quick Start Guide*, Ministry of Justice, World Wide Web, www.justice.gov.uk/guidance/bribery .htm. Site visited 6 September 2011.

Greenawalt, K. (1987) *Conflicts of Law and Morality*, Oxford: Oxford University Press.

Greenslade, R. (2011) 'The actor, the ex-News of the World executive and a broken-downFerrari,…', Greenslade Blog. *The Guardian.co.uk*, 9 July 2011, World Wide Web, www.guardian.co.uk/media/greenslade/2011/jan/03/hughgrant-newsoftheworld/. Site visited 6 September 2011.

Gregory, M. and Rufford, N. (1994) *Dirty Tricks: Inside Story of British Airways' Secret War Against Richard Branson's Virgin Atlantic*, London: Little Brown.

Greimas, A. (1987) *On Meaning: Selected Writings in Semiotic Theory*, trans. Paul J. Perron and Frank H. Collins , London: Frances Pinter.

Griffiths, P. (2011) 'Ethical objections to Fairtrade', *Journal of Business Ethics*, May: 1–17.

Griseri, P. (1998) *Managing Values*, London: Palgrave.

Grolin, J. (1998) 'Corporate legitimacy in risk society: The case of Brent Spar', *Business Strategy and the Environment*, (7) 213–22.

Groom, B. (2011) 'City pays out £14bn in bonuses', *The Financial Times*, 19 July 2011, World Wide Web, http://www.ft.com/cms/s/0/e2673ae-b22a-11e0-9d80144feabdc0.html. Site visited 29 July 2011.

Gross, J. (1987) *Oxford Dictionary of Aphorisms*, Oxford: Oxford University Press.

Grove-White, R. (2005) 'Environmentalism: A new moral discourse for technological society?', in Milton K. (ed.), *Environmentalism: The View from Anthropology,* London, UK: Routledge and Taylor & Francis e-Library.

Gudex, C. (1986) *QALYs and their Use by the Health Service*, Discussion paper No. 20, Centre for Health Economics, York: Centre for Health Economics, University of York.

Guerrera, F. (2001a) 'Hit squad to tackle animal rights activists', *FT.com*, 27 April.

Guerrera, F. (2001b) 'Huntingdon seeks nominee structure to protect holders', *Financial Times*, 12 May.

Gustafson, A. (2000) 'Making sense of postmodern business ethics', *Business Ethics Quarterly*, 10 (3), 645–58.

Habermas, J. (1999) On the Pragmatics of Communication, edited M. Cooke, Cambridge: Polity Press.

Haidt, J. (2003) 'The moral emotions', in Davidson, R.J., Scherer, K.R. and Goldsmith, H.H. (eds), *Handbook of Affective Sciences*, 852–70, Oxford: Oxford University Press.

Haley, G.T. and Haley, U.C.V. (1998) 'Boxing with shadows: Competing effectively with the Overseas Chinese and the Overseas Indian Business Networks in the Asian Arena', *Journal of Organisational Change Management*, 11 (4), 301–20.

Hampel Committee (1998) The Hampel Committee report. Avaialble on the World Wide Werb http://www.ecgi.org/codes/documents/hampel_index.htm

Hansen, J., Sato, M., Kharecha, P., Beerling, D., Masson-Delmotte, V., Pagani, M., Raymo, M., Royer, D.L. and Zachos, J.C. (2008) *Target atmospheric CO2: Where should humanity aim?* World Wide Web, http://www.columbia.edu/~jeh1/2008/TargetCO2_20080407.pdf.

Harding, L. (1999) 'The fall of Aitken: from Eton and Oxford to the Ritz and the Old Bailey', *Guardian*, 9 June: 4. *Guardian* and *Observer* on CD-ROM.

Harding, L. (2004) 'Delhi schoolboy sparks global porn row', *Guardian Online*, 21 December.

Hare, R. D, (1991) The Hare psychopathology Checklist Revised, New York: Multi-Health Systems.

Harford, T. (2007) *The Undercover Economist*, London: Abacus.

Harrington, M. (1965) *The Accidental Century*, Harmondsworth: Penguin.

Harrington, S. (2003) 'Stringing us along?' in *AccountancyAge.com*, World Wide Web, http://www.accountancyage.com/Features/1137242. Site visited 13 September 2004.

Harris, C. and Michaels, A. (2004) 'Shell Board blames crisis on human failings', *FT.com*, 19 April, World Wide Web, http://www.FT.com. Site visited 12 June 2004.

Harris, J.E. and Reynolds, M.A. (1993) 'Formal codes: The delineation of ethical cilemmas', *Advances in Public Interest Accounting*, 5, 107–20.

Harris, L.C. and Ogbonna, E. (1999) 'Developing a market oriented culture: A critical evaluation', *Journal of Management Studies*, 36 (2), 177–96.

Hartley, R.E. (1993) *Business Ethics: Violations of the Public Trust*, Chichester: John Wiley & Sons.

Harvey, D. (1989) *The Condition of Postmodernity*, Oxford: Blackwell.

Harzing, A.-W. (2000) 'An empirical test and extension of the Bartlett and Ghoshal typology of multinational companies', *Journal of International Business Studies*, 31 (1), 101–20.

Hawkes, S. (2007) 'A little white lie that meant one of Britain's top businessmen had to be shown the door', *The Times*, 2 May: 6.

Hazlitt, W. (2004) *William Hazlitt on 'The Pleasure of Hating'*, London: Penguin Books.

Head, J. and Lucas, R. (2004) 'Employee relations in the non-union hotel industry: a case of "determined opportunism"', *Personnel Review*, 33, (6) 639–710.

Heal, M. (1970) *The Social Responsibilities of Business: Company and Community, 1900-1960*, USA: Cleveland.

Heelas, P. and Morris, P. (1992) (eds) *The Values of the Enterprise Culture: The Moral Debate*, London: Routledge.

Hegel, G.W.F. (2003) *The Phenomenology of Mind*, trans. J.B. Baillie, a reprint of the 1910 2nd, revised edn, New York: Dover.

Heidegger, M. (1959, translation 2000) *Introduction to Metaphysics*, trans. G. Fried and R. Polt, Yale: Nota Bene.

Held, D. (1987) *Models of Democracy*, Oxford: Polity Press.

Held, D. and McGrew, A.G. (2000) *The Global Transformations Reader: An Introduction to the Globalization debate*, Cambridge: Polity Press.

Helin, S. and Sandstrom. J. (2010) Resisitng a corporate code of ethics and the reinforcement of management control', *Organisation Studies*, 131 (5), 583–604.

Helson, R. and Wink, P. (1992) 'Personality Change in Women from the Early 40s to the Early 50s', *Psychology and Ageing*, 7 (1), March.

Henn, M. and Foard, N. (2011) 'Young people, political participation and trust in Britain', *Parliamentary Affairs*, 64 (4) 1–21.

Herman, S.M. (1994) *The Tao at Work: On Leading and Following*, San Francisco: Jossey-Bass.

Hillman, A.J. and Keim, G.D. (2001) 'Shareholder value, stakeholder management, and social issues: what's the bottom line?', *Strategic Management Journal*, 22, (2) 125–39.

Hills, J. (2012) *Getting the Measure of Fuel Poverty: Final Report of the Fuel Poverty Review*, CASE report 72, London: London School of Economics and Political Science, Department of Energy and Climate Change (DECC).

Hindustan Times (2004) 'Ambanis told to talk', *The Hindustan Times*, 2 December: 1.

Hirst, P. and Thompson, G. (1996) *Globalisation in Question*, Oxford: Polity Press.

Hobbes, T. (1968) *Leviathan*, Harmondsworth: Penguin.

Hobbes, T. (n.d.) (ed.) M. Oakeshott, *Leviathan or the Matter, Forme and Power of a Commonwealth Ecclesiastical and Civil*, Oxford: Blackwell.

Hoffman, W.M. and Moore, J.M. (1990) *Business Ethics: Readings and Cases in Corporate Morality*, London: McGraw-Hill.

Hofstede, G.H. (1991) *Cultures and Organisations. Software of the Mind*, London: McGraw-Hill.

Hofstede, G.H. (2001) *Culture's Consequences*, 2nd edn, London: Sage.

Hogarth, R. (1980) *Judgement and Choice*, New York: John Wiley & Sons.

Holbrook, M.B. and Hirschman, E.C. (1982) 'The experiential aspects of consumption: Consumer fantasies, feelings, and fun' *Journal of Consumer Research*, 2 (September) 132–140.

Holden, N.J. (2002) *Cross Cultural Management. A Knowledge Management Perspective*, Harlow: Pearson Education.

Holland, L. and Gibbon, J. (2001) 'Processes in social and ethical accountability: External reporting mechanisms', in Andriof, J. and McIntosh, M. (eds), *Perspectives on Corporate Citizenship*, 278–95, Sheffield: Greenleaf Publishing.

Hollinger International Inc. (n.d.) Hollinger International Inc. home page, World Wide Web, http://www.hollingerinternational.com/. Site visited 15 September 2004.

Home Office (2000) *Reforming the Law on Involuntary Manslaughter*, London: The Home Office.

Hope, C. (2004) 'Shell advised to retreat from Nigeria', *Business Telegraph*, 11 June.

Hopwood, A. (1974) *Accounting and Human Behaviour*, London: Prentice-Hall.

Hosking, P. (2004) 'Ousted Shell chief takes FSA to court', *The Times*, 17 September, Business section: 25.

House of Commons (2004) *The Future of the Railways*, Select Committee on Transport, seventh report, HC 145, London: The Stationery Office, World Wide Web, http://www.guardian.co.uk/business/story/0,3604,821285,00.html. Site visited 3 November 2004.

Hunt, G. (1995) *Whistleblowing in the Health Service: Accountability, Law & Professional Practice*, London: Edward Arnold.

Hunt, G. (1998) *Whistleblowing in the Social Services: Public Accountability and Professional Practice*, London: Edward Arnold.

Husserl, E. (1931) *Ideas: General Introduction to Pure Phenomenology*, trans. W.R. Boyce-Gibson, London: George Allen & Unwin.

Husserl, E. (1965) *Phenomenology and the Crisis of Philosophy: Philosophy as Religious Science and Philosophy and the Crisis of European Man*, trans. Q. Lauer, New York: Harper Torchbooks, Harper & Row.

Ibeanu, O. (2000) 'Oiling the friction: Environmental conflict management in the Niger Delta, Nigeria', *Environmental Change and Security Project Report*, Issue 6, Summer.

IBFAN (International Baby Food Action Network) (n.d.) *How Breast Feeding is Undermined*, World Wide Web, http://www.ibfan.org/english/issue/bfundermined01.html. Site visited 17 February 2002.

Ibrahim, H. and Samad, F.A. (2011) 'Agency costs, corporate governance mechanisms and the performance of public listed family firms in Malaysia', *South African Journal of Business Management*, 42 (3), 17–25.

Independent Police Complaints Commission (IPCC) (2004) *IPCC decision on Superintendent Dizaei*, World Wide Web, http://wwwipcc.gov.uk/news/pr160604_dizaei. Site visited 8 February 2005.

Institute of Alcohol Studies (1997) *The Co-op and Iceland ban alcopops*, Alcohol Alert 1997 No. 1, World Wide Web, http://www.ias.org.uk/resources/publications/alcoholalert/alert199701/al199701_p4a.html. Site visited 3 March 2008.

Institute of Business ethics (IBE) (2002) Demonstrating Corporate Values - Which standard for your Company? London: IBE.

International Chamber of Commerce (ICC) (1997) *International Code of Advertising Practice*, World Wide Web, http://www.iccwbo.org/home/statements_rules/rules/1997/advercod.asp. Site visited 13 March 2002.

International Labour Organization (ILO) (2004) *Codes of Conduct for Multinationals*, World Wide Web, http://www.itcilo.it/english/actrav/telearn/global/ilo/guide/main.htm. Site visited 17 February 2002.

International Monetary Fund – IMF (2008) *The Fiscal Implications of Climate Change*, Fiscal Affairs Department, IMF.

Investor Responsibility Research Centre (IRRC) (2004) *Investigation of governance at Hollinger reveals 'corporate kleptocracy'*, IRRC news item 10 September World Wide Web, http://www.irrc.org/index.html. Site visited 15 September 2004.

IPCC (2007) *Climate Change 2007: Synthesis Report. Contribution of Working Groups I, II and III to the Fourth Assessment Report of the Intergovernmental Panel on Climate Change*, Geneva, Switzerland: UN.

IRC (International Relations Centre) (1998) *The Fair Trade Movement: Making Commerce Work for the Poor Majority*, Bulletin No. 50, World Wide Web, http://www.irc-online.org/content/bulletin/bull50.php. Site visited 22 December 2004.

Jackall, R. (1988) *Moral Mazes: The World of Corporate Managers*, New York: Oxford University Press.

Jackson, T. (2009) *Prosperity Without Growth: Economic for a Finite Planet*, London: Earthscan, Dunstan House.

Jaeger, A.M. and Kanungo, R.N. (eds) (1990) *Management in Developing Countries*, London: Routledge.

Jankowicz, A.D. and Dobosz-Bourne, D. (2003) 'How are meanings negotiated? Commonality, sociality, and the travel of ideas', in Scheer, J. (ed.), *Crossing Borders, Going Places*, Giessen: Fischer-Verlag.

Jensen, T., Sandstrom, J. and Helin, S. (2009) 'Corporate codes of ethics and the bending of moral space', *Organisation*, 16 (4), 529–45.

Joergens, C. (2006) 'Ethical fashion: Myth or future trend?', *Journal of Fashion Marketing and Management*, 10 (3), 360–71.

Johannes Paulus PP II (1993) *VeritatisSplendor*, World Wide Web, http://www.vatican.va/holy_father/john_paul_ii/encyclicals/documents/hf_jp-ii_enc_06081993_veritatis-splendor_en.html. Site visited 6 September 2011.

John Paul II (1991) *CentesimusAnnus: Encyclical Letter of the Supreme Pontiff John Paul II on the One Hundredth Anniversary of RerumNovarum*, World Wide Web, http://listserv.american.edu/catholic/church/papal/jp.ii/jp2hundr.txt. Site visited 11 June 2001.

Johns, H. and Ormerod, P. (2007) *Happiness, Economics and Public Policy*, London: IEA (Institute of Economic Afairs).

Johnson and Johnson (n.d.) *Our Company, Our Credo*, World Wide Web, http://www.jnj.com/our_company/index.htm. Site visited 2 December 2004.

Johnson, G. (1994) *University Politics*, Cambridge: Cambridge University Press.

Jones, J.E. and Pfeiffer, J.W. (eds) (1974) *The 1974 Handbook for Group Facilitators*, Iowa City: University Associates.

Jonsen, A. and Toulmin, S. (1988) *The Abuse of Casuistry*, Berkeley: University of California Press.

Jos, P.H. (1988) 'Moral autonomy and the modern organisation', *Polity: The Journal of the North-Eastern Political Science Association*, XXI (2), Winter.

Joyce, J. (1996) *Portrait of the Artist as a Young Man*, London: Penguin.

Jung, C.G. (1953) *Psychological Reflections, An Anthology of the Writings of C.G. Jung*, J. Jacobi (ed.), London: Kegan Paul.

Kahneman, D. (2011) *Thinking Fast and Slow*, London: Allen Lane Penguin.

Kahneman, D., Slovic, P. and Tversky, A. (eds) (1982) *Judgement under Uncertainty: Heuristics and Biases*, Cambridge: Cambridge University Press.

Kaler, J. (1999) 'What's the good of ethical theory?' *Business Ethics – A European Review*, 8 (4), 206–13.

Kanter, J. (2007) *Carbon trading: Where greed is green*, The New York Times, 20 June, World Wide Web, http://www.nytimes.com/2007/06/20/business/worldbusiness/20iht-money.4.6234700.html?_r=3. Site visited 19 April 2012.

Kanungo, R.N. and Mendonca, M. (1996) *Ethical Dimensions of Leadership*, London: Sage.

Kapner, F. (2004a) 'A hole dug over 30 years', *Financial Times*, 20 February, Companies section: 26.

Kapner, F. (2004b) 'Fast-track Parmalat trial rejected', *Financial Times*, 25 March, Companies section: 30.

Kapner, F. and Minder, R. (2004) 'Police arrest three more of the Tanzi family', *Financial Times*, 18 February, Companies International section: 28.

Kapner, J. (2004): 'A hole dug over 30 years, Companies Section', *Financial Times*, 20 February 2004, p. 26

Kaptein, M. (2011) 'Towards effective codes: Testing the relationship with unethical behavior', *Journal of Business Ethics*, 99, 233–51.

Kärreman, D. and Alvesson, M. (1999) 'Ethical Closure in Organisational Settings – the Case of Media Organisations', paper presented at the 15th EGOS Colloquium, *Organisations in a Challenging World: Theories, Practices and Societies*, The University of Warwick, 4–6 July.

Keats, R. (1993) 'The moral boundaries of the market', in Crouch, C. and Marquand, D. (eds), *Ethics and Markets: Co-operation and Competition within Capitalist Economies*, 6–20, Oxford: Blackwell Publishers.

Keay, J. (2000) *India: A History*, London: HarperCollins.

Kell, G. (2004) *Gearing Up: From Corporate Responsibility to Good Governance and Scalable Solutions in SustainAbility*, New York: UN Global Compact.

Kelman, H. (1961) 'The process of opinion change', *Public Opinion*, 25, 57–78.

Kemm, J.R. (1985) 'Ethics of food policy', *Community Medicine*, 7, 289–94.

Kerr, C., Dunlop, T.J., Harbison, F. and Myers, C.A. (1960) *Industrialism and Industrial Man*, Cambridge, MA: Harvard University Press.

King Committee on Corporate Governance (2002) *King Report on Corporate Governance for South Africa (King II)*, Parklands, South Africa: Institute of Directors in Southern Africa.

King, C. (2001) 'Providing advice on whistleblowing', in Lewis, D.B. (ed.), *Whistleblowing at Work*, London: The Athlone Press.

Kirchenbaum, H. (1977) *Advanced Value Clarification*, La Jolla, CA: University Associates.

Kirk, G.S. (1974) *The Nature of the Greek Myths*, Harmondsworth: Penguin.

Kirkpatrick, J. (1994) *In Defense of Advertising: Arguments from Reason, Ethical Egoism and Laissez-Faire Capitalism*, Westport: Greenwood.

Kjonstad, B. and Willmott, H. (1995) 'Business ethics: Restrictive or empowering', *Journal of Business Ethics*, 14, 445–64.

Klein, J. G., Craig Smith, N. and John, A. (2002) 'Why We Boycott: Consumer Motivations for Boycott Participation and Marketer Responses', *Centre for Marketing*, Working Paper 02-701, UK: London Business School.

Klein, N. (2000) *No Logo*, London: Flamingo.

Kleveman, L. (2003) *The New Great Game. Blood and Oil in Central Asia*, London: Atlantic Books.

Klonoski, R. J. (1991) 'Foundational considerations in the corporate social responsibility debate', *Business Horizons*, 34 (4), 9–18.

Knights, D. and Willmott, H. (1999) *Management Lives: Power and Identity in Work Organizations*, London: Sage.

Koehn, D. (1994) *The Ground of Professional Ethics*, London: Routledge.

Kohlberg, L. (1969) *Stages in the Development of Moral Thought and Action*, New York: Holt Rinehart and Winston.

Kohlberg, L. (1984) *Essays in Moral Development, Volume 2, The Psychology of Moral Development*, New York: Harper and Row.

Koretz, G. (2001) 'Why Americans work so hard. How pay inequality galvanizes effort', *Business Week*, issue 3736, 6 November.

KPMG, 2011, *KPMG International Survey of Corporate Responsibility Reporting 2011*, KPMG International, Switzerland.

Kraus, P. and Britzelmaier, B. (2011) 'Corporate governance and corporate performance: A German perspective', *International Journal of Management Cases*, Vol. xx, no. 00 327-340.

Kumar, N. (2011a) 'Secretive trader prepares to open up', *Business, The Independent*, 25 January: 34.

Kumar, N. (2011b) 'Glencore sails straight into FTSE with £6.7bn Flotation', Business, *The Independent*, 15 April: 31

Kumar, N.S. and Rao, U.S. (1996) 'Guidelines for value based management in Kautilya's Arthashastra', *Journal of Business Ethics*, 15 (4), 415.

Kurtz, L. (2009) 'Socially responsible investment and shareholder activism', in Crane, A., McWilliams, A., Matten, D., Moon, J. and Siegel, D.S. (eds), *The Oxford Handbook of Corporate Social Responsibility*, 249–80, Oxford: Oxford University Press.

Kurucz, E.C., Colbet, B.A. and Wheeler, D. (2009) 'The business case for corporate social responsibility, in Crane, A., McWilliams, A., Matten, D., Moon, J. and Siegel, D.S. (eds), *The Oxford Handbook of Corporate Social Responsibility*, 83–112, UK.

Lambur, M., Rajgopal, R., Lewis, E., Cox, R. and Ellerbrock, M. (2003) *Applying Cost Benefit Analysis to Nutrition Education Programs: Focus on the Virginia Expanded Food and Nutrition Education Program*, Virginia Cooperative Extension, publication no. 490–403, World Wide Web, http://www.ext.vt.edu/pubs /nutrition/490-403/490-403.html. Site visited 2 March 2005.

Lane, J.-E. (1995) *The Public Sector. Concepts, Models and Approaches*, 2nd edn, London: Sage.

Lariba.com (2001) *Lariba Concept*, World Wide Web, http://www.lariba.com/ concepts.shtn. Site visited 20 August 2001.

Larson, M.S. (1977) *The Rise of Professionalism: A Sociological Analysis*, Berkeley, CA: University of California Press.

Lawson, N. (2008) 'The economics and politics of climate change: An appeal to reason, *Centre for Policy Studies*.

Layard, R. (2006) *Happiness: Lessons from a New Science*, London: Penguin.

Lee, T.A. (1984) 'Company financial statements: An essay in business history 1890–1950' in Lee, T.A. and Parker, R.H., (eds), *The Evolution of Corporate Finanacial Reporting*, 15-29, New York and London: Garland Publishing Inc.

Legge, K. (1995) *Human Resource Management: Rhetoric and Realities*, London: Macmillan.

Legge, K. (1998) 'Is HRM ethical? Can HRM be ethical?' in Parker, M. (ed.), *Ethics & Organisations*, 150–72, London: Sage.

Lenke, S. and Davies, G. (1995) 'Cultural, social and organizational transitions: the consequences for the Hungarian manager', *Journal of Management Development*, 14 (10), 14–31.

Lessnoff, M. (1986) *Social Contract*, London: Macmillan.

Levi, M. and Linton, A. (2003) 'Fair trade: a cup at a time?', *Politics & Society*, 31, 3: 407–32.

Levitt, T. (1956) 'The lonely crowd and the economic man', *Quarterly Journal of Economics*, February: 109.

Lewis, D.B. (2000) *Whistleblowing at Work*, London: The Athlone Press.

Lewis, D.B. (2001) *The Management of Non-Governmental Development Organisations*, London: Routledge.

Liedtka, J. (1991) 'Organisational value contention and managerial mindsets', *Journal of Business Ethics*, 10, 543–57.

Lindblom, C.E. (1977), *Politics and Markets: The World's Political-Economic Systems*, New York: Basic Books Inc.

Locke, J. (1952) *The Second Treatise of Government*, The Library of Liberal Arts.

London, B. (1932) *Ending the Depression Through Planned Obsolescence*, World Wide Web, https://commons.wikimedia.org/wiki/File:London_(1932)_Ending_the_depression_through_planned_obsolescence.pdf. Site visited 19 April 2012.

Lord Davies, E. (2011) *Women on Boards, February 2011*, Department for Business, Innovation and Skills, UK Government.

Lovell, A.T.A. (2002) 'The vulnerability of autonomy that denies the exercise of moral agency', *Business Ethics: A European Review*, 11 (1), 62–76.

Lovell, A.T.A. and Robertson, C. (1994) 'Charles Robertson: In the Eye of the Storm', in Vinten, G. (ed.), *Whistleblowers*, 146–73, London: Chapman and Hall.

Low, C. (2009) 'Cornerstone investors and initial public offerings on the stock exchange of Hong Kong', *Fordham Journal of Corporate & Financial Law*, 14, 3.

LSE (2011) 'Glencore Raises $10bn in London's Largest Ever International IPO', *News Release 22/11, LSE,* 24 May.

Lundberg, M. and Squire, L. (2003) 'The simultaneous evolution of growth and inequality', *Economic Journal*, 113, 326–44.

Lyons, D. (1984) *Ethics and the Rule of Law*, Cambridge: Cambridge University Press.

Lyotard, J.-F. (1988) *Le Postmodernisme Expliqué aux Enfants, Correspondance 1982–85*, Paris: Editions Galilée.

Mabbott, J.D. (1967) *The State and the Citizen*, 2nd edn, London: Hutchinson and Co.

Machado, A. (1988) *Selected Poems*, trans. Alan S. Trueblood, Cambridge, MA: Harvard University Press.

Machiavelli, N. (1950) *The Prince and the Discourses*, introduction by M. Lerner, New York: Modern Library.

MacIntyre, A. (1967) *A Short History of Ethics: A History of Moral Philosophy from the Homeric Age to the Twentieth Century*, London: Routledge.

MacIntyre, A. (1987) *After Virtue: A Study in Moral Theory*, London: Duckworth.

Mackie, J.L. (1990) *Ethics: Inventing Right and Wrong*, Harmondsworth: Penguin.

Maclagan, P. (1996) 'The organisational context for moral development: questions of power and access', *Journal of Business Ethics*, 15 (6), 645–54.

Maclagan, P. (1998) *Management & Morality*, London: Sage.

Maclagan, P. and Snell, R. (1992) 'Some implications for management development of research into managers' moral dilemmas', *British Journal of Management*, 3, 157–68.

Maguire, K. (2000) 'Clarke admits BAT link to smuggling', *Guardian Unlimited*, 3 February, World Wide Web, http://www.newsunlimited.co.uk/bat/article/0,2763,131957,00.html. Site visited 24 August 2001.

Mahesh, V.S. (1995) *Thresholds of Motivation*, New Delhi: Tata McGraw Hill.

Mahoney, J. (1990) *Teaching Business Ethics in the UK, Europe and the USA: A Comparative Study*, London: The Athlone Press.

Malhiason, N. (2004) 'BP's pipeline to nowhere: Georgia halts oil giant's $2.4b project', *The Observer*, 25 July.

Mallin, C. A. (2010) Corporate Governance, 3rd. edition, Oxford: Oxford University Press

Marcuse, A.H. (1991) *One-Dimensional Man*, 2nd edn, London: Routledge.

Margolis, J.D. and Walsh, J.P. (2003) 'Misery loves companies: rethinking social initiatives by business', *Administrative Science Quarterly*, 48, 268–305.

Marx, K. (1963) *The Eighteenth Brumaire of Louis Bonaparte*, first published 1852, International Publishers.

Marx, K. and Engels, F. (1962) 'Critique of the Gotha Programme' in *Selected Works*, vol. II, Moscow: Progress Publishers.

Maslow, A.H. (1987) *Motivation and Personality*, 3rd edn, New York: Harper Collins.

Mathews, M.C. (1988) *Strategic Intervention in Organizations*, Sage Library of Social Research, No. 169, London: Sage.

Matthews, J.B., Goodpaster, K.E. and Nash, L.I. (1991) *Policies and Person: A Casebook in Business Ethics*, 2nd edn, London: McGraw-Hill.

May, B. (2005) 'Under-informed, over here', 'Life', *Guardian*, 10.

McCauley, R. (2003) '"Going large" on shorts costs pub chain its late license', *Scotsman.Com News*, World Wide Web, http://news.scotsman.com/topics.cfm?tid+585&id+1236132003. Site visited 5 June 2007.

McCornack, S.A., Levine, T.R., Solowczuk, H.I., Torres, H.I. and Campbell, D.M. (1992) 'When the alteration of Information is viewed as deception: an empirical test of information manipulation theory', *Communication Monographs*, 59, 17–29.

McDonald, G. and Nijhof, A. (1999) 'Beyond codes of ethics: an integrated framework for stimulating morally responsible behaviour in organisations', *Leadership & Organisation Development Journal*, 20 (3), 133–46.

McGreal, C. (2001) 'Crucial drug case opens in Pretoria', *Guardian*, 6 March: 17.

McGuiness, R. (2008) 'Tesco may lead ban on super-strength drinks' *Metro*, 25 February, 5.

McIntosh, M., Thomas, R., Leipziger, D. and Coleman, G. (2003) *Living Corporate Citizenship. Strategic Routes to Socially Responsible Business*, Harlow: FT Prentice Hall.

McKinley, A. and Starkey, K. (1998) *Foucault, Management and Organization Theory: From Panopticon to Technologies of Self*, London: Sage.

McKinsey & Co (2007) 'Women matter: gender diversity, a corporate performance driver', World Wide Web, http://www.mckinsey.com/locations/swiss/news_publications/pdf/women_matter_english.pdf.Site visited 8 August 2009.

McLuhan, M. and Powers, B.R. (1989) *The Global Village. Transformations in World Life and Media in the Twentieth Century*, Oxford: Oxford University Press.

McMylor, P. (1994) *Alisdair MacIntyre: Critic of Modernity*, London: Routledge.

McWilliams, A. and Siegel, D. (2001) 'Corporate social responsibility: a theory of the firm perspective', *Academy of Management Review*, 26 (1), 117–27.

Meade, J.E. (1973) *Theory of Economic Externalities: The Control of Environmental Pollution and Similar Social Costs*, Leiden: Sijhoff.

Meikle, J. (2001) 'Professor quits over tobacco firm's £3.8m gift to university', *Guardian*, 18 May: 6.

Meirovich, G. and Reichel, A. (2000) 'Illegal but ethical: an inquiry into the roots of illegal corporate behaviour in Russia', *Business Ethics: A European Review*, 9 (3), 126–35.

Miceli, M.P. and Near, J.P. (1992) *Blowing the Whistle: The Organisational & Legal Implications for Companies and Employees*, New York: Lexington Books.

Michaels, A. (2001) 'Inside Track: Big pharma and the golden goose: interview Hank Mckinnell, Pfizer: Cheaper drugs would mean less money to spend on research and innovation, Pfizer's chief tells Adrian Michaels', *Financial Times*, 26 April.

Mihil, C. (1990) 'Thatcher shuns out of court deal for haemophiliacs with HIV', *Guardian*, 9 November: 2.

Mill, J.S. (1971) *Utilitarianism*, Harmondsworth: Penguin (reprint of 1861 edition).

Mill, J.S. (1998) *On Liberty and other Essays*, (ed.) John Gray, Oxford: Oxford University Press.

Milmo, C. (2001) 'Watchdog warns Virgin over misleading adverts', *Independent*, 30 May.

Minnesota Center for Corporate Responsibility (2001) *The Global Sullivan Principles*, World Wide Web, http://tigger.stthomas.edu.mcer/SullivanPrinciples.htm. Site visited 26 October 2001.

Mitchell, R. K., Agle, B. R. and Wood, D. J. (1997) 'Toward a theory of stakeholder identification and salience: defining the principle of who and what really counts', *The Academy of Management Review*, 22 (4), 853–86.

Mokhiber, R. (1998) 'The death penalty for corporations comes of age', *Business Ethics*, 12, November–December.

Monks, R.A.G. (2003) 'Equity culture at risk: The threat to Anglo-American prosperity', *Corporate Governance: An International Review*, 11 (3), July, 164–70.

Moore, G. (2001) 'Corporate social and financial performance: an investigation in the UK supermarket industry', *Journal of Business Ethics*, 34 (3, 4), 299–315.

Moore, G. (2003) 'Hives and horseshoes, Mintzberg or MacIntyre: what future for corporate and social responsibility?', *Business Ethics: A European Review*, 12 (1), 41–53.

Moore, G. and Robson, A. (2002) 'The UK supermarket industry: an analysis of corporate social and financial performance', *Business Ethics: A European Review*, 11 (1), 25–39.

Moore, O. (2000) 'Day of peace plea to sugar factory', *Great Yarmouth Mercury*, 7 July.

Moray Sustainability Forum (2005) *Moray Sustainability Forum: The Rough Guide to Moray's Future*, Keith, Banffshire: Moray Sustainability Forum.

Morgan, O. (2004) 'Dutch helm disease gets blame at Shell', *Observer*, 25 April.

Mortished, C. (2004) 'Deutsche Bank attacks Yukos court protection', *The Times*, Business section, 30 December: 43.

Moskvitch, K. (2012) *Unused e-waste discarded in China raises questions*, BBC, 20 April, World Wide Web, http://www.bbc.co.uk/news/technology-17782718. Site visited 23 April 2012.

Mounce, H.O. (1997) *The Two Pragmatisms: From Peirce to Rorty*, London: Routledge.

Murphy, L.B. (2001) *Moral Demands in Non-ideal Theory*, Oxford: Oxford University Press.

Myers, A. and Dehn, G. (2000) *Whistleblowing: The first cases and practical issues*, World Wide Web, http://www.pcaw.co.uk/news/press/_14.html. Site visited 17 February 2002.

National Institute of Health (n.d.) The *Hippocratic Oath*, Available on the World Wide Web, http://www.nlm.nih.gov/hmd/greek/greek_oath.htm. Site visited 14 September 2011.

National Snow & Ice date Centre, World Wide Web, http://nsidc.org/cryosphere/frozenground/methane.html. Site visited 19 April 2012.

NICE (National Institute for Clinical Excellence) (2001) *Interferon Beta/glatiramer Speculation*, World Wide Web, http://www.nice.org.uk/nice-web/article.asp?a=1370. Site visited 23 May 2001.

NICE (National Institute for Clinical Excellence) (2002) *NICE issues guidance on drugs for multiple sclerosis*, World Wide Web, http://www.nice.org.uk/article.asp?a=27619. Site visited 7 March 2002.

Niebuhr, R. (1932) *Moral Man and Immoral Society*, New York: C. Scribner.

Nisbet, R.A. (1953) *The Quest for Community*, Oxford: Oxford University Press.

Nolan Committee (1995) *Standards in Public Life, Volume 1. First Report of the Committee on Standards in Public Life*, London: HMSO.

Noland, J. and Phillips, R. (2010) 'Stakeholder engagement, discourse ethics and strategic management', *International Journal of Management Reviews,* British Academy of Management, 12 (1) 39–49.

North, D.C. (1990) *Institutions, Institutional Change and Economic Performance*, Cambridge, UK: Cambridge University Press.

Nozick, R. (1974) *Anarchy, State, and Utopia*, New York: Basic Books.

Oberman, W.D. (2000) Book review of Mitchell: 'The Conspicuous Corporation', (1997) *Business and Society*, 329(2), 239–44.

Observer (2000) Leader article 'The mob should never rule', 17 September.

Observer (2001) 'Beware – you've got mail', 7 January, World Wide Web, at *Guardian Unlimited*, http://www.guardian.co.uk/freespeech/article/0,2763,418935,00.html. Site visited 18 March 2004.

Observer (2004) 'Noble gesture', 2 September.

OECD (Organisation for Economic Co-operation and Development) (2000) *The OECD Guidelines for Multi-national Enterprises*, World Wide Web, http://www1.oecd.org/daf/investment/guidelines/mnetext.htm#6. Site visited 12 December 2001.

OECD (Organisations for Economic Cooperation & Development) (2005) *OECD Guidelines on the Corporate Governance of State-owned Enterprises.* Available on World Wide Web http://www.oecd.org/dataoecd/46/51/34803211.pdf

Ofcom (Office of Communication) (2007) *Young people and alcohol advertising. An investigation of alcohol advertising following the changes to the advertising code*, London: Ofcom.

Ojefia, I.A. (n.d.) 'The Nigerian State and the Niger Question' *22nd Annual Conference of the Association of Third World Studies*, Americus, Georgia, World Wide Web, http://www.deltastate.gov.ng/oyefia.htm. Site visited 17 December 2004.

Osman Gürbüz, Aybars, A. and Kutlu, O. (2010) 'Corporate governance and financial performance with a perspective on institutional ownership: empirical evidence from Turkey', *Journal of Management Accounting Research*, 8 (2), 21–37.

Outhwaite , W. (1994) *Habermas. A Critical Introduction*, Cambridge: Polity Press.

Owen, D. L. and O'Dwyer, B. (2009) Corporate social responsibility: The reporting and assurance dimension, in Crane, A., McWilliams, A., Matten, D., Moon, J. and Siegel, D.S., (eds) *The Oxford Handbook of Corporate Social Responsibility*, 384–409, UK: OUP.

Owen, D. L. and O'Dwyer, B. (2009) 'Corporate social responsibility: The reporting and assurance dimension, in Crane, A., McWilliams, A., Matten, D., Moon, J. and Siegel, D.S. (eds), *The Oxford Handbook of Corporate Social Responsibility*, 384–409, Oxford: Oxford University Press.

Owusu, K. and Ng'ambi, F. (2002) *Structural Damage: The causes and consequences of Malawi's food crisis*, Report for World Development Movement. http://www.wdm.org.uk/resources/reports/debt/structuraldamage1610202.pdf.

Pagels, E. (1982) *The Gnostic Gospels*, Harmondsworth: Penguin.

Painter- Morland, M. (2011) 'Moral decision-making', in M. Painter-Morland and R. ten Bos (eds), *Business Ethics and Continental Philosophy*, 117–140, Cambridge: Cambridge University Press.

Paris, G.A., Savage, G.W. and Seitz, G.H. (2004) *Report of the Investigation by the Special Committee of the Board of Directors of Hollinger International Inc. (The Breeden Report)*, Washington DC: US Securities and Exchange Commission, World Wide Web, http://www.sec.gov/Archives/edgar/data/868512/000095012304010413/y01437exv99w2.htm. Site visited 16 September 2004.

Parker, A. (2004) 'Audit team had "lack of warnings": Hollinger Inquiry', *Financial Times*, 2 September: 28.

Parker, M. (1998a) 'Business ethics and social theory: Postmodernizing the ethical', *British Journal of Management*, 9, September: 27–36.

Parker, M. (1998b) 'Against Ethics', in Parker, M. (ed.), *Ethics & Organisations*, London: Sage.

Parsons, T. (1999) 'The traditional square of opposition', *The Stanford Encyclopedia of Philosophy (Spring 1999 Edition)*, Zalta, Edward N. (ed.), World Wide Web, http://plato.stanford.edu/archives/spr1999/entries/square/. Site visited 25 October 2003.

Passmore, J. (1984) 'Academic ethics', *Journal of Applied Philosophy*, 1 (1) 63–77.

Pateman, C. (1985) *The Problem of Political Obligation: A Critique of Liberal Theory*, New York: John Wiley & Sons.

Paul, K. and Lydenberg, S. (1992) 'Applications of corporate social monitoring systems; types, dimensions, and goals', *Journal of Business Ethics*, 11 (1) 1–10.

Pava, M.L. (1999) *The Search for Meaning in Organisations: Seven Practical Questions for Ethical Managers*, Westport: Quorum Books.

Pereira, J. (1989) *What does Equity in Health Mean?* Centre for Health Economics, Discussion paper No. 61, York: Centre for Health Economics.

Peston, R. (2011a) *Browne not going to Glencore*, BBC Business News Blogs, 14 April, World Wide Web, http://www.bbc.co.uk/blogs/thereporters/robertpeston/2011/04/browne_not_going_to_glencore.html. Site visited 12 February 2012.

Peston, R. (2011b) *Is US right about UK's financial tragedy?*, BBC Business News Online, 6 June, World Wide Web http://www.bbc.co.uk/news/business-13677012. Site visited 12 February 2012.

Peters, G.P., Minx, J.C., Weber, C.L. and Edenhofer, O. (2011) 'Growth in Emission Transfers via International Trade from 1990 to 2008', *Proceedings of the National Academy of Sciences of the United States of America*, 108 (21), 8903–8.

Peters, T.J. and Waterman Jnr, R. (1982) *In Search of Excellence*, New York: Harper Row.

Petrick, J.A. (2000) 'Global human resource management competence and judgement integrity: towards a human centredorganisation', paper presented at Third Conference on Ethics and Human Resource Management, Towards a Human Centred Organisation, Imperial College, London, 7 June.

Petrick, J.A. and Quinn, J.F. (1997) *Management Ethics. Integrity at Work*, London: Sage.

Pilger, J. (2001) 'Spoils of a massacre', *Guardian Weekend*, 14 July: 18–29.

Pilling, D. and Timmins, N. (2000) 'Medicines arbiter delays decision on beta-interferon clinical excellence. Multiple Sclerosis Society angry that drug ruling is only likely after election', *Financial Times*, 23 December.

Planet Ark (2004) 'Shell says it unwittingly fed conflict in Nigeria', World Wide Web, http://www.planetark.com/avantgo/dailynewsstory.cfm?newsid=25486. Site visited 1 November 2004.

Plant, R. (1992) 'Enterprise in its place: the moral limits of markets', in Heelas, P. and Morris, P. (eds) *The Values of the Enterprise Culture: The Moral Debate*, London: Routledge, 85–99.

Plender, J. (2004) 'The insidious charms of Shell's dual votes: But just one factor in the foul up', *Financial Times*, 21 June: 22.

Pojman, L.P. (1998) *Classics of Philosophy*, Oxford: Oxford University Press.

Pollitt, M. and Ashworth, H. (2000) 'Beet lorry victory for villages', *Eastern Daily Press*, 21 July: 63–77.

Porter, M.E. and Kramer, M.R. (2002) 'The competitive advantage of corporate philanthropy', *Harvard Business Review*, December: 56–68.

Porter, M.E. and Kramer, M.R. (2006) 'The link between competitive advantage and corporate social responsibility', *Harvard Business Review*, December: 78–92.

Porter, M.E. and Kramer, M.R. (2011) 'Creating shared value', *Harvard Business Review*, February: 62–77.

Portman Group (2008) *Code of Practice on the Naming, Packaging and Promotion of Alcoholic Drinks*, 4th edn, World Wide Web, http://www.portman-group.org.uk/?pid=18&anp;=level4. Site visited 12 August 2008.

Post, J., Frederick, W.C, Lawrence, A. and Weber J. (1996) *Business and Society: Corporate Strategy, Public Policy and Ethics*, New York: McGraw-Hill.

Press Association (2005) 'Bar staff face fines for serving drunks' *The Guardian Online*, World Wide Web, http://society.guardian.co.uk/drugsandalcohol/story/0,8150,1450399,00.html?gusrc_rss. Site visited 10 August 2006.

Preston, L. and O'Bannon, D. (1997) 'The corporate social-financial performance relationship. A typology and analysis', *Business and Society*, 36 (4), 419–29.

Preston. L.E. and Sapienza, H. J. (1990) 'Stakeholder management and corporate performance', *Journal of Behavioral Economics*, 19 (4) 361–75.

Preuss, L. (1999) 'Ethical theory in German business ethics research', *Journal of Business Ethics*, 18, 407–19.

Proctor, E.K., Morrow-Howell, N. and Lott, C.L. (1993) 'Classification and correlates of ethical dilemmas in hospital social work', *Social Work*, 38 (2), 166–77.

Project Management Profession (1996) *Code of Ethics for the Project Management Profession*, World Wide Web, http://www.pmi.orh/pmi/mem_info/pmpcode.htm.Site visited 4 May 2002.

Public Administration Select Committee (2009) *Lobbying: Access and influence in Whitehall, First Report of Session 2008–09*, London: The Stationery Office, House of Commons.

Pusey, M. (1987) *Jürgen Habermas*, London: Routledge.

Ramesh, R. (2004) 'Bhopal is still suffering, 20 years on', *Guardian*, 29 November, available at *Guardian Unlimited*, World Wide Web, http://www.guardian.co.uk/international/story/0,,1361551,00.html. Site visited 25 January 2005.

Ramming, I., Kleinwort, D., Carbon Trade and Finance (2008) AAU Trading and the Impact on Kyoto and EU Emissions Trading. Before the Flood or Storm in a Tea-cup?, Greenhouse Gas Markets Report, Geneva: IETA.

Rand, A. (1995) *Philosophy: Who Needs It?* New York: Signet/Penguin USA.

Rand, A. (2007a) *The Fountainhead*, London: Penguin.

Rand, A. (2007b) *Atlas Shrugged*, London: Penguin.

Rangarajan, L.N. (ed.) (1992) *Kautilya: The Arthrashastra*, New Delhi: Penguin Books India.

Rao, E.M. (2000) 'Human resource management: The road to neo-Taylorism in Management Thought', in Saini, D.S. and Khan, S.A. (eds), *Human Resource Management. Perspectives for a New Era*, New Delhi: Response Books, Sage.

Raphael, D.D. (1970) *Problems of Political Philosophy*, London: Methuen.

Ravallion, M. (2004) *Looking Beyond Averages in the Trade and Poverty Debate*, World Bank Policy Research working paper 3461, Washington DC: World Bank Development Research Group.

Ravallion, M. and Chen, S. (2004) *China's (Uneven) Progress against Poverty*, Policy Research Working paper 3408, Washington, DC: World Bank, World Wide Web, http://econ.worldbank.org/files/38741_wps3408.pdf. Site visited 10 January 2005.

Rawls, J. (1971) *A Theory of Justice*, Cambridge, MA: Harvard University Press.

Rawls, J. (1999) *A Theory of Justice*, (revised edn) Cambridge, MA: Harvard University Press.

Redclift, M.R. (1984) *Development and the Environmental Crisis: Red or Green Alternatives?*, London: Methuen.

Redclift, M.R. (1987) *Sustainable Development: Exploring the Contradicitons*, London: Routledge.

Redfern Report (2001) *The Royal Liverpool Children's Hospital Report*, House of Commons Parliamentary Papers, World Wide Web, http://www.rlcinquiry.org.uk/. Site visited 6 May 2002.

Reece, D. (2011) 'Maintaining a culture of success could be a major challenge for Glencore', Business, *The Daily Telegraph*, 5 May: 2.

Rees-Mogg, W. (2004) 'Not quite as Black as he's been painted', *Mail on Sunday*, 5 September: 59.

Rehbein, K., Waddock S. and Graves S. (2004) 'Understanding shareholder activism: which corporations are targeted?' *Business and Society*, 43 (3) 239–67.

Reitaku Centre for Economic Studies (1999) *Ethics Compliance Management Systems. ECS 2000. Ethics Compliance Standard*, Reitaku Centre for Economic Studies, World Wide Web, http://www.ie.reitakuu.ac.jp/~davis/assets/applets/ecs2k-e.pdf. Site visited 12 December 2004.

Rest, J.R. (1986), *Moral Development: Advances in Research and Theory*, Praeger, New York.

Rifkin, J. (1999) *The Biotech Century: How Genetic Commerce Will Change the World*. London: Phoenix.

Rigby, E. (2007) 'Tesco protest vote on chief pay', *Financial Times*, 30 June, Companies: 18.

Ritzer, G. (1993) *The McDonaldization of Society*, California: Sage.

Roberts, J. (2003) 'The Manufacture of Corporate Social Responsibility: Constructing Corporate Sensibility', *Organization*, 10 (2), 249–65.

Robertson, D. (2011a) 'Hayward and polar explorer in line to join new Glencore board', *The Times*, 12 April: 35.

Robertson, D. (2011b) 'New concerns about friends in high places', Business, *The Times*, 15 April: 41.

Robertson, D. (2011c) 'A team of close-knit professionals, or is it just the old pals act?', Business, *The Times*, 25 April: 32 and 33.

Robertson, D., Carter, D. and Gupta, G. (2011) 'Dark side of City's secretive new giant', *The Times*, 19 May: 1, 16, 17

Robins, J. (2004) 'Should business bat for apartheid?', *The Times*, Law section, 28 September: 5.

Rokeach, M. (1973) *The Nature of Human Values*, New York: The Free Press.

Rorty, R. (1985) 'Habermas & Lyotard on postmodernity', in Bernstein, R. (ed.), *Habermas and Modernity*, Cambridge: Cambridge University Press.

Rorty, R. (1989) *Contingency, Irony and Solidarity*, Cambridge: Cambridge University Press.

Rorty, R. (1990) *Philosophy and the Mirror of Nature*, Oxford: Blackwell.

Rorty, R. (1992) 'The Pragmatist's progress', in Eco, U. with Richard Rorty, Johnathan Culler and Christine Brooke-Rose, (eds.) Stefan Collini (1992) *Interpretation and Overinterpretation*, Cambridge: Cambridge University Press.

Ross, W.D. (1930) *The Right and the Good*, Oxford: Oxford University Press.

Rotter, J.B. (1966) 'General expectancies for internal versus external control of reinforcement', *Psychological Monographs; General and Applied*, 80, 1–28.

Rousseau, J.-J. (1913) *The Social Contract*, London: J.M. Dent & Sons Ltd.

Rowley, T., Moldoveanu, M. (2003) 'When will stakeholder groups act? An interest- and identity-based model of stakeholder group mobilization', *Academy of Management Review*, 28 (2), 204–19.

Royle, T. (2000) *Working for McDonald's in Europe: The Unequal Struggle?*, London: Routledge.

Rubin, S. (2004) 'Hollinger trial to test dual-class structures', *National Post*, 18 February.

Russell, J. (2005) 'The glue is coming unstuck', *Guardian*, 23 April: 20.

Russell, J.B. (1985) *The Devil in the Middle Ages*, Cornell: Cornell University Press.

Sahay, S. and Walsham, G. (1997) 'Social structure and managerial agency in India', *Organisation Studies*, 18 (3), 414–44.

Said, E.W. (1978) *Orientalism*, London: Routledge, Kegan Paul.

Sainath. P. (2011) 'Bribes: A small but radical idea', *The Hindu*, Online edition 21 April, World Wide Web, http://www.hindu.com/2011/04/21/stories/2011042157861000.htm. Site visited 12 September 2011.

Saini, D.S. and Khan, S.A. (eds) (2000) *Human Resource Management: Perspectives for the New Era*, New Delhi: Sage.

Sarason, S.B. (1986) 'And what is the public interest?' *American Psychologist*, August, Vol. 4, 8, 899–905.

Sawyer, G.C. (1978) *Business and Society: Managing Corporate Social Impact*, Boston, MA: Houghton Mifflin.

Schafer, H. (2005) 'International corporate social responsibility rating systems: conceptual outline and empirical results', *Journal of Corporate Citizenship*, 20, 107–20.

Schein, E. (1992) *Organizational Culture and Leadership*, San Francisco: Jossey-Bass.

Schein, E. (1993) *Career Anchors: Discovering your Real Values*, revised edn, San Diego: Pfeiffer.

Schein, E.H. (1985) *Career Anchors: Discovering Your Real Values*, San Diego, CA: University Associates.

Schell, J. (1982) *The Fate of the Earth*, London: Picador, in association with Jonathan Cape.

Scholte, J.A. (2000) *Globalisation: A Critical Introduction*, London: Palgrave.

Schreier, M. and Groeben, N. (1996) 'Ethical Guidelines for the Conduct in Argumentative Discussions: An Exploratory Study', *Human Relations*, 49 (1), 123–32.

Scruton, R. (2000) *Animal Rights and Wrongs*, 3rd edn, London: Metro.

Seedhouse, D. (1988) *Ethics: The Heart of Healthcare*, London: John Wiley & Sons.

Sen, S., Gürhan-Canli, Z. and Morwitz, V. (2001) 'Withholding consumption: a social dilemma perspective on consumer boycotts', *Journal of Consumer Research*, 28 (3), 399–417.

Senge, P.M. (1990) *The Fifth Discipline. The Art and Practice of the Learning Organisation*, London: Century.

Seymour, L. (2003) 'Talisman is out ... What now?' *Review: The North-South Institute Biannual Newsletter*, Winter 2002–2003: 5, World Wide Web, http://www.nsi-ins.ca/english/pdf/review_winter_2002.pdf. Site visited 6 April 2005.

Shan, Y.G. and McIver, R.P. (2011) 'Corporate governance mechanisms and financial performance in China: panel data evidence on listed non-financial companies', *Asia Pacific Business Review*, 17 (3), 301–24.

Shaw, W.H. and Barry, V. (1998) *Moral Issues in Business*, 7th edn, Belmont, CA: Wadsworth Publishing Company.

Shell Group (2004) *Notes to corporate governance arrangements, Shell Annual Report 2003*, World Wide Web, http://www.shell.com/html/investor-en/reports2003/st/g/g8.html. Site visited 13 September 2004.

Shrader, C., Blackburn, V. and Ilse, P. (1997) *Journal of Management Issues*, 9, 355–72.

Sibun, J. and Ebrahimi, H. (2011) 'Glencore's float hit by concerns on transparency', Business, *The Daily Telegraph*, 15 April: 1

Silk, C. (1999) 'Why did Kitty Genovese die?', *The Navigator. An Objectivist review of Politics and Culture*, World Wide Web, http://www.objectivistcenter.org/navigator/articles/nav+silk_why-kitty-genovese-die. Site visited 8 March 2005.

Simon, H.A. (1952) 'Comments on the theory of organizations', *American Political Science Review*, 46, 1130–39.

Simon, H.A. (1953) 'Notes on the observation and measurement of political power', *Journal of Politics*, 15, 500–16.

Simon, H.A. (1955) 'A behavioural model of rational choice', *Quarterly Journal of Economics*, 69, 99–118.

Simon, H.A. (1983) *Reason in Human Affairs*, Oxford: Basil Blackwell.

Simpson, D. (2005) 'Caring big business or a wolf in sheep's clothing?', *Online Opinion* (email journal), World Wide Web, http://www.onlineopinion.com.au/print.asp?article=2913. Site visited 17 January 2005.

Sinclair, A. (1993) 'Approaches to organisational culture and ethics', *Journal of Business Ethics*, 12, 63–73.

Singer, P. (1983) *Hegel*, Oxford: Oxford University Press.

Singh, J.P. (1990) 'Managerial culture and work-related values in India', *Organisation Studies*, 11 (1), 75–101.

Skapinker, M. (1998) 'BA says sorry to Branson', *Financial Times*, 17 May.

Skapinker, M. (2001) 'Michael Skapinker examines the issues raised by Luc Vandevelde's recent decision to turn down a generous pay bonus', *FT.com*, 4 May, World Wide Web, FT.com. Site visited 23 June 2004.

Skinner, A.S. and Wilson, T. (1975) *Essays on Adam Smith*, Oxford: Clarendon Press.

Sklair, L. (1995) *Sociology of the Global System: Social Change in Global Perspective*, Hemel Hempstead: Harvester Wheatsheaf.

Slade, G. (2007) *Made to Break: Technology and Obsolescence in America*, Cambridge, MA: Harvard University Press.

Slapper, G. and Tombs, S. (1999) *Corporate Crime*, London: Longman.

Sloan, K. and Burnett, A. (2004) *Enlightenment: Discovering the World in the Eighteenth Century*, London: British Museum Press.

Smircich, L. (1983) 'Concepts of culture and organisational analysis', *Administrative Science Quarterly*, 28, 339–58.

Smith, A. (1776/1982) *An Inquiry into the Nature and Causes of the Wealth of Nations*, with an introduction by Skinner, A., London: Penguin Books.

Smith, A. (2000) *The Theory of Moral Sentiments* (originally published 1799), New York: Prometheus Books.

Smith, H. (2011) 'Met chief quits as hacking scandal claims more scalps', *Metro*, 18 July 2011, 1.

Smith, J.E. (n.d.) *Moral terminology and Proportionalism*, The Archdiocese of Detroit.Available on the World Wide Web. http@//www.shms.edu/aodonline-sqlimages/shms/faculty/smithjanet/Publications/MoralPhilosophy/Moralterminology.pdf. Site visited 23 January 2012.

Smith, M. (1977) *A Practical Guide to Value Clarification*, La Jolla, CA: University Associates.

Smith, N.C. (1990) *Morality and the Market: Consumer Pressure for Corporate Accountability*, London: Routledge.

Smith, N.C. (2003) 'Corporate social responsibility: whether or how?', *California Management Review*, 45, 4: 52–76.

Smith, N.C. and Cooper-Martin, E. (1997) 'Ethics and target marketing: the role of product harm and consumer vulnerability', *Journal of Marketing*, 61 (3), 1–20.

Smithers, R. (2008) 'Asda bans shooters to deter binges', *The Guardian*, 26 February, news section: 5.

Snell, R.S. (1993) *Developing Skills for Ethical Management*, London: Chapman and Hall.

Snell, R.S. (2000) 'Studying moral ethos using an adapted Kohlbergian Model', *Organisation Studies*, 21 (1), 267–95.

Soeken, K. and Soeken, D. (1987) *A Survey of Whistleblowers: Their Stresses and Coping Strategies*, Laurel, MD: Association of Mental Health Specialties.

Sokal, A. and Bricmont, J. (2003) *Intellectual Impostures*, London: Profile Books.

Solomon, R.C. (1993) *Ethics and Excellence: Cooperation and Integrity in Business*, Oxford: Oxford University Press.

Spaemann, R. (1989) *Basic Moral Concepts*, trans. T.J. Armstrong, London: Routledge.

SpeakersUK (2005) *home page*, World Wide Web, http://speakers-uk.com/. Site visited 15 February 2005.

Spurlock, M. (2004) *Super Size Me*, film, Samuel Goldwyn Films.

Srivastva, S. and Cooperrider, D.L. (1988) 'The urgency for executive integrity', in Srivastva, S. (ed.), *Executive Integrity: The Search for High Human Values in Organisational Life*, 1–28, San Francisco: Jossey-Bass.

Standerwick, K., Davies, C., Tucker, L. and Sheron, N. (2007) 'Binge drinking and sexual behaviour and sexually transmitted infection in the UK', *International Journal of STD and AIDS*, 18, 810–13.

Starzl, T.W. and Dhir, K.S. (1986) 'Strategic planning 2,300 years ago', *Management International Review*, 26 (4), 70–8.

Stauffer, N. (2008) *Carbon emissions trading in Europe: lessons to be learned*, MITei, World Wide Web, http://web.mit.edu/mitei/research/spotlights/europe-carbon .html Site visited 19 April 2012.

Sterman, J.D. and Sweeney, L.B. (2002) 'Cloudy skies: Assessing public understanding of global warming', *Systems Dynamic Review*, 18 (2).

Stern, N. (2006) *Stern Review on the Economics of Climate Change*, London: HM Treasury.

Sternberg, E. (1996) 'A vindication of whistleblowing in business', in Brindle, M. and Dehn, G. (eds), *Four Windows on Whistleblowing*, 24–39, London: Public Concern at Work.

Sternberg, E. (2000) *Just Business: Business Ethics in Action*, 2nd edn, Oxford: Oxford University Press.

Stevens, B. (1994) 'An analysis of corporate ethical code studies: "Where do we go from here?"', *Journal of Business Ethics*, 13, 63–9.

Stewart, D.W. (1984) 'Managing competing claims: An ethical framework for human resource decision making', *Public Administration Review*, 44 (1), January/February, 14–22.

Stibbe, A. (2011) *The Handbook of Sustainability Literacy: Skills for a Changing World,* Devon, UK: Green Books.

Stiglbauer, M.(2010) 'Transparency and Disclosure on Corporate Governance as a Key Factor in Companies' Success: a Simultaneous Equations Analysis for Germany', *Problems and Perspectives in Management,* 8 (1), 161-173.

Stiglitz, J. (2004) *Globalisation and its Discontents*, London: Penguin.

Stokes, E. (1959) *The English Utilitarians and India*, Oxford: The Clarendon Press.

Storvik, A, and Teigen, M. (2010) *Women on Board: The Norwegian Experience*, Berlin: Friedrich- Ebert – Stifling International Policy Analysis.

Stylianou, A.C., Winter, S. and Giacalone, R.A. (2004) 'Accepting unethical information practices: the interactive effects of individual and situational factors', paper presented at the *Academy of Management Conference: OCIS division*, New Orleans, August.

SustainAbility (2004) *Gearing Up: From Corporate Responsibility to Good Governance and Scalable Solutions*, New York: UN Global Compact.

SustainAbility (2005) *The Changing Landscape of Liability: A Director's Guide to Trends in Corporate, Environmental, Social and Economic Liability*, London.: Sustainability.

SustainAbility, Ketchum, United Nations Environment Programme (UN-EP) (2002) *Good News & Bad: The Media, Corporate Social responsibility and Sustainable Development,* World Wide Web, http://www.grainesdechangement.com/docs/medias/Good-News-and-Bad.pdf Site visited 19 April 2012.

Tait, N. (2003) 'Cleared police chief accuses Met of witch-hunt', *Financial Times*, 16 September: 5.

Taki (2004) 'A publisher and a gentleman', *The American Conservative*, 15 March. 31–33

Tawney, R.H. (1966) *Religion and the Rise of Capitalism*, Harmondsworth: Penguin.

Taylor, A. (2006) 'No justification for fat cat salaries say Unions', *Financial Times*, 28 December, National News: 3.

Taylor, C. (2001) 'How to be diverse. The need for a "looser" us to accommodate "them"', *Times Literary Supplement*, No. 5116, 20 April: 4.

Taylor, D. (2001) 'E-mail: good, bad and ugly', *Computer Weekly*, 8 March.

Taylor, M. and Saarinen, E. (1994) *Imagologies: Media Philosophy*, London: Routledge.

Tencatti, A., Perrini, F. and Pougtz, S. (2003) 'New tools to foster corporate socially responsible behaviour', *European Business Ethics network – 16th Annual Conference*, Budapest, 29–31 August, World Wide Web, http://ethics.bkae.hu/html/documents/Tencattietalpapernew.doc. Site visited 9 December 2004.

Terazono, E. (2011) *Xstrata's Paper Billionaires*, FT.com, 5 May, World Wide Web, http://www.ft.com/cms/s/0/cc290680-76a3-11e0-bd5d-00144feabdc0.html#axzz1mGJT5pv0. Site visited 12 February 2012.

Terjesen, S. and Singh, V. (2008) 'Female Presence on Corporate Boards; a Multi-country study of environmental context', *Journal of Business Ethics*, 83 (1), 55–63.

Terjesen, S., Sealy, R., Singh, V. (2009) 'Women Directors on Corporate Boards: A review and a research agenda', *Corporate Governance: An International Review*, 17 (3), 320–37.

Terry, M. (1975) 'The inevitable growth of informality', *British Journal of Industrial Relations*, 1 (3), 76–90.

Tester, K. (1991) *Animals and Society: The Humanity of Animal Rights*, London: Routledge.

Texas Instruments (1999) *Ethics in the Global Market*, World Wide Web, http://www.ti.com/corp/docs/company/citizen/ethics/market.shtn. Site visited 12 November 1999.

Texas Instruments (2001) *The TI Ethics Quick Test*, World Wide Web, http://www.ti.com/corp/docs/company/citizen/ethics/quicktest.shtml. Site visited 19 November 2001.

The Cabinet Office (2004) *The Civil Service Code*, World Wide Web, http://www.cabinetoffice.gov.uk/propriety_and_ethics/civil_service/civil_service_code.asp. Site visited 2 December 2004.

The Chartered Institute for Personnel and Development (CIPD), 'Diversity and equality', World Wide Web, http://www.cipd.co.uk/hr-topics/diversity-equality.aspx. Site visited 19 April 2012.

The Corner House and 14 other NGOs (2003) *Review of the Environmental Impact Assessment for the Baku-Tbilisi-Ceyhan oil pipeline*, World Wide Web, http://ifiwatchnet.org/doc/btceiareview.pdf. Site visited 28 November 2004.

The Economist (2012a) 'Prometheus unsound: America's Supreme Court wallops the biotech industry', 24 March, World Wide Web, http://www.economist.com/node/21551087?frsc=dg%7Ca. Site visited 19 April 2012.

The Economist (2012b) 'Apple and the American economy', 23 January, 13:46 by R.A. http://www.economist.com/blogs/freeexchange/2012/01/supply-chains. Site visited 19 April 2012.

The Guardian (1999) Leading article: 'Mr Aitken pays the price', 9 June: 21. Guardian and Observer on CD-ROM.

The Guardian (2002) 'Sweatshop campaigners demand gap boycott', 22 November, World Wide Web, http://www.guardian.co.uk/uk/2002/nov/22/clothes.globalisation. Site visited 19 April 2012.

The Guardian (2004a) 'Damned in detail – but let off lightly', Guardian Unlimited, 25 August, World Wide Web, http://www.guardian.co.uk/online/news/0,12597,1377968,00.html. Site visited 21 December 2004.

The Guardian (2004b) 'Solitary part-timer conducted group audit', Guardian, 25 August: 22.

The Guardian (2008) 'Northern Rock under fire for Chief's £760,000 payout' by Inman P., Wearden G. and Treanor, J., 1 April: 27.

The Guardian (2011) 'Canada pulls out of Kyoto protocol', 13 December, World Wide Web, http://www.guardian.co.uk/environment/2011/dec/13/canada-pulls-out-kyoto-protocol?INTCMP=SRCH. Site visited 19 April 2012.

The New York Times (2012) 'In China, human costs are built into an iPad', 25 January, by Charles Duhigg and David Barboza, World Wide Web, http://www.nytimes.com/2012/01/26/business/ieconomy-apples-ipad-and-the-human-costs-for-workers-in-china.html. Site visited 19 April 2012.

The Telegraph (2011a) *'Cotswold Geotechnical fined £385,000 in first corporate manslaughter conviction'*, World Wide Web, http://www.telegraph.co.uk/finance/yourbusiness/8331262/Cotswold-Geotechnical-fined-385000-in-first-corporate-manslaughter-conviction.html. Site visited 5 November 2011.

The Telegraph (2011b) 'David Cameron rewrites conference speech after credit card gaffe', 5 October, World Wide Web, http://www.telegraph.co.uk/news/politics/conservative/8808294/David-Cameron-rewrites-conference-speech-after-credit-card-gaffe.html. Site visited 19 April 2012.

The Telegraph (2011c) 'Rebekah Brooks has driven News of the World 'into the dirt'', *The Telegraph online*, 7 July, World Wide Web, www.telegraph.co.uk. Site visited 6 September 2011a,2011b,2011c.

The Times of India (2004) 'CBI struggling to extradite Anderson', 20 July, World Wide Web, http://timesofindia.inditimes.com/articleshow/784941.cms. Site visited 25 January 2005.

The World Commission on the Ethics of Scientific Knowledge and Technology (COMEST) (2005) *The Precautionary Principle*, Paris: UNESCO, World Wide Web, http://unesdoc.unesco.org/images/0013/001395/139578e.pdf. Site visited 14 September 2011.

Thomson, A. (1999) *Critical Reasoning in Ethics. A Practical Introduction*, London: Routledge.

Thompson, A. (2005) 'The mail went undercover in a pub to discover the truth about Britain's new drink laws. We found a cynical drive for bar profits and to hell with the consequences', *Daily Mail*, 29 November, 26–27.

Thorpe, V. (2011) 'Hugh Grant and Steve Coogan join war on the red tops', *The guardian.co.uk*, 9 July, World Wide Web, www.guardian.co.uk/media/2011/jul/09/hugh-grant-steve-coogan-news/print. Site visited 6 September 2011.

Tilney, L.H. (2000) 'Peter Pan and the big bad wolf', *Financial Times*, 5 August, Book section: 4.

Time (2010) *More Warming Worries: Methane from the Arctic*, 4 March, World Wide Web, http://www.time.com/time/health/article/0,8599,1969767,00.html. Site visited 19 April 2012.

Times Online (2009) 'Satyam: Ramalinga B Raju's resignation letter'. Available on the World Wide Web, http://business.timesonline.co.uk/tol/business/industry-sectors/technology/article5467583.ece. Site visited 5 February 2010.

Times, The (2011) 'Resource management; A huge corporation's launch on the UK stock market requires more information', Editorial, 15 April: 2

Tinker, T. (1985) *Paper Prophets*, Eastbourne: Holt, Reinhart and Winston.

Titmuss, R.M. (1970) *The Gift Relationship: From Human Blood to Social Policy*, London: Allen & Unwin.

Todd, E. (2003) *After the Empire*, New York: Columbia University Press.

Toffler, B.L. (1991) *Managers Talk Ethics: Making Tough Choices in a Competitive World*, New York: John Wiley & Sons.

Torchia, M., Calabrò, A. and Huse, M. (2011) 'Women Directors on Corporate Boards: From Tokenism to Critical Mass', *Journal of Business Ethics*, 102, 299–317.

Transparency International (2002) *Bribe Payers Index 2002*, World Wide Web, http://www.transparency.org/policy_research/surveys_indices/bpi/bpi_2002. Site visited 13 February 2005.

Transparency International (2006) *Bribe Payers Index 2006*, World Wide Web, http://www.transparency.org/news_room/latest_news/press_releases/2006/en_2006_10_04_bpi_2006. Site visited 13 February 2008.

Transparency International (2007) *Corruption Perceptions Index 2004*, World Wide Web, http://www.transparency.org/policy_research/surveys_indices/cpi/2007. Site visited 12 April 2008.

Trevino, L.K. (1986) 'Ethical decision making in organisations: A Person-Situation Interactionist Model', *Academy of Management Review*, 11 (3), 601–17.

Trevino, L.K. and Youngblood, S.A. (1990) 'Bad Apple in Bad Barrels: A causal analysis of ethical decision-making behaviour', *Journal of Applied Psychology*, 75 (4), 378–85.

Tripathi, R.C. (1990) 'Interplay of values in the functioning of Indian organisations', *International Journal of Psychology*, 25, 715–34.

Trompenaars, F. and Hampden-Turner, C. (1993) *Riding the Waves of Culture. Understanding Cultural Diversity in Business*, 2nd edn, London: Nicholas Brealey.

Truscheit A. and Otte, C. (2004) 'Sustainable games people play: Teaching sustainability skills with the aid of the role-play 'NordWestPower'', *Greener Management International*, (48) 51–6.

Tsogas, G. (1999) 'Labour standards in international trade agreements: A critical assessment of the arguments', *International Journal of Human Resource Management*, April, 10 (2), 351–75.

Turner, C.T. (2001) *The Real Root Cause of the Ford–Firestone Tragedy: Why the Public is Still at Risk*, Public Citizen and safetyforum.com, World Wide Web, http://www.citizen.org/fireweb/index7.htm. Site visited 3 June 2001.

United Kingdom Central Council for Nursing, Midwifery and Health Visiting (UKCC) (1996) *Code of Professional Conduct*, World Wide Web, http://www.ukcc.org.uk/codecon.html. Site visited 8 May 2002.

United Nations – Environmental Programme (UN-EP) (2008) *Emerging Challenges, Methane from the Artic: Global Warming Wildcard*, World Wide Web, http://www.unep.org/yearbook/2008/report/Emerging.pdf. Site visited 19 April 2012.

United Nations – Framework Convention on Climate Change (UN-FCCC) (2006) *Report of the Conference of the Parties Serving as the Meeting of the Parties to the Kyoto Protocol*, Montreal: UN.

United Nations - World Institute for Development Economics Research (UNU-WIDER) (2006) *The World Distribution of Household Wealth*, Helsinki, Finland: UN.

United Nations (1948) *Universal Declaration of Human Rights*, World Wide Web, http://www.un.org/Overview/rights.html. Site visited 8 February 2002.

United Nations (1951) *Measures for the Economic Development of Under-Developed Countries: Report by a Group of Experts appointed by the Secretary-General of the United Nations*, Department of Economic Affairs, New York: UN.

United Nations (1989) *Convention on the Rights of the Child*, World Wide Web, http://www.unicef.org/crc/crc.htm. Site visited 30 March 2002.

United Nations (2007) *Sustainable Development Innovation Briefs: CSR and Developing Countries,* Issue: 1, NY: Department of Economic and Social Affairs.

United Nations (n.d.) *The United Nations Global Compact,* World Wide Web, http://www.globalcompact.org. Site visited 12 May 2008.

United States District Court: Southern District of New York (2003) *Opinion in the case of Pelman and Bradley against McDonald's Corporation*, World Wide Web, http://tajnedokumenty.com/MDpelmandismissal.html. Site visited 29 September 2004.

van Buitenen, P. (2000) *Blowing the Whistle. One Man's Fight Against Fraud in the European Commission*, London: Politico's Publishing.

Vardy, P. and Grosch, P. (1999) *The Puzzle of Ethics*, revised edn, London: Fount.

Varley, P. (1998) *The Sweatshop Quandary: Corporate Responsibility on the Global Frontier*. Washington: Investor Responsibility Research Centre (IRRC).

Veblen, T. (2009) *The Theory of the Leisure Class*, Oxford: Oxford World's Classics, OUP.

Verbeke, W., Ouwerkerk, C. and Peelen, E. (1996) 'Exploring the contextual and individual factors on ethical decision making of salespeople', *Journal of Business Ethics*, 15, 1175–87.

Verbos, K. A., Gerard, J, A., Forshay, P.R., Harding, C.S., Miller, J. S. (2007) 'The positive Ethical Organization; Enacting a Living Code of Ethics and the Ethical Organization', Journal of Business Ethics , Vol. 76, 17-33.

Viswesvaran, C. and Deshpande, S.P. (1996) 'Ethics, success and job satisfaction: A test of dissonance theory in India', *Journal of Business Ethics*, 15 (10), 1065–9.

Vogel, D. (2005) *The Market for Virtue: The Potential and Limits of Corporate Social Responsibility,* Washington, DC: Brookings Institution Press.

Vroom, V.H. (1964) *Work and Motivation*, New York: Wiley.

Wakefield, J. (1999) 'Surfing results in sacking', *ZDNet UK News*, 16 June, World Wide Web, http://news.zdnet.co.uk/intrnet/0,390220369,2072304,00.htm. Site visited 18 March 2004.

Wallach, M.A. and Wallach, L. (1983) *Psychology's Sanction for Selfishness: The Error of Egoism in Theory and Therapy*, San Francisco: W.H. Freeman and Company.

Waller, M. (2011) 'Favourite for Glencore's job 'walked away at last minute', Business, *The Times*, 18 April: 31

Walzer, M. (1983) *Spheres of Justice: A Defence of Pluralism and Equality*, Oxford: Martin Robertson.

Warren, R.C. (1993) 'Codes of ethics: Bricks without straw', *Business Ethics: A European Review*, 2 (4), 185–91.

Warwick-Ching, L. (2007) 'Farepak: The indebted road from butcher's shop to administration', *Financial Times*, 7 December, Companies Section: 23.

Watchman, R. (2004) 'FSA probes scandal of "missing" Shell reserves', *Observer*, 14 March.

Watson, T.J. (1994) *In Search of Management. Culture, Chaos and Control in Managerial Work*, London: Routledge.

Watson, T.J. (1998) 'Ethical codes and moral communities: The gunlaw temptation, the Simon Solution and the David Dilemma', in Parker, M. (ed.), *Ethics & Organisations*, 253–69, London: Sage.

Watson, T.J. (2002) *Organising and Managing Work. Organisational, Managerial and Strategic Behaviour in Theory and Practice*, Harlow: Pearson Education.

Weaver, M. (2000) 'Chummy protest hides drivers' grim resolution', *Daily Telegraph*, 14 September.

Webb, T. and Thompson, S. (2012) 'Glencore Chief waives his £1.8m bonus 'because it's unecessary'', *The Times*, 6 March: 37.

Webley, S. and More, E. (2003) *Does Business Ethics Pay?*, London: Institute of Business Ethics (IBE).

Weick, K.E. (1995) *Sensemaking in Organizations*, London: Sage.

Weick, K.E. (2001) *Making Sense of the Organization*, Oxford: Blackwell.

Weitzman, H. (2006) 'The bitter cost of 'fair trade' coffee', *The Financial Times*, 8 September 2006.

Welford, R. (1995) *Environmental Strategy and Sustainable Development: The Corporate Challenge for the Twenty-first Century*, London: Routledge.

Wells, M. and Ramesh, R. (2004) 'BBC reputation hit by Bhopal interview hoax', *The Guardian*, 4 December: 1.

Werhane, P.H. (1999) *Moral Imagination and Management Decision-making*, New York: Oxford University Press.

Weybrecht, G. (2011) *The Sustainable MBA: The Managers Guide to Green Business*, Chichester, England: John Wiley & Sons Ltd.

White, G. (2011a) 'Abu Dhabi to become major shareholder in Glencore', Business, *The Daily Telegraph*, 4 May: 1.

White, G. (2011b) 'Glencore float will create five new billionaires', *Business*, *The Daily Telegraph*, 5 May: 1.

Whysall, P. (2000) 'Addressing the issues in retailing: A stakeholder perspective', *International Review of Retail, Distribution and Consumer Research*, 10 (3), 305–18.

Wilde, O. (1996) *A Woman of No Importance*, Harmondsworth: Penguin.

Wilkinson, J. (2007) 'Fair Trade: Dynamics and dilemmas of a market oriented global social movement', *Journal of Consumer Policy*, 30: 219–39.

Williamson, J. (1978) *Decoding Advertisements: Ideology and Meaning in Advertising*, London: Marion Boyars.

Willmott, H. (1998) 'Towards a new ethics? The contributions of poststructuralism and Posthumanism', in Parker, M. (ed.), *Ethics and Organisations*, London: Sage.

Wilson, B. (2004) 'Proximate cause and fries to go', *Times Literary Supplement*, 24 September: 17.

Wilson, J. (1999) 'Aitken "will not be a priest" ', *The Guardian*, 10 June: 10.

Wilson, T. and Skinner, A.S. (1976), *The Market and the State: Essays in Honour of Adam Smith*, Oxford: Clarendon Press.

Windsor, D. (2001) 'Corporate citizenship, evolution and interpretation', in Andriof, J. and McIntosh, M. (eds), *Perspectives on Corporate Citizenship*, 39–52, Sheffield: Greenleaf Publishing.

Windsor, D. (2006) 'Corporate social responsibility: three key approaches', *Journal of Management Studies*, 43 (1), 93–114.

Wines, A.W. and Napier, N.K. (1992) 'Towards an understanding of cross-cultural ethics: A tentative model', *Journal of Business Ethics*, 11, 831–41.

Winfield, M. (1990) *Minding Your Own Business: Self-regulation and Whistleblowing in British Companies*, London: Social Audit.

Winstanley, D. and Woodall, J. (eds) (2000) *Ethical Issues in Contemporary Human Resource Management*, London: Macmillan.

Winstanley, D., Clark, J. and Leeson, H. (2001) 'Approaches to Child Labour in the Supply Chain', paper presented at *4th Conference on Ethics and Human Resource Management: Professional Development and Practice*, Middlesex University Business School, 20 April.

Winter, R. (1989) *Learning from Experience. Principles and Practice in Action Research*, Lewes: Falmer.

Wolf, M. (2000) 'Sleepwalking with the enemy: Corporate social responsibility distorts the market by deflecting business from its primary role of profit generation', *Financial Times*, 16 May: 21.

Wollstonecraft, M. (1995) *Wollstonecraft: A Vindication of the Rights of Man and a Vindication of the Rights of Woman and Hints* (Cambridge Texts in the History of Political Thought), (ed.) S. Tomaselli. Cambridge: Cambridge University Press.

Wood, D. J. and Logsdon, J.M. (2001) 'Theorising business citizenship' in Andriof, J. and McIntosh, M. (eds), *Perspectives on Corporate Citizenship*, 39–52, Sheffield: Greenleaf Publishing.

Wood, D.J. and Logsdon, J.M. (2001) 'Theorising business citizenship', in Andriof, J. and McIntosh, M. (eds), *Perspectives on Corporate Citizenship*, 83–103, Sheffield: Greenleaf Publishing.

Wood, Z. (2008) 'Investors' anger rises after M&S reshuffle', *The Observer*, 16 March, Business & Media: 1.

Woodall, J. and Douglas, D. (1999) 'Ethical Issues in Contemporary Human Resource Development', *Business Ethics: A European Review*, 8 (4), October, 249–61.

Woodbury, M. (1998) 'Email, voicemail, and privacy: What policy is ethical?', paper presented to *The Fourth International Conference on Ethical Issues of Information Technology*, Erasmus University, The Netherlands, 25–27 March, World Wide Web, http://www.cpsr.org/~marsha-w/emailpol.html. Site visited 18 March 2004.

Woodcock, M. (1979) *The Team Development Manual*, Aldershot: Gower Press.

Woodcock, M. (1989) *50 Activities for Team Building*, Aldershot: Gower.

World Bank (2002) *Globalization, Growth and Poverty*, Washington DC: World Bank.

World Commission on the Social Dimension of Globalization (2004) *A Fair Globalization: Creating Opportunities for All*, Geneva: International Labour Organization.

Wyschogrod, E. (1990) *Saints and Postmodernism*, Chicago: University of Chicago Press.

Wyver, J. (1989) 'Television and postmodernism', in Appignanesi, L. (ed.), *Postmodernism: ICA Documents 4*, London: Free Association Books.

Yang, A.A. (1998) *Bazaar India: Markets, Society, and the Colonial State in Gangetic Bihar*,Berkeley: university of California Press.

Yeung, L.N.T., Levine, T.R. and Nishiyama, K. (1999) 'Information manipulation theory and perceptions of deception in Hong Kong', *Communication Reports*, 12 (1), 1–13.

Young, K. (1977) 'Values in the policy process', *Policy and Politics*, 5, 1–22.

Young, R., West, P. and Sweeting, H. (2007) 'A longitudinal study of alcohol use and antisocial behaviour in young people' *Alcohol and Alcoholism*, 43 (2), 204–14.

Zakhem, A. (2008) 'Stakeholder management capability: A discourse-theoretical approach', *Journal of Business Ethics*, 79, 395–405.

Zwolinski, M. (2007) 'Sweatshops, choice and exploitation', *Business Ethics Quarterly*, 17 (4), 689–727.

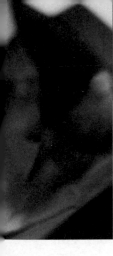

Index